WESTMAR COLLEGE LIBRARY

D1091444

Sexual
Decisions

Sexual Decisions

Milton Diamond
John A. Burns School of Medicine,
University of Hawaii

Arno Karlen

Little, Brown and Company
Boston   Toronto

BF
692
.D52

Copyright © 1980 by
Milton Diamond and Arno Karlen

All rights reserved. No part of this book may be
reproduced in any form or by any electronic or
mechanical means including information storage
and retrieval systems without permission in writing
from the publisher, except by a reviewer who may
quote brief passages in a review.

Library of Congress Catalog Card No. 79-88188

First Printing

Artist: Arthur Polonsky
Medical illustrations: Kathleen Hagelston

Published simultaneously in Canada by Little,
Brown & Company (Canada) Limited

Printed in the United States of America

CREDITS

Figure 2-1: top left, The Bettmann Archive; bottom left, Massachusetts Historical Society; right, Jim Jackson. Figure 2-2: top, Culver Pictures; bottom left, The Granger Collection; bottom right, Burt Glinn, Magnum. Figure 2-3: Program of Human Sexuality, University of Minnesota.

Figure 3-1: Jim Jackson. Figure 3-2: top right, Laird Sutton, Institute for the Advanced Study of Human Sexuality; bottom right, Jim Jackson. Page 36: bottom left, from *Love and Hate* by I. Eibl-Eibesfeldt, © 1970 by permission of the publisher R. Piper and Co., Verlag.; top right, Jim Jackson; bottom right, from *Love in Action* by F. Henriques, © 1960, by permission of the publisher, E. P. Dutton.

Chapter 4. Lines from "The Wild Old Wicked Man" reprinted with permission of Macmillan Publishing Co., Inc., M. B. Yeats, Miss Anne Yeats, and the Macmillan Co. of London and Basingstoke from *Collected Poems* by William Butler Yeats. Copyright 1940 by Georgie Yeats, renewed 1968 by Bertha Georgie Yeats.

Figure 4-2: Jim Jackson. Figure 4-3: Drs. Phyllis and Eberhard Kronhausen. Figure 4-4: top, from *Men and Apes* by R. and D. Morris © 1966, by permission of Mrs. Ramona Morris; bottom, Jim Jackson. Figure 4-5: Laird Sutton, Institute for the

Advanced Study of Human Sexuality.

Figure 5-1: adapted from A. C. Kinsey et al., *Sexual Behavior in the Human Male* (W. B. Saunders, 1948).

Figure 6-1: top, Christa Armstrong, Photo-Researchers, Inc.; bottom, Bob Adelman, Magnum.

Chapter 7. Fig. 7-1 from Milton Diamond, "Human Sexual Development: Biological Foundations for Social Development" in F. A. Beach, ed., *Human Sexuality in Four Perspectives,* © 1976, 1977 by the Johns Hopkins University Press. Reprinted by permission of the publisher, The Johns Hopkins University Press.

Figure 7-2: left, Courtesy of Med Com; right, M. Diamond. Figure 7-4: top, Jeff Albertson, Stock, Boston; bottom, Guy Gillette, Photo-Researchers, Inc. Figure 7-5: Danny Lyon, Magnum.

Figure 8-1: Massachusetts Dept. of Public Health. Figure 8-2: Massachusetts Dept. of Public Health. Figure 8-3: left, Camera MD; right, Massachusetts Dept. of Public Health. Figure 8-4: left, Camera MD; right, Massachusetts Dept. of Public Health.

Chapter 9. Fig. 9-1 adapted from A. C. Kinsey et al., *Sexual Behavior in the Human Male,* p. 200. (W. B. Saunders, 1948). Reprinted by permission of the Institute for Sex Research.

98729

Figure 9-2: top, The Granger Collection, bottom right, from "Attempts to Modify Penile Erection." by Montjoy © 1974 *The Psychological Record,* by permission of the publisher. Figure 9-4: left, *Boccacio 70;* top, Jim Jackson; bottom, Burk Uzzle, Magnum.

Chapter 10. "A Boy's Puberty" reprinted with permission of Macmillan Publishing Co., Inc. from *Manchild in the Promised Land* by Claude Brown. Copyright © Claude Brown, 1965. "A Girl's Puberty" excerpted from *Anne Frank: Diary of a Young Girl.* Copyright 1952 by Otto H. Frank. Reprinted by permission of Doubleday & Company, Inc. and Vallentine, Mitchell & Co. Ltd.

Chapter 12. Fig. 12-3 adapted from A. C. Kinsey et al., *Sexual Behavior in the Human Female,* p. 488. (W. B. Saunders, 1953). Reprinted by permission of the Institute for Sex Research.

Figure 12-1: top left, Wide World Photos; top right, UPI; bottom left, right, Steve Dain. Figure 12-2: The Granger Collection. Figure 12-4: top left, Photo-Researchers, Inc.; bottom left, Magnum; top right, Joel Gordon; bottom right, Martin A. Levick, Black Star.

Chapter 13. "somewhere i have never travelled, gladly beyond . . ." is reprinted from *Viva, Poems by E. E. Cummings,* with the permission of Liveright Publishing Corporation and Granada Publishing Limited. Copyright 1931 and renewed in 1959 by E. E. Cummings, "23rd Street Runs into Heaven" from Kenneth Patchen, *Collected Poems.* Copyright 1939 by New Directions Publishing Corporation. Reprinted by permission of New Directions. "For Anne Gregory" and "A Last Confession" reprinted with permission of Macmillan Publishing Co., Inc., M. B. Yeats, Miss Anne Yeats, and the Macmillan Co. of London and Basingstoke from *Collected Poems* by William Butler Yeats. Copyright 1933 by Macmillan Publishing Co., Inc., renewed 1961 by Bertha Georgie Yeats. "may i feel said he . . ." is reprinted from *No Thanks* by E. E. Cummings, Edited by George Firmage, with the permission of Liveright Publishing Corporation and Granada Publishing Limited. Copyright 1935 by E. E. Cummings. Copyright © 1968 by Marion Morehouse Cummings. Copyright © 1973, 1978 by Nancy T. Andrews. Copyright © 1973, 1978 by George James Firmage. "Passionate Love" is excerpted from "Seizure" in *Sappho,* Lyrics in the Original Greek with Translations by Willis Barnstone. Copyright © 1965 by Willis Barnstone. Reprinted by permission.

Figure 13-1: University of Wisconsin Primate Lab. Figure 13-2: top, Charles Harlbutt, Magnum; bottom left, Cary Wolinsky, Stock, Boston; bottom right, Cynthia Benjamins, Black Star. Figure 13-3: Jules Feiffer © 1974.

Figure 14-1: top left, Christa Armstrong, Photo-Researchers, Inc.; top right, John Veltri, Photo-Researchers, Inc.; bottom left, James H. Karales, Peter Arnold; bottom right, Franz Furst.

Figure 15-1: from *Love and Hate* by I. Eibl-Eibesfeldt, © 1970 by permission of the publisher R. Piper and Co., Verlag. Figure 17-3: Henri Cartier-Bresson, Magnum.

Figure 18-1: Dr. Ryuzo Yanagimachi, University of Hawaii. Figure 18-2: left, Dr. David Philip, Rockefeller University; right, Dr. Ryuzo Yanagimachi, University of Hawaii. Figure 18-6: top, Bob Combs, Photo-Researchers, Inc.; bottom left, Elizabeth Hamlin, Stock, Boston; bottom right, Jean-Claude LeJeune, Stock, Boston. Figure 18-7: left, Lawrence Frank, Black Star; right, Buddy Mays, Black Star.

Chapter 19. Fig. 19-4 courtesy of Ortho Pharmaceutical Corporation, Raritan, N.J.

Page 425: Reproduced by Special Permission of *Playboy* magazine, copyright © 1973 by Playboy. Figure 20-2: The Bettmann Archive.

Figure 21-2: top, Franz Furst; middle, Louis Goldman, Photo-Researchers; bottom, Marvin E. Newman, Woodfin Camp & Assoc. Figure 21-3: top, Ed Lettau, Photo-Researchers, Inc.; bottom left, Charles Gatewood; bottom right, Ellis Herwig, Stock, Boston.

Figure 22-1: Leif Skoogfors, Woodfin Camp & Assoc. Figure 22-2: left top, left bottom, The Granger Collection; right top, Sherry Suris, Photo-Researchers, Inc.; right bottom, Martin A. Levick, Black Star. Figure 22-3: top left, The Granger Collection; top right, Michael Hanulak, Photo-Researchers, Inc., bottom, Elliot Erwitt, Magnum.

*Love and thanks
to our wives, parents, and children,
whose generous decisions
have helped us so much
in writing this book.*

Foreword

A decade ago college courses devoted to sexuality were uncommon. More common were courses on marriage and the family under the aegis of the sociology or home economics department. Sex was usually discussed in these courses, but with rare exceptions it was overly intellectualized and sterilized. Though it is hard to imagine sex as dull, it often was. It was not relevant to students' lives, to their current or anticipated sexual decisions.

Since then courses on human sexuality have proliferated, increasing the need for superior textbooks. What I found in *Sexual Decisions* are two things: sexual information is organized more clearly than in other texts and it is presented in such a way as to provoke in the reader an inner dialogue about his or her feelings and attitudes. The title of the book asserts the authors' aim to engage each reader in a review of sexual behaviors in which choices or options are available. Students are far more interested in these nodal points of sexual behavior than they are in the facts of sexual plumbing, though goodness knows plenty of misinformation about *that* is abroad and requires correction, and this textbook does that, too, and does it well. But more important to students are the ethical choices, weighing consequences and determining the impact on oneself and others of one decision or another. The authors highlight the

choices that face every human being, and students will appreciate this emphasis.

Fundamentally, in any sexual situation, intelligent, responsible, satisfactory, and, yes, pleasurable sexual decisions are formed out of a background of information that feeds a person the correct cues. The information presented here has been researched by two scholars in the biological and behavioral sciences. Their backgrounds allow them to integrate a great variety of disciplines, adding to our understanding of a complex subject. We cannot understand sexual behavior without possessing a basic knowledge of its biological underpinnings. Animal behavior and experimentation as a reconnaissance arm of human inquiry must be included as must psychology, for we must know about the interplay of thoughts, feelings, attitudes, and behavior. The individual is a member of a society, so sociology and anthropology make important contributions. The most important aspects of sex are couple-related, so we have to know how sex affects relationships with others and how love, intimacy, bonding, and marriage affect sex. Ethics, theology, philosophy, and the law also touch on sexuality. To integrate these disciplines, these different perspectives, is a difficult assignment, but one the authors have carried out admirably.

While I have made some general comments

on the splendid way in which the authors have integrated material from so many diverse sources, and have expressed my belief that the text will help the student greatly in learning about sexuality, I have said little about the text's specific content. I would like to draw attention to four subjects: theories of sexual development, couples, love, and homosexuality.

Ordinarily, theories of psychosexual development are presented one dimensionally, emphasizing one viewpoint, whether psychoanalytic or sociological, cognitive or behavioral. The authors of *Sexual Decisions* have avoided that trap. They have outlined the major theories, giving the research findings that support or detract from each theory. This is an excellent aid to the student.

Textbooks on sexuality often lack a section on couples and marriage, as if sex is dissociated from bonding or coupling. Mistakenly, the emphasis is on the individual rather than on the interactive patterns that affect sex so profoundly. Sexual dysfunction occurs as a consequence of disharmony between two people far more often than it causes disharmony, although after a while a vicious cycle results. This textbook takes this fact into account, and explores the dynamics of relationships in depth.

Along with the chapter on relationships is a chapter dealing with a neglected ingredient of relationships, love. Rarely do textbooks on sexuality devote so much space to love and its myriad meanings. By and large scientists have confused the subject. Recognizing this, the authors have turned to literary sources, acknowledging that great writers' insights into love are more penetrating than those of scientists or other academics. This contribution of Diamond and Karlen alone is worth reading.

These days, homosexuality is a difficult subject to treat dispassionately. No treatment of the subject will please everyone. The authors have presented the subject in considerable detail and with an excellent review of the literature. More importantly, they have presented it with fairness and sensitivity.

I have written of the value of this book for college students. While they may be the primary audience, the book will also be helpful as a basic text for students in the health professions—medicine, nursing, social work—as well as for those graduate students learning to become marital and sex therapists. I do not wish to exclude the general reader—the intelligent reader who wishes to be well informed on a subject vital to everyone's well-being. That reader will find this book informative, extremely well written, and certain to grab his or her attention.

Harold I. Lief

Professor of Psychiatry and
Director, Marriage Council of Philadelphia
University of Pennsylvania School of Medicine

Preface:
Our Approach

Sexuality is part of being human, a complex potential we all develop to some degree. The kind and degree of development depend on one's biological inheritance and psychological and social experience. Many people do not reach their full potentials: they cannot engage in sexual and sex-related activities with satisfaction for themselves and their partners. Or they may act without seeing the possible consequences for themselves and society.

Too often, interest in human sexuality centers on personal and social problems—population control, venereal disease, illegitimacy, and rape. Such concern is quite justified, but most people are more interested in day-to-day sexual expression and close relationships. The study of politics does not center on war, nor the study of economics on bankruptcy. The study of sex should center not only on problems but on daily feelings, acts, and decisions.

We make decisions about sex-related matters every day. Some are minor, others have great personal, interpersonal, or social consequences, and they involve deep needs. We hope to offer information and perspectives people can use in making their decisions as intelligent, prudent, and satisfying as possible.

Too many sexual decisions are made under stress and without knowledge of the facts, options, and consequences. No one recommends

such choices in politics, in economics, or even in buying a car; we see no reason to be content with them in sexual matters. We hope to present a background for better decision making, and information that helps one become a more satisfied and satisfying sexual individual and partner, sensitive to the needs of oneself, of others, and of society.

Many texts on sexuality closely follow the borders of the disciplines on which they draw. The biological aspects of sex are presented as if they had no psychological implications, and the psychological and social aspects as if they had no physical limits. In life, the biological, psychological, and social aspects of sex are intertwined; we think they should be integrated as much as possible in a text. A biological statement about breast size or penis size has psychological and social implications, and attitudes about contraception must deal with physical realities. We try to discuss such aspects together, believing that an interdisciplinary view of sexuality can broaden students' approaches to human behavior and values—perhaps even enlarge their views of health, biology, psychology, sociology, anthropology, ethics, and other disciplines.

If we organize some material in new ways, it is because we believe new models are needed. For instance, in discussing anatomy, we distinguish the reproductive system (organs involved in procreation) from the sexual system (organs usually thought of as erotic). Obviously the oviducts are part of the reproductive system but not of the sexual system, and the mouth is part of the sexual system but not of the reproductive system. We also try a new model in our discussion of love, using psychological, evolutionary, historical, literary, and cross-cultural perspectives, and addressing common questions many people in our society ask.

We also offer information on such important concerns as orgasm, sexual play and techniques, marriage and family, sex roles, and relationships—each of which is ignored or slighted in some texts. We assume that most readers who want information on human sexuality will welcome special attention to these subjects. And we discuss what is normal and what is unusual in sexual behavior, which developmental patterns and behaviors are typical, and a variety of ethical positions. In doing so, we draw on a wide range of disciplines, to aid both understanding and individual decision making.

Our references are by no means exhaustive. We give sources for all data and for material that often rouses interest or debate. Since our task is essentially to synthesize and integrate what is known and believed about sexuality, some stated views and conclusions are ours and do not necessarily reflect the interpretations of others.

We begin each chapter with questions, some common and some too rarely asked. At the end of each chapter, we suggest questions and subjects for discussion that involve basic information and common sexual decisions. These, we hope, will allow readers to review the material in the chapter, to explore how they might react to real situations and, on the basis of growing knowledge and experience, make the decisions that are best for them.

The word "best" raises questions of values, ethics, and even legality. We present these issues as part of the groundwork for decision making. We discuss different moral and ethical views, but usually avoid taking a stand in favor of any moral or ethical school of thought. If we have a consistent position, it is that one should try to understand the roots and consequences of a sexual situation, and that this is best helped by education, not indoctrination. We believe that

---

I lose my respect for the man who can make the mystery of sex the subject of a coarse jest, yet when you speak earnestly and seriously on the subject, is silent.

—Henry David Thoreau,
"Writings of Henry David Thoreau" (1906)

I would rather have all the risks which come from free discussion of sex than the great risks we run by conspiracy of silence.

—Dr. C. G. Lang,
Archbishop of Canterbury

---

each adult, given a full range of facts and values, can make decisions suitable to himself or herself; if someone else makes a different decision, it is a subject for inquiry and discussion, not necessarily for moral judgment. Especially in our pluralistic society, the alternative to responsible personal decisions is to make sexual watchdogs of the state or of each other. We find it ambitious enough to hope for decisions based on knowledge and responsibility.

This is not to say that we, the authors, do not have our own views. Where we have strong convictions, we present them. But as information accumulates and time passes, individuals and society change. We have seen our own and others' views alter. We hope that what we offer about sexuality provides tools for examining and evaluating social and individual change, without preaching or proselytizing.

Furthermore, we do not agree on all points: no two people could possibly do so on all the matters raised in a comprehensive book on human sexuality. We will share these differences with the reader when honesty and relevance demand. In fact, we hope that the occasional dialogue between us will show students how writers in any field continue to examine and debate issues, as their readers do.

The book begins in Part I with a brief discussion of the scope and functions of sexuality and with an introduction to the study of sex and to the concept of sexual decision making. The book goes on to five major areas of sexual interest—the person (Part II), sexual behavior (Part III), the couple (Part IV), reproduction (Part V), and society (Part VI).

Part I, The Foundation, presents the foundations of sexology—the scientific study of sex-uality. Then it shows how sex research can be evaluated and how knowledge can be applied in making decisions (Sexual Learning and Decision Making).

Part II, The Person, explores the body (The Sexual System), its functions (Sexual Responses and Mechanisms, Orgasm), and development as a male or female (Sexual Development). This section also discusses the effects of drugs, hormones, and alleged aphrodisiacs (Sex-Active Substances) and of physical illness (Physical Health and Dysfunction).

Part III, Sex Behavior, introduces methods and concepts of studying sex behavior and contains chapters on Autoeroticism, Early Genital Behavior, and on the most common forms of Adult Genital Behavior. The section concludes with a chapter covering Other Sex Behaviors.

Part IV, The Couple, presents chapters meant to clarify decisions about emotional and sexual relationships (Love, Relationships and Marriage, Sexual Techniques). Another chapter, Psychosexual Health and Dysfunction, discusses both individual and interpersonal concerns.

Part V, Reproduction, offers chapters on The Reproductive System, Reproduction, and Sex Without Reproduction. These subjects involve some of the most important sexual decisions individuals and couples make, decisions that bring far-reaching changes in one's own life, affect and are affected by major social institutions, and may involve bringing a new person into the world.

Part VI, Society, presents sexuality in a broader setting. Chapters on What Societies Say and on Gender Roles place our society's sexual attitudes and behaviors in historical and cross-cultural perspectives. The final chapter, The Law, Morality, and Ethics, discusses the psychological and social consequences of sexual decision making.

In life, these five areas often overlap, but we think the arrangement has some merit both conceptually and as a learning device.

Sex can be a serious matter. It can also be fun. We have tried for balance in tone and sources; to achieve this, we have drawn on a variety of literary and artistic material, items from the press, and our own and others' observations. All of this is presented as simply and straightforwardly as possible, for we feel that any book, especially one about so important a part of life, should be clear and enjoyable.

Our comments would not be complete without acknowledgment of those who have reviewed all or part of the manuscript and provided constructive suggestions. We wish to thank John Delamater, University of Wisconsin; Alan G. Glaros, Wayne State University; Fred Humphrey, University of Connecticut; Roger Libby, University of Massachusetts; Harold I. Lief, University of Pennsylvania; Gerhard Neubeck, University of Minnesota; Peter A. Wish, Framingham State University.

To accompany *Sexual Decisions*, we have developed a manual for instructors with a variety of discussion and text questions, reading and film suggestions, and student projects.

Brief Contents

Contents

Part I · The Foundation

Part II The Person

Part III

Sex Behavior

Part IV   The Couple

Part V   Reproduction

Part VI Society

Part I

The Foundation

This section lays the foundation for understanding and using sexology as a science. First we present the scope of human sexuality, its pervasiveness, and its many functions and meanings. Then we show how sexology has developed as a scientific field and present sex research and education in a historic context. After this background, we show how sexology can be a practical aid in making everyday decisions. We also discuss some ways to conceptualize sexuality, the methods of sexology, the interpretation of data, and social and scientific aspects of decision making.

1

The Scope of Sexuality

The Meanings of "Sex"

Our society is in debate: is there or is there not a sexual revolution? Is increasing openness about sex a blessing or a curse? Have gender roles changed too much or too little? Is sexual permissiveness making relationships better or worse? More and more people, whatever their views, express a desire to know more about every aspect of human sexuality. The result has been a flood of books, films, and television programs on whether to do "it," how to do "it," how not to catch "it"—on everything from rape to roles to rare sexual variations. Despite all the discussion, it remains difficult to distinguish opinion and fantasy from fact.

When people hear the word sex, what usually comes to mind is genital play, coitus, or reproduction. But consider what sex means in the following sentences.

1. "Do you believe in *sex* before marriage?" Sex means coitus, whether done for love, for pleasure, or for both.
2. "*Sex* is for making babies." Here sex means that coitus is justified only by reproduction.
3. "That's a *sexy* dress." In this sentence, sex means erotic appeal.
4. "There shall be no *sex* discrimination." Here sex denotes both biological sex (being

male or female) and gender role (what society expects of males and females).
5. "His *sexual* feelings were strong." Here sex means a drive or motivating force.
6. "Is she homo*sexual* or hetero*sexual?*" In this case, sex means orientation in erotic and love partners.
7. "*Sex* education should be given in schools." Here sex may include anatomy, physiology, development, reproduction, love, coitus, venereal disease—almost anything involving eroticism, reproduction, or gender.

These are only some of the meanings of sex; obviously a concise definition hides more than it clarifies. In the wider and more accurate sense, sex means all the physical, emotional, and social implications of being male or female.

Sexual expression is, of course, basic to reproduction, but reproduction fails to account for most sexual activity—masturbation, viewing pornography, much social behavior, and even most coitus. If the only purpose of sex were reproduction, nonmarital and even marital coitus would be far less frequent. Coitus after menopause and by sterile couples would not occur; neither would homosexuality or prostitution. The uses of sexual expression are so numerous and important that without it, life would be simpler and unimaginably drearier.

3

The Functions of Sex

Thinking of sex as any action or interaction that rises from being male or female, consider these functions:

Sex for pleasure. To most of us, there is an inherent reward in genital response and in much body contact and sexual fantasy.

Sex for tension release. After satisfying erotic experiences, most people feel deep relaxation, a relief from tension both sexual and nonsexual. Coitus and masturbation are often used to release tensions arising from school, work, or home.

Sex in barter. Sex is often exchanged for nonsexual gains, from short-run material rewards such as a date, dinner, gift, or prestige to long-run rewards such as companionship and economic, social, and emotional security. Sex is often bartered for love.

Sex in commerce. Prostitution is the most obvious example. Sex is also used in advertising as an inducement to buy goods or services.

Sex for love. Many people consider love the only justification for coitus. Certainly love helps make it deeply rewarding. Today, our society generally asumes that sex will follow love. In our past and in other societies, especially where marriages were arranged, sex was thought a way to help *create* love.

Sex for companionship. We are gregarious creatures, and friends may share many things. Erotic exchanges often express or enhance companionship; sometimes they simply drive away loneliness and help someone make it through the night.

Sex as duty or obligation. Coitus is seen virtually everywhere as a marital right, and marriage counselors often hear, "I do my duty" and "I oblige my spouse."

Sex as a weapon or reward. If someone wants coitus, a potential partner can give it as a reward or withold it as a punishment, openly or indirectly using it as a means of control.

Sex as recreation. Sex can be a game with no goal but pleasure. Some view this disapprovingly as hedonism; others approve it as liberated humanism. As in many contact sports, people are sometimes hurt—for instance, if the encounter is merely fun for one partner but a serious involvement for the other, or when partners play by different rules.

Sex to affirm gender identity. People have neuter identity only in theory, and sexual acts and relationships can help confirm one's sense of maleness or femaleness, in others' eyes and one's own.

Sex for ego enhancement or for status. A satisfying sexual encounter gives most people a strong feeling of general ego enhancement. They feel more successful sexually and in a larger sense, as individuals. This can come not only from receiving pleasure but from giving it. Sex may also confer prestige—if one has many lovers, is wanted by many people, or catches a partner with high status.

Sex for intimacy. A sexual encounter can produce a kind or level of intimacy unattainable any other way. Many people look to coitus to establish or cement intimacy and trust.

Sex for communication. A look, touch, or caress can say things that words cannot. Sexual contact can be used to express feelings, to bridge a gap between people, or to cement a relationship. Like other kinds of communication, it can also be misused, be misunderstood, or reveal things one didn't intend to reveal.

Sex can be a vehicle for these and many other emotions and needs, from lust and power to tenderness and joy. Any need or motive may predominate on a given occasion, but several may act simultaneously. Sometimes they are contradictory, as when a person uses sex as a reward and wants tenderness and understanding in return. We believe that no purpose or motive is necessarily better or more mature than another.

Sex as Love

Sex is a biological expression of love. If the sexual act is accompanied by feelings of hostility or contempt for the sexual partner, this ambivalence denotes the dissociation of the individual's conscious feelings from his instinctive behavior.

—Alexander Lowen, *Love and Orgasm* (1967)

Sex Without Love

Love and sex are sometimes mutually exclusive. Deep love does not necessarily ensure good sex, and sex may sometimes be more erotic without love.

—Arnold A. Lazarus

Sex for Love

"And do you love me?" she said, placing her hand around his swollen sex. "Do you really still love me?"

He did not have the courage at that moment to provoke a scene, he was resigned to avow anything—and Paula knew it. "Yes, I do."

"Do you belong to me?"

"To you alone."

"Tell me you love me, say it."

"I love you."

She uttered a long moan of satisfaction. He embraced her violently, smothered her mouth with his lips, and to get it over with as quickly as possible immediately penetrated her. . . .

When finally he fell limp on Paula, he heard a triumphant moan. "Are you happy?" she murmured.

"Of course."

"I'm so terribly happy!" Paula exclaimed, looking at him through shining tear-brimmed eyes. He hid her unbearably bright face against his shoulder.

—Simone de Beauvoir, *The Mandarins* (1956)

Conceptual Schemes

Progressive and Parallel Levels

One way to approach a complex subject is to divide it into manageable areas, examine them one at a time, and then try to create an overview and synthesis. For instance, one can divide human sexuality into areas of *increasing complexity.* In this book, we consider first the individual, then the couple, the family, and society. Each area adds to knowledge of the next; understanding individuals helps one understand how couples interact, which helps one understand a family and society.

Another way is to examine *parallel levels* of equal complexity, such as sexual patterns, sexual mechanisms, sexual identity, sexual orientation, and reproduction (Diamond, 1973, 1977b). Any aspect of an individual's, a couple's, or a society's sexuality—from behavior to individual and social attitudes—can be described in these terms. Later we will deal with these areas in detail; here let us consider them briefly.

Sexual Patterns. These are behaviors that result from being male or female. Many sex-related patterns (gender roles) are related to biological sex differences, such as physical strength. These patterns are clear in nontechnological societies, where men most often do the heaviest and most dangerous work, such as hunting and fighting, and women do other kinds of labor, such as planting and child care. Though these patterns are sometimes not as striking in developed societies, they still exist. However, some behaviors that distinguish males and females are socially learned. Some

are public, such as choices of clothes, work, play, and social interaction. Others, such as choice of coital positions, are private. Still others, such as erotic fantasies, are still more private. Some, such as which sex should wear a skirt, seem purely symbolic rather than functional.

Sexual Mechanisms. These are physiological processes involved in sexual arousal, coitus, and orgasm. Some mechanisms are obviously sexual, such as erection of the penis or the nipples, vaginal wetting ("lubrication"), pelvic thrusting, orgasm, and ejaculation. They can be affected by physiological factors, such as aging, fatigue, nutrition, hormones, and drugs. Although innate, these mechanisms are also influenced by personal experiences and social learning. For example, being stroked on the inside of the thigh may lead to penile erection or vaginal wetting, but lack of privacy or an upsetting word can inhibit the response.

Sexual Identity. This conviction that one is male or female develops very early in life and is deep and persistent. Sexual identity usually corresponds to biological sex, but it should be distinguished from gender role. Society and an individual may disagree on which behaviors and traits are masculine or feminine, but this does not affect sexual identity. A nurturant male maintains his male identity, even if society calls his behavior feminine. Even if society considers a male effeminate, he and society know he is biologically male; and a woman considered masculine remains female.

Sexual Orientation. A small proportion of people are attracted not to people but to objects *(fetishism)* or to other species *(bestiality),* but

6

almost everyone, at some time in life, is attracted to another person as a love or sex partner. Whether the partner is of the same or the other sex is called sexual orientation. A minority of people have homosexual (same-sex) rather than heterosexual (other-sex) relationships; some have both, simultaneously or at different times in their lives. Societies are almost always concerned with orientation and with a sexual partner's age, race, religion, social class, educational class, and life-style.

Sexual Reproduction. Western society has long publicly considered reproduction the chief legitimate reason for coitus (although there has been a more permissive informal standard). There is some disagreement about whether reproduction is a single instinct in humans, but procreative capacity—the ability to have and rear children—is entwined with many other aspects of sexuality. Reproduction directly involves such matters as whether, how, and why people procreate; what procreation means to them; how they control their reproductive potential; and how they deal with problems of sterility and overpopulation.

Behavior, Attitudes, and Knowledge

Another way to organize the study of sexuality is to distinguish what people *know* from what they *feel* and what they *do*. Behavior, attitudes, and knowledge are not always in concert. A couple may know many scientific facts about premarital coitus, believe it to be wrong, but do it nonetheless. A woman may know little about abortion, approve of it for others, but not seek it herself. One must also distinguish covert from overt values; a person may intellectually and publicly approve of open marriage but object strongly when it involves people close to him; or he may secretly condone such an arrangement for himself while condemning it in public. The reasons for such disparities may be complex or simple, hidden or obvious. Were we to understand fully the relationships among sexual knowledge, overt and covert attitudes, and behavior, we would know immensely more about human sexuality.

Biology, Psychology, and Culture

One popular way to organize information on sexuality is to divide it into the academic fields from which the information is drawn: biology and medicine, psychology and psychiatry, sociology and anthropology (Katchadourian and Lunde, 1975). This has the advantage of presenting consistent data. Biological material is compared with other biological material, not psychological or social findings. But sexology involves many disciplines with different perspectives and concerns. For example, in studying sexual orientation, a biologist may want to understand how heterosexual and homosexual patterns develop in evolution and how they are or are not adaptive to our species. A psychologist's primary concern may be how an individual becomes heterosexual or homosexual, and how he or she copes with other individuals and society. A sociologist may be most interested in how sexual orientations affect society and are affected by it. Each of these approaches may seem to exclude the others; actually, all can add to a comprehensive understanding of the many aspects of sexology.

Overview

Sexuality involves the whole fabric of human feelings, thoughts, and actions as they affect and are affected by society. We all see ourselves as males and females, are affected socially and emotionally by our gender roles, and develop erotic and reproductive patterns. Some people argue that sex, unlike other basic behaviors, such as eating, can be postponed or even avoided. However, even those who exist without coitus cannot avoid being sexual in other ways. The parallel with eating is a good one: one can exist without eating meat or by eating one meal a day or five, but eat one must. People may restrict or expand their sexuality, but sexual they are.

There is no general agreement on how to study sexuality. The terms sex and sexuality have myriad meanings and implications, and sex serves so many functions that people are bound to disagree about how to approach it. Furthermore, our information about sexuality comes from many sources, each with its own viewpoint and biases.

We think it best to seek an integrated, interdisciplinary view of sexuality, for knowledge about sex is used in making decisions without regard for theoretical categories. For convenience, we will present sexuality in areas of increasing complexity; when it is useful, we will also consider parallel areas. But however information is presented, the reader is encouraged to relate it to other knowledge and to the realities of sexual life and sexual decisions, past, present, and future.

2

Sexual Learning and Decision Making

Is sex education necessary? Is it new?

How do most people learn about sex?

How do ideas about sexuality today differ from those of the past?

Has there been a sexual revolution?

Are all sex studies reliable? Which ones can I use in making a sexual decision?

What important sex research and sex education remains to be done?

At first thought, a text on human sexuality seems superfluous. Since humans, like other creatures, have reproduced for millions of years without help from texts, a book such as this might be merely a formal exercise. But the idea of simple animal sex drive is misleading. Most higher animals need some learning and experience to court, mate, and raise their young, and human sexuality far exceeds theirs in extent and complexity. In fact, people have always been taught about sex, and even told what sort of decisions to make.

Learning about Sex

In sexually permissive societies, learning about sex is gradual and open. Young children see physical sex differences and may be allowed to experiment with themselves and each other. They hear adults discuss sex and perhaps witness sexual and sex-related acts, from petting and coitus to childbirth and childrearing. Adolescent boys may be initiated by experienced women, girls by experienced men.

Restrictive societies pass on such information later in life, in measured amounts and often covertly. Through much of Western history, sexual knowledge and activity have been discouraged or forbidden except within marriage, and kept as far as possible from the eyes, ears, and reach of the young. But this, too, is sex education: it teaches that there are sexual secrets to be learned, and that they are important yet shameful. This makes learning about sex sporadic, furtive, and often rooted more in myth than in observation and experience.

Some societies have dispensed information on sexual hygiene and erotic techniques at puberty. In Japan, instruction was once given at marriage, through "pillow books," so called because they were placed beneath the pillows of bridal beds, which gave erotic information in words and pictures. The Chinese produced books of sexual instruction some 2,000 years ago. About 1,500 years ago in India, Vatsyayana (1963) composed the *Kama Sutra* (Kama is the Hindu god of love, a *sutra* is a text), full of ingenious elaborations of love-

9

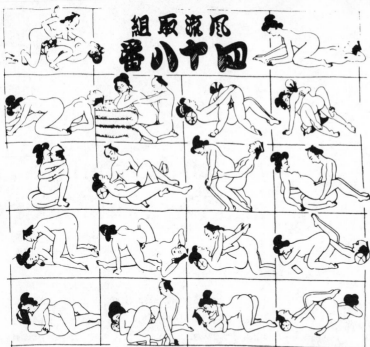

風流艶組
四十八番

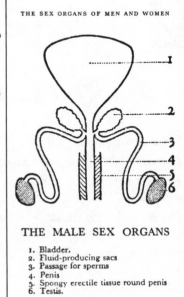

THE MALE SEX ORGANS

1. Bladder.
2. Fluid-producing sacs
3. Passage for sperms
4. Penis
5. Spongy erectile tissue round penis
6. Testis.

CHAPTER VII.

THE ANATOMY AND PHYSIOLOGY OF GENERATION IN WOMAN.

SO far, our thoughts have been with the choice of a perfect union between the man and woman—a union from which the birth and growth of love so surely follows. Yet a something is necessary to the higher perfecting of this union, and the complete elevation and intense enjoyment of this love; and this something is a baby—typical, in its beauty, and purity, and innocence, of the perfect joining together of the man and woman, and of an intensified peace, happiness and love that angels might envy, and that approaches in its exercise the very gates of Paradise.

To a right carrying out of this desire for a new existence, a knowledge of the anatomy and physiology of the reproductive system is essential; and a thorough study of these

10

Figure 2-1 / *Every society teaches about sexuality, both directly and by implication. In Japan, books on erotic technique (top) were placed under the pillows of brides' beds; the message was that sexual pleasure should be learned, but only after marriage. Early in this century, many Western books spoke of coitus only as an act of reproduction (bottom left), and in presenting the sexual system (bottom right) left out parts people might recognize and enjoy.*

making. In the Arab world, in the eleventh century, Sheik Nefzaoui (1964) performed a similar service in *The Perfumed Garden.*

This century has seen a flood of "marriage manuals" and, more recently, sex manuals (with marriage optional). Few have the artistic charm of the best pillow books, and perhaps few are more accurate and helpful. We still leave most people's early learning about sex to chance—to children's imaginings and gossip and to fragments of fact and misinformation stolen from adult talk, books, and entertainment. It seems a poor start in an era of so many sexual choices and challenges.

Only a few generations ago, vast numbers of Americans and Europeans entered marriages arranged by their families or limited by the choices of small communities. Many wed in their middle teens and became parents soon after. An extended family of sisters, brothers, grandparents, uncles, and aunts might pass on a wealth of knowledge, folklore, and daily help. Today the majority of young people seek partners on their own and must resort to on-the-job learning about love, sexuality, marriage, and parenthood. The explosion of public talk about

sex may hinder as well as help, for it abounds with inaccuracies and contradictory urgings.

In our changing, pluralistic society, deciding about sex-related issues has obviously become a more complex part of life. It is not surprising that over the past century sexology has emerged as a science, seeking something beyond lore and muddled conviction. We will briefly review how sexual attitudes, behavior, and research have evolved, and now require that each person find his or her own path.

The Historical View

From Dogma to Science

If one compares the sexual behavior and rules of societies around the world (see chapter 20), Western society is not among the most restrictive or the most free (Ford and Beach, 1951). But throughout history, Western sexual restrictions have varied, becoming more or less narrow, their enforcement more or less zealous (Karlen, 1971). This century's permissive trend has led some historians to call our restrictive past Victorian, puritanical, or Judeo-Christian. None of these terms is accurate. The outlook we call Victorian existed millenia before Queen Victoria; the Puritans had no monopoly on scarlet letters; the mainstream of Judaism has in many ways affirmed sexual expression; and the Christian view of sex has changed many times.

Many early Christian writers made paganism synonymous with pleasure seeking. Actually, their pagan predecessors ranged from sensual to ascetic (Bullough, 1976; Karlen, 1971). Some of the religions that competed with early Christianity called for celibacy, even castration;

11

others allowed prostitution and homosexual acts in their temples (G. Taylor, 1954). Judaism had a few ascetic splinter groups, but its Old Testament celebrated the beauty of the body and of sexual expression in marriage; it did not consider abstinence and virginity virtues in themselves (Patai, 1959).

Christianity became the dominant religion of the West and helped set its sexual code, but only after long debate. Some sects held extreme pro- or anti-sexual views. Apparently some included nudity and lovemaking in their rites, finding in the body and its pleasures a manifestation of the highest beauty and love (Brinton, 1959). Others believed that the soul reaches perfection by escaping from flesh and pleasure; they said even procreation could not justify sex, and the most zealous castrated themselves (Bullough, 1976). During the Middle Ages, a majority Christian view did emerge; it made chastity a moral ideal (although dissident sects have occasionally reappeared). The Western clergy were to be celibate; other Christians, unable to reach that goal, should accept Saint Paul's concession that it is better to marry than to burn. However, the only justification for sexual activity was reproduction; masturbation, adultery, oral-genital acts, coitus when conception is impossible, and homosexuality were all considered sins (T. Cole, 1966).

During the late Middle Ages, some of this dogma became civil law (Lea, 1966). Laws and ideals, of course, do not always reflect what people do. Premarital coitus, adultery, and homosexuality did occur, in some times and places rather commonly. The reurbanization of Europe, beginning in the late Middle Ages, changed many people's sex and family lives (Karlen, 1971). The modern state emerged and

started taking control of sex away from the church. People cautiously began to do research on the reproductive system.

The Reformation also modified views of sex and marriage. Martin Luther thought sexual impulse so strong that to attempt celibacy was to fall for a trick of the Devil. Marital sex might show our imperfection, he said, but "God winks at it!" (W. Cole, 1966). John Calvin went further, calling marital coitus "pure, honorable, and holy." The Puritans, in their return to Biblical fundamentals, praised marital love—and marital sex—with almost Hebraic enthusiasm. When a member of the Puritan First Church of Boston rejected coitus with his wife to punish himself for his sins, the congregation expelled him for unnatural and un-Christian behavior (E. Morgan, 1966).

Science and Sex

Scientists of the sixteenth century knew little more about human sexuality than had the ancient Greeks and Romans. Then the anatomy and physiology of the sexual and reproductive systems were slowly explored by Anton van Leeuwenhoek, Gabriello Fallopio, and others. During the seventeenth and eighteenth centuries, the microscope revealed that most higher plants and animals reproduce sexually, through the union of a sperm and an egg. But some felt that saying even flowers reproduced this way was blasphemous and obscene (Wendt, 1965). And the chief argument about human reproduction was whether the mythical homunculus—a fully formed human of sub-microscopic size—lay awaiting growth inside the sperm or the egg.

An extensive hunt for knowledge about

human sexuality did not begin till eighteenth-century utopian philosophers such as Jean Jacques Rousseau and Denis Diderot had called for both a return to nature and a leap toward science. They claimed that life could be perfected by liberal reform of love, sex, and marriage. Rousseau called for the end of arranged marriages and of love's contamination by money and property. Diderot (1956) imagined an erotic utopia in the South Seas that still seems radical today.

These thinkers took two important new attitudes. First, they cast aside the old belief that impulses, especially sexual ones, are destructive and must be controlled. Natural impulses, they said, are good and should be expressed; it is society's restriction that subverts human joy and perfection. At their most enthusiastic, they implied that every woe, from war to pimples, would vanish if sex were liberated from brittle custom and vengeful piety. They were the opposite numbers of the religionists who preached that rejecting sex brought one halfway to heaven.

Second, the "light" of the Enlightenment was a blend of reason and relentless optimism. No longer should poverty, plague, war, and inequality be considered facts of life, like the weather, or acts of God. Reason and science would study them, and feeling would set them right. This would also be true of sexual problems and discontents.

Sex in Utopia

PERMISSIVE UTOPIA

Is there anything so senseless as a precept that forbids us to heed the changing impulses that are inherent in our being? . . .

May a father sleep with his daughter, a mother with her son, a brother with his sister, a husband with someone else's wife? Why not? Marital fidelity is a will-of-the-wisp; modesty, demureness and propriety are a retinue of imaginary devices. The gap which divides a man from a woman would be crossed first by the more amorously inclined of the two.

Religious institutions have attached the labels "vice" and "virtue" to actions that are completely independent of morality. But the untamed heart will not cease to cry out against its oppressors.

—Denis Diderot, condensed from
*Supplement to Bougainville's
"Voyage"* (1772)

RESTRICTIVE UTOPIA

The groundwork of this corporeal beauty is nothing else but phlegm and blood and humor and bile . . . when you see a rag with any of these things on it, such as phlegm or spittle, you cannot endure looking at it; are you then in a flutter of excitement about the storehouses and repositories of these things?

—Saint John Chrysostom, *Letters to Theodore*
(fourth century)

In my flesh dwelleth nothing good. . . . It is good for a man not to touch a woman. Nevertheless . . . it is better to marry than to burn.

—Saint Paul, First Epistle to the Corinthians

In heaven there will be . . . no resumption of voluptuous disgrace between us.

—Tertullian, *To His Wife*
(third century)

The Victorian Period

Advocates of erotic joy were still a minority at the turn of the nineteenth century, and the West was about to enter the restrictive era that bears Victoria's name. The few scientific writings on sex at that time tended to equate traditional sin with medical sickness. Most were influenced by the first widely read secular work about sex in the Christian West, *Onania, or the Heinous Sin of Self-Pollution*, probably written around 1717 by an anonymous London quack. It went through eighty editions in a half century, only to be succeeded in popularity by a volume of similar title and views by Samuel Tissot (1760), the eminent Swiss physician to the Pope. Tissot made *Onania's* folklore conventional medical wisdom—that sexual "excess," especially sexual solitaire, lead to physical and mental ills from eye disease and tuberculosis to melancholy, impotence, perversion, imbecility, epilepsy, madness, and death (Comfort, 1970; Hare, 1962).

In the first half of the nineteenth century, the medical sex-information book became popular. It was usually an essay on the anatomy and physiology of the genitalia mixed with medical, religious, and ethical warnings against any sex acts but marital coitus, done in moderation. Unlike early clerics, who had called woman a temptress and hell the wages of sex, Victorians made sex a male monopoly and the price of lust illness. Dr. William Hammond, Surgeon General of the United States Army during the Civil War, said that nine-tenths of the time, "decent" women experience no sexual pleasure (Marcus, 1964). Men who expended much sperm were said to risk madness and death (Haller and Haller, 1974). We do not know

how many people agreed with these books, but probably a large number did.

Victorian pseudosexology had one positive result; it further established that human sexuality lay within the province of science. Until the nineteenth century, many offenses against sexual norms had been commonly considered the work of the devil (Foucault, 1973). Then, as the rudiments of psychiatry developed, courts began asking physicians whether sex offenders were criminals who should be jailed or victims of mental illness who needed treatment. This question prompted Richard von Krafft-Ebing's landmark book *Psychopathia Sexualis* (1965).

Krafft-Ebing, a German neurologist and psychiatrist, produced this ponderous volume in 1886; the case histories, from his own observations, were in Latin to protect the unlearned, and in many places sale was limited to physicians and jurists. But the contents soon became known, and people learned of cases of bizarre sexual behavior from ritualized sadism to rare fetishisms. It was the most peeped-at book of its time, and it set a new standard for studying sex. Krafft-Ebing was the first person to attempt a full review of sexual knowlege; then he related it to such important new fields as evolution, genetics, psychiatry, and social science, and welded all this into a comprehensive theory. Standardized observation and experiment still lay in the future, but sex had become the subject of interdisciplinary study.

Today Krafft-Ebing sounds thoroughly Victorian. He warned ominously against sexual excess, said that a normal woman feels little sexual desire, and gave the blessings of God and science to the mores of his social class and era. Nevertheless, *Psychopathia Sexualis* was a revolutionary work. It concluded that many uncommon sex behaviors were results of hereditary weakness and should be treated rather than punished, in that time a dangerously liberal position. Some people whose perversions Krafft-Ebing described were otherwise decent and respectable. They could no longer be merely objects of outrage, disgust, or dirty jokes; their conditions cried for the physician's understanding and care and for society's compassion.

Other researchers were going to work—Paolo Mantegazza in Italy, Jean Charcot in France, Albert Moll in Germany, Richard Burton in England, and others from Russia to Spain to the United States (Karlen, 1971). At the turn of the century, the Berlin physician Magnus Hirschfeld conducted the first large-scale study of sex behavior, a questionnaire survey of 10,000 people; he also formed an Institute for Sex Research in Berlin, the first organization of its kind. In England, the writer and physician Havelock Ellis had begun to publish his seven-volume *Studies in the Psychology of Sex* (1936). It surpassed Krafft-Ebing's book in scope and imagination, and it introduced several generations of English-speaking scientists and laymen to the study of sexuality.

Freud and the Twenties

In 1905, Viennese neurologist and psychiatrist Sigmund Freud produced the first edition of *Three Essays on the Theory of Sexuality*. This and his other writings changed Western thought as deeply as had the works of Darwin and Marx (for a fuller explanation of Freud's thought see chapter 7). Freud said that uncon-

scious sexuality lies behind much nonsexual behavior; that everyone has the potential for all sexual patterns; and that sexual feelings are crucial to human development from infancy on. The idea of childhood sexuality especially horrified people; the Victorians believed that sexual feelings emerged only at puberty, and mostly in males. Freud was called a madman, a sex fiend, a Viennese libertine. Even Ellis and many other sex researchers were hostile.

But Freud's work soon attracted followers. Karl Abraham, Carl Jung, Alfred Adler, Wilhelm Stekel, and other psychoanalysts contributed new observations and theories about sex; soon their accounts of curing sexual problems began appearing, and sex moved decisively from the theological framework of virtue and sin to the medical framework of sickness and health.

Much of society was ready to accept that change in the 1920s. The anti-Victorian reaction had already given birth to sexology in the upper-middle class and among scientists and social observers. Now massive social changes made that reaction, and sexology itself, public property. Those who have seen the sexual revolution of the Sixties and Seventies need only stretch their imaginations a bit to envision the possibly greater one of the Twenties. World War I had left disillusionment and hedonism in the United States and Europe. Great social changes had been building for decades—urbanization, mass education, greater social and economic independence for women. One after another, the radical causes of early anti-Victorianism became major social movements—a single sexual standard for men and women, birth control, divorce, eroticism in the arts and mass media.

15

THE SEVEN DEADLY WHIMS

NEW LIPS TO KISS
FREEDOM FROM CONVENTIONS
A NEW WORLD FOR WOMEN
NO MORE CHAPERONS
LIFE WITH A KICK IN IT
THE SINGLE MORAL STANDARD
OUR OWN LATCHKEYS

HOUSEWIVES ARE UNPAID SLAVE LABORERS!

TELL HIM WHAT TO DO WITH THE BROOM!!

Figure 2-2 / *A century of sexual revolution has seen a different emphasis at each peak of activity. Before 1920, women's fight for the vote held center stage (top, a suffragette struggles against arrest in London). By 1920, that battle had been won in the United States, and movie star Gloria Swanson (bottom left) was willing to be identified with the rising call for erotic emancipation. In 1970, another round began (bottom right), a widespread protest against traditional gender roles.*

In the United States, the urban, native-born children of rural and foreign parents felt a generation gap probably greater than any of later decades. Young people could live away from home, economically independent, seeking their own paths to love, sex, and marriage. The dating system and adolescent youth culture came into existence. Popular journalism, with only some exaggeration, portrayed "flaming youth" and "liberated women" who scorned traditional standards by drinking from flasks, snorting cocaine, spooning at shockingly early ages, and careening around at night with strangers in automobiles, which were sometimes called brothels on wheels.

One strong force for change was the feminist movement, which in a half century had been transformed from a radical-fringe effort into a strong social force. By the early Twenties, women could vote in the United States, the United Kingdom, and several other Western countries. The movement then turned increasingly to fighting for personal choice in birth control, divorce, and sexual conduct. Such women as Margaret Sanger, Marie Stopes, and

Elise Ottesen-Jensen helped make contraception, and sexuality in general, areas of greater personal choice for women.

As always, science both created and reflected social attitudes. Victorian physicians had said that unrestrained sex caused physical and mental disease. A century later, the idea was being reversed. In the Twenties, some doctors were saying that sexual repression created mental and physical ills. For instance, a French physician studied inmates of a Paris asylum and portentously announced that two-thirds of them were celibate (Karlen, 1971). The press popularized such ideas; many people now wanted to hear that science proved sex to be an instinct demanding satisfaction, a cause and a sign of health. They were accepting what sociologists would later call "permissiveness with affection"—the idea that love rather than marriage makes coitus legitimate (I. Reiss, 1967).

The most popular new guide to sex was *Ideal Marriage,* by the Dutch physician Theodoor Van de Velde (1930). It was not called *Ideal Sex;* the author wasn't sure he approved of coitus for widows, let alone those not yet married (Karlen, 1979). But he did suggest that couples keep their sexual relationship exciting with oral-genital and other sex play that many doctors still called perversions. He also said women not only could but *must* be sexually active, joyful, and orgasmic. Victorian gynecologists had called this pathological; Van de Velde, at the other extreme, claimed that every time a woman felt sexual excitement without reaching orgasm she suffered "injury to both body and soul." His emphasis on female orgasm and on extended, inventive sex play became a model for subsequent marriage manuals.

17

The Emergence of Modern Sexology

Modern Landmarks of Research

Sex research was barely becoming legitimate around 1920; it still was not respectable. Institutional backing had been almost entirely for research in such problem areas as prostitution and venereal disease. Then in 1921 the National Research Council of the National Academy of Science formed a Committee for Research in Problems of Sex (NAS-CRPS). It was financed largely by the Rockefeller Foundation and consisted of eminent physicians, psychologists, biologists, and anthropologists. For decades it backed important studies on subjects from marriage counseling to physiology, including the landmark research of Robert Yerkes, Edgar Allen, Frank A. Beach, William C. Young, and Alfred C. Kinsey (Aberle and Corner, 1953). It provided support to gynecologists, social workers, penologists, and psychologists; to sociologists and anthropologists studying childhood, adolescence, and the family around the world; and to researchers studying animal behavior. The NAS-CRPS disbanded after forty years, when government funding began making its support less necessary.

In the Thirties the revolution in sexual behavior almost stopped, but scientific and social changes continued. Sex education and planned parenthood were being adopted in many communities, and counseling for sex and marriage problems became part of health care and social services. An explosion of biological research produced new knowledge about reproduction, the neurohormonal system, and genetics. It seemed to some that an Enlightenment dream was coming true in science and society. Lewis

Terman (1939), an eminent psychologist and sex researcher, said in the late Thirties that if present trends continued, no American girl would reach the marriage bed a virgin in 1960. His prediction was off by almost 50 percent (see chapter 11). The work of Alfred C. Kinsey would soon show how many false assumptions about sex were widespread, how many questions were unanswered, and how much hostile resistance remained to sex research (Pomeroy, 1972).

Kinsey was a zoologist at Indiana University, and like many biology teachers, he was asked by students about human sexuality. When he sought answers, he learned that more was known about the sexual behavior of some insects than that of people. But this lack of knowledge had not prevented many experts from dispensing their guesses and convictions as facts. They labeled people normal, underactive, or hypersexual without knowing what was, in the statistical sense of the word, normal—what most people did.* In 1938 Kinsey began trying to find out.

Aided eventually by several collaborators (Paul Gebhard, Clyde Martin, and Wardell Pomeroy), Kinsey interviewed more than 18,000 people over two decades. The results were the most extensive, reliable studies of sex behavior ever done. *Sexual Behavior in the Human Male* (1948) and *Sexual Behavior in the Human Female* (1953) contained something to surprise everyone and discomfort many.

Kinsey learned that half the women in the

---

* It is very important to distinguish this from the other senses of the word "normal," which are "healthy" and "acceptable." The scientific meaning is "most common," without implications about health or sickness, right or wrong.

18

United States were nonvirgins at marriage; that one wife in four had coitus outside marriage; that about one man in ten had a significant amount of homosexual experience during his life; that some women's capacity for orgasm is greater than men's. He also showed that the startling range and variety of human sexuality—some people experiencing orgasm once or twice a year, others ten or twenty times a week—and the tendency to consider oneself more or less normal, account for a great deal of sexual dispute. Kinsey et al. (1948) concluded:

"The possibility of an individual engaging in sexual activity at a rate remarkably different from one's own is one of the most difficult for even professionally trained persons to understand."

When Kinsey began his work, some scientists showed timidity or disapproval, even said the results should not be published. But when the first volume appeared, it instantly became a best-seller and lowered the barriers against discussing sex in public. By its contents and the debate it provoked, Kinsey's work probably

---

Marriage Manuals:
From "Thou Shalt Not" to "Thou Must"

The sexual act is an exhausting one. . . . Locally there is an overexcitation, irritability, and possibly inflammation. The digestion becomes impaired, dyspepsia sets in, the strength is diminished, the heart has spells of palpitations.

—Henry G. Hanchett, *Sexual Health* (1887)

The frequency with which sexual intercourse can be indulged without serious damage to one or both of the parties depends [on] . . . constitutional stamina, temperament, occupation, habits of exercise, etc. Few should exceed the limit of once a week; while many cannot safely indulge oftener than once a month.

—Dr. R. T. Trall, *Sexual Physiology and Hygiene* (1897)

The sex instinct has other high purposes besides that of perpetuating the race, and sex relations may and should be indulged in as often as they are conducive to man's and woman's physical, mental and spiritual health.

—William J. Robinson, *Woman, Her Sex and Love Life* (1917)

When the wife does not secure an orgasm, she is left at a high peak of sexual tension. . . . Repeated disappointments may lead to headaches, nervousness, sleeplessness, and other unhappy symptoms of maladjustment.

—Oliver Butterfield, *Sexual Harmony in Marriage* (1964)

---

had more effect than any in the field since Freud's. Some scientists criticized Kinsey's research methods; others felt he was one of the century's greatest innovators (Pomeroy, 1972). Three decades of subsequent research have shown that he was accurate more often than not—considering the difficulty of his project, an extraordinary feat.

Some people objected to Kinsey's work on moral grounds; Claire Booth Luce used the odd phrase "statistical filth" (Geddes, 1954). These critics felt that since sex without love is wrong, so is the study of sex as "mere" behavior. Similarly, some scientists feared that Kinsey's "cold and clinical" data might morally or emotionally damage readers, perhaps encourage them to divorce sex from emotion (Geddes, 1954). They ignored the fact that emotional convictions about how sex should be had always prevented research on how it is. Kinsey did not consider emotion unimportant; he simply devoted himself to the staggering task of finding basic facts of behavior. To those who feared that his figures might damage the public, Kinsey et al. (1953) replied, "The restriction of sexual knowledge to a limited number of professionally trained persons, to physicians, to priests, or to those who can read Latin, has not sufficiently served the millions of boys and girls, men and women, who need such knowledge to guide them in their everyday affairs." A public-opinion poll showed that five out of six laymen approved of Kinsey's work.

Kinsey began observing sexual response, but the task was unfinished when he died in 1956. The effort was picked up by gynecologist William Masters and Virginia Johnson (first Masters's assistant, later his collaborator and his wife). They watched and measured sexual response, aided by new technology, including miniaturized equipment that allowed them to observe events within the vagina. Their book *Human Sexual Response* (1966) presented the first extensive description of sexual arousal and climax. Their *Human Sexual Inadequacy* (1970) showed how this knowledge had helped them develop new treatments for sexual problems. Their first book, like Kinsey's, brought some complaints about clinical dehumanizing of sex. But again much of the resistance subsided, and the findings were accepted as the best basic knowledge available.

To most people today, sex research means Kinsey, Masters and Johnson, and a handful of others. Their contribution, while great, is a small fraction of the important work in the field. Since the early Fifties, a new field loosely identified as sexology has been taking shape. Increasingly, more people bear the academic or professional label sexologist; since sexuality involves our bodies, minds, society, and species, its study includes sociology, anthropology, clinical and experimental psychology, psychiatry, animal behavior, biology, and dozens of subspecialties. Formal recognition of sexology as an interdisciplinary science arrived in 1979 with the formation of The American College of Sexologists, which develops standards for the certification of sexologists.

For two decades, research on sexuality has been extensive, and increasing acceptance of it is shown by Federal agencies, which are replacing private foundations as the chief sponsors. This blossoming of research coincided with the so-called sexual revolution of the Sixties and Seventies. The sociosexual changes of the Twenties had resumed. The women's movement, almost dormant for decades, again became an important social force. The mass media kept repeating that a new, liberated era was making youthful copulation and middle-age swinging the major national sports. The revolution was probably overstated; as in the Twenties, talk and attitudes shifted more than behavior. For instance, one study of college students (Freedman, 1965) revealed that only 59 percent of those who said they approved of premarital coitus had experienced it. But there have been significant changes (see chapters 10 and 11). More people now begin sexual activity earlier; divorce and perhaps extramarital coitus have increased; sexual activity by the unmarried is more accepted. Some religious groups have modified their views on sex and, like many legal and medical societies, suggested easing restrictions on sexual behavior between consenting adults. Some laws controlling abortion, contraception, and sex behavior have been changed. Sex and marriage counseling are now parts of many clergymen's training. A new sort of sex-information book has become popular, which says that sex need not be legitimized by love, let alone marriage.

The Present

One effect of these changes has been a widespread belief that sex research is ready to close its books. All is known, there has been a sexual revolution, and society is fully informed. But often this air of knowledgeability hides ignorance about basic sexual anatomy and physiology, myths about sexual behavior, and conflicts about relationships. Our society still has no fully effective programs to combat overpopulation and venereal disease, let alone complex problems of gender roles, relationships, and life

conduct. Much discussion and depiction of sex in the media ignores recent scientific knowledge and is more entertainment than information.

This residue of ignorance and problems shows in our crowded clinics and counseling offices, in continuing debates about gender roles, sex education, female orgasm, homosexuality, and unusual life styles, from open marriage to communes. Perhaps more than ever, people ask uneasily, "How should I feel and act to be a healthy, happy man or woman?" They seek help in making sexual decisions. It has been estimated that one out of six visits to a physician's office results directly or indirectly from a sex or marriage problem (Burnap and Golden, 1967). In 1971 Masters and Johnson estimated that despite a half century of sexology, education, and counseling, at least half the married people in this country live with some degree of sexual dysfunction.

Sex research has left its infancy, but is still in its youth and often difficult to finance. Still, research, teaching, and clinical work are continuing. The Institute for Sex Research, founded by Kinsey at Indiana University, continues under the direction of Professor Paul Gebhard, one of Kinsey's collaborators. Masters and Johnson continue their work in St. Louis. The international Society for the Scientific Study of Sex (SSSS), founded in the late 1950s, provides seminars and discussion and publishes *The Journal of Sex Research*. Research, teaching, and publishing efforts are being continued by The Sex Information and Education Council of the United States (SIECUS), The American Association of Sex Educators, Counselors, and Therapists (AASECT), The International Academy of Sex

Figure 2-3 / *One of the most dramatic changes in teaching human sexuality is "sexual attitude reassessment." In courses for undergraduates, medical students, and marital-enrichment groups, participants see multimedia presentations of the full range of sexual behaviors and relationships, such as the film above. Then they may discuss these in small groups led by experienced group leaders. This allows for consideration and discussion of sex behavior and provokes conscious examination of one's own attitudes and values.*

Research, Planned Parenthood, and many institutions and individuals in Great Britain, Scandinavia, Holland, Germany, Japan, Czechoslovakia, and a few other nations.

Formal Sex Education

We began this chapter by asking whether a book on human sexuality is necessary or even useful. We saw that human sexuality is uniquely complex, that all societies teach about it somehow, and that interdisciplinary study of it has been growing for a century. In our changing society, many people are seeking ways to obtain this knowledge; one sign is the steadily growing student demand for sexuality courses. Yet bitter conflict has recurred over whether or how to teach about sex.

Sex education has become widespread in the United States and in parts of Europe. However, it is usually optional and, for younger students, subject to parental approval. It is rarely given much before puberty, and sometimes it proselytizes for sexual conservatism (McCary, 1973) or liberalism (Haeberle, 1978).

Opponents still claim that sexuality courses threaten society; advocates say that they offer too little too late. The debate usually ends in passionate arguments over "promiscuity," illegitimacy, the alleged breakdown of the family, abortion, sexual deviance, civil rights, politics, even patriotism. Yet neither side has proven that sex education, for sixth graders or postgraduate students, has greatly affected sex behavior or society. A study of 545 students at the University of Missouri (Wiechman and Ellis, 1969) found no relationship between sexuality courses and erotic behavior. It is hardly surprising that one semester in a classroom did not shatter twenty years of family and social influence.

Some preliminary evidence (Diamond, 1976; Gordon, 1976) does, however, suggest that sexuality courses may alter attitudes and thus have an indirect but important influence on future learning and decision making by giving students more options to choose from and greater sensitivity to their own and others' sexuality. Courses have made some people feel better about themselves and deal better with sexual problems (Diamond, 1976; Neubeck and Mason, 1977). It is a clinical truism that sexual ignorance contributes to many physical and emotional ills, and cogent arguments have been offered that allowing people to learn more about sexuality and confront their needs and values encourages responsible sexual behavior (Calderone, 1965; Libby, 1974; Schiller, 1977). For these reasons, many organizations now encourage sex education, among them the National Council of Churches, the Synagogue Council of America, the U.S. Catholic Conference, the National Educational Association, and the American Medical Association (Gordon and Libby, 1976).

So despite lack of conclusive evidence, we and some others (for example, Scales, 1978) believe that sexuality courses can not only add to one's knowledge but help one make more informed, rewarding decisions about oneself, others, and important social issues.

Some people object on religious or moral grounds to discussing such options as premarital or extramarital coitus, contraception, and abortion. Sometimes this expresses a fear that discussion will lead to increased sexual behavior, which is presumed to be personally or socially destructive. We regret such boycotting of knowledge or ideas.

Convictions about sex range from idealizing chastity to calling for unlimited eroticism. We feel that many moralities, attitudes, and life-styles must be accepted or tolerated, especially in a pluralistic society. This requires open and enlightened discussion of many sexual practices and attitudes. A person who wants his own convictions and choices respected must respect those of others. If one doesn't believe in certain sexual choices for oneself, one needn't make them.

Data and Methods

There is often confusion about the nature of science, facts, and values. Science is not a code of behavior or a way of life. It is a method, a way of gathering and testing information. Like any method, it is subject to error, misuse, and faddism. Usually it provides not definitive data but an approximation of truth. As in much of life, we must often act on partial or even contradictory evidence when making sexual decisions. In studying sexuality, always bear in mind these three points (Diamond, 1975a):

1. *Every fact is colored by attitudes or emotions, for a person and for society.* Attitudes and emotions affect the way facts are gathered, evaluated, and used. Question all material given as fact—ask its source and reliability and the reason for its presentation.
2. *We talk about populations and trends, but must deal with individuals.* Any individual may differ in some ways from the population as a whole, yet be average in other ways. If someone differs from or resembles the majority, ask how, why, and with what effect.
3. *We must always distinguish what is from what might be or "should" be.* Sometimes we aren't sure what is, and what should be is constantly under debate.

The information in this book comes from interviews, clinical reports, questionnaire surveys, field and laboratory observations, experiments, and personal experiences. Each source has advantages and disadvantages.

Direct observation gets around many people's tendency to exaggerate what might enhance them and to hide or ignore what causes them guilt, embarrassment, or vulnerability. Masters and Johnson (1966) used direct observations to study sexual response, as did Laud Humphreys (1975) in studying homosexual behavior in public places. If observations are followed by interviews, as in both of these studies, the findings are even more useful.

This method has drawbacks. It is time-consuming, so the number of subjects is limited. The kind of information gathered by observation alone is also limited; for instance, one can learn which coital positions are used, but without interviews one cannot learn why, whether they are satisfying, or whether they differ from those used in the past. Also, the subjects may or may not differ from others who, by choice, design, or unavailability, are not observed. Interviews, of course, are as good as the interviewer and interviewee make them.

No major study has yet used observation and *experiment* to learn about sexual response. Experiment manipulates one factor of a situation at a time, to see its effect. For example, would men respond faster to a new sexual partner than to a familiar one? This "Coolidge effect" occurs in other mammals (Michael and Zumpe, 1978) and might exist to some extent in humans. Experiment is used in animal research, and it allows study of possible cause-and-effect relationships. For instance, the classic work of Phoenix et al. (1959) used guinea pigs to show that much adult sex behavior is organized by the hormones before birth. And Harry Harlow's (1974) famous research with monkeys showed how adult sexual behavior is affected by their early relationships with their mothers and peers. (See chapters 7 and 13.)

Without experimentally manipulating a situation, one can find *correlations* (relationships) between data or events, but not causation. If a high correlation existed between sun-spot activity and masturbation frequencies, one could

not assume that masturbation caused sun spots or vice versa; other research would be needed to prove whether one leads to the other.

Surveys, interviews, and *depth clinical studies* also provide information about sex. *Surveys* gather data on many people; *depth interviews* gather more data about fewer people; *depth clinical studies* produce even more information on still fewer people. The modern landmark interview studies of sexuality were conducted by Gilbert V. Hamilton (1929), who interviewed 200 married people, and Kinsey et al. (1948, 1953), who interviewed about 18,000 men and women. The classic depth clinical studies were those of Freud (1959), who gathered intimate information on individuals over months or years.

Depth interviews and clinical studies allow one to study feelings, motives, and individual development. Furthermore, they tend to be more accurate than questionnaires. This is not necessarily because people make mistakes or lie on questionnaires, but because selective memory and mental editing about emotion-laden subjects can distort initial answers. During an interview, however, as people feel more comfort and trust, they often remember events they had forgotten for years and change their earlier responses. Skilled interviewers and clinicians become sensitive to body language, voice quality, and other signals of anxiety that suggest an area should be explored further. They also use cross-checks, or different questions seeking the same information; if answers to cross-checks conflict, interviewers keep exploring.

The Kinsey studies used extensive interviewing with cross-checks. They remain, in our view, the most complete and reliable source of data on sexual behavior. They have been criticized (Cochran, Mosteller, and Tukey, 1954) on methodological and other grounds (Pomeroy, 1972). They are not based on a complete or representative sample of the population, but they are far closer to that ideal than any other study. The strongest criticism of them today is that they are some thirty years old, but no study since Kinsey's even approaches them in sample size, diversity, or depth. Furthermore, many small but careful studies done after them came up with similar findings (see chapters 9 through 12). We believe that the figures for some sex behaviors have changed since the Kinsey studies appeared, as some questionnaire studies suggest, but that the changes vary from one behavior to another and are significant but not vast.

Questionnaire surveys provide the greatest amount of data on sexual attitudes and behavior. These were pioneered by Magnus Hirschfeld; M. J. Exner, a physician who in 1915 surveyed male college students; and Katharine Davis (1929), a social worker who surveyed college women. The best known recent questionnaire surveys are those of Vance Packard (1968), Melvin Zelnik and John Kantner (1972), Robert C. Sorenson (1973), Morton Hunt (1974), and Shere Hite (1976).

Questionnaires allow one to gather much standardized information from many people, and they are relatively inexpensive. However, there are many drawbacks. A questionnaire may ask clumsy or vague questions or fail to elicit important information. There is little or no control over who responds, and no way to tell whether or how the respondents compare to nonrespondents. For example, Hite's study (1976) was compiled selectively from about 3,000 replies to 100,000 questionnaires distributed (a 3 percent rate of return). There are similar problems in the survey of Packard

(1968) and the oft-cited one by Hunt (1974), which is based on only 2,000 responses to 10,000 questionnaires (20 percent return) sent to people selected at random from phone books. Many surveys done recently by magazines, such as *Psychology Today* (Athanasiou, Shaver, and Tavris, 1970) and *Redbook* (Levin and Levin, 1975) have some value, but some deficiencies as well. Respondents may differ from non-respondents not only sexually but in being younger or older, more or less educated, more liberal or conservative, etc.—all factors that affect sex behavior. Kinsey and his colleagues, in comparison, sometimes managed to obtain 100 percent samples (entire small communities).

Sampling is crucial to a study; people tend, correctly or not, to generalize to the population at large. Data gathered from 200 college women in Iowa about contraceptive practices may not apply to college women in Atlanta or San Francisco, to noncollege women, or to women five years older or younger. In a large-scale study of every hospital with a maternity ward in Hawaii (Diamond, unpublished data), it was found that depending on which hospital was looked at, and when, it seemed that the majority of patients having abortions or babies were variously Roman Catholic or Protestant, Japanese or Caucasian, married or single. Investigators using any one hospital for their research would produce a distorted picture. That probably would not stop some scholars or readers from generalizing to the entire nation.

For these reasons, we often briefly mention the samples and methods of studies we cite in this book. Writers must be selective in presenting material; we have chosen studies we consider accurate or at least significant. Where researchers disagree, we have tried to see that the major positions are presented. Where we feel the evidence is preponderant in one direction, we have been less generous in giving all the contrary views. Some of our governing rules have been:

1. *Human sexuality follows evolutionary trends.* Humans differ from other creatures in the extent and complexity of symbolic and sexual behavior, but there are also some strong patterns of evolutionary continuity. When a study reports that human behavior or development is quite unlike that of other higher species, we tend to be cautious or even doubtful. For example, in almost all mammalian species, males are much more likely than females to initiate sexual activity; the same finding in humans shows biological continuity. The burden of proof falls on someone who suggests the opposite.

2. *Human sexuality follows historical and cultural trends.* We believe that societies tend to remain stable in their basic sexual values and behaviors. If someone reports a quick, dramatic break with entrenched attitudes and behaviors, we await firm evidence that the change is real and involves many people.

3. *We give greatest weight to studies that reveal cause and effect rather than correlations, and to those that rest on careful study in depth.*

Decision Making

We put decision making at the heart of this book because doing so reflects reality. Humans are nature's farthest experiment in leaving sexuality to learning and choice. Some sexual decisions are made for us before or soon after birth, by our genes, family, society, and environment. We are all male or female, tied to schedules of growth and change, socialized, and shaped by intimate relationships. But each person ultimately decides about relationships, sexual behavior, contraception, marriage, parenthood, childrearing, and how to respond to others' sexuality.

Often sexual decisions are not made rationally or even consciously; rarely are they made with full knowledge of all the choices and their consequences. Often reflection might dictate other choices. Sometimes people decide on the spur of the moment, on impulse, on a dare, or out of avoidance, fear, hope, or hopelessness. Sometimes people decide by default. To remain ignorant is itself a decision. So is refusing to decide: a situation drifts until others define or even force what could have been a free choice.

We can understand the emotions and pressures that lead to avoiding difficult decisions, but such passivity is hardly the most rewarding path. We all deplore negative, passive decision making in politics, education and public health. We hope that in sexuality, as in other important matters, people will gather as much information as possible, consider the practical and ethical implications of a situation, and follow a course based on more than drift or impassioned prejudgment.

As we shall see throughout this book, decision making is shaped in part by personality, family influences, education, religion, social class, educational level, and many other factors. Peers are an important source of information and attitudes in late childhood and adolescence (J. Elias and Gebhard, 1969), perhaps for some people more important than family attitudes (Hauser, 1969). That puts even more responsi-

26

bility on each person to make important decisions on matters from erotic activity to mate selection and marital goals (Luckey, 1970). Students of sexuality can sometimes predict what the majority of a particular group is likely to do, but not any given person. That is always ultimately the individual's decision.

Overview

Science has too often been looked to for solutions to the world's problems. Sex research has been asked to prove that certain sexual attitudes and behaviors are healthful or unhealthful, destructive to society or beneficial. But science is not an ethical code, a way of life, or even a source of sure answers on many factual issues. It is a method, as good as the way it is used. If sexology deserves serious regard as a science rather than as a pulpit for the sexual right or left, it must provide knowledge, examine attitudes and values and, if it presumes to recommend, do so only on the basis of reliable data.

We have discussed the universality of sexual learning and sexual decision making. In the chapters that follow, we present basic information and theory about sexuality and describe the practical and ethical implications of various choices. Each of us is responsible for his or her own choices. We hope that those choices can be wise and joyful.

Review, Discuss, Decide

1. What have been the sources of your sex information in the past? Today? Could they have been better or different? If so, how?
2. Has this chapter changed any of your ideas about sexology and sex education? If so, how?
3. Can you identify any sexual attitudes or values you think reflect your religious, ethnic, or social background?
4. How does our society indirectly teach about sexuality?
5. How likely is it that formal sex education will affect people's lives? What was the effect of any past instruction on your life?
6. How many sexual decisions can you think of that most people make?
7. What might affect decisions about having coitus, getting married, or getting divorced?
8. Can you think of an example of each of the three basic sexological rules given on page 23?

Part II

The Person

This section starts by offering information and a vocabulary about the male and female sexual systems. We then describe basic sexual processes. There are separate chapters on orgasm and sex-active substances, because they are common concerns and, to many people, major ones.

Many people are dissatisfied with or uncertain about their own or their partners' bodies and sexual functioning. This can affect sexual confidence, behavior, and satisfaction. Much folklore and many commercial enterprises (legal and illegal) capitalize on these problems. There are also many ways to alter some body parts and sexual processes. Decisions about using any of these means should be made with knowledge of their real effects. Many are dealt with in the chapter on sex-active substances.

We all develop sexually from embryos to infants, children, adolescents, and adults. In some ways, males and females develop similarly, in others differently. Chapter 7 presents some findings and theories about sexual development. These may help one decide how to view one's physical and psychosexual nature and growth, and may influence decisions on how to deal with one's children.

This section ends with a chapter on physical health and dysfunction. It has been estimated that about one person in ten of those in their teens, twenties, and thirties have physical problems that affect them sexually. Here we also review sexually transmitted (venereal) diseases, which have reached epidemic proportions, especially among teenagers and young adults. It seems that more people than ever, by default or ignorance, risk sickness with sexual activity. Full information may help people make more healthful and satisfying decisions about their well-being.

3

The Sexual System

Are my breasts big enough?

Why does one testicle hang lower than the other?

How do I know if my hymen is still intact?

Is my penis big enough to satisfy a woman?

Do I urinate through my vagina?

Can the clitoris become erect?

Are most men's nipples erotically sensitive?

Most of us are at least a little concerned with the adequacy of our looks and our bodies. And we may be familiar with our bodies without really understanding them. This is especially true of the sexual parts; most of us have at least a small, perhaps unrecognized gap in our knowledge of the male and female sexual systems. The results can be important, influencing our health and sexual satisfaction, and that of our partners. Physical self-consciousness and concern about the size, shape, and functioning of one's sexual system can distort body image, create shyness, and produce emotional static that interferes with sociosexual communication. And people cannot discuss human sexuality or make intelligent decisions about it without thorough, myth-free knowledge of its physical basis.

In our society, most people are raised to hide their genitals, even to feel ashamed of looking

at them closely. Later in life this discomfort may fade, only to be replaced by shame at admitting ignorance about one's own or others' genitals. If you have never looked closely at your own body, do so with the help of a hand mirror. If you have a sexual partner, looking closely at each other will give you more information than any diagram. And remember that a diagram is a composite of many findings; an individual may be somewhat different and still be normal.

The Concept of Sexualia

Biology and medicine divide body structures into systems according to their functions, such as digestive, excretory, and reproductive. Some organs serve several functions; for instance the penis is a sexual, reproductive, and excretory organ. Traditionally, texts on human sexuality describe the *genitals,* or *genitalia* (structures involved in sex activity and reproduction), dividing them into male and female, external and internal. This ignores two important facts: most sexual expression takes place without reproduction, and modern technology allows reproduction without sexual expression.

It seems philosophically and biologically logical to us to distinguish the *sexual system,* the parts of the body we associate with sexual ex-

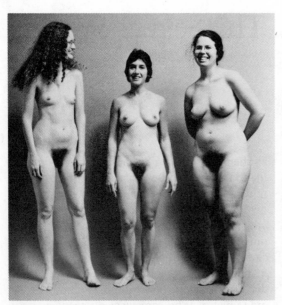

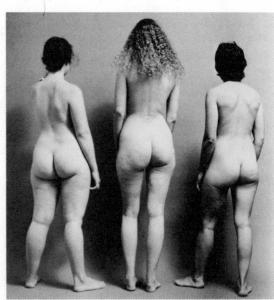

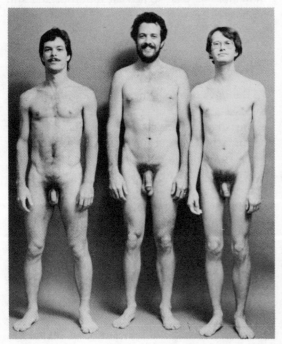

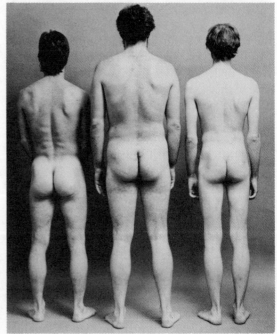

Figure 3-1 / *The variety of human physiques is enormous, and many people have unresolved doubts about how normal, attractive, or adequate their bodies are, especially the sexualia. Simply seeing this variety may ease doubts as no words can.*

pression, from the *reproductive system,* the parts involved in procreation. Some parts of each system are not part of the other, and some organs belong to both. We discuss the reproductive system in chapter 17. Here we talk about only what we call the *sexualia,* or sexual system, the parts of the body we think of primarily as erotic. The *primary sexualia* are the external and internal genitals that can be erotically stimulated by touch; they are different in males and females. The *secondary sexualia*—mouth, anus, skin, and other nongenital areas with erotic sensitivity—are similar in both sexes. The basic anatomical descriptions are agreed on; references and further information are in any standard text. Primary sources used for the responses discussed below are Kinsey et al. (1948, 1953) and Masters and Johnson (1966).

Before we proceed, some comments on language are called for. Poet Robert Graves told of a soldier shot in the buttocks who was asked by a visitor where he had been wounded and replied, "I'm sorry, ma'am, I don't know: I never learned Latin." Like him, we have slang and idiomatic words for the sexualia and sex acts, and we learn early that these are "dirty." Some people find them difficult to use in public situations, such as a classroom; certainly no one wins medals for social finesse by using them everywhere. More socially acceptable euphemisms such as "privates" and "it" are not only vague but self-conscious, and by their deliberate avoidance send a negative message about

sexual organs and acts. Medical terms, on the other hand, strike some people as formal or unpleasantly clinical. We will usually use the scientific vocabulary; it is most widely accepted in public discussion, and people who want to read more on sexuality will need it. Actually, many of these words have graphic origins in Latin and Greek, which we will often give to make the words easier to understand and remember. But since many people know only the vernacular terms, we mention them as well.

Primary Sexualia: Male

The main male sexualia are the penis and scrotum (external sexualia) and the testes, or testicles (internal sexualia).

The Penis

The penis (Latin: tail), or *phallus* (Greek: penis) ("prick," "peter," "tool," "organ," or "cock"), is the male copulatory organ. It consists of three parallel cylinders *(corpora)* of erectile tissue bound tightly by tough connective tissue, all surrounded by skin. The three cylinders are attached to the pelvis and function as a single structure. The two cylinders on the upper side have relatively large spaces between their cells, so they are called *corpora cavernosa* (Latin: cavernous bodies). When the penis is flaccid, these are only potential spaces; when blood fills them, the penis becomes *tumescent* (swollen), larger, and erect. When flaccid (soft), it can be greatly manipulated, twisted, or folded without pain. When erect, it increases in size and becomes fairly rigid and limited in motion. Some primates and almost all other mammals—from cats to deer, rodents to

33

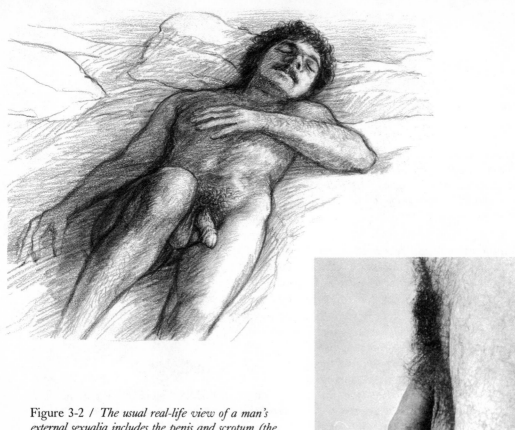

Figure 3-2 / *The usual real-life view of a man's
external sexualia includes the penis and scrotum (the
sac behind the penis). Compare with the female
sexualia (Figure 3-3). At right, above, an
uncircumcised penis. Below, a circumcised penis;
removal of the foreskin permanently exposes the glans
and corona.*

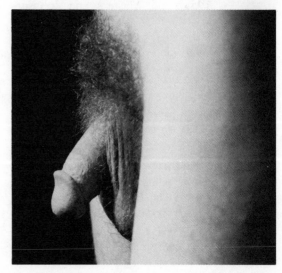

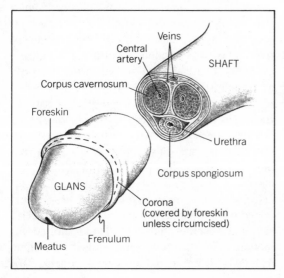

whales—have a bone within the penis. Humans do not.

At the base of the penis, the two corpora cavernosa diverge to the sides and attach to the pubic bones. They are covered by the *ischiocavernosus* muscles, which slow the drainage of blood from the penis and prolong erection.

The third cylinder, the *corpus cavernosum urethra* (or *corpus spongiosum*), on the under side, is spongy; even when the penis becomes erect, it remains unrigid. This provides a soft protective cushion around the *urethra*, which runs the entire length of the penis. Urine and semen travel through it (normally not simultaneously) and exit through the opening *(meatus)* at the head of the penis. Near the base of the penis, the *corpus urethra* is fixed within the *bulbocavernosus* muscle, which helps eject semen and urine from the urethra and stop urine flow. The urethra and corpus urethra can be felt and their outline seen on the under side of the erect penis.

The *glans* (Latin: acorn), or head, of the penis consists of the expanded end of the corpus urethra. It looks like a knight's helmet and has a rim called the *corona* (Latin: crown). The narrow area between the glans and the shaft is the *neck* of the penis. The *frenulum*, a thin band of skin, is near the corona on the under side of the penis.

The skin covering the body of the penis is loose and flexible. On an uncircumcised penis, it forms a hood over the glans called the *prepuce*, or foreskin. Normally the foreskin can be easily drawn back to expose the glans. This can be prevented by adhesions between the glans and prepuce or by too small an opening in the prepuce. A physician can (and should) remedy either condition in a simple office procedure. In extreme cases, the prepuce clings tightly around the glans, a condition called *phimosis* (Greek: muzzling); circumcision is necessary to relieve this (see chapter 8).

Circumcision is the removal of the prepuce to expose the glans fully and permanently. This is not medically necessary for most males, but in the United States and many other countries, it is recommended for hygienic reasons and done routinely in the hospital soon after birth. There are several arguments for circumcision, primarily that it makes it easier to clean the glans and remove *smegma*. This cheesy substance is an accumulation of dead skin cells, dirt, and fluid from small glands in the neck and corona (the fluid acts as a lubricant between prepuce and glans). Smegma can become smelly and irritating, and it may harbor organisms conducive to disease (Licklider, 1961). (See chapter 8.)

Circumcision is also a religious practice. Among Jews, it is a rite performed when a boy is eight days old that affirms the Hebrews' covenant with God, first made by Abraham. Muslims also perform ritual circumcision, when a boy is seven to thirteen years old.

The argument for retaining the foreskin is that it protects the glans, and that it is natural to have one. Many people believe that circumcision makes the penis either more or less sensitive; no conclusive evidence exists one way or the other (Masters and Johnson, 1966). Penile sensitivity may well depend more on a person's nervous endowment, learned patterns of sexual response, and feelings in a given situation than on the presence of a foreskin.

The skin of the penis and scrotum (see below) is highly *erogenous* (sensitive to sexual stimulation). The sensitivity is greatest at the head, frenulum, and corona; it decreases down the shaft of the penis. The shaft, though less

Phallic Worship and Abhorrence

The word *testify* comes from the word *testis:* among the ancient Egyptians, the eighteenth-century Dutch (below), and some other peoples, a man held his testes or penis when speaking under oath, as in our society we put a hand over the heart. The male external genitals, more visible than the female, have been portrayed more often in art. Actually, many carvings and pictures of phalli may not have been objects of so-called phallic worship, but symbolic or magical displays of aggression (Eibl-Eibesfeldt, 1974; Wickler, 1973). Some of man's primate relatives display their erect penises (right) as symbolic threats to rivals and territorial intruders. There is a striking parallel in the way phallic carvings (below right) are set up to repulse evil spirits from homes and fields in Africa, Asia, and rural Europe. The ancient Romans, among others, wore phallic amulets to ward off evil influences. However, some societies and religions have shown abhorrence of the male genitals. Many ancient religions of the Eastern Mediterranean demanded that priests and even laymen undergo castration—amputation of the testicles, and sometimes the penis as well. This practice passed into early Christianity and occurred sporadically into the eighteenth century; it occurred even later in the Skopzi sect of the Russian Orthodox Church.

sensitive to touch, is more sensitive to pressure. The scrotum is less responsive than the penis. For most males, the penis is the prime focus of sexual sensation during masturbation, petting, and coitus.

Most males are concerned about penis size, and many believe that bigger is better. There is wide variation, but the average adult penis is 8 to 12 centimeters long and 2.5 to 3.0 centimeters in diameter when flaccid (Masters and Johnson, 1966; Dickinson, 1949); when erect, it is almost twice as long (12–18 centimeters) and slightly greater (about 0.5 centimeters) in diameter. It seems that a penis which is short when flaccid increases relatively more in erection than a longer one, and that erect penises vary less in size than flaccid ones. Penis size has no known relation to body build or the amount of masturbation or other sexual activity.

One myth about penis size is that a long, thick penis is more satisfying to women. There seems to be no consistent relationship between penis size and the ability to satisfy a woman. In fact, a large penis disturbs some women, who fear (realistically or not) that they cannot accommodate it. However, just as some men are aroused by large breasts, some women respond erotically to a large penis.

There is no safe, proven way to increase penis size except in those rare cases where the organ is small because of a deficiency of androgens (male hormones); these men may be helped by hormone therapy.

The Scrotum and Testicles

The *scrotum* is a sac that hangs below the body and behind the penis. It contains the two *testicles,* or *testes,* and their attached *spermatic cords.* Heat and relaxation make the scrotum hang loose and low; this distension makes its surface smooth. Cold and sexual arousal make the scrotum contract toward the body, making it compact and its skin furrowed. This tightening and slackening of the scrotum is related to sperm production, which requires a lower temperature than that within the body.

The *testes,* ("balls," "jewels," "nuts") are the two egg-shaped *gonads* within the scrotum. Each is about 4 centimeters by 2 centimeters and has a separate compartment to cushion and protect it. The testes hang at different heights; usually the left is lower than the right, but the reverse is not rare. This seems to reduce their bumping against each other during ordinary movement. Even slight pressure to the testes can cause exquisite and lasting pain. If the pain is great enough, it can render any male helpless. Although books on self-defense and the martial arts suggest a blow to the testes to stop an assailant, this is difficult to accomplish; they are small and somewhat protected targets and draw close to the body for protection under stress conditions. Besides producing sperm cells (see chapter 18), the testes provide the body with androgens, or male hormones (mainly *testosterone*). Androgens organize and activate sexual behavior (see chapter 6) and male body development.

One of the commonest testicular problems is *cryptorchidism* (Greek: hidden testicles). The testes normally develop inside the body before birth and descend into the scrotum some time after the seventh fetal month. In 2 to 5 percent of males, one or both testicles fail to descend by birth. In most cases, they soon descend without medical treatment. But if descent is delayed beyond several months, it can be induced by certain hormonal drugs or, if these fail, by surgery. If this condition continues for long without a physician's attention, sterility may result, since normal body temperature hinders the formation of sperm cells. After the testicles descend, there need be no further concern.

The *spermatic cords* can be felt in each compartment of the scrotum. They allow the products of the testicles to pass to the penis. In most men they are not erotically sensitive.

Primary Sexualia: Female

The primary female sexualia are the inner and outer labia, vestibule, clitoris, and breasts (all external), and the vagina (internal). The word *vulva* (Latin: covering) includes all the external sexualia. The slang terms "pussy" and "snatch" are usually used for the vulva, but sometimes for the vagina as well.

These sexualia, except for the breasts, lie within the cradle of bones called the *pelvis*. In females the pelvis tilts more horizontally than in males, and anteriorly (toward the front) it becomes a bony prominence, the *pubic symphysis*. The *mons veneris* (Latin: mount of Venus), or *mons pubis,* is a deposit of fatty tissues that acts as a protective cushion over the pubic symphysis in both males and females. After puberty, pubic hair ("bush," "beaver") covers the mons, so little of the genitals can be seen from a front view; what is seen is called the *pudendum* (Latin: shameful). The usual textbook diagram of the external sexualia is rarely seen in real life.

The Labia

The *labia majora* (Latin: large lips) are fatty deposits covered with skin and, after puberty,

with hair; they look like parallel rolls of tissue and extend from the mons to the anus, covering the vaginal entrance. The *labia minora* (small lips) lie parallel to and within the labia majora, covering the vaginal outlet. They remain without hair throughout life. Along with the clitoris (see below), the labia are the female's most sensitive erotic areas. Anteriorly, the labia minora cover the clitoris as its prepuce, or foreskin.

The Clitoris

The *clitoris* (Greek: that which is hidden; plural, *clitorides*) ("clit" or "button") is a small female phallus. It has no urinary function and therefore no urethra. Like the penis, it has two corpora cavernosa attached to the pubis, and they become engorged with blood and swollen during sexual excitement. However, in only a few women does the tumescent clitoris become truly erect and protuberant. The size of the clitoris varies from 0.5 to 2.5 centimeters in length and from .2 to 1 centimeters in diameter (Masters and Johnson, 1966). In women who receive androgens in medical treatment or produce excess androgens because of illness, the clitoris grows larger and protrudes markedly during erotic excitement or by reflex.

Enclosed by the labia minora and protruding away from the pubis, the clitoris seems located to receive a concentration of erotic stimuli. In fact, receiving erotic stimulation seems to be its only function. Despite its erotic importance, the clitoris often goes unrecognized by many women and men. Perhaps because of this, our society has fewer myths about the size of the clitoris than about that of the penis. Recently

many sex and marriage manuals have tried to make up for past omissions by writing as if the clitoris alone were erotically important to females.

Like the penis, the clitoris has a *glans* and a *frenulum.* The glans does not protrude much in most women; often it remains completely hidden by the overlying prepuce. It can be exposed by manipulation, but this is not essential for stimulation. Sensitive to touch, pressure, and stretching, the clitoris receives stimuli originating some distance away, even when, during arousal, it remains buried by the engorged surrounding tissue.

Some feminists argue for female circumcision, to allow greater, more direct stimulation of the clitoris (Rathmann, 1959). Most health professionals, male and female, disagree (Seemans, 1973; Oliven, 1965). A small number of gynecologists, sexologists, and feminists have recommended that for women who find clitoral stimulation unexciting or painful, a blunt probe be passed between the glans and prepuce to

Figure 3-3 / *The usual real-life view of a woman's external sexualia reveals only the breasts and the hair-covered mons and labia majora. Only by spreading the legs and separating the labia can the external sexualia be seen entirely. Compare with the male sexualia (Figure 3-2).*

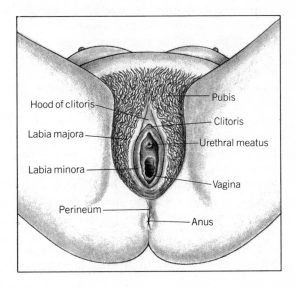

expose the glans for stimulation or cleansing (L. Clark, 1963, 1967; Hartman and Fithian, 1972). Others, equally qualified and concerned about female sexual response, are not convinced of the need (Kline–Graber and Graber, 1975; Kaplan, 1974). Exposing the glans may make it uncomfortably sensitive.

In some women, the clitoris has exquisite erotic sensitivity. A few men complain that their glans penis is too sensitive; many more women sometimes find direct touch on the glans or even the body of the clitoris distracting, even painful. Therefore while many females enjoy clitoral stimulation, many others prefer stimulation of the labia minora, vaginal vestibule, and mons (Masters and Johnson, 1966).

The Vestibule and Hymen

The *vaginal vestibule,* or entrance, is a basin-shaped area. Its walls are the labia minora, its floor a thin sheet of tissue in which appear the openings of the urethra and vagina. In most women, the vestibule is erotically responsive.

In young virgins, a large part of the vestibule floor consists of the *hymen* (Greek: the god of marriage), a thin membrane that may cover much of the vaginal opening. The hymen is the subject of many fallacies and traditions, and a source of many personal and social difficulties. Many people believe that an intact hymen reflects virginity. This and the high value given to premarital chasity create pressure on some women in some societies, such as Japan and Italy, to undergo surgery reconstructing the hymen, to give it the appearance of being intact. But the vestibule floor, and especially the hymen, varies widely from small and thin to very thick and resistant. Virginity as a fact of behavior is one thing; as a state of the hymen it can be something else. Some hymens stretch quite easily; in most virgins, the hymen allows passage of a vaginal tampon or inspecting finger. In others, the hymen may be pierced or completely broken by accident or experimentation. Or the hymen may remain more or less intact, covering the vaginal opening, until coitus takes place or even later: a woman with a very stretchable hymen can have coitus and reach the hospital delivery room with her hymen only partly perforated.

Some hymens defy penile penetration; inserting a series of increasingly large devices called dilators may enlarge the hymeneal opening. If the hymen is too resistant, a physician can cut it (a simple office procedure) to prevent frustration at first coitus. In rare cases, the hymen is completely intact at puberty, preventing menstrual fluids from exiting freely, which creates gynecological problems; then a physician must pierce the hymen. Remnants of the hymen are usually permanent features of the vaginal opening. These remains vary greatly in extent, size, number, shape, and sensitivity.

The vestibular floor surrounds the vaginal opening and the urethral meatus, the opening for the outflow of urine. Worry about urine getting into the vagina is rarely warranted; a healthy person's urine is generally sterile.

The vestibule also contains the ducts from the *vulvovaginal glands* (also called *Bartholin's glands*). These were once thought to provide fluids for lubrication during coitus; now their function is in doubt. Like the appendix and wisdom teeth, they are most notable as sites of irritation and infection.

The Vagina

The *vagina* (Latin: sheath) ("cunt," "slit," "hole," "snatch," and in some regions "cock") is not a cylindrical receptacle, as it is often pictured, but a flexible potential space that can conform to the size and shape of almost any cylindrical object that enters it, as an elastic glove does. At rest, the vagina has an average depth of about 8 centimeters in *nulipara* (women who have not given birth); it distends and elongates with stimulation. Extremes exist, but a normal vagina usually accommodates a large or small penis equally well.

The walls of the vagina consist of *rugose* (wrinkled) muscle tissue. Most of the vaginal muscles are involuntary; voluntary vaginal contractions are caused primarily by the muscles encircling the vaginal opening, the bulbocavernosus muscles, and those of the *pelvic diaphragm.*

Some women's vaginas have stretched after childbirth; since the urethra passes through the same muscles as the vagina, some then find urinary control more difficult. This problem can be helped by a combination of counseling and exercises that strengthen the bulbocavernosus muscles, the *pubococcygeus muscle,* and the pelvic diaphragm. These exercises also help many women who for reasons other than childbirth complain of being "too loose." They improve urine control, vaginal muscle strength, and muscle tone, and give women a clearer awareness of their vaginal response (Kline-Graber and Graber, 1978; Kegel, 1952). And they can obviously add to their partners' pleasure.

To perform these exercises, a woman bears down hard as if to stop urine flow and holds the muscle tension briefly; this is repeated during short periods several times a day. The value of such exercises was known in sixteenth-century India. They were recommended in the erotic text *The Ananga Ranga* "... ever strive to close and constrict the Yoni [vagina] until she holds the Linga [penis] ... acting as the hand of the Go-pala-girl, who milks the cow. This can be learned only by long practice ... so lovely and pleasant ... is she who constricts."

The vagina itself is not very sensitive. Therefore many routine gynecological procedures produce no pain, only a slight sensation of pressure. Just inside the vagina, where a ring of pelvic diaphragm muscles surrounds and supports the vaginal entrance, most women are sensitive to pressure and stretching; many, when stimulated here, are erotically aroused. Some are especially responsive to pressure on the vaginal walls at about the four and eight o'clock areas, at a depth of two finger joints. Some women also find quite erotic the pressure of deep vaginal penetration, which stimulates the *cervix* (neck) of the uterus, the portion of the womb that protrudes into the vagina. Others find such stimulation painful. If pain on vaginal penetration persists, a physician should be consulted.

The Breasts

In some societies, the female breasts *(mammae)* arouse little erotic interest. In others, such as our own, they can be so sexually arousing that covering or uncovering them in private or in public becomes an erotic drama.

One of women's commonest worries about body appearance is weight distribution, particularly in their hips and thighs, but breasts are clearly also important. A survey found about 25 percent of the respondents dissatisfied with their breasts and 9 percent very dissatisfied (Berscheid, Walster, and Bohrnstedt, 1973). Both the size and shape can cause concern. The most common complaint is breasts women consider too small. However, few women desire breasts so large that they exceed familiar standards and steal attention from the rest of the body and the personality. Despite myth to the contrary, there is no more relationship between breast size and sexual capacity than between penis size and sexual capacity—unless a person is so convinced of the idea that it becomes a self-fulfilling prophecy.

The female breast varies greatly in size and shape. It extends from the collar bone down to the sixth rib, and from the midline of the chest into and below the armpit. It is filled with fat and with loose, soft tissue. How much the breasts protrude depends on their size, their support by connective tissues, a woman's age and *parity* (the number of children she has borne), and the care she has taken of them. Women, especially large-breasted ones, who do not support their breasts with brassieres will eventually have more pendulous breasts.

On the surface of the breast is the *nipple,* surrounded by a pigmented *areola.* The nipple contains the exits of ducts from milk glands and has involuntary muscles that cause nipple erection. It also contains many *sebaceous glands,* which secrete an oily substance that helps keep the nipple supple and prevent its skin from cracking. The areola's size varies widely and does not depend on breast size; this area serves as a target for a nursing baby. To many women's consternation, it seems to sprout hairs more than the rest of the breast. These can safely be plucked by women who find them disturbing.

Breast development is one of the first signs of female puberty. Some women's breasts remain unusually small *(micromastia).* Usually this is hereditary, for breast size is genetically determined. The breasts can also shrink after women give birth, because of loss of breast tissue. Many small-breasted women try to build up their breasts with exercises or hormone creams, but in vain. Exercises do build up back muscles and thus increase over-all girth, and they may tighten breast support, but they cannot greatly change breast size. Hormone creams may help only in those few cases caused by hormone deficiency, and those should be treated by a physician. Women who are realistically concerned about themselves can rest assured that many men find small breasts erotically exciting.

Very large breasts *(macromastia)* may make a woman feel overwhelmed by the attention they receive. In extreme forms, macromastia may lead to medical problems. The weight of the breasts, if poorly distributed, may be a physical burden for small women, putting stress on nerve and blood supplies to the shoulder and arm and causing neck pains (Kaye, 1973). Surgery can reduce breast size, but this, like most cosmetic surgery, should be done only after consultation with a psychotherapist.

Breast development sometimes occurs on one or both sides in men *(gynecomastia)* and may be quite disturbing. This is not uncommon in prepubescent boys, but it is usually temporary. In adulthood the condition may be associated with liver disease or alcoholism. The basic cause of the problem should be found; removing the excess tissue is routine surgery.

In some women, one breast has a different size or shape than the other. If this is disturbing, it can be dealt with by padding and altering clothing. Other common variations are inverted (nonprotruding) nipples and extra nipples. These usually do not interfere with nursing and need not cause major concern. Any embarrassment they create should be treated like that resulting from any other common but rarely discussed variation.

Many women find stimulation of their breasts and nipples moderately arousing, as do a minority of men. The nipples and areolae are more sensitive than the surrounding areas, but some women and many men do not find even nipple stimulation appealing. A small number of women can be brought to orgasm by breast and nipple stimulation alone (Kinsey et al., 1953).

Secondary Sexualia

Most sexual encounters begin with a kiss, a touch, a caress, yet the mouth and skin are often ignored as sexualia. We consider as *secondary sexualia* these and other nongenital areas often involved in petting, masturbation, and coitus.

The Mouth

Many mammals, including our primate relatives, engage in some sort of oral-oral or oral-genital contact; so do virtually all human societies (Ford and Beach, 1951). Most sex play in our society includes kissing and often other oral acts. Deep kissing ("French kissing," "soul kissing"), in which one partner's tongue enters the other's mouth, can be pleasurable in itself and as an oral expression of intended or concomitant genital penetration. Some women can reach orgasm by kissing alone (Kinsey et al.,

1953); no men are known to be that responsive to kissing, but probably few like to do without it. Almost every sort of oral stimulus can be felt as erotic. For some people, the mouth and tongue rival the genitals in erotic significance.

Many peoples do not kiss as we do; some societies prefer "nose kissing"—not merely nose rubbing but gentle mutual nuzzling and exchange of breath. Others carry mouth-to-mouth eroticism farther than we. The Kwakiutl Indians of North America and the Truk and Trobriand Islanders of the Pacific suck each other's lips and exchange saliva when kissing (Ford and Beach, 1951).

The Anus, Anal Canal, and Rectum

The anus, anal canal, and rectum are the terminal parts of the digestive system, but Kinsey et al. (1953) reported that perhaps half or more of all heterosexuals have used them erotically at least once in their lives. So have a larger proportion of male homosexuals.

The *anus* ("asshole") is a round opening in the cleft of the buttocks. The skin around it has many sweat glands and, in many men but fewer women, the area around it is endowed with hair. In both sexes, the skin around the anus is highly pigmented and forms folds that radiate from the orifice.

The *anal canal* is the bottom part of the large intestine. The anus and anal canal are heavily surrounded, internally and externally, by ring-like muscles *(sphincters)* that normally keep these structures closed. The anal canal widens into the *rectum*. The rectal lining reabsorbs and conserves water, drying the feces. It also provides a mucoid lubrication to smooth passage of the feces. An unlubricated or sharp object can damage this sensitive area; rectal examinations by physicians are always performed with the aid of a lubricant.

Sensitivity to pain and other stimuli is mostly limited to outer parts of the anal area. Inside the rectum, as within the vagina, stretching and pressure are easily felt, but not pain and touch; internal damage, infection, or cancer can progress without warning. The anal region, vagina, and penis share the same trunk line of nerves. This common input toward the central nervous system helps explain why both males and females may find anal stimulation erotic. There is wide variation in anal responses and in how people feel about them, probably at least as much because of psychological and cultural forces as because of nerve receptors (see chapter 12).

The Perineum

The term *perineum* refers to the entire pelvic floor or, more specifically, to the region between the anus and the vulva or penis. The perineal skin is supplied by the same nerves as the genitals and in many males and females is erotically sensitive to pressure. The pressure can be external, as in horseback riding, or internal, as in deep vaginal or anal penetration.

The Buttocks and Thighs

Contractions of the buttocks ("ass") have been said to "reflect, more than any one factor, the development of the nervous and muscular tensions which are involved in erotic arousal" (Kinsey et al., 1948). The *gluteal muscles* there are large and powerful, and with those of the

lower back are largely responsible for pelvic thrusting during coitus. The large thigh muscles often tense rhythmically along with the gluteal muscles during sexual excitement; the tension is transmitted to the genital region, where it contributes to over-all sexual response. Some males can reach erection by tensing their buttock and thigh muscles and may even reach orgasm this way. A larger number of women respond sexually to tensing those muscles; in fact, it is a not uncommon way for females to masturbate (Kinsey et al., 1953).

The skin of the inner thigh is more erotically sensitive to touch than the skin over the buttocks. The buttocks seems more responsive to pressure.

The Skin

For many people, close body contact is the most pleasurable part of sexual expression, even of coitus. From the time of birth, there seems to be a hunger for skin contact between infant and parent. This contact creates feelings of contentment, security, warmth, and nurture (Montagu, 1973), and its absence has been implicated in infant illness and death (Bowlby, 1966). The desire for body contact continues throughout life and brings the same reward. A touch, hug, or caress can show many kinds of erotic and nonerotic closeness.

Lack of such contact can be a problem between sexual partners, leading to such complaints as, "He never touches me enough, all he wants is sex," or "She doesn't hold or caress me in public, only when we're in bed." These complaints may rise not only from culturally learned romantic desires but from a biological need. Of course they also reflect a desire to see coitus as part rather than all of sexual communication, and to see oneself as a person as well as a sexual partner. In North American and northern European societies (as compared to Mediterranean, Slavic, and Latin ones), many people are wary of touching and being touched; they are taught to make little contact unless there is sexual intent.

The sensory input from the skin goes simultaneously to the brain, which places the stimuli in an erotic or nonerotic context, and to reflex centers; both can cause sexual response. For example, pressure against the perineum—from horseback riding or from a lover's hand—may cause penile erection or vaginal wetting. Which skin contacts are erotic varies a great deal from person to person (see chapter 4).

Genital Hair

Hair is part of the skin, and each follicle has touch receptors. After puberty, part of the external genitals of most men and women is heavily endowed with hair. In most men it grows in the shape of a shield *(escutcheon),* with its upper border pointing to the navel. In women the top of the escutcheon is relatively flat. These hairs are highly sensitive to touch or motion. Seeing pubic hair is erotic to most men and some women. Several centuries ago, false pubic hair pieces *(merkins)* were sometimes used.

Other Erogenous Zones

Erogenous zones are parts of the body where touch, pressure, temperature, and other stimuli are sexually exciting. Most are skin areas of the primary and secondary sexualia, but variations in biological makeup and individual conditioning cause wide differences. Many people find stimulation of the neck, eyes, ears, or legs sexually arousing. The skin of the feet, arms, armpits, abdomen, and navel may be especially erogenous. While genetic factors and nerve receptors are no doubt involved, so are the situation, social traditions, and individual experience, and each person's response is difficult to predict. There are women who have been brought to orgasm by only having their eyebrows stroked or by having pressure applied to their teeth; no men are known to respond in such ways (Kinsey et al., 1948, 1953).

Overview

Everyone needs accurate, complete information about the male and female sexual systems. Even many sexually experienced people have areas of ignorance or doubt about their bodies, their partners' bodies, and their ability to give sexual satisfaction. We have described the parts of the body involved in sexual expression. In doing so, we have discussed not only anatomy but some myths and doubts that cause many people anxiety or lack of self-acceptance.

We have also discussed some common health problems and concerns associated with the sexualia. This information should make it easier to communicate with a sexual partner and, if the need arises, with a physician. It should also help one answer questions like the following, which occur in daily life.

Review, Discuss, Decide

To give an idea of how to apply the information in this chapter to decision making, here are some questions about the sexual system. A number of them involve sexual relationships and sexual behavior. Some discussion and suggestions follow the first two. Answer or discuss the remaining ones yourself.

1. How am I better off by knowing sexual anatomy? Isn't sex more than just body parts?

   Of course sex is more than body parts; but people pay a price for not knowing enough about them. Hesitating to talk about the sexualia because of ignorance or shame can permit the progress of physical disorders (breast cancer, venereal disease, hernia). It can also inhibit social and intellectual communication. And knowing about the sexualia allows greater freedom in exploring oneself and one's partner, which increases sexual satisfaction and emotional communication. Each person must decide when and how to use knowledge of the sexualia, but first the knowledge and vocabulary should be there for one to draw on.

2. How can I tell what would be sexually most pleasurable for me and my partner?

   Since sexual response varies somewhat among individuals, experiment with kinds of stimuli and areas of response. Partners must find verbal or other ways of saying "I like this," "Please try that," "Do you like this?" or "Would you like me to try that?" Regardless of what the majority of people like or dislike, partners can find what pleases them both only by consideration, experimentation, and communication.

3. What advantages or disadvantages are there in grouping sex-related structures as "sexualia" rather than "genitalia"?
4. Were you brought up to know the names and functions of the sexualia? Would you educate children differently? Why?
5. Is there a connection between penis size and ability to give a woman pleasure? Between breast size and female sexual capacity? How do men and women respond to the idea or the

reality of a large or small penis? Of large or small breasts? Might knowing the answers affect a person's sexual experience? How?

6. What would you say to a young woman who fears that her vagina is too large or too small? That her breasts are too large or small?

7. Can you tell whether a female is a virgin from how intact her hymen is? How would you respond to concern about this on the part of her or her partner, family, or friends?

8. What are the real and imagined advantages or disadvantages of circumcision?

4

Sexual Responses and Mechanisms

What is involved in having an orgasm?

Do men and women have similar or different sexual responses? How?

How do my thoughts or attitudes influence my sexual response?

As I get older, will I stay as sexually responsive as I am now?

How much of sex response is learned?

One commonly hears such complaints as:

"We both wanted sex to last a long time, but it was over so fast we were both disappointed."

"I couldn't tell whether my partner was turned on, and that turned me off."

"We had been planning to get away by ourselves, but when we finally did, I couldn't get it up."

"I was very embarrassed the first time. I was anxious to please him, but I just couldn't relax. I felt terrible."

"Everything seemed okay, but I couldn't come. She felt rejected, and I couldn't explain it to her or understand it myself."

Solving such problems involves understanding why the mental and physical aspects of sex are not coordinated. To do so, one must consider some of the mechanisms of sexual response.

Basic Concepts

A *physical (somatic)* aspect of sex is external and obvious—erection of the penis or nipples, vaginal wetting ("lubrication"),* orgasm. It may be situational or phenotypic. If the penis becomes erect in erotic circumstances—say, because of a genital caress—the response is *situational* (appropriate to the situation). If not, it is *phenotypic* (sexual in appearance only); for instance, erection caused reflexively by a full bladder does not happen in a sexual encounter and usually doesn't feel erotic.

The *mental (psychological)* aspects of an act or response can be *cognitive* (intentional) or *instinctive* (reflexive). Deliberately touching another person's genitals is a cognitive act. Penile erection and vaginal wetting are reflexive; they can happen without one knowing why.

The mental aspects of sex—thoughts, feelings, and fantasies—may be learned or spontaneous. They are not always obvious; someone thinking about sex play may look no different from someone who isn't. The mental aspects of sex may or may not be arousing, and they vary for each person and among individuals. Some

---

* The words sweating and wetting are accurate descriptions of a process that has many functions. We use them unless referring to lubrication for coitus.

people fantasize easily and frequently, others rarely and with difficulty.

When the mental and somatic aspects of sex do not work together smoothly, the result can be very disturbing. A man may want coitus but not have an erection; a woman may want coitus but not lubricate adequately; a person may want orgasm but be unable to reach it. Also, many people aren't sure whether their partners have reached arousal or climax; some aren't sure whether they themselves have. Therefore they want to know the signs of arousal and orgasm. Understanding the sexual response cycle can help solve such difficulties.

The Sexual Response Cycle (SRC)

One of the major contributions of William Masters and Virginia Johnson (1966) has been to detail the physical changes involved in genital activity. They divide sexual response into four phases—excitement (arousal), plateau, orgasm and resolution (Table 4.1). For descriptive purposes, we add the resting phase (see below). These phases are the same for most people most of the time from early childhood on, and they constitute the *sexual response cycle* (SRC).

Most often a person is sexually at *rest*—involved in schoolwork, a job, play, talking, sleeping. When a person is not aroused, the penis is flaccid, the vagina relatively dry and relaxed. As sexual interest develops, because of psychological or physical stimuli, *excitement*, or *arousal*, begins. In both men and women, this is marked by an increasing flow of blood *(vasocongestion)* to the genitalia and rising muscular

tension *(myotonia)*, also primarily in the genital region. Vasocongestion and myotonia are the main signals of sexual arousal. They cause penile erection and vaginal sweating. This sweating is the female counterpart of penile erection; the clitoris becomes engorged and sometimes enlarged, but in most women does not become erect (Kinsey et al., 1953; Masters and Johnson, 1966). These processes usually are not under control; wishing doesn't necessarily bring them about or help them go away.

It is not always clear what leads to sexual excitement. Sometimes the cause seems obvious, such as seeing an attractive person, petting, or viewing a sexually explicit movie. But usually it isn't clear what stimulates someone to seek a partner, to be aroused at one time rather

Table 4.1/*Elements of sexual response*

I. Aspects

  Psychological (mental)
    Cognitive: nonarousing, arousing
    Instinctive (reflexive): nonerotic, erotic

  Somatic (physical)
    Phenotypic
    Situational

II. Phases

  Resting
  Excitement
  Plateau
  Orgasm
  Resolution (includes postorgasmic)

III. Mechanisms

Arousal		Sensory stimuli
Copulatory	*involves*	Erection, sweating
Orgasmic		Ejaculation, muscle contractions

Figure 4-1 / *The full sexual response cycle goes from the resting state through orgasm and back to rest. However, the cycle is not always completed, and the degree, strength, and pattern of response vary among individuals, and may differ for each person from one occasion to another.*

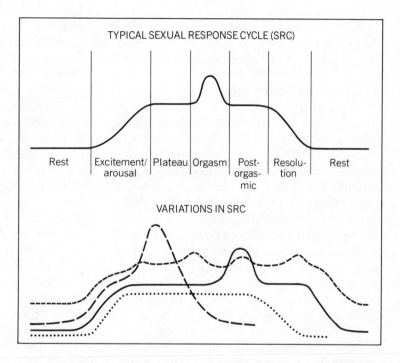

than another, or to start feeling "horny" while doing something unerotic.

Regardless of what starts sexual excitement, it continues only if psychological or physical stimuli persist. If excitement rises, one enters the *plateau phase;* vasocongestion and muscle tension level off, but sexual interest remains high. The plateau may be short or long, depending on the stimuli and a person's desire, social training, and constitutional endowment. One person may strive to reach orgasm quickly; another may have little control over it; another may enjoy greatly extending the plateau phase (see Figure 4.1).

From the plateau phase one can go on to the *orgasmic phase.* This is relatively brief. Psychological and muscle tension rapidly increase, as do body activity, heart rate, and breathing. Then there is a sudden release. This rapid buildup and sudden release of sexual tension is called *orgasm,* or *climax.* Orgasm can be triggered psychologically (by fantasy) or somatically (by stimulation of any part of the body), but it usually results from stimulation of the penis, scrotum, and testes in males and of the clitoris, vagina, and uterus in females. But no matter what region is stimulated, the chief site of pleasure is ultimately the brain, the main area of release the pelvis. Any part of the body may be fondled while one thinks about sex or love, or both, and the body responds. That is why it has been said that the most important sex organ is not between the legs, but between the ears.

51

For men, orgasm usually involves ejaculation (called "shooting" or "coming," although the later term is also used for orgasm in both men and women). There is no such event for women or prepubertal boys.

The time immediately after orgasm *(postorgasm)* is different for males and females. Males tend to become passive and unresponsive *(refractory)* to further sexual stimuli, and the penis becomes limp *(detumesces)*. They quickly pass through the *resolution phase* to the resting phase. Often this involves a period of sleep. Some females also resolve quickly toward sleep, but many remain sexually responsive and rarely show an immediate refractory period. They may return to the plateau stage, invite more stimulation, and go on to orgasm again *(multiple orgasm)* before passing back to the resting phase. Multiple orgasms occur only rarely in males (see chapter 5).

After orgasm, both males and females go through the resolution phase and return to the resting phase. They experience mental and physical relaxation and a feeling of well-being. Many people report psychological satisfaction or relaxation without apparently reaching orgasm. Others say that not reaching orgasm causes frustration. If one partner's resolution phase brings sleep and the other is still aroused, the situation can be frustrating indeed.

The SRC of some males may differ slightly from the one just described (Kinsey et al., 1948), but men are more consistent than females, both as a group and as individuals from one time to another. Except in old age or when sick, most males, having reached the plateau stage, rarely stop short of orgasm. Typically a young male in the resting phase can be quickly aroused by a thought or incident. With stimulation by himself or a partner, he strives intensely for rapid increase in pleasure, wanting to move quickly through the plateau to orgasm. He approaches climax with rapid, heavy breathing and pelvic thrusting. Orgasm is usually short and explosive; it brings ejaculation, vocal noises, the end of thrusting, and brief loss of awareness. (The French call this *le petit mort*, "the little death," and in sixteenth- and seventeenth-century English poetry the word "die" often had the same double meaning.) Orgasm is usually followed by rapid loss of erotic interest, return to the resting phase, and often by sleep.

Women are more variable. Some have an SRC like the typical male one: excitement rises quickly through the plateau to an explosive orgasm, with a great deal of involuntary movement and noise. The woman may thrash about and cry or scream, even laugh or sob uncontrollably; she may look and sound as if she were in pain. A smaller number of men also do this. The first time this is experienced or seen, it can be frightening to the person or the partner. Resolution may occur quickly or the woman may return to the plateau, in some cases ready for another orgasm.

For other women, perhaps the majority, arousal builds more slowly, the plateau is prolonged, and orgasm less dramatic but powerful. For still others, orgasm seems not a climax but a passing over to a more relaxed condition, with little movement and noise and a slow resolution. For a number of women, perhaps 10 to 30 percent, orgasm never occurs; for many, if not most, it is intermittently absent (Gebhard, 1970; Giese, 1970; Kinsey et al., 1953). A woman may experience different patterns at different times. No pattern is better than another, and noise and energy of expression do not necessarily correspond with satisfaction.

Sexual Mechanisms

It has been traditional in psychology and ethology (the study of normal animal behavior) to think in terms of *drives,* or forces, leading to specific behaviors. Scientists spoke of a hunger drive or a sex drive that creatures strove to reduce (Hull, 1943). In studying sexual activity, the classic idea of drive is usefully replaced by the concepts of *arousal, copulatory,* and *orgasmic mechanisms* (Beach and Jordan, 1956; Beach and Whalen, 1959; McGill, 1965). The three mechanisms share some characteristics, but each has something unique. These internal mechanisms react to external, specific stimuli called *releasing factors* (Tinbergen, 1951).

Arousal mechanisms are set off when the brain interprets such releasing factors in sight, sound, touch, smell, and thought. These mechanisms leave a person turned on or turned off; they interact to bring one from the resting phase to orgasm. *Copulatory mechanisms* are involved in genital activity; among them are penile and nipple erection, vaginal sweating, and pelvic thrusting. Among *orgasmic mechanisms* are ejaculation in males and muscle contractions in males and females.

The sensitivities, or *thresholds,* of these mechanisms depend on biological factors, but they can be modified by cultural forces and individual development. For instance, nature prepares males to be aroused by the sight of female buttocks and breasts (releasing factors); but one man may be more or less easily aroused for genetic or hormonal reasons; his society may teach him to give special erotic attention to the breasts or to prefer large or small breasts; his individual development may make him respond more or less to such influences.

All three kinds of mechanisms interact to produce the sexual response cycle. Consider a person at the resting phase. Sight, smell, hearing, and other stimuli are elaborated by thought, memory, or fantasy; an odor, the gesture of a hand, the expression in someone's eyes, becomes sexually arousing. If the arousing stimuli are sufficient, excitement rises, and copulatory mechanisms come into action; if a sufficient level is not reached, the person returns to rest. Then the copulatory mechanisms are affected by positive and negative influences. If the stimuli keep increasing, and vasocongestion and myotonia proceed, the threshold of orgasmic mechanisms is passed, and climax is possible; if not, the person returns to rest.

Many mental and physical factors affect arousal, copulation, and orgasm. Rest, relaxation, a sense of well-being, and androgens (male hormones) all lower thresholds for these mechanisms, making their activation more likely. Hunger, fatigue, depression, and progesterone (a female hormone) usually raise the thresholds and have the opposite effects.

Emotions strongly affect all these mechanisms. Anxiety, shame, or preoccupation with a problem at home, school, or work, can interfere with arousal. A person who feels rejected may not respond to sights, sounds, and words that would be arousing at other times. Individual learning and experience also have effects; having had a sexually restrictive background may make it difficult to be aroused by a genital caress. Cultural influences also color a person's response. Suppose a couple is kissing, and the man caresses the woman's thighs. She accepts the kisses as affectionate but withdraws from the caress, having been taught that it shows impersonal desire. He, raised differently or exposed to other attitudes, thought it showed not only sexual excitement but emotional intimacy.

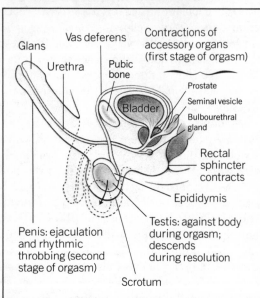

Figure 4-2 / *During the excitement phase of the SRC, the penis rises, thickens, and stiffens. Rhythmic contractions of the sexual system occur at orgasm, and semen is ejaculated.*

Image labels (Figure 4-2):

- Glans
- Urethra
- Vas deferens
- Pubic bone
- Contractions of accessory organs (first stage of orgasm)
- Prostate
- Bladder
- Seminal vesicle
- Bulbourethral gland
- Rectal sphincter contracts
- Penis: ejaculation and rhythmic throbbing (second stage of orgasm)
- Epididymis
- Testis: against body during orgasm; descends during resolution
- Scrotum

With another couple, the interpretations might be reversed.

The Processes of the SRC

All living creatures strive for *homeostasis,* a stable, or balanced, condition. Many parts of the sexual response cycle disturb homeostasis; they resemble the stress ("fight-or-flight") reactions a person feels when threatened. The eyes dilate, the heart and lungs work harder and faster, the muscles tense. Blood shifts to the parts of the body that will need it most. After the emergency, the body returns to a relaxed state.

Many of these changes take place automatically during and after sexual excitement. As arousal occurs, the autonomic nervous system (ANS) increases muscle tension and increases blood flow to the sexualia, filling and swelling the tissues and making them red and warm. This vasocongestion and myotonia are automatic; they can not be brought about just by willing them, nor can they always be willed away.

Male Processes

Penis. There are three penile processes in the male SRC. These are erection, ejaculation, and detumescence.*

Penile *erection* ("hard on," "boner") is one of the first signs of male sexual arousal. Stimuli to the penis, inner thigh, bladder, or scrotum

* Unless otherwise indicated, the following descriptions are based on the landmark work of Masters and Johnson (1966) and on personal and clinical impressions.

can cause erection even in the absence of erotic thoughts or feelings. Touch, warmth, vibration, combined wetness and pressure, sights, smells, and sounds can also lead to erection. In themselves they probably have no specific powers and depend on psychological readiness.

The erection reflex is generated when arousing sensations from the brain or body reach an erection center in the lower part of the spinal cord. Nerves then relay impulses that set off vasocongestion. Blood fills the corpora cavernosa; this puts pressure on the veins, slowing the departure of blood from the penis. Erection remains fully or nearly complete until orgasm is over.

Despite a host of humorous stories, the penis almost never becomes locked in a vagina so that withdrawal is impossible. A survey of scientific literature has revealed only one confirmed account (Oliven, 1974), associated with spasmodic contractions of the vagina. In dogs, wolves, and foxes, such a lock does occur, because of engorgement of the posterior part of the penis after penetration; the surrounding vaginal tissues prevent withdrawal until ejaculation and detumescence have taken place.

Ejaculation is the spasmodic release of sperm and semen from the testes and accessory glands through the urethra and out the penis. Like erection, it is largely reflexive. Ejaculation is not the same as orgasm and does not always happen along with it, but usually they occur together.

Ejaculation has two phases, *emission* and *ejaculation proper*. During emission, the accessory glands and the vas deferens empty semen into the dilated urethra. Men are usually aware

---

Nocturnal Emissions

Considering the frequency of male masturbation (chapter 9), nocturnal emissions, and other noncoital orgasms, some men may ejaculate more often outside the vagina than in it.

Nocturnal emissions ("wet dreams") are reflex ejaculations that occur during sleep. Sometimes they are accompanied by erotic dreams. These emissions are common in boys, especially from the start of puberty through early adolescence. But nocturnal emissions do not end with adolescence. Almost all males have erotic dreams, and orgasm occurs in many of them. About half the married men interviewed by Kinsey et al. (1948) still had nocturnal emissions, which accounted for 3 to 5 percent of their total orgasmic outlet. For single men, nocturnal emission accounted for 5 to 12 percent of orgasmic outlet. Nocturnal emissions cease after age fifty.

Females also have nocturnal orgasms, usually with erotic dreams, but less often than males do. These orgasms do not, of course, leave the telltale signs of emission.

that this has happened and that ejaculation proper is inevitable; they "know they are coming" and cannot prevent it. In ejaculation proper, strong reflex muscle contractions in the vas deferens and urethra propel the semen outside the body. There are some six to eight rhythmic contractions in healthy young men, first at intervals of 0.8 seconds, then more weakly and at longer intervals.

Detumescence is the return of the penis from erection to a flaccid state during the resolution phase. It usually begins after orgasm and ejaculation, but can occur earlier. At first, detumescence is rapid; then the penis empties of blood more slowly, until it is limp. Detumescence usually happens regardless of efforts to maintain erection, which can frustrate one or both partners.

Scrotum and Testes. Sexual excitement produces myotonia in the scrotum; it tightens, rises toward the body, and loses its loose, saclike appearance. Vasocongestion makes the scrotum warm and reddish and causes the testes to increase 50 to 100 percent in size. Before and during orgasm, the testes are pressed firmly against the body.

Resolution brings a reversal of vasocongestion and myotonia; the scrotum and testes return to their normal position, size, and color. The speed of return varies among individuals, but it also seems related to the intensity and duration of the excitement and plateau phases. Prolonged vasocongestion of the testes may become painful, a condition commonly called "blue balls." It can occur whether or not there has been orgasm.

Female Processes

Vagina. As erection signals male sexual arousal, three vaginal changes signal female excitement — vaginal sweating, expansion of the inner two-thirds of the vaginal barrel, and

---

Lubrication

Lubrication is necessary for coitus, and usually vaginal fluids do the job. But in some women, especially after menopause, there is too little sweating for satisfactory coitus. This does not necessarily show lack of erotic interest or excitement, any more than copious fluids always reflect intense arousal. Estrogen levels, vaginal infections, and a number of drugs can influence wetting. The need for artificial lubrication should not automatically be thought a sign of sexual uninterest or inadequacy by either partner.

The most common lubricant, always available but not long-lasting, is saliva. Most soaps and vegetable oils irritate the vagina or turn rancid. Petroleum jelly and petroleum oils feel greasy and tend to damage rubber contraceptives. Some condoms are prelubricated, and some vaginal foams and jellies contain lubricating agents. Water-soluble lubricants helpful for coitus are sold without prescription at drug stores.

---

reddening of the labia. All depend on vasocongestion and myotonia.

As soon as ten to thirty seconds after arousal begins, the vaginal walls start a sweatinglike process called *transudation*. The fluid *(transudate)* is clear, slightly slippery, nonoily, and has a distinctive aroma and taste. It seems to have at least three functions: it lubricates the penis and vagina, its alkalinity neutralizes the usually acidic vagina, and its moisture, like its alkalinity, aids sperm survival.

Recall that at rest the vagina is only a potential space, like an unfilled glove. With excitement, the deeper portion begins to balloon, creating a space greater than is needed for the penis, perhaps providing a receptacle where semen can collect. As vasocongestion increases, the vagina's normal pink deepens to red, and its inner two-thirds balloon further *(tenting)*. Meanwhile, the outer third narrows and tightens; it is now called the *orgasmic platform*.

During orgasm, tenting continues, and the orgasmic platform contracts strongly and rhythmically. Recall that in men, orgasmic contractions occur at intervals of 0.8 seconds, then more weakly and at longer intervals. In women, the contractions may continue far longer than in men. More intense and prolonged contractions are felt as a longer, more intense orgasm. Vaginal wetting may increase before and during orgasm, but women, as we noted, do not ejaculate. In some women, more stimulation can cause repeated orgasm.

Resolution brings a reversal of all the changes described above. For many reasons, resolution may take a long time. Often this results from prolonged arousal not followed by orgasm; vasocongestion remains, creating *chronic pelvic congestion*. Severe discomfort and frustration can continue until congestion ends.

This "lower-back ache" is the female equivalent of blue balls.

Clitoris. Although the clitoris is highly sensitive, its response seems undramatic during the excitement phase. It becomes more sensitive to touch and pressure, and there is vasocongestion but not usually erection. Changes are difficult to see during the plateau phase, when the clitoris disappears under its hood. (It may disappear and reappear as excitement waxes and wanes.) This retraction may be a protective mechanism; many women complain that direct stimulation of the clitoris is unpleasant and painful. During resolution, there are changes similar to penile detumescence. In chronic pelvic congestion, the clitoris may remain engorged and very sensitive.

Labia Majora and Minora. The labia majora and labia minora react differently during the SRC. Both are influenced by the woman's *parity* (how many children she has borne).

In *nulipara* (women who have had no children), the myotonia of excitement makes the labia majora flatter and thinner, and they remain that way through plateau and orgasm. In *unipara* (who have had one child) and even more in *multipara* (who have had more than one child), the labia have developed an extensive network of blood vessels. During excitement, this network becomes congested, and the labia swell two to three times in size.

The labia minora show color and size changes rather like those seen in the sex skin of some nonhuman primates. With excitement, they double or triple in size and become reddish-purple. When the legs are apart, the labia may develop a gaping appearance. A return to normal occurs during resolution, first rapidly and then slowly.

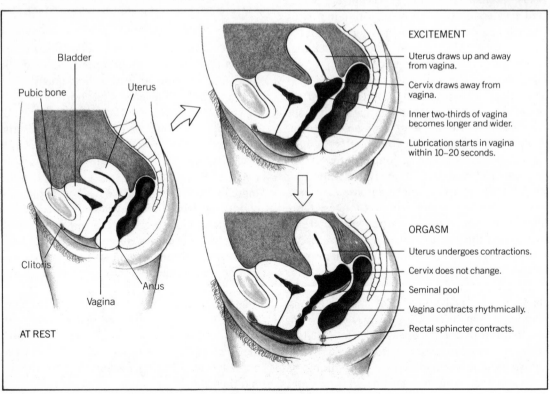

Bladder

Pubic bone

Uterus

Clitoris

Vagina

Anus

AT REST

EXCITEMENT

Uterus draws up and away from vagina.

Cervix draws away from vagina.

Inner two-thirds of vagina becomes longer and wider.

Lubrication starts in vagina within 10–20 seconds.

ORGASM

Uterus undergoes contractions.

Cervix does not change.

Seminal pool

Vagina contracts rhythmically.

Rectal sphincter contracts.

Figure 4-3 / *Changes in the female internal sexualia occur at each stage of the SRC (bottom). Some external changes, such as curling or flaring of the fingers or toes, were noted by artists (as in this Japanese scroll, ca. 1830) long before researchers described the SRC in detail.*

Uterus. Changes and movements of the uterus play a dramatic part in some women's SRC and in their awareness of their response. During arousal, the uterus lifts upward, becomes engorged with blood, and contracts (vasocongestion and myotonia again). The elevation continues into the plateau phase and is then maintained. During orgasm, the uterus contracts along with the orgasmic platform. Whether a pumping or sucking action occurs, as if to aid sperm transport, is debated (Masters and Johnson, 1966; Fox, Wolff, and Baker, 1970). Within five to ten minutes after orgasm, the uterus returns to normal size and position.

Responses Shared by Males and Females

Females' breasts and skin are more sexually responsive than males'. The other responses described below, however, are more alike than different in males and females.

Breasts. Erection of the nipples, caused by reflex muscle contraction, is an early sign of sexual arousal in women. It occurs in about half of all men. The nipple may also become erect because of nonerotic stimulation, such as cold.

Vasocongestion enlarges the female breast and areola during the excitement and plateau phases, especially in women who have never given birth or suckled. In men and in women whose breasts are large from nursing, no changes appear. As the breast enlarges, the nipple seems to retract; actually, it does not pull back, the breast swells out. No noticeable changes occur during orgasm. During resolution, the breast and areola quickly return to normal.

Skin. During the SRC, 70 to 75 percent of women and about 25 percent of men show a *sex flush*, a blush of vasocongestion across the chest, breasts, back, and neck. This develops during the transition from excitement to plateau and is clearest at orgasm. With resolution, it quickly disappears. This striking event went unrecognized until Masters and Johnson (1966) described it, surprising scientists and laymen alike.

Muscular-Skeletal Systems. Unlike the sex flush, muscle tension and body movement have

---

The Sex Skin

Animals have many ways to show that they are sexually receptive. Some female primates do so by a *sex skin,* an area of the buttocks that becomes swollen and bright red in response to increased sex-hormone levels in the blood. The sex skin is largest and brightest when a female is sexually most receptive. In some animals, a second patch of skin on the face or chest mimics the first, raising the chance of getting the message across (see also Figure 4-4).

Figure 4-4 / *In most mammalian species, the male mounts the female from behind; in some, when she is sexually receptive, visual "targets" develop on her rear to help arouse and guide him. The gelada baboon, which spends much time squatting instead of on all fours, duplicates its signal of sexual readiness on its chest. The development in humans of upright posture and language requires frequent face-to-face contact; not surprisingly, humans are among the few species that mate face to face. Some researchers see no functional explanation for the roundness of women's breasts except as similar mimicry, repeating the round contour of the buttocks, which have long been primate arousal targets. The areolae are assumed to be visual targets for nursing infants.*

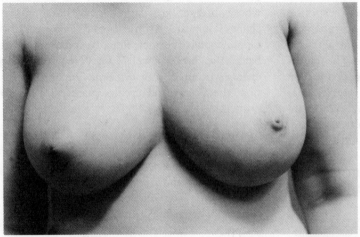

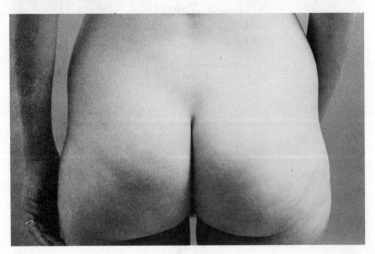

long been noticed and talked about as parts of the SRC. Over-all muscle tension and activity increase in both males and females during arousal and into the plateau phase, especially in the thighs and buttocks and around the mouth and in the neck's "strap" muscles. These apparent signs of stress show not discomfort but a reaching for sexual release. With impending orgasm, muscles in the limbs contract, and the toes extend, curl, or flare *(carpopedal spasm)*.

Orgasm brings a peak in muscle tension and activity. There may be dramatic movements of the entire body, especially the pelvis, or else rigorlike tenseness and tremors. Resolution brings rapid relaxation. These actions vary greatly from person to person and according to age, sexual experience, health, and other factors. Sometimes the most important element is how free a person feels to let go during arousal and orgasm. Much body movement during genital activity is reflexive, but some is learned, even practiced. Many people restrict their movements because of guilt, ignorance, or embarrassment. Others enhance their activity as an expression of eroticism. Some therapists advocate practicing movement and muscular response until they become automatic.

Other Systems: Cardiovascular, Respiratory, Digestive, Excretory. Sexual excitement involves the entire body, especially through reflexive stress responses. As excitement rises, the heart rate may double and blood pressure rises greatly. Blood is shunted away from the digestive and excretory systems to the genital and respiratory systems. The rate and depth of breathing increase greatly. Many so-called love sounds are those of a pounding heart and heavy, labored breathing.

Although digestion stops, the mouth and anus may be very active. Saliva may flow freely. The anus tightens; this and the cessation of rectal processes prevent defecation during coitus. During orgasm, the anus may pulsate; the strength of these contractions reflects the intensity of orgasm.

Urination is almost impossible during sexual activity; kidney functions are much reduced, and in males the sphincter at the base of the bladder constricts to keep urine from passing through the urethra. The release of this sphincter after sexual activity often brings an urgent need to urinate. Some women occasionally release urine during orgasm because of spasmodic relaxation of the sphincters of the bladder and urethra. This is more common in women who have borne children.

Influences on Sexual Responses and Mechanisms

The Influence of the Genes

The mating behavior of all species is highly *stereotyped*. In the social sciences, stereotyped means widespread and socially learned. In biological science, it means determined by the genes and activated through hormones, enzymes, the nervous system, and experience. For instance, a social scientist would call the American association of tea with feminine or genteel behavior a social stereotype. A biologist would call the mewing and rolling of a female cat in heat stereotyped.

Through evolution, each species has developed a distinctive, stereotyped mating process. The processes of most higher species, however, have many common elements. Although there are many ways of courting, there are relatively few ways to use the sexualia.

Animal breeders have long known that cows can be bred to give much or little milk, horses to run fast or slow. Animals can also be bred for many kinds of sexual behavior. Researchers have bred guinea pigs, rats, chickens, and other animals that do much sexual mounting or little, that stay in heat (estrus) for many hours or few, that ejaculate quickly or after a long time (Goy and Jackway, 1959; Hale and Schein, 1962; McGill, 1965).

There is some evidence that humans also inherit stereotyped courtship and coital mechanisms. Clues to the existence of such inherited mechanisms are found in such genetic conditions as *Klinefelter's syndrome*. The cells of a Klinefelter male have not the usual XY sex chromosomes but XXY—an added female chromosome. The Y chromosome produces a male phenotype; he has testes and a penis. However, the extra female chromosome seems related to the Klinefelter male's low sex drive (Raboch, Mellan, and Starka, 1975).

Most genetic effects on sexual and sex-related behavior are milder and more subtle, and many are still disputed. Among the best-known genetic studies of human sexuality are those of Franz Kallmann (1952a, 1952b, 1953). Kallmann studied sets of twins, one of whom, in each set, was known to be homosexual. Kallmann compared monozygotic twins (identical, with identical genes) and dizygotic twins (fraternal, who are genetically no more or less alike than other siblings). He reported that in almost all monozygotic twins, but few dizygotic ones, if one twin was homosexual so was the other. It did not seem to matter that some pairs of mono-

zygotic twins had been reared in different homes. This implied a strong genetic factor in their sexual orientation.

However, the matter is far from settled. Both the methods and interpretations of this study have been widely criticized (Ellis, 1963), and some researchers reported opposite results (Heston and Shields, 1968; Mesnikoff et al., 1963; Rainer et al., 1960). Beach has said that the chances of a direct genetic cause for homosexuality are "probably one in a thousand" (quoted in Karlen, 1971). Of course, an indirect genetic influence may exist. In recent years, a promising approach has been the study of interaction traits through *behavior genetics*.

Behavior genetic experiments with rats give intriguing insight into a common human situation. Male rats were selected for being sexually active at one time of day and housed with females that were active at another. Unless synchronized by light changes, these pairs of rats would not mate (Richter, 1970). Many couples, similarly, have conflicting preferences for when to have coitus—before sleep at night, on awaking in the morning, or during the day. Work schedules, privacy, and social customs may be important influences, but innate preferences may exist.

Aging

Almost every mental and physical aspect of each phase of the SRC changes with age. The changes are slow and subtle from year to year, but unmistakable over long periods. The effects of age on various sexual acts are discussed in chapters 9 and 11; here we cover only sexual response.

No particular age separates youth, middle

age, and old age. The effects of aging vary according to constitution, physical condition, personality, and attitudes. Sexual aging is also related to having a receptive partner: men and women who have steady sexual partners seem more likely to retain normal physiological processes than those who don't (Masters and Johnson, 1966).

Physical Aspects: Men. Many young men are concerned about becoming erect too readily and ejaculating too quickly; in later life, the opposite often happens. With age, a man becomes slower to have an erection, begin coitus, and reach orgasm; erection, orgasm, and ejaculation have less force and intensity. He is also more influenced by the situation and his changing emotions.

Each phase and mechanism changes at its own rate. Orgasm is the first to weaken and, in some men, fade away. Erectile ability is next to decrease and perhaps eventually disappear. Arousal mechanisms are likely to last longest. In some older men, all sexual response ceases for days or longer, as if there were an extended refractory period. After age fifty, many men increasingly find that the flesh won't always follow where the spirit leads:

There is progressive decline in penile sensitivity (H. Newman, 1970).
From age fifty on, erection takes two or three times longer to occur than in the forties.
After age sixty, a lost erection is difficult to regain.
Orgasm is much less vigorous, and ejaculation is felt as a single rather than a two-stage

---

Age and Passion

> Grow old along with me!
> The best is yet to be,
> The last of life, for which the first was made. . . .
>
> — Robert Browning,
> "Rabbi Ben Ezra" (1864)

"Kind are all your words, my dear,
Do not the rest withhold.
Who can know the year, my dear,
When an old man's blood grows cold?

I have what no young man can have
Because he loves too much.
Words I have that can pierce the heart,
But what can he do but touch?"

> — William Butler Yeats,
> "The Wild Old Wicked Man" (1938)

Aging Changes

Her years are in her favor, for she knows
Tricks that a novice never could disclose.
Yes, she is sixty; but still full of fire,
She'll do, my friend, whatsoever you desire.

> — Louis Untermeyer,
> "Sexuality and Aging" (1975)
> Adaptation from the Greek Anthology

What is needed most for a man to continue to feel like a man when he is older, is to treat him like one.

> — Simone de Beauvoir,
> *The Second Sex* (1960)

event. Ejaculation may become more a seepage than a shot.

Detumescence follows ejaculation immediately. Nocturnal emissions are less frequent.

Masters and Johnson (1966) have observed:

With rare exceptions the male over 60 years old usually will be satisfied completely with one, or at the most, two ejaculations a week regardless of the number of coital opportunities or the depth of his female partner's sexual demand. Many cannot redevelop penile erection for a matter of 12 to 24 hours after ejaculation. Those who achieve a relatively early return to ejaculation may have lost their ejaculatory urge and are perfectly content to serve their female partners to the completion of the women's sexual demands without recurrent ejaculatory interest.

Physical Aspects: Women. An aging woman must contend with more physical changes influencing sexual response than a man. Men still produce male hormones and sperm in middle and old age, though in decreasing amounts; a marked decrease occurs only in the seventies. Women's ovaries, however, produce markedly less of the female hormones with menopause (between ages forty-five and fifty-five), and ovulation stops completely. This starts changes in the sexual and reproductive tissues. The most apparent ones are the loss of firm fat deposits at the pubis, hips, and breasts and reduced vasocongestion and myotonia. Other changes are:

The vaginal walls become thinner and less able to expand, so coitus may become painful.

About five years after menopause, vaginal wetting decreases greatly in most women (though some still lubricate adequately).

After age sixty, vaginal wetting may not occur for one to three minutes after arousal, instead of within ten to thirty seconds.

During orgasm, the orgasmic platform contracts more briefly and less intensely.

After orgasm, resolution is relatively quick and complete.

Severe uterine cramps may accompany orgasm and persist afterward. Estrogen replacement may give some relief.

Many of these changes parallel those in men. However, their extent and the time of their appearance can differ in a couple. Partners who cannot admit to these changes and have difficulty adjusting to them may feel frustration and conflict. But for those who adjust, sex may remain as satisfying in old age as at any other time in life. People who value body contact, physical intimacy, and genital expression may find that coitus and orgasm become less important, and physical closeness more satisfying for its companionship, affection, and warmth.

Effects on Coital Frequency. Kinsey et al. (1948) found that on the average, men want coitus about half as often at age fifty as they did during their teens. For seventy-year-old men, the commonest (median) orgasmic frequency is down to a bit less than once a week, but many healthy older men and women remain coitally active in their seventies. Those vigorous in early life are more likely to be active later; the inactive tend to become less active still (though there are exceptions). One long-term study of men and women past sixty (Pfeiffer, Verwoerdt, and Wang, 1968) found that the median age for stopping coitus was sixty-eight for men and sixty for women. But this is not always

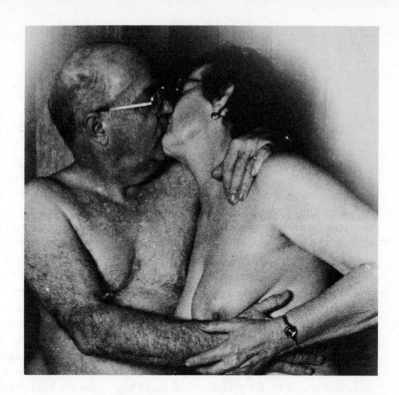

Figure 4-5 / *A fact of erotic life our society long avoided is the need for love and sex in the later years. It was under almost complete taboo even in medical literature until the mid-1960s, and it still causes as much avoidance as empathy.*

because people want to stop. Older people, especially women, who have lost their spouses find it difficult to find new partners and privacy. And coital frequency does not invariably decline with age. The study also showed that 15 percent of the people increased their sexual activity as they aged.

In later-life sexuality, as in most physical activities, it seems that "Those who don't use it, lose it." The sexual tissues stay more fit if kept active. Masters and Johnson (1966) found women in their seventies who still produced vaginal wetting and who showed little vaginal shrinkage. These women had engaged in coitus or masturbation at least once or twice a week most of their adult lives. Women who did so once a month or less during the decade after menopause had difficulty accommodating the penis when they did try. Sexual mechanisms also last longer and remain stronger in people with regular partners. Masters and Johnson (1966) concluded that a woman or man needs only good general health and an interested, in-

teresting partner to have a gratifying sex life even into the eighties.

Social and Psychological Factors. Adulthood, middle age, and old age are as much social conventions as biological conditions. A person defines them differently at ages ten, twenty, forty, and seventy, and the definition of old age varies from one culture to another. In some, a woman of thirty-five may have borne a dozen children, seem tired and worn, and be thought old by herself and her community. In our society, a woman that age may have borne only one child, enjoy the benefits of leisure, makeup, even cosmetic surgery, and take for granted her continuing youthful attractiveness.

The subject of later-life sexuality was strictly taboo in our society until the middle sixties. At best, sexually active older people received snickering recognition as dirty old men and women. The usual rationale for this attitude was that age brought a dignity that sex somehow offended. Some people also believed the

65

myth that eroticism dies in midlife, as if sex were a fixed reserve that could be used up. Avoiding the facts of later-life sexuality may also be a carry-over of childhood reluctance to see one's parents and others their age as sexual beings (Pocs et al., 1977).

Many people's sexual activity dwindles for nonphysical reasons, such as boredom with their partners, entrenched marital conflict, or shame at feeling or seeming like a dirty old man or woman. Others fear being found unattractive and rejected; they withdraw on the principle that it is better to quit than be fired. People who find much of their feelings of pride and worth in being sexually attractive may be devastated by aging. Menopause makes some women—and some women's partners—feel that love and sex are behind them, even that their femininity has perished. Furthermore, middle age is for many people a time of peak nonsexual pressures—job, career, childrearing, the leaving of children, midlife crisis and readjustment. The resulting depression and anxiety can easily interfere with sexual activity.

These factors affect men as well as women. Any man may have trouble reaching erection or orgasm and then avoid coitus rather than risk another ego-shattering experience (although the problem may be easily reversible). Although this can happen at any age, it is increasingly common from midlife on. Fatigue, depression, and other physical and psychological stresses can then more easily overcome arousal mechanisms. This is sometimes erroneously attributed to "male menopause," but men undergo nothing like the relatively rapid end of ovulation and shift in hormone balance.

Yet the psychological influences that dampen later-life sexuality for some can enhance it for others. Life experience makes many people more accepting of themselves and their partners. They tend to become less impetuous and less vulnerable to feeling sharp frustration. In men, the speed and urgency of sexual response less often overrides the emotions. They react more as women usually do, influenced as much by mood, emotion, and ambience in a sexual encounter as by sexual drive. Aging brings complementary changes in many women. Through their thirties and forties, many become less inhibited sexually, more playful and aggressive. Menopause may end fear of pregnancy; the moving out of children or the diminished need to add to family income can allow sexual and emotional blossoming. With such changes, many couples find themselves more sexually compatible than ever before. This may explain the significant minority of people whose sexual activity increases with aging (G. Newman and Nichols, 1960; Pfeiffer, Verwoerdt, and Wang, 1968; Verwoerdt, Pfeiffer, and Wang, 1969).

Our society is only beginning to accept that people of all ages need to give and receive love, physical pleasure, and the self-affirmation of satisfying sexuality. Many older people, like many youngsters, lack the money, facilities, privacy, and full social permission that make sexual relationships easier to form and maintain. It is ironic that many people still have difficulty finding new partners and sexual opportunities when they are most adult.

Overview

In this chapter, we described basic sexual mechanisms and responses and some theoretical ideas and models that put them in perspective. These descriptions and models are meant not as prescriptions but as ways to see how and why certain sexual responses do or don't happen. This approach may seem to make sex too mechanical—in sex, as in tennis and skiing, one can engage in the activity without knowing the mechanics—but appreciation and performance often do improve with understanding of the fundamentals. That this is true will become apparent in trying to answer the questions below.

In the next chapter, on orgasm, we will focus on one sexual response that today provokes a great deal of interest and emotion.

Review, Discuss, Decide

1. How are the sexual response cycles of males and females similar? How are they different?
2. How do male orgasmic experiences vary? Female experiences?
3. Which physical and psychological factors can interfere with sexual response? Which ones can aid response?
4. How can aging affect sexual response?
5. What is your reaction to sexual activity among the middle aged and the old? Have your ideas or attitudes ever changed?
6. How might sexual decisions and life-styles adopted by young adults affect sex activity in middle and later life?
7. Does this chapter's attention to biological factors lessen the importance of psychological or social factors in sexual response? Explain.

5 Orgasm

Are men's and women's orgasms different?

How can I tell whether I've had an orgasm? Whether my partner has?

Should a person fake an orgasm?

Does prolonging coitus help a woman reach orgasm?

Can all women have multiple orgasms? Can men?

Many people think of orgasm as a goal for themselves and their partners, and reaching it takes on special importance. During or after coitus, they may ask, "Did you come?" A common reply is, "Couldn't you tell?" The important issues raised by these questions are often avoided.

Reaching and Recognizing Orgasm

Despite all the signs described in chapter 4, orgasm is not always obvious. Comparing orgasms to fireworks, tidal waves, and symphonies isn't helpful. Even many regularly orgasmic people don't recognize their experiences in these descriptions.

Almost all males masturbate in early adolescence, so from then on they recognize their orgasms by sensation and ejaculation. They, like women who have quite dramatic orgasms, may find it difficult to accept some women's difficulty reaching climax or knowing whether they have.

Also, women's orgasms don't always have signs they and their partners easily recognize. Some people have said (Hastings, 1966a) that if one doesn't know whether one has had an orgasm, one hasn't. However, there may be a discrepancy between the physical signs of orgasm, which can be measured, and unmeasurable feelings that accompany it.

Women can show physical signs of arousal without feeling aroused (Heiman, 1975), just as men can have pleasureless erections. Also, some women do not reach a peak experience but remain in a state like the plateau phase of the SRC. For any man or woman, a state of sexual tension followed by feelings of tension release, relaxation, and completion, and a desire to talk, rest, cuddle, or sleep suggest that orgasm has occurred.

Some signs of orgasm can be easily detected by instruments or by a bystander, but recognizing them in the dark or while sexually involved may be impossible. Some men recognize their partners' orgasms, but many do not. To avoid problems, it is easiest if partners indicate, verbally or nonverbally, whether a climax has occurred and—sometimes another matter—whether either wants to continue.

Coitus does not always bring orgasm for both partners, even if both are usually orgasmic. Orgasm is often faked, mostly by women but occasionally by men. To fake or not to fake orgasm is both an emotional and ethical question. Some say that faking could make orgasm less likely on future occasions, leave one partner sexually frustrated, or distort the relationship through dishonesty. It can certainly prevent one partner from trying to help the other to reach orgasm. Women do most of the faking, so many see it as a way of salvaging men's egos, perhaps at women's expense (Masters and Johnson, 1975). The issues and answers may be different for occasional or regular faking.

Another view is that both partners' egos are involved, and not reaching orgasm may suggest sexual failure or incompetence by either or both of them. Also, both partners want to be considered able to give pleasure. Since many people are often insecure about sex, total honesty is probably a rarity, and it may not always be the kindest course. There is often some compromise, a mixture of honesty, tact, and practicality.

Thoughts and feelings can aid or hinder orgasm, both regularly and on any occasion. People may have thoughts and fantasies unrelated to what their bodies are doing—for instance, not concentrating on the real sexual act or partner but imagining others. This is common during masturbation, and perhaps more common during coitus than most people admit.

Satisfaction, whatever it means to a given person, is usually the first concern in sexual activity. Some men and more women are sometimes satisfied by coitus without orgasm. Even never experiencing orgasm *(anorgasmia)*

or reaching it rarely has little importance to some people (Gebhard, 1966; Wallin and Clark, 1963). However, it may become a sore point in a relationship or a source of worry or low self-esteem. All the factors involved in anorgasmia are not known. Many anorgasmic people have had strict religious upbringings (Masters and Johnson, 1970), feelings of sin and guilt about sexual pleasure (Kinsey et al., 1953), ignorance of their own sexual potential, and general sexual inhibitions. Often education, training, or therapy can make orgasm possible and desirable (Barbach, 1975; H. Kaplan, 1974; Masters and Johnson, 1970). Some people can reach orgasm but don't want it; they see it as losing control, not worth the effort, or undesirable with a resented or unloved partner.

Types of Orgasm

Much debate has centered on whether more than one type of female orgasm exists. The question is often asked, "Is there a difference between vaginal and clitoral orgasm?" This phrasing rises from Freud's idea that in women, psychosexual maturity is associated with a shift in erotic focus from the clitoris (stimulated in masturbation) to the vagina (stimulated in coitus). But neither this nor any other theory accounts for all the varied reports of women and men. Three major types of female orgasm have been described.

Single Model

Kinsey and his colleagues (1953) were among the first to seriously question that a physiological difference exists between clitoral and vaginal orgasms. Then the research of

Masters and Johnson (1966) showed that the physiological response of orgasm is the same regardless of how it is caused, whether by stimulation of the clitoris, vagina, breasts, thigh muscles, or even the ears. This is the single-model theory, described in the preceding chapter. It is perhaps the best researched sort of orgasm, both physiologically and psychologically.

Double Model

Some researchers say that all orgasms are not identical or are not described by the Masters and Johnson model. Many women distinguish two types of orgasms, brought about in different ways. For example, Seymour Fisher (1973) reports that women describe orgasms brought on by clitoral stimulation as warm, ticklish, electrical, and sharp, and those triggered by vaginal stimulation as throbbing, deep, and soothing. Fisher also reports that some women prefer one type of stimulation to others; some even experience one type as unpleasant or painful. In attaining orgasm, he says, about two-thirds of women "ascribed relatively more importance to direct clitoral as compared to vaginal stimulation." Fisher does not consider either kind of orgasm a sign of psychosexual maturity.

Cecil and Beatrice Fox (1969) describe responses that fit this double model: some women have one or more orgasms before the man's climax and one soon after; the one after ejacu-

---

Missing or Faking Orgasm

These are experiences involving orgasm reported to us by men and women.

A woman of twenty-two: "I had an affair with a guy for about six months. When we were breaking up, he said something that obviously had been eating away at him, that I'd never had an orgasm with him. It wasn't true, and I told him so. But he didn't believe me."

A man of fifty: "Once when I was having intercourse for the second time in a night, I kept reaching the edge of orgasm but couldn't quite make it. Finally I just stopped trying and slumped. The woman thought I'd come. After all, they can't usually feel the ejaculation, they go mostly by body movements. That's when I realized a man can fake it. I've done it a few times, for one reason or another, and I don't think they knew."

A woman of twenty-nine: "I never had an orgasm until I'd been married a few years. Until then I always felt I was a failure, so I did what I imagined women do when they're coming—thrashed around and clawed men's backs and moaned. I was trying very hard to be a good lay. I wonder how many of them knew I was faking."

A man of thirty-five: "When a woman fakes it, am I supposed to be a gentleman and pretend I don't know? Sometimes I suspect that if I don't let on, they actually resent me afterward. They secretly wanted a man to see through their act and *do it* for them. But I never let on. Why bruise an ego?"

A man of twenty-two: "I know I'm not the smoothest lover, so when my partner climaxes, I feel like the world's greatest stud, and I feel much closer to her. If she ever let me know she was frustrated, I think it would damage our relationship. I'm not sure I could handle it."

A woman of twenty-four: "Three times in my life I've been to bed with guys who couldn't keep their erections or couldn't reach orgasm. I don't think I've ever felt so awful and so guilty. Do men feel like that when women don't come?"

lation is always satisfying. Fox and Fox (1971) say that spasmodic contractions of the vagina occur with orgasm when a penis is inside it, creating a sensation of inward suction. Orgasm without a penis in the vagina does not provide that sensation. This description is based on observations of only one couple, but the authors have heard similar accounts; the description may or may not apply to many people.

Triple Model

Irving Singer (1973) offers a *triple model*. The first type of orgasm, the *vulval orgasm*, resembles that described by Masters and Johnson. It consists of involuntary rhythmic contractions of the outer third of the vagina, the vulva, and the orgasmic platform. It does not vary with the stimuli that cause it. The second type, the *uterine orgasm*, involves repeated movements of the uterus, with stimulation of the abdominal nerves. Since only deep penile thrusts or similar deep vaginal stimulation sets off these nerves, this orgasmic response is unique. The third, a combination of the first two, is called a *blended orgasm*.

Theory and terminology seem to have come full circle since Freud distinguished between clitoral and vaginal orgasms. Later research said that such a distinction and the values often attached to it were false. In recent years, however, some research again suggests that psychological and physical factors combine to produce various kinds of orgasm, not measurably different but subjectively so. Also, when two people's entire bodies are involved, many mingled sensations are involved.

Most people are content to enjoy their or-

The Hite Report

As research and discussion of orgasm grew, a study of 3,000 women (who responded to 100,000 questionnaires distributed) by Shere Hite (1976) attracted wide attention. Her work added little to the basic data of Kinsey et al. (1953), Masters and Johnson (1966), Fisher (1973), and others. However, the first-person accounts made the material interesting to many readers. In reviewing her work, Hite (1977) said: "I found that [70 percent] of women do not [regularly] reach orgasm as a result of intercourse. An unrealistic expectation has placed a great burden on women (and men). . . . Women know very well how to have orgasms when they stimulate themselves—easily, quickly, and with great physical pleasure. Eighty-two percent of the women in the study had masturbated, and 95 percent of those achieved orgasm. Women are not dependent on men to have orgasms, yet in sex they are taught to act as if they are. Why is there such a stigma on . . . masturbation? . . . Why shouldn't women give themselves orgasms, while their partners are cooperating by kissing them, etc.? I am advocating that women take power over their own bodies and their own sexual lives."

gasms without such close scrutiny. Furthermore, various women describe their orgasms as fitting the single, double, or triple model or even as being quite different. It is when people say one kind of orgasm is better or preferred that problems arise. Then it may be important to keep in mind that a more clitoral (or vulval, or single-model) orgasm is usually caused by masturbation or by manual or oral stimulation; a more vaginal orgasm usually results from penile penetration.

Many men report similar orgasmic differences; they experience one sort of sensation and satisfaction from orgasms caused by manual or oral manipulation, another from orgasms caused by coitus. Also, occasionally a man's peak pleasure occurs without ejaculation; loss of erection follows, along with the loss of urgent desire for coitus and a tendency to talk, rest, snuggle, or sleep.

The intensity of orgasm, as measured by the strength of muscle contractions, differs in various types of orgasms. Orgasms from masturbation are usually more intense. However, intensity is not necessarily a measure of how much satisfaction is felt. Most people prefer the total body involvement and emotional intensity of coital orgasm, even though it is often physically less intense.

Sex Differences in Orgasm

There are more individual orgasmic differences among women than men. From 10 to 30 percent of women never climax; about 14 percent can have continuous or repeated climaxes (Kinsey, et al., 1953; Gebhard, 1970; Raboch, 1970; Masters and Johnson, 1966). Either extreme is exceptional for a healthy man; if a man

is anorgasmic for a long period, he is probably physically or psychologically ill. Many men, however, are occasionally anorgasmic (Hunt, 1974).

A very small number of men are capable of multiple orgasms similar to women's—one orgasm after another without resolution phases in between (Robbins and Jensen, 1978). Slight detumescence follows the first orgasm, but the man returns to a plateau and then to orgasm. When this happens, the final orgasm is felt as the best, and it alone is followed by resolution.

Are orgasms felt differently by men and women and by singly and multiply orgasmic women? Like any subjective experience, this question cannot easily be settled, but most men reach coital orgasm more easily than women, and are more likely to continue coitus until orgasm does occur. Women prefer that coitus result in orgasm, but they are more likely than men to enjoy coitus without climax (Gebhard, 1966; Wallin and Clark, 1963). However, Hite's (1976) view that coitus "was never meant to stimulate women to orgasm" is not generally accepted. Neither is her belief that direct clitoral stimulation is always necessary. Probably most women are satisfied with one orgasm. Those who experience multiple orgasms usually feel satisfaction after one, two, or a few. Only a minority desire more than five, even if capable of more.

Another major difference between the sexes is that men reach their highest orgasmic frequency from age fifteen to twenty-five (Kinsey et al., 1948); from then on, there is a gradual decline. Women's orgasmic frequency peaks between thirty and thirty-five (Kinsey et al., 1953), when men's is already declining.

In male orgasm, sensation is primarily in the penis. Stimulation elsewhere can heighten pleasure but rarely results in orgasm. Female orgasm is most often focused on the clitoris, but the source may also be the vagina, breasts, or other parts of the body. For about one woman in fifty and one man in a thousand, orgasm can be brought about by fantasy alone (Kinsey et al., 1953).

What accounts for the orgasmic differences between the sexes? One argument is that they are cultural. Advocates of this view say that females' sexuality is more controlled and repressed than males' and takes longer to develop. Females, they say, are sheltered more and have fewer opposite-sex contacts. Kinsey's data show that in women, sexually restrictive backgrounds and lack of higher education cor-

relate with difficulty reaching orgasm and with reaching it less often. In males, these factors correlate with sexual behavior (see chapter 11), but not with impaired orgasmic ability. In women, experience often makes a difference in reaching orgasm, whether through learning or the loss of inhibitions. The likelihood of female orgasm also seems related to the length of marriage; women report more frequent orgasm after five years of marriage than in the first year (Wallin and Clark, 1963; Kinsey et al., 1953).

Some differences, however, may not be entirely cultural. Cultural forces can hardly create the capacity for multiple orgasm in many women but almost no men. And if culture accounts for women's responses developing more

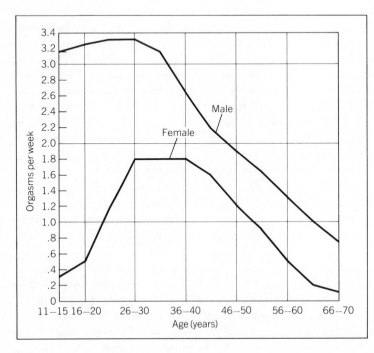

Figure 5-1 / *Mean orgasmic frequencies of males and females, whether from coitus, masturbation, or other sex behaviors.*

slowly, it should make men, who receive more sexual encouragement from peers, show increasing orgasmic frequency. But men's orgasmic frequency decreases with age. The best explanation for differences between the sexes and individuals seems to be a combination of physical, cultural, and psychological differences.

Cultural and Social Influences

The variety of patterns of female orgasm among societies and among groups within our society indicates strong cultural influence on female response. In the very repressive atmosphere of some Irish villages, female orgasm is almost unknown (Messenger, 1971). Among many Polynesian peoples, virtually all women experience orgasm (D. Marshall, 1971). Unfortunately, few cross-cultural studies mention multiple orgasm (Gebhard, 1971); knowing whether there is cross-cultural variety would suggest a great deal about the nature of female response. Margaret Mead (1949) has concluded that "the human female's capacity for orgasm is to be viewed much more as a potentiality that may or may not be developed by a given culture." But it still has not been proven that all women have the same orgasmic capacity. Variations are probably the result of biosocial interaction.

Anthropologist Paul Gebhard (1971) believes that "in all societies, the majority of young females require longer duration of coitus to reach orgasm than the majority of young males; a number of ethnographies report intentional delaying by the male to insure female orgasm or complaints by females that males ejaculate too quickly." However, in some societies this gap between the sexes narrows quickly. Among the Mangaians of Polynesia, (D. Marshall, 1971) men teach sexual techniques to young girls. Their aim is for the woman always to have one or two orgasms and then for the partners to have one simultaneously. This does not take prolonged efforts; Mangaian girls soon begin to reach orgasm quickly through vigorous, straightforward coitus.

There are also differences among women from various backgrounds in our society. Whether women experience orgasm regularly or at all correlates somewhat with their educational level (often an indicator of social class) in the United States (Kinsey et al., 1953) and Czechoslovakia (Raboch, 1970). Kinsey et al. (1953) found that by the fifth year of marriage, 31 percent of women with grade school educations usually or always reached climax in marital coitus; for women who had gone to graduate school, the figure was 43 percent. Women's religion and devoutness made little difference. However, the proportion of women who never experienced orgasm decreased from 33 percent of those born in the 1890s to 22 percent of those born in the 1920s. Kinsey et al. (1953) and other researchers (for example, C. Adams, 1966) have found that coital techniques make relatively little difference in whether women reach orgasm.

Masters and Johnson (1975) have confirmed Kinsey's conclusion that the belief in male responsibility for female orgasm is a middle-class attitude. Middle-class men are likely to try to delay their own orgasms in an effort to help women reach theirs; men from lower social classes are likely to think a man should reach orgasm whenever he feels ready for it. Some researchers think that because of this attitude, fewer women in the lower classes reach orgasm, and fewer do so often (Rainwater, 1971). Yet as we have noted, female anorgasmia probably depends more on a woman's background and development than on her partner's coital technique. Anorgasmia, of course, can also have physical and psychological causes.

Simultaneous Orgasm and "Giving Orgasm"

Simultaneous orgasm—both partners reaching climax at the same time—has been much recommended. Some couples strive to attain it, even consider its absence a sign of sexual incompatibility. For others it is not important. It became part of marriage-manual wisdom about a half-century ago, with the increased emphasis on sexual equality and on the desire or even alleged necessity for female coital orgasm.

Some people, however, think it better if each person finds pleasure in his or her own way. For example, one partner may enjoy prolonging the excitement or plateau phase, but the other may like reaching orgasm quickly. During orgasm, most women desire deep, forceful vaginal penetration and sustained clitoral stimulation, either direct or indirect, but men tend to stop thrusting during orgasm and to pull back the pelvis. These desires seem to conflict; therefore many people may be more satisfied by *non*simultaneous orgasm, each partner offering the other the most possible pleasure during climax.

Simultaneous orgasm may either heighten or limit sexual pleasure. Idealizing it seems like saying that a meal is enjoyable only if two people finish it at the same moment. Perhaps each would be better finishing at his or her own pace, the only stipulation being that neither leave the table before the other has finished.

For some people, the desire to give another an orgasm occasionally outweighs the wish to reach orgasm themselves. This desire comes largely from changing ideas about the nature of female eroticism (Masters and Johnson, 1975). A century ago, many men and women thought that women had little or no erotic desire and that sex is something men do *to* women. Women could show duty or love by providing orgasms to men. During the first few decades of this century, many people began to say that normal women could or even should enjoy sex. Apparently many did not know how, so men should help them learn. Sex then became something men do *for* women. If a woman didn't have an orgasm, her partner might be thought inept. In the last two decades, many people have come to believe that women's eroticism is independent of men's. This makes sex something men do *with* women. In short, women are now considered responsible for their own orgasms.

This shift of responsibility is not welcomed by every woman or man. If a woman is responsible for her own orgasm, she can no longer blame her partner for its absence, nor can he feel proud if she has one. If he is inept, she can teach him how to please her or she can please herself. She must also admit her own sexual desires to herself and others, something not all women like to do and not all men are comfortable dealing with. We suggest that no one gives another an orgasm, but that often one can certainly help.

The Function of Orgasm: An Hypothesis

Humans are among the most erotic of all creatures. Only in humans and perhaps dolphins (Tavolga, 1966) are both sexes excitable, active, and orgasmic all year around, even during pregnancy and lactation and when fertility is past. The clitoris seems to play a special role in humans (Masters and Johnson, 1966): with evolution to an upright posture and the widespread use of ventral (belly-to-belly) coitus (also common in dolphins and whales) (Tavolga and Essapian, 1957), direct or indirect clitoral stimulation may make orgasm more likely.

Male orgasm, like other physical functions, probably evolved because it had a function—to reinforce the pleasure of ejaculation, increasing the probability of coitus and therefore of reproduction. It is tempting to assume that female sexual response is important in promoting reproduction, and some animal behavior supports the view (Diamond, 1970; 1972). Females of a few species (such as cats, rabbits, and turkeys) seem to show orgasm; there is a sudden release of sexual tension followed by relaxation. But orgasm as we know it seems absent or rare in most female animals, even nonhuman primates (Ford and Beach, 1951).

One possible explanation of human female anorgasmia is that female orgasm is a relatively new evolutionary development. Because it is

---

Adept or Inept in Bed

The "sexual revolution" of the past half century has stressed foreplay and prolonged coitus to induce female orgasm. Theodoor Van de Velde's *Ideal Marriage* (1930) is the classic marriage manual of that school. One of his followers (Street, 1959) wrote, "Foreplay should never last less than fifteen minutes even though a woman may be sufficiently aroused in five." More recently, "Dear Abby" (Van Buren, 1977) reflected that tradition in her response to a letter about men who commit adultery "because they have a Frigidaire in the kitchen and a 'Frigid Dear' in the bedroom." Abby replied, "There's no such thing as a 'Frigid Dear'—only clumsy men."

A cross-cultural survey (D. Marshall and Suggs, 1971) reveals this to be a cultural bias of the Western middle class. In Polynesia, they say, "there is relatively little foreplay [but] orgasm is achieved virtually universally and without difficulty [although] the direct Polynesian approach to coitus resembles in many respects that in a number of [poor Western areas], in which female dissatisfaction with sex runs high." In fact, Kinsey et al. (1953) suggested that "the use of extended and varied techniques may, in not a few cases, interfere with the female's attainment of orgasm" by preventing a steady, vigorous build-up of excitement. Passion itself is often an aphrodisiac, calm an anaphrodisiac.

---

not yet deeply rooted, it can perhaps be cultivated or repressed. Another possible explanation, based on reinforcement theory, is that occasional reward can drive people harder than regular reward. It would thus be biologically adaptive for females to keep seeking orgasm, ensuring a relatively regular supply of sperm to help ensure conception.

Overview

We have looked at some descriptions of orgasm and personal questions about it. Deciding whether one's partner has had an orgasm, has faked one, and is or is not satisfied requires sensitivity and has major consequences. Orgasm has important real and symbolic meanings and satisfactions. The getting, giving, and sharing of orgasm also have psychological and social meanings that can enhance or endanger a sexual relationship.

Orgasm is clearly adaptive in evolutionary and biological terms in males; we can only guess that its function in females is to create a pleasure bond to hold couples together through the long child-raising period. Since female orgasm is probably a relatively new evolutionary development, it is more vulnerable to social and psychological influences.

Review, Discuss, Decide

1. What are some signs that a partner has reached orgasm?
2. If you are sexually active, can you identify your own orgasmic pattern among those described in this chapter? If you are not orgasmic, what stage of the SRC do you reach?
3. Does it matter to you whether you or your partner has an orgasm? Why?
4. To what extent do you think people are responsible for their own and their partners' orgasms?
5. What do you think of faking orgasm?
6. What are the advantages and disadvantages of simultaneous orgasm? Of taking turns at orgasm?
7. How many differences and similarities can you find in male and female orgasmic patterns? What causes the differences?
8. How have ideas about vaginal, clitoral, and other kinds of orgasm changed?

6

Sex-Active Substances

What can I use to turn on a person sexually?

How will marijuana or cocaine affect me sexually?

Will saltpeter or anything else decrease my own or my partner's sex drive?

What can I take to increase my sexual abilities?

Will vitamin E or hormone injections help?

Is Spanish fly safe?

Since the beginning of history, and probably long before, people have sought *aphrodisiacs* (from Aphrodite, the Greek goddess of love), substances to arouse love or sexual desire and enchance sexual performance. Probably with less urgency, they have sought *anaphrodisiacs,* substances to turn off love and eroticism. Certainly the idea of sex-active substances was familiar a few thousand years ago. In Genesis, Leah, aging and feeling unloved, used mandrake plants to arouse her husband Jacob: "And Jacob came out of the field in the evening, and Leah went out to meet him and said, Thou must come in unto me; for surely I have hired thee with my son's mandrakes. And he lay with her that night."

Controlling Sexual Response

A person may actually want only one of the many alleged effects of a sex-active substance— to make another person fall in love, to increase one's own potency, or to reach orgasm faster or slower. A man may want something to decrease a woman's reluctance (reduce her threshold of arousal), but be quite disturbed if it also delays her orgasm. A woman may want something to strengthen her partner's erection but be unhappy if it also arouses him more often or leads him to have coitus with others.

A sex-active substance may affect one or several of the mechanisms involved in arousal, coitus, or orgasm. It probably does so through the hormones' actions on the nervous system (Beach, 1948; Bancroft, 1978) or by influencing chemical messengers of the nervous system, such as serotonin and norepinephrine (Zitrin, Dement, and Barchas, 1973; Myerson and Malmnas, 1978). Many mood-altering drugs (see below) are believed to affect sexuality by such means. Most aphrodisiacs intended for women are meant to stimulate arousal, most intended for men to aid excitement or make coitus longer or more vigorous.

Most anaphrodisiacs are aimed at decreasing

79

a man's arousal or a women's performance demands. However, no potion, powder, or drug can selectively and safely turn a person on or off, although some drugs, hormones, and other substances do have sexual effects.* Nevertheless, lore and literature describe many alleged aphrodisiacs and anaphrodisiacs. Some drugs, hormones, and other substances do have sexual effects (Ellinwood and Rockwell, 1975). Belief in them and hope of finding others remain so widespread that many people must at some time decide whether to seek or use a real or alleged sex-active substance.

Belief in the sexual value of such substances was once explained by the *doctorine of signatures* or by *homeopathic magic,* the ideas that a body organ or function is helped by a substance that looks like it or has similar properties. For instance, a rhinoceros horn looks like a penis, and peppers create a sensation of heat (MacDougald, 1961). Sometimes people use dangerously high amounts of such substances, assuming that if one swallow helps, two will be better.

When aphrodisiacs seem successful, it is usually because they induce erection or warm or burning feelings in the sexualia—actually, local irritation and reflex vasocongestion, which may be interpreted as sexual arousal. The substance may be rubbed on the sexualia and cause inflammation. If it is swallowed, the body excretes it through the urinary system, and blood flow to the pelvic region is stimulated; this often causes pain, and occasionally serious

---

* These directly or indirectly alter chemical messengers within the brain, such as serotonin and epinephrine. It is thought that increased serotonin inhibits sexual activity in males and that decreased serotonin enhances sexual performance.

damage to the kidneys or other parts of the body.

A popular American folk preparation for decades has been *aspirin in Coke.* If this combination has any effect, it is only because a person expects and perhaps wants it to. Willingness to take a drug for its desired effects probably accounts for the positive results reported about many alleged aphrodisiacs. Of course, a truly effective drug works whether or not a person knows its nature or desired effect. This is judged by *double-blind tests:* neither the person administering the drug nor those taking it know who receives the substance and who receives an inert substitute, or *placebo.* This checks for the *placebo effect,* an imagined or psychosomatic response resulting solely from belief that the treatment will work.

Aphrodisiacs

Many *folk preparations* around the world are made from plant or animal structures that resemble a penis, testes, vagina, or breast; some are actually made from such organs. Various peoples use powdered rhinoceros horn, elephant tusk, oysters, radishes, ginseng, mandrake root, water buffalo penis, or sheep or bull testicles ("Rocky Mountain oysters," "prairie oysters").

Two of the best-known aphrodisiacs are Spanish fly and yohimbine. *Spanish fly* (Cantharides) is the common name for a powder made from a species of beetle named *Cantharis vesicatorea.* The preparation, usually taken mixed with a liquid, can cause erection through reflex vasocongestion, but also severe pain, irritation, and even ulcers in the abdomen and urinary tract. Spanish fly may have gotten its reputation when farmers, seeing the anguished moans and movements of cattle sick from eating dead beetles, thought the cattle were in heat. Spanish fly is extremely dangerous.

Yohimbine, a drug made from the bark of the African yohimbé tree, has a mixed record as sexual stimulant. In animal tests it has failed to increase sexual arousal or performance (D. Johnson and Diamond, 1969), and no double-blind studies show it to be effective in humans. There are, however, reports of increased and prolonged genital feelings and erection. Yohimbine used to be available by prescription in a commercial preparation that also contained testosterone (see page 87) and *strychnine,* which acts as a poison if taken in more than very small amounts and reduces nervous-system thresh-

olds to certain stimuli. Double-blind tests resulted in a report that it helped induce erection (Margolis and Leslie, 1966), but doubt remains about the effectiveness of yohimbine alone. The drug has been removed from the market.

Alcohol is widely thought to decrease sexual inhibitions. In small amounts it does indeed reduce tension and inhibitions. Since preoccupation and stress greatly deter eroticism, alcohol, by reducing them, may increase sexual interest, activity, and enjoyment. There is no evidence, however, that alcohol directly stimulates sexual behavior. It cannot cause desire for an unwanted partner or act, induce erection, or positively affect other copulatory mechanisms. Taken in large amounts, alcohol depresses emotion and sexual desire in both men and

---

Passion: Rites and Recipes

Aphrodisiacs and magic to produce love and sexual desire were well known in ancient Greece and Rome and during the Middle Ages. Honey, onions, and oysters have been considered aphrodisiacs in many times and places, from ancient Rome to pre-Victorian England. When the potato was brought to Europe from the New World, some people thought it was a sexual stimulant. In many places, a person's hair, blood, spittle, or nails have been used in love magic and potions. Czech peasants used to bake hair from the armpits into little cakes; whoever ate one was supposed to fall in love with the person from whose body the hair came. Human sperm has also been widely used. The people of central Sumatra thought elephant sperm a powerful aphrodisiac; certainly a man who dared obtain it might score points for motivation alone. Some Caribbean people and blacks in the United States (especially those with roots in

the West Indies) use spells, often with prayers and special candles, to influence others' love and desire.

Solomon Islanders believed in a convenient dual-purpose magic (Blackwood, 1935): "To make a woman love you get some leaves of the plant rarakot and powder some sisiwa [powdered lava] on to them, rub the two together and smear the mixture on to a piece of tobacco which you then give to the woman you desire. Then take a little more sisiwa and make it hot over the fire. As she smokes the tobacco, and as the sisiwa gets hot, so she will become warmed towards you and the next day she will come to you. She will be hot with desire for you, and you will copulate and copulate and copulate. When you are tired of her and want the affair to come to an end, take a little sisiwa and put it into water; her passion will then be cooled."

women and produces impotence in men (Jones and Jones, 1977). Of course, the amount of alcohol that constitutes moderate or too much varies from person to person.

Many users of *marijuana* (cannabis, "grass," "dope," "pot") claim that it enhances sexual pleasure and makes coitus last longer. Marijuana may change time perception, so that coitus and orgasm seem prolonged, and to many people longer is better. But marijuana is not an aphrodisiac. Like alcohol, it tends to reduce inhibitions, but has no power to induce amorous or sexual desire in an unwilling person or to induce or maintain erection (Ewing, 1972). The situation in which marijuana is used and the feelings of those using it probably have much to do with the effects.

According to one study (Kolodny et al., 1974), prolonged marijuana use by men decreases testosterone and reduces sperm production, apparently without affecting sexual activity. Further studies may show a decrease in sexual behavior after long use; such a trend was appearing at the end of the study. Some researchers (Hembree et al., 1976) have found such negative effects, but others (Mendelsohn et al., 1974) have not. However, another study showed that marijuana use correlated with a higher probability of coital orgasm in women (Kolodny et al., 1977). Much more research is needed to fully understand the effects of marijuana on sex, but that may not happen soon: unfortunately, Congress has denied government funds for such research (Holden, 1977).

Two drugs developed for nonsexual purposes have drawn interest as possible aphrodisiacs. One, *L-dopa* (levo-dopa), is used to treat Parkinson's disease, a kind of palsy; it brought not only relief from the disease but renewed sexual desire. However, when L-dopa was given to neurologically healthy men who complained of insufficient erection and *libido* (sexual drive), there were few positive effects. It is now thought that the sexual effect first reported was a result of improved general health (Benkert, 1973).

The other drug, *PCPA* (p-chlorphenylanine), was developed to treat schizophrenia, but an aphrodisiac effect was reported in the first study of its effects on animals (Tagliamonte et al., 1969). Some animals seem to respond sexually to PCPA, but others do not (Zitrin, Demant, and Barchas, 1973). Studies of PCPA's sexual effects on humans are few, the results uncertain; the doses needed to bring about even mild effects in men caused adverse side reactions, including retarded ejaculation (Benkert, 1972; Zitrin, Dement, and Barchas, 1973). Apparently PCPA cannot predictably and safely induce desire or potency in men. No studies have appeared of the drug's effects on women.

Animal testicular extract is one of the oldest alleged aphrodisiacs in medical literature. Injections of extracts from dogs and guinea pigs were described as rejuvenators by the famous physician Charles Brown-Séquard in 1889; "monkey gland" treatments won much publicity. No more reliable or long-lasting are the modern counterparts—injections of cells from animals' testes, hypothalamus, placenta, or embryonic tissue. Such "rejuvenation" treatment, considered unethical in this country, is available in Europe and elsewhere, and the press often reports on the rich and famous seeking it. While some transient hormone effects may occur, there is no known reason for such treatments to work except by the placebo effect.

Amphetamines, antidepressants, and stimulants

("uppers," "speed") energize many or most users and have been reported to increase sexual desire and potency as a side effect. The effects vary with dosage and are not always predictable. At the usual prescription doses, these drugs rarely have sexual effects. At higher doses, potency may increase, but orgasmic ability decrease; in some people, however, multiple orgasms result (H. Kaplan, 1974). But positive sexual effects seem to diminish with use, and anarousmia develops. Menstrual disorders may also result from high doses. It seems that when drug use stops, normal sexual and reproductive functions return.

Cocaine ("coke," "snow"), which is extracted from the coca leaf, is usually inhaled like snuff, but occasionally is taken intravenously. The resulting high often brings a great energy and a sense of power and increased sexual interest and ability. However, extended use can lead to *priapism* (prolonged, painful erection), usually with inability to reach orgasm (Oliven, 1974). In women, cocaine tends to decrease vaginal secretions. Cocaine was once used medically as an anesthetic; some couples rub the powder on the penis to reduce sensation and prolong coitus.

Amyl nitrate ("poppers," "snappers," "amies") is a vasodilator used medically to increase blood flow to the heart. The "popper" (usually a liquid-filled glass vial) is usually opened and inhaled at the start of sex play or just before orgasm. It increases heart blood flow and perhaps genital vasocongestion. Users say they enjoy orgasm more and have a brief subsequent high. The high probably comes from a drop in blood pressure in the brain caused by blood shifting to the heart and internal organs; this produces a light-headed feeling that may be pleasant but can cause fainting. A similar but smaller high is claimed to result from using menthol inhalers. For people with heart disease, blood-pressure problems, or glaucoma, the increased blood pressure and shift of blood concentration can be dangerous.

Butyl nitrate ("butyl," "rush," "locker room") is now used more widely than amyl nitrate in erotic situations because it is not a prescription drug. It has the same effects and is sniffed repeatedly during sexual activity. Some

---

Jokes as Aphrodisiacs

In *Rationale of the Dirty Joke* (1968), George Legman writes: "Many people feel, and will state, that the telling of dirty jokes has an aphrodisiacal effect on persons of the desired sex, or at least on the tellers themselves. And that they tell dirty jokes as part of their approach." When such an approach seems successful, the reason may not always be the sexual content of the jokes. Many women say that a sense of humor is one of the most attractive qualities in men, and some find playful teasing almost irresistible. Many men find humor equally attractive in women. The laugh and smile may be two of nature's best aphrodisiacs.

people experience not only a high but impotence or anorgasmia from repeated use. Function returns after drug use ends.

The use of "amies" and "butyl" seems especially common in some group-sex and male homosexual circles.

Vitamin E has a wide reputation for sexual effects. A deficiency of vitamin E causes blood problems, not sexual ones, but several studies have linked this deficiency to impaired animal fertility; reproduction improves after vitamin E is administered. There are no verified claims that vitamin E improves human sexual performance. A double-blind study of the possible sexual effects of vitamin E on normal couples found feelings of well-being after both partners took high doses (1,000 IU per day) for a month. There was a small but statistically insignificant increase in libido and the frequency of masturbation, but none in the frequency of coitus. Couples taking the vitamin believed their sexual experiences were better while using it. The researchers caution, however, that some people taking vitamin E become depressed and tense (Herold, Mottin, and Sabry, 1979).

Perfume and cosmetics have been used for thousands of years to enhance the scent and appearance of the body and increase others' sexual interest. Coloring the lips draws attention to them, and before women had eye shadow, eye liner, and false lashes, they used the plant extract belladonna (Italian: *bella* = pretty; *donna* = women) to dilate the pupils. Some ethologists believe that bright, full lips and wide eyes may be biologically rooted signals to stimulate sexual desire (Eibl-Eibesfeldt, 1974; Morris, 1969). Sometimes, however, the motive for using cosmetics is personal or social, not erotic; people often want to

be attractive or desirable without being available.

People have used perfumes for at least a couple of thousand years. Sometimes the reason may have been chiefly erotic, but when bathing was less frequent, scents were used to mask undesirable body odors. Of course, natural odors, even when quite strong, can also be attractive and sexy. However, there is no conclusive evidence yet that natural human secretions act as *pheromones,* air-borne substances that act like hormones to produce reactions in others. In many species, pheromones signal sexual readiness, activate egg and sperm production, and induce mating (Bronson,1968). Evidence for their presence in primates, including humans, is put forward by some researchers Michael, Bonsall, and Zumpe, 1976), but refuted by others (Goldfoot et al., 1978).

Anaphrodisiacs

When partners' sexual desires are different, one may want to decrease the other's libido or coital ability. People have also wanted to dampen the sexuality of ships' crews, prisoners, schoolchildren, and sex offenders. For these reasons, anaphrodisiacs have been and still are in demand. Three timeworn suggestions are push-ups, a cold shower, and "a good sleep"; Plato and Aristotle recommended walking barefoot.

Saltpeter (potassium nitrate) is probably the best-known substance believed to inhibit sexual desire and ability. There is no evidence that it does more than increase urine flow unless one takes too much, which can be fatal. Its reputation may have come from its early use to bring

Figure 6-1 / *Cosmetics and perfumes to draw and hold erotic attention are used all over the world and have been found in the remains of civilizations which far predate ancient Egypt.*

down fevers, with the faulty reasoning that it could reduce the "heat" of sexual desire.

Opium, heroin ("junk," "horse," "H"), *morphine,* and other *opiates* (poppy derivatives and their synthetic relatives, such as *methadone*) act as sedatives and pain relievers; they also quickly decrease sexual interest, potency, and orgasm (Chein et al., 1964; Jones and Jones 1977). In addicts, these drugs replace sex as a focus of interest or desire. During coitus, women who take opiates are usually very passive. Also, these drugs inhibit ovulation. Some addicted men, though impotent, act as recipients in homosexual encounters. Heroin users, male and female, may engage in prostitution to get money to buy the drug.

Barbiturates ("downers," "reds," "goofballs"), like alcohol, initially decrease inhibitions, thus raising the probability of sexual activity. With increased use, impotence and lack of libido develop. These drugs generally put one down emotionally, physically, and sexually, as their slang name implies.

LSD (lysergic acid diethylamide, "acid") is one of the most widely used hallucinogens. It alters thought and perception and is not easily categorized as "good" or "bad" for sex. The kind and duration of effects, sexual and nonsexual, vary widely. Many people experience pleasant results, and some report an enriched sexual life, but bad trips also occur, resulting in destructive or self-destructive behavior, and sometimes in permanent mental damage. Coitus while under the influence of LSD is often described not as more erotic but as "different" or "interesting." Orgasm is reported as "more pronounced and encompassing as an experience," but "detached" and "out there" (H. Kaplan, 1974).

Cyproterone and *cyproterone acetate* are strong drugs that inhibit the action of testosterone, rapidly decreasing arousal, the functioning of copulatory mechanisms, and sperm production. They are used medically as anaphrodisiacs outside the United States but are not legally available here. The drugs present ethical problems. It has been recommended that people who have committed such sex crimes as rape and child molestation receive not imprisonment but these antiandrogenic drugs to reduce their sexual desire—or at least that they be given this option (Money, 1970). Debate continues about whether such acts deserve punishment, medical treatment, or psychiatric treatment. One argument against the drug is that removing a person's ability to perform sexually is cruel and unusual punishment, a sort of chemical castration. The past abuse of castration as a treatment of real and alleged sexual offenders makes the objection a serious one.

Tobacco use has been related to sexual performance. Several clinical reports suggest that when heavy smokers give up cigarettes, they experience increased sexual interest and activity for several weeks (Ochsner, 1971). Whether this results from increased general well-being or a substitution of one gratification for another remains unclear. A recent review of research concludes that smoking is not harmful to sexual behavior or fertility (Sterling and Kobayashi, 1975).

Hormones

Hormones are not usually considered aphrodisiacs or anaphrodisiacs; unlike most such substances, they exist naturally in the body and, when administered, take days or weeks to produce effects. Nevertheless, when swallowed or injected, some hormones have more effect on sexual behavior and reproduction than any other substances (Young, 1961). The effects of hormones on development and on nonsexual behavior is discussed in chapter 7. Here we will discuss their influence on sexual behavior.

Androgens

Androgens, or male hormones (testosterone, testosterone propionate, androstenodione, etc.), activate sexual drive and performance in both males and females. A normal male usually produces enough androgens in his testes; additional amounts have little or no sexual effect, except eventually to reduce his own androgen and sperm production. When androgens are given to a man whose production of them is deficient or who has been castrated, or to a woman, there is almost always a rise in sexual desire. This desire is not necessarily converted into action, but when it is, it occurs with greater vigor and leads to stronger orgasm. This occurs in both sexes, but especially in men (Salmon and Geist, 1943; Waxenberg, Drellich, and Sutherland, 1959).

Besides their sexual effects, androgens help maintain a male's muscle tone, hair patterns (on head, face, and body), voice tone, sperm production, and reproductive tract—in fact, almost every male physical and behavioral trait. They enhance general activity levels, aggressiveness, perseverance, territoriality, and dominance. In contrast, castration, loss of androgens with aging, and taking antiandrogens (such as cyproterone) all decrease these characteristics (Bremer, 1959; Laschet, 1973).

This link with secondary male traits limits the use of androgens by women. When given male hormones, they may show not only in-creased sexual desire, but also acne, voice deepening, greater hairiness and muscle development, and clitoral growth (Diamond and Young, 1963).

Although administered androgens masculinize women, they do need them in small quantities. These they normally produce, primarily in their adrenal glands, but also in their ovaries. If a woman's ovaries are removed, her production of estrogens slackens; her sexual activity may then increase, because the androgen still produced by her adrenals are not balanced out by estrogens. If the androgen-producing adrenals are removed (for instance, to treat certain types of cancer), sexual arousal and orgasmic capacity decline. The decrease is greater than if the vagina, uterus, or breasts are removed (Waxenburg, Drellich, and Sutherland, 1959), even though most people associate these organs with sexuality more than the adrenals.

Administered androgens increase sexual interest and vigor, but they never change sexual orientation. Giving androgens to a male or female homosexual will not make him or her heterosexual; it only makes it more likely that the person will engage in sexual activity with someone of the same sex (Hoffman, 1977).

Estrogens

The effects of estrogens on human sexual activity are less clear than those of androgens. In mammals, estrogens are normally crucial to a female's sexual receptiveness and behavior, including the *lordosis* (crouched presentation of the hindquarters) necessary for copulation. Without estrogens (for instance, after castration), almost any nonhuman mammal soon ceases receptive behavior and copulation.

Extra estrogens seem to have little effect on

women's sexual behavior, but there may be indirect effects. Additional estrogens will upset a normal woman's menstrual cycle; this is how oral contraceptives work (see pages 408–12 for a discussion of oral contraceptives and sexual behavior).

Estrogens keep the female sexual tissues healthy and functioning well. They also seem to enhance feelings of well-being and self-satisfaction. This is noticeable when they are present in higher amounts, as during certain phases of the menstrual-ovarian cycle (see chapter 17). Estrogen deficiency, which occurs after menopause, makes vaginal tissues thin and less elastic, lubrication slower and scantier. Fat deposits, which contribute not only to a female appearance but to coital comfort (as on the mons veneris and buttocks), tend to diminish. Estrogen replacement reverses these effects and tends to make women more sexually receptive.

Males given estrogens develop secondary female characteristics, such as larger breasts (gynecomastia) and rounded hips (caused by local fat deposits). Muscles soften, hair and beard growth decrease, and libido and potency wane. Even very small doses produce these effects; men working in factories producing oral contraceptives have experienced such changes because of inhaling microscopic amounts.

As normal females produce some androgens, normal males produce some estrogens, in their testicles. The reason is not clear, however, and no functional problem has been associated with a male's loss of estrogens. Some medical problems, such as long-term alcoholism, in which the liver's normal excretion of estrogen falters, can cause a buildup of the hormone, leading to breast development and decreased libido and potency (Rubin et al., 1976). Increased estrogens and therefore feminization may also result from tumors of the testes.

Progesterone

Progesterone (*pro* = for, *gester* = gestation, *one* = hormone) seems to decrease sexual arousal in both sexes. Women given extra progesterone seem calmer and less sexually active. Like any sex hormone, progesterone acts in relation to all other sex hormones: if a person has a high level of estrogens or androgens, it takes more progesterone to produce effects. The relatively high levels of progesterone during late pregnancy and the luteal phase of the menstrual cycle are believed to cause the reduced sexual interest and activity common at those times.

In men, progesterone acts as an antiandrogen, inhibiting sperm production, sexual arousal, and potency. These hormones have been tested as male contraceptives, but they cause loss of sexual function (Heller et al., 1958).

Other Hormones

Gonadotropins are hormones produced in the pituitary gland and placenta that stimulate the gonads to produce sex hormones described above. Giving a woman LH (luteinizing hormone) leads to the creation of progesterone (see chapter 17); the progesterone then acts as it would if given directly. In men, LH is called ICSH *(interstitial cell stimulating hormone),* because it stimulates androgen-producing cells in the testes. Administering it has the same effect as administering androgens. FSH *(follicle stimulating hormone)* stimulates ovarian follicle growth and the associated estrogen production. LH and FSH are given to some people with fertility problems.

Thyroxin, produced by the thyroid gland, increases general activity and well-being. Normally it does not affect sexuality, but libido and sexual activity are low in many people with low levels of thyroxin, and administering the hormone renews sexual interest and activity.

Prescribed Drugs

Psychotropic drugs, such as tranquilizers and relaxants, account for more than half of all prescriptions in the United States. They fall into three major categories: *antipsychotic drugs* (for example, Thorazine and Stelazine), used to treat such psychoses as schizophrenia; *antianxiety drugs* (for example, Librium and Valium), used to relieve anxiety and relax muscles; and *antidepressants* (for example, Flavil and Tofranil), used to combat depression.

Since these drugs are usually given to people who are not functioning at their best, analyzing the sexual effects is difficult, but some impressions exist (H. Kaplan, 1974; Story, 1974). Antipsychotic drugs tend to decrease libido, potency, and orgasm. Antianxiety drugs act like alcohol; low doses reduce inhibitions and increase libido, but the muscle-relaxing effects decrease potency and orgasm. Antidepressants similarly raise libido and potency in some individuals, but lower them in others.

Any drug that affects the nervous system or blood pressure can be suspected of influencing sexual behavior—directly, by acting on the brain, or indirectly, by affecting vasocongestion or myotonia. For example, some *antihyperten-sion* drugs (which lower blood pressure) can produce depression and impotence (Howard, 1973). Other drugs that affect the nervous system can inhibit potency but leave libido intact.

Practical and Ethical Decisions

All the drugs and substances mentioned in this chapter should be approached with caution and skepticism; some should arouse alarm. Prescription drugs should be taken only if and as directed by a doctor. Taking many of the nonprescription substances is even riskier. Effective and safe sex-active drugs may eventually be developed. However, they might introduce new problems: they could encourage sexual interest but not sexual activity, or stimulate activity with inappropriate partners or at inopportune times.

Changing someone's sexual behavior without influencing feelings or attitudes toward the behavior poses serious ethical questions about sex-active substances. Should they be used without the recipient's knowledge and permission? Informed consent is a legal as well as a moral issue. To use another's body or mind in ways he or she might object to requires utter conviction that the end justifies the means. Such conviction is often suspect. And using one's own body in potentially harmful or socially disapproved ways calls for more than casual thought. Short-term benefits must be weighed against possible long-term dangers. So-called aphrodisiacs and anaphrodisiacs should not be taken or given indiscriminately, we believe, even if the person is aware of receiving them.

Overview

This chapter covered the common and some less common substances usually thought to affect sexual interest and performance. All the hormones and many of the other substances directly or indirectly alter chemical messengers within the brain (Zitrin, Demant and Barchas, 1973). The hormones are thought to act on specific regions of the central nervous system, affecting the likelihood of any behavior.

Research on sex-active substances will surely increase. However, greater knowledge probably will not replace the folklore and individual hit-or-miss experiments of the past and present. There is still more word-of-mouth wisdom about the subject than there is scientific literature. The studies that do exist suggest that few substances can alter sexual response without detrimental effects. Deciding whether to use any substance to modify sexual processes should involve careful consideration of both the physical effects and the ethical implications.

Review, Discuss, Decide

1. What would you expect to be the sexual effect of alcohol? Marijuana? Heroin? LSD? Testosterone? Progesterone?
2. If you have used any substance mentioned in this chapter, did it have any effects? How does one distinguish a placebo effect?
3. If sexual expression is as natural, pleasurable, even ecstatic as many people say, why alter it? What is being sought in the use of these substances?
4. Would you like to experiment with any of these substances? If so, which ones and why?
5. What ethical issues are involved in giving someone an aphrodisiac or anaphrodisiac without his or her knowledge and permission? With knowledge or permission?
6. Would your answer to the previous question be different if the person were a lover? A patient? A stranger? A convicted sex offender?
7. Would you want these substances used on you without medical approval or without your knowledge? Would your age or marital situation make a difference?

7

Sexual Development: Starting Out Male or Female

How are males and females similar at birth, and how are they different?

Which sex differences that appear through life have a biological basis? A social basis? Both?

How are "male and female" different from "masculine and feminine?"

How does a person become heterosexual or homosexual?

Through most of history, people have taken for granted that a person is born male or female and develops into a man or woman. Like the movements of the sun and the changing of the seasons, this required no more explanation than a "how-it-came-to-be" story in religion or mythology. During the past century, scientific research and social ferment have changed that. Few aspects of sexuality have a greater hold on public curiosity and concern today—or have generated so many conflicting theories and social efforts. Understanding one's development is a major part of understanding one's sexuality, and it has implications about what is appropriate, desirable, or possible in manhood and womanhood. It has consequences for life-styles, personal commitments, childrearing, education, medicine, and public policy.

In its fullest sense, sexual development means everything in body, mind, and behavior that rises from being male or female. A person's views about maleness and femaleness are deeply influenced by his or her personality, family, ethnic and social background, and life experience. It is easy to take these views as rules of nature, because they are so deep a part of one's sense of oneself and the world. And one can find authorities to back up almost every view—not only because of conflicting theories but because scientists, like everyone else, are products of their experience and society. Various experts have claimed that sex differences are rooted firmly in biology, in social conditioning, in emotional and mental growth, or in interacting physical, social, and psychological factors.

In this chapter we review some of the basic findings that must be considered in any theory of sexual development; then we review some of the competing theories. These findings and theories may help you decide whether certain factors were important in your upbringing and may influence how you choose to interpret your own life and rear your children. A detailed discussion of social variations in adult behavior and gender roles—the results of this development—is in chapters 11, 12, and 21.

Sex and Gender

Most one-celled organisms reproduce by dividing. Not very far up the evolutionary ladder, animals developed *sexual dimorphism* (*di* = two, *morph* = shape), division into different forms, male and female, that must carry out a sexual act (uniting sperm and egg) to reproduce. In more complex creatures, sexual dimorphism involves nongenital anatomy and behavior as well. One need only compare the appearance of the male and female of most higher species, including human beings, to see how extensive sexual dimorphism becomes.

Being male or female is a physical fact called *sex;* behavior that results directly from one's sex is *sex-linked.* For instance, a female dog, regardless of training, squats to urinate, while a male lifts a leg to do so; most human males stand to urinate, and most females sit or squat.

The social concomitants of sex are called *gender.* Behavior thought socially appropriate for a male or female is *masculine* or *feminine* and is called *gender-role behavior* (the less accurate phrase *sex-role behavior* is also widely used). Definitions of gender role vary somewhat from society to society. For instance, in the United States greeting a person of the same sex with a kiss is widely considered feminine, but in many other societies, no such distinction is made. However, some aspects of gender role are similar in most societies (see chapter 21).

Many behaviors are neither solely sex-linked nor purely social; gender roles often elaborate on biological tendencies. One of the great controversies of our day is the distinction between sex-linked behavior (biological, so referred to as male or female) and gender-role behavior (social, so referred to as masculine or feminine). Unfortunately, this is often discussed as an either/or choice between biology and society, or nature and nurture, with the implication that one or the other is somehow better. Often the argument is emotionally charged by a feeling that recognizing the existence of sex-linked behavior may be used to justify social inequalities. As Frank Beach (1977a) has said, "Any concept of sexuality would be impossible without the accompanying concepts of male and female ... *there cannot be sexuality without sex....* We must comprehend differences between male and female before we can grasp differences between masculine and feminine."

A small number of people claim that most differences between the sexes besides those in their sexual and reproductive systems have social origins. Another minority sees a firm biological basis for most of the differences. Both views, we believe, face overwhelming evidence that biology, society (or environment), and individual experience interact throughout life to create both differences and similarities. Biological forces set a range of potentials, and a person's development within family and society determines how fully the potentials are realized. This theory of *biosocial interaction* (or *biased interaction*) is especially useful in describing the earlier part of life, in which much adolescent and adult development is rooted (Beach, 1977a; Diamond, 1965, 1977b, 1979a). This theory underlies much that follows.

Sexual Differentiation

Sexual development begins at fertilization, when the ovum, with an X chromosome, unites with a sperm carrying either another X, to produce a female, or with a Y, to produce a male (see chapter 17). The fertilized egg contains all the genetic guidance the person will ever have. It contains more than 500,000 genes, which influence myriad aspects of development, including hair color, height, perhaps sensitivity to sound and visual stimuli, even elements of behavior and personality (Fuller and Thompson, 1967). The genes bear these directions in biochemical messengers (DNA and RNA) as a computer carries programmed instructions that direct an entire assembly line.

During its first few weeks, the human fetus has a *genital tubercle* (a groove topped by a bud of tissue), apparently *undifferentiated* (not yet male or female) *gonads,* and two duct systems, the *Müllerian* and *Wolffian.* Around the sixth or seventh week, the genes trigger *differentiation* as a male or female. In a female, the undifferentiated gonads become ovaries, in a male, testicles; then the fetus's own sex hormones interact with its genes to direct much of the process.

Except in quite rare cases (see pages 95–96, 104–105), the rudimentary sexual tissues develop into either male or female *analogous tissues*—a penis or clitoris, vulva or scrotum, ovaries or testes (Jost, 1958). A female's Müllerian duct develops into female internal reproductive organs; the Wolffian duct atrophies and disappears; the tubercle changes, the groove becoming a vulva and a clitoris. In a male, the Wolffian duct develops into the male internal reproductive system; the Müllerian duct atrophies; the genital groove closes to become a scrotum, and the genital bud grows into a penis.

Once the gonads have become testes or ovaries, the fetus's own hormones (as well as those entering its bloodstream from the mother) have an *organizing,* or *sensitizing,* effect on the developing brain and nervous system (Diamond, 1977b). The words organizing and

---

From Without to Within

For thousands of years, many people have believed that events in a pregnant woman's life could affect the fetus—for instance, that if a cross-eyed person stared at her, the baby might be born cross-eyed. Several such magical beliefs have existed about the sexual activity of the mother. L. Ron Hubbard, the founder of Scientology, has said that the fetus hears and records all the words and sounds its parents made during coitus, and that these influence its behavior after birth (Hubbard, 1950). There is no evidence to support this idea, and most scientists deny that it is possible. Nevertheless, animal research suggests that some outside events do affect an unborn child. If a pregnant female rat experiences great stress, her male offspring show less-than-average mounting (male behavior) and above-average lordosis (female behavior) (I. Ward, 1972). Stress affects the body's hormonal balance, and hormonal changes in a mother's blood may affect a fetus. Although such an effect has not been shown in humans, it may exist.

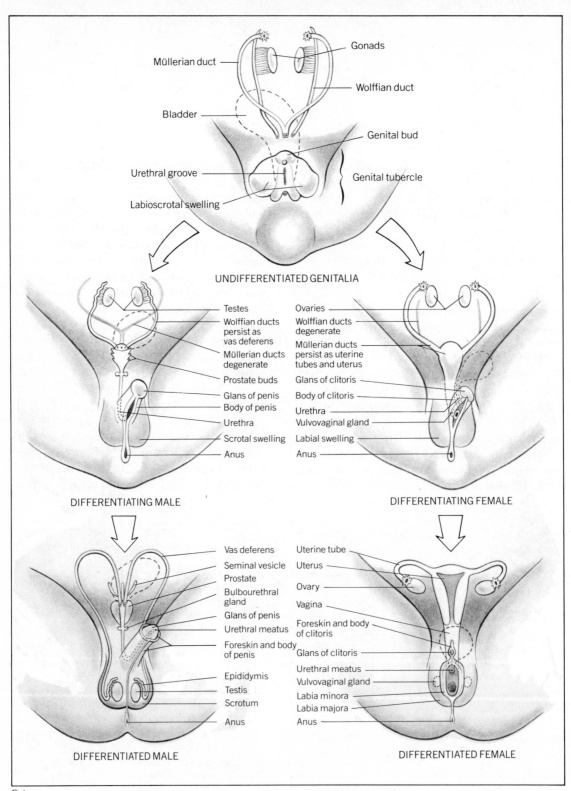

MÜllerian duct — Gonads

Wolffian duct

Bladder

Genital bud

Urethral groove

Genital tubercle

Labioscrotal swelling

UNDIFFERENTIATED GENITALIA

Testes
Wolffian ducts persist as vas deferens
Müllerian ducts degenerate
Prostate buds
Glans of penis
Body of penis
Urethra
Scrotal swelling
Anus

Ovaries
Wolffian ducts degenerate
Müllerian ducts persist as uterine tubes and uterus
Glans of clitoris
Body of clitoris
Urethra
Vulvovaginal gland
Labial swelling
Anus

DIFFERENTIATING MALE

DIFFERENTIATING FEMALE

Vas deferens
Seminal vesicle
Prostate
Bulbourethral gland
Glans of penis
Urethral meatus
Foreskin and body of penis
Epididymis
Testis
Scrotum
Anus

Uterine tube
Uterus
Ovary
Vagina
Foreskin and body of clitoris
Glans of clitoris
Urethral meatus
Vulvovaginal gland
Labia minora
Labia majora
Anus

DIFFERENTIATED MALE

DIFFERENTIATED FEMALE

Figure 7-1 / *Before the end of the first trimester, a fetus has developed undifferentiated genitalia (top). Then the genes trigger differentiation. In a male (left center), the rudimentary female system atrophies, and the male system continues toward full basic development (left bottom). In a female (right center), the male system atrophies, and the female system goes on toward complete basic development (right bottom).*

sensitizing are really metaphors for a process still incompletely understood. In some way, the embryo's gonads—producing mostly androgens in a male, but nothing yet in a female—predispose the nervous system to respond in certain male and female ways throughout life. For obvious ethical reasons, one cannot experiment with people to learn how this happens, but animal research and medical studies offer strong clues (Diamond, 1965, 1968, 1977b, 1979a).

Some human sex-linked differences seem to be rooted in hundreds of millions of years of evolutionary development; they are automatic in virtually all higher animals. For instance, in most or all higher species, males show more aggressive behaviors, such as threat, attack, and rough-and-tumble play, than females. Females show more appeasing and submissive behavior and more lordosis. The hormonal influence on these behaviors is dramatic. If males of any species, including humans, are castrated, the male behavior decreases—in some cases slowly, but inevitably (Beach, 1948; Bremer, 1959). If they are then given androgens, the behavior resumes. If a female is castrated (spayed or ovariectomized), she ceases to show lordosis. If she is then given estrogens, lordosis reappears.

Differentiation of the human nervous system

begins about six weeks after fertilization and continues till the end of puberty. In a female, the absence of prenatal androgens helps set the biological clock that at puberty will launch and maintain her menstrual cycle. In a male, prenatal androgens set no cycle, but establish a *tonic* (continuous) process of hormone and sperm production (Diamond, 1977b; Whalen, 1968). After an individual has been sensitized, additional hormones will produce sex-linked traits more powerfully throughout life. For instance, doses of androgens make facial hair grow in prepubertal girls, but make more of it grow faster in boys; doses of estrogens make breasts develop in boys, but they develop more and faster in girls (Burns, 1961).

Certain medical accidents have provided further clues about sexual differentiation. In the 1950s, some pregnant women took a synthetic hormonal drug to prevent miscarriage; no one knew that it would have the same effect on fetuses as a dose of male hormones. Girls were born with masculinized genitals (an enlarged clitoris, fused labia that looked like a scrotum, and other abnormalities). The genital effects were surgically corrected, and the children raised as normal girls. Some years later, it turned out that all the girls, though heterosexual, had been considered tomboys by themselves and others—very active and aggressive in many ways, from choice of games to sexual behavior (Ehrhardt and Money, 1967). The researchers inferred that prenatal hormones masculinized not only the girls' genitals but their nervous systems, and thus their behavior.

Similar results appeared in girls whose own adrenal glands produced abnormally high amounts of androgens before birth because of a disorder called the adrenogenital syndrome (see

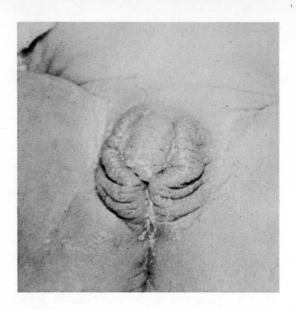

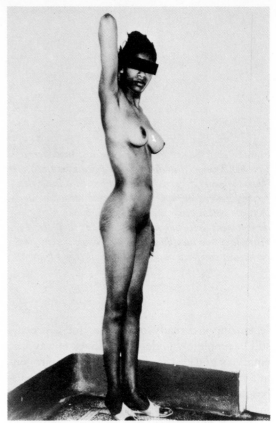

Figure 7-2 / *Two rare anomalies throw light on normal development. In the adrenogenital syndrome (left), excessive androgens masculinize the appearance of a genetic female. In the testicular feminizing syndrome (right), a genetic male cannot respond to his own androgens; not only his body, but his nervous system is to some degree feminized.*

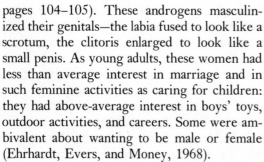

pages 104–105). These androgens masculinized their genitals—the labia fused to look like a scrotum, the clitoris enlarged to look like a small penis. As young adults, these women had less than average interest in marriage and in such feminine activities as caring for children: they had above-average interest in boys' toys, outdoor activities, and careers. Some were ambivalent about wanting to be male or female (Ehrhardt, Evers, and Money, 1968).

Similar inferences have been drawn from studies of males who lacked fetal androgens; they later showed feminine physical and behavioral traits. Furthermore, some males born with low testicular hormone function later show low sex drive and activity—perhaps, some suggest, as much because of early neuroendocrine effects as low adult androgen levels (Dia-

mond, 1965; 1977b; Meyer-Bahlberg et al., 1974).

Some researchers think early hormonal effects on the nervous system may influence sexual arousability, sexual identity, sexual orientation, and many other responses and activities (Diamond, 1976a; Reinisch and Karow, 1977). The technical difficulties of proving or disproving this are compounded by complex individual and social variations. Furthermore, many behaviors exist to different degrees in both males and females; a neurohormonal influence may exist, but elude proof. But it seems clear that before birth, the genes and the hormones do, to some degree, affect the nervous system and thus behavior, producing a male or female bias for reacting to other individuals and the social environment.

One indication that a behavior is genetically sex-linked is that similar traits exist in most close evolutionary relatives of humans. Some are characteristic of virtually all mammals—for example, the female reproductive cycle and the male's greater size and aggressiveness. Some sex-linked qualities are not limited to either males or females, but exist more in one sex than the other; that is, they are not polar opposites but tendencies stronger in one sex or the other. Generalizations about these traits hold true for large populations but not necessarily for a given person. For instance, human females, like almost all mammalian females, can be aggressive, at times more aggressive than some males; but males, as a group, show more aggression more often. And males may nurture the young, but more females do so more often. Societies shape and emphasize these natural tendencies to some degree, and often institutionalize and reinforce them in unique ways. Therefore there are cross-cultural variations in the *form* and *extent* of some sex-linked behaviors, but broad consistencies remain.

These facts make some people react with uneasiness. They fear that admitting any biological influence on gender development means saying that society and individuals cannot make free choices. But few scientists today believe in a simple, inflexible genetic basis for behavior and personality traits. They speak rather of *interaction traits,* which result from the influence of environment on a *range of genetic potential.* For instance, a person may be capable genetically of growing to be anywhere from five to six feet tall; infant care, nutrition, exercise, climate, and other factors determine what point in that range will be reached. Two people with the same potential for a quality or skill—dexterity, aggression, verbal or spatial ability—may show differing degrees of that quality because of social, family, and individual factors. Furthermore, a better endowed person may neglect his potential, a less endowed one excel because of high motivation or social reward. A host of interpersonal influences also exist; many people act differently toward first- and last-born children, males and females, tall people and small people. Clearly much of development is not a matter of either nature or nurture but of interaction between the two (Diamond, 1977b; Kagan, 1977).

Childhood Development

A researcher in child development, Jerome Kagan, has written (1976), "The developmental psychologist is puzzled by the increasing differences between the sexes that accompany maturation, for males and females are more similar during the first week of life than they will ever be again."

At birth, the most obvious sign of a baby's sex is its genitals, but many other differences exist (Ounsted and Taylor, 1972). Some differences begin before birth and persist throughout life. For instance, males are more vulnerable to disease and death. It is probably to compensate for this that 120 or more males are conceived for every 100 females (the *primary sex ratio*). Fewer males survive gestation; about 105 boys are born for every 100 girls *(secondary sex ratio).* More boys are born with developmental defects, and one-quarter to one-third more die by age one, chiefly of immunity disorders and infectious diseases. Males remain more susceptible to disease, and their life span is shorter. This basic vulnerability may be related to genes on the Y chromosome (Teitelbaum, 1976).

Though more vulnerable, males are bigger and stronger. They grow faster than females in the later part of gestation, and at birth are an average of 5 percent heavier and 1 to 2 percent taller. A greater proportion of their bodies is muscle and bone; females have more skin and fat. The height difference persists until ages eleven to thirteen, when girls temporarily catch up to or slightly surpass boys. Then at puberty boys outgrow girls again.

At about age six, boys start to acquire the characteristic male body form, with shoulders wider than the hips and a large, muscular chest. At around the same age, girls start to show typical female fat deposits at the buttocks and hips. In both sexes, the development of these traits accelerates greatly at puberty.

Males and females are born with a lasting difference in their potential for muscular strength and sustained exertion *(vital capacity)*. At birth, a male's muscle mass is only a little larger than a female's, but his muscular capacity is 10 percent greater. His muscle mass and vital capacity shoot farther ahead from ages seven to nine, and even more during puberty and early adolescence. Males also have a higher basal metabolism from birth, and from the second month of life consume more calories (Teitelbaum, 1976).

While the evidence is not clear (Maccoby and Jacklin, 1974), boys' body movements, both before and after birth, seem more rapid and vigorous. Boys seem to be more restless before they are fed and to fall asleep more readily afterward (Teitelbaum, 1976). They

are more irritable than girls and cry more (Moss, 1967); that may be why they are pacified and given attention more often than girls, though maternal handling does not quiet infant males as easily as it does females (C. Hutt, 1972; Moss, 1967).

Although boys are born bigger and stronger, girls develop faster, over-all and neurologically. Newborn girls are physically as mature as four- to six-week-old boys (C. Hutt, 1972). They are able to sit, crawl, walk, and talk before boys. Their teeth come in earlier, and their bones finish growing sooner. They become socially and sexually mature earlier, as do females in many higher species.

The cerebellum, the part of the brain responsible for balance and coordination, is considerably larger in females from birth on. This probably helps account for females' greater grace, fine coordination, and delicacy of movement. Sex differences also exist in the cerebral cortex, the largest part of the brain; similar surgery there affects males and females differently (Lansdell, 1962; McGlone, 1978). The right hemisphere of the cortex has greater control over space perception, the left hemisphere over verbal functions. Girls seem to have more efficient left hemispheres and faster verbal growth; boys seem to have more efficient right hemispheres and better spatial and large motor abilities (Buffery and Gray, 1972; Kimura, 1967; D. Taylor, 1969).

Females are more sensitive from birth to touch, pain, and some tastes (Bell and Costello, 1965; Lipsitt and Levy, 1959). These physical sensitivities seem to have a counterpart in emotional sensitivity. Such sensitivities may be associated with the greater empathy and imagination found in older girls and women (Bard-

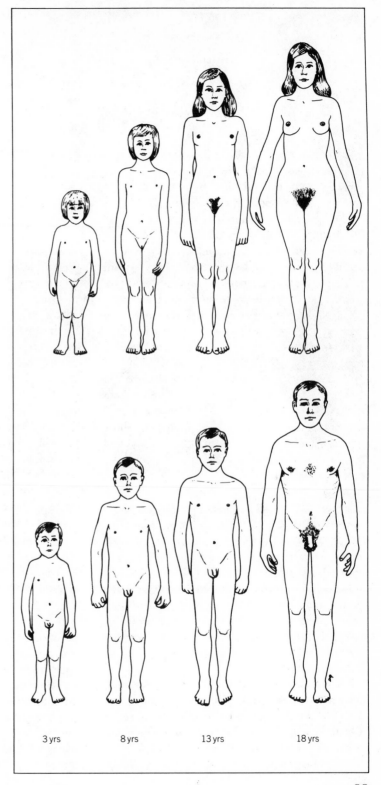

Figure 7–3 / *In childhood, males are taller and heavier than females. Late in preadolescence, girls catch up in height. During adolescence, males' relative height, weight, and muscle development increase. By adulthood, males have wider shoulders and chests; females have wider hips.*

3 yrs 8 yrs 13 yrs 18 yrs

Figure 7-4 / *In preadolescence the sexes begin to play apart more than together. Boys tend to form gangs and teams, and they engage in much competitive and rough-and-tumble play. Girls tend to play less aggressively, in twos and threes. This tendency appears cross-culturally and in many higher social species.*

wick, 1971). Even as infants, girls are more responsive than boys to the cry of another baby (Simner, 1971). At five or six months, girls pay more attention to photographs and pictures of faces; boys prefer watching geometric forms, especially new or complicated ones (Garai and Scheinfeld, 1968). As preschoolers, girls are more empathic than boys about the problems of others (Hoffman and Levine, 1976). In other words, girls seem more responsive to people, boys to things.

When only three days old, girls have finer hearing, males more discriminating vision. Later in life, males seem to depend more on visual sexual stimuli, females on verbal, auditory, and tactile stimuli (Money, 1973). This has also been observed in many other mamma-

lian species (Buffery and Gray, 1972), and is probably an evolutionary trend.

In early childhood, many of these differences increase. As one might expect, boys make use of their greater strength, endurance, and spatial abilities. As early as seven months of age, they show more aggression than girls; at two, the difference is great. Boys' play is exploratory, wide-ranging, and aggressive; they run, climb, and wrestle more often than girls. Girls more often choose play activities that involve relationships, use small muscles, and require fine dexterity—hopping, jumping, playing house, mothering dolls. The only play involving motion that girls engage in more than boys are passive ones, such as riding a swing (Teitelbaum, 1976; Maccoby and Jacklin, 1974).

This is not to say that such behaviors are entirely independent of rearing. An individual's amount and ways of expressing aggression may be influenced by family structure, parental permissiveness, and cultural patterns (R. Sears, 1951, 1965; P. Sears, 1951). Still, most boys are more aggressive more often regardless of upbringing. Some fifty studies of children in the United States over four decades have shown boys and men to be more aggressive and hostile than girls and women (Maccoby and Jacklin, 1974). Cross-cultural studies show that boys direct more aggression at other boys than at girls; that they elicit more aggression; and that they retaliate with more aggression (C. Hutt, 1972). These patterns also exist in most higher species.

Boys of three and four are more active, competitive, and aggressive at play than girls; girls spend more time in cooperative games. Girls are also much more likely to care for and protect younger children; boys interacting with children of other ages usually try to attach themselves to older boys and join their activities (McGrew, 1972).

From a few years of age on, both boys and

Evolving as Male and Female

Man's acquisition of an erect posture and bipedalism freed the upper limbs, which then could be developed for tool-using and hunting. The development of a large brain necessitated a larger pelvis in the female, but still some brain development had to be deferred until after birth, in fact up to the second decade. The infant's immaturity and dependence were protracted; more parental care and nursing were required. The young could no longer be easily transported; the females and young had to adopt a less mobile mode of life. This meant greater distinction between the roles of males and females. Males traversed wide spaces hunting in packs or groups; females remained within their territory, nurturing the young. Good vision and sense of direction were of advantage to the hunter; so were agility and strength. Since hunting was a group activity, both the propensity for aggression and the ability to derive pleasure from the company of other males would be a distinct advantage for the males. Conversely, the skills of nurture and repair would be advantageous to the females. The evolutionary heritage of modern man then probably predisposed the males to be more aggressive, more exploratory, more vigorous and more group-oriented, and the females to be relatively more passive and dependent, more nurturant, more verbal. There is considerable evidence for differences in sensory and executive skills which enable these predispositions to be manifest.

—condensed from Corinne Hutt, *Males and Females* (1972)

girls tend to play with children of their own sex. Girls usually form intimate twos and threes, boys larger groups; boys, though more competitive, seem more eager and able to play in groups (Tiger, 1969). In no society have girls developed team games such as baseball, football, and soccer, except in emulation of boys (Diamond, 1977b). This tendency remains throughout childhood and, to different degrees in various societies, in adulthood. Like girls, women tend to form small intimate groups; like boys, men tend to form clubs and societies.

Table 7.1 / *Sex differences in toys, play, and interests*

Age	Sex	Pattern	Age	Sex	Pattern
13 months	M	Play with nontoys, bang rather than manipulate them.	9–11 years	M	Prefer games with forceful physical contact, propelling objects through space, complex team games.
	F	Play with blocks and toy animals, manipulate rather than bang them.		F	Prefer verbal games, realistic noncompetitive games, games for one player.
2–4 years	M	Play with blocks, push toys.	12–17 years	M	Know more terms about money, autos, motorcycles.
	F	Play with dolls, paint, cut, glue, sew.		F	Know more terms about clothes, fashions, appearance, boys, popularity.
4 years	M	Choose masculine toys and prefer pictures of masculine activities.	18 years	M	Preferred occupations: engineering, agriculture, technology
	F	Choose feminine toys and prefer pictures of feminine activities.		F	Preferred occupations: social, religious, educational.
6–8 years	M	Prefer many occupations, in this order: football player, policeman, doctor, dentist, priest, scientist, pilot, astronaut.	18–20 years	M	College students' goals: academic distinction, career requiring postgraduate study.
	F	Prefer few occupations, in this order: teacher, nurse, housewife, mother, stewardess, salesgirl.		F	College students' goals: appreciation of ideas, establishing own values, developing relationships with males, finding a spouse, learning to get along with a variety of people, preparing for immediate career.
7–12 years	M	Express wish for material possessions, money.			
	F	Express wish for another person.			

Adapted from Maccoby and Jacklin, *The Development of Sex Differences* (1974).
Sources of items, in order, are: S. Goldberg and Lewis, 1969; Clark, Wyon, and Richards, 1969; R. Sears, Rau, and Alpert, 1965; Looft, 1971; Ables, 1972; Rosenberg and Sutton-Smith, 1960; Nelson and Rosenbaum, 1972; Monday, Hout, and Lutz, 1966–1967; Constantinople, 1967.

Some argue that social conditioning accounts for many of these differences. However, the differences reviewed here have been observed with striking regularity in many different societies and in other higher species (D'Andrade, 1966; Freedman, 1974; C. Hutt, 1972; Tiger, 1969). For instance, a study (B. Whiting and J. Whiting, 1975) of children in six cultures (India, Okinawa, the Philippines, Mexico, Kenya, and the United States) showed that in all these very different societies, girls show "nurturance and responsibility, and this combination is essentially the definition of what a mother is to her children. . . . Girls exhibit this at an earlier age and more than boys do. Conversely, in each of these six cultures, boys are characterized by more physical attack, more physical aggression, than are girls."

Such patterns appear in most other mammals, including primates. For instance, young male rhesus monkeys form same-sex play groups and chase, wrestle, and climb more than females the same age (Phoenix, Goy, and Resko, 1968). And rhesus females just emerging from infancy are protective of newborn rhesus monkeys; males the same age are indifferent or hostile to newborns (Harlow, 1974).

Scientific and social arguments have arisen about the reasons for two common childhood sex differences, toy preference and play patterns. Boys and girls choose and use toys differently the majority of the time (see Table 7.1), but not all the differences are those most people would expect. At thirteen months, boys play with dolls more than girls do (Kaminski, 1973), though by age two, girls prefer dolls more (A. Clark, Wyon, and Richards, 1969). From age two on, boys play more often with blocks and with nontoys, such as door knobs

and electrical outlets (S. Goldberg and Lewis, 1969). The question is whether they do so because society says these are boys' toys. Maccoby and Jacklin (1974), after an extensive review of research on the subject, concluded that "there is no obvious reason why pre-school girls should be spending more time in painting, drawing, cutting paper, or manipulating play dough (since few modern mothers make bread, and professional artists are frequently male). If these activities become labeled as more appropriate for one sex, then, it seems possible that it is because children of one sex choose to do them rather than vice versa."

Developing Sexual Identity

By the time a child is two and a half to three, it has developed its *sexual identity,* a deep, life-long conviction of being male or female. In its simplest sense, this is knowing "I am a boy" or "I am a girl." By four or five, this expands to include a sense of one's future as a man or woman, father or mother. It then becomes entwined with other developments but should not be confused with them—*gender identity* (how society views one as a male or female), *gender role* (social ideas of how males and females should act), and *sexual orientation* (also less accurately called sexual preference or object choice).

Typical Development

Sexual identity normally seems a fact of life, like the color of one's eyes, and it is virtually irreversible. Gender identity, as a function of society, is more flexible. Gender role and sex-

103

ual orientation develop later, and they are more easily shaped by society and individual experience. Some children feel anxiety or resentment over their gender roles. A tomboy may find aspects of the feminine role constricting; a timid boy may find the masculine role demanding. But discomfort with gender role, even wanting to be like the other sex, only very rarely changes a child's conviction of being male or female. Neither does atypical orientation; most homosexuals, like most heterosexuals, know and value their biological sex (Karlen, 1971).

A minority of researchers believe sexual identity rises from biological forces alone; some others claim people are born sexually neutral* and develop both sexual identity and gender identity through learning or conditioning alone. We believe that in this, as in so many aspects of sexuality, there is probably an interplay among biological, social, and psychological forces.

Some early sexual development is influenced by learning. Just after birth, parents and doctors look at an infant's genitals, pronounce a *sex assignment* (call the child male or female), and name and rear the child accordingly. In some ways boys and girls are raised alike, in others differently. For instance, they are similarly encouraged to go to school, but males are more often encouraged to think of a career, females of marriage. This subject demands far more study than it has received. Some apparent similarities in the treatment of the sexes may mask subtle differences; for instance, the different kinds and degrees of discipline given to boys

* We use the word neutral rather than "bisexual," which has other connotations.

and girls may affect such behaviors as aggression and its control. However, some differences, such as the traditional blue blankets for boys and pink ones for girls, may have more symbolic importance for adults than real impact on children.

During its first few years, a child becomes capable of speech and develops a sense of "I" as separate from "mother." Still developing, more mobile, in contact with more people, the child begins to distinguish *me* from *them, like me* from *not like me, girls* from *boys,* and *women* from *men.* He or she increasingly associates such qualities as aggression and nurture with one sex or the other. Probably through observation, imitation, and socialization, the child begins to learn its gender role.

Gender roles, however, are not entirely learned. From infancy, boys and girls evoke different responses from adults, and they respond differently in turn. It seems logical that boys feel a greater urge to use their larger muscle mass, and more satisfaction in spending their higher activity level in forceful play. Similarly, girls apparently have a greater desire for cooperative and nurturing play and find more satisfaction in it. Parents and other adults can encourage or discourage such tendencies, but cannot easily erase them. Many such sex differences persist through childhood and into adult life (see chapters 8, 9, 10, and 21).

*Atypical Development:
Hermaphrodites and Transsexuals*

Study of two rare disorders, *hermaphroditism* and *transsexualism* (see chapter 12), has recently shed light on sexual identity and gender identity. Hermaphrodites are people with both male and female gonadal tissue. Only a very few cases fit the strict definition—having a pair of ovaries and a pair of testicles or one of each. The word *pseudohermaphrodite* is used for the more common (but still rare) cases in which the external genitals differ from genetic sex or the internal sexual and reproductive organs.

For instance, a female with the *adrenogenital syndrome* has female chromosomes, gonads, hormones, and internal sex organs; but because of a genetic anomaly, excess fetal androgens cause the labia to fuse into a scrotum, the clitoris to overdevelop. At birth such a girl may look like a boy with a small penis. The parents assume that the child is a boy and raise her accordingly. At puberty, however, her biological sex is revealed, when she begins to develop breasts.

Male or Female

In a community in Central America, a genetic defect caused eighteen males to be born without penises. They were assumed to be girls and raised accordingly, but at puberty they started to develop penises and respond behaviorally to their own hormones. Despite their rearing, all the boys rebelled against their female status and assumed male identities and life patterns. They felt sexually attracted to girls (Imperato-McGinley et al., 1974, 1979). Biological forces apparently overcame their learned gender identities.

Another report (Money and Ehrhardt, 1972) is sometimes cited to defend the opposite view of how sexual identity develops. It describes twin boys who were circumcised by cautery; the penis of one was accidentally burned off. On the assumption that sex identity is learned, the decision was made to raise the penectomized boy as a girl. The report assessed his situation when he was about eight years old; he was said to identify as female and, aside from tomboyish behavior, acted like a girl. The other twin identified as male and behaved normally.

This was taken by some to show the power of rearing and socialization over biology. However, the penectomized boy was also castrated (which removed his source of androgen), had surgical reconstruction to enhance a female appearance, and received female hormones; in short, everything possible was done to defeat his male biological potential and enhance female appearance and function. Time has shown, however, that even with such alteration of biological and social forces, a typical female identity has not developed. The psychiatrist now in charge of the case has said: "At the present time [at age 15] . . . she does display certain features that would make me suspicious that she will ever make the adjustment as a woman" (Williams and M. Smith, 1979).

There are also male pseudohermaphrodites. One type, because of a genetic anomaly, is born with the *testicular feminizing syndrome,* or *androgen insensitivity syndrome.* From prenatal life on, this genetic male cannot respond to his own androgens, so he fails to develop external male genitals, and his nervous system is not masculinized. At birth he looks like a female; his testicles, hidden in his groin, produce androgens, but his body does not react to them. Like most pseudohermaphrodites, he is likely to be raised in accordance with his genital appearance, though it contradicts his genetic sex. Female body development occurs at puberty, but there is no menstruation and no pubic or axillary (armpit) hair.

Sexual identity, called by some "core gender identity" (Stoller, 1968), seems to start becoming fixed at eighteen months. According to some researchers (Money, Hampson, and Hampson, 1955), a girl raised as a boy has, by age two and a half, developed lifelong male identity, mannerisms, fantasies, play preferences, self-image, and interests. Surgical correction leaves her feeling not like a female but like a castrated male being pressured into homosexuality. Therefore some such people have been surgically treated to make their sexualia match their gender identity rather than their genetic sex. According to Money, Hampson, and Hampson, after age four only a few children whose gender identity was ambiguous could adapt to change to their genetically correct sex without undergoing severe mental disturbance, even psychosis. Other clinicians, however, say that some misassigned individuals welcome change to their genetic sex (J. Brown and Fryer, 1964; Dewhurst and Gordon, 1963; Stoller, 1965, 1968).

There are researchers, we noted, who have concluded that people are born psychosexually neutral, or nearly so, and that sexual and gender identity are mostly learned (Money and Ehrhart, 1972). Some of them say that *sex typing,* the social association of certain traits with one sex, is what makes people feel male or female (Gagnon and Simon, 1973). But a large number of researchers disagree. Many children whose sex was misassigned at birth feel discomfort and doubt about their ascribed sex; this doubt may become so strong at puberty that the child, despite its rearing, insists on belonging to its true biological sex (Diamond, 1978; Imperato-McGinley et al., 1974, 1979). Some such children find change (with surgery and hormones if necessary) satisfying (Diamond, 1965, 1979a), even in late childhood.

Other interesting results have come from studies of *transsexualism.* Most transsexuals, male and female, seem physically normal; however, they believe that they really belong to the other sex. A male transsexual feels that his penis is a mistake of nature, as a sixth toe would be; he thinks he is a female trapped in a male body. A female transsexual feels the same way about her breasts and menses (Stoller, 1968). It is transsexuals who seek sex-change surgery, to make their bodies conform to their sexual identities (for example, Christine Jorgensen, Rene Richards, and Jan Morris).

A depth psychiatric study of transsexual children and their parents (Stoller, 1968) suggests that reversed sexual identity arises largely from physical and emotional messages the child receives from the mother that prevent normal separation and independence. This seemed further evidence that sexual identity is largely learned, in the family. However, in a few of Stoller's cases, and in a majority of those reported by Benjamin (1966), the children's biologically correct sexual identity eventually asserted itself despite childrearing pressures to the contrary. A number of more recent studies (Šipová and Stárka, 1977; Dorner et al., 1976) support the idea that biological forces play a part in transsexualism. It may be that there is more than one source of transsexualism, and that biological and family-forces interact in different degrees in various cases.

Theories of Development

No one theory fully explains male and female development, but several have particular strengths in dealing with certain stages, ages, or aspects of development. Various ones have risen and fallen in popularity over the decades; people have tried to make each a total explanation, sometimes creating sharp scientific and popular argument. We have already discussed early development in terms of biosocial interaction, a theory we find especially helpful in understanding prenatal and early-life development. Other major theories are:

1. Psychoanalytic (Freudian)
2. Cultural adaptation (Neo-Freudian)
3. Learning theory (differential reinforcement)
4. Differential socialization
5. Role modeling and sex typing
6. Cognitive learning
7. Social scripting

Psychoanalytic (Freudian) Theory

From the 1890s through the 1930s, Sigmund Freud created the theory and technique of *psychoanalysis* (analysis of the mind). The re-

currence of certain thoughts and feelings in patients and nonpatients led Freud to infer the existence of a universal pattern of psychosexual development. This was the first comprehensive theory of development.

Like many scientists of his time, Freud tried to explain behavior as the result of drives, or instincts, conceived as energy forces like electrical or hydraulic power. In 1905, in his *Three Essays on the Theory of Sexuality* (1962), Freud set forth the concept of *libido,* a drive toward reproduction, erotic pleasure, and general well-being. As electricity can charge a spot, said Freud, libido can make any part of the body an *erogenous zone* (erotically responsive area). In normal development, libido concentrates first at the mouth (the *oral stage* of the suckling infant), then the anus (the *anal stage* of toddlerhood), and then the clitoris or penis (the *phallic stage* of the late preschool years). Various experiences can *fixate* (hold) libido at any stage, arresting sexual and personality development. Residues of the early libidinal stages account for oral and anal eroticism in normal adults.

Freud's belief that sexual feelings and activities are normal in childhood made him an outcast in his time. Freud further scandalized people by saying that a child's love and desire are normally directed at the parent of the opposite sex. This creates rivalry with the same-sex parent, and fear of punishment and retaliation. Freud called this triangle the Oedipus complex. (Psychoanalytic theory later suggested a comparable triangle in girls, the Electra complex.) Healthy development, he said, occurs only if a child resolves the desires and rivalries that occur within the family.

Freud said that sexual feelings, like much early-childhood experience, are pushed from memory at about ages five to seven. From then until puberty, there is a *latency period,* when sexual drive is *sublimated* (transformed into nonsexual drives), as the child is educated and socialized. At puberty, genital libido surges, and as the transition to adulthood approaches, erotic interest shifts from one's own body (masturbation) and the family (incest) to coitus with people outside the family. For girls, Freud thought, this also begins a shift of primary erotic response from the clitoris to the vagina, and a corresponding change in the type of orgasm (see chapter 5).

In the early 1920s, Freud (1961, 1959) developed what came to be known as *ego psychology,* which eventually influenced many writers on psychosexual development. He divided mental activity into three aspects. The *id* (Latin: it) is the instinctual self. A small child is almost pure id, full of primitive impulses such as lust and aggression. The growing child develops an *ego* (Latin: I), a sense of his own identity, as the world limits his impulses; he learns to defer pleasures and control impulses. He *introjects* his parents' voices so that they seem his own; now he himself will feel that his emotions and behavior are right or wrong. The child has begun to develop a *superego.* The superego is rather like the usual idea of conscience, but it is partly unconscious, often working without the person being aware of it.

The division of mental activity into *conscious* and *unconscious* is crucial to Freudian theory. Freud said that often people act on unconscious thoughts and urges, even when they seem most rational. He also said that it is natural to feel *ambivalence*—to have conflicting or even op-

Oedipus and Incest

Freud kept finding in his patients' memories, dreams, and fantasies a family triangle reminiscent of that in Sophocles' play *Oedipus Rex.* In the play, Oedipus unknowingly murders his father and marries his mother. After discovering this, he blinds himself out of guilt, and his mother hangs herself. A similar triangular story from Greek mythology, that of Electra, offers a female counterpart.

Freud believed that the Oedipal complex is universal (whether an individual can recall it or not), and that many emotional problems stem from a failure to resolve the guilts and anxieties that arise from desiring one parent and seeing the other as a rival. A major study of a non-Western society soon supported tne idea that intense, erotically tinged relationships within the family are a crucial part of development, though not necessarily on the Oedipal model (Malinowski, 1929; see chapter 20), but there is still no conclusive proof. Freud's theory does offer explanations of the particular horror in which incest is held in virtually all cultures, and of many sexual behavior patterns and emotional conflicts in children and adults.

posed feelings at one time. Many people simultaneously feel love and hate, fear and rage, passivity and aggression, and such conflict has consequences in development, sexuality, and relationships.

Clinical experience convinced Freud that a child *identifies* to some degree with both parents. Identification goes beyond imitation, to a sense of feeling one with another person. He believed that all infants first identify with their mothers; boys must switch to identifying with their fathers. This difficult separation from mother and positive identification with father must be reinforced, so males value their hard-won sexual identity more than females. This helps explain why males everywhere seem to show more *sex fixedness* than females; why they seem to stubbornly place a higher value on maleness than on femaleness; and why in all societies more men than women suffer dysfunctions of sexual identity and sexual orientation. Masculinity, being harder to achieve and maintain, is more vulnerable, and therefore more strongly bolstered and defended.

Another aspect of Freudian thought bears on sexual development. Small children think magically, without adult concepts of time, reality, or cause and effect. They may imagine that the absence of a penis means one was removed or that one will eventually grow. A male's fear that vulnerable parts of the body, especially the genitals, will be injured or mutilated is called *castration anxiety;* the female counterpart, a general fear of being destroyed, is called *aphanasis.* Freud also believed that girls experience *penis envy.* This is not merely a child's "I want one, too!" but an association of the anatomical differences with males' higher social status and greater assertiveness. Such fears and associations can be associated with a wide variety of feelings and experiences, and persist in the unconscious of adults.

Few people have had so great an influence on modern thought as Freud. Even many who oppose psychoanalytic theory accept certain Freudian concepts: that early nuclear-family relationships, laden with love, desire, and competition, shape the personality; that identification, ambivalence, and unconscious motives are part of life; that the sexual and nonsexual aspects of life are inseparable. Freudian ideas— and a good bit of pseudo-Freudianism—are commonplace. One often hears a cold, controlling woman described as "castrating," and a seductive male as a "neurotic Don Juan" or a "latent homosexual." In discussions of sexual development, only the theories of conditioning and differential socialization have been so used and misused.

Freud's concept of instincts, common in his day, has been dropped by many biologists today. The idea of sublimation has been ably argued against (Kinsey et al., 1948). Studies have confirmed the existence and importance of childhood sexuality, but revealed that latency is not a universal stage of development but a trend more prominent in sexually restrictive societies (Kinsey et al., 1948; Ford and Beach, 1951). Scientific opinion now widely rejects the idea of a progression from "immature clitoral" orgasm to "mature vaginal" orgasm, although some researchers have recently made similar distinctions of types of orgasms (see chapter 5). Many clinicians do not find the same developmental patterns in their patients that Freud found, nor do they interpret what they find as he did.

Oddly, some "Freudian" concepts that are

opposed today were not believed or stated by Freud at all. He has sometimes been accused of biological determinism, but he pioneered the understanding of emotional and interpersonal experience, and therapy to alter dysfunctional early-life learning experience. His phrase "anatomy is destiny" has erroneously been taken to mean that innate differences should relegate women to rigidly defined gender roles and second-class status. Freud actually said that men and women are products of both their anatomy and upbringing and that a happy life comes from accepting this complex interaction and using it to one's advantage. He has also been accused of being antihomosexual and considering homosexuality an illness. But he did neither. He once wrote (1951), "Homosexuality is assuredly no advantage, but it's nothing to be ashamed of, no vice, no degradation, it cannot be classified as an illness; we consider it to be a variation of the sexual function produced by a certain arrest of sexual development."

Other Psychoanalytic Theories

Many psychoanalysts have produced influential observations and ideas on sexual development, though few have created full, systematic theories. Carl Jung (1972), for instance, said that a boy's early identification with his mother leaves a feminine self in his unconscious; similarly, a girl's partial identification with her father creates an unconscious masculine self. Helping to create a view now widespread, Jung said that to the extent that men fear their female "shadow" selves, and women their male selves, they pay a toll in emotional discomfort.

Alfred Adler (1964) put more stress on the social environment than on instincts. Since everyone is born helpless and dependent, said Adler, life begins with a need to master one's environment and win security and self-esteem. From the first relationships in life, a child learns to feel secure or insecure, confident or timid, lovable or worthless. A timid person—a small frail boy, an unattractive and graceless girl, a child intimidated by parents or siblings—may feel unable to live up to his or her ideal picture of masculine or feminine success, and as a result develops an *inferiority complex*. Attempts to *compensate* for real or imagined inadequacies will show in his or her *life-style*. Since both sexes see males as more powerful, effective, and prestigious, some women compensate by undervaluing their femininity and overvaluing masculine traits *(masculine protest)*. In most men, he said, and many women, neurosis is an insecure and desperate attempt to be a "real man." In stressing the *social embeddedness* of sexual development Adler anticipated learning theory and the theory of differential socialization (Adler, 1978).

Ego psychology, created by Freud and developed by many others, assumed that personality and behavior develop through continuing adaptation to life situations. It opened the door to explorations of psychosexual development, particularly by a number of woman analysts, including Melanie Klein, Helene Deutsch, Clara Thompson, Karen Horney, and Anna Freud (Sigmund Freud's daughter). Their work is too varied and complex to be detailed here (for an overview see Thompson, Mazer, and Witenberg, 1955), but they were less bound by the attitudes of Freud's generation and milieu—middle-class Central Europe of the late nineteenth century. They created a more positive and detailed view of female development, and their work has had extensive influence.

Further contributions came from Harry Stack Sullivan, an innovative American analyst (see chapter 14). He stressed the importance of imaginary figures to whom children (and adults) relate—for instance, a personal picture of a dream girl or ideal man. He was also interested in male *preadolescent chumship*. Between about eight and twelve, peers become enormously important. Recent anthropological and ethological studies have shown that preadolescent friendships are also important in other societies and species (Tiger, 1969). More research on the subject may reveal a great deal about sexual development in both males and females.

Erik Erikson's eight-stage scheme of life development (1959, 1963, 1968) is now widely appreciated. Although he sees libidinal forces underlying development, he stresses social forces as well. He believes that throughout life one keeps defining and redefining one's identity, often by going through a period of *identity crisis*. He sees puberty and adolescence as especially important times of development. Erikson believes that achieving sexual intimacy with others depends on learning when to trust and when not to trust, when to be independent and when self-confident, when to feel shame and when doubt.

Cultural Adaptation (Neo-Freudian Theory)

The emphasis of ego psychology on interpersonal relations (Sullivan, 1968) and social influences continues in the work of the psychiatrists and psychologists who have been called *neo-Freudians* or *cultural adaptationists*. They accept Freud's idea that unconscious ideas, sometimes sexual or sex-related, lie behind much apparently nonsexual behavior. But they add the converse—nonsexual motives lie behind much sexual behavior. They have explored such patterns as having coitus out of a need to dominate or be dependent, to conquer or be cared for. This approach has had strong if dif-

---

Freud: A Modern Misappreciation

Freud might have been moved to laughter or exasperation by many distorted popularizations of his ideas. A good fictional example is in Peter De Vries's novel *Comfort Me With Apples* (1968). A middle-aged poet named Gowan McGland (a caricature of the Welsh poet Dylan Thomas) gave readings from campus to campus, always drunk and seeking new girls to seduce. Female students who had not read Freud but thought they knew what he had said pityingly told McGland that he didn't have to try to seduce them; they understood that he must be a latent homosexual trying to prove his masculinity. The more they "understood" him, the harder he tried; the harder he tried, the more they gave compassion, not passion. The lecherous McGland was reduced to howling frustration, undone by the distorted shadow of Freud.

111

fuse influence on psychiatry, clinical psychology, child psychology, marriage counseling, and psychiatric social work. It has also explored how children's development continues through interaction with family, peers, and society. In the United States, there have been major contributions by Sandor Rado, Abram Kardiner, Leon Saltzman, Lionel Ovesey, Rollo May, and Herbert Hendin (Karlen, 1971). To some extent, it is compatible with the theories of differential socialization and cognitive development. It is largely through the adaptational approach that integrated cross-cultural and historical studies of psychosexual development have been done.

Learning
(Differential Reinforcement) Theory

One theory, now centuries old, is that a person is born a *tabula rasa,* a clean slate on which experience writes its lessons. In classic experiments early in this century, Ivan Pavlov (1960) taught dogs to salivate at the sound of a bell associated with feeding, rather than at the sight of food; this proved, he felt, that in higher animals a great deal of behavior is *conditioned,* or ingrained through learning. *Learning theory, behaviorism, operant conditioning,* and other terms have been used for later experiments and theories based on conditioning (by John B. Watson, B. F. Skinner, and others). Learning theory has contributed valuable knowledge, but has also been criticized for oversimplifying human experience and ignoring its social and emotional complexities.

According to learning theory, sex-typed behaviors develop from the different ways boys and girls are conditioned. Boys receive *positive*

reinforcement (rewards of encouragement and praise) for wearing masculine clothing and for not fearing rough-and-tumble play. They receive punishment, shaming, or the withholding of praise for wanting to cook or wear a dress, being weak or fearful, and being passed over in competitive games. Similarly, girls are conditioned to be quiet, compliant, and considerate, and to avoid assertion, competitiveness, and sex play. More sophisticated forms of learning theory note subtle punishments and rewards for sex-typed behavior, such as social expectations, parental warmth or distance, nonverbal communication, and adult responses to a child's dependence, independence, aggression, and genital activities (Maccoby and Jacklin, 1974).

Two principles of learning are generalization and discrimination. Through *generalization* one reacts to a new situation as one did to a previous one that it resembles or evokes. For example, a woman whose first coitus was a rape or was unpleasant and frustrating might generalize and find later coitus unpleasant because it reminds her of the first experience. Through *discrimination* one learns to react to one situation or experience and not to another. For instance, a person learns by being rewarded or rejected to discriminate when it is and is not appropriate to make a sexual advance.

Learning theory seems logical and has intuitive appeal. Experiments have shown that conditioning affects many behaviors in experimental animals and to some degree in people. While there is little direct evidence of its role in sexual development, the different clothes and hair styles of males and females are obvious examples of learned sex differences; so are many patterns of sexual approach and response seen in dating and courting.

However, learning theory explains only part of sexual development. People are not clean slates at birth. Some things seem more inherently rewarding for one sex or the other. There are sex differences and response biases that increase as people mature, some of which contradict conditioning as a basis for many sex differences. Aggression is an example. Males everywhere are more aggressive than females; learning theory would say that boys are conditioned to be aggressive, girls not to be. Most studies, however, show that young boys are not praised more than girls for aggressiveness, and girls are not praised more than boys for being cooperative. The aggression of preschoolers of both sexes is treated the same way by parents (Sears, Rau, and Alpert, 1965); if anything, parents and teachers react more harshly to displays of temper in boys (Lambert, Yackley, and Hein, 1971; Newson and Newson, 1968).

Doubtless the concepts of conditioning and reinforcement have human applications, but anthropological studies show some broad cross-cultural similarities in sex behavior and gender roles (see chapters 11 and 21). Why should so many males and females in so many different cultures learn the same things? We suggest it is because they are biased to accept some things more than others (Diamond, 1977b). Kagan (1977) says, "Psychological differences between the sexes are, in large measure, the result of differential socialization; nevertheless, [their general similarity] across many cultures suggests that different societies are responding in the same way to biological differences in size, bodily proportion and normal life functions. As a result, they are constructing similar sets of psychologically limiting sex role standards."

Differential Socialization

This theory proposes that culture is the major force in sex typing, working first through parents and then the rest of society. This approach shares much with learning theory, but it places more emphasis on the social context that guides conditioning (Bandura and Walters, 1963). Experimental evidence is scant, but observations of parents and children do give some support to the theory (Block, 1977), and it has gained wide popular acceptance.

In some ways, parents and society do treat boys and girls differently, but observations offer some surprises about how and with what effects. From early life on, for instance, girls are treated as if they were more fragile than boys; boys are played with more roughly (M. Lewis, 1972; Kagan, and Levine, 1971; Moss, 1967; Pederson and Robson, 1969; Tasch, 1952). Yet observation shows that infant boys and girls receive equal amounts of parental warmth and protection. Around elementary-school age, however, differences emerge in how children think they are treated. From about age nine to late adolescence, girls say they receive more parental affection, empathy, support, and acceptance than boys (Armentrout and Burger, 1972; Bronfenbrenner, 1960; Hoffman and Saltzstein, 1967). Perhaps this feeling accounts for the common adult belief that girls are treated more warmly. Another reason for that belief may be that boys, who are increasingly aggressive as they grow older, receive more rebukes along with the warmth.

It is widely assumed that gender roles are taught by parents, by allowing boys more freedom and encouraging girls to be more dependent. Yet some of the obvious differences in

113

adult male and female behavior do not seem to be taught in childhood. Actually, mothers discourage dependence and infantile behavior equally in boys and girls of three to four (Baumrind, 1971). Parents do not allow five-year-olds of either sex to go further from home, make more noise, treat household objects differently, watch television more, or avoid bedtime more (Sears, Maccoby, and Levin, 1957). Most studies have found no difference in how parents treat boys' and girls' exploration, self-sufficiency, independence, neatness, and general disobedience (Baumrind and Black, 1967; Hatfield, Ferguson, and Alpert, 1967). The few studies that do report differences say that boys from three to thirteen are restricted more than girls (Armentrout and Burger, 1972; Radin, 1973).

Still, boys seek independence more than girls, resist supervision more, and show greater hostility to peers. Being more aggressive, they are punished more for aggression, and in their teens feel that they are subject to greater psychological control than girls. Neither fathers nor mothers, though, encourage or praise aggressiveness in boys more than in girls. This may vary according to social class; most studies are done with middle-class families, which tend to expect all their children to resolve problems by talk rather than physical action, and to cooperate rather than compete (Lapidus, 1972; Williams, 1973). There is one parental difference: fathers are more concerned if a son is not aggressive, and they punish both sons and daughters more severely than mothers do.

Research bears out an important piece of traditional wisdom about differential socialization: mothers say they find it easier to punish sons than daughters (Block, 1972). Boys re-

ceive more restriction and physical punishment from both parents at all ages (Bronfenbrenner, 1960; Siegelman, 1965; Simpson, 1935). It may be that boys provoke punishment more than girls or that girls avoid punishment by responding more quickly to parental requests (Minton, Kagan, and Hein, 1971). But there may also be an inherent reluctance to hurt girls. In most higher species, aggression against females is less frequent and less forceful than against males (Moyer, 1976).

The term *rehearsal* is now widely used for children doing or playing at things they will do in later life; the assumption (possible but unproven) is that parents' sex-type play, and this typing prepares children for adult gender roles. We have seen that boys play more with certain toys (trucks and cars), girls with others (dolls and houses); also, boys more than girls avoid opposite-sex toys (Hartup and Moore, 1963). When asked how they would react to their daughters playing with boys' toys, parents say they would not be concerned. But when asked about a son choosing feminine toys and activities, parents are concerned and negative; fathers especially discourage what they consider feminine choices by their sons (Fling and Manosevitz, 1972; Lansky, 1967). Even feminists trying to rear their children without regard to traditional gender roles admit reluctance to encourage feminine games and goals in sons, though willing to encourage masculine ones in their daughters (Gelder and Carmichael, 1975). They are not worried that their daughters might be considered tomboyish or masculine, but they are concerned that their sons might seem sissyish or feminine.

Differential socialization suggests that socialization alone makes males more sexually assertive than females. But the evidence suggests that socialization affects certain aspects of sexual behavior far more than others. In most or all societies, virtually all boys begin masturbating in early adolescence, do so more often than girls, and are more likely to take sexual initiatives (see chapter 10). This eludes purely social explanation. Studies of four- and five-year-olds in the United States (Sears, Maccoby, and Levin, 1957; Sears, Rav, and Alpert, 1965) and England (Newson and Newson, 1968) show that parents do not treat boys and girls differently in giving information about genital activity, allowing masturbation, or permitting nudity and the sight of nudity. (They also react the same way to one child's sexual activity with another whether the partner is of the same or the opposite sex.) In short, parents do not seem to foster a double standard in children. To be sure, this research does not take into account the effect of attitudes outside the home, but parents are a strong initial influence.

If parents do not encourage young boys to experiment sexually, and young girls to avoid sex behavior (Maccoby and Jacklin, 1974), any such early differential socialization must come from other sources, such as peers. Among three- and four-year-olds, boys do receive more

---

Male and Female

A woman knows how to keep quiet when she is in the right, whereas a man, when he is in the right, will keep on talking.

—Malcolm de Chazal

All women become like their mothers. That is their tragedy. No man does. That is his.

—Oscar Wilde

Nature has given women so much power that the law has very wisely given them little.

—Samuel Johnson

Most men who rail against women are railing at one woman only.

—Remy De Gourmont

The great question that has never been answered, and which I have not yet been able to answer despite my thirty years of research into the feminine soul is "What does a woman want?"

—Sigmund Freud

What Is Woman? Only men worry over the mystery of women; women do not, because they are not mystified. If women wished, they could ask about the mystery of men's sexuality, which may not be so clear as some would have us think.

—Robert Stoller

Women have served all these centuries as looking glasses possessing the power of reflecting the figure of man at twice its natural size.

—Virginia Woolf

Anyone who says there are no differences between the sexes has never had her wrist twisted by a man.

—Mary McCarthy

Nothing is so useless as a general maxim.

—Thomas Babington Macauley

reinforcement from their male peers for whatever they do, girls more from their female peers (Charlesworth and Hartup, 1967).

At the approach of puberty, girls are warned more than boys of sexual dangers (real and imaginary) and are more often chaperoned. Girls receive messages from parents and other adults about harm from strangers that link the ideas of sexuality and assault. Strong effects of differential socialization are suggested by cross-cultural evidence: in sexually restrictive societies, almost all sexually active girls become inactive during puberty, while in less restrictive societies they do not (see chapter 20). However, the majority of pubertal boys become sexually active; social restrictions have far less effect on them, which suggests a biological force is at work (see chapters 9 and 10).

Several studies show differences in expectations of older boys and girls, but not in the ways many people would assume. Fathers expect boys to go to college more than they do girls (Tasch, 1952); mothers are more concerned with girls' intellectual achievement than with boys' (Buck and Austrin, 1971). It is not clear what effects these parental expectations and concerns have; presently more women than men are entering colleges.

Clearly boys and girls are socialized differently in many ways (Mischel, 1966). The question is which long-term differences are affected. Apparently differential socialization affects girls' pubertal and adolescent sex behavior, and sex typing is somewhat stronger for boys than for girls. But differential socialization may be more important for how adult behavior is performed in frequency and style than for whether it develops at all.

Role Modeling and Sex Typing

Several theories of sexual development draw on the ideas of *role modeling* and *sex typing*. These processes are assumed to involve identification with and imitation of people of the same sex, especially the parent. It is easy to accept that a little girl watches her mother cook, feed, and nurture, and uses her as a model, and that a boy identifies with and emulates his father. The question is why children choose the models they do.

Infants and toddlers everywhere are raised chiefly by their mothers and other females. Yet by the time they are toddlers, the vast majority of children imitate the parent of the same sex. Adults are quite aware of this; many unmarried parents try to see that same-sex models are present for their children. But even children who live in one-parent households are exposed to adults of both sexes, and some degree of same-sex identification and modeling occurs.

Identification is a psychoanalytic concept that has been widely adopted, even by many people who reject most psychoanalytic thought, including some proponents of role-modeling theory (Lynn, 1969). Freud, we noted, said that while a girl goes on identifying with her mother, a boy must shift to identifying with his father. The effort at making this switch, Freud said, gives males great emotional investment in their sexual identity. It may explain boys' greater sex fixedness. Given a choice, males from preschool age to adulthood are less willing than females to engage in other-sex activities. Men choose masculine tasks over feminine ones even if it means working for less pay

(Bem, 1975); this finding is striking, for men are more likely than women to seek the most money possible in work choices. Women are more often neutral about choosing sex-typed activities; many would rather satisfy personal preferences than make more money.

The question remains: why and how does a child pick one parent to identify with and model itself after? Children spend most of their first five or six years with adult females, and there is no evidence that fathers are more available to sons than to daughters in those years. Yet by age six, almost all children's behavior is strongly sex typed for life; males have modeled after males, females after females. Modeling does not seem to occur in sexual identity or orientation. Probably most transsexuals and homosexuals are brought up in heterosexual families, and probably few children raised by homosexuals and transsexuals follow by modeling (Green, unpublished paper).

In a review of research on role modeling, Maccoby and Jacklin (1974) conclude that it "plays a minor role in the development of sex-typed behavior. This conclusion seems to fly in the face of common sense and to conflict with many striking observations of sex-typed role playing on the part of children."

It does seem common sense that a child identifies with and emulates the parent of the same sex. Perhaps common sense is wrong about this or perhaps further study is needed. Much research on roles and role modeling measures only one behavior or attitude, through limited observations or questionnaires. It may fail to take into account many other factors, from body language to feelings and attitudes that appear only in depth interviewing.

Cognitive Learning

The theory of *cognitive learning,* or *self-socialization,* holds that children progressively imitate gender-role behavior as their sexual and gender identities grow along with their other mental capacities (Kohlberg, 1966). That is, social training and reinforcement can only affect whatever concepts already exist in a child's mind at a given age.

According to this theory, a child's gender identity is not yet firm at three or four. Children identify with other children of the same sex, but still classify all adults as grownups, not by sex. They have simplified and distorted pictures of masculinity and femininity, and may still think that changing clothes or hair style may change one's identity. As ability to deal with abstract ideas increases, the child begins to think of sex differences across age lines. By about age six, the child's *gender constancy* has increased; he or she identifies with adults of the same sex and understands better what society considers masculine and feminine.

Kohlberg says that "sexual development starts directly with neither biology nor culture, but with cognition. . . . This patterning of sex-role attitudes is essentially 'cognitive' in that it is rooted in the child's concepts of physical things—the bodies of himself and others—concepts which he relates in turn to a social order that makes functional use of sex categories in quite culturally universal ways." This means that a boy first conceives of himself as a boy, then thinks "I am a boy, therefore I want to do boys' things," and then feels that doing so is rewarding. This is unlike learning and socialization theories, which say the child's mental

Figure 7-5 / *Social scripting theory underscores the cross-purposes at which the sexes work in adolescence. Males, seeking sex, learn that they must adapt to females' desire for intimacy and romance. Females learn that to keep males in relationships, they must accept increasing degrees of eroticism.*

pattern is, "I am rewarded for doing boy things, and I want to do what is rewarding."

It is logical and consistent with research findings to say that a child's choice of sex models and life-styles depends on his or her ability to understand the models, their qualities, and social ideas of what is masculine and feminine. We do know, for example, that kindergarten children hold strongly to their masculine or feminine values regardless of punishment or reward. And the values associated with these roles actually determine what is considered a reward (Epstein and Leverant, 1963). Such findings back up the cognitive theory that identity is a cause rather than a product of social learning and modeling (Kohlberg, 1966).

This theory does not, however, account for many sex differences that appear in the first few years of life. Much sex-typed behavior develops before gender constancy is strong, and identifying with peers does not seem an adequate explanation. In an attempt to explain this contradiction, Kagan (1977) suggests that an infant develops mental pictures *(cognitive schemata)* of experiences that later allow it to recognize past events. Kagan and others (Diamond, 1977b; 1979a) believe that this capability develops differently in males and females—at different rates, with different responsiveness

to various stimuli, and obviously with different results.

Social Scripting

Some sociologists explain sexual development with the concepts of *social roles* and the behavioral *scripts* for those roles. Children, they say, begin early in life to learn male and female behavior patterns from parents, peers, television, books, and myriad other sources (Gagnon and Simon, 1973). Scripting theory uses the ideas of learning theory and differential reinforcement; it sometimes acknowledges a biosocial force but minimizes it.

Two developers of scripting theory, William Simon and John Gagnon (1969), say that much sexual behavior is not experienced as erotic until a child learns to see it that way. They point out that prepubertal sexual behavior proceeds to coitus or to a long sexual relationship in only a small minority of children. Perhaps, they say, the child does not yet have enough of a sexual script to see its experience as sexual in the adult sense. Adults often do not clarify the issue: children may be taught shame and guilt in confusing ways, without fully grasping the sexual aspects of "Keep your dress down" and "Lock the bathroom door." Children will

118

comply, yet only with additional experiences and learning will they come to realize the sexual connotations.

During puberty, according to this theory, children realize that they have a sexual capacity, and they now watch more closely how adults use their sexual capacities and deal with physical needs. By doing so, youngsters develop their own scripts for later use. Meanwhile, puberty has set boys and girls on different courses. According to Simon and Gagnon (1969), boys are sexually driven and preoccupied, but pubertal girls seldom report feeling sexually deprived. Girls are trained to respond to romantic rather than erotic words and actions, and develop a greater capacity than boys for intense emotional relationships. Furthermore, girls are taught that there are personal and social dangers in becoming too committed to active sexuality during adolescence.

During adolescence, dating leads boys and girls to learn each other's wants and differences. The process is not smooth, because their scripts have them at cross-purposes. Boys primarily want erotic satisfaction, and learn that to obtain it, they must develop relationships, which they may come to value. Girls primarily want love, and through relationships learn to accept and perhaps to value eroticism. Thus through adolescence both sexes expand their scripts. "Ironically," say Gagnon and Simon (1973), "it is not uncommon to find that the boy becomes emotionally involved with his partner and, therefore, lets up on trying to seduce her, at the same time that the girl comes to feel that the boy's affection is genuine and, therefore, that sexual intimacy is permissible."

Scripting theory has many attractive aspects, especially in describing adolescence. However, it often fails to take into account the biosocial factors that create the same developmental patterns in different cultures. And while scripting theory emphasizes that males and females are socialized differently, it does not fully consider that in some ways they are socialized similarly, nor does it explain why they apparently learn different things with different ease. Finally, while scripting may seem a convincing interpretation of many people's experience, it is unsupported by strong clinical or experimental evidence. It may be calling the results of development its causes.

Most important, the sociological perspective of human sexuality is useful but not comprehensive. People do act out roles and follow social scripts, but some behavior seems quite individual. The description of behavior as roles, scripts, and rehearsal is a dramatic metaphor; some of life does seem a social theater, but some does not. And the existence of universal or near-universal behavior patterns suggests a biosocial basis for some aspects of development.

Overview

Humans are born with sex differences and the basis of a sexual identity. These interact with social influences through mental development, learning, and physical maturation. To say that gender identity is wholly or even largely learned implies that parents or society can produce any behaviors desired in either sex (Skolnick, 1978). Children are flexible, but learning does act on a person already biased toward male or female behaviors and responses. All people do not learn the same things with equal ease or skill.

Furthermore, some things are best learned during *critical learning periods* that are biologically determined. Human children, for instance, have an optimal time for learning language; they will never again do so as quickly and easily. There is apparently a critical learning period for establishing sexual identity, from age one and a half to age three. Learning gender identity and gender role may continue into puberty. In fact, the word learning is not fully accurate in this context; it is not the only alternative to innate. People cannot speak or walk at birth, but they are biologically prepared to "learn" walking and talking at certain ages—the best word is *develop.*

One cannot raise children contrary to their biological sex with impunity, but that does not argue against allowing as many choices as possible in gender development. We believe that people should have flexibility in decisions that do not endanger their basic well-being (Diamond, 1978, 1979a).

Each theory of sexual development has strong points in dealing with certain aspects or periods of development. Learning theory and differential socialization theory help account for some gender-role behaviors and some mechanisms by which they develop. Role modeling and sex typing theories explore identification and imitation, which seem crucial to sexual development. Cognitive learning theory stresses that an influence can act only on given mental capacities at any time in life. Scripting theory brings in clear focus many social aspects of development, especially those at work during puberty and adolescence. All these theories have evidence to draw on, and all are to some degree intuitively attractive, perhaps because

today we are accustomed to seeking answers in social influences and learning processes, and because each describes commonly perceived realities.

We ourselves evaluate the evidence on human sexuality development somewhat differently. Diamond is most impressed by the theory of biosocial interaction. It is consistent with evolutionary evidence and has the support of animal experimentation and medical data. It shows continuity in development from conception through the early years, and to some degree through later periods. It provides a conceptual link between biological potential and social reality, and it accounts for cross-cultural consistencies in the development of basic physical and behavioral sex differences. It also provides a framework on which learning and socialization theories can build, for example, by suggesting that males and females inherently find different behaviors rewarding and different models attractive. It also allows for individual variation without calling for elaborate and untestable theory.

Karlen sees great value in this theory, especially in studying the early years, but gives equal weight to cultural adaptation (neo-Freudian) theory and considers the two compatible. Psychodynamic studies are the only long-term observations of individuals that synthesize conscious and unconscious feelings and motives, link early experience and complex adult experience, and allow for both biological and social influences. While not subject to experimental proof, this theory has provided insight into the subtle complexities of feelings, intimate relationships, life-style, and social adaptation. It is also compatible with cross-cultural evidence and to some extent with learning and cognitive theories.

120

However, no one or even two theories are wholly adequate to explain human sexual development, and we see some merit in the others. Sexual development is so entwined with the rest of human development that only an integrated approach can do it justice. Despite some gaps and inconsistencies, a rough overview is possible. Biosocial interaction says that males and females are born with a tendency to interact with the world in certain ways. Learning, modeling, identification, and cognitive development all play important roles in development. There are also many social and family forces—maternal care, family relationships, religious and economic influences—and quite individual emotional events that the adaptational approach seeks to understand.

If one delves into scientific and popular writings on sexual development, one is struck by the fierce defense of boundaries between academic disciplines and the great emotional stake people have in particular theories. Some writers on development seem to be talking about people as regulated machines, without loves, hates, fears, fantasies, and ambivalence. Others seem to discuss emotions or roles that exist outside bodies that feel desire, pleasure,

and pain. Still others ignore historical, ethnic, and other cultural influences. Those who seek to fully explain development by biology, learning, or social influence alone are ignoring a great deal of evidence. And they present an impoverished view of the complexities of human feeling, behavior, and potential.

If one studies a variety of societies, one finds many patterns of gender roles and sexual behavior. Some societies offer many choices; some limit individual choice sharply. The same can be said of families; the family is, for the child, a sort of micro-culture. There is no proof that any social pattern ultimately creates happier human beings. We believe that in our society, rigid social and parental forces that minimize free choice may hinder the development of a flexible and rewarding self. We would like to see an environment for sexual development that offers the richest possible banquet of experiences from which to choose, without fear of losing love, self-love, and acceptance (Diamond, 1978). The society and family must also, of course, offer guidelines and limits. Which ones, and to what extent, remains one of the most debated issues of our times.

Review, Discuss, Decide

1. How many examples of external sexual dimorphism can you see in human males and females?
2. What are the effects of a fetus's hormones on its own nervous system? What evidence do we have of those effects? How much is known of the mechanisms by which sex hormones organize the developing brain?
3. Can you give an example of an interaction trait?
4. How are boys and girls similar at birth and how are they different? Which differences change over the years?

5. What are the differences between sexual identity and gender identity? What are sex role and gender role? What is sexual orientation?

6. When does sexual identity develop? Is it reversible?

7. How do you think your upbringing influenced your masculinity or femininity?

8. How would you like to see children raised with regard to gender roles? Why?

9. In what aspects of life other than sexual development have the ideas of conditioning and reinforcement been used? Do your reactions to gender-role conditioning have any relation to your ideas of other conditioning?

10. What do studies show to be the similarities and differences in how parents raise boys and girls?

11. Do you feel you learned any sexual scripts? Have you any doubts about the theory of scripts? About which behaviors are scripted and which may rise from biosocial forces or individual experience?

12. Which psychoanalytic or neo-Freudian concepts match your experience or that of others you know? Which do not?

13. Does your experience make you agree or disagree with the idea that preadolescent peers are important in sexual development? Are peer relationships different for preadolescent boys and girls. Are they different in the teens?

14. Is any theory of development especially convincing to you? Why? Which are less convincing, and why?

15. Can any of the developmental theories be used destructively? Which ones, and how? If a theory backed by strong evidence could be misused, what should the scientist, teacher, or student do or say about it?

8

Physical Health and Dysfunction

Do men need genital examinations? Why do women?

How can I prevent, detect, or cure myself of venereal disease?

Is breast or uterine cancer related to sexual activity?

How do illness and medication affect sex activity?

At least one person in five will at some time experience disease or dysfunction of the sexualia. The effects can be far-reaching and involve the psyche as much as the body. The social stigma of venereal disease and other sexual problems has kept many people from being candid with partners and from seeing health professionals. Breast cancer, uterine cancer, and conditions demanding genital surgery often place severe strains on self-image and sexual relationships. All of these conditions call for knowledgeable, objective decisions.

This chapter begins with descriptions of the male and female genital examinations. It goes on to cover sexually transmitted (venereal) diseases, and then physical conditions that can affect sexuality.

The Genital Examination

Both males and females should have regular physical examinations that include the sexual and reproductive systems. Unfortunately, the embarrassment of the patient, the physician, or both often makes this a cursory once-over. Genital examinations commonly occur at birth and puberty but are needed more often. They are especially important for women, who are more susceptible to such asymptomatic ("silent") problems as gonorrhea, breast tumors, and uterine cancer. Men's silent ills—asymptomatic syphilis and rectal cancer—are far less common.

In any genital examination, a physician looks for pain, sores, discharges, abnormal growth, and changes in the shape, color, or feel of the sexualia. A person who discovers any of these himself should promptly have them checked by a physician.

The Male Examination

Genital discharges and pains in males, unlike several kinds in females, are never routine. Discharges, itches, and rashes often indicate venereal disease, and pain often signals herniation or constricton. They must always be diagnosed and treated.

Doctors look especially for growths in the scrotum, testes, and spermatic cords. They check for *cryptorchidism,* or failure of one or both testes to descend, and for *hydrocoele,* a fluid-filled cyst in the testes or cords (this is easily drained). An uncircumsised penis is checked for *balanitis,* an infection of the glans caused by poor cleaning under the foreskin, and for *phimosis,* a constriction of the prepuce that hinders its full retraction. Balanitis is treated by antibiotics and cleaning, phimosis by cutting the prepuce or by circumcision.

Herniation is a weakness of the abdominal muscles that allows a portion of intestine to project into the scrotum. This common problem can be corrected surgically. The physician checks for it by placing a finger over the most common place for herniation to occur (where the spermatic cords enter the abdomen) and asking the patient to cough. The cough creates abdominal pressure and reveals the presence of hernia.

A physician also checks for hemorrhoids and unusual growths of the prostate and rectum. Tumors of the reproductive system occur more often in older than in younger men (though far less often than in women). Most common are tumors of the prostate; they are rare in men below fifty, but become common with advancing years. These are best detected by feeling the prostate through the wall of the rectum. The growth pinches off the urethra, so the most common symptom is difficult and frequent urination.

Both cancerous and benign tumors are treated by surgery, the former by radiation and hormones as well. The relatively slow growth and limited spread of prostate cancer make fatalities rare, but difficulty urinating and the possibility of the cancer spreading usually make surgery necessary. Five to forty percent of men become impotent after such operations, because the autonomic nerves of the penis have been severed. The risk depends on the extent and cellular nature of the cancer, the surgeon's skill, and the technique used (Madorsky, Drylie, and Finlayson, 1976).

Retrograde ejaculation sometimes follows prostate surgery. The sperm is ejaculated into the bladder (where urine is stored) because the sphincterlike action of the urogenital diaphragm closes off the penile urethra. The semen gives urine a milky color. Retrograde ejaculation is also common in diabetes (Oliven, 1974). It is rare in normal males, in whom it may result from learning to masturbate so that no semen shows or from pressing hard on the base of the penis as a contraceptive method *(coitus obstructus).*

The Female Examination

Most of the female reproductive system is internal, therefore more difficult to examine than the male system, and more subject to problems. Perhaps the most common problems are vaginal discharges and vaginal infection *(vaginitis).* At some time, most women experience a whitish vaginal discharge, *leukorrhea* (*leuko* = white; *rhea* = flow), the vagina's response to infection or an acid-alkaline imbalance. It often results from poor hygiene or irritating devices and chemicals (some vaginal sprays or harsh douches). Treatment must deal with the infection or irritant.

Breast Examination

Women should routinely examine their breasts at least once a month. The best time is a week after menses. Since many women's partners fondle their breasts, men should also understand breast examination. At first it may seem awkward, but practice makes it easy.

1. Stand or sit upright in front of a mirror. Compare the breasts, looking for any change in size, shape, or color. Note any dimpling or change in skin texture on the breast or nipple. Gently press each nipple and check for discharge.
2. Standing or sitting in front of a mirror, raise the arms over the head and repeat the inspection.
3. The rest of the examination is aimed at detecting any lump or thickening. Lie down on a bed, put a pillow or bath towel under the left shoulder, and your left hand under your head. Hold the fingers of the right hand together and flat; press gently against the left breast with small circular motions to feel its inner, upper portion, starting at the breastbone and going outward to the nipple. Also feel the area around the nipple.
4. With the same gentle pressure, feel the low, inner part of the breast. Here you may feel a ridge of firm tissue; this is normal.
5. Bring the left arm down to the right side, and with the fingers still held flat, feel the left armpit.
6. Feel the upper, outer portion of the left breast from the nipple to where the arm is resting. Check this area twice; it is where tumors most often occur.
7. Feel the lower, outer portion of the breast, from the outer part of the nipple.
8. Repeat the entire procedure on the right breast, using the left hand.

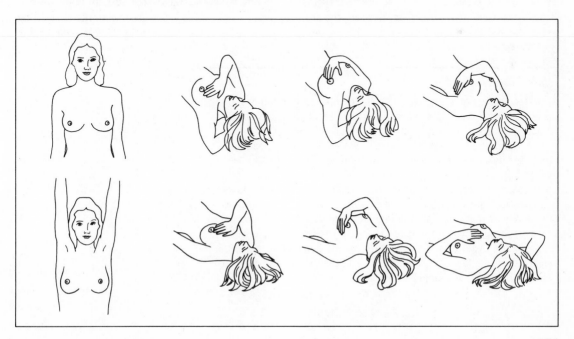

Another common infection that can be caused by irritation or poor hygiene is *cystitis,* or infection of the bladder. This can become chronic and painful. The urethra dilates during sexual excitement, and sometimes stays that way for a long time. A woman's urethra is short (less than 5 centimeters), and when dilated allows infectious organisms to pass to the bladder more easily than a male's. Therefore when women suddenly become coitally active—for the first time or after a period of inactivity—they may suffer *"honeymoon cystitis."* This infection can be painful and usually causes a frequent feeling of having to urinate. The treatment is frequent voiding, drinking large amounts of water, and prescribed antibiotics.

Unusual pains are more common in women than men, and less easy to treat. Those caused by structural changes, such as uterine tilting (tipped uterus), can often be treated by surgery, but the results are uncertain. If not very severe, this problem is sometimes best managed by changing coital positions or by pain-control drugs such as aspirin.

The most serious problems are cancer of the uterus and breast. Cancer may attack any part of the uterus, but it occurs more often at the cervix, less often in the endometrial tissue. In later stages, it is visible with the aid of a light and a medical instrument called a speculum. A *Papanicolaou smear* ("Pap test") is the usual method for detecting cervical cancer before a tumor is visible. It is a routine part of a female genital examination. A physician or medical technician scrapes the cervix with a small, smooth spatula and smears the material collected on a glass slide. This is quick, simple, and painless. The smear is then examined under a microscope for precancerous or cancerous cells. Women should have this test at least once a year; some authorities recommend that it be done every six months after age thirty-five.

After Mastectomy

A mastectomy is not a physically debilitating operation, but one you are unlikely to forget. Learning to live in a world that idolizes the female breast is not easy. At the beginning one lives with feelings of sexual inadequacy, and the endless questions: Why me? How did this happen? What did I do wrong? Am I less of a woman? Am I cured? Will I live long enough to worry less?

As the wound heals, so does the rage, diminishing the need to ask unanswerable questions that only interfere with living. Time gives each of us the hope that scientists will find more answers and it allows me to share my thoughts to help reduce the fear of cancer so people won't run from their symptoms but seek care. And perhaps it may make the way a little easier for other victims for me to say that if you must learn to live with cancer, you can.

—Nina Diamond,
Newsweek, November 29, 1976

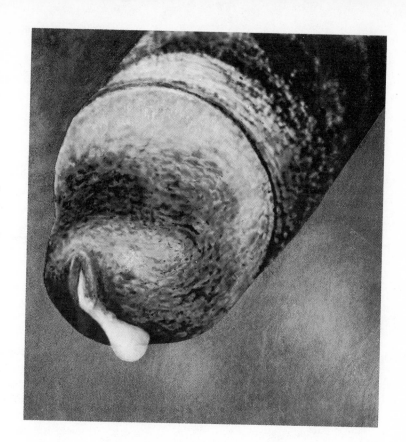

Figure 8-1 / *In men, gonorrhea usually causes pain and a pus filled discharge from the penis. Many women show no such symptoms and become "silent" carriers of the disease.*

Many people think this test also detects venereal disease, but it does not.

About one woman in fifty suffers cervical cancer. There is now evidence that it is affected by coitus, perhaps by transmission of a virus. Women who don't have coitus don't develop cervical cancer (see page 134). Treatment, by surgery, radiation, or both, depends on how early the cancer is detected and where it is located. Cancer of the endometrium, the lining of the uterus, is less common and is not thought to be sexually transmitted. Treatment is like that for cervical cancer. Uterine cancer and persistent uterine bleeding are the most common reasons for *hysterectomy* (removal of the uterus). After abortion and appendectomy, hysterectomy is the most common surgical procedure in this country—although cancer is not the only reason for doing it, and many people believe it is often done unnecessarily.

Breast cancer is the most common cancer in women; it strikes about one in every thirteen and is one of the leading causes of death among women (Levine et al., 1974). Its cause is unknown. The earlier it is detected, the more likely is successful treatment. New techniques, such as special X-rays and sensitive heat-detecting equipment, are being used to detect breast tumors in mass screening programs and in private physicians' offices. But one of the most effective means is still self-examination. If tumors are treated early and properly, the chance for success is high; about 85 percent of women treated early will be alive five years later. Too many women die needlessly of this common disease.

Most lumps are harmless, but both benign and malignant tumors are painless, so all must be checked immediately by a physician. If tumors are found and *mastectomy* (surgical removal of a breast) is recommended, it is a good idea to swiftly seek second and third opinions before a decision is made (Culliton, 1977) and to take advantage of new diagnostic techniques. The operation itself is not debilitating, but psychological and social readjustment may be difficult (Asken, 1975); a pilot study (D. Frank et al., 1978) has shown a decrease in sexual activity. There is damage to a woman's feelings of body integrity, body image, and femininity. With time and, in some cases, counseling, such feelings can diminish, as can terror of cancer (Wabrek, Wabrek, and Burchell, 1979). The greatest danger is that fear of surgery or of not adjusting after mastectomy makes some women delay seeking medical help or carrying through treatment.

Sexually Transmitted Disease (STD)

Venereal disease (named after Venus, Roman goddess of love) is an infection transmitted by sexual contact. Many people now prefer the term *sexually transmitted disease* (STD). One reason is that the term VD is stigmatized by its association with nonmarital coitus, which makes some people reluctant to seek help. We will use both terms, usually limiting the older term to what are now sometimes called the "classic" venereal diseases (see below).

The best known VDs are syphilis and gonorrhea, but some others are just as common. And these diseases do not just affect the genitals; they may involve the rectum, anus, mouth, throat, and eyes. Still other parts of the body may be involved, but only by the disease spreading from a primary site. Some nongenital diseases are also spread by sexual activity.

This chapter presents clues for recognizing certain diseases transmitted sexually and non-sexually. However, all self-diagnoses should be confirmed by a physician, and treatment based on the specific needs of each case. Most medicines for these diseases require prescriptions, and the best treatment methods change with advances in medical knowledge. Therefore self-diagnosis and self-treatment are inadequate and sometimes dangerous.

Venereal Disease (VD)

The five classic venereal diseases are *gonorrhea, syphilis, chancroid, granuloma inguinale,* and *lymphogranuloma venereum.* They are spread not only by coitus but by oral-genital and anal-genital contact. Dirty toilet seats and towels and other nonsexual means of transmission are very rare; the microbes that cause these diseases soon die outside the body.

Gonorrhea (gon = genitals; *rhea* = flow) ("clap," "gleet," "strain," "morning drip," "morning drop") is one of the country's most serious common diseases. It affects more than 500,000 teenagers each year; one in ten people from age fifteen to twenty-five now contract gonorrhea. Historical records show that this was not much different in the 1930s and 1940s (McFalls, 1973; Darrow, 1976).

The bacterium that causes gonorrhea *(Neisseria gonococcus)* lives in the mucous membranes of the mouth, anus, urethra, and vagina. Not every sexual contact with an infected partner transmits the disease. A man has a 20 to 50 percent chance of catching gonorrhea from a single exposure, a woman about one chance in two. Despite some reports to the contrary, there is little evidence that using oral contraceptives raises the odds for women (Darrow, 1975).

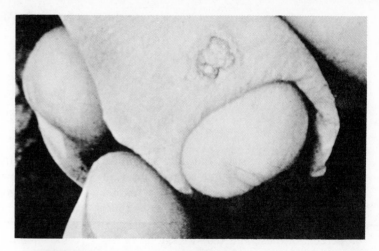

Figure 8-2 / *A chancre is the first sign of syphilis. It appears at the site of infection and is visible on the penis, vulva, or mouth; it sometimes occurs and remains undetected in the vagina or the rectum.*

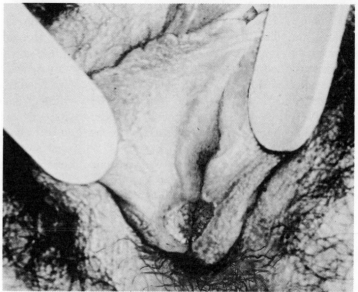

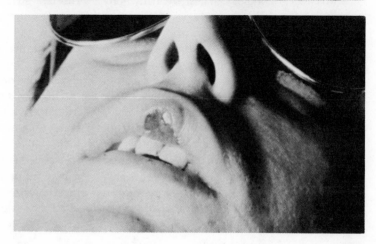

Men commonly start showing symptoms within two to ten days after contact, often in three to five days. There is a burning sensation during urination and a white discharge (pus) from the penis. These signs appear in a lucky 85 percent of those infected—we say lucky because the pain makes them seek medical help. The unlucky 15 percent suffer damage and may spread the disease without knowing it. In women the signs are about the same, but the percentages are reversed: 80 to 85 percent of those infected don't know it. The discharge may be within the vagina and go unnoticed; the vagina is relatively insensitive to pain, so there is little discomfort unless the urethra becomes infected.

You cannot look at yourself or your partner and be sure whether either of you has gonorrhea. However, it is easily diagnosed. Smears are painlessly taken from the penile meatus or uterine cervix, the anus, and the throat, and applied to bacterial culture plates. If the germs are present, they will grow within several days.

Untreated gonorrhea can destroy many body tissues, leaving scars within the vas deferens or ovarian tubes, causing sterility. Men with long-untreated gonorrhea develop scar tissue in the urethra, which must be penetrated mechanically to allow urine to pass; this is very painful and must be repeated periodically throughout life. Women with long-untreated gonorrhea may develop *pelvic inflammatory disease* (PID), which is both painful and dangerous. It may cause partial obstruction of the ovarian tubes, leading to life-threatening ectopic pregnancy, in which the fertilized egg is implanted not in the uterus but in the tubes. PID can also cause total obstruction and sterility.

Oral-genital and anal-genital intercourse can transmit gonorrhea to the mouth or anus. Oral gonorrhea sometimes leads to hoarse, red throat, anal gonorrhea to an anal discharge. Anal infections are usually painless, so they become unknown reservoirs for further spread of the disease.

Arthritis may result from gonococci traveling through the bloodstream to the joints. Long-standing gonorrhea can also cause heart disease and thus death. It also sometimes leads to blindness; during birth, a baby passing through an infected vagina can get the germs in its eyes and become blind within days. This used to be quite common; now every state requires that newborns' eyes be preventively treated with penicillin or silver nitrate. The danger of blindness is not limited to birth. At any age, people can transfer gonococci to the eyes with their fingers and cause blindness.

A single massive injection of penicillin usually cures gonorrhea, as does treatment with ampicillin or a recently developed type of penicillin in pill form. However, several highly resistant strains of gonococci have developed, so retesting after treatment is advisable. Some of these strains are susceptible to other antibiotics, but new strains have appeared that resist all drugs, and these are rapidly spreading throughout the world (Culliton, 1976).

Unlike many other infections, STDs do not leave recovered victims immune. Vaccines are being sought, with some promising results, but they will raise ethical and social problems. If scientists do develop an STD vaccine, how can it be used or even tested without stigmatizing the subjects. Some would say that only "immoral" people need it. What might the public reaction be to a recommendation that all high-

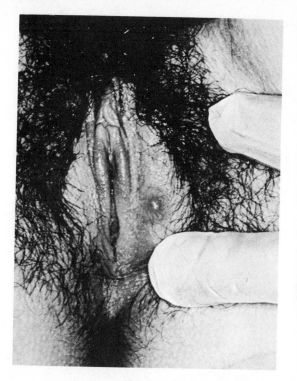
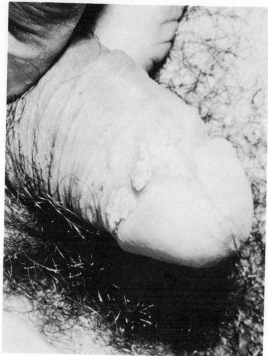

Figure 8-3 / *Herpes genitalis, an increasingly widespread viral infection, is painful and long-lasting in both women and men.*

school students be vaccinated against STDs? Or that tax funds be used for this purpose?

Syphilis ("syph," "pox," "bad blood," "lues," "haircut") has been one of the most feared and devastating diseases of recent centuries. A century ago, syphilitic paralysis *(paresis)* and insanity was responsible for more than half the chronic cases in United States mental hospitals. Public concern diminished after the discovery and use of penicillin in the Thirties and Forties, but syphilis remains a very serious problem. More than 100,000 cases were reported in North America in 1975. Most people getting married in the United States are required to take a blood test for syphilis. More than one person in ninety who takes the test has the disease (Curtis, 1972).

Syphilis is caused by a corkscrew-shaped organism *(spirochete)* called *Treponema pallidum* (*Treponema* = turning thread, *pallidum*

= pale). This protozoan (one-celled animal) usually enters the body through a mucous membrane or a break in the skin; it then enters the bloodstream and travels throughout the body. Every organ is susceptible to its effects. It causes skin sores and rashes and, more important, can affect the heart and brain, causing paralysis, insanity, and death. Infants born to syphilitic mothers are likely to be infected and to have visual and hearing difficulties, notched teeth, and bent "saber" shins.

Detection is difficult. Syphilis has been called "the great imitator" because it affects many organs and may mimic a host of diseases. The primary stage occurs in the two to four weeks after infection occurs. A sore called a *chancre* develops where the spirochete entered the body. This round, hard, rubbery ulcer with raised edges may appear on the penis, vulva, or mouth; if in the vagina or anus, it usually goes unnoticed. Most chancres are painless and disappear three weeks after their appearance, with or without treatment.

If the infection is not treated, it progresses

131

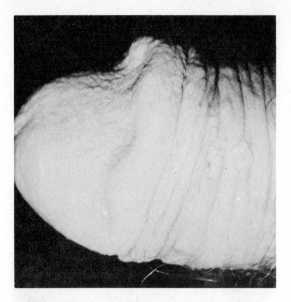 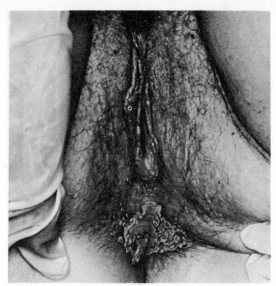

Figure 8-4 / *"Venereal warts" result from a virus that can be sexually transmitted. Like all growths, they should be examined by a physician; they may require surgical removal.*

after several weeks or months to the secondary stage. This causes any, all, or none of the following symptoms: low fever, sore throat, reappearance of chancres, skin rash, hair loss (hence the slang term "haircut"), and muscle and joint pains. These symptoms may come and go for a year or two. The disease then enters a latent phase followed by a tertiary stage. An infected person can no longer infect others, but the germs continue to penetrate and destroy blood vessels, the brain, the spinal cord, bone, and muscle.

The only sure way to diagnose syphilis is a blood test. A blood sample is taken from a vein in the arm and examined under a microscope for the presence of spirochetes. To control the spread of syphilis, most states require a premarital and a pregnancy blood test, although some people consider this an invasion of privacy. Many hospitals now require that this test be made on admission.

The treatment at any stage of the disease is antibiotics (usually penicillin, but sometimes tetracycline or erythromycin). During treatment and for at least a month afterward, the

patient must avoid sexual contact. Tests for the disease must be made every three months for at least a year, since treatment makes the spirochete difficult to detect.

Because *chancroid ("soft chancre"), lymphogranuloma venereum (LCV, "tropical bubo"),* and *granuloma inguinale ("Donovan's disease")* are seen in the United States much less often than gonorrhea and syphilis, they are called the *minor venereal diseases.* These microbial and viral infections cause skin sores or swellings that may or may not be painful. Detecting these and other STDs depends on being suspicious of any genital lesion or pain. Diagnosis is done by microscopically examining material from the lesion. Treatment varies, but sulfa drugs and tetracycline are most often effective.

Other STDs of the Genitals

Nonspecific urethritis, or *nongonococcal urethritis* (NGU), resembles gonorrhea and is perhaps more common. Its cause is unknown, and it can occur without sexual contact. Symptoms may be mild, severe, or absent in both sexes; regardless, one can transmit the disease. It responds best to tetracycline.

Herpes genitalis has become one of the most common and serious STDs. It is caused by herpes simplex, a virus similar to that which causes cold sores on the lips. After two to twenty days, the genital site of infection may itch or burn. Then blisters develop and ulcerate. They may heal without treatment, but they reappear unpredictably and are highly contagious. The disease may never be fully cured, but the discomfort can be reduced by applying an anesthetic cream (xylocaine) or ointment (zinc oxide). When the disease is dormant, it is not contagious.

Herpes genitalis is worse for women than men; it may develop in the uterus without their knowledge. However, herpes sores on the labia are painful, especially during urination. The herpes virus is suspected of being a causative factor in cervical cancer. It can also infect infants during birth and may be fatal to them, so caesarean delivery is often receommended to an infected mother.

Condyloma acuminatum ("venereal warts") is a viral infection that causes warts, especially in

---

The Origins of VD

The histories and origins of gonorrhea and syphilis are still debated. For centuries, it was argued whether they were manifestations of one illness. The matter was resolved in 1793 when the Scottish physician Benjamin Bell inoculated some of his students with material from VD patients and learned from their reactions that he was studying two distinct diseases. Unfortunately, another fifty years passed before Philippe Ricord inoculated over 2,500 subjects and thereby convinced the medical and public community (U.S. Department of Health, Education, and Welfare, 1968).

Gonorrhea was described in the Bible, and the Greek physician Galen named it in the second century. A famous example of popular and medical knowledge of the disease in the eighteenth century is in the journal of James Boswell (1950), who told with drama and bitter humor how he caught it from an actress with whom he was infatuated.

The history of syphilis is less clear. At one time, the most popular theory was that Columbus's crew brought it to Europe from the New World. The first cases in Europe were recorded around 1494 to 1495, when soldiers from France and other countries were besieging Naples. They allegedly consorted there with prostitutes who had been with

Columbus's sailors; when the soldiers returned home, they started the disease's spread throughout Europe. It got its name from a poem of 1530, *Syphilis,* by Fracastorius of Verona, in which a fictitious Caribbean shepherd named Syphilis was punished by the sun god for impiety by being made this new plague's first victim.

In recent decades, many scholars have doubted the New World origin of syphilis. Some guess that it existed in Europe and the Near East long before Columbus's time, but had been lumped together with other diseases that cause skin lesions under such names as "leprosy" and "ulcer." They guess that syphilis, like such infections as measles and influenza, has periods of greater and lesser virulence, and that around 1500 it became more severe and was mistaken for a new disease (Rosebury, 1973).

Another theory has been gaining acceptance—that syphilis eveolved from a nonvenereal spirochete (the one causing the tropical diseases pinta and yaws) as humans evolved from warm-weather villagers to temperate-climate town dwellers, and in the course of this became more virulent (Bullough and Bullough, 1977; Rosebury, 1973).

moist genital areas. These are at best uncomfortable, and medical treatment is required. The warts are removed, and in uncircumcised men often the prepuce as well, so that there is no unnecessary repository for the virus.

Cervical cancer, as noted earlier, is influenced by coitus, but there is reluctance to

Figure 8-5 / *The crab louse (top) and the mite (bottom) are small parasites that can be transmitted sexually or nonsexually.*

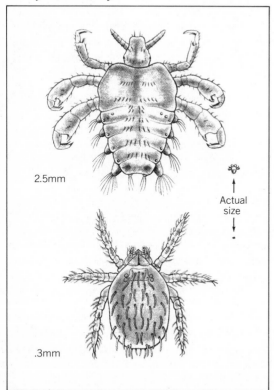

2.5mm

Actual
size

.3mm

call it an STD because of the stigma attached to such diseases. Some physicians and educators fear that treatment may be put off, as often happens with VD, if the disease is associated with sex. Also, cervical cancer occurs in middle- and upper-class people; some mistakenly think that STDs occur only among the poor and uneducated.

Women who start coitus early in life and have many partners are more likely to develop cervical cancer than those who start later and have few partners (Rotkin, 1973). A study of 900 women with genital herpes revealed a rate of cervical cancer eight times higher than that of an uninfected control group (Nahamias et al., 1969). Women who don't have coitus never develop cervical cancer; a study of some 13,000 nuns failed to reveal a single case (Novak et al., 1970).

An important causative factor may well be a herpes virus or modified DNA agent transmitted by coitus, perhaps interacting with some other factor. It was once thought that women whose sexual partners were circumcised at birth, and whose penises are therefore easier to clean and less likely to harbor viruses, run a low risk of cervical cancer, but this is no longer certain (Rotkin, 1973).

Genital Diseases Transmitted Sexually or Nonsexually

Candidiasis (monilia, yeast)

Candidiasis (monilia, vaginal thrush, "yeast") is caused by yeastlike fungus cells called *candidia* or *monilia* that are found everywhere in the environment and in the mouth, vagina, or intestines of at least 50 percent of healthy people. If these cells multiply in the vagina or under the foreskin, they produce severe itching and a thick, white, "cottage cheese" discharge. Women are especially sensitive to monilia during periods of high progesterone levels—pregnancy, the luteal phase of the menstrual cycle, and when using certain oral contraceptives. Treatment is with fungicidal salves or suppositories.

Trichomoniasis

This common vaginal infection (also called "trich") is caused by a protozoan called *Trichomonas vaginalis*. The symptoms are itching, a yellow-green discharge (which may stain undergarments), and strong odor. Diagnosis is by microscopic examination of the discharge to identify the parasite. Men rarely show signs of trichomoniasis, but they can harbor it under the foreskin and transmit it. It is treated with Flagyl, taken orally. During pregnancy, vaginal suppositories are preferred, to protect the fetus. The patient must avoid alcohol, since the drug and alcohol can interact to cause nausea, cramps, and dizziness.

Pediculosis pubis (crab lice)

This common problem, popularly called "crabs" or "crab lice," is infestation of pubic and other body hair with tiny blood-sucking parasites related to common body lice. The lice are transmitted by contact with an infected person or with contaminated bedding or clothes; this is one STD that can be transmitted by a dirty towel or toilet seat. Washing with ordinary soap will not get rid of crab lice. One must use a special benzene agent, usually in ointment form.

Scabies (ticks, mites)

Scabies (ticks, mites) is caused by mites, animals smaller than the periods printed on this page. Female mites burrow into the skin and deposit feces and eggs, which cause itching, welts, and extreme sensitivity to touch. Scabies is treated with benzene agents.

Jock Itch, Panty Itch

This is caused by a fungus *(Tinea cruris)* related to those which produce ringworm and athlete's foot. The skin in the genital area may scale, redden, crack, and itch severely. The cracks can become infected. Fungicidal powders and salves are available to treat it.

Infectious Mononucleosis

This viral disease ("mono," "kissing disease," "glandular fever") causes fever, headaches, chills, sore throat, swollen lymph glands, weakness, and general discomfort. It is transmitted by deep kissing but also in many other ways. After two to four weeks of rest, vitamins, and a bland but balanced diet, there is usually improvement. However, severe complications can develop, and fatalities occasionally occur.

Hepatitis B

Only recently has this viral disease been recognized as sexually transmitted. Now it is considered one of the most prevalent STDs, especially among homosexual men who practice anal intercourse (Szmuness et al., 1975). Hepatitis B causes fever, chills, and long-lasting general discomfort; symptoms may persist for months, and in rare cases the disease is fatal, but the illness is usually self-limiting. A vaccine for hepatitis B may well be developed (Wiesner, 1978). If it is, this will be the first vaccine for an STD.

Preventing, Detecting, and Treating STDs

Prevention and Detection

Most sexually active people know about venereal diseases, but don't always take steps to avoid them (Darrow, 1977; Hart, 1976). This decision may be prompted by embarrassment, unwillingness to "ruin the mood," or willingness to take the gamble. It is indeed a gamble.

These guidelines can help in both the prevention and detection of STDs.

1. *Be suspicious.* Someone with many partners is obviously exposed more to infection. Many people are unknowing carriers of VD. And "nice" people from "good" homes can give and get it. Picking partners carefully is the most effective and most widely used way to avoid VD (Darrow, 1976).
2. *Take preventive measures.* Washing the genitals with soap and water before sexual contact helps prevent several VDs (Walker, 1926). Washing, douching, and urinating soon afterward also help. Special products available at pharmacies (e.g., Progonasyl) and some contraceptive foams are also ef-

fective. Using a condom prevents penile transmission of diseases; of course many STDs can also be caught by contact with the mouth, anus, or an infected skin area.
3. *When in doubt, check it out.* Be suspicious of any bump, sore, pain, discharge, or discoloration of the genitals, anus, or mouth, in yourself or your partner. Remember that these may develop from three days to three months after contact. At any inkling of a problem, go to a private physician or public clinic, and be specific about your symptoms and concerns. Have your partner do the same.
4. *Check dyspareunia (painful coitus).* Rule out the possibility of disease or an anatomical problem before assuming that the cause is psychological.
5. *Do not transmit VD.* It is obviously unethical to have sexual relations when you can transmit VD. And by infecting a partner, you set yourself up to be reinfected.
6. *Fear not.* Tests for VD are quick, simple, and relatively painless. The same is true of treatment.

Incidence and Transmission of VD

All STDs except cervical cancer can be spread by homosexual as well as heterosexual contact. In fact, the commonest source of syphilis today is thought to be homosexual relations, in which protective measures are very rarely taken.

There seems to be a much higher rate of STD in lower socioeconomic levels (Brooks, Darrow, and Day, 1978). This may be caused by poor hygiene, reluctance to seek treatment, inability to pay a private doctor and use a clinic, or greater tolerance of or resignation to discomfort. However, the class differences in STD rates may also partly reflect doctors' tendency to report VD more in poverty cases than in middle- and upper-class patients. It has been guessed that almost 90 percent of private patients with VD are "protected" by their physicians and not reported to public-health centers (Sagarin, 1974)—actually, not usually a kindness to the patients, those close to them, or society. Public health agencies try to check out all of an infected person's sexual contacts, to ensure treatment and stop the spread of the disease. Courts have begun to recognize the right to sue for damages if a partner knowingly transmits VD (*Time*, 31 May 1976).

VD is most often contracted in sexual relations with someone who is not an exclusive partner. The more people one has relations with, the greater the possibility of contact with an infected partner. Of course, one's spouse or regular partner may then become infected.

Treatment

All cases of STD demand treatment. This helps not only the patient but partners, preventing a ping pong effect of mutual reinfection. If you do have an STD, don't treat yourself or use patent medicines or home remedies. Few nonprofessionals can accurately diagnose STDs, and non-prescription drugs rarely cure them. Take prescribed drugs and other measures as directed by the physician, even after symptoms disappear, since infection may still exist. Abstinence is a must until cure is complete; otherwise the disease will be spread to others. Masturbation is also often discouraged, to prevent trauma to healing tissues. Honesty requires telling all recent partners to seek examinations. This may be very difficult, but failing to do so is harmful to others and risky to yourself. An infected partner can reinfect you.

In almost every state, confidential examination and treatment for any STD is available to people of all ages, from both private physicians and public health facilities. In some places, local laws require that a minor's parents be notified, but most clinics will consider the minor's best interests if he or she thinks that would create severe difficulties. Treatment at clinics is often free or very cheap, since many are federally subsidized. This has become a minor political issue; some people don't want to "subsidize sin" with public funds. But the government has recently tended to conclude that the toll of STDs in illness and misery outweighs such considerations. Some people welcome STDs as a check on population growth. Moral objections aside, VD does not accomplish this. Sterility usually occurs after people have already had their families (McFall, 1973).

Handicaps, Illness, and Sexuality

Almost every illness has a sexual aspect. Fatigue, pain, and decreased vigor lessen one's capacity for full sexual expression. As many as 10 percent of all people and 50 percent of those over fifty may be in some way handicapped, yet their own and their partners' sexual concerns have been dealt with seriously only in the past decade. Many people, in giving up sexual expression, have also given up vital opportunities for warmth, touching, companionship, and love. They need no longer pretend that illness or disability destroys sexual desire or expression (Diamond, 1974a). A disabled or ill person and his partner may feel, or be made to feel, that it is selfish and trivial to add sex to serious health concerns. But of course the matter is not added, it is already there. A person with any illness or handicap should explore all of its sexual implications. Some physicians fail to do so; then it is up to the patient to ask.

Some of the sexual concerns of people with disfigurements, heart disease, diabetes, blindness, arthritis, and partial paralysis are like those of the healthy and able-bodied, but they arise more often and more acutely—self-consciousness, poor self-image, guilt, unrealistic expectations about sexual performance, and poor communication with partners. And present or potential sexual partners may have emotional difficulties dealing with the problem. Full medical information and good communication are essential to keep the relationship alive, sexually and otherwise. This may take unusual courage. It can be difficult enough to admit being uncomfortable about one's own or a partner's weight, shape, or scars, let alone a handicap or disease, but it is the first step toward finding a satisfying way to deal with it.

The handicapped person must cease to blame himself for physical limitations beyond his control. He must also be helped to dwell on what is still possible, not on what is no longer possible. And he should be encouraged to explore new ways to fill his own and his partner's sexual needs—in some cases, oral-genital and manual stimulation, new coital positions, or the use of such devices as vibrators.

We cannot discuss every physical problem that affects sexuality, but some are so common that they warrant a few words.

Disfigurements

Scars from accidents, burns, and surgery, amputation, severe obesity, and other problems in appearance can have lasting and severe effects on sexuality—more through self-consciousness, impaired body image, and social difficulties than by directly impairing sexual function. This may be true whether the disfigurement was suffered in childhood or in adult life. Often counseling, with or without the aid of surgical and cosmetic measures, can be a great help. So can sexual acceptance by a loving partner and the support of another person who has come to terms with the same problem.

Diabetes

This disease affects 5 percent of our population, and if present trends continue, the number will double every fifteen to twenty years. Sometimes unexplained impotence and retrograde ejaculation are early signs of diabetes; as the disease progresses in men, impotence becomes more likely (Ellenberg, 1977). In both sexes, orgasmic ability may be impaired, although desire is not. Diabetes also changes the vaginal environment, predisposing one to Candidia and other infections. Fortunately, many diabetics do not have these problems, which seem related more to the duration of the illness than how well it is controlled (Schiavi, 1979). The reasons for losing potency or orgasm are not clear, but the damage to nerves and blood vessels caused by diabetes may play a role (Schiavi, 1979).

Nervous System Problems and Stroke

Most major neurological problems affect sexual expression (Horenstein, 1976). Polio, industrial and auto accidents, military wounds, and sports injuries have left quite a few people, many of them young, with spinal cord damage causing paralysis and loss of sensations in the lower body *(paraplegia)* and in the arms as well *(quadraplegia)*. Stroke can also leave a person partially or severely paralyzed and with sensory damage. Someone suffering loss of sensation may not know his sexualia are being touched unless he sees it happen.

With spinal cord problems, ejaculation may be impossible for men and orgasm impossible for both men and women. In some men, erection can be produced by very strong stimulation; this depends on the extent of the injury. For men who cannot achieve erection, other means of sexual expression are advised. Orgasm and satisfaction for both men and women may be reported as psychic phenomenon: some adults with spinal-cord injuries say they can concentrate on sensation from a neurologically intact part of their bodies, reassign that sensation to their sexualia, and experience it in fantasy as orgasm. Using that technique, some spinal cord injured men report multiple orgasm (T. Cole, 1979). For some unknown reason, spinal cord injury is followed by infertility in men but not in women.

Parkinson's disease causes severe tremors and robs people of free, controlled movement. Cerebral palsy, multiple sclerosis, spina bifida, and other neurological problems also deny people full body mobility and function. Drugs and physical therapy provide some help for certain problems, but deficits may remain. The suggestions given below for arthritis and mobility problems also apply to many nervous system problems.

Mental Retardation

About 3 percent of our population have IQs below 70, the usual definition of retardation. The sexual maturation of most of these people is normal, though somewhat delayed. Parents and guardians are rightly concerned about both their sexual exploitation and their sexual deprivation. Another problem is that the incidence of STDs among the retarded is three times that in the normal population (Kempton, 1973).

There is also great concern about the retarded not preventing conception—a difficult idea and practice to teach them. Sterilization is highly controversial; if it is not performed, a retarded woman can at least be fitted with an IUD (Hall, 1975). Decisions about sterilization should allow for the fact that few of the severely retarded marry, but a majority of the slightly retarded (IQ 55 to 70) do. Society has a serious dilemma about protecting the rights of the mentally retarded to sexual expression, marriage, and children while protecting the rights of their children and the rest of society (Hall and Sawyer, 1978).

Cardiac and Vascular Problems

Problems of the heart and blood vessels affect some 5 to 10 percent of our population, yet research on their sexual concerns is scanty. Until quite recently, many people were routinely told to reduce or avoid sexual activity after a heart attack, and even today quite a few stop sexual activity out of fear (Tuttle, Cook, and Fitch, 1964).

Sexual activity does increase blood pressure and heart rate, but few people die of heart attacks during coitus—and fewer still of those who have it regularly with familiar partners. With new partners, people may try new things or try to display their prowess; the stress and anxiety may be more taxing than coitus itself. Experienced people often undergo less cardiac stress and hypertension during coitus with regular partners than they do during a brisk walk around the block or when feeling a strong emotion such as anger or grief.

Many people can safely resume sexual activity a few months or even a few weeks after a heart attack if they do so under careful medical supervision. The patient and his or her partner should discuss both general and sexual rehabilitation with a doctor. Physical conditioning will strengthen the heart; as a rule of thumb, when the person can walk a few blocks briskly, routine coitus can probably be resumed (Wagner, 1975). *Angina* (chest pain) during coitus can be prevented by medication (nitroglycerin).

Arthritis and Other Mobility Problems

Arthritis is an inflammatory disease of the joints that makes movement difficult and painful. Though often thought of as a problem of the old, it can strike at any age. So can such mobility problems as lower-back disorders and joint injuries. Sexual difficulties arise because of pain and limited movement; people may have

difficulty thrusting, stroking, or supporting weight.

While spontaneous sex has its pleasure, so does planned sex, and mobility problems benefit from planning. Arthritis is often worse in the morning and when one is fatigued; coitus can be planned for the late morning or early evening. A warm shower relieves the pain and stiffness of arthritis or an injured back. Finding new coital positions and new kinds of stimulation (oral or with a vibrator) may increase satisfaction. Close body contact and soft stroking may be particularly welcome to someone whose body is a source of pain and inconvenience.

Impaired Sight and Hearing

Impaired sight and hearing have no direct effect on sexual performance, but they may greatly affect a person's sexual self-image, and they limit communication. Since sexual messages are usually indirect, the decreased communication must somehow be overcome. Participating in social activities with sighted and hearing persons helps the blind and deaf understand common sexual cues. In attempting sexual communication, directness must be chanced and tolerated despite anxiety, embarrassment, or a desire for tact. Once a relationship has been established, many partners develop a private sexual vocabulary; sexual performance is then usually satisfactory (Fitz-Gerald and Fitz-Gerald, 1978).

Overview

Some of the problems discussed in this chapter are best dealt with in advance, by prevention. The STDs can generally be avoided; the surest way is to have completely exclusive relationships, but many do not choose this. Using condoms, soap and water, and caution in choosing partners can help a great deal.

Other problems are best dealt with by detection. Routine periodic examinations by oneself and a physician often reveal tumors, STDs, and other problems. Regrettably, many physicians are uncomfortable with genital and rectal examinations, so we recommend finding a physician or clinic that is thorough and humane about such matters.

People who are told they require major treatment, such as surgery, should seek second opinions before making final decisions. Treatment methods change rapidly, and differences of opinion are common. The success of treatment should never be taken for granted. Cancers always require follow-up examinations, and STDs don't always respond to drugs as anticipated. New strains of bacteria and viruses are constantly challenging medical skills, sometimes successfully.

Finally, several ethical considerations should be kept in mind. Engaging in sexual activities to express love, companionship, or pleasure entails some degree of trust. That trust is violated if a disease is knowingly transmitted or even if suspicion of one is ignored. It takes great honesty and courage to tell a partner about the possibility of disease; this is one of the more difficult but necessary aspects of sexual life. While it disturbs us to raise the specter of illness or death in relation to love and pleasure, venereal diseases are not like bad colds. They can have devastating effects.

To maintain sexually rewarding lives, the ill and handicapped must admit that sexual concerns are important and legitimate, and then concentrate on the sexual abilities that remain rather than those that are gone. More medical and counseling help is becoming available. However, our society is only beginning to think about the needs for affection and sex of the mentally retarded and those institutionalized for handicaps. As science continues to save and prolong the lives of more people, the sexual needs of the ill and handicapped will demand new knowledge, new attitudes, and new social and personal decisions.

Review, Discuss, Decide

1. How often should one have a physical examination that includes genitalia, breasts, and anus? What should be looked for?
2. What are the typical signs of gonorrhea in males? In females?
3. Which sexually transmitted diseases can make silent carriers of males? Of females?
4. How does one conduct a breast examination? Where are tumors most common?
5. What is a Pap smear? What does it reveal? What does it not reveal?

6. What are some of the sexual concerns of people with diabetes, arthritis, heart conditions, back problems?
7. What preliminary steps can a handicapped person take to deal with his or her sexual concerns?
8. What are some of society's ethical and practical concerns about STDs? About sexuality and the mentally retarded?

Part III

Sex Behavior

Behavior means, simply, what people do, the acts they perform. Sex behavior is one of the first things to enter most people's minds when they hear the phrase sexual decision. Shall I? With this person? In what circumstances? How often? Some sex behaviors, such as masturbation and fantasy, though of almost universal concern, do not directly involve other people. But most other sex behaviors involve partners, and they affect and are affected by society. Decisions about them often seem immediate and intimate, but are guided by many forces of which most people remain unaware. Understanding those forces can make decisions about sex behavior freer and more truly individual. Furthermore, it is difficult to make satisfying and unpressured decisions if one mistakenly believes one's own or one's partner's behavior is either rare or common.

First we will discuss the concepts, terms, and methods of studying sex behavior, and then sexual behaviors that do not involve partners (autoeroticism). Then we will detail what people do sexually as they grow toward maturity (early sex behavior) and in adulthood (adult sex behavior). Finally we will look at the less common sex behaviors (other sex behaviors). Along the way, we will examine some of the implications of these behaviors for individuals, for relationships, and for society.

9 Autoeroticism

Do most people masturbate? When do they start?

How do most people masturbate?

How often do most people masturbate? How much might be excessive?

What are the physical and mental effects of masturbation?

Do people masturbate after marriage?

Are orgasms during sleep common?

What sort of sexual fantasies are normal?

Masturbation and sexual fantasy are a large part of many people's erotic lives, and part of nearly everyone's. They introduce almost all males and females to genital sexuality and are common ways of finding relief from sexual tension. Autoeroticism is also a matter of individual and social concern, and seeing it in historical and cross-cultural perspective makes our society's present attitudes more understandable.

Autoerotic acts are the first sexual behaviors we will study; we will begin by discussing the concepts, terms, and methods of studying sexual behaviors. These concepts will also be used

in the chapters on early genital behavior, adult genital behavior, and other sexual behaviors.

Studying Sex Behavior

Since most people are curious about sexual behavior, one would think a great deal is known about it, but that is far from the truth. One reason is that many people, generalizing from their own experience, assume they already know what others do. Another is the gap between what people do and what they say they do. Also, sex-behavior research is still relatively new and has often run into public and scientific resistance.

In the late 1930s, Alfred Kinsey began his first massive *quantitative* study of human sexual behavior; some scientists objected that behavior is meaningless without its *qualitative* emotional context (see chapter 2). This may be true when one tries to understand an individual; but one cannot understand a person if one mistakenly thinks his or her behavior pattern unusual or common. If nothing else, counting noses makes us aware of how much some sexual behaviors vary. One person may reach orgasm several times a day, another never in a lifetime. There may be more quantitative and qualitative variety in sexual behaviors than in most other aspects of life.

Which Behaviors to Study

Some behaviors are easy to define, count, and study. Has a person ever had coitus? With how many partners? Was contraception used? Other behaviors are difficult; should one class together as petting both a quick feel in early adolescence and prolonged adult genital play?

Also, some behaviors are different in men and women. For instance, from puberty on, almost all men want to carry sexual activity through to orgasm. Women's excitement often lacks such urgency; even a sexually active, experienced woman may reach orgasm rarely or never. Therefore reaching orgasm is a different measure of men's than of women's sex behavior (Kinsey et al., 1953).

Furthermore, most men have a rather regular frequency of orgasm throughout life. A woman may have days or months of intense sexual activity, with or without orgasm, and then a long period of inactivity. Therefore similar orgasmic frequencies for men and women don't always represent similar behavior patterns. Taking these factors into account, Kinsey and his colleagues created some concepts that have become standard in sex research (see below).

Many important questions about sex behavior remain unanswered. For example, how often people decline sexual opportunities may be as significant as how often they accept. Who starts or instigates sexual activity, how, and why may be as important as how often. But we still know very little about these matters (Kirkendall, 1967a).

Concepts and Terms of Behavior Study

Certain concepts and terms are standard in studying sex behavior. One of these is *incidence,* or how many people have performed an act. For instance, if twenty people out of 100 have ever had coitus, the *cumulative incidence* of coitus in the group is 20 percent. If only fifteen of those twenty are presently having coitus, the *active incidence* is 15 percent.

Frequency is how often something happens, usually expressed as an average. A person who has coitus six times in two weeks has a weekly frequency of three. *Averages* of frequency can be calculated two ways. A *mean* is reached by adding figures and dividing the total by the number of figures. A mean often gives a distorted picture, because it is skewed by extreme highs and lows. Suppose one person has coitus thirty times a month, and six others have frequencies of one, two, three, four, and five. The mean would be seven, an unrepresentative figure for most of the individuals. A mean can also give a false impression of frequency over time, especially for females, some of whom go months or years without an orgasm and then have dozens within days.

Therefore, another sort of average is often used, the *median.* This is the midpoint of an array of figures. For instance, if one learns how often people have coitus and arranges the figures from highest to lowest, the middle figure is the median. Half the people have coitus more often, half less often. A few extreme highs and lows do not change the median, as they do the mean, so the median more nearly expresses what we hope to know from an average. In the example above, the median would be four.

Kinsey and his collaborators, Paul Gebhard, Wardell Pomeroy, and Clyde Martin (1948), introduced the useful ideas of *total sexual outlet* and *proportion of outlet*. Outlet is usually counted in sex acts leading to orgasm. If a person has coitus twice a week and masturbates once, his total outlet is three per week; coitus is two-thirds of that outlet, masturbation one-third. Total outlet is obviously less easily calculated for acts that don't lead to orgasm.

There is no neat boundary between generations or social eras, but one can try to measure change over time. Kinsey et al. compared peo-

Figure 9-1 / *Note that until the extreme upper range, not more than 2 to 10 percent of males have the same frequency of total sexual outlet.*

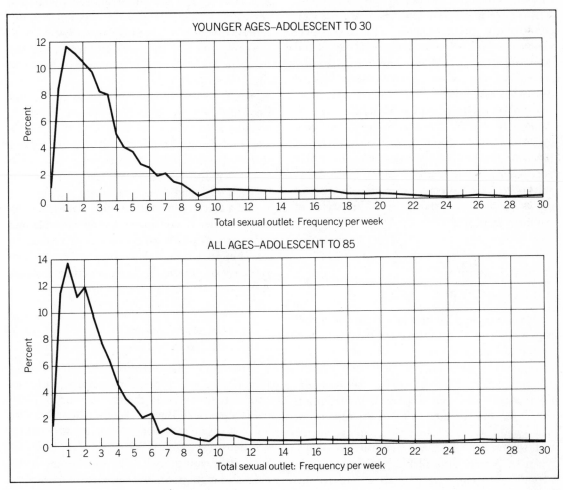

ple by decade of birth (1890–1900, 1900–1910, etc.) and found some striking changes and continuities. This type of analysis is still used.

A very important influence on sexual behavior is *social class*. This is difficult to define; income, occupation, status, parents' income and occupation, all fail as single criteria. Kinsey et al. found the best single measure of social level was the amount of schooling one completed. Few people from poor families attain high income, status, and education; few upper-level people drop far below their families' social and educational world. When one compares the sexual behavior of people who have finished primary school, high school, and college, there are differences from early childhood on. Obviously people don't know at five or fifteen how long they will go to school and adjust their sex behavior accordingly. The sex-behavior differences that correlate with education levels probably reflect the differences created by the income, occupation, status, and life-style of parents, peers, and self.

Masturbation: The Background

Many people automatically think of sexual activity as involving two people. However, two of the commonest sexual behaviors are *autoerotic* (*auto* = self)—masturbation and fantasy. *Masturbation* is deliberate sexual self-stimulation, usually aimed at orgasm. Sexual tension can make one irritable and easily distracted; males and females masturbate to relieve sexual and sometimes nonsexual tension, especially when no partner is available. (Mutual masturbation and having the genitals stimulated by another person are discussed under petting in chapter 11.) *Fantasy*, or imagined scenes and events, may accompany masturbation or exist by and for itself. Another solitary sex behavior is involuntary *nocturnal orgasm*; in postpubertal males this is accompanied by seminal emission.

In our society, masturbation often provokes shame, guilt, and fears of mental and physical damage. Until recently it was one of the least studied and understood of all sex behaviors, shrouded in scientific as well as popular myth. This is unfortunate, because masturbation is an important part of early self-discovery, and for many people is a bridge from inexperience to sexual relationships.

Some young people masturbate without knowing the word or without relating the term to their behavior. Many people of all ages use the euphemism "playing with oneself." Boys learn expressions that describe male more than female masturbation, such as "jerk off," "whack off," and "beat your meat"; girls have no such terms. This reflects the almost universal difference in how males and females talk and learn about masturbation, which is related to whether, when, and how they do it. In few aspects of eroticism do the sexes differ so much and understand each other so little.

The Cultural Legacy: Sin and Excess

The word masturbation probably comes from Latin and means "to pollute with the hand." It was used in the first century A.D. by the Roman poet Martial (1860), who wrote, "Is your hand safe and sound? Well use it, then you will not want a whore. Why pay for what your hand gives you gratis?" The word entered the English language in the seventeenth century.

People convinced that masturbation is harmful or immoral have called it self-abuse, and since the eighteenth century it has also been called onanism, through misinterpretation of the Biblical story of Onan.

Self-stimulation appears in the art and literature of ancient Babylon, Israel, Egypt, India, Greece, and Rome. Western attitudes have varied over the centuries from amused tolerance to harsh punishment. The Jewish, Christian, and Moslem faiths have traditionally condemned masturbation. The Christian ban was embedded in the view that nonreproductive sex acts are sinful. Many medieval penitentials—the manuals advising clerics how much penance to prescribe—classed masturbation among the mortal sins. The penance was generally greater for adults than for children and might be as much as several years (deMause, 1974; Karlen, 1971). But perhaps then, as now, masturbation was more shrugged at than punished by some people.

Few medical works of the Renaissance mentioned masturbation, but some called it normal or even beneficial for children. The sixteenth-century anatomist Gabriel Fallopius (for whom the Fallopian tube, or oviduct, is named) urged parents to "be zealous in infancy to enlarge the penis of the boy" by massage (deMause, 1974). Guittoncino de'Sinibaldi, a popular seventeenth-century medical writer, said that sexual activity could improve the mood, the complexion, and in some cases epilepsy, and that abstinence could cause "spermatic fevers" (Comfort, 1970).

Such views were drowned out during the eighteenth century (Hare, 1962). The anonymous book *Onania* (see chapter 2) claimed that masturbation led to epilepsy, madness, "lying, forswearing, perhaps murder." In 1760 the Swiss physician Tissot wrote that the "crime of masturbation" wasted precious semen, paving the way for tuberculosis, impotence, and blindness. Since sexual activity rushed blood to the

The Sin of Onan

Onan's sin, described in Genesis 38, was not masturbation but defiance. Onan, a nephew of Joseph, had a brother named Er, who was struck dead by God for an act of wickedness shortly after being married. Onan's father told him to marry Er's widow and "raise seed to thy brother." (This may reflect the ancient custom of the levirate, by which a man marries his brother's widow or has her as a secondary wife.) Apparently Onan didn't want to raise children bearing his brother's name, for "when he went in unto his brother's wife . . . he spilled [his seed] on the ground." (He probably performed *coitus interruptus*, withdrawing from the vagina before ejaculation.) God struck Onan dead for his disobedience. Only in the eighteenth century was Onan's act linked with masturbation, probably because Onan was struck dead after a noncoital ejaculation, and masturbation was becoming a fearsome, even fatal, act in many people's minds. The term onanism was used widely into this century.

brain, excess also caused nervous weakness, melancholy, fits, idiocy, and paralysis. When Benjamin Rush wrote the first American text on psychiatry in 1812, he probably reflected general medical opinion in claiming that sexual "intemperance" caused a host of ills and "fatuity and death" (Comfort, 1970). In 1863 the Scots physician David Skae set forth the idea of masturbatory insanity as a distinct disease (Zilboorg, 1941).

This attitude toward masturbation and excess had ancient roots. One source was fear of losing emotional control; another was anxiety over postejaculatory feelings; a third was magical thinking about sperm (Karlen, 1979a).

Like people in a number of societies, many Westerners have feared that orgasmic loss of self-control may destroy all mental controls, releasing tides of lust and aggression. This view was expressed by Saint Augustine (1957), who compared lust to a fit of rage and said that orgasm set man farthest from rationality, and thus from God. With the development of science, these traditional ideas were translated into medical terms. Health meant abstinence, control, and reason; illness meant excess, loss of control, and loss of reason (the traditional definition of insanity). These ideas are not dead.

Many people fear that letting go in sex means going crazy—a fear commonly involved in orgasmic dysfunction. Of course conscious control does fade during orgasm, but briefly and harmlessly.

Another source of masturbation guilt has been anxiety over postejaculatory feelings. In societies around the world, men have variously interpreted the sudden physical and emotional relaxation that often follows orgasm. Some feel it as a pleasant afterglow. But guilt, anxiety, and fear of passivity may make men experience it as fatigue, disgust, or depression. Therefore, some men have feared ejaculation as a cause of weakness or loss. More than 2,000 years ago, Hippocrates worried that loosing too much sperm could leave men frail or even paralyzed from damage to the spine (Comfort, 1970).

This vague connection of semen with vitality and the nervous system has echoed through Western history. People have thought of sperm as a vital essence limited in supply, and have feared depletion through excess. For instance, some athletic coaches still needlessly urge pregame abstinence.

These fears of madness, weakness, and loss probably played a part in the soaring eighteenth- and nineteenth-century fear of mastur-

---

"The Masturbator"

During the first half of the nineteenth century, doctors became convinced that they could identify the masturbator, a child bearing such special signs as downcast eyes, pale skin, and a brooding, vacant expression. The French physician Claude-François Lallemand, a refiner of sexual scare theories, wrote (1853) that the masturbator "has no other interests; he loves no one; he is attached to no one; he shows no emotion before the grandeur of nature or the beauties of art . . . [he is] dead to the call of his family, his country, or humanity."

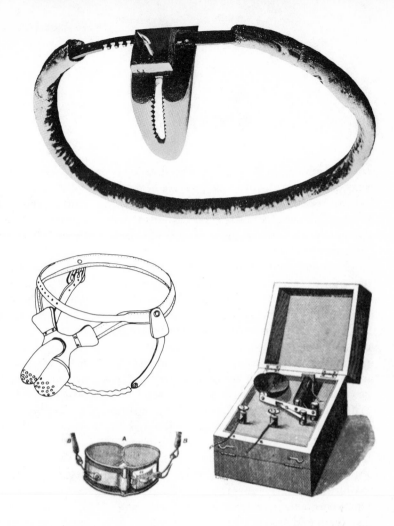

Figure 9-2 / *In the late Middle Ages and after, there were devices to keep females from coitus, such as this "chastity belt" from thirteenth-century France (top). In the nineteenth century, there arose a whole industry to prevent male masturbation (center) and even nocturnal emissions (below right)—the latter by devices that set off an alarm when the swelling of erection closed an electrical circuit in a band around the penis.*

bation; so, apparently, did the Victorians' stress on sexual, emotional, and social controls. Historian Steven Marcus (1964) says this emphasis was a frantic effort by the growing middle class to control both itself and people it feared might not control themselves—the unsocialized young, the "backward" poor, the "self-indulgent" rich, "primitive" non-Westerners. Perhaps masturbating children were especially threatening to parents anxious about suppressing their own sexuality (Kern, 1974).

The campaign against masturbation became more widespread and intense through the nineteenth century. Many children were forbidden to eat spicy foods, wear tight clothes, and keep their hands in their pockets. Identifying mas-

turbators became an unofficial subspecialty of medicine (Karlen, 1979a, 1971). Doctors even hoped to prevent nocturnal emissions, which were said, through loss of semen, to cause softening of the brain. The French physician Claude-François Lallemand (1853) announced a new disease, spermatorrhea, or involuntary loss of sperm, which he said caused listlessness, nervous ills, and premature death.

Soon sexual excess was thought to cause "degeneracy" and "neurasthenia." The former meant degeneration of the genes, said to produce a variety of sexual aberrations—hence the term "sexual degenerate." Neurasthenia meant irritation and weakness of the nervous system; it was often used where "nervous" or "neu-

151

rotic" might be applied today. The theory became widespread that degenerated genes caused neurasthenia, which caused masturbation, which caused further neurasthenia and eventually perversion (homosexuality), madness, and paralysis.

How could children be saved? A spartan life was a start—exercise, cold showers, no idle time or solitary play. The eminent physician William Acton (1857) suggested that parents douse infants' genitals with cold water and dress children in straitjackets; he said the "ordinary practice of sleeping with the hands bound behind one's back should not be ignored even by grown men." Acton did not dwell on the perils of female masturbation, for he considered the idea that healthy women had sexual feelings "a vile aspersion." They had coitus only to make babies and gratify their husbands, thus saving their spouses from whores. Worries about girls masturbating were less of death (they lost no vital sperm) than of nymphomania (see page 237) and madness (Karlen, 1979a). Some females were made to wear chastity belts that allowed excretion but prevented coitus and masturbation (Comfort, 1970).

Sexual restraint became an industry. Between 1856 and 1919 fourteen antimasturbation devices were granted United States patents (Mountjoy, 1974). Parents made children sleep in mittens and manacles and wear genital cages. The ingenious Dr. Lallemand, having invented spermatorrhea, devised a preventive, a spike-lined ring that fitted around the flaccid penis; erection set off a bell to waken the sleeper and his parents. Restraining devices were sold as late as the 1920s, and many mental hospitals used them to prevent the self-abuse that allegedly had put many patients there.

When restraints failed, medical measures were taken. Some doctors blistered the penis with mercury, making it too painful to touch; others performed circumcision without anesthetic (Haller and Haller, 1974). In 1858, Dr. Isaac Brown of London developed clitoridectomy (surgical removal of the clitoris) for use on girls considered incorrigible masturbators. The final solution was castration (Karlen, 1971). Removing the testes or ovaries was expected to reduce excessive sex drive and rid the world of degenerated genes. In the 1890s, many states allowed castration of young "confirmed masturbators." In 1899 Dr. Harry Sharp of Indiana State Reformatory announced that he had created a neater sterilization technique for this purpose, which he called *vasectomy* (see pages 417–18).

Of course there was no evidence, then or now, that masturbation or the ills blamed on it are caused directly by the genes or gonads. Yet tens or hundreds of thousands were castrated all over the Western world during the early decades of this century. Then in Nazi Germany, uncounted Jews, Gypsies, political prisoners, blind people, and homosexuals were castrated as degenerates before being murdered. The practice continued on a small scale into the 1950s in Europe and the United States and probably is still performed now and then (Haller and Haller, 1974; Karlen, 1971).

Much of this seems semicomic, grotesque, or brutal. It is worth review because it infected many otherwise intelligent and humane people, including the grandparents and even the parents of many who read these pages. And it shows how intense a campaign was waged against autoeroticism—and, by implication, all eroticism. It is not strange that we still feel an indirect impact. The old fears have persisted in milder, subtler forms.

Havelock Ellis and Freud, early in this century, were among the first to discourage the vigilante pursuit of autoeroticism, but they still had some reservations. Ellis (1936) reached the then shockingly liberal conclusion that "in the case of moderate masturbation in [genetically] healthy, well-born individuals, no seriously pernicious results necessarily follow." This still left vague terrors about the exact meanings of "moderate," "well-born," "seriously pernicious," and "necessarily." Freud (1962) said masturbation is natural in small children and at puberty, but that healthy, mature people abandon it for coitus. Some sexual reformers still feared it could fixate females on "immature clitoral orgasm" (Singer, 1973), and males on sex without partners. The price of sexual solitaire had shrunk from blindness and insanity to mere immaturity and maladjustment.

Kinsey et al. (1948, 1953) revealed that many people masturbate frequently without apparent ill effects. They concluded that the attempt to control masturbation was the keystone of society's effort to control all sexuality. Many people, they pointed out, still tried to limit masturbation on allegedly scientific grounds, although their real objections were moral.

In the past few decades, more and more health professionals have spoken of masturbation as harmless or positively healthful. Nevertheless, a residue of old attitudes makes masturbation one of the most discomforting and least discussed subjects in all age groups, even among many laymen and professionals who consider themselves knowledgeable and uninhibited (Karlen, 1979a). We will examine the alleged and known effects of masturbation, but first we must briefly examine what it is, how it is done, by whom, how often, and with what attitudes and feelings.

Techniques of Masturbation

Since masturbation is usually solitary, few people know how others do it. Most males (Kinsey et al., 1948) grasp the shaft of the penis with one hand and stroke, rub, or pump it, often with a milking motion and often bringing light or occasional friction against the glans and corona. Some lightly stroke the very sensitive ventral surface of the penis, especially the frenulum. A few briefly stroke or pull the glans, but it is so sensitive that usually sustained friction becomes painful.

A small number of males rub the penis against a pillow or other object, perhaps simulating coitus. Still fewer have other, very individual ways of masturbating, such as inserting objects in the urethra or anus; the latter is often accompanied by homosexual fantasies (such insertions are physically dangerous). Self-fellation (*fellatio* is oral stimulation of the penis) is a common boyhood fantasy and the subject of many jokes, but only two or three men in a thousand can do it (Kinsey et al., 1948).

As males approach orgasm, they make the movements as fast as possible, but when ejaculating most grip the penis almost spastically—just as, during coitus, they cease thrusting and withdraw slightly or plunge as far into the vagina as possible. About one-tenth of men (Masters and Johnson, 1966) keep stroking or pumping the penis during orgasm; they also continue thrusting during coital orgasm.

Some males prolong masturbation for half an

153

hour or more to draw out the pleasure. The majority, however, reach climax as quickly as possible. During adolescence and young adulthood, this takes from less than one minute to a few minutes, in later life a bit longer.

Sexual fantasies can create excitement leading to masturbation, and many or most males fantasize during self-stimulation. Many use erotic books and pictures; the so-called men's magazines and pornography often serve this function.

Females' masturbatory techniques are far more varied, probably because of their anatomy and social development. First, they have more potential orgasmic triggers in their bodies than males (see chapter 5). Second, far fewer girls than boys exchange sexual information; therefore females are more likely to discover masturbation on their own. The result is much greater individual variation. Masters and Johnson (1966), after observing hundreds of women, wrote that no two masturbated in identical fashion.

The great majority of females who masturbate (84 percent) depend chiefly on stimulating the clitoris, the labia, or both. Some rhythmically rub or press the entire mons with the hand; some stroke with one finger between the labia, occasionally contacting the clitoris; others rub the clitoral shaft rather gently. Most continue rubbing the clitoris or mons during orgasm, just as they continue to thrust or seek male thrusting in coital orgasm (Masters and Johnson, 1966).

About 10 percent of those who masturbate sometimes rub their genitals against a pillow, chair, or bed. Another 10 percent sometimes cross their legs and press their thighs together rhythmically. Some 5 percent use muscle tension and pelvic thrusting. Others draw one leg

up under them and rock the vulva against the heel. A small number can reach orgasm merely by stimulating their breasts or buttocks, and 2 percent can do so by fantasy alone, something very few males say they can do (Kinsey et al., 1953). Some females direct a stream of water on the clitoris and vulva, and lately the use of a vibrator has become popular. A very few insert small objects in the urethra or anus; as for males, such insertions are very dangerous.

Most males fantasize coitus when masturbating, and some simulate it, so many assume that females do the same by inserting fingers or a penislike object in the vagina. There are innumerable jokes about women playing with bananas, cucumbers, and candles, and some occasionally do so. But only one-fifth of females who masturbate use vaginal insertions, usually while massaging the more sensitive mons or clitoris. Barely two-thirds of females fantasize when masturbating, and only half of these do so regularly. Some fantasize only after years of masturbating. Kinsey et al. (1953) found that only rarely do they excite themselves with erotic pictures or books as they masturbate; however, some people believe that this is becoming more common.

Some females prolong masturbation to draw out the pleasure; the multiorgasmic may do so until they have had several or dozens of orgasms. The majority, however, reach climax only once, in four minutes or less (Kinsey et al., 1953).

The Biological Background

Many mammals touch their genitals with their paws, hands, mouths, or other parts of their bodies (Ford and Beach, 1951). Female spider monkeys, for example, touch the clitoris

Dildos and Other Devices

The masturbation device most widely depicted and written about is the dildo, or artificial penis (French *godmiché;* Greek *olisbos,* pl. *olisboi*). It is used by some women in many societies and inserted anally by some male homosexuals. The Chukchee women of Siberia masturbate with the large calf muscle of a reindeer, Tikopian women of the Pacific with a banana or manioc root (Ford and Beach, 1951). In Western antiquity, craftsmen made dildos of wax, ivory, and precious metals, and the Greek playwright Aristophanes claimed that the women of the city of Miletus were famous for the leather *olisboi* they made (Ellis, 1936).

Some dildos are hollow, to allow the passage of warm liquid, simulating ejaculation. Penis-shaped vibrators are sold in drugstores and other shops today, and some men and women masturbate with vibrators strapped to the back of the hand. The counterpart of the dildo for heterosexual men is the inflatable, life-size female doll of rubber or vinyl with a simulated vagina—like other masturbatory devices, sold by mail order and in certain stores.

Japanese women have long used another device, called *rin-o-tama* or *ben-wa* balls. They place in the vagina two hollow metal balls; one is empty, the other contains pellets of mercury or lead. The women then swing, rock, or walk, and the rolling and bumping of the pellets and of the two balls against each other send waves of vibrations through the vagina.

with their prehensile (grasping) tails. But calling such behavior masturbation is often a human projection. A male dog licking its genitals may merely be cleaning itself. Actually, rather few species deliberately masturbate to orgasm—among others, horses, dogs, and several primates—and virtually all animals that do are males. Captive monkeys and apes sometimes mesmerize children at zoos by masturbating, stimulating the penis with hand, foot, or mouth. Male rhesus monkeys have been seen masturbating in the wild even when females were nearby (Ford and Beach, 1951). Occasionally female primates manipulate their genitals, but less often than males and not to orgasm.

Self-stimulation, then, has a stronger evolutionary basis in human males than females (Kinsey et al., 1953). This is apparent not only in animal-behavior studies but in men's and women's masturbation patterns throughout life, as the following comparison shows.

Masturbation: Behavior

Male Behavior

In our society, few young children go beyond sporadic sexual play; one-tenth of boys masturbate to orgasm before age nine. At nine or ten, puberty brings a rise in sex hormones (gonadotropins and steroids), and soon sexual excitability and activity start to surge. From about a year before the signs of puberty* till the middle teens, the majority of boys feel a sexual urgency greater, Kinsey et al. believed (1948), than they will ever feel again, and probably greater than most females feel at any age. Masturbation daily or several times a day for weeks at a time is not uncommon. There is a correlation between the pubertal rise in testosterone and this sexual activity (Ramsey, 1943b). Boys who reach puberty early are sexually more active throughout life than those who mature late (Kinsey et al., 1948).

Not all males masturbate, and some do so rarely; they may have little sex drive or be very inhibited. Some experience orgasm only by nocturnal emissions (see chapter 4). But masturbation is a major part of sexual self-discovery for most boys, and for two out of three it causes the dramatic event of their first ejaculation. Half of all boys in their thirteenth year have masturbated to orgasm; more than four-fifths have done so by age fifteen, and nine-tenths by their late teens. Eventually well over 90 percent of males masturbate, the majority regularly, at least during their teens. In 1974, Hunt found the 1948 figures of Kinsey et al. almost unchanged.

In permissive societies, boys express pubertal sex urges with girls (Gebhard, 1971). Our society expects them to wait; during early adolescence, masturbation is their main sexual outlet. At sixteen to twenty, many men find sexual partners, but almost nine-tenths still masturbate. Through adult life, fewer masturbate, and they do so less often, but about half of all single

---

* Puberty, often thought of as the rather abrupt advent of ejaculation or menses, is a complex process that takes three or four years, from about nine to thirteen years in girls and eleven to fifteen in boys (Oliven, 1974). The words puberty and adolescence are often used interchangeably; more precisely, *puberty* is a physical process, *adolescence* the transition to full reproductive and social maturity. To some extent, adolescence is governed by social ideas of maturity, and in our society may fill an entire decade or at least the teen years.

men still masturbate at age fifty, and a tenth of married men at fifty-five (Kinsey et al., 1948).

Some males masturbate infrequently, others several times a day for years or decades. This means that some masturbate several thousand times as often as others. In the early teens, the average frequency is about twice a week (mean 2.5, median 1.8), but almost one-fifth of boys average four to seven times a week or more. In the middle teens, these figures drop by about a third; then they decrease slowly but steadily throughout life. At fifty, single men masturbate half as often as in adolescence, married men less often. Men with the highest orgasmic frequencies still masturbate almost daily at age fifty.

Educational Level. Educational (social) level is the strongest social correlate with male masturbation. Boys with only grade-school educa-

tions are sexually more active than those who go on for higher education, but fewer of them masturbate (84 percent, compared to 96 percent of the college-bound). Furthermore, they start coitus earlier, and they stop or reduce masturbating when coitus becomes available. They tend to scorn masturbation as a sign of failure to find sexual partners. By age twenty, 40 percent of them have already stopped masturbating, and less than a third ever masturbate after marriage. Little could surprise them more than the extent to which college-educated men (or any grown men) could even think of masturbating when they have wives at home (Kinsey et al., 1948).

During the years sixteen to twenty, when many of the grade-school-level males have coitus and marry, the great majority of college-level males still substitute masturbation for coitus. They masturbate twice as often as

Figure 9-3 / *The cumulative incidence of masturbation was found by Kinsey et al. to differ greatly in males and females. Recent studies suggest little change, although some females who masturbate may begin a bit earlier.*

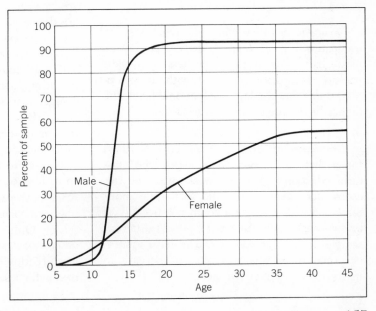

157

grade-school males, and the difference increases with age. After marriage, masturbation is 20 to 30 percent of grade-school males' sexual outlet and 60 to 70 percent of college males'. The figures are even higher for men in professions, most of whom have postgraduate degrees. Men at all levels may masturbate when their wives are pregnant, menstruating, or sick; but especially at the upper educational levels, some do so when coitus is available, for the sake of variety. In masturbatory behavior and attitudes, high-school-educated males are a bit more like the grade-school than the college group.

There are three other important social influences on masturbation.

Devoutness. Religious devoutness has very little effect on whether males ever masturbate (Hunt, 1974; Kinsey et al., 1948), but religiously active males masturbate two-thirds less often than religiously inactive ones.

Occupational Level. Men who reach a given occupational level tend to have that level's masturbation pattern, regardless of their parents' occupations. Almost without exception, the higher a man's occupational level, the higher his frequency of masturbation.

Generation of Birth. Kinsey et al. (1948) found that the proportion of males who masturbated hadn't changed much over the decades, but younger men did so a little more often and with less moral conflict, especially at lower social levels. In Hunt's (1974) different sample, these changes seemed to have continued, and there was a significant increase in masturbation by married men.

Female Behavior

Female masturbation patterns show major biological and social differences. First, far from all females masturbate. Kinsey et al. (1953) found that at thirteen (at the time of their study, the average age of first menstruation), only 15 percent of girls had done so. The incidence rose steadily until age thirty-five and then more slowly into the forties, until finally about two-thirds had masturbated, most of them to orgasm. Hunt (1974) found that 60 percent of his female subjects eighteen to twenty-four were masturbating; but like Kinsey et al., he estimated that almost 40 percent will never masturbate, and almost identical results come from a study of college women (Arafat and Cotton, 1974).

The majority of girls who masturbate before puberty discover the act on their own. Since girls tend not to share sexual information, many are unaware that anyone else does what they are doing, so masturbation remains a more secret, personal experience than for boys (see Table 9.1). During the teens, self-discovery is still girls' commonest way to learn about masturbating; some 60 percent start that way, compared to some 30 percent of boys (Kinsey et al., 1953). Next most common is talk or reading (sometimes of books or lectures meant to discourage masturbation). Only one-tenth of girls learn to masturbate by seeing other girls do it; four times as many boys learn by seeing other boys masturbate. In fact, some girls see boys masturbate and then experiment themselves. Only 3 percent first masturbate with other females. A number of women discover masturbation on their own as late as their thirties or forties. As Table 9.1 shows, this is very

158

different from male experience. Hunt (1974) reports a much higher early incidence and frequency of female masturbation than did Kinsey et al. This difference, if it applies to the whole population, may result from the greater availability of talk and information about sex.

Boys' shared information does not fully account for these differences between the sexes. Although many girls feel increased sexual interest at puberty, most who were sexually active before puberty cease until the middle teens (see chapter 10). This is true of very few males, and the difference seems to have hormonal as well as social causes. Boys who reach puberty early have high sexual levels throughout life; in females there is less relationship between the age of puberty and sex behavior. Some girls learn about masturbation but wait months or years before trying it; few males delay.

Women may have coitus because a partner wants it, but in masturbation they themselves choose to seek erotic pleasure. Also, masturbation is the one sex act in which most women usually reach climax—perhaps partly because some feel anxiety or inhibitions during coitus, partly because in masturbation they needn't adjust to a partner's needs and techniques. Most women who fail to reach orgasm by masturbating have made only one or two desultory tries, whether from lack of interest, lack of pleasure, or emotional and social inhibitions. Therefore, masturbation is a good indicator of many women's erotic desire and expressiveness (K. B. Davis, 1929; Kinsey et al., 1953).

Women's masturbation frequencies are very different from men's. Some masturbate only once or twice a year, and many quite sporadically. Some go years without doing so, because of sexual satisfaction with partners or lack of interest. The median frequency for single women over twenty is once every two-and-a-half to three weeks; for married women it is once a month.* These frequencies remain the same (or in some women rise) from the twenties into the fifties, while male frequencies decline. During any given year, only 20 percent of all females who ever masturbate do so, compared to 30 percent of married men and 75 percent of single men.

In almost every social level and age group, masturbation is females' second most frequent genital act—in youth second to petting, in adulthood to coitus. As for males, it is the largest source of premarital orgasm. After marriage, it provides only about one-tenth of women's orgasms until age fifty; then the incidence and frequency of masturbation rise, probably because of husbands' decreased interest in coitus (see chapter 5). After divorce or widowhood, masturbation usually remains above premarital levels.

Several of the social influences on male masturbation also affect females, but not all in the same ways. Among these are educational level, devoutness, and generation of birth.

Educational Level. Females' masturbation patterns are strongly influenced by education, and in the same way as males'. The higher their education, the more likely it is that they will masturbate. Of married women in their early twenties, 11 percent of those with grade-school

* Mean and median masturbation figures are farther apart for females than for males. About 4 percent of females masturbate fourteen or more times a week at some time in their lives; some reach twenty or even a hundred climaxes within an hour. The means are therefore two to three times above the medians.

educations masturbate in a given year, compared to 31 percent of those with college educations. As with males, parents' vocation makes little or no difference: the daughters of doctors and of ditch diggers are equally likely or unlikely to masturbate.

Girls with only grade-school educations begin coitus earlier than the better educated;

Table 9.1 / *Male and female masturbation*

	Females	Males		Females	Males
Learning to masturbate*			Decade of birth: incidence	About 10% increase from 1890s to 1920s.	Some increase, but only in lower educational level.
Self-discovery	57%	28%			
Verbal and printed					
sources	43	75			
Petting	12	—			
Observation	11	40	Decade of birth: frequency	Little or no change.	Slight increase.
Homosexual contact	3	9			
Cumulative incidence			Religious background: incidence	Much lower in devout.	Somewhat lower in devout.
By age 12	12	21			
By age 20	33	92			
Ever during life	62	92–97			
Trend of active incidence	Increases into middle age.	Decreases after teens.	Religious background: frequency	No relationship.	Somewhat lower in devout.
Frequency			Fantasy while masturbating		
Individual variation	Very great.	Less than females.	Almost always	50%	72%
			Sometimes	14	17
Lifetime trend	Uniform to mid-fifties.	Decreases after teens.	Content of fantasy	Occasionally surpasses experience.	Usually surpasses experience.
Educational level: incidence			Relation to educational level	None.	More common in better educated.
Grade school graduates	34	89			
High school graduates	59	95			
College graduates	57–63	96			
			Techniques		
Educational level: frequency	No relationship.	Higher in college group.	Genital manipulation	84%	95%
			Other	Not uncommon.	Uncommon.

Source: Adapted from Alfred C. Kinsey, W. B. Pomeroy, C. E. Martin, and P. H. Gebhard, *Sexual Behavior in the Human Female* (Philadelphia: Saunders, 1953).
* More than one source may be named.

they have a greater fear that masturbation is morally or physically harmful; and many stop masturbating when coitus begins. As with males, the behavior of high-school-educated females lies between that of the grade-school and college groups. However, educational level does not affect how often females masturbate; males' frequencies rise sharply with education.

Devoutness. Devoutness reduces the incidence and frequency of masturbation more in females than in males; 41 to 51 percent of devout females masturbate, compared to 67 to 75 percent of the religiously inactive (Hunt, 1974; Kinsey et al., 1953). As with males, religious adherence rather than denomination makes the difference. But once a woman starts masturbating, devoutness does not influence how often, as it tends to do in males. Masturbation is actually a larger part of the devout woman's total outlet, for she has less sexual activity with partners; perhaps masturbation seems a lesser evil. Devoutness has a little less influence as the years pass and experience increases (Kinsey et al., 1953).

Generation of Birth. In each generation from 1890 to 1929, Kinsey et al. (1953) found that slightly more women masturbated, for a total rise of 10 percent. Further increases may have happened since then, but this is not certain. Hunt (1974) reports an accumulative incidence of 94 percent for males and 63 percent for females, almost identical to the Kinsey et al. findings of 92 percent and 62 percent. The age of first masturbation may have fallen some two years, to about fifteen and a half (Gagnon and Simon, personal communication).

The Cross-Cultural View

In most societies anthropologists have studied, adults apparently masturbate rarely. However, many people deny or underestimate masturbation; it is usually solitary and often secret, and widely looked down on as childish or a sign of failure. Female masturbation is more disapproved or more secret in some societies, so information on it remains scantier, but it seems that more males than females masturbate almost everywhere, and that they do so more often (Ford and Beach, 1951). This corresponds to trends in other higher species, as described earlier.

The Kgatla of southern Africa are exceptional in that masturbation seems more common among women than men. This is also true of the Lesu, a very permissive people of New Ireland. Hortense Powdermaker (1971), in her famous study of Lesu, wrote:

A woman will masturbate if she is sexually excited and there is no man to satisfy her . . . [she] sits down and bends her right leg so that her heel presses against her genitalia. Even young girls of about six years may do this quite casually as they sit on the ground. The women and men talk about it freely, and there is no shame attached to it. It is a customary position for women to take, and they learn it in childhood. They never use their hands for manipulation.

The use of dildos and other vaginal insertions is reported more in preliterate societies than in the West (although reliable data are scanty). For instance, in Africa, Azande women are said to use phalli made from wooden roots (Ford and Beach, 1951); and although lonely or frustrated Kgatla wives usually masturbate manually, some hide from their husbands the rag-covered sticks they use as penis substitutes (Schapera, 1941).

Some permissive societies allow or encourage children to masturbate. Some also allow it for adolescents and adults, especially those without partners, but even some permissive cultures disapprove of masturbation after childhood; they expect coitus to take its place. The very permissive Trobianders consider masturbation unworthy of an adult (Malinowski, 1929). The Bala of the Congo accept masturbation in boys and girls but fear that if grown men do it often, it destroys their interest in women (Merriam, 1971). This idea has been held by some Westerners.

Some societies condemn all masturbation. Kwoma boys of New Guinea learn not to touch their genitals even when urinating; adults who masturbate are considered sick, sinful, or deficient (Ford and Beach, 1951). But even in the most restrictive cultures, many or most males and some females masturbate anyway, in secrecy, shame, and fear. Since rules against nonmarital coitus are even stronger than those against self-stimulation, masturbation may be far commoner in restrictive than in permissive societies (Gebhard, 1971).

In our society, masturbation has been condemned but secretly practiced. Nothing with the scope and depth of the Kinsey studies has been done in other Western nations, but small-scale investigations suggest similar patterns in Northern Europe. In Germany 80 percent of boys and 25 percent of girls masturbate before reaching fifteen (Giese, 1970; Sigusch and Schmidt, 1973). As in the United States, the boys begin regardless of sociosexual experi-

ence, many girls only after feeling pleasure in petting or coitus. German girls, especially those with higher education, now begin masturbating earlier than they did a few decades ago, as do those in the United States.

Effects and Attitudes

About half of all adults in the United States still condemn masturbation (Levitt, Albert, and Klassen, 1973) and would discourage a twelve- or thirteen-year-old child from doing it (W. Wilson, 1975). A study of university students (Arafat and Cotton, 1974) found that about 30 percent of the men and 40 percent of the women who masturbated felt guilty or depressed or feared becoming insane. Another such study (Greenberg and Archambault, 1973) produced figures of 40 percent and almost 50 percent; these results are almost identical with those reported by Kinsey et al. a few decades ago. Despite talk of a sexual revolution, masturbation fears and guilts are obviously pervasive and deep. Attitudes among health professionals, though, have shown some change. A nationwide study in the early Seventies showed that 15 percent of male and female medical students thought masturbation could cause mental problems, compared to some 50 percent a decade earlier (Lief and Karlen, 1976).

Masturbation is now widely thought a normal, even helpful part of sexual development (Gadpaille, 1975). And there is now rather strong evidence of what masturbation does *not* do. There is no relationship between masturbation and any mental or physical illness, major or minor, in males or females (Kinsey et al., 1948,

1953). That is, the effects of masturbation are no different than those of any other genital act. Orgasm from any sexual act is often followed by relaxation, but not by damaging loss of energy. And most healthy males produce more sperm than they could expend by even the highest known rates of sexual activity.

Furthermore, one person's excess is another's norm. Kinsey et al. (1948), after noting that some males' orgasmic rate is once a week, others' twice a day, said: "Like many other physiological functions, erotic response depends upon a remarkably foolproof mechanism. When one reaches the limit of physiological endurance he no longer responds erotically." Females also have a physiological limit—irritated sexualia.

Some people's belief that masturbation causes or reflects emotional immaturity seems to express theoretical conviction or moral disapproval. The too shy or asocial person who retreats from sexual partners probably has inner conflicts of which such withdrawal is a reflection, not a cause (A. Ellis, 1963). Concern that masturbation may condition girls to respond only to their own clitoral manipulation, and boys to think only of their own pleasure, is now thought unjustified (Gebhard, 1960; Singer, 1973). Most people who masturbate would usually rather have a partner. Masters and Johnson (1966) found that women who have masturbatory orgasms are more likely to reach coital orgasms as well.

In recent decades, some people have written that masturbation causes no harm other than the guilt it may provoke. This seems true, but it is like telling someone facing a gun that he has nothing to fear but fear itself (Karlen, 1979a). In our society, some guilt and shame over masturbation probably exist in the great majority of people; its depth and extent should not be underestimated. One psychiatrist (Gadpaille, 1975) describes a common experience of clinicians and sexologists when he writes that

One Man's Excess

Masters and Johnson (1966) found that many of the men they studied thought masturbation in excess might cause weakness and neurosis, yet none could give an example from his personal knowledge, and none could define excess. Their own masturbatory frequencies varied from once a month to two or three times a day. Each defined excessive as somewhat more than his own rate: "One man with a once-a-month masturbatory history felt once or twice a week to be excessive, with mental illness quite possible as a complication. . . . [The man] with the masturbatory history of two or three times a day wondered whether five or six times a day wasn't excessive and might lead to a 'case of nerves.' No study subject among the 321 questioned in depth expressed the slightest fear that his particular masturbatory pattern was excessive. . . . Certainly there is no accepted medical standard defining excessive masturbation."

masturbation is by far the most difficult topic for adolescents to discuss: "It remains taboo and shameful even though young people can talk about other typical and even atypical sexual activity."

For some people, guilt rises from a religious belief that masturbation is a sin. But probably many more feel vague discomfort they cannot explain, probably rising from early psychological and social influences. A child learns early from parents and society that genital play is shameful, even punishable; if the child continues in secret, he or she worries whether it is damaging and feels further fear and guilt. Also, children's masturbation fantasies may involve forbidden and fearsome feelings and ideas, such as incest, rage, dominance, submission, and punishment (including castration). Guilt over these fantasies may become inseparable from guilt over masturbation.

At puberty, as sexual interest and activity quicken, masturbation often involves fantasies about orgies, harems, enslavement, torture. As in early childhood, such fantasies add to guilt. Also, physical change at puberty brings concern about new, uncontrollable events such as ejaculation and menstruation; some adolescents associate semen with pus or milk, menstrual blood with injury, and relate these ideas to genital acts (Gadpaille, 1975). In fact, at all times in life, sexual activity may be a vehicle for a wide range of emotions, which become mentally entwined with behavior. If people use masturbation to relieve or distract themselves from anxiety, the emotional conflict behind that anxiety may enshroud autoeroticism.

Throughout early life, then, frightening and guilt-laden feelings and fantasies may make masturbation a source of worry and self-con-

tempt. Many young people count their orgasms and try to have fewer of them or to stop masturbating entirely—often only to fail, suffer remorse, try again, and fail again. Some fear that the expression in their eyes or the shape and color of the penis or labia can reveal that they masturbate (Oliven, 1974). Kinsey et al. learned that half the females who had ever masturbated said that at least initially they felt low self-esteem and conflict with their moral codes (1953), and some of the males (1948) lived in continual conflict and fear of discovery and disgrace.

Many people are embarrassed about admitting masturbation, even if they have no available partner; such an admission is even more difficult for the adult who does have a partner. Few married people admit solitary masturbation to each other; each fears that the other will see the act as a sign of sexual dissatisfaction. It may indeed reflect dissatisfaction, but it may also reflect other needs or merely an easy acceptance of masturbation. Some counselors and therapists recommend that couples communicate freely about masturbation, even masturbate in each other's presence. However, when partners become that comfortable with autoeroticism, they have probably already reached a high level of sexual communication, acceptance, and self-acceptance.

A growing number of experts, we have noted, believe that masturbation is a normal part of a child's discovery, acceptance, and enjoyment of his or her body; that it brings familiarity and mastery over new sexual responses and capacities; that it offers practice for sexual response with partners later in life (Gadpaille, 1975). From clinical experience and studies of non-Western societies, they infer that autoeroticism is necessary for healthy adult sexuality; limiting it, they claim, often causes guilt, conflict, sexual dysfunction, and fear of orgasmic release (Barbach, 1976). Many marriage counselors and sex therapists now suggest a variety of masturbatory techniques in treating sexual dysfunctions (LoPiccolo and Lobitz, 1978; Heiman, LoPiccolo, and LoPiccolo, 1976).

Occasionally autoeroticism does justify concern. In the rare cases where it is continual or socially inappropriate, the cause is usually severe emotional disturbance or a hormonal or neurological illness, any of which may be treatable. Many of the small proportion of adults who prefer masturbation to sex acts with partners are very shy and inhibited or have a paraphilia that does not call for a partner (for example, some kinds of fetishism and transvestism). Such problems usually call for professional help.

Children who feel bored, lonely, or anxious sometimes comfort or distract themselves by handling their genitals. This behavior may become habitual or compulsive. Their tension may result from loss of a loved person, birth of a sibling, coping with school, or conflicts in their families. If the tension passes, so may compulsive self-stimulation. The behavior may often be a greater problem to anxious adults than to the child (Gadpaille, 1975).

In later childhood and adolescence, similar pressures may produce compulsive masturbation—loneliness, conflict with parents or peers, school or social worries. Again, the problem is not masturbation but the conflicts that make it guilt-laden or pleasureless. As Warren Johnson (1968) has put it, "if an individual is watching television too much because this represents relief from pressures or because there are no other satisfactions available in life, then the problem is obviously not his addiction to television but the pressures or the absence of other satisfactions."

Whether any amount of masturbation should cause concern remains a judgment for which no rules exist. We suggest that the important factor is usually the emotions that motivate, accompany, or follow the act—anxiety, shame, defiance, guilt, instead of pleasure and satisfaction. If the source of conflict is fear of masturbation's effects, the answer is simple, if difficult to accept at once: evidence abounds that there is no need to worry. If one is convinced that a given person's masturbation involves emotional conflicts, it is a matter for thought, discussion, and perhaps professional consultation.

Fantasy

A *fantasy* is an imagined scene or event. The ability to infuse sexuality with imagined stimuli and goals is one of the most important influences on human sexuality. Sexual fantasies probably occur to some extent in virtually everyone and range from fleeting images to prolonged, intricate daydreams. They may be vague or vividly detailed, pleasurable or disquieting, a major or minor part of one's sexual life.

Few things can arouse such feelings of privacy, shame, and anxiety as sexual fantasies. This is especially true of fantasies that accompany masturbation. About 70 percent of males and 50 percent of females who masturbate almost always fantasize while doing so (Kinsey et al., 1948, 1953). Some masturbatory fantasies

Figure 9-4 / *Erotic fantasy is highly individual, but for many men (left) it focuses on acts and partners desired, not already experienced. For many women it centers on past experience, or sometimes (right) on erotic situations with a vaguely imagined partner or partners. Besides such fantasies, often associated with arousal and masturbation, there exists in art and in life (bottom) the play of imagination on sexual themes, often as whimsical as it is erotic.*

are quite individual, even eccentric, but most are about seeing, giving, or receiving sexual pleasure. They may involve partners or situations that are imaginary or real, long past or recent or hoped for.

In sex as in other aspects of life, fantasy often rides far beyond reality, to include behavior one would never engage in because of the reactions of partners or society—rape, sexual domination, orgies, incest, homosexual acts, being a prostitute. This is not the only reason for guilt or anxiety over sexual fantasy. We noted above that masturbation may be accompanied by feelings of inadequacy, fear, or rage, and that sexual fantasy and masturbation may be used as distractions from disturbing emotions. Thus negative feelings about masturbation, sexual fantasies, and nonsexual conflicts may all tinge each other. Some people feel guilty about having fantasies about another partner during coitus; such fantasies, like ex-

travagant masturbation fantasies, are probably more common than most people care to admit.

Fantasy has been explored in depth by psychoanalysts and other researchers. It begins early in life and serves many purposes. Some fantasies provide imagined pleasures; these can be a substitute for action, a retreat from threatening situations, or fictitious triumphs over a frustrating reality. Many clinicians believe that if fantasies regularly serve such functions as psychological escape, defense, and repair, they can shape sexual desire and response—affecting anything from the type of partner to whom one is attracted to the sort of sexual activity one prefers (Rado, 1969). Robert Stoller (1975) believes that fantasy, "the vehicle of hope, healer of traumas, protector from reality, concealer of truth, fixer of identity, restorer of tranquility, enemy of fear and sadness, cleanser of the soul," also plays a major part in the formation of paraphilias (see chapter 12).

There is wide agreement that fantasies are important in the performance of paraphilias (Walker, 1978), but not everyone agrees that they are crucial to their formation (Goleman and Bush, 1977).

Sexual fantasy tends to follow different patterns in males and females. Many more females than males (31 percent compared to 16 percent) never have them (Kinsey et al., 1953); many more males than females have them often (37 percent, compared to 22 percent). In fact, some males may have difficulty reaching orgasm without help from fantasy or visual stimulation (Kinsey et al., 1948). Males also have more erotic dreams than females (W. Wilson, 1975). It is not surprising, then, that males are more often aroused by a potential partner before any relationship or physical contact occurs (Kinsey et al., 1953).

Males' and females' fantasies also tend to differ in content (Barclay, 1973). Males' are more directly sexual than romantic, more physically detailed, and usually involve being in control of a sexual encounter or being sexually desired. A male's fantasies may draw on experience, but more often they are about things he would like to do and partners he would like to have (Kinsey et al., 1948). Males with higher educations fantasize more than those with less; there is a similar but less pronounced difference among females (Kinsey et al., 1948, 1953; Masters and Johnson, 1979).

Although some females have very explicit fantasies about sex acts, they are more likely than males to fantasize about sexual relationships or situations, and with less sharp detail (Kinsey et al., 1953). Often the fantasy partner is a friend, movie star, or sports hero; sometimes it is a stranger. Most females' fantasies, unlike most males', draw on past experience; someone who hasn't gone beyond petting isn't likely to go further in her fantasies. But even many quite experienced women imagine scenes that sexually do not go as far as coitus.

Females' fantasies are more varied and individual than males', but certain themes are common (Friday, 1973; Hunt, 1974). Being loved or happily married and having a joyous sexual experience with a spouse or lover is a common fantasy (Hunt, 1974): "We finally marry after knowing each other for several years. Our honeymoon night is so exciting and romantic we try to recreate the setting repeatedly throughout our marriage." Another common theme is being abducted, dominated, degraded, prostituted (as in the film *Belle de Jour*), or raped (Hariton, 1973; Friday, 1973). In such fantasies, the female is not really harmed; she sees herself as overwhelmed or as so desirable that the male can't restrain himself. For some females, this fantasy may be a way of shedding guilt about erotic thoughts (sex occurs against their wills). Obsessive, disturbing rape fantasies may also occur at times of emotional stress (Ovesey, 1969). Another common female fantasy is nursing and caring for a desirable male; although the imagery is not sexual, she feels the situation as erotic (Barclay, 1973).

Such lack of visual genital focus in many female fantasies raises questions about sex differences and pornography. It has been argued that only cultural training prevents females from responding to the sort of pornography that excites most males. However, Kinsey et al. (1953) said that perhaps it is conditioning that makes some females respond to it as males do; males naturally respond more to visual stimuli, females to emotional or situational ones, so it is not surprising that females don't respond to the same material. Actually, the problem may be a failure to recognize male and female pornography for what they are (Stoller, 1975). Males are sexual "watchers," females much less so. Probably most females are puzzled about precisely how and why explicit pornography can arouse males. Yet males are equally puzzled about what arouses females in the romantic and vaguely (or directly) sadomasochistic themes of many films and novels—what Stoller (1975) calls "favorite-harem-of-the-sultan" and "supergirl-frustrating-droves-of-roaring-studs." Males and some females fail to call such fantasy female pornography because it is not always or primarily visual and genital.

Sexual fantasy usually need not arouse shame or anxiety. Today many sex therapists encourage cultivating sexual fantasy, especially in nonorgasmic women. We would add that although fantasy is not harmful, neither is it obligatory. Some people who experience little or no sexual fantasy are quite responsive with partners.

Overview

Masturbation is the chief orgasmic outlet of both males and females during adolescence, and for many through the college years or even later in life. Petting and masturbation are sometimes encouraged, directly or indirectly, as substitutes for coitus (I. Reiss, 1967). The effort seems successful in some cases; masturbation doesn't reduce the desire for coitus, but it often reduces the feeling of immediate need for it. Some other societies, such as the Mar-

quesas Islanders, also encourage adolescent masturbation to discourage premarital coitus (Davenport, 1965).

The major Western religions continue to condemn masturbation, on the grounds that it diverts people from reproductive sexuality and creates habits of egocentric pleasure-seeking. Today some clergymen and religious groups, like the majority of health professionals, consider masturbation normal, acceptable, or helpful to sexual development.

A moral and emotional dilemma confronts people with religious, ethical, or emotional aversions to both non-marital coitus and masturbation. They must choose between two evils or remain abstinent. Many schools, hospitals, prisons, and other institutions still expect abstinence of the unmarried, and often of the married. This is our society's official, or public, morality. Yet the capacity for abstinence varies, and in most people it has limits.

The situation is often complicated by the lack of a single clear sexual standard. There is a gulf between public and private standards, and attitudes vary among social, ethnic, and age groups. For instance, public values may say that masturbation is wrong, private values that it is natural among the sexually deprived and children; still, the partnerless and the young may be shamed or punished for masturbating.

Masturbation may be tolerated or approved for the young and for solitary adults, but even in most permissive societies, it is thought second-best or childish for the mature (Ford and Beach, 1951). In restrictive societies, it is condemned as immoral, unhealthful, or indulgent. In our society, the word masturbation (and its slang synonyms) are used loosely for any fruitless activity, another reflection of it being con-

169

sidered less than ideal. Perhaps masturbation will always carry such connotations to some degree.

Attitudes about autoeroticism are relaxing in our society, but they remain entwined with values about childhood sexuality, nonmarital coitus, and sexual expression in general. Too little is yet known about what masturbation means at a given time in a person's life. Studies of our own and other societies rarely tell when people masturbate or how they feel about it. The act may be a physical release almost devoid of emotion; an angry substitute for coitus, with feelings of failure and self-contempt for not winning a partner; an exquisite pleasure and a physical and emotional release; a young man's safeguard against reaching orgasm too fast with a woman a few hours later; a gesture of sexual self-affirmation by a woman raised to deny her sexuality to herself.

The majority of people do masturbate, it does no harm, and it probably helps psychosexual development in many or most people. It certainly need not bring guilt, anxiety, and suffering. A second-best aura may well continue to cling to adult autoeroticism, so it takes efforts at social and individual acceptance to balance the powerful tradition of shame and guilt.

Review, Discuss, Decide

1. Suppose a friend confided that he or she masturbated daily and was concerned about the effects. What would you think or say? Suppose it were twice a day, once a month, or never—would your response be different? Why?
2. Could you tell anyone your erotic fantasies, especially masturbation fantasies? If not, why not?
3. What were you taught, directly or indirectly, about masturbation? Consider attitudes and nonverbal communication as well as words and books. By parents? Friends? Others?
4. What are the differences between masturbation by males and females in occurrence and frequency? In techniques?
5. What understanding or misunderstanding can exist between the sexes because of these differences?
6. How do educational level, devoutness, and other social factors influence masturbation?
7. What generalizations can be made about male and female sexual fantasies?

10

Early Genital Behavior

At what age can children first feel sexual excitement? Can young children have orgasms?

How much sex play is normal in children?

Are boys' and girls' sexual activities similar in infancy and childhood?

What are the effects of childhood genital exploration and play?

Should parents allow their children to engage in sexual play?

How might my early sexual experience or lack of it have influenced my life?

Western tradition has long put sexual awakening at puberty. Many people still believe children are "innocent," and that sexual knowledge and activity can lead them to harmful excess. In 1905, Freud's *Three Essays* (1962) (see chapter 7) contained a section headed "Infantile Sexuality," which said that erotic feeling and acts are normal from birth onward. It is difficult now to imagine how revolutionary this was, and the rage and resistance it provoked in scientists and laymen alike. But in our time of greater frankness, the subject still creates anxiety and controversy, and children's genital behavior may still be called delinquent, sick, or just bad. Even many permissive parents do not actively prepare their children for adult sexual-

ity, assuming that they will have somehow learned when the time comes or will "do what comes naturally." Scientists have great difficulty doing research on what children know about sex, let alone their behavior. The evidence we do have suggests that erotic response exists from very early life, although erotic behavior does not develop the same way for everyone.

From Infancy to Puberty

Infancy

Most boys and girls show genital feelings and behavior in infancy or even earlier. Penile erections occur in the womb. From the day of birth, boys may have erections at times of excitement, frustration, hunger, sleep, urination, and bowel movements, and perhaps by reflex (Martinson, 1973). These last from half a minute to an hour and often appear pleasurable.

Freud thought the first year of life a time of oral eroticism, and that there is a sexual element in suckling and thumb sucking. Some oral behavior does indeed involve erection and rhythmic body movements leading to orgasm, and after nursing, male infants show a relaxation similar to that which follows sexual satisfaction (Newton and Newton, 1967). It now seems most accurate to say that much oral behavior is inseparable from sex and affection, and that all three are entwined in psychosexual development.

It has been said that because the penis is exposed to stimulation by clothes and washing, and in some societies to stroking by adults to quiet fretfulness, boys experience more early arousal than girls. This seems likely, but infant girls also receive sexual stimuli. For weeks after birth, their genitals may remain swollen by traces of maternal estrogen and progesterone; this may cause local sensations (Gadpaille, 1975). When parents bathe little girls, they often do (and should) clean between the labia, which may be erotically pleasing.

Orgasm can occur in both sexes as early as one month of age (Kinsey et al., 1953). We do not know why this happens in some infants and not in others. Perhaps infants' genetic and hormonal thresholds of arousal vary; parental care and handling doubtless have effects. And once erotic response does occur, it may cause a child to seek further pleasure.

As soon as infants can control their hands, they squeeze and rub every part of the body, exploring shape and sensation. Boys first touch the scrotum often, then become more interested in the penis. Many girls try inserting a finger in the vagina, but eventually most find the mons or clitoris a source of greater pleasure (Gadpaille, 1975). Thereafter, many rub the penis or vulva against a pillow, a toy, the edge of a crib, or an adult's body; some clearly reach orgasm by self-manipulation or by rhythmically rocking the body. Infants rarely seem to have erotic intent in handling their genitals until about the tenth month, but from then until age three, masturbation to orgasm occurs in a significant minority of children (Kinsey et al., 1948, 1953).

Sometimes children rock and stimulate themselves when tense, frustrated, or withdrawn, as a distraction from inner discomfort or a painful environment. However, genital play sometimes reflects not tension or unhappiness but contentment. Infants with good maternal relationships show more genital play than those in orphanages and institutions (Spitz, 1965). Infants also show hugging, pelvic thrusting, and other attachment and erotic behaviors, especially when they feel secure (Lewis, 1965).

Clearly many sexual and attachment behav-

Oral Sexuality

In the late nineteenth century, a Hungarian pediatrician named S. Lindner (Kern, 1973) wrote that the sucking impulse is universal and can lead to "delirious sucking," creating "voluptuous points in erotic life." An illustration showed a little girl sucking her thumb while masturbating. Freud had heard of Lindner's work when he put forward the ideas of childhood sexuality and oral eroticism. Sucking is indeed instinctive, and recent research confirms that it is often accompanied by vaginal contractions in infant girls and erection and pelvic thrusting in boys.

---

iors develop in concert throughout infancy. We know that primates, and very probably humans, may not reach normal sexual maturity if these early behaviors are stunted (Bowlby, 1969; Harlow, 1974). Therefore many researchers consider genital play a necessary part of early development.

Toddlers: The Age of Exploration

At one and a half to two, when children become mobile toddlers, their coordination and mental capacity grow; so does their fascination with their own and others' bodies. Unless adults prevent it, they leave their genitals exposed. They want to examine other children and adults, ask questions, touch, compare. These explorations may be genital, oral, and anal.

At three and four, sexual identity is usually set (see chapter 7), and sexual curiosity sharpens. Children ask where babies come from and why the sexes are different. With more understanding of sex pleasures and greater sensory and motor capacities, they increase their genital activity. They share their fascination with the rise and fall of erection and how objects can disappear into the vagina and rectum. Boys inspect each other and compete at who can urinate farthest. Girls have far less social sexual play, but some do get together to insert fingers or objects in their vaginas. Boys and girls play "house" and "doctor"—games apparently reinvented by each generation.

The upsurge of genital play around ages four to six sometimes reflects a search for pleasure rather than curiosity, especially if children are sexually stimulated or taught by adults or older children. Now sexual fantasies may ac-company masturbation; these fantasies often involve parents and other adults. Nevertheless, show-and-tell remains commoner than sustained effort at orgasm. By age five, about one-tenth of boys and one-twentieth of girls have experienced orgasm (Kinsey et al., 1948, 1953).

More sexual play occurs from two to five than most adults remember (Kinsey et al., 1948). Some of this is incidental to other play and quickly forgotten. Some is *repressed,* or stricken from conscious memory, because of anxiety or guilt. Having forgotten some of their own past, adults may consider normal sexual play excessive or fail to distinguish eroticism from exploration.

Parental Influence and Restrictions

Only a few generations ago, many parents punished and terrified children for any genital behavior (see chapter 9), verbally or nonverbally teaching that it is harmful, sinful, or shameful. Today fewer parents tell children that they are wicked or making themselves sick, but few fully shed the anxiety over childhood sexuality which they themselves learned early in life. Some feel they know better than to inhibit early eroticism, but fear encouraging it; they send subtle signals of sexual avoidance that contradict their declared attitudes. And truly permissive parents realistically fear the reactions of neighbors and society at large.

Also, many people attribute adult motives to children's behavior. Some toddlers take coital positions without fully understanding their meaning to adults (Bowlby, 1969); parents may react as if the children did understand. When two children of the same sex explore each other's genitals, a parent may be horrified at their "homosexual" play, though the children were curious rather than aroused.

When infants touch their genitals, many mothers automatically push their hands away (Sears, Maccoby, and Levin, 1957). When preschoolers do so, parents may express discomfort through body language—facial expression, tone of voice, or tense awkwardness in handling the child. Some parents try to shield their children from all sexual information and stimuli; they give boys and girls separate rooms and reprove all "immodest" behavior. They teach by example when they conceal their own bodies and speak vaguely of genitals as "it" or "there," and many consciously or unconsciously avoid touching their children's erogenous areas, even avoiding hugging.

Some parents send contradictory messages. A mother may gently fondle a child's genitals when bathing him, yet slap his hands when he does so himself. Or when the child touches himself or the mother, she may suggest another activity. Even more subtly confusing messages come from many parents who intend to be permissive; when the child touches his genitals, they avoid looking or mentioning it. The child is left to wonder, "Why don't they look or talk to me when I touch it?" Certainly they don't smile approvingly, as when he touches or names other parts of his body. Without conceptualizing the message, the child receives it: sexuality somehow brings loss of attention, approval, and perhaps love.

It is widely assumed that such strictures are stronger for girls, but several studies in the United States and England reveal that both sexes are equally forbidden nudity, masturbation, and sexual play in early childhood (Maccoby and Jacklin, 1974). The double standard seems not to appear until late preadolescence, when much crucial sexual development has already occurred.

Psychological and cross-cultural research suggests that strict sexual prohibitions create deep and lasting guilt. Such taboos probably prevent many people—especially women, whose less urgent drive is apparently more easily influenced by social pressures—from accepting sex even in marriage (Kinsey et al., 1953; Masters and Johnson, 1970). Societies that tolerate or encourage children's sexual interest and activity seem to suffer less impotence, anorgasmia, and other sexual dysfunctions than restrictive societies (Ford and Beach, 1951; Marshall and Suggs, 1971; Money and Tucker, 1975).

Nevertheless, some child-development experts still disagree on how social and family nudity affects children. Some think it overstimulates them to see the bodies and genitals of other children, adults, and especially parents. Probably more agree that children are disturbed by the *primal scene* (their witnessing of parental coitus); this may cause a troubling mixture of desire, jealousy, and fear (Freud, 1953). It is often misinterpreted as well; a child may confuse the groans and clutching of coitus with violent attack. Paradoxically, the misunderstanding may be greatest if the parents have emphasized to the children the affectionate side of sex.

There are indeed children with disturbing memories of witnessing adult genitals, nudity, and coitus, but there is no evidence that this is true of all or even most children (Gadpaille, 1975). Their curiosity is satisfied in permissive societies, where they see nudity and even parental coitus from infancy on, without apparent damage (Ford and Beach, 1951). However, in our relatively restrictive society, some self-consciousness and ambivalence are almost inevitable in all but the most permissive parents. The effects of nudity, of exposure to adult sexuality, and of childhood sexual behavior may depend as much on parents' and others' ease or discomfort as on the behavior itself.

Preadolescence

Argument continues about the Oedipus complex and latency period and their role in preadolescent sexual behavior (see chapter 7). Most children's sexual interest and behavior increase around ages four to seven; very many

Figure 10-1 / *Many children engage in sexual comparisons and exploration. Usually the motive is as much curiosity as pleasure, though a minority engage in sustained sex play.*

reveal fantasies about the parent of the opposite sex, ranging from vague infatuation—"I want to marry Mommy or Daddy when I grow up"—to strong, specific sexual desire (Oliven, 1974). Such feelings tend to cause conflict and guilt and may be a cause of sexual amnesia— people remembering erection, clitoral sensation, or erotic desire as having first occurred at seven or ten, though these are very common far earlier (Freud, 1953; Martinson, 1973). Almost 60 percent of men remember preadolescent heterosexual play, but 70 percent of boys do (Kinsey et al., 1948).

The idea of the latency period has fared poorly (Kinsey et al., 1948, 1953). Freud (1962) saw that genital activity seemed to diminish during the early school years and inferred that from then until puberty, sex drive is sublimated into intellectual and social growth. However, in permissive societies (and in most primate species), sexual expression develops through childhood and into puberty without interruption (Ford and Beach, 1951). Even in our relatively restrictive society, many preadolescent children continue genital play (Broderick, 1966; Broderick and Weaver, 1968; M. Lewis, 1965), and apparently without in any way stunting their mental and social development. Latency, to the extent that it exists, is now widely considered a product of social restrictiveness, not a natural phase of development.

However, there is a phase of development that bears on prepubertal sex behavior in humans everywhere, and in their evolutionary ancestors. As many higher social animals become independent of their mothers, they form same-sex play groups and show sporadic but increasingly frequent sexual play within and outside those groups (Tiger, 1969). Although some preadolescents have brief heterosexual crushes, most feel their greatest affections outside the family for same-sex buddies and best friends. These same-sex peer bonds seem crucial to sexual development (see pages 111, 253). If primate juveniles fail to make bonds with their peers and play with them, sometimes sexually, they never reach normal adult sexuality (Harlow, 1974). Many clinicians believe this is also true of humans, and predict psychosexual problems for the child who is a loner or plays mostly with children of the other sex (Bieber et al., 1962; Green, 1974; Sullivan, 1968).

Boys' Sex Behavior. Kinsey et al. (1948) estimated that almost all boys engage in genital play at some time; it is greatest from age eight to puberty. Until about age nine, much of this play is exploratory or results from talk about anatomy and reproduction—"What does it look like?" and "How do babies get born?" This is a search for the education most parents avoid giving their children.

Pairs and groups of preadolescents may explore, touch, or masturbate themselves or each other. Less commonly, they try oral, anal, and other kinds of sexual play. Their playful or earnest attempts at coitus sometimes succeed, but many result only in *genital apposition,* pressing or rubbing the genitals together while clothed or unclothed. Some children, especially boys, attempt sex acts with farm animals or domestic pets.

The predominance of same-sex friendships and play makes much of this sex behavior homosexual in a literal sense, but usually it involves little or no homosexual arousal. Some 40 to 60 percent of boys experience some same-sex erotic activity. Their commonest act is ex-

Figure 10-2 / *In preadolescence and early adolescence, many pairs and groups of boys compare their genitalia and play, sometimes competitively, at masturbatory games. For the majority this is one of many kinds of group play rather than an expression of homoeroticism.*

posing and comparing their genitals. Next most common is group and mutual masturbation, which half to two-thirds of boys have done by age eleven (Kinsey et al., 1948; Ramsey, 1943b).

It is a common misconception that many boys are initiated to homosexual or heterosexual acts by adults. Usually sexual play occurs first with age mates. Though many boys finger their genitals frequently, the great majority do not discover masturbation entirely on their own. They see friends masturbate or are told or taught how to reach orgasm by older males—or in some cases, by older females. As puberty approaches, more boys masturbate themselves or each other in groups (the "circle jerk" of summer camps and junior high school). Some are goaded by curiosity, competitiveness, or by fear of being thought a sissy or chicken. Far fewer boys attempt oral-genital acts; by preadolescence most already sense that this is socially taboo. A small number try anal intercourse, but usually they fail and end up performing *interfemoral intercourse*, thrusting the penis between another's thighs.

177

Figure 10-3 / *In late preadolescence and early adolescence, many girls are deeply preoccupied with the changes in their bodies and physical functions.*

Such male-male behavior begins, on the average, early in the ninth year. For most boys it does not lead to adult homosexual behavior; in fact, many adult homosexuals recall no same-sex acts in childhood. Parents should not brand occasional sexual play with other boys as perverted or as homosexual in the adult sense (Gadpaille, 1975).

About 40 percent of boys recall preadolescent heterosexual play, but this number reflects sexual amnesia, and the true figure is almost surely higher (Kinsey et al., 1948). Much of this behavior is only sexual exhibition, but for four-fifths of these boys it leads to touching or manipulating a girl's genitals, and in half to inserting fingers or small objects into the vagina. Oral-genital acts are likely only if the boy is taught by a grown woman.

In late preadolescence, one-fourth of heterosexually active boys have attempted coitus, and many have succeeded. There are striking differences between boys from different social classes. Three times as many from lower social levels try coitus, far more succeed, and they have more partners. In part, this may be because they receive more sexual information from older boys and men and have more experience with older girls.

Girls' Sex Behavior. Young girls' genital behavior is quite different. Only half (Kinsey et al., 1953) recall any sexual play with others before puberty, and only one-fifth remember genital play (although, again, the real figures are almost surely higher). For many of those girls, sexual play is limited to one or a few acts

---

A Boy's Puberty

K.B. must have been real shy when he came to Wiltwyck, because he used to beg me to tell him about the girls I knew. Late at night when I was sleepy and tired of lying all day and half the night, I would listen to K.B. tell me about Linda. For the six months that my bed was next to K.B.'s, I went to sleep hearing about Linda. After a week of hearing about Linda, I had to meet her just to see if she was as fine as K.B. said she was. K.B. said she was real dark skinned, had long hair, wore lipstick, had "titties, little ones, but tits just the same," had a pretty face, and was real fresh. K.B. said he had done it to her one time up on the roof, and he used to tell me about it so much and in so many different ways that it had to be a lie.

Most of the time, K.B. couldn't think about anything but girls, and anybody who could tell him a good lie about girls could get him to do things. Sometimes when I wanted K.B. to help me steal something, I would have to promise to tell him about a real pretty, real fresh girl. K.B. was always trying to jerk off, and he said he shot one time; but I didn't see it, so I didn't believe it. But about a year after K.B. and I had moved to Aggrey House, I heard K.B. come tearing down the stairs yelling as loud as he could. It was around one in the morning. He woke everybody in the first-floor dormitory. I was awake and wondering what was going on, when K.B. came running into the dormitory with his dick in his hand and yelling, "Claude, I did it! I did it!" When he

reached my bed and yelled out, "Man, I shot," all the beds in the dormitory started jumping, and everybody crowded around my bed with flashlights before K.B. stopped yelling.

Some guys just said things like "Wow" or "Oh, shit," but Rickets said, "Man, that's the real stuff."

Horse said, "Man, that ain't nothin' but dog water."

K.B. said, "That ain't no dog water, man, 'cause it's slimy."

Horse, who was always talking about facts, said, "Man, that can't be scum, 'cause scum is white."

Knowing that scum was white, most of the guys said that Horse was right and that it was just dog water. I said that dog water was more than he ever made. Horse went heading for the bathroom saying he was going to show me what the real stuff looked like. Everybody followed Horse and watched and cheered him on while he tried for the real stuff. Horse only made dog water, just like K.B., but nobody paid much attention—everybody was trying to jerk off that night. It was a matter of life and death. After what seemed like hours of trying and wearing out my arm, I shot for the first time in my life. A lot of other guys did it for the first time too, but some cats just got tired arms.

—Claude Brown, *Manchild in the Promised Land* (1971)

of genital exhibition. Half the girls who try this go on to handling the male genitals. Vaginal insertions are made by about a fifth of the sexually active girls, usually in play with other girls rather than with boys. Few perform oral-genital acts. Seventeen percent attempt coitus, but many, for lack of knowledge or persistence, achieve only genital apposition.

Most girls who reach orgasm by twelve do so by masturbating, not through sexual play with partners. A little more than one-tenth of girls masturbate before age twelve, the major-ity by fingering the clitoris but many by rhythmic rocking. The great majority learn to masturbate on their own, without the help or example of other girls or elders.

Only one-third of girls (compared to one-half of boys) engage in same-sex erotic play before puberty, and most of that is mutual exhibition. For two-thirds of them, exhibition leads to genital play, and for one-fifth to vaginal insertions. Most girls feel little or no arousal during this "homosexual" play, only curiosity.

One girl in three engages in heterosexual

A Girl's Puberty

Yesterday I read an article about blushing by Sis Heyster. This article might have been addressed to me personally. Although I don't blush very easily, the other things in it certainly all fit me . . . [including the statement] that a girl in the years of puberty becomes quiet within and begins to think about the wonders that are happening to her body.

I experience that, too, and that is why I get the feeling lately of being embarrassed about Margot, Mummy, and Daddy. Funnily enough, Margot, who is much more shy than I am, isn't at all embarrassed.

I think what is happening to me is so wonderful, and not only what can be seen on my body, but all that is taking place inside. I never discuss myself or any of these things with anybody; that is why I have to talk to myself about them.

Each time I have a period—and that has only been three times—I have the feeling that in spite of all the pain, unpleasantness, and nastiness, I have a sweet secret, and that is why, although it is nothing but a nuisance to me in a way, I always long for the time that I shall feel that secret within me again.

Sis Heyster also writes that girls of this age don't feel quite certain of themselves, and discover that they themselves are individuals with ideas, thoughts, and habits. After I came here, when I was just fourteen, I began to think about myself sooner than most girls, and to know that I am a "person." Sometimes, when I lie in bed at night, I have a terrible desire to feel my breasts and to listen to the quiet rhythmic beat of my heart.

I already had these kinds of feelings subconsciously before I came here, because I remember that once when I slept with a girl friend I had a strong desire to kiss her, and that I did do so. I could not help being terribly inquisitive over her body, for she had always kept it hidden from me. I asked her whether, as a proof of our friendship, we should feel one another's breasts, but she refused. I go into ecstacies every time I see the naked figure of a woman, such as Venus, for example. It strikes me as so wonderful and exquisite that I have difficulty in stopping the tears rolling down my cheeks.

If only I had a girl friend!

—Anne Frank, *The Diary of a Young Girl* (1944)

play before age twelve, compared to 40 percent or more of boys. Most of these have only one or a few experiences, and only one-third go farther than sexual exhibition. Only half of these girls try genital manipulation with boys; it is far more often exploratory than masturbatory. Oral-genital contact and vaginal insertion when playing with boys are uncommon. For every heterosexually active girl in preadolescence, there are seven boys. Kinsey et al. (1953) inferred that girls who are sexually active then must have many male partners, perhaps because some are admitted to groups of boys.

In summary, 30 percent of girls try sexual play with boys, 33 percent with other girls, and 15 percent with both. All these figures are lower than those for boys. In late preadolescence, boys' and girls' behavior become increasingly different. There is probably a biosocial basis for this, since in many societies and in our close evolutionary relatives, juvenile males outstrip females in aggressiveness and genital play. As Harlow (1974) puts it, "human males not only display more of everything than females, but also meander to maturity through masturbatory marvels. Males in our society have obviously written their own sexual development script by hand."

This male-female difference, however, is much greater in sexually restrictive societies. Where social controls do not interfere, both girls and boys show unbroken development from infantile self-discovery through juvenile experimentation to adult sexuality, with males always more active than females, but not as much as in restrictive cultures (Ford and Beach, 1951). In our society, girls more than boys are taught to curb or deny sexual interests

and activity when puberty arrives—to conceal their bodies, not arouse boys, not feel aroused themselves, and avoid or even fear body contact with males.

Puberty and Adolescence

Our society's sexual messages to young adolescents are complex and contradictory. Boys are told by parents to curb their sexuality, but by peers to score; girls are told by parents to be modest, yet by peers to be popular and sexy—but not too sexy. The restrictive message does not affect boys' behavior as much as it does girls'—probably because of boys' greater drive for orgasmic release. While boys' genital activity keeps increasing, there is a dramatic break in girls'.

Two-thirds of all boys with genital experience continue sexual play without a break through late preadolescence and puberty; only 13 percent of girls with experience do so. Half of all boys with coital experience continue, compared to about one girl in twenty. Eight percent of women recall having engaged in heterosexual play at age five through seven, but only 3 percent recall doing so just before adolescence, compared to one-fifth of boys.

The strength of cultural influences on early sexual behavior also shows in the great differences among social levels (Kinsey et al., 1948, 1953). Blue-collar boys are more likely than white-collar boys to continue all sexual activities from childhood into their teens. For instance, about three-fourths of blue-collar boys who have coitus before adolescence continue into their teens; only one-fifth of white-collar boys do so. For girls the reverse is true. Fewer blue-collar than white-collar girls engage in sexual play with others in preadolescence, and they are less likely to continue into adolescence. Blue-collar girls are more closely monitored by parents and peers.

Kinsey et al. (1953) found that the differences between the sexes seen in preadolescence widen during adolescence. Most recent research confirms this. For instance, a study of several hundred teenagers (Offer, 1969; Offer and Offer, 1975; Offer and Simon, 1975) found no significant change since the Kinsey reports. Others (Simon, Berger, and Gagnon, 1972; Sorenson, 1973) confirm that adolescent coital behavior has not substantially changed.

Figure 10-4 / *Percent of boys and girls who are sexually active before adolescence and continue to be during adolescence. There is a striking break in activity for most girls, but for most boys there is not.*

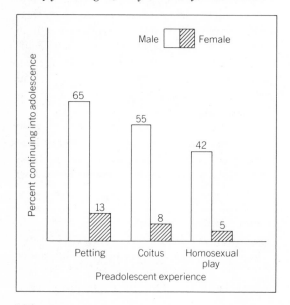

W. Wilson's (1975) study of 2,500 adults reports (adjusting for some methodological differences) that coitus is now starting slightly earlier, but adolescent attitudes and other sexual behaviors are quite similar to those reported decades earlier. Hunt's (1974) data differ somewhat, showing an earlier beginning for many sexual behaviors, but Hunt used different methods and may draw on a different sort of population. This lack of change may seem surprising in the light of so much talk of sexual revolution, but recall that there are often great gaps between what people do, what they say, and what they think (V. Elias, 1978).

This is not to say that adolescent sex behavior has not changed since Kinsey's time. Petting now begins earlier (see chapter 11). A recent study of more than 10,000 women in Hawaii showed that the mean age of first coitus had dropped over many years from the early twenties to eighteen (Diamond, unpublished). And some writers (Libby, 1977b) think recent changes in attitudes indicate changed behavior, chiefly females' greater willingness to experiment with and enjoy their sexuality. We ourselves suspect that somewhat more people engage in sexual activities a little earlier, but that the change is slow rather than dramatic.

Sexual Contact with Adults

Probably virtually all societies discourage or forbid extensive sexual play between adults and small children. However, the allowable age varies; in some permissive societies, it is in preadolescence. And despite formal strictures, there are records of adult-child sexuality through Western history.

One woman in four recalls being approached

sexually in childhood by someone at least five years older than herself (Kinsey et al., 1953). Usually it was a verbal approach or genital exhibition; one-fifth of the incidents involved genital fondling, and only 3 percent involved coitus. Some of the girls were four or five, but most were ten or older. Only one-fifth of the girls had contact more than once, and only about 5 percent more than ten times, many because they collaborated in or invited sexual play.

Parents tend to think of child "molesters" as violent strangers. Actually, cajoling and bribes are far commoner than threats and force, and half the adults who have sexual contact with children are parents' friends, neighbors, or relatives living in the home (Gebhard et al., 1965). (Sexual contact with relatives is dis-

cussed in chapter 12.) It is also with such people that sexual play is likely to continue. Even some children initially forced into sexual activity soon collaborate because of the pleasure, attention, or affection they receive. Also, as we noted, coitus is uncommon; even among men convicted of sex offenses against children, only 6 percent attempt coitus, and only 2 percent succeed (Gebhard et al., 1965).

There are no comparable figures about boys, but sometimes baby sitters, adolescent neighbors, older female relatives, and domestic employees stimulate and instruct them in sex. Kinsey et al. (1948) suspected that homosexual contacts with adults are commoner than heterosexual ones. However, he did find that some boys (many more from blue- than white-collar backgrounds) begin coitus with help from older

---

Sex with Adults

Many of the ancient Greeks and Romans used child prostitutes and concubines. Brothels full of boys and girls have been described during the past 150 years from London to India—Lawrence Durrell's *Alexandria Quartet* describes one in Cairo in the 1930s. They may still exist in some impoverished nations. In recent centuries, many children's sexual contact with adults has been at home, especially with servants and nursemaids. Lloyd De Mause writes (1974):

"Sexual use of children after the eighteenth century was widespread among servants and other adults and adolescents. Cardinal Bernis, remembering being sexually molested as a child, warned that chambermaids and 'even young ladies brought up in the chateaux dare with a child that which they would be ashamed to risk with a young man.' A German doctor said nursemaids and servants carried out 'all sorts of sexual acts' on children 'for fun.' Even Freud said he was seduced by his nurse when he was two. . . . When one learns that as late as 1900 there were still people who believed venereal disease could be cured by sexual intercourse with children, one begins to recognize the dimensions of the problem more fully."

---

females. Adults may consider them lucky rather than victims, feeling that males should learn about and experience sex despite formal sanctions against it. People worry much more that genital experience will cause girls physical, emotional, or moral damage, and perhaps affect later sexual and marital life. Actually, little is known about the effects of sex acts between children and adults.

Kinsey et al. (1953) found that women who, as children, had had sexual contact with adults had variously been interested, pleased, or frightened; about 80 percent were upset at the time, but only a small number seemed seriously disturbed as adults. Some follow-ups show few or no ill effects for a large majority of females (Bender and Blau, 1937; Bender and Grugett, 1952; Rasmussen, 1943). Many experts now believe that the hysteria and cross-examinations of parents and authorities can disturb a child far more than the flash of an exhibitionist or some incidents of touching or fondling (Gebhard et al., 1965).

Such conclusions surprise many people; perhaps they forget that genital acts may not greatly startle a child, may satisfy his or her curiosity, may even be sought after. Kinsey et al. (1953) noted that "The contacts had often involved considerable affection, and some of the older females in the sample felt that their pre-adolescent experience had contributed favorably to their later socio-sexual development."

Sometimes, however, sexual contact with adults is clearly disturbing or damaging (Bender and Grugett, 1952). The child may feel guilty, and an adult's sustained, intense orgasm-seeking may upset a preschooler or preadolescent. Furthermore, child-adult relations are so strictly taboo in our society that many of the adults may be psychologically disturbed. Even if the child cooperates, the adult's power and authority make that less than full consent. Since one cannot predict which children will be damaged, society holds the adult responsible for risking the child's well being. The legal age of sexual consent is sixteen or older in most states, although lowering it has often been suggested (MacNamara and Sagarin, 1977).

The Cross-Cultural View

In all societies, children learn some sexual restraints, such as the incest taboo and the etiquette of avoiding genital exposure. In permissive cultures, limits are relatively few, and children's sexual behavior resembles most primates'. Infants and preschoolers explore their own and each others' bodies. Then curiosity leads to action; they try masturbatory play alone and with other children of both sexes. Older children and adults give sexual instruction deliberately or by example. Finally, imitations of and attempts at coitus lead to adult sex behavior. During puberty, most children begin to make coitus their primary genital activity. Many researchers (Ford and Beach, 1951) believe this pattern of development is grounded in our biosocial nature.

The term permissive implies consent or toleration, but many societies actively encourage sexual expression. Among the Hopi Indians and the Alorese Islanders of the Pacific, mothers fondle infants' genitals during suckling and at other times, to soothe or give them pleasure; there are also verbal reports of this among some rural poor in the United States. Some societies allow children to go naked, publicly masturbate and engage in sexual play with other children, observe adult sexual behavior, and join adult discussions of sex. Children in the Trobriand Islands traditionally began coitus as young as ten, and it has been reported that the Ila-speaking people of Africa have no virgins older than that (Ford and Beach, 1951). In some societies, sexual play becomes private as childhood progresses, but more as a matter of etiquette than of morality or health.

Some societies even consider early genital play essential to health and development. The Chewa of Africa think genitally inactive children won't become fertile adults. The Lepcha of India believe girls won't mature without coitus; they engage in it regularly at eleven or earlier, sometimes with older males (Ford and Beach, 1951). Some societies permit coitus between late-preadolescents and adults; others disapprove only mildly, chiefly because they think it shows the adult couldn't attract an adult partner (Gebhard et al., 1965).

The Marquesans of Polynesia (Suggs, 1966) start preparing children for adult sexuality in infancy. A few weeks after birth, a girl's mother begins giving her vagina herbal medication to increase muscle tone and suppress odor, and she massages the mons veneris to give it a flat appearance—all qualities prized in women. By three, boys have learned to masturbate by watching older boys; female masturbation occurs but is one of the few secretive sex acts among Marquesans. Children sleep beside their parents, who try to conceal coitus only when their offspring reach seven or eight.

By then, of course, the children are quite knowledgeable. Boys and girls are playing mother and father, with genital apposition and much giggling. The boys, who form loosely knit gangs, gather in the bush for masturbation contests to see who can reach orgasm first; sometimes there is mutual masturbation. Preadolescent sexual play is surreptitious, but only because children are now expected to understand that sex is a more or less private activity. In precolonial days, Marquesan children probably began coitus at ten or eleven, some perhaps earlier. Today it starts in the early teens.

Restrictive societies fear that early genital activity harms body, mind, or both (see chapter 9), and some that it violates morality. They try to keep children away from sexual knowledge and stimulation. In the Caroline Islands, as in much of the West, sex is not discussed in children's presence. If a Kwoma woman of New Guinea sees a little boy with an erection, she beats him on the penis with a stick. Chiricahua Indian children are whipped if caught at genital play. Some young Westerners are still told babies are brought by the stork, a hospital, or God; the Chagga of East Africa say they come from the forest (Ford and Beach, 1951). The restrictive parents of rural Ireland (Messenger, 1971) conceal their own and their children's genitals, treat defecation and urination as shameful, and even whip household pets for setting bad examples by licking their genitals (some American parents do this to dogs that mount and thrust). Boys and girls are kept separate as much as possible, and their play with both sexes may be monitored. Most societies that, like ours, discourage childhood sexual play also try to prevent premarital coitus.

Despite these efforts, many or most children engage in some genital play, even in very restrictive societies. But in restrictive cultures they do it less, keep it secret, and feel shame

185

and guilt. This remains true to some degree for most Americans.

Many cultures, subcultures, and families don't fall neatly into the category restrictive or permissive. Some set restraints but enforce them weakly; the Alorese, and some Americans, object to older children's genital play but may not punish those who do it in private. Some make a strong distinction between the sexually mature and immature; in the Caroline Islands, girls are strictly forbidden coitus before puberty but enjoy great sexual freedom afterward (Ford and Beach, 1951).

The West has had a double standard; attitudes toward boys' genital behavior have varied, but maturing girls have been trained to be modest or even prudish, to fear and avoid genital activity, even to consider it merely a marital duty. This remains true in much of the West and in many non-Western societies as well (Rainwater, 1971). Where girls and boys are unequally restricted, it is usually boys who have greater freedom (Ford and Beach, 1951).

Values and Childrearing

Basic sexual attitudes and behavior patterns are molded during the first decade of life, and they affect adult sexuality. During the past century, much of the West has been less firm in its traditional restrictiveness. Some experts on childrearing believe that further change is needed; they point out that permissive societies show fewer sexual dysfunctions (Gadpaille, in press). Clinical and cross-cultural evidence seem to favor some easing of our restrictions on genital behavior in childhood, when crucial psychosexual development occurs.

But abrupt changes in childrearing are unlikely. Even people with permissive intentions retain some of the restraints of their own upbringing, if only in vague or rationalized forms. They subtly or openly transmit these to their children. And regardless of their liberalism or conservatism, most parents want to prohibit or limit premarital genital activity (Libby and Nass, 1971). Furthermore, a child raised in a permissive home will eventually face conflict with values outside the home. But greater sexual fulfillment is increasingly sought in our society, and early-life restrictions may ease somewhat in decades to come.

Overview

For many people, genital activity that can lead to orgasm starts in the crib. There is a rather predictable progression of sex behavior through childhood and adolescence. The incidence and frequency of sex behavior increase; in many cultures and in different levels of our society, this increase is dramatically different for boys and girls. Findings from anthropology, sociology, and ethology agree that these male-female differences probably reflect a biological tendency modified by social influences.

It is widely said now that childhood play is rehearsal for adult activities. We believe that besides satisfying curiosity and bringing pleasure, early genital play may well serve such a function. But exploring oneself and others and engaging in sexual play have other functions as well. In infancy and childhood, they probably foster a positive acceptance of one's physical and emotional self and of physical intimacy (Bowlby, 1969). In puberty and adolescence, they are probably necessary ways for boys and girls to learn to trust each other, be intimate, and find pleasure in each other (Sorenson, 1973; Adler, 1978).

Parents, in deciding how to raise their children, must consider that early genital behavior lays a foundation for adult genital behavior, and perhaps for broader psychological and social development. They must also face the conflict between this and traditional restrictiveness.

Review, Discuss, Decide

1. How do you view your own childhood genital behavior? How does it match what researchers have reported?
2. Can you recall how you felt about various sex behaviors, feelings, and fantasies as a child? How do you feel about them now?
3. What are the main similarities and differences in boys' and girls' sex behavior in the few years before adolescence? In early adolescence?
4. Would you raise children as you were raised? Differently? How and why?
5. Might boys' and girls' early genital behavior, or lack of it, affect their sexuality later in life? How?
6. Would you vote to lower or raise the age of consent for sexual activities? To what age? Why?
7. Would you like to see our society become more or less permissive about early sexual behavior? Why?

11

Adult Genital Behavior

Are men's and women's sex behavior different? How?

How many men and women are still virgins when they enter college? When they leave?

How does a person's social background influence sex behavior?

Has sex behavior changed much in the past decade?

Is adultery becoming more common?

Are people who have coitus before marriage more likely to have it outside marriage?

Is adultery a common reason for divorce?

This chapter describes the most common sexual behaviors of adulthood, petting, or sex play, and coitus. Later chapters will describe in detail how these are done (chapter 15, "Sexual Techniques") and the relationships in which they often occur (chapter 14, "Relationships and Marriage"). Here we stick mostly to the basic facts of who does what with whom, how often, and under which social influences. We also look at these behaviors in biological, historical, and cross-cultural perspectives. Since our society gives so much importance to whether these acts occur before, within, or outside marriage, we will look at these distinctions and their implications for individuals and society.

Petting

From Light Petting to Foreplay

Petting ("making out") is kissing, caressing, and other erotic contact short of coitus. It ranges from brief hugging and kissing to hours of elaborate play involving the entire body. It may be done for pleasure as an end in itself, as a prelude to coitus *(foreplay),* or after coitus; in any case, it may or may not be enjoyed by both partners. Until about a decade ago, many people distinguished *light petting* (kissing and caressing without any touching of the genitals, or "necking") from *heavy petting* (caressing the girl's breasts, mutual masturbation, oral-genital play, and genital apposition). These terms are being replaced by less specific phrases such as "making out," but many young people still distinguish between petting above the waist and below the waist (Wagner, Fujita, and Pion, 1973).

Many higher species perform mutual stimulation (nuzzling, stroking, licking) before coitus. In humans, as in most species, it is usually the male who starts sexual contact and becomes more aroused and demanding (Ford and Beach, 1951). However, only humans regularly and intentionally pet to orgasm. They occasionally do so out of preference, but

Figure 11-1 / *Many recent books on sexuality and erotic techniques have encouraged women to be more active and take more initiatives in foreplay.*

usually as a substitute for coitus—because of moral or religious conviction, fear of pregnancy or of violating social sanctions, limited sexual interest, or emotional conflict and anxiety about the act or the partner.

In our society, petting is usually exploratory rather than aimed at orgasm until the early teens (Martinson, 1973). During or soon after puberty, petting tends to develop in a sequence, from kissing to deep kissing (inserting the tongue in the partner's mouth), touching

the female breast, kissing the breast, touching the female genitals, touching the male genitals, genital apposition, and perhaps oral-genital intercourse. The great majority of women allow their genitals to be touched before they reciprocate. At first, many reciprocate only if asked to; with increasing experience, more do so without being asked or take the initiative. Most women say that handling the male genitals doesn't excite them, although some enjoy it and a few experience orgasm as a result (Kinsey et al., 1953). However, most petting originates with males and is meant to excite females. Males' attempts to stretch the limits of sexual play, and females' continued if diminishing resistance, often give adolescent relationships an adversary tone that may persist in later years.

190

Extended petting without orgasm leaves many people very excited and frustrated; some females and many males masturbate as soon as possible to relieve the tension. Prolonged excitement can cause pain in the testicles ("blue balls," see page 56) or, in females, pelvic congestion (page 57).

Factors Affecting Petting

Kinsey et al. (1948) found strikingly different attitudes toward petting among young men at different social levels: "With the better educated groups, intercourse versus petting is a question of morals. For the lower level, it is a problem of understanding how a mentally normal individual can engage in such highly erotic activity as petting and still refrain from actual intercourse."

Almost 60 percent of college-educated males had petted to orgasm, but only about 30 percent with a high-school education and 15 percent with a grade-school education had. However, the frequencies at all social levels were the same, a median of three to five times a year. Petting to orgasm accounted for only 3 percent of all males' total sexual outlet and was done most in their early twenties. Petting without orgasm happened at all levels about once every few weeks.

Over 90 percent of women (Kinsey et al., 1953) had petted by age twenty-five. Less than 40 percent had ever reached orgasm that way; the median frequency was four to six times a year, for 4 to 18 percent of their total outlet—much more than for men. As in men, petting to orgasm reached its height from the middle teens to middle twenties and was progressively replaced by masturbation and coitus. The

number of women who petted didn't vary by educational level; but because more educated women married later, they petted more often and reached orgasm more often that way.

The age when girls began petting had little relationship to when they reached puberty. Boys, in contrast, began petting at or soon after the onset of puberty.

The chief restraint on women's petting was devoutness. It didn't stop many from petting or make them do it less often, but it did limit how far they went; fewer devout women petted to orgasm.

Petting began earlier among Kinsey's younger subjects. Women born before 1900 began petting at a median age of eighteen; those born two decades later started before sixteen. This reflected the rise of the dating system. As society became increasingly urban and prosperous, more people went to school through their teens and early twenties; they spent more of their sexual maturity single, perhaps away from home. Petting became most middle-class adolescents' introduction to sexual play, in a society that was increasingly middle-class (Kinsey et al., 1953). Since the Twenties, open petting and sex-revolution rhetoric, as much as increased coitus, have made many think that college students were sexually wild, even though the less educated were having coitus far more than they.

Today discussions of petting strike some people as almost quaint. Most experienced people had done extensive petting before marriage even three decades ago. Certainly sex-behavior research tends to concentrate on coitus. And in adulthood, when deciding "to" or "not to" may not always seem momentous, it is easy to smile at the passionate, uncertain gropings of adolescence. Although petting starts earlier, it remains most people's gradual education—sometimes joyful, sometimes painful—about their own and others' bodies, love, sex, and the etiquette and politics of sexual encounters. It often still involves months or years of struggle to justify erotic feelings that contradict the social sanction against early coitus. Novelists and poets have observed and interpreted adolescent sexuality with more care and accuracy than most scientists. Little in sexology tells as much about the early passage to love and sexuality as the drama of Turgenev's *First Love* (1956) or the satire of Philip Roth's *Portnoy's Complaint* (1969).

Some parents still fear that petting is the path to early coitus; others hope it will be a substitute for coitus. But many people have come to see such experience as natural and as preparation for later sexual relationships.

Petting, however, is not entirely an experience of youth. Kinsey et al. (1953) revealed that extramarital petting is rather common: "At many an upper-level social affair, at cocktail parties, at dances . . . married males may engage in such flirtations and physical contacts with other men's wives, sometimes quite openly and without being restrained by the presence of other spouses." This, they said, was done increasingly, and sometimes by people who wouldn't think of having extramarital coitus. Some felt that even the heaviest petting was not infidelity.

Oral-Genital Sexuality

Using the tongue, lips, and mouth to stimulate the male genitals is called *fellatio*. Orally stimulating the female genitals is called *cunni-*

Figure 11-2 / *Oral stimulation of the sexualia has been increasingly accepted; it is now probably practiced by a majority of adults in the United States.*

lingus. There are many slang terms for oral-genital contact—"eat," "blow," "muff dive," "suck," "go down," "give head"; the phrase "69" is used for mutual oral-genital play.

In many mammalian species, males stimulate females orally, although the reverse is rare (Diamond and Henderson, 1980). Kinsey et al. (1953) said, "The human is exceptional among the mammals when it abstains from oral activities because of learned social proprieties, moral restraints, or exaggerated ideas of sanitation."

Attitudes toward oral-genital sex vary greatly among societies. Cunnilingus probably occurs less regularly than fellatio in our culture and probably in most others. That fellatio is practiced in a society does not mean that cunnilingus is, but in almost all societies where there is cunnilingus, there is fellatio (Gebhard, 1971). The greater prevalence of fellatio may result from males' desire for a greater amount and variety of sexual stimulation and their greater initiative in seeking it.

Some people object to oral-genital contact as indecent, unnatural, unsanitary, or disgusting. Many find it acceptable only in a love relationship. Some are embarrassed by having their genitals seen close up or by unsureness about how to perform orally. The taste and smell of both sex's genital secretions, especially women's, are surrounded by folklore and hostile jokes. Many couples fear ejaculation in a woman's mouth because she may gag or dislike the taste (such reactions often fade with expe-

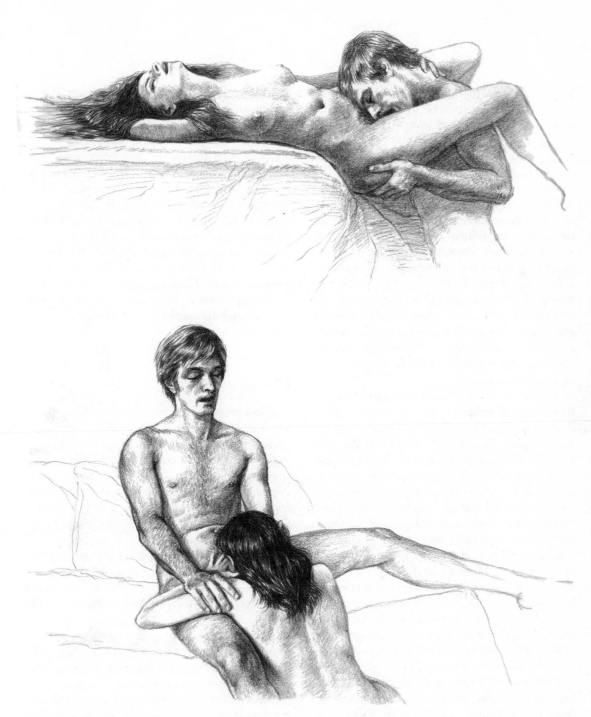

rience). One partner's desire for oral sex and the other's refusal may be felt as a deep personal rejection and create severe conflict. Many men go to prostitutes or seek other partners for the oral sex their wives will not perform (Kinsey et al., 1948, 1953).

Attitudes toward oral sexuality vary by social level. Men with higher education tend to accept oral eroticism, from deep kissing to cunnilingus and fellatio (Hunt, 1974; Kinsey et al., 1948). Many less educated men find it disgusting or perverted. Kinsey et al. found that about 45 percent of college-educated men had ever performed cunnilingus on their wives, but less than 5 percent of grade-school educated men had. Many less educated men also considered kissing or sucking the breasts infantile or perverse; this was true of far fewer men with higher educations.

Kinsey et al. (1948, 1953) found that all forms of oral sexuality had increased a great deal during the first half of this century. Two decades later, Hunt (1974) found that the percentage of men who practiced cunnilingus had again risen, from 45 percent to 66 percent. Kinsey et al. (1953) found that the number of college-educated women who had fellated their husbands had risen from 29 percent of those born before 1900 to 57 percent of those born a few decades later. Hunt (1974) found a figure of 72 percent. Hunt's sample may well have been weighted with people more accepting of oral sexuality (Kirby, 1977); another study (Curren, Neff, and Lippold, 1973) found no great change in their high school sample. We believe there may well have been some change, though how much is uncertain.

One reason for rejecting oral-genital contact has been its association with homosexuality since Greco-Roman times (Karlen, 1971). Of course far from all oral-genital contact is homosexual, but cunnilingus is common among the great majority of women with extensive lesbian experience (Kinsey et al., 1953). About 50 percent of males with any homosexual experience have been brought to orgasm orally by other males, and about half as many have fellated other males (Kinsey et al., 1948).

Oral-anal contact ("rimming") was widely considered rare and repulsive in Kinsey's time. More than one-quarter of Hunt's (1974) sample had experienced it, most of them with their spouses. Again, Hunt's sample may have been more exploratory than society at large, but some change has probably occurred.

Coitus

Most people's first association with the word sex is *coitus*, or vaginal intercourse ("fucking," "screwing," "balling," "making it," "humping"). It is the most common and desired adult sex act; all over the world, it accounts for the greater part of most adults' sexual outlet (Ford and Beach, 1951; Marshall and Suggs, 1971).

The words coitus and intercourse are often used interchangeably. Coitus is properly used only for entry of the penis into the vagina. Intercourse is also used for other kinds of genital contact—oral, anal, *interfemoral* (between the thighs), and *intermammary* (between the breasts).

In our society, marital coitus is the only approved sex behavior, and sexology has paid much attention to when coitus first occurs and whether it is between spouses. Sexuality is a continuous life experience, and some cultures are less concerned than ours about whether coitus occurs before, within, or outside marriage. But our society's distinctions affect behavior, so we will discuss premarital, marital, extramarital, and postmarital coitus, in that order.

One should keep in mind that despite shifts in the average age of marriage, the period of premarital coitus has always been relatively short in most people's lives—recently about five or six years for most men and one or two years for most women (Hunt, 1974).

Premarital Coitus

Males. In virtually all societies, most men probably have coitus before their teens are past (A. Reiss, 1971). The chief reason seems to be postpubertal males' strong drive for orgasmic release. If they don't reach this release one way, they seek another; so if men's sex behavior has changed in recent times, it has not been in whether they have orgasms, but how and with whom.

When Kinsey et al. (1948) compared males born in each decade from the 1890s on, they found that the incidence and frequency of premarital coitus had changed little; however, there had been a shift in their partners. The proportion of men who had ever visited a prostitute had not changed, but men born later used prostitutes less often and had coitus more with women from their own social backgrounds. This trend has continued (Hunt, 1974).

Kinsey et al. (1948) found that about 70 percent of men had visited a prostitute at least once, one-fifth did so more than a few times a year, and prostitutes were common as first

---

Premarital Coitus in Colonial New England

In much of colonial New England, the ban on nonmarital coitus was strictly enforced. Marital coitus, though often praised, was discouraged during the Sabbath, and giving birth on Sunday was frowned on, since it was taken as a sign that conception occurred on a Sunday. (In Judaism, by contrast, marital coitus has been thought a way to fulfill the Sabbath by strengthening the family, and a birth on the Sabbath has been considered a blessing.) Open displays of affection might be punished as lewd and unseemly. A record remains of a colonist who was put in the stocks for two hours for kissing his wife at the doorstep of his house when he returned from a three-year voyage.

Fornicators (those who engaged in premarital coitus) were expected to confess their sin publicly in church and marry. Many must have felt obliged to do so, for any child born within seven months of marriage would be refused baptism, and the couple would be excluded from the religious (therefore from almost the entire) community. Such confessions were entered in church records, and they were not uncommon. In one church, one-third of those baptized in the years 1761 to 1771 had confessed to fornication (Calhoun, 1917).

partners. Hunt later found (1974) that almost 10 percent of college-educated men under thirty-five still had their first coitus with a prostitute; for those without a college education, the figure was only 5 percent. Kinsey et al. (1948) reported that prostitutes accounted for some 10 percent of single men's coitus, but only about 2 percent of married men's. Hunt (1974) estimated that single young men in the 1970s visited prostitutes half as often or less as had those in the Forties. Like Kinsey et al., Hunt attributes this trend to the growing attitude among both sexes that "decent women" are interested and willing.

Kinsey et al. found dramatic differences in coital behavior according to social level, age of puberty, devoutness, urban or rural background, and generation of birth. For instance, in the youngest generation they studied, somewhat more males were having coitus than those in previous generations—40 percent of those up to age fifteen, about 70 percent of those fifteen to twenty-five. Most single men's frequencies were irregular, about once every two weeks for the entire population, but at lower educational levels perhaps twice a week.

There were dramatic differences by social level. About two-thirds of college-educated men had coitus before marriage; the figures were 85 percent for high-school men and 98 percent for grade-school men. Coitus was never more than one-fifth of the total outlet of single college-level men, but was as much as two-thirds of the outlet of the less educated. In other words, through much or most of adolescence, college-educated males experienced sex more as masturbation and petting than as coitus; the less educated might find this incomprehensible or even "perverted." Many college-level men had premarital coitus only with

one or a few women, and that sporadically. Many of the less educated had coitus as often as two to four times a week, with many partners.

Males who reached puberty early tended to have higher sexual frequencies throughout life. This apparently biological influence, interacting with others such as social class, produced enormous variation in coital experience. By their late teens, 86 percent of less-educated men who had reached puberty early were having coitus; less than 33 percent of college men who reached puberty late were doing so. A study that compared college students over thirty years (Finger, 1975), found a higher incidence and frequency of coitus among young men in the Seventies, but with fewer partners—perhaps an oddity of this particular sample or perhaps reflecting a greater linkage of coitus with extended, intimate relationships.

At all social levels, coital incidence and frequency were lower among the devout. They were also lower among farm boys than urban boys, probably because of fewer potential partners and perhaps because of stricter religious and social views in rural communities.

To the extent that men's premarital sex behavior has changed, one important reason has apparently been that more people receive higher education and enter middle and upper social strata, where premarital coitus starts later and happens less often. Since the great majority of men reach a certain number of orgasms one way or another, this implies a shift from early coitus to petting, masturbation, and other coital substitutes—hardly the sexual revolution so widely assumed to have taken place.

Some researchers, however, feel there has been a rather abrupt change in the 1970s. A summary of research in 1966 (I. Reiss) concluded that all studies from the Fifties till then showed no change in behavior but a change in attitudes; premarital coitus was becoming more acceptable but not more common. But Hunt (1974) reported that in his sample, 95 percent of men eighteen to twenty-four years old had had premarital coitus—a significant increase over Kinsey's figures. The increase was largest among the college-educated—who, having been the least active, had the most room for change.

Females. Of all sex behaviors, female premarital coitus is the one most discussed as a social and personal issue. Many social scientists believe that this results from concern about pregnancy and the social "licensing" of child bearing. In some cultures, both sexes have relative freedom in sex play during childhood and adolescence. But our culture, like many others, tries hard to restrict coitus, especially by adolescent girls and unmarried young women. If sex is to be limited, females' less demanding orgasmic drive seems more easily managed than males'.

Therefore many people were shocked when Kinsey et al. (1953) revealed that nearly 50 percent of women who married by age twenty had had premarital coitus. But the shock was lessened by further details. For example:

Only 3 percent of unmarried females had had coitus by age fifteen, 20 percent by age twenty.

More than half the nonvirgins had had only one partner, in most cases their future husbands; only 13 percent had had six partners or more. Kinsey et al. (1953) noted that even people with restrictive values may make some allowance for premarital coitus with a future spouse.

Age of first coitus was closely related to age of marriage; many who began coitus early also married young. For only one-fourth of nonvirgins had coitus extended over four years or more; it had been regular for very few. Almost 30 percent had had coitus ten times or less, and it had pushed many of them toward marriage.

Before age twenty, the median frequency of premarital coitus was only once every five to ten weeks, after that once every three weeks. Although many women had coitus often for a while, they might go months or years without it. Relatively few had coitus with the regularity typical of very many men.

Social level was the strongest influence on premarital coitus in men, and at first glance this also seemed true of women. Those with only grade-school educations started coitus five or six years younger than those who went on to graduate school (18 percent and 1 percent, respectively, started by age fifteen). However, the less-educated women married much earlier; if one adjusts the figures for age of marriage, the differences between social levels disappear (Kinsey et al., 1953). Only 30 percent of the grade-school women had premarital coitus, compared to 47 percent of the high-school educated and 60 percent of college educated women. But obviously women who postponed marriage for education spent many more years as single adults. And higher education may also be associated with being or becoming sexually more liberal. These trends were the opposite for males, who with more education had less premarital coitus. Women's coital frequency did not vary by educational level.

Devoutness had the same effect on women as

on men, but more strongly. By almost any measure, from frequency of coitus to incidence of orgasm, very devout women were sexually less active than the moderately devout, who in turn were less active than the nondevout.

The most important influence turned out to be decade of birth. There was a dramatic break in the behavior of females born after 1900—the teenagers and young adults of the late Teens and Twenties. They and later generations of women were more likely to be sexually active with men they loved or liked. There was a leap of ten, fifteen, or twenty percentage points for most sexual behaviors. This difference cut across such influences as devoutness and educational level. Younger women were sexually more assertive, and less restrained about oral eroticism. Two to three times as many were having premarital coitus during any five-year period of their lives. Fewer females were completely inactive sexually. Of women still single at twenty-five, 36 percent had had coitus, compared to 14 percent of the previous generation. More married women tried a variety of coital positions, and more experienced orgasms.

Yet certain things did not change. Once women began a sexual practice, they did it no more often: we noted that females began petting to orgasm two years earlier (at sixteen), but they did so no more often. The proportion who reached coital orgasm before marriage was unchanged. Half or more of the younger nonvirgins had had coitus only once or a few times, many anticipating marriage or to hasten it.

The Twenties brought successes for the feminist and birth-control movements, much talk of free love and antipuritanism, the popularization of psychoanalysis; it was an age, said Viennese satirist Karl Kraus, when if a man walked the boulevard with a woman, he was considered her lover; if with a man, a homosexual; if alone, a masturbator (Karlen, 1971). There was a generation gap at least as great as in later decades, between rural and immigrant parents and their native-born, city-bred children, who were creating changes in courtship, life-style, family size and structure, and childrearing.

There was no sweeping sexual revolution, but the mass media created a picture of massive change, as they would again in the Sixties and Seventies (V. Elias, 1978; Karlen, 1971). In the Thirties, noted psychologist Lewis Terman (1939) predicted that by 1960 no American bride would be a virgin: he turned out to be wrong by a wide margin. The regulation of sexual behavior is fundamental to all societies, and deeply set and deeply felt in individuals. It is no surprise that a massive change in attitudes brought a smaller shift in behavior.

In fact, most people's lifelong sex-behavior patterns are predictable by their middle teens. They themselves may be surprised at what they do, but someone who knew their backgrounds could have predicted those surprises. Kinsey et al. (1948) said: "Upper-level individuals like to think that they have become more liberal, sexually emancipated, free of their former inhibitions, rational instead of traditional in their behavior, ready to experiment with anything. It is notable, though, that such emancipated persons rarely engage in any amount of actual behavior which is foreign to the pattern laid down in their youth ... the change in the form of a generation's rationalizations has not affected its overt behavior one bit."

Recent Changes. This historical perspective is important when we ask whether a sexual revolution has occurred since the Kinsey data appeared. We saw in the previous chapter that early, noncoital behaviors have changed little. Some researchers believe there has been a great change in coital behavior since the middle or late Sixties. Others think there has been only moderate change—perhaps as much as in the Twenties, perhaps less.

Researchers at the Institute for Sex Research (founded by Kinsey) tried in the middle Sixties to recreate as closely as possible Kinsey's college-age sample. Sexual revolution was already, according to the mass media and popular opinion, an established fact. Some significant changes were found, but they were far from revolutionary (Gagnon and Simon, personal communication). Petting and masturbation began a year or so earlier, but still relatively few college students had had coital experience in high school. In the Forties, 20 percent of college women had been nonvirgins; in the Sixties, the figure had risen to 25 percent (50 percent of seniors). For most, coitus was still commonly limited to close relationships. The age of first coitus had dropped, but so had the age of marriage; the old relationship between the two ages was unchanged.

Several subsequent studies (R. Bell and Chaskes, 1970; Broderick, 1966; K. Davis, 1972; Kaats and Davis, 1970) concluded that the premarital coitus figure had risen to 40 to 45 percent in college women, and that commitment to marriage had become less important as a precondition (Kaats and Davis, 1970).

However, in an interesting questionnaire study at a Midwestern university (Jackson and Potkay, 1973), only 10 percent of the women said they had had premarital coitus at sixteen or earlier. When asked how many women on campus they thought were virgins, they estimated 45 percent. The actual figure was 57 percent. Almost 80 percent of the students had *underestimated* the number of virgins on campus. This supports the idea (McCary, 1967) that there has been more change in sexual attitudes than in sex behavior.

Studies of college students—unfortunately, most done by questionnaire rather than the more reliable interview method—vary according to the college, the region of the country (Packard, 1968), and the particular group of students (volunteers, a psychology class, a complete or partial dormitory sample). A study at a small church-related college in the Midwest and at a university in the Southeast (Lewis, 1973) showed that two-thirds of the women were virgins (compared to 37 percent of the men). Only 11 percent had had two or more coital partners (males, 39 percent). Obviously any sexual revolution had only brushed these schools in passing.

The most recent and reliable major study of premarital female coitus (Zelnik and Kantner, 1972, 1977) surveyed more than 4,600 young women from fifteen to nineteen in a nationwide sample. By age nineteen, 46 percent had had premarital coitus (40 percent if only white females were considered, as in the Kinsey figures). Premarital coitus had risen markedly, but as in Kinsey's day, few of the white women and fewer of the black ones had had many partners; some 60 percent had had only one, the man they hoped to marry. Again we see moderate change, not a dramatic break with the past.

We have noted that a study of more than 7,000 women up to age fifty in Hawaii in 1971 showed that the age of first coitus had slowly decreased, without a distinct break in any period, to eighteen (Smith et al., 1973). In recent decades there have been several changes besides age of first coitus:

More men and women believe in permissiveness with affection (I. Reiss, 1960, 1967), accepting sexual contact with people one loves or likes. For some people, this means sex within committed love relationships; for others it seems to include what novelist Saul Bellow (1969) has called "fellatio with friendly strangers."

Females begin masturbating earlier (Simon and Gagnon, personal communication), and perhaps fewer rarely or never experience orgasm (Hunt, 1974).

Physical maturity continues to arrive earlier; this correlates with boys beginning orgasmic acts younger and girls starting sexual contacts earlier.

The social-class differences observed by Kinsey et al. still exist (Rainwater, 1965, 1971), but may be less pronounced (I. Reiss, 1975).

As in the Twenties, real change has apparently taken place, but has probably been overestimated. Attitudes and rhetoric have again probably outrun behavior. Kinsey et al. (1953) found that in the Twenties, a majority of college women approved of coitus with a person one loved, but only a minority had done it ("I just haven't found the right man yet"). Similarly, in the Sixties, the majority of students in one study (Freedman, 1965) said they approved of premarital coitus, but little more than half of those who approved had done it. In the Seventies, many researchers and clinicians believe, there has been no basic change in the trend of the previous half century.

Research in Europe over the past two de-cades shows similar patterns (Luckey and Nass, 1969.) A study of 2,000 teenagers in England (Schofield, 1965) revealed that the frequencies of petting and coitus were similar to or perhaps lower than in the United States. German teenagers start coitus younger than in the past, and young women masturbate earlier: "Basically today's sixteen and seventeen-year-old boys and girls behave the same way as the nineteen and twenty-year-olds ten years ago" (Sigusch and Schmidt, 1973).

Some studies in Scandinavia show higher nonvirginity rates than those in the United States (Linner, 1967), but perhaps partly for special reasons. It was long traditional in parts of Sweden for engaged couples to prove their match was fertile, then marry after the hoped-for pregnancy. Furthermore, the "permissiveness with affection" standard has gained much ground in the past half century, with less effective public resistance by conservative minorities than in many other Western nations. The results are high but easily misinterpreted rates of premarital coitus and illegitimacy. Changes in Sweden and Denmark have probably been roughly like those in the United States. Despite talk about free love and promiscuity, some observers think there is less casual premarital coitus in Stockholm than in New York or Los Angeles (Karlen, 1971).

Marital Coitus

Coital Behavior. Many people perform coitus before, outside, or after marriage, but the universal institution of marriage involves the right to coitus with one's mate (Goode, 1964). In some restrictive societies, marital coitus is the only formally approved sex behav-

Figure 11-3 / *Coitus is adults' most common and desired erotic act in virtually every society.*

ior, as it has been through much of Western history.

There are many widespread restrictions on marital coitus (Ford and Beach, 1951). In a number of societies, people avoid it during menstruation, much of pregnancy and lactation, after childbirth, when either partner is ill, or even when other relatives are sick. Some also forbid coitus during certain religious occasions (Christian Lent and Jewish Yom Kippur), to

men before hunting or battles, to women before or while sowing crops, or to people engaged in certain crafts, such as men who are smelting iron.

Despite all these restrictions, the majority of married people almost everywhere probably limit their sexual activity largely to marital coitus. It accounts for about 85 percent of American married men's total sexual outlet and about 80 percent of married women's (Kinsey et al., 1953). The remainder is accounted for by masturbation, extramarital relations (including homosexual ones), and to a lesser extent other behaviors.

Coital frequency varies greatly among couples and societies—most commonly from two to five times a week (Gebhard, 1971), but there are high and low extremes. Among the Bosongye of Africa, even older adults report having coitus more than seven times a week (Merriam, 1971); the Cayapa of Ecuador consider twice a week frequent (Altschuler, 1971). In the United States, the median frequency of young married couples is about two and a half times a week (Kinsey et al., 1948, 1953). By age thirty, it is about twice a week, by fifty once a week, by sixty every twelve days. Of course, these figures conceal enormous variations, and the means are higher, especially until middle age, because a substantial minority of men have orgasmic frequencies of five to ten times a week, and it is usually the man's desire that keeps coital frequency high (see below). Furthermore, some couples are active at certain periods, inactive at others. But many couples probably do form coital habits and follow more or less regular frequencies for long periods.

One of Kinsey's most interesting findings (1953) has been oddly ignored: over several generations, coital frequency decreased from an average 3.2 times a week to 2.6. The only apparent explanation was that the greater emphasis on women's sexual wishes and satisfaction made men give more consideration to their wives' desire—or lack of it. Since then, there has been even greater emphasis on female orgasm and a single sexual standard. It would be interesting if so-called sexual revolution and liberation have reduced the frequency of marital coitus. W. Wilson (1975) found frequencies unchanged, and Hunt (1974) found them higher, but neither used samples and methods like Kinsey's. Data from more than 20,000 women in Hawaii from 1970 to 1974 were similar to Kinsey's, except that the median frequency remained 2 to 3 times a week from age 25 to 40. It decreased to about once a week from age 41 to 50 (Diamond, unpublished).

Aging is the greatest influence on coital frequency, but it affects men and women differently. Besides the physical changes (see chapter 4), there are behavioral ones. Masturbation and extramarital coitus remain a significant part of some married men's total outlet; marital coitus remains women's most frequent and consistent sexual activity, for a greater part of their outlet. In fact, it is women's only sex behavior that approaches male masturbation and coitus in regularity.

We stress again that averages do not reveal the great range of variation in sex behavior at any age. Some 10 percent of men from fifteen to thirty have less than one orgasm a week, and almost one-third have more than three. Some women go years without an orgasm, while others don't go one day.

Marital Adjustment. Few wives want coitus more often than their husbands; few husbands wish their wives were less desirous (Kinsey et al., 1953). In very few societies are wives said to instigate coitus more often than their husbands (Whiting and Child, 1941). In other words, men's desire helps make coitus regular, but women's restraints help limit its frequency—especially among the better educated in our society, who give increasing importance to a woman's desire rather than expecting her to accommodate the man. In some couples, though, the reverse happens; the woman loses inhibitions, and the man's interest wanes because of aging, boredom, or antagonism. Kinsey et al. (1953) concluded that in many marriages

... The male may be most desirous of sexual contact in his early years, while the responses of the female are still undeveloped and while she is still struggling to free herself from [inhibitions]. But over the years most females become less inhibited and develop an interest in sexual relations which they may then maintain until they are in their fifties or even sixties. But by then [the man's interest in coitus, especially] with a wife who has previously objected to the frequencies of his requests, may have sharply declined ... Most of [this decline] may have represented physiologic aging; part of it may have been the product of a failure to work out effective relations in the earlier years of marriage; and part of it may have been a product of the fact that a number of the males—especially the better-educated males—were engaging in extra-marital coitus ... in their forties and fifties at the expense of coitus with their wives.

This is especially likely to happen among the college educated. For men with little education, marital coitus rises from 80 percent of total sexual outlet early in marriage to 90 percent at age fifty. For the college educated, it falls from 85 percent to 60 percent.

Women do not vary this way by educational level until their middle twenties (Kinsey et al., 1953). From then on, marital coitus is a little less of college-educated women's outlet—by their forties, 60 to 65 percent, compared to 73 to 80 percent for high-school-educated women. This resembles, on a smaller scale, the trend seen in men, but as we shall see in discussing extramarital coitus, the reasons are different.

Of all Kinsey's findings, few had the impact of his discovering a correlation between premarital and extramarital coitus. Only 13 percent of women who had been virgins at marriage had extramarital partners; 29 percent of the nonvirgins did. Some people took this as evidence that premarital coitus leads to adultery. But both behaviors may have some other common source; a correlation does not prove cause and effect. A long-term study of 161 couples married twenty years or more showed no evidence that premarital coitus had any ill effects on marriage (Ard, 1974). The subject requires further research.

Extramarital Coitus

Behavior and Sanctions. The terms adultery, extramarital coitus, and infidelity have different emphases. *Adultery* is a legal term meaning coitus by a married person with someone other than his or her spouse. *Extramarital coitus* describes the behavior without any legal or moral connotations. (*Postmarital* more accurately describes coitus by the separated, widowed, and divorced.) Such behavior may or may not mean being *unfaithful,* or showing *infidelity;* these words imply a breach of an understanding that no extramarital relations will occur. Some couples openly or tacitly accept extramarital coitus, so adultery is not always infidelity.

After love and marriage, perhaps no sexual theme has a larger place in literature, song, and anecdote than adultery. It has usually been shown as tempting and exciting, yet sinful and ill-fated. Kinsey et al. (1948) said that no sex behavior caused so much evasion and dishonesty in their subjects. Virtually all societies try

203

to limit coitus largely to marriage; a very few, such as the Toda of India, may more or less permit extramarital coitus (Ford and Beach, 1951).

We are used to thinking of marriage as sexually exclusive, but many societies allow secondary partners or plural marriage—in all but a handful, for men but not women (see chapter 20). Some societies allow *concubinage*, an institution that existed in medieval Europe and continues in parts of Asia and Africa. In effect, the concubine is a secondary mate who lacks many of a wife's privileges.

Many societies allow wives some form of extramarital coitus, but in most their choice of partner and circumstances is limited, and the husband's permission may be needed. Restrictions on adultery are almost universally more strict for wives than for husbands (Marshall and Suggs, 1971). Yet few married men easily take advantage of their theoretical liberties (Ford and Beach, 1951). They must compete with unmarried men, and it can be difficult for married men and women to find time, funds, and places to meet discreetly.

Some cultures have "wife lending"—one man allows another sexual access to his wife on certain occasions—or long-term wife exchanges. These arrangements usually occur where men must be away from home for long periods (trading, hunting, or fishing), and usually everyone involved must give permission (Ford and Beach, 1951). Some cultures permit extramarital coitus on certain festive and religious occasions.

Formal sanctions do not, of course, always reflect daily life. The Bena of Africa condemn adultery severely, but for them, write Ford and Beach (1951), "undetected extramarital seduc-

tion is the spice of life. If one mate does apprehend the other in an affair there is likely to be a furious outburst of temper in which the offending partner bears the brunt of the fierce attack. But the tantrum is soon over and both partners renew the game, with the recently caught one determined to be less careless on the next occasion." In some societies, people detected in such liaisons are very harshly punished. A spouse's reaction in American society may be anything from indifference to murderous rage. Revenge for adultery has been the West's most common crime of passion.

Extramarital coitus raises questions beyond possessiveness and jealousy. Does it weaken the marital bond, disrupting trust and intimacy? Might it strengthen some aspects of a relationship? Will it make a partner neglect obligations to spouse, children, and community? Does it interfere with harmonious childrearing? Will pregnancy result? Will there be resentment over raising the children of another biological parent? Society may punish both the spouse and the extramarital partner; the Biblical punishment was for both offenders to be stoned to death. Almost everywhere, adultery can be grounds for divorce. In our society, with its strong condemnation of coitus outside marriage, such behavior has enormous disruptive potential, and in many states it is illegal.

Incidence and Frequency. In our society, most people limit extramarital affairs, to avoid emotional ties they fear might disrupt their marriages (Hunt, 1974). As a result, extramarital coitus is usually sporadic, happening only once or a few times with any partner, and commonly at intervals of months or years. There are some extended, intimate affairs, but one-night stands and brief liaisons are more common. Some people's frequencies may average out to once a week or two, but the year's total may well have occurred on one trip or during a few weeks of summer vacation (Kinsey et al., 1948).

About half of all married men told Kinsey et al. (1948, 1953) that they had extramarital coitus at least once by age forty, as did one-quarter of women. In any five-year age group (for instance, people from thirty to thirty-five), about one-third of married men were having extramarital coitus. Prostitutes accounted for 8 to 15 percent of this activity. Hunt (1974) found extramarital incidence about the same, but contact with prostitutes much reduced.

There were striking differences between social levels. Men from lower levels had extramarital coitus more often and with more partners, for a larger amount of their total outlet. In their teens, 45 percent did so, at age forty 27 percent, and at age fifty, 19 percent. Over that span, the mean frequency dropped from more than once a week to once every two weeks. Most of these contacts were brief and without lasting involvement.

The pattern of the college-educated was just the opposite: only 15 to 20 percent had extramarital coitus early in their marriages, but 27 percent had done so by age fifty, and the mean frequency increased from once every two or three weeks to almost once a week, for an increasing proportion of total outlet. These men might have only one or a few extramarital partners, and affairs that lasted for years.

This fits the general pattern of lower-level men being sexually active early in life but less so in midlife, and upper-level males starting in midlife to do what lower-level men did when young.

Kinsey et al. (1953) found that less than 10 percent of women at all levels had extramarital coitus in their late teens. By age forty, almost one-third of college-educated women had done so, compared to 24 percent of high-school women, and even fewer grade-school women. About 40 percent of all these women had only one extramarital partner, another 40 percent two to five partners. After age forty, very few women had extramarital coitus for the first time.

Devoutness affected extramarital coitus more than any other background factor. For instance, only 7 percent of religiously active Protestant women had extramarital coitus by their early thirties, but 28 percent of the religiously inactive did.

Decade of birth, the strongest influence on premarital coitus, had less effect on extramarital relations. By age forty, 22 percent of the women born before 1900 had extramarital coitus; 30 percent of those born after 1920 did so. There was an especially large increase in women ages twenty-one to twenty-five (from 4 percent in the pre-1900 generation to 12 percent of the 1920–1929 generation). There was little subsequent change (Kinsey et al., 1953), but a similar shift may have occurred in the past decade; Hunt (1974) found a figure of 24 percent (compared to 32 percent of men).

From 1900 to 1950, the frequency of extramarital coitus was unchanged, yet extramarital coitus rose from 3 percent of women's total outlet in the early Twenties to 14 percent in the late Forties (Kinsey et al., 1953). In that period, we noted, the frequency of marital coitus dropped. Apparently if husbands or wives had less coitus together, adultery was now a more common substitute.

Most women's extramarital partners were married men close to them in age. Married women in their late thirties and forties are preferred as partners by many married men (Kinsey et al., 1953). Kinsey et al. also commented that many younger women become very upset after engaging in extramarital coitus, and many men fear the consequences of that disturbance. Fewer older women become upset, and many are sexually sophisticated; therefore many men prefer them as sexual partners, as Benjamin Franklin suggested (see page 208).

Impact on Marriage. It is a truism in our society that the great majority of women must feel some emotional involvement with a man to have coitus with him, and that most men find sexual outlets, if not with their wives then elsewhere. There is evidence for the idea that men are more likely to seek regular sexual activity and a variety of outlets and partners. Twice as many men as women have extramarital coitus. Almost three-quarters of the men Kinsey et al. (1948, 1953) interviewed expressed a wish for extramarital coitus; far fewer women said they wanted sexual variety before or during marriage. Similar findings have come from other researchers (Terman, 1939).

Perhaps it is a lifetime of social training that makes women want variety less than men, but a biological tendency may well be involved. In most mammalian species, sexual response is strongest in new circumstances and with new partners. Monkeys long caged together be-

---

Adultery, Crime of Passion, and Temporary Insanity

Before the Civil War, divorce was exceptional (Cable, 1969), although adultery had been both a crime and an affront to society. A wife was supposed to look the other way if her husband took a lover, although adultery was grounds for divorce for both husbands and wives. A husband, however, was seen by society as justified in inflicting any punishment on his adulterous wife or her lover. In 1859, Congressman Daniel Sickles shot and killed his wife's lover in a duel. Sickles admitted the murder and was acquitted, with public approval. His plea was temporary insanity. It was the first time this defense had been used.

After the Civil War, attitudes changed. Adultery was no longer seen as a justification for violence, but was socially more accepted as a cause for divorce by either spouse. Between 1878 and 1898, twice as many divorces were granted on a wife's complaint as on a husband's. Adultery was given as the cause less often than desertion, but this may have reflected social pressures and embarrassment as much as reality.

Until recently, adultery remained virtually the only grounds for divorce in many states, and some couples had to rig faked adultery scenes, photographed by private detectives. The laws governing adultery and divorce have been easing, and the Model Penal Code proposed by the American Law Institute does not make adultery a crime.

---

come aroused less often and mate less vigorously, like many married couples; with new partners, both the male and the female may become more aroused and vigorous again. This is called the "Coolidge effect" (Michael and Zumpe, 1978), and in many species it is stronger in males than in females. In humans, said Kinsey et al. (1948), this is one of the commonest sources of conflict between the sexes.

Most males can immediately understand why most males want extramarital coitus ... many females find it difficult to understand why any man who is happily married should want to have coitus with any female other than his wife. The fact that there are females who ask such questions seems, to most males, the best sort of evidence that there are basic differences between the two sexes.

The desire for variety for its own sake, they said, was expressed even by many men who said that for moral or social reasons they had not had extramarital coitus and would not, however much they desired it. A smaller proportion of women found sexual variety as interesting. Hunt (1974) found that the second most common reason women gave for avoiding extramarital sex was that they never had the desire or interest or never took advantage of opportunities.

At every social level, women are more likely than men to accept a spouse's extramarital acts. At lower social levels, where such behavior takes place most, many wives expect their husbands to play around at times and say they don't object as long as they don't know the details. In some middle- and upper-level marriages, extramarital coitus occurs with the spouse's knowledge; it is sometimes even encouraged as part of a mutual arrangement to have separate sex

lives in addition to marital coitus, though rarely instead of it (Kinsey et al., 1953). Some husbands encourage their wives to have coitus with other men—to justify their own extramarital behavior, as part of mate swapping, to watch for their own pleasure, or to have entree into group sex.

Reactions to a spouse's extramarital activity often depend on its nature, the partner or partners involved, and the motives. It is one thing to spend half an hour with a prostitute or stranger, another to carry on a long love affair. Also, it may matter whether the reason was the spouse's physical illness or disability or a desire to wound or humiliate. Among the reasons women gave Kinsey et al. (1953) for having extramarital coitus were:

To find new and perhaps more exciting or skillful sex partners.
To gain social status through contact with certain men.
To accommodate a respected or valued friend.
In retaliation for the husband's adultery.
In retaliation for real or imagined (nonsexual) mistreatment by the husband.
To assert independence from the husband.
To find greater emotional satisfaction.

Many women found it impossible to have emotional involvements outside marriage; many who did felt guilty and were deeply troubled. There was less apparent suffering among those who accepted their acts as a form of pleasure (Kinsey et al., 1953).

Even in scientific works, Kinsey et al. pointed out, extramarital coitus is often evaluated morally, with the assumption that it always damages marriages. They said they had histories of long extramarital relationships that seemed not to have damaged the marriages—unless the spouse found out, which might bring a suit for divorce. In fact, they felt that some people's sexual adjustment in marriage had been helped by extramarital experience, by learning new techniques or attitudes that reduced inhibitions. Hunt (1974) also reports that many in his survey found that affairs helped their marriages. It was when the nonmarital partner became very important emotionally that trouble often arose.

Many researchers and clinicians have assumed that extramarital coitus indicates an unhealthy marriage. Others say that boredom, chronic marital strife, and stresses from within and without the marriage can lead people to seek extramarital partners, not necessarily with harmful results (we discuss this more fully in chapter 14). This remains a matter of clinical impression or personal conviction. In any case, many people indirectly accept extramarital coitus ("I don't want to know if anything happened"), especially as a sexual safety valve for men, as long as it doesn't cause neglect or disruption of the marriage and family.

Kinsey et al. (1953) questioned more than 400 people who had had extramarital coitus and whose marriages had ended in divorce. Only 14 percent of the women and 18 percent of the men thought that their extramarital acts had been a major factor in the breakups of their marriages. Another 20–25 percent thought it

---

How to Choose a Mistress

Among Benjamin Franklin's writings was a letter, written in 1745 and long kept from public view, on how to choose a mistress. It first appeared in complete form in a biography of Franklin by Phillips Russell in 1926. Franklin starts and ends by encouraging marriage to satisfy sexual needs, but he counsels choosing older women as mistresses:

1. Because they have more Knowledge of the World and their Minds are better stor'd with Observations, their Conversation is more improving and more lastingly agreeable.
2. Because when Women cease to be handsome, they study to be good. To maintain their Influence over Men, they supply the Diminution of Beauty by an Augmentation of Utility.
3. Because there is no hazard of Children, which irregularly produc'd may be attended with much Inconvenience.

4. Because thro' more Experience, they are more prudent and discreet in conducting an Intrigue to prevent Suspicion.
5. . . . covering all above the waist with a basket, and regarding only what is below the Girdle, it is impossible of two Women to know an old from a young one. And as in the dark all Cats are grey, the Pleasure of corporal Enjoyment with an old Woman is at least equal, and frequently superior, every Knack being by Practice capable of Improvement.
6. Because the Sin is less. The debauching a Virgin may be her Ruin and make her for Life unhappy.
7. Because the Compunction is less. The having made a Young Girl miserable may give you frequent bitter Reflections; none of which can attend the making an old Woman happy.
8. (thly and Lastly) They are so grateful!

had been a contributing factor. However, men and women who knew of their spouses' adultery viewed it differently. Half of the men thought their wives' sexual activity the chief factor leading to divorce; another third thought it an important factor. Only one-quarter of the women thought their husbands' extramarital activity was a factor, and half saw it as a moderate factor. That is, twice as many men as women felt the effects had been drastic. More recent research (Schwartz, 1973) confirms that both sexes consider a woman's sexual activity outside a relationship more dangerous than a man's. Kinsey et al. (1953), like some other researchers, saw males' greater jealousy as typically mammalian (see chapter 15).

Postmarital Coitus

The sexual patterns of the widowed and divorced tend to differ. Most divorced people need sexual and emotional experiences more gratifying than those of their unsatisfying marriages (Hunt, 1966). Some use sex to restore their self-esteem; others, who were erotically frustrated before the divorce, become sexually very active afterward. Widows and widowers tend not to feel as sexually deprived or to need as much ego enhancement. Also, grief and enduring love for the dead spouse often make new liaisons difficult to start and guilt-ridden.

The median coital rate of the divorced men Hunt (1974) studied was a little higher than that of married men. That of sexually active divorced women was the same as married women's. The divorced men had had a median of eight partners, women a median of four. This is a good bit higher than the Kinsey et al. findings (1953) and may suggest social changes.

However, Gebhard (1966) found that both divorced and widowed women had higher orgasm rates after marriage than during marriage, a result of increased experience and of rebounding from poor marriages or illness. Hunt (1974) comments that for the divorced, postmarital sex "often involves powerful physical pleasure but lacks comparable emotional fulfillment. For many men and even more women, coitus with a loved partner is more totally rewarding than coitus with a sexually more exciting but unloved partner."

Overview

In discussing all sex acts, from masturbation to the less usual ones taken up in the next chapter, one must bear in mind the point of studying sex as a behavior. It provides real rather than guessed norms and shows the enormous range of individual variation. Numbers, of course, are guideposts in our knowledge, not prescriptions for living, and neither more nor less means the same as better or worse.

The incidences and frequencies of sex behaviors are not dull figures but keys to the nature of human sexuality. They depend in different ways and degrees on biological and cultural inheritance, gender role, age, generation, devoutness, rural or urban upbringing, and social level. There are probably other differences that have not been studied (ethnic background) or cannot be quantified (family relationships). We believe that a greater understanding of the differences (especially those between the sexes) may ultimately offer ways of reducing conflicts between partners.

We suspect that few people decide on a sexual act being part of their lives or how often to do it. However, discomfort about one's own or another's behavior may be changed by greater understanding of it. In some cases, such knowledge gives a feeling of permission about performing or not performing certain acts.

It is true, as many point out, that sex behavior takes place in the context of a relationship, whether it be casual or intimate. The psychological and interpersonal aspects of sex behaviors demand detailed attention. But with the information of this four-chapter sequence on sex behaviors, such attention can be given without interference from myths or ignorance about what most people actually do. Before going on to relationships, then, we will use the fourth of these chapters to look at some less common but often discussed sex behaviors.

Review, Discuss, Decide

1. What are some of the quantitative and qualitative differences between men and women in petting and coitus?
2. What are some social influences on sexual activity? When in life do they start having effects?
3. Why are the distinctions between premarital, marital, extramarital, and postmarital sex useful or necessary. Could they be detrimental?
4. How does marital sex behavior vary with age? Educational level? In various societies?
5. Are premarital and extramarital coitus affected the same ways by various social influences?
6. Are you surprised or not surprised by any evidence about change or lack of it in sex behavior over this century? If so, in what way, and why?
7. What do you predict would be the results of a study of sex behavior in your home neighborhood, school, or other area or institution you know? How much might individuals differ? How much might averages and ranges of variation differ from one group to another? Might they differ much from the findings of Kinsey and his colleagues?

12

Other Sex Behaviors

What are the differences between homosexual, transvestite, and transsexual behaviors?

How do people with such behaviors function sexually and in society?

Are these behaviors as common in women as in men?

Are peepers and exhibitionists dangerous?

How common is incest?

What are bestiality, fetishism, and sadomasochism?

What causes these patterns? Can they be treated? Should they be?

Most of the behaviors covered in the previous three chapters are practiced by many people in many societies; some are virtually universal. Here we deal with behaviors that are *deviant* in both senses of the word: they are not done often by most people in any society, and are generally disapproved or, at best, tolerated. We include in this category paraphilias in sexual identity (transsexualism), gender role (transvestism), sexual orientation (predominant or exclusive adult homosexuality), and some other relatively uncommon acts, such as incest, bestiality, pedophilia, sadomasochism, voyeurism, and exhibitionism.

The Debate over Terms

In recent years there has been sharp controversy over the terms for these behaviors, a debate that reflects turmoil in science and in society. As regular adult patterns, all of these acts come under the definition of dysfunction we give in chapter 16; although their presence does not necessarily mean a person is sick in the common sense of the word, they are often biologically and socially maladaptive.

It is true that social and scientific definitions of health and function have changed over the years. Only half a century ago, many authorities called oral-genital intercourse a perversion; today many authorities accept or recommend it. But in virtually all societies, the acts discussed in this chapter are considered somewhat deviant or dysfunctional when they are predominant adult behaviors.

The most common word for these behaviors over the past century has been *perversion* (Latin: turned the wrong way), because they were thought to result from a misdirection of sexual instincts. Stoller (1975) still uses the word, for he believes that a perversion is a fantasy put into action and that it usually contains open or unconscious desire to hurt, dominate, or humiliate others. However, he says, he cannot bring himself to use the word pervert because of its condemnatory ring and the persecution of people so labeled. We, the authors, use the word deviance because it seems scientifically most accurate, but we avoid the word deviant for the same reason as Stoller.

For quite a while, sexologists have urged society not to view these behaviors as sins or as crimes. Therefore they have sought blander words. The phrase *sexual deviance* is common, usually in its statistical sense, meaning a minority practice, though it sometimes also implies social disapproval. The terms *sexual variation* and *sexual alternative* are now commonly used, especially by people who feel the behaviors they discuss are only "different." These terms often seem to imply that incest, fetishism, and homosexuality are emotionally and socially neutral choices. We do not believe this is realistic. Recently the word *paraphilia* has gained popularity (*para* = alongside, *philia* = love), and we find it acceptable.

Definitions

Many people do not accurately distinguish homosexuality, transvestism, transsexualism, and hermaphroditism.

A small number of people are born with genetic, hormonal, or other conditions that give them some physical traits of each sex; these are *hermaphrodites* or, more commonly, *pseudohermaphrodites* (see chapter 7). But even most pseudohermaphrodites seem predominantly either male or female and are *heterosexual* (attracted to people of the other genetic sex).

Most *transsexuals* appear physically normal but believe they belong to the opposite sex, and some may seek "sex-change" surgery. The majority are sexually inactive much of the time.

212

Figure 12-1 / *Some transsexuals obtain "sex-change" surgery and alter their social identities. The results of surgical and hormonal treatment vary from poor to startlingly effective; genetic sex, of course, remains unchanged. One well-known transsexual, formerly Dr. Richard Raskind (top), has appeared as Renée Richards in women's professional tennis tournaments; the woman shown (bottom left) went through comparable treatment and is now Mr. Steve Dain.*

They do not consider themselves homosexual if they have partners of the same sex, since they believe they belong to the opposite sex. Transsexualism is variously estimated to be anywhere from three to nine times more common in males than females (Benjamin, 1966; Stoller, 1968).

Transvestites get sexual and emotional pleasure from dressing or disguising themselves as the opposite sex. Some but not all are homosexual. The great majority are men.

Far more common than all of these together are *homosexuals,* men and women who desire people of their own sex as erotic and love partners. The great majority are not hermaphrodites, transsexuals, or transvestites. Although effeminate male homosexuals and mannish female homosexuals draw society's attention, they are a minority of homosexuals. There are probably more male than female homosexuals in most or all societies; in our society, the ratio is about two to one (Karlen, 1971).

Hermaphroditism is a physical variant, transsexualism a sexual-identity deviance, transvestism a gender-role deviance, homosexuality a sexual-orientation deviance. Although homosexuality is most common, the nature of these behaviors is made clearer by considering transsexualism and transvestism first.

Transsexualism

This rare reversal of sexual identity usually involves no detectable disorder of the genes, gonads, or sexualia. A male transsexual believes that he is a woman trapped in a man's body, a female transsexual that she is a man in a woman's body (Diamond, 1978; Green and Money, 1969; Stoller, 1977). He may wear women's clothes or have male sexual partners, but he is not a transvestite or homosexual in the usual sense; he is less interested in sex behavior than in sexual identity. An erection may only remind him of the penis he wishes to lose. Above all he wants a female body, female status under law, and recognition as a female by society; he may want to marry and adopt children. He lives with frustration and anxiety, and if he can't live according to what he considers his true nature, he may threaten to mutilate himself or commit suicide and eventually do either.

The even rarer female transsexual wants to be rid of menstruation and her breasts, to dress and live and be recognized as a man. Like the male transsexual, the female denies being homosexual, feeling she does not belong to her sex of birth.

Transsexualism was named and defined in 1949 (Cauldwell) and first reached wide attention in 1952, when a young American named George Jorgensen underwent "sex-change" surgery in Denmark, returned to the United States as Christine Jorgensen, and set off an avalanche of publicity. This ignited not only scientific debate about the benefits, the legality, and the morality of such surgery but thousands of requests for it (Anderson, 1956; Hamburger, 1953).

Of course no one can be converted to the other sex genetically, and hormonal and surgical efforts vary in effectiveness. A male-to-female procedure begins by administering estrogens, usually for six months, a year, or longer, during which time the individual lives as a female. Then in a series of operations the penis and testicles are removed, artificial breasts are implanted, and an artificial vagina created. Electrolysis to remove body and facial hair, plastic surgery to reduce the Adam's apple, and other treatments help create a female appearance. All of this is expensive and painful. At the end, the person is not a genetic female and cannot bear children, but the change in most cases is usually welcome and life saving. To an onlooker, the results are sometimes startlingly effective, sometimes sadly unconvincing.

There are comparable procedures for female transsexuals. After months of androgen treatment and of living as a male, the woman's breasts and internal sexualia are removed, a scrotum is surgically created from labial tissue and filled with artificial testicles, and an artificial penis is created by implants and skin grafts. The penis is not large or normally functional.

Such surgery has been done illegally in many places for decades. It has been done legally in the United States for about two decades in some half dozen research centers. Presently it is available in many clinics and hospitals. No one knows how many people have been treated, but the number is at least several thousand.

Opinions on these procedures are inseparable from views of transsexualism, and there is great controversy over both. Some believe there may be a biological basis or contributory factor in transsexualism (Benjamin, 1966;

Šipová and Stárka, 1977). Diamond (1974, 1977b) believes transsexualism is due to a prenatal variation in development. Others believe that psychological influences outweigh biological tendencies in development (Money, 1968).

Stoller (1968) has found a pattern in his studies of child transsexuals and their mothers. The mothers wrapped the children in a cocoon of intimacy and never encouraged normal separation. The fathers were physically or emotionally distant, and the children never went through the normal male process of breaking infantile identification with their mothers. This does not explain female transsexualism; symbiosis with the mother should promote strong female identity in children of both sexes. Few female transsexuals have been studied, but Stoller (1975) reports that some had absent or distant mothers and fathers who were unusually intimate and nurturing. This parallels his observations of male transsexuals.

Should a physician cooperate with a person's belief in belonging to the opposite sex? Some experts believe that by definition, a transsexual is delusional or deeply disturbed (Socarides, 1975). A large number do seem intensely unhappy and disturbed in many ways (Green, 1974). Yet Stoller (1968) has said that some are surprisingly without inner conflict, and suggests that there may be more than one path to transsexualism.

Some child transsexuals have been effectively treated by psychodynamic therapy, but virtually no adults have (Stoller, 1975). Behavior-modification techniques have also been unsuccessful in changing transsexuals (Marks, Gelder, and Bancroft, 1970). For some, allowing surgery may be kinder than insisting that they live in suffering and in conflict

with society, perhaps becoming victims of their own poor surgical skills or committing suicide (Diamond, 1974b, 1965; Green and Money, 1969). There is little large-scale or long-term follow-up research on surgically treated transsexuals, but several studies (Benjamin, 1966; Fish, 1978; Hastings and Markland, 1978; Pomeroy, 1968) conclude that the majority are far happier than before. There are also reports of people who regret it deeply afterward (Jayaram et al., 1978; Socarides, 1975). Because of the ethical and scientific problems involved, many physicians still will not associate themselves with the surgical treatment of transsexuals. Although very rare, transsexualism has captured the public imagination. It has also drawn much attention from researchers, because it may offer insight into normal sex-identity development.

Transvestism

Cross-dressing, or wearing the clothes normally worn by the opposite sex, occurs occasionally in normal young children, in some adults' dreams and behavior, and in the art, drama, and mythology of many eras and societies. As a regular behavior or a condition of erotic satisfaction, it is called *transvestism* (also eonism) and is a gender-role paraphilia.

Women's use of masculine fashions may be seen as cute, chic, or merely eccentric. But when most women wear men's clothes, they leave no doubt of their biological sex, by the cut of the clothes, the way they wear them, and the use of feminine accessories. They are not trying to pass as men. And unisex styles do not put men in women's clothes. When a man dresses as a woman, it usually provokes laughter, as in such plays and films as *Charlie's Aunt* and *Some Like It Hot.* ("Drag," an old show-business term for male cross-dressing and effeminate behavior, has been adopted by much of society.) We have seen (chapter 7) that there is greater sex-fixedness in males; also, that society accords greater prestige to men and the masculine role (see chapter 20). As a result, a male who even partly adopts feminine appearance is usually ridiculed.

When cross-dressing is done by either sex in earnest, it is likely to bring mockery, hostility, and social penalties (Karlen, 1971). The Old Testament said that if either sex dressed as the other, "their blood shall be upon them." In many Western nations and many of our states, cross-dressing is illegal.

The word transvestite was coined by the German sex researcher Magnus Hirschfeld (1910). Until his work on transvestism appeared, it was widely assumed to be an expression of homosexuality. Hirschfeld pointed out that many transvestites are heterosexual, a fact later confirmed by many others (Benjamin, 1966; Prince and Butler, 1972; Stoller, 1975). In fact, there are many varieties of transvestism. Since most transvestites by far are men, we will discuss them first.

A small proportion of transvestites are on the border of transsexualism. Besides disguising themselves as women, they have facial and body hair removed and may even take estrogens, but they don't seek surgery. Some are effeminate homosexuals. A transvestite who is good at passing for the opposite sex may perform as a female impersonator and associate with other transvestites, effeminate homosex-

uals, and male prostitutes. Some even work as "female" prostitutes; either they make clear that they are really men or they take customers to dimly lit places and, using menstruation as an excuse, perform fellatio (Karlen, 1971).

However, even most extreme transvestites do not doubt their biological sex and do not want to change it. As the transsexual is preoccupied with sexual identity, the transvestite is preoccupied with gender role. Some spend hours before mirrors rehearsing feminine gestures, in order to pass as females. Like transsexuals, they may be relatively inactive sexually, their sexual release limited to masturbating while cross-dressed, while having transvestic fantasies, or while viewing transvestite pornography.

Many transvestites seem unexceptionally masculine and heterosexual (Prince and Butler, 1972). They are married, have children, and find homosexuality abhorrent. Yet they sometimes or often feel anxious when not wearing women's clothing (for instance, panties) beneath their masculine garb. Others secretly dress as women at home; some eventually get their wives to help them learn feminine gestures and how to use makeup, but for the majority cross-dressing remains a guilty secret. Some are potent with women only if they wear a particular item of female clothing or imagine themselves to be women. But many, as we said, are more interested in femininity than in sex behavior, and their pursuit of female appearance may become obsessive (Beigel, 1967; Beigel and Feldman, 1963; Stoller, 1975). Some are especially interested in one item of women's clothing and are borderline fetishists (see pages 239–40).

216

Figure 12-2 / *Some transvestites, such as this man from Thailand (top), are so successful at sexual disguise that they win transvestite beauty contest prizes. Transvestism is sometimes called eonism, for the Chevalier d'Éon (bottom), a French nobleman who had passed as a woman for so long that after his death in 1810, an autopsy was done to dispel the rumor that he was actually a woman who had sometimes dressed as a man.*

Clinical material (Rubinstein, 1964) shows other, significant themes in the fantasies, memories, and dreams of some transvestites, which are reflected in transvestite pornography. In much of this pornography, the male hero is compelled by a cold, tyrannical woman to become her slave and dress as a female. Eventually he is accepted as a woman by the women around him. Then he triumphantly reveals himself to the world as a male. This is, in fact, the usual conclusion of a female impersonator's act—revealing at the end that he is male. In fact, transvestism often seems a way of keeping threatened masculine identity by hiding it behind skirts (Beigel and Feldman, 1963).

To most people, transvestism is puzzling, especially in heterosexuals. Many transvestites explain that their parents wanted a girl or that older female relatives dressed them as girls. In some cases this is true, but some transvestites admit to saying so only because they feel it is an answer others expect and understand (Beigel and Feldman, 1963; Beigel, 1967).

Clinical histories show that some transvestites came to feel in childhood that being male cost them love and security. A number felt displaced in their mothers' affections by rival sisters; this was more likely to happen if the mother seemed hostile to masculinity. The child concluded, "I'm not loved or secure as a

---

A Female Transvestite:
Humanizing the Paraphilias

Psychoanalyst Wilhelm Stekel had a gift for showing how even apparently bizarre paraphilias can be tortuous, symbolic paths to finding what everyone wants—to love and be lovable. He described a patient who was a female transvestite of thirty-four. She had love affairs with other women, but these were nonphysical; her pleasure came from cross-dressing. Her father had died when she was two; her mother remarried and had two sons, who took much attention away from her. The stepfather often told the girl that she was unattractive. With a child's reasoning, she decided that if she were a boy, her mother and stepfather would give her love and attention. She envied and resented males because they seemed to have stolen her parents' love. She had dreamed she would grow up to be a man, but when her first menses arrived, she settled for dressing in the clothes of a stepbrother; this caused her first orgasm. To her, clothes remained the chief symbolic difference between the sexes. At thirty-four, she still felt that being a woman meant being ugly and rejected. Through transvestism, said Stekel, she sought what any woman wants, to be lovely and loved. In her fantasies, through the wondrous resilience of the human mind, "her injured narcissism found a way to pleasure and to beauty." The needs and feelings, if not the behavior, are familiar to anyone.

---

male, but I would be if I were a female." Transvestites commonly speak of the advantage of being female (Beigel, 1967).

There are a very few women transvestites (Stoller, 1975). But just as there have been some famous cases in history of men passing as women in society for years, there are a few of women passing as men (H. Ellis, 1936). The classic study of female transvestism (Stekel, 1964) revealed a pattern similar to one often found in male transvestites—a harsh, cold mother, a distant father, and envied siblings of the opposite sex.

Optimism about ridding patients of transvestism has traditionally been slight, and many transvestites claim to be content with their lives. However, there have been some changes through psychodynamic and behavioral therapy (Green and Money, 1969; Marks, Gelder, and Bancroft, 1970). Beigel (1967), who had success with hypnotherapy, said that the key is convincing the transvestite that he has depreciated his own sex, feels it endangered his security and happiness, and believed that the other sex is inevitably happier.

Homosexuality

Homosexual (Greek: *homo* = same) behavior can have many patterns, origins, and emotional and social meanings. Some people perform many homosexual acts but do not think of themselves as homosexual. At the other extreme are people who have strong homosexual desires but never act on them. Anna Freud (1951) suggested that the term homosexual is best used for people whose fantasied sexual partner is of the same sex, regardless of whether this fantasy is acted on or not. Later we will further distinguish between homosexuality as a behavior, as an identity, and as a sociosexual pattern.

"Homosexual" Behavior in Animals

References to homosexual behavior in animals are common, but almost all are actually about mounting and lordosis as ritualized behavior for nonerotic purposes. For instance, male baboons (DeVore, 1965) express both dominance and cooperation by mounting each other. They may or may not have erections, but there is no genital contact. Females of some species, such as cattle and guinea pigs, mount each other under certain circumstances, but the reason may not be erotic gratification (Beach, 1968; Hanby, 1974). Apparently reliable accounts of homosexual behavior in animals, with intromission and ejaculation, are extremely rare. Homosexuality, as we use the word of people, is uniquely human (Karlen, 1971; Stoller, 1975).

Homosexuality as a Human Behavior

Three decades ago, Kinsey et al. (1948, 1953) estimated that 4 to 6 percent of men are predominantly or exclusively homosexual most of their lives, and about 10 percent have a significant amount of homosexual behavior during at least three consecutive years. More than one man in three (37 percent) has had at least one homosexual experience. The figures are one-half to one-third as high for women. Some people think that these numbers are a bit high, others a bit low; they are still the best ones we have.

Unfortunately, these high cumulative incidence figures lump together frequent oral and anal intercourse between men, a single incident of mutual masturbation by thirteen-year-old boys, and exploratory caressing of each other's breasts by pubescent girls. Of the 37 percent of men, half had their homosexual experience between ages twelve to fourteen and never again; much of it was limited to joint or mutual masturbation. For many women, homosexual experience was exploratory, and for half it was limited to a year or less.

Kinsey et al. (1948) created a seven-point scale going from exclusive heterosexuality

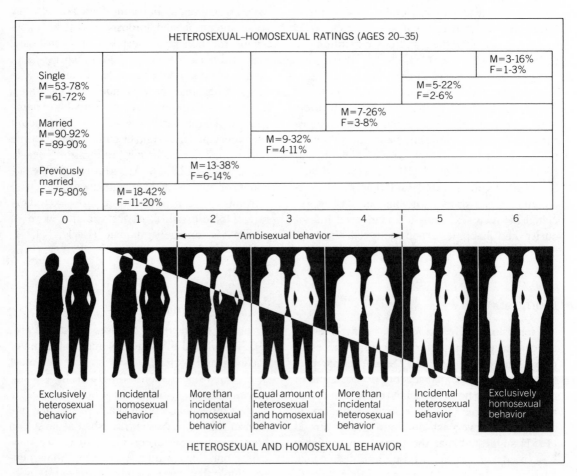

(zero) to exclusive homosexuality (six), which can be used to rate behavior, fantasy, or both. The scale reminds one that homosexual and heterosexual acts and images are not mutually exclusive; the word *bisexuality* ("bi," AC–DC) is sometimes used to describe their coexistence in a person. One author (Karlen) prefers not to use the term in this sense; it could apply equally to someone whose behavior is 99 percent homosexual or 99 percent heterosexual, so it may obscure as much as it reveals. Very few people in our society (or any society studied in this regard) sustain anything like an equal balance of same-sex and other-sex partners for a long period of time. Most are predominantly heterosexual or homosexual over years and decades (Karlen, 1971; Kinsey et al., 1948, 1953).

One of Kinsey's most surprising and ignored findings is that the proportion of males and females with any kind or amount of homosexual experience did not change from about 1900 to 1950 (Kinsey et al., 1948, 1953), despite the so-called sexual revolution of the Twenties. Despite another wave of permissiveness in the

Sixties and Seventies, and a great deal of public rhetoric about homosexuality and "bisexuality," there has been little or no significant change since the Kinsey studies (Karlen, 1978). In the middle Sixties, John Gagnon and William Simon tried to replicate Kinsey's college-age sample and found no significant increase in male or female homosexual behavior in their 2,000 subjects (personal communication). The studies of Morton Hunt (1974) also echo Kinsey's findings. The fixedness of these figures is taken by some (e.g., Diamond) to suggest a biological influence on sexual orientation; others (e.g., Karlen) think wide differences among societies and among social classes within our society suggest the contrary.

People surprised by these findings should recall that throughout Western history, people have been claiming that homosexuality is more widespread and more open (Karlen, 1971). If it had been true even half the time, there might not be anyone around today to discuss it. Kinsey et al. guessed that most young people are unaware of the homosexuality around them. As their awareness increases, they think they are seeing something new come into existence.

Over the centuries, people have guessed that homosexuality is more common in one social class or another. Kinsey et al. found that at age nineteen, the same proportion of males with grade school and with college educations had had a homosexual experience—almost 30 percent. But among those who finished high school, the figure was 45 percent. Interestingly, this segment of society, which has the highest amount of homosexuality, also condemns it the most.

Religion and devoutness affect many sex-

Figure 12-3 / *The majority of people in our society are mostly or entirely heterosexual or homosexual in orientation, but the two are not always mutually exclusive. Kinsey et al. viewed orientation as a continuum and devised a seven-point scale to describe it, from 0 (entirely heterosexual) through 3 (equal homosexual and heterosexual activity for at least three consecutive years) to 6 (exclusively homosexual). The "Kinsey scale" can be used to describe psychological as well as behavioral orientation, though this is obviously difficult to quantify beyond an estimate.*

221

behavior patterns, and Kinsey et al. (1948) found that homosexuality was one of them. For instance, they found homosexuality almost nonexistent among Orthodox Jews, and learned that the devout of all faiths have fewer homosexual contacts than the religiously inactive. We have never heard of anyone investigating whether these figures partly reflect ethnic differences, and we suspect they may (Karlen, 1978).

It is often said that homosexuals exist in all walks of life. There are indeed homosexual physicians, athletes, Congressmen, soldiers, hairdressers, and criminals (R. Smith and Garner, 1977; Weinberg and Williams, 1971, 1974). A disproportionate number of homosexuals take jobs in certain tolerant professions, and they have been accused of forming self-serving cliques. These professions, however, employ only a small proportion of all homosexuals. It is questionable that now or in the past the creative arts have contained a very high proportion of homosexuals or that creativity is related to homosexuality (Karlen, 1971). It does seem true, though, that there are many homosexuals in the performing arts. Green and Money (1966) suggest not that homosexuals are drawn to the performing arts because it is tolerant, but that a propensity for role playing is sometimes a factor in homosexuality.

Male and Female Homosexuals

Only 13 percent of women have ever had a homosexual experience leading to orgasm, compared to 37 percent of men. Only 2 to 3 percent are predominantly or exclusively homosexual *(lesbian)* most of their lives, compared

to 4 to 6 percent of men. While 50 percent of men say they have ever responded physically or emotionally to someone of their own sex, only 28 percent of women do. These findings contradict the popular idea that more women than men have and accept homosexual feelings and behavior.

The differences between male and female homosexuals' behavior and attitudes are much like those between male and female heterosexuals'. The women have sexual relations less regularly than men and with fewer partners. Kinsey et al. (1953) found that only 4 percent of lesbians had had ten or more sex partners, compared to 22 percent of homosexual men. More than half had had only one partner, another fifth only two. And women's homosexual behavior, like their heterosexual behavior, started later in life than men's. A. Bell and Weinberg (1978), with different methods and samples, found that 40 percent of lesbians and 70 percent of homosexual men had had more than 100 partners, and 28 percent of the men had had more than 1,000.

Lesbian acts occur almost entirely among the yet unmarried, the formerly married, and the never married. Only about one woman in a hundred is homosexually active while married (Hunt, 1974; Kinsey et al., 1953). This destroys the old myth of secret lesbianism among married women. However, about 10 percent of men who have been married have had homosexual experience while married (Kinsey et al., 1948).

Women's devoutness (Kinsey et al., 1953) plays a predictable restraining role. But differences between generations, so striking in women's heterosexual behavior, correlated little or not at all with homosexual behavior. Educational level affects homosexual behavior as it does heterosexual. Those who postpone marriage for a higher education have more years as single adults and are more likely to experience a variety of sex acts.

Like heterosexual women, lesbians do not quickly develop fully orgasmic sex lives, and many are sexually inactive for long periods. Eventually, though, most lesbians do become orgasmic, through cunnilingus (about 80 percent) or genital apposition (50 percent). Using a dildo or other penis substitute is extremely rare. Most lesbians do not want a substitute penis any more than a real one.

In many other ways, the sex and love lives of male homosexuals tend to be typically masculine, those of lesbians typically feminine. Two men bring together their greater tendency toward regular orgasmic release, two women their greater desire for intimate, long-lasting relationships. The male homosexual world often proclaims the beauty, nobility, even superiority, of homosexuality, but often it seems sex-obsessed. For many men there are orgies in steam baths, anonymous quickies in doorways and public toilets (L. Humphreys, 1975), and use of male prostitutes.

Many homosexuals of both sexes report establishing satisfying lives and relationships (A. Bell and Weinberg, 1978), but male homosexuals do not have as many long-term relationships as female homosexuals or as heterosexuals (Westwood, 1960). English sociologist Michael Schofield (1965) found that only half of the "best adjusted" of his homosexual subjects had had an affair longer than one year. Some say this is because society discourages same-sex relations and gives them no support (Hoffman, 1968, 1976). Others say the reasons are inherent in male homosexuality. Many homosexual men divide their intimates into exclusive categories of friends and sex partners, often seeking strangers of other classes and races. Long-term couples tend to become roommates bound by companionship and domestic ties, ceasing to be bed partners and finding sex outside the relationship (Leznoff and Westley, 1963; Sonnenschein, 1968).

Like male heterosexuals, male homosexuals often affirm their masculinity through sex and dominance; like female heterosexuals, lesbians often affirm their femininity through love and intimacy. While the lesbian world often proclaims its social and sexual rights, it often seems obsessed with romance. Like heterosexual women, lesbians tend to consider sexual aggressiveness and having many partners unfeminine and offensive; they tend to avoid anonymous encounters and partners from different social and ethnic backgrounds (Bass-Hass, 1968; Martin and Lyon, 1972; Sawyer, 1965). Long-lasting, monogamous arrangements are more common among lesbians than among male homosexuals. In prisons, women form relationships more from emotional than sexual need, and even form extensive pseudofamilies (Giallombardo, 1966; Ward and Kassebaum, 1965). There is very little lesbian prostitution.

Many lesbians regard homosexual men as promiscuous and sexist bad boys. As a group, the men return the coolness. Despite some individual close relationships and joint political efforts, the male and female homosexual worlds seldom touch, and then rarely comfortably or for long (Karlen, 1978).

223

Sociosexual Patterns

There are lifelong exclusive homosexuals, people whose homosexual behavior is episodic, and many gradations in between. Among people who are predominantly homosexuals are a minority of effeminate males (perhaps 10–15 percent) and mannish females; militant group-joiners and isolated "closet" homosexuals; sadomasochists and "leather freaks"; "chicken hawks" interested in children and youths; people who adapt to homosexuality temporarily or permanently in prison; social circles of middle-aged professional women and of young strippers and go-go dancers; and many people who apparently differ little from their heterosexual neighbors (Karlen, 1978). We speak for convenience of homosexuals, but there are many homosexual patterns and life-styles.

In the past decade or so, the word "gay" has passed beyond homosexual circles to describe anyone or anything homosexual. So has the word "straight" for people and things heterosexual. The so-called gay world is most extensive and visible in big cities, which offer more partners, tolerant professions and neighborhoods, and anonymity. However, one should not underestimate the extent of the homosexual scene in smaller cities and towns (A. Bell and Weinberg, 1978; Gerassi, 1966; Karlen, 1971). Kinsey et al. (1948, 1953) found only slightly less homosexuality in rural than in urban areas; the difference seemed to result in large part from the anonymity and the availability of more partners in cities.

Gay bars are one of the most visible and important parts of the homosexual subculture. Many young people, especially soon after "coming out" (revealing themselves) as homo-

Figure 12-4 / *Many homosexual individuals and couples now seek—sometimes demand—society's acceptance of their erotic relationships. Homosexual organizations have made massive protests against the restrictions they often face in hiring, housing, military service, and other aspects of public life.*

sexuals, plunge frantically into the bar-and-party scene, seeking friendship, understanding, love, and sex (in various orders). They make friends, meet lovers, and learn gay slang and etiquette and perhaps a defensive homosexual ideology (Hooker, 1965). The gay bar is a secure oasis in a straight world, but above all it is a busy pickup point (Hoffman, 1976). Especially in large cities, some bars are tense "meat racks," matched in sexual competitiveness only by the most predatory singles bars for straights. Many lesbian bars, though more socially oriented, may have an intense air of erotic predation, but lesbians do not typically "cruise" (seek pickups) in public places, as homosexual men do (Saghir and Robins, 1973). Large cities such as New York, San Francisco, and Chicago have specialized bars for homosexual leather fetishists, sadomasochists, and transvestites.

The three most common and obvious roles in the male gay scene are "swish," "butch," and boyish (Karlen, 1978). The swishy role is a caricature of feminine seductiveness or gentility; it blends imitation and parody. At the opposite pole is the hypermasculine butch role. In its extreme form, it involves body building, wearing leather clothes, and perhaps affecting a menacing swagger. Between these is the more common boyish role, with its Peter Pan manner, meticulous grooming, and absence of dis-

plays of male aggressiveness. That these are roles is evident from the way they can be quickly turned on or off, as situations demand. There are similar roles among female homosexuals, from the hyperfeminine "femme" to the emerging "baby butch" to the pseudomasculine "dyke." To our knowledge, none of these roles has been thoroughly studied. However, not all homosexuals play any of these roles, and some find them offensive.

Many homosexuals, especially lesbians and male secret homosexuals, rarely enter this world of bars, dancing, clubs, partying, and public role playing. Some associate in small circles, especially after age thirty and in small towns; some live in secrecy and isolation; some are shy and inhibited. And after entering close relationships, homosexuals tend to drop out of the bar-and-party scene; they may return to it when the relationship breaks up (Sonnenschein, 1968).

Those who live in the gay scene tend to start dropping out around ages thirty to thirty-five. The strong homosexual emphasis on youthful good looks means that as men grow older, they must often pay for sex, and women must compete hard for younger partners. There is also a reaction to the squalid side of gay life—impersonal sex, prostitution, venereal disease, abuse of alcohol and drugs, desperation, paranoia, and suicide. All of these often make the word gay seem a cruel euphemism (Hatterer, 1970). Efforts to change this atmosphere probably have not altered life much for the majority of homosexuals (Karlen, 1978).

Other Types of Homosexual Behavior

Latent. Many predominantly heterosexual people occasionally have homosexual images, fantasies, dreams, and behavior. Classic psychoanalytic theorists (Freud, 1962) considered these to be outbreaks of the homosexuality latent in all people because of a bisexual instinct system. But the concept of latent homosexuality is under increasing criticism. Leon Salzman (1965), in a classic critique, said that the concept of latency implies either dormancy (a hibernating bear is a dormant bear) or potential (an acorn is a potential oak). But few scientists now accept that there is a unitary homosexual instinct dormant in us, awaiting release. Of course, some people are potentially homosexual: the simple proof is that some do become homosexual. But more people become heterosexual, and latent heterosexuality is spoken of only jokingly. People can develop tuberculosis, but we don't speak of humans as latent tuberculars. The idea is used only about homosexuality, and it may often reflect emotional views rather than scientific clarity. Some people do have homosexual desires that they find unacceptable and therefore repress or deny. To these people alone might the concept of latent homosexuality be applied. Homosexual behavior and mental content in the predominantly heterosexual is better explained by many of the following concepts.

Substitutive. Substitutive homosexuality occurs when no heterosexual partner is available. It is jokingly tolerated in many societies and subcultures. It often happens in prisons and other one-sex living situations; Kinsey et al. (1948) suggested it was common among cowboys. However, it is not inevitable in such situations. The great majority of men and women living in military barracks do not have homosexual relations; Kinsey et al. (1948) found no increase in homosexual behavior during World

War II, when many people served in the armed forces. Even in prisons, where homosexuality may involve a significant minority of men, a great deal of it is forced (homosexual rape) and seems more a symbolic act of dominance than of sexual desire (MacNamara and Sugarin, 1977). Deprivation seems only one factor in substitutive homosexuality. In the past it has been assumed that people who turn to homosexuality in prison drop it when heterosexual partners become available; this is not always true (Sagarin, 1976).

Exploratory. Some homosexuality happens out of curiosity or adventuresomeness; there are people who try homosexual acts chiefly to find out what they are like. Sometimes more than one motive is involved; some women experiment with other women primarily out of narcissistic curiosity, to know what they themselves feel like to a man (Karlen, 1971).

Ideological. Ideological homosexuality is a new concept that has risen largely because of some feminists' belief that women should have homosexual experience. The primary motivation is said to be less erotic than political. However, there is no way of knowing whether many people who claim to perform ideological acts would not have done so anyway.

Pseudohomosexuality. The concept of pseudohomosexuality, developed by psychiatrist Lionel Ovesey (1969), is now widely used in counseling and therapy. He formulated it through studying heterosexuals who experienced homosexual thoughts, dreams, or fantasies, but without physical arousal. Such events often cause anxiety, even panic; this is one of the commonest reasons for men seeking counseling on campuses. It occurs in women but is far more common in men.

As noted in chapter 7, adaptational (neo-Freudian) theory sees nonsexual motives behind much sexual thinking and behavior. Feelings of dominance and submission are especially likely to be put in sexual metaphors ("I was shafted," "I screwed him"). Sometimes, because of stress, performance demand, or conflict, sexual or nonsexual, such images appear in dream or fantasy. If these images of "shafting" (or other homosexual acts with the same emotional overtones) are taken literally, the result is often a rush of anxiety and the question, "Does that mean I'm homosexual?" Fear of being homosexual may also occur when people doubt that they are adequately masculine or feminine in any sexual or nonsexual way.

Sometimes sexual metaphors of power and submission coincide with sexual arousal and are acted out. This is now a widely accepted explanation for some predominantly heterosexual people performing homosexual acts at times of stress; typically such acts puzzle the person and are ego-alien ("It doesn't seem like me thinking and doing that"). Pseudohomosexual anxiety and such ego-alien homosexual behavior often respond well to counseling or psychotherapy (Ovesey, 1969).

The Historical and Cross-Cultural View

It is often said that homosexuality has appeared in all times and places, but in some societies it is virtually unknown (Karlen, 1971; Malinowski, 1929). In fact, the incidence of homosexuality has varied among societies and through history (Bullough, 1976; Karlen,

1971). However, homosexuality has never been a majority adult behavior and has nowhere been fully approved. Contrary to popular views, it was not fully accepted by law or most of society in ancient Greece (Flacelière, 1962; Karlen, 1971; Lacey, 1968). It was illegal in the Greek city-states and tolerated chiefly by part of the leisured upper class (Karlen, 1971; Marrou, 1956).

The Greek pattern of homosexuality was one also found in some non-Western societies. A man was not considered homosexual or unmasculine if he took the role of penetrator with a "nonman," a category including both women and boys. This is true in the Marquesan Islands, where most or all men engage in such behavior (Davenport, 1965). There, as in ancient Greece, sexual relations between two grown men would be viewed as unnatural, wrong, or a sign of sociosexual inadequacy.

In an attempt at a cross-cultural survey, Clelland Ford and Frank Beach (1951) found that in twenty-eight of seventy-six societies on which reports were available, adult homosexual acts were absent or so rare or secret that they remained unknown. Lesbianism apparently existed in only seventeen. Forty-nine societies, Ford and Beach said, approved some form of homosexuality for some members of the community.

This finding has often been quoted; unfortunately, the authors do not say whether homosexuality means occasional group masturbation by boys or regular anal intercourse by adults. Neither do they say whether approved means enthusiastically praised or ignored as a misdemeanor. They note that some cultures "make special provisions for the adult male homosexual, according him a position of dignity and importance," referring to *berdaches* (transvestite homosexuals) and *shamans* (magicians or priests, in some societies homosexual). Some homosexuals did traditionally take such roles in certain societies, but their position was not necessarily dignified or enviable (Karlen, 1971; Devereaux, 1963). In no society is homosexuality the preferred outcome of childrearing. We suspect that this is partly because most predominant homosexuals relinquish (or feel forced to relinquish) the social roles of spouses and parents, and the rights, privileges, and responsibilities that go with them (Karlen, 1971). It is also partly because parents generally believe their children will be happier with the heterosexual orientation of the majority.

Societies obviously vary in how they define homosexuality. In some societies, one may perform many homosexual acts without being labeled a homosexual. In our society, even one homosexual act may earn someone a homosexual label. Societies also vary in how they react to homosexuals. In traditional Navaho society, homosexuals might receive only mild and occasional negative attention. In medieval Europe, they were burned at the stake, and today they may be denied employment, ostracized, or imprisoned.

Origins of Homosexuality

Throughout Western history, the idea has recurred that there is some quality of each sex inside the other (Delcourt, 1961). The theory became popular in the nineteenth century that all people are constitutionally bisexual (Freud, 1962; Krafft-Ebing, 1965), and that this was the chief source of homosexuality. But it is now generally believed that sexual differentiation, including a tendency in sexual orientation, is set before birth (see chapter 7). However, the idea of innate bisexuality has always had a ring of truth to many people. This may be because all children identify to some degree with parents of both sexes, so that there is a residue of cross-sex identification, more or less conscious, in most people.

Over the past century, there have been many claims that homosexuality has constitutional roots other than in a potential for bisexuality. Arguments for a genetic basis (Kallmann, 1952a, 1952b, 1953) exist, but at most the relationship is believed to be indirect (Karlen, 1972). There have also been many claims of an endocrine factor. One recent review of these (Meyer-Bahlburg, 1977) shows that some studies have found different levels of sex hormones (e.g., testosterone, estrogens), in homosexuals than in heterosexuals, but others did not. However, all studies of certain other hormones (e.g., etiocholine, androstenodione) showed that these were consistently different in homosexuals. Studies on the effects of prenatal hormones strongly support the theory of prenatal influence (Ehrhardt, 1975; Phoenix et al., 1959; Reinisch and Karow, 1977; Yalom, Green, and Fisk, 1974). That prenatal hormones may contribute to the development of sexual orientation (by biasing the nervous system in its reactions to environmental influences) is a position one of us has held for some time (Diamond, 1965, 1968, 1977b, 1979). This is still an area for vital research.

The other author (Karlen) feels that constitutional factors may predispose some people to have difficulties in psychosexual development, and that the final result depends on individual development. But since homosexuality is uniquely human, it is best explained by the distinctly human influence on sex—the enlarged cerebral cortex that permits many kinds of learning and mislearning. The readjustment of many homosexuals to heterosexuality and the variety of homosexual patterns among individuals and cross-culturally also point to predominantly developmental origins of many or most instances of homosexuality.

A study of the patients of more than seventy psychoanalysts of different theoretical persuasions revealed a pattern in the lives and families of about two-thirds of male homosexuals (Bieber et al., 1962). The prehomosexual boy tended to be timid, a loner, and not comfortable in nonsexual relationships with other males. He may well have been overprotected and raised in an antisexual atmosphere. The mother was "close-binding and intimate" with him but not necessarily affectionate; the father was emotionally distant or openly hostile. The study concluded that it usually takes two parents to help create homosexuality in a child, and a warm relationship with the father makes it virtually impossible. Similar backgrounds were found for many in the control group of psychosexually disturbed heterosexuals, but not as strongly or consistently. Similar findings have come from many depth clinical studies (Green, 1979; Hatterer, 1970; Socarides, 1968). Many find comparable family backgrounds, particularly a critical or cold mother and a distant father, in many lesbians (Karlen, 1971).

The most common adaptational view of homosexual orientation is that it is a *phobic* (fearful) reaction to the genitals of the opposite sex. Among the reasons for this reaction may be maternal deprivation, the lack of a warm relationship with the father, competition problems with siblings and peers, feelings of masculine or feminine inadequacy, and difficulty relating warmly but nonsexually to others of one's own sex. These and other factors may interact to produce different homosexual patterns—as psychoanalyst Clara Thompson (1963) first pointed out, there are many homosexualities.

A study of more than 1,500 male homosexuals from a socio-psychological perspective (A. Bell, Weinberg, and Hammersmith, 1980) confirms that during preadolescence and adolescence, many who became homosexual "felt different" from their peers. This study does not strongly support the finding (Bieber et al., 1962) that homosexuality is often associated with a particular constellation of family relationships, but its methods of investigating this were not comparable. There are some other sociological studies of homosexuality which view it as a learned role. However, we know of no families or peer groups that offer homosexuality as a preferred role; furthermore, most homosexuals become aware of and enter the homosexual subculture after developing homosexual behavior and identities (Dank, 1971; Whitam, 1977, 1978).

It is sometimes said that the origins of homosexuality do not matter, only the social realities faced by homosexuals. However, if homosexuality is rooted in psychosexual conflicts rather than in prenatal neuroendocrine programming or in social roles, this cannot fail to affect one's view of sexual orientation and of childrearing.

Health, Dysfunction, and the Politics of Science

Most homosexuals, like most other people, more or less come to terms with finding friends and lovers, making a living, aging, and the other usual demands of life. But there is great

scientific and social controversy about whether homosexuals as a group are more neurotic or self-destructive than heterosexuals, and if they are, whether this is inherent in homosexuality or results from society's reaction to them.

Some who have studied homosexual populations offer evidence for homosexuals' relative normality (A. Bell and Weinberg, 1978; Weinberg and Williams, 1974). Others claim that although some signs of maladaptation exist, they result from social pressures and are not inherent in homosexuality (Hoffman, 1968). Some (Hooker, 1957, 1965; Simon and Gagnon, 1967) portray homosexuals as being little or no different from heterosexuals except in their sexual partners. Some of these studies have been criticized for their methods, samples, and assumptions (Karlen, 1978; Whitam, 1977); the matter is not settled.

Another claim of homosexual normality has come from some sociologists using the concepts of *deviant career* and *sexual scripts*. Fundamentally, they say (Becker, 1963; Gagnon and Simon, 1967; Goffman, 1968; Polsky, 1969; Weinberg and Williams, 1974) that society labels a person homosexual, and that people labeled deviant for any reason—homosexuals, drug users, jazz musicians, prostitutes, the handicapped, members of ethnic minorities—respond by flaunting their deviance and live up to the majority's expectations.

These concepts are intuitively attractive, but for homosexuality are not supported by research. One major study of homosexuals that tested this viewpoint (Weinberg and Williams, 1974) found that homosexuals' unhappiness was not proportionate to the social disapproval they met. We, like some others (Whitam, 1977), suggest that a sociological view can contribute much to understanding homosexuality, but is not by itself adequate. Humans are not only social creatures but biological and psychological ones.

A large body of clinical evidence (Bieber, 1962; Storr, 1964; Ovesey, 1969; Hatterer, 1970) finds both sexual and nonsexual conflicts in many or most homosexuals. The most common psychodynamic view is that conflict is usually inherent in the development of homosexuality (Socarides, 1968; Stoller, 1975). It has been argued that such results reflect only people who seek treatment, and that they are "the sick ones." However, research suggests that nonpatients and those who seek treatment differ less in degree of conflict than in factors influencing who asks for help during crises (Hendin, Gaylin, and Carr, 1965).

Many nonclinical studies also find inner conflict in homosexuals. One study of lesbians in West Germany (Schäfer, 1976) revealed that less than half wanted to be homosexual, and one in four had tried to commit suicide at least once. In this country, Bell and Weinberg (1978) found that one homosexual man in five had attempted suicide at least once, compared to one heterosexual man in twenty-five. A depth interview study of nonpatient college students showed much conflict and self-dissatisfaction among those who were homosexual, stemming largely from inner and interpersonal sources (Hendin, 1977).

One of us (Karlen) believes that although a number of homosexuals cope as well with life over-all as many heterosexuals, homosexuality is more often than not rooted in inner conflict and takes an inner toll. The other author (Diamond) believes that social pressures account for most if not all of these difficulties.

But both of us agree that homosexuality is not a measure of human worth, and that society usually loses by segregating homosexuals, let alone punishing them. Homosexuality is not contagious, and social fears about it seem to us greatly exaggerated. Neither, however, do we think it fair to portray homosexuality as a neutral path, let alone an enviable one. One pays some price, often a heavy one. We believe that society can afford to lighten this burden.

Unfortunately, the question of homosexual adaptation has been sharply politicized, and the scientific community polarized, before conclusive evidence is in. One of the arguments has been over therapy and the possibility of change to a heterosexual orientation.

There is a myth that no homosexual can change his or her behavior. About one-fourth of people with extensive homosexual experience leave it behind on their own (Pomeroy, 1972). Not surprisingly, more do so with counseling or therapy. Since the early 1950s, there has been a growing scientific literature reporting surprisingly similar results. Therapists who do not believe change is possible do not work to that end, and they rarely report it. Therapists who do believe it is possible rather consistently report that about one homosexual in three who voluntarily undergoes therapy makes a full heterosexual adaptation; another third change to a partly heterosexual pattern; some others remain homosexual but may feel improvement in their nonsexual problems. Such figures come from both behavior therapists (Feldman and McCullough, 1971) and psychodynamic therapists of various schools (Bieber et al., 1962, Hatterer, 1970). There are systematic follow-ups of very few kinds of counseling and therapy, but one of former homosexuals (Lief and

Mayerson, 1965) confirms claims of lasting change.

Many homosexuals, like many heterosexuals, seek therapy because of anxiety, depression, suicidal feelings, work problems, or other nonsexual difficulties. Probably the majority position among therapists today is to aim for change in sexual orientation only if the patient requests it. However, some who enter therapy for nonsexual reasons later decide to try to change their orientation, and some do so (Hatterer, 1970). Change is most likely in people who have at least some memory of heterosexual arousal (Bancroft, 1977; Bieber et al., 1962; Feldman and McCullough, 1971).

Some homosexuals are hostile to the idea of change, and some mental-health professionals have condemned homosexuality. Conflict between both groups has grown in recent years; this has politicized many issues, raising passions, but clouding facts.

Since the early Fifties, homosexual organi-

zations (sometimes called homophile groups or the homophile movement) have increasingly campaigned for the decriminalization of homosexual behavior, which is still illegal in the majority of states, and for homosexuals' civil rights. These groups, such as the Mattachine Society, Society for Individual Rights, Gay Rights Task Force, Gay Activists Alliance, and Daughters of Bilitis, constitute a tiny minority of homosexuals, but they have had some influence on social policies (Karlen, 1978).

In the past few decades, the American Psychiatric Association and many other professional groups have also urged decriminalization (MacNamara and Sagarin, 1977). However, many homosexual groups have taken issue with them for not endorsing homosexuality as healthy and for saying it sometimes changes through therapy. Prominent in this polarization was the 1973–74 decision of the American Psychiatric Association (with about half its members voting) to remove from its list of dis-

---

Incest Aversion

Human incest aversion may have biological roots in the regulation of primate society. In most species with long mateships, the territorial male drives away or intimidates all potential rivals, including his growing male offspring. And a female is unlikely to mate with a male less dominant than herself, thus excluding her sons. Therefore, Irven DeVore points out, parent-child (especially mother-son) incest is very infrequent in higher primates (Karlen, 1971).

This sounds like an animal version of the Oedipal complex. Certainly many close relatives are sexually attracted to each other, consciously and/or unconsciously. There is an argument that this is counteracted by familiarity, which may dull sexual attraction, particularly among siblings (Talmon, 1964).

To these observations and theories one might add George Bernard Shaw's—that the incest taboo reflects a natural and healthy aversion to all relatives.

---

orders homosexuality with which a person is not dissatisfied (*ego-syntonic* homosexuality). Some members privately admitted that they voted this way on social and humanitarian grounds, although they still considered homosexuality a dysfunction or disorder.

In 1977, a survey of several thousand APA members reversed the 1975 vote; two-thirds of those polled said they considered homosexuality a disorder (Lief, 1977). Apparently many were dissatisfied with some uses to which the formal APA decision had been put (Lief, 1977, personal communication). For instance, some were disturbed that a number of homophile groups, quoting the APA decision, recommended that all teenagers with sexual conflicts receive counseling from homosexual activists as well as from mental-health professionals. And despite evidence to the contrary, many homosexual groups informed the public that changing from homosexuality to heterosexuality is impossible.

Like many professionals involved in human sexuality, we believe that therapy should be forced on no one. We also believe that full and accurate scientific information should be available to the public, and that those who might consider therapy, for sexual or nonsexual problems, should be allowed to decide in a free and fully informed way whether to seek it.

Incest

Cultural and Biological Background

Incest (Latin *incestum:* unchaste or spoiled) is sexual contact between people too closely related to marry and between certain other kin (variously designated from society to society).

The common definition of incest as coitus with close kin ignores noncoital and homosexual acts.

The family exists in all societies, and nowhere is sexual contact allowed between any of its nuclear members except husband and wife (Murdock, 1949a; K. Weinberg, 1976). Neither, of course, may they marry, since marriage always involves the right to sexual access. The definition of incest varies from society to society, but everywhere it extends beyond the nuclear family, usually according to ties of *designated kinship* ("not blood" kin) rather than *consanguinity* ("blood"). Although incest is relatively uncommon, we will give it more than passing attention, for it provides a prototype for the social restriction of sexuality (see chapter 20).

Our society, like all others, reacts to incest with such aversion, even horror (K. Weinberg, 1976), that many nineteenth-century scientists thought the feeling instinctive. Inbreeding (reproduction by closely related people) was said to cause sterility, physical deformities, and mental defects. Kirson Weinberg (1976) quotes one authority who claimed that sibling marriages would make humans a "race of pygmies."

However, incest does occur occasionally among some animals (Ford and Beach, 1951), and inbreeding may bring out beneficial as well as damaging genetic traits from both parents; animal breeders have long used it for that purpose. There is now some evidence that human inbreeding does raise the frequency of infant deaths, malformations, and physical and learning deficits (Adams and Neel, 1967; Schull and Neel, 1965; Seemanova, 1971; Stevenson et al., 1966). However, it has been argued (Dobzhansky, 1970), that any such effects are probably too small for most people to have noticed through history. Some societies' incest laws encourage inbreeding—for instance, by banning coitus with stepsiblings but encouraging first-cousin marriages (Murdock, 1949a). This supports the theory that even if incest aversion has biological roots, the deepest prohibition is probably social.

Incidence and Participants

Because incest is guiltily hidden, its frequency is unknown. Only about two convicted incest offenders per million people are reported in the United States each year, but most researchers think incest is far more common (K. Weinberg, 1976). Studies of two small (and perhaps atypical) groups of women revealed rates as high as 15 percent (DeMartino, 1969; Halleck, 1962). It has been guessed that first-cousin incest is most frequent, involving perhaps 3 to 4 percent of the population; less frequent, in descending order, are incest with siblings (3 to 4 percent according to Hunt, 1974), aunts, siblings-in-law, uncles, fathers, and mothers (Gebhard et al., 1965). Mother-son incest is most rare according to all studies.

Most incest behavior consists of brief, sporadic investigation by siblings and cousins in childhood; few of them have coitus. Sibling incest often begins when an older brother—or, less often, an experienced older sister—initiates sexual games. Some researchers suspect that crowded homes promote sibling incest, especially if the children share a bedroom, but this is not certain (K. Weinberg, 1976).

Most incest research is done with father-daughter cases that ended in the father's imprisonment. Too often the research doesn't distinguish daughters and stepdaughters; in one study (Maisch, 1972), roughly half of the cases involved stepdaughters. MacNamara and Sagarin (1977) say that coitus with a brother- or sister-in-law or a mother- or father-in-law probably isn't rare, and to many participants "are extramarital rather than incestuous events." For this reason, the American Law Institute recommends that sexual relations between adults whose ties are legal rather than genetic should not be considered incest. Canadian and Swedish law-reform commissions have made similar recommendations, distinguishing "true incest" from "statutory incest" (Maisch, 1972). The Swedish commission also suggests that true incest be decriminalized for partners older than eighteen.

Two studies of incest with daughters and stepdaughters report that many of the men were poor, badly educated, and unemployed (Gebhard et al., 1965; K. Weinberg, 1976); another (Berest, 1968) claimed that almost all were emotionally disturbed. Yet another (Cavallin, 1966) says that most had average intelligence and education and worked steadily. It may be that poor, uneducated, and antisocial men are more often discovered and jailed. Hunt (1974) reasons so, since he found incest more common among the college educated.

An extensive study by the Institute for Sex Research (ISR) found striking differences between men convicted of incest with younger and older daughers (Gebhard et al., 1965). Most of the offenders with daughters under twelve had grown up in poor, disorganized, affectionless homes. Three-fourths were "passive, shy, emotionally and often financially dependent on their wives." The majority were preoccupied with sex but not very active sexually and considered themselves unhappily married. They lacked confidence socially and sexually, and almost all started incest at a time of marital stress. It isn't always clear where parental authority ends and intimidation begins, but few of these fathers used open threat or force. Most bribed and persuaded, and they limited themselves to genital fondling or oral-genital contact. Such relationships may go on for many years if undetected (Oliven, 1974).

Many men who began incest when their daughters were twelve to fifteen fit no psychological or social category. Coitus occurred in three-quarters of these cases, and half the daughters were willing or passive. But a number of fathers who had incestuous relations with daughters over sixteen did fit a pattern. They were devout, held conservative social and sexual views, and had been psychologically and sexually restrained since childhood. Yet these moralistic, inhibited men had histories of violence, impulsiveness, and excessive drinking as well as incest.

Most of these men were poor, uneducated farmers and ranchers of low-average intelligence. They lived in isolated mountain subcultures where morality was often rigid in public but violated in private. Many considered any postpubertal girl a legitimate sexual object, especially a nubile stepdaughter. A similar pattern may exist in some rural parts of Sweden and Japan (Kubo, 1959; Reimer, 1940).

The ISR study found that coitus occurred in 90 percent of cases of incest with older daughters. Often this was a continuation of incest begun in the girl's early adolescence. In some cases, the partner was a seductive adult stepdaughter. Less than one older daughter in ten actively resisted, and more than half, in the researchers' opinion, passively cooperated or actively encouraged the father. Many fathers first became involved with the oldest daughter living at home and then had coitus with successive daughters as they matured (Gebhard et al., 1965).

Only about half the incest cases were reported by mothers. Some seemed to look the other way as long as possible, apparently willing to let the daughters be their sexual substitutes. Some knew, but feared the father's violence or the economic effect of his desertion or imprisonment. Resentment eventually made some wives go to authorities or drive the girl from home.

Much remains to be learned about some mothers' tacit collaboration. One small study (Garrett and Wright, 1975) showed that wives of convicted incest offenders were better educated than their husbands and, like the wives of some alcoholics and rapists, seemed to relish their roles as martyrs to socially "inferior" husbands. They used the sex offense to bolster the sense of moral and social dominance that seemed fundamental to their marriages.

Effects

Surprisingly little is known about the long-term effects of incest or any other adult-child sex behavior. Some writers (Meiselman, 1978; Sloane and Karpinsky, 1969) find a variety of neurotic and sexual conflicts in many young participants in incest; some of these difficulties become acute or reach a therapist's attention only many years after the event. Kirson Weinberg (1976) says the incestuous father's jealous attempts to keep himself the daughter's only partner often isolates her from peers and disrupts her social and sexual development. However, he points out that some daughters reciprocate the father's affection and eroticism and are content with the relationship.

Several decades ago, Lauretta Bender and her colleagues did follow-up studies on people who had had a variety of sexual contacts with adults in childhood, including incest (Bender and Blau, 1937; Bender and Grugett, 1952). Some of the children had "deep confusion" about their sexuality. However, Bender stressed that many had sought and enjoyed the sexual contact, which "did not necessarily forecast maladjustments." In a small study of nonpatient women (DeMartino, 1969), half with incestuous experience felt it had affected them adversely.

Many now believe (K. Weinberg, 1976) that children who experience incest may be injured less by the event than by the reactions of family, society, and authorities. MacNamara and Sagarin (1977) suggest the contrary, that one might expect children to react adversely to adults' failure to prevent incest. They also point out that while young victims must be protected, reports of incest must be investigated carefully, for children can have flights of fantasy, be spiteful or vengeful, or misinterpret a nonsexual situation.

The effects of incest probably depend on the ages of the people involved, their relationship, the entire constellation of family relationships, the social milieu, whether the incest is discovered, and many other factors.

Pedophilia and Lolitaism

Pedophilia is predominant erotic attraction to children, male or female or both. We distinguish this from desire for young adolescents (see below). Almost all pedophiles are men (Money and Ehrhardt, 1972).

A small number of pedophiles fit the cliché of an old "degenerate" who assaults children in playgrounds. There are pedophiles of all ages, from the teens on (McCaghy, 1971). The Institute for Sex Research found the largest number of convicted offenders against children are stepparents and other relatives, neighbors, or family friends, and few use force (Gebhard et al., 1965). Many of the children involved are passive or encouraging, and some of the relationships are affectionate. Sexual contact is usually limited to fondling, masturbation, or oral genital contact (see chapter 10).

Many men convicted of contact with children, the study found, preferred teenagers but would settle for a younger partner. Only one-quarter to one-third were true pedophiles. Some were heterosexual, some homosexual, and some interested in both sexes. Quite a few fit the common clinical characterizations of pedophiliacs as sexually timid and emotionally disturbed. A number were neurotic, psychotic, alcoholic, or lacked adequate social controls; a higher proportion of the homosexual pedophiles were repeaters and seemed very deeply disturbed. Psychotherapy is sometimes successful with pedophiliacs (Toufexis and Karlen, 1974), as was movingly shown in the film *The Mark*.

The *Lolita syndrome,* or *nympholepsy,* is compulsive attraction to girls in puberty and early adolescence. It was classically portrayed in Vladimir Nabokov's novel *Lolita* (1972); the protagonist, Humbert Humbert, was obsessed with pubescent girls—nymphets, he called them—and began a long affair with his seductive stepdaughter of twelve, Lolita. This is indeed the commonest sort of relationship found among sex offenders against minors (ages twelve to fifteen) by the ISR study. The authors of that study found, as Humbert argued in his defense, that very many men are attracted to young adolescents, and only strong social sanctions prevent them from acting. In many permissive societies, it is common for men to take such girls or even younger ones as partners. And the majority of convicted offenders against minors are not nympholepts; they merely come from certain rural and urban-poor subcultures that do not separate biological and legal maturity, but assume, "If they're big enough, they're old enough." Few seemed to have marked emotional problems. Neither did the other large group of offenders, the "near-peers"—for instance, a boy of seventeen who had coitus with a girl of fifteen.

A small number of the offenders were indeed nympholepts and had repeatedly sought young adolescents. This group was composed of more homosexuals than heterosexuals. Some of these Humberts had sought youths on whom to lavish affection and gifts, with sex perhaps a second motivation.

A review of psychological studies of Lolitas and Lolita-seekers (Toufexis and Karlen, 1974) found that many of the men are married to women who reject and control them, sexually and otherwise; they approach young girls because they think the chances of rejection and control low. The ISR study found homosexual offenders against minors striking among sex offenders in their consistent pattern of having had very poor relationships with their parents, especially their fathers. Psychiatric studies often stress the problems of the men, but many

of the seductive adolescents are also disturbed; a striking number learned early to use seductiveness to win the attention and affection they lacked, having had physically or emotionally absent fathers in early childhood. Individual and group psychotherapy for both Humberts and Lolitas has often been successful (Toufexis and Karlen, 1974); the results with homosexual youth-seekers are less clear.

Nymphomania, Satyriasis, Promiscuity, Don Juanism, Frigidity

We have seen that many apparently healthy people have orgasmic frequencies of less than once a month, others more than once a day; and some have had only one coital partner, others have had hundreds. We also saw that people tend to consider their own behavior normal and to call less deficient, and more excessive. Thus there is no satisfactory definition of such terms as hypersexual, undersexed, frigid, nymphomania, satyriasis, promiscuity, and Don Juanism. Our society has tended to define "too much" sexual activity or "too many" partners rather strictly, and to see deviations as a disorder, a moral failure, or both (Karlen, 1979).

Nymphomania (Greek: nymph = beautiful young divinity; also bride) is usually defined as excessive sexual desire in a woman. It is often used by parents, police, clinicians, or peers for any female who is sexually active, and by men whose partners are more desirous than they. Truly continual sexual excitement occurs rarely, in people suffering certain physical or mental disturbances (Oliven, 1974).

The male equivalent of nymphomania is *sa-*

tyriasis (Greek: satyr = mythical creature serving the god of pleasure and fertility). Some women call their partners satyrs for wanting coitus more often than they or for admitting that they enjoy the thought or reality of having more than one partner. Like nymphomania, satyriasis is far more often a moral judgment than a scientific reality. The rare occurrences of constant desire or excitement are usually results of physical or emotional disorder. Satyriasis should not be confused with *priapism* (Greek: Priapus, god of male sexual power), a rare condition of constant erection that results from certain tumors, infections, and neurological and blood diseases. The erections are pleasureless, and without medical attention may last for days or longer and eventually become very painful. If priapism goes untreated, permanent damage may result (Oliven, 1974).

Promiscuity means having "too many" erotic partners and is applied to both sexes, but more often to women; the term *Don Juanism* (for the mythical seducer) is also used for men. *Frigidity*, a word used exclusively for women, means lack of interest in sex or inability to feel arousal or pleasure. Often the words imply compulsion or other neurotic motivations; one often hears such pseudopsychology as "That Don Juan must be a latent homosexual" and "A woman who sleeps with that many men must be frigid."

It remains a matter of argument whether any given amount of erotic desire, activity, or partners constitutes a problem for an individual or those around him. Some people have high or low sexual frequencies, many or few partners during certain periods of their lives. Sometimes high activity seems a search for new experience or response, especially in youth, after an unsatisfying relationship, or at other times of life

change. Stress, anxiety, and depression can reduce sexual interest in normally responsive people.

Sexual activity has been called excessive or promiscuous when it is compulsive, hostile, or relatively joyless. Some people do seek many partners out of a need to control and demean others (Stoller, 1977); others do so chiefly to feel attractive or worthwhile, to win attention and care, or for tangible rewards. Sometimes an anorgasmic woman feverishly tries many partners in the hope that one will bring her to climax; an impotent man may try many women in the hope of getting an erection. And sometimes emotional conflict or sexual dysfunction is quite apparent and seems to justify the terms we are discussing—for instance, in a man who seeks a new partner literally every day but usually turns away when "conquest" is assured, and is impotent or anorgasmic when coitus is attempted (Stoller, 1977).

We suggest that using sex to try to solve such nonsexual problems as low self-esteem or fear of dependence is rarely satisfying for long. And because behavior widely labeled promiscuous or frigid is generally looked down on, it can bring feelings of guilt, shame, self-contempt, frustration, and deviance. Still, it remains to be shown that even in these situations, the sexual activity itself (or lack of it) is harmful. The problem is, we suggest, the insecurity or conflict that underlies the behavior.

We believe that the terms discussed in this section are best avoided unless they can be better defined. They have often been used to brand both healthy and troubled individuals as sick, delinquent, or criminal and to subject them to penal or even surgical brutalities (Karlen, 1971).

Fetishism

The French psychologist Binet coined the term *fetishism* in 1888 (H. Ellis, 1936) to describe predominant or exclusive sexual interest in an inanimate object *(fetish)* or a part of the human body. The fetish must be present for sexual gratification to occur. The most common fetishistic objects—hair, hands, feet, shoes, underwear, leather clothing, and handkerchiefs—are not sexually arousing to most people. Fetishism occurs almost exclusively in men.

In some people, fetishism is entwined with transvestism or sadomasochism (see below) and may involve bondage with chains and manacles. Fetishism may also overlap with *coprophilia* (being excited by feces), *urolagnia* (being excited by watching urination or being urinated upon—a "golden shower"), or other paraphilias. Many fetishists are also emotionally disturbed in nonsexual ways.

A foot fetishist may be aroused only by looking at or touching women's feet. He reaches orgasm by doing so in reality or fantasy and by masturbating. Many fetishists collect their fetishes (panties, gloves, shoes), and some find satisfaction in stealing them from stores and homes (MacNamara, 1961).

Fetishism has drawn great scientific interest because it may offer a model for a variety of sexual patterns in which a compulsive fantasy takes over the sexual stage. Some people (DeLora and Warren, 1977; Katchadourian and Lunde, 1975; Kinsey et al., 1953) say there is a continuum of sexual preference ranging from mild preferences—being a "leg man" or "ass man"—to fetishism. They attribute preferences to childhood experience or social conditioning, perhaps through one critical learning experience. For instance, if a boy is sexually aroused and happens to see a pair of shoes, he may become sexually fixated on shoes.

This leaves questions. Why should it happen to males but almost never to females? Why to one person and not another? Why one object and not another? Many common fetishes, such as red spike-heeled shoes, are rarely seen by most children; how can they be the basis of conditioning, let alone such one-shot learning?

There is a major difference between a sexual preference and a compulsive sexual fixation that minimizes or excludes partners. It is common, probably universal, for men to be attracted by breasts, thighs, buttocks, and hair. Some are especially aroused by one of these parts of the body, which is sometimes called *partialism* (Binet called it *petit fetishisme*). A small number of men are impotent unless this part of the body or some particular garment is visible during coitus (Oliven, 1974); such cases seem to lie on the borderline between partialism and fetishism.

True fetishism is sexual obsession with an object or body part rather than interest in a partner; sexual release usually comes from fantasy and masturbation. In a classic portrait of fetishism, Stekel (1964) described how a fetishist tends to progressively withdraw from sexual contact with people, while the fetish becomes so loaded with emotional and symbolic meaning that it is the worshipped object of an "erotic monotheism" that carries the fetishist away from reality. The word fetishism was well chosen: anthropologists use it for an object believed to have supernatural power.

There have been many psychiatric studies of fetishism (Freud, 1959; Stekel, 1964; Storr, 1964; Gillespie, 1964; Stoller, 1975). To simplify them in brief summary, a child whose psychosexual development is already disturbed may associate sexual desire with guilt, rage, desire for a parent, or other unacceptable feelings and desires. If the conflict becomes too intense, unacceptable urges (incest, guilt, rage) are mentally disowned, and sexual desire is fastened on a "safe" symbolic object—for instance, the shoes worn by the desired person. The unconscious mental formula is, "I don't want to do anything nasty with people, I just like their shoes." Thus genital function continues under a safe fiction. The fetishist's collection of symbolic objects, said Stekel, is a symbolic harem. Such thinking is, of course, unconscious and magical. To explain his behavior to himself, the fetishist may enlarge on some early incident when he desired the symbolic object, giving the impression of having been traumatized or conditioned by the event.

Exhibitionism

Exhibitionism is obtaining erotic gratification from displaying the genitals. Virtually all exhibitionists are men, and theirs is one of the commonest sex offenses (Rosen, 1964).

Some say that the wish to display the body is universal, and the provocatively dressed woman, the stripper, and the man who shows his erect penis in the subway are at the high end of a continuum. But as we said in discussing fetishism, there is an important difference when the act becomes a sexual end in itself. Usually when a woman displays her body, she wants to attract attention or arouse desire. The exhibitionist wants to shock unwilling witnesses; that is why, if married, he displays himself to a stranger who is not a potential sex partner. In a public place or before a window, he flashes open his clothing (hence the term "flasher"). This act and the reaction are usually sufficient satisfaction for him; at most, he may masturbate afterward (Storr, 1964).

The exhibitionist is rarely the dirty old man or sex fiend of popular imagination. The ISR study of sex offenders (Gebhard et al., 1965) found that more than half the exhibitionists had started in their late teens, and 90 percent by age twenty-five. Even many of the married ones were sexually rather inactive. Many had acted at times of stress or failure—say, after rejection by a spouse or employer. The ISR group and other researchers (Ellis and Brancale, 1956) have concluded that flashing is the act of an insecure man whose ego has been damaged by feelings of sexual or nonsexual failure.

Some clinical reports find that the exhibitionist, feeling unable to assert himself normally with women, tries to affirm his masculinity through others' reactions to his genitals. This explains his need (Stoller, 1977) "to upset the observing woman and later civil authorities; only then has he forced society to attend to the fact that he unquestionably is male, is masculine, and has a penis." Clinicians and penologists also point out the element of hostility in his effort to shock, though the aggressive feelings may be unconscious. But MacNamara and Sagarin (1977) note that some flashers have also been convicted for voyeurism (see below) or rape. They say that the danger of most exhibitionists has been exaggerated, but the potential for danger should not be ignored out of well-meaning sympathy for the psychologically disturbed. Fortunately, the treatment of exhibitionists by individual and group psychotherapy is often effective (Rosen, 1964).

Perhaps psychologically related to the flasher are the compulsive obscene phone caller and the *frotteur* (French: one who rubs), who touches or rubs against others in crowded places. There is not enough research to show their true motives and whether a significant number of them have histories of other kinds of sexual intrusion or aggression.

Voyeurism

The *voyeur* (French: looker; "peeper") finds sexual satisfaction in spying on scenes of nudity, excretion, or sex behavior (Karpman, 1954). Voyeurism is also called *scoptophilia* (Greek: *skoptein* = to look). Virtually all voyeurs are men.

Again, one must distinguish normal from dysfunctional acts. Most men and many women are sexual "lookers"; especially in societies such as ours, which are secretive about sex, strong curiosity commonly remains in adulthood, and many people would take advantage of chances to watch others' bodies and sex play. But the voyeur does so compulsively, risks shame and arrest repeatedly, and makes it a substitute for sexual relationships (Stoller, 1977). He almost always spies on strangers and may masturbate while doing so. He may prowl and wait for hours to be able to spy through a window (Gebhard et al., 1965). Homosexual peeping occurs, but it rarely receives attention from the law or researchers.

The voyeur is widely considered sexually timid, more a pitiable nuisance than a threat (Ellis, 1962). Many voyeurs do feel inadequate and are inept at making sexual relationships (MacNamara and Sagarin, 1977). Some apparently have a great deal of bottled-up ag-

gression; a significant minority have committed other crimes, such as burglary, arson, and rape (Yalom, 1960).

The argument has been made that voyeurism is a victimless crime; another is that even public looking—staring and whistling on the street—should be considered an offense. Reactions in public are an arguable matter, but the voyeur's spying often is a deliberate and usually planned invasion of privacy in the home. The minority of voyeurs who commit other sexual and nonsexual crimes require that one not automatically consider all voyeurs benign (MacNamara and Sagarin, 1977).

Bestiality

Bestiality, or *zoophilia,* is sexual contact with animals. Virtually all religious and legal codes condemn it. The Old Testament prescribed the penalty of death, and legal records from the Middle Ages (Karlen, 1971) tell of men convicted of bestiality and burned at the stake with such partners in sin as sheep and geese. As late as 1750, a Frenchman was hanged for copulating with a she-ass; the animal was acquitted on the grounds that she had not been a willing partner (Ford and Beach, 1951).

In our society, bestiality is sometimes tolerated in children, adolescents, and the sexually deprived. It usually occurs not because of great sexual interest in animals but as an experiment or because no human partner is available. Most societies, says Clellan Ford (1973), feel that bestiality is "if not wrong, at best inadequate and a last resort."

Sexual relationships with animals are a common theme in art, mythology and folklore around the world (Ford and Beach, 1951). There are cave paintings that show men having coitus with animals. However, the idea often has more symbolic or magical significance than erotic meaning. In Greek mythology, the god Zeus had intercourse with Europa as a bull and Leda as a swan. In reality, mating of one species with another is rare. Impregnation of a human female by a male animal or of a female animal by a human male is impossible.

Several decades ago (Kinsey et al., 1948), about 17 percent of males raised on farms had orgasmic contact with an animal; the figure was only 2 to 4 percent for urban males. A more recent study (Hunt, 1974) found an over-all incidence of 4.9 percent and attributed the decline to the large drop in rural population. Contact is usually with sheep, calves, and other large animals of placid temperament, but also with household pets, especially dogs. Only a few men and older boys engage in bestiality fairly frequently. Most people do so only once or a few times.

Some boys have sexual contact with animals because they see other boys do so or are taught to by them. This rarely happens with girls, who generally don't discuss sexual activities as much as boys. Still, Kinsey et al. (1953) found that 3 to 4 percent of females had had sexual contact with animals—as with males, most only once or twice, during preadolescence or adolescence. (Hunt's 1974 finding was about 2 percent.) Often this contact did not lead to orgasm or even excitement. Most of the girls' acts were with dogs or household pets—touching the animal's genitals, masturbating it, or having it lick their genitals. Only two of almost 6,000 women interviewed had had coitus with an animal, in both cases a dog (Kinsey et al., 1953). How-

ever, 18 percent of females told Kinsey et al. that they had been aroused at some time by watching animals mate.

Sadomasochism

Sadism is the enjoyment of inflicting pain or humiliation on others. The word is often used in a general psychological sense, sometimes in a specifically sexual sense. The sadist's satisfaction may come not only from inflicting pain but from a feeling of domination. The word comes from the name of the eighteenth-century writer the Marquis de Sade, whose sexually explicit novels such as *Justine* (1966) are unsurpassed models of sadism as a behavior and a state of mind.

The converse of sadism is *masochism,* desire for or pleasure in pain or humiliation. This, too, is often used in either a broad psychological or specifically sexual way. The word was coined by Krafft-Ebing in *Psychopathis Sexualis,* after Sacher-Masoch, the nineteenth-century author of *Venus in Furs* (1965) and other fiction about sexual masochism. Sadism and masochism often coexist; a person who practices one may also practice the other.

Sadism and masochism ("S and M"), like fetishism, have raised popular and scientific curiosity. Some people have pointed out that there is aggression and sometimes violence or pain in many species' courtship and mating; similarly, many people scratch, squeeze, bite, and roughly handle their partners when sexually excited, and some like having this done to them. They suggest that there is a continuum from people who occasionally give or receive a "love bite" to sadomasochists. But we believe

Figure 12-5 / *To a person who is not a fetishist or sadomasochist, it may be puzzling that drawings such as these, from publications for fetishists (left) and for sadomasochists (right), produce erotic excitement. But it is precisely the focus on an object or on a situation of pain or dominance, rather than on a partner, that defines these paraphilias.*

there is a difference between someone who is rough when aroused and someone for whom potency or sexual satisfaction can occur only when accompanied by torture, humiliation, or even injury to a sexual partner or oneself.

There is no way of knowing how many sadomasochists there are, but they are apparently relatively rare. Many find partners through ads in "underground" newspapers. There are female prostitutes who specialize in "domination," "English culture," or "discipline," code names for catering to the needs of masochists; some, usually with agreed-to safeguards, will fill the needs of sadists. Others specialize in "bondage" and "domination" ("B and D")— being tied, shackled, humiliated, and in some cases tortured.

Like other paraphilias, sadomasochism is more common in males. Gebhard (personal communication) says that outside the largest cities, if a female sadomasochist becomes known in the underground network of those who seek partners for such practices, she may receive phone calls and letters from men for one or two hundred miles around. Hunt (1974) and Kinsey et al. (1948, 1953) give rough estimates of how many people engage at least occasionally in sadomasochistic practices—about 6 percent of males and 4 percent of females. However, the figures may be different for occasional or mild experimentation with sadomasochistic behavior. Definitions of the terms vary, and these numbers may well be high.

Conditioning and learning theories have the same drawbacks in explaining sadomasochism as in explaining fetishism. Psychodynamic theories (Bieber, 1966; Stoller, 1975) for the two phenomena, though complex, are fundamentally similar to those for fetishism: such behavior substitutes normally nonerotic or semierotic acts or objects for genital union, as a result of guilt or anxiety. Sadomasochism sometimes responds to psychodynamic therapy (Panken, 1973).

Other Paraphilias

From Krafft-Ebing's *Psychopathia Sexualis* (see chapter 2) to recent psychiatric journals, researchers have written about paraphilias that strain most people's credulity: coprophilia and urolagnia, foreskin fetishism, necrophilia, sadomasochistic rituals carried out in bizarre costumes or circumstances. Most people cannot imagine how anyone finds these sexually exciting, let alone how they become the only way a person can be sexually aroused or potent.

We said that understanding fetishism could serve as a model for understanding other paraphilias. A broad range of clinical material (Rosen, 1964) suggests that in many of them, a compulsive substitution of an object or ritual for coitus is unconsciously thought of as a safe way of expressing sexuality without suffering guilt, anxiety, or inadequacy.

Overview

Some sex acts are done by only a small number of people as a predominant adult behavior. Since society has a stake in promoting the family as a reproductive and survival unit, it tends to discourage them and to have sanctions against them, from mild disapproval to severe penalties. Many seem compulsive and rooted in internal conflict, though some may have constitutional components.

Some of these behaviors are controversial, and the most controversy today is about homosexuality. The matter has been sharply politicized among scientists and laymen, and disagreement continues about the nature and social implications of homosexuality. There are apparently different developmental paths to homosexuality, and many homosexual patterns and life-styles.

Some people have said (Ullerstam, 1966) that even the most bizarre paraphilias should be socially accepted and scientifically viewed as neutral as long as there is no harm to a partner. We believe that paraphilias often indicate not only sexual but nonsexual emotional conflicts. There is an important difference between finding a woman sexy when she wears high heels or lacy panties and preferring a shoe or panties to a woman. Even if the person reaches orgasm and receives sexual pleasure, many possibilities for a rich emotional, sexual, and social life are precluded. Furthermore, the paraphilias often demand a social price, from ridicule to imprisonment. The degree of acceptance by society changes with time but not necessarily toward more permissiveness.

It has been claimed that there is free choice in the practice of paraphilias. True, one can freely decide to have intercourse while dressed in the clothes of the opposite sex or engage in homosexual activities; indeed, some people do so out of curiosity or novelty. We believe, however, that most people who regularly engage in these practices—and certainly those who find sexual release through them only—act out compulsions. How our society will allow individual freedom without jeopardizing the institutions it feels may be threatened remains to be seen. The cross-cultural evidence suggests that full social acceptance is very unlikely.

Review, Discuss, Decide

1. What are the differences in meaning and implication between the terms deviance, perversion, paraphilia, and dysfunction? Would you prefer some term other than deviance or paraphilia? If so, which one, and why?
2. What are fetishism, sadomasochism, and incest?
3. Distinguish between heterosexual, homosexual, bisexual, hermaphrodite, transsexual, and transvestite.
4. Do you think your view of the behaviors described in this chapter would be influenced if you participated in any of them?
5. Which behaviors do you consider the most deviant? In which sense of the word? Why?
6. Do you see society substantially changing its view of any of these behaviors in the next fifty years? How, and why? What forces might be most influential?
7. Should any sexual deviations be punishable? Why? How?
8. What would you say to a friend who revealed to you that he or she practiced common or rare deviations?

Part IV   The Couple

As we saw in Part II, The Person, and Part III, Sex Behavior, many major decisions, although they involve others, are primarily individual. But eventually, for most people, sexuality involves two people interacting—a couple. This section views the interactions and concerns of couples, in long- and short-term erotic and love relationships. There are three chapters about matters that concern every couple—love, relationships and marriage, and sexual techniques. We hope that these will give readers not only information but understanding helpful in making important and often difficult decisions about entering, sustaining, and ending relationships.

This section concludes with a chapter on psychosexual health and dysfunction. Few relationships are without some strain and conflict; couples must identify their difficulties, resolve them, or seek aid if it is needed or desired. Such decisions require the clearest thinking and feeling, but they are often impeded by uninformed convictions and emotional interference. Clarifying the issues is the first step in improving the chances for a satisfying outcome.

13　Love

Can I love him without being in love with him?

How do I know if I'm really in love?

If she really loved me, wouldn't she sleep with me?

Should we get married because we're in love?

Should we split up because we aren't in love any more?

Can I love more than one person at a time?

Just because we went to bed, why does he have to fall in love?

Many of the most common and deeply felt questions that come up in discussing sexuality are about love. Yet love is the part of sexuality about which we have the least information and the fewest answers—and often a pressing need for crucial personal decisions. Psychologist Harry Harlow (1974) has said:

There is and always will be a desperate need for learning to love. In the area of love the lowly layman should not stand in awe of the professionals, since there is objective evidence to suggest that psychologists, psychiatrists, psychoanalysts, and social workers are either unaware or afraid of love, in fact or in fancy.

Harlow combed psychological literature from 1950 to 1970 and found only a handful of articles, and those were about theoretical rather than real love. "For all practical purposes," he observed, there were "no experiments on love and no scientific essays on developmental love."

The contrast with daily life is startling. Imagine a Martian sent to earth to observe what people feel, say, and do about love. He would be in a frenzy of note taking. He would find love in most people's thoughts, fantasies, and conversations, in films, songs, books, television, and roadside billboards. The bemused Martian would record the words "God is love" above a church door; a mother's whispered "I love you" to her infant; two people who met only hours ago whispering the words in a motel room. He might now be as confused about the meanings of love as most people.

We recently saw a decade in which many people thought love a universal cure. "Love children" experimented with love and eroticism, hoping to save themselves and society. Society is not yet saved, and many individuals seem quite unredeemed. Still, our society believes deeply in the need for love, and in love's power. Poets and novelists remind us that the search for personal and social salvation through

249

love is not new; science is just starting to pay attention to it.

Science has faltered before love because it is not measurable. Furthermore, the word love covers a vast variety of feelings and relationships. Speaking of *bonds,* or *affectional systems,* in primates, Harlow says there are at least five basic kinds of love—the mother's love for her infant, the infant's love for its mother, peer (age-mate) love, heterosexual love, and paternal love.

The complexity and duration of human bonds distinguish us from other creatures, but studies of higher animals' bonds do provide some basic concepts to work with. We will look at these animal bonds and then see how they have been elaborated by humans. Then we will see how love has been described and analyzed in history, literature, and other societies. Finally, we will try to relate all of this to common concerns in our time and culture. We will reach no simple definition of love, but the discussion may provide some insight for future decisions.

Bonding in Higher Animals

Kinds and Purpose of Bonds

Most higher animals are social; they live in families, packs, or herds, and they gain obvious advantages from group hunting and defense and from dividing many tasks of survival. Sociability also allows the young to learn from their elders and peers. This permits more flexible, varied responses to a changing environment. Long, intimate bonds, then, are means of

survival, increasingly important as creatures become more complex and creative in their ways of adapting.

Higher social animals show bonds between adult male and female, parent and offspring, young peers, old and young, male and male, female and female, dominant and subordinate individuals, individuals and social groups. These are the same types of relationships in which people feel some of their strongest loves and loyalties. But only in the highest species does anything like human feeling seem to be involved, and even in them, the foresight and feeling of human relationships probably aren't present. The bonds that exist have been programmed genetically through natural selection. But in higher animals we probably see ties of which human loves are vast elaborations.

Ritualization

Bonding is aided by *ritualization,* the transfer of nonverbal language from one situation to another. The behavior acquires a formalized, exaggerated quality that makes its symbolic meaning clear. For instance, a gull chick stimulates its parents to feed it with a food-begging noise. Courting adults also use this noise; but the adult voice, the situation, and the addition of a head-tossing motion show that the noise is not a request for food. It brings the male and female closer by eliciting their nurturing reactions. The male may, in fact, feed the female; if he does, the pair will probably mate (Tinbergen, 1951, 1965). It may be more than social convention that humans often carry on courtships over offerings of food and drink.

Humans also ritualize an infant feeding be-

250

havior in courtship: they convert the infant's sucking reflex into kissing. After infancy, touching pursed lips to another's body conveys many meanings other than "feed me." A little girl kisses her doll, heads of state kiss on a public occasion, passionate lovers kiss deeply during coitus, a flirt lightly brushes the lips of a near-stranger—and more often than not, at least, people recognize the different messages.

Another example of ritualization is grooming, or cleaning another's body. Primate mothers groom their infants, and mutual grooming becomes a ritualized way for adults to affirm sexual, cooperative, and protective bonds. Such physical "caring for" often occurs in human love, as when lovers brush dust from each other's clothes and scrub each other in the shower or tub.

Ritualization also expands the language of aggression and cooperation, which are crucial to forming affectionate and erotic bonds. In most higher species, males are more aggressive than females; females cope with the males through flight and appeasement behavior. Aggression increases with sexual maturity and is particularly strong at reproductive periods, when there are territory and young to protect. For mating to occur, the male's pugnacity must be checked or he may attack potential mates; and the female must accept his body weight while in a vulnerable position, not flee from it. It is largely through ritualized behavior, both innate and learned, that they manage to form a bond and make love rather than war.

In the ritualized behavior of courtship, it is clear that neither is really attacking or fleeing, and eventually the two become accustomed to each other. The parallel with courting humans'

showing off and coyness makes people smile at films of animal courtship. The animals, of course, do not parody humans; the people are watching the evolutionary sources of their own behavior.

Sex, Power, and Aggression

Adult bonding has important roots in ritualized behavior during the *juvenile* period, between infancy and puberty. Males and females learn to use and limit aggression and cooperation; without this learning, social life would be impossible. In most social species, young males begin to form a "pecking order" or some other, more complex dominance hierarchy. In many primate species, the dominant males are not simply the strongest but the most cooperative and protective (DeVore, 1965). In some species, females also establish a dominance order; in others, they derive their status from their mates. Many researchers believe that humans learn the basis of adult same-sex and other-sex relationships in similar ways; and that some adult's problems with assertion, cooperation, trust, love, and sex are rooted in poor relations with childhood peers (Harlow, 1974; Karlen, 1971; Bieber et al., 1962).

Higher animals express dominance and subordination toward both sexes with ritualized fragments of sex behavior. Soon after birth, a male primate shows mounting and pelvic thrusting, a female lordosis. They ritualize these movements in many situations. For instance, when male baboons vie for dominance, the contest ends when one presents his rear, as a female presents herself sexually. It is as if he were signalling, "Don't attack a vulnerable fe-

251

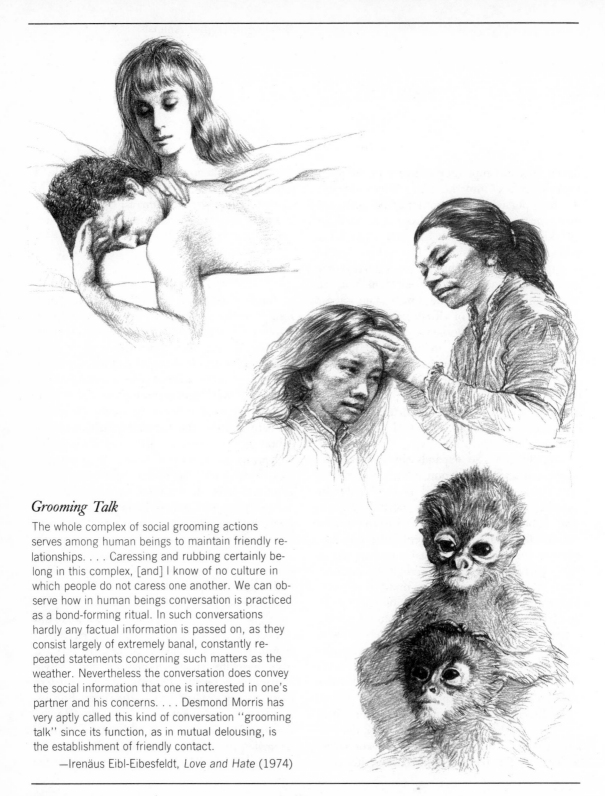

Grooming Talk

The whole complex of social grooming actions
serves among human beings to maintain friendly relationships. . . . Caressing and rubbing certainly belong in this complex, [and] I know of no culture in
which people do not caress one another. We can observe how in human beings conversation is practiced
as a bond-forming ritual. In such conversations
hardly any factual information is passed on, as they
consist largely of extremely banal, constantly repeated statements concerning such matters as the
weather. Nevertheless the conversation does convey
the social information that one is interested in one's
partner and his concerns. . . . Desmond Morris has
very aptly called this kind of conversation ''grooming
talk'' since its function, as in mutual delousing, is
the establishment of friendly contact.

—Irenäus Eibl-Eibesfeldt, *Love and Hate* (1974)

252

malelike creature." The winner usually mounts and makes a few perfunctory pelvic thrusts, as if announcing, "I'm on top, you've been shafted." There is no genital contact, but this has been misperceived as homosexual behavior (De Vore in Karlen, 1971).

It may not be mere social convention that in language, humans' most extensive communication system, sexual metaphors often express power relationships. Such phrases as "I've been shafted" and "screw you" are used without regard for a person's sex, to express dominance rather than eroticism.

Because of their ideals about sex, love, and society, some people are upset to see how primate bonding is linked with aggression, appeasement, and status. It remains to be proven how much these connections hold true for humans, though there is strong clinical evidence that erotic acts are often seen as expressions of dominance and submission. In fact, some psychologists believe many internal and interpersonal conflicts rise from confusing the affectional, erotic, and symbolic aspects of sexual relationships (Jonas and Jonas, 1975; Maslow, 1962; Ovesey, 1969).

Bonding and Sequential Learning

Further clues about human loves emerge from research showing how *sequential learning* replaces rigid programming in higher species. Harlow (1974), trying to learn what binds mother and infant rhesus monkeys, isolated monkeys at birth and raised them with substitute mothers, such as wire dummies equipped with feeding bottles. Later he combined various amounts of real and substitute mothering with a variety of peer contact.

Unmothered monkeys acted much like psychotic children; they crouched passively or huddled in corners, cried, grimaced, and rocked back and forth with their hands over their faces. As adults, they failed to form relationships with other monkeys. The males attacked rather than courted females. If they did try sexual contact, they seized the female's body from the wrong direction and thrusted against her back or side. The females would not present their hindquarters or accept a male's weight. Harlow wrote, "Their hearts were in the right place, but nothing else was . . . we had developed not a breeding colony, but a brooding colony."

From such experiments, Harlow concluded that there are the five basic bonds mentioned earlier, and that each is a preparation for the next. First mother and infant establish a bond through mutual cues and satisfactions. Thus the infant builds enough security and confidence to separate from her and enter peer relationships. If deprived but not crushed by inadequate mothering, it may reach normal development through peer bonds. Some peer bonds are between male and female, but the majority are between members of the same sex.

Sexual maturity brings a transition to heterosexual bonds. Of course, failure to develop these precludes experiencing parental bonds. With great patience and effort, Harlow got some of his unmothered female monkeys to mate and bear infants. But they ignored, abused, or beat their babies, none of which would have survived without human intervention.

If each bond is built on those before it, adult love and sex bonds are not magic or good chemistry or instinct. Even in rhesus monkeys, they result from step-by-step development and learning.

253

Figure 13-1 / *Psychologist Harry Harlow, in his famous experiments with rhesus monkeys, found that an infant deprived of mothering (top left) cowered much like a human infant deprived of warmth and care. When grown (bottom left), it was unable to interact with other monkeys, remained isolated, and turned its aggression on itself. If a deprived female, with human help, managed to mate and bear an infant (bottom right), it neglected or even severely abused its offspring.*

The Survival Value of Love and Sex Bonds

A minority of higher animals form long-lasting breeding bonds. Nonhuman primates are more selective and stable in mating than most other mammals, but even most of them pair for only hours, days, or seasons, in what has been called sequential monogamy or "Hollywood mating." Few creatures' bonds approach humans' in length, and none approach them in complexity.

We draw the conclusion that love and sex bonds have expanded *together* in our species because they provide an evolutionary advantage. Long, even lifelong bonds, reinforced by eroticism, help join creatures who must raise offspring through the longest, most demanding childhood in nature. This may explain why female sexual responsiveness is so much greater and more frequent in humans than elsewhere in nature, and why the father-child bond, weak or brief in most species, is highly developed in people (Eibl-Eibesfeldt, 1974).

The physical and emotional pleasures of a loving sexual relationship are thus as functional as our lungs, brains, and hands. They are part of the vast, varied bonding system that preserves us as individuals, families, and societies.

Paths of Human Love

Freudian Insights

Despite differences in viewpoint and terms, researchers in many fields agree that a person's capacity for love develops through phases, each dependent on those before. Early in this century, Freud (1962) said that one experiences strong attachments from infancy on, and that these are often erotically tinged. Stunted or distorted love between mother and infant, he said half a century before Harlow's experiments, damages the ability to love and trust later in life. Clinical studies have borne this out (Bowlby, 1969). Freud stressed that early feelings of dependence and bliss remain part of love: "There are thus good reasons why a child sucking at his mother's breast has become the prototype of every relation of love." Through the mechanism of *transference,* the feelings associated with important early relationships are carried over to later ones. Each lover, said Freud, brings along to a new relationship the ghosts of important past loves, such as parents, siblings, friends, and lovers.

Freud also elaborated psychiatrist Eugene Bleuler's term *ambivalence:* in love, people often feel such contradictory feelings as lust and tenderness, cravings for dependence and dominance, and urges that are parental and infantile, reverent and playful. Lovers, with the best intentions, may blindly compete, clutch, reject, or overestimate each other—all at the same time.

Freud also pointed out the importance of *narcissism,* or self-love, in love relationships; people often love others who resemble themselves physically or emotionally, or may project onto the beloved an idealized self-image. Later, Abraham Maslow (1962) spoke of the converse, *deficiency-love,* which seeks to remedy a deficiency in the self through the beloved's positive attributes. This is very different from love based on realistically appreciating the other's qualities.

255

Post-Freudian Views

Freud's development of ego psychology in the 1920s (see chapter 7) created new avenues for understanding love. Students of the mind and behavior focused increasingly on how people cope with society and with others, and on how love and sex form part of an individual's coping pattern.

Harry Stack Sullivan (1953) coined the term *interpersonal relations.* He expanded the idea that love involves ghosts of past attachments; he said it may also call up imaginary figures such as a "dream girl" or "prince charming," and personifications such as "the law" and "respectability." He emphasized preadolescent learning: between eight and twelve, he said, a child finds chums of the same sex and for the first time considers another's happiness as important as his own. This nonerotic love is one's first true love outside the family; if it doesn't develop, especially in boys, adult heterosexual love and sexual function may fail to develop. (This, of course, anticipated Harlow's findings.) Sullivan also stressed that people can love others only to the extent that they can love themselves.

Karen Horney's books (1937, 1939, 1942) are widely read today; they explore in detail how people relate to each other in love—basically, she said, by moving *toward* others, *away* from others, and *against* others. A healthy person, she said, feels all three urges but manages to keep them in satisfying balance.

Erich Fromm, a psychoanalyst and sociolo-

Figure 13-2 / *The capacity for love, loyalty, and commitment seems to be built upon the early basic bonds that develop between mother and child, father and child, and siblings and peers.*

gist, has stressed the need for intimacy and meaning in mass society. His *The Art of Loving* (1956) has been widely read on campuses for many years. Fromm stresses respect and caring; in fact, his view of love sometimes seems more altruistic than passionate, even semi-mystical: "Love is not primarily a relationship to a specific person; it is an *attitude,* an *orientation of character.* . . . Immature love says: '*I love you because I need you.*' Mature love says: '*I need you because I love you*' . . . love is primarily *giving,* not receiving."

Erik Erikson (1968) developed the idea of redefining one's sense of *identity* throughout life. Adolescence, he says, is especially important in identity formation, and falling in love then "is by no means entirely, or even primarily, a sexual matter. . . . To a considerable extent, adolescent love is an attempt to arrive at a definition of one's identity by projecting one's diffused ego-image on another and by seeing it thus reflected and gradually clarified. This is why so much of young love is conversation."

Sullivan, Fromm, and many others say or imply that certain kinds of love are best. Clinical experience and perhaps wisdom lie behind their views, but not necessarily truths one can apply to everyone. Psychiatrists Laplanche and Pontalis (1973) have with some justice called their views directly or indirectly moralistic, setting up convictions as scientific standards of mental health.

Among today's experts, there are many views of what love is and should be. There have been some new observations and therapeutic techniques, particularly in marriage and family therapy, communication-system therapy, and problem-centered counseling. Still, the most common expert views of love are little different than they were a few decades ago, after the innovations of ego psychology. These views range from seeing love as a cure for pain and conflict to calling it immature or a neurotic delusion. Most of these views are very different from the love celebrated by films, television, songs, verse, fairy tales, and friends. Is it most of society or the experts who are out of touch with life?

We think the varieties of love have been observed best by poets and novelists. In their work, we see that most of what is said on love today actually fits a handful of very old views.

The Variety of Loves: An Inheritance

The ancient Hebrews celebrated love and sex as long as they took place within marriage.

The *Song of Songs* proclaims, "Many waters cannot quench love, neither can the floods drown it." This sounds like modern romanticism, but the psalmist would have been astounded to hear that love comes before all else: "if a man would give all the substance of his house for love, it would utterly be condemned." Obviously finding the word love in other times and places doesn't mean finding our own views and values. Even today, people often create comedy or tragedy by giving the word different meanings.

Philia, Eros, and Agape

The ancient Greeks distinguished between *philia* (brotherly love), *agape* (spiritual or altruistic love), and *eros* (physical desire and infatuation). The Homeric (Mycenaean) Greeks,

---

Healing with Love

For people concerned with love, mental-health professionals seem to have used it rather little. An exception was Sandor Ferenczi (1950, 1952), who believed that a doctor should be the warm "good parent" many of his patients lacked. Sometimes when patients were reliving childhood anguish, he took them in his arms or on his lap. Most therapists believe that such use of love is easily abused by patient or therapist, intentionally or unintentionally, and that it is not always the most effective therapy. But Ferenczi did help break down the distant, authoritarian quality of early psychoanalysis, and today he has many knowing or unknowing disciples—therapists, especially in some forms of group therapy and sensitivity training, who encourage the open expression of loving concern or even of sexual feeling within the therapeutic session (see McCartney, 1966; Shepard, 1971). The recent codes of ethics drafted for the American Medical Association and the American Association of Sex Educators, Counselors and Therapists forbid sexual activity between therapist and patient.

who flourished more than 3,000 years ago, prized *philia;* in their warrior culture, the bond between comrades in arms was treasured but apparently not erotic (Flacelière, 1962). Passionate heterosexual love was considered a destructive madness. But Homer (1946) and, we assume, his contemporaries did believe that a wonderful mingling of attachments can grow in marriage. Ulysses, returning to his wife Penelope, expresses *companionate love* when he says, "There is nothing better or more precious than the perfect sympathy between husband and wife at the domestic hearth . . . the pinnacle of happiness."

The first Western celebrations of *passionate love* that have survived are in the verse of Sappho (1965), of the isle of Lesbos, who lived in the seventh century B.C. Though her name and that of her home became synonymous with female homosexuality *(sapphism, lesbianism),* some of her poetry celebrates heterosexual love. She was lyrical, despairing, jealous, tender, tempestuous, driven by needs no one could have filled. It is her frenzy caused by *eros* that dominates Western ideas of love today.

By the time of Plato, a couple of centuries later, Greek ideas of love had changed. Warrior-society *philia* was now sometimes joined with *eros* in male homosexual love. Women's social position was low, and marriage widely seen as a social requirement but not necessarily passionate or companionate (Karlen, 1971). Plato's *Symposium* (1956) is an alleged record of a conversation about love among Socrates and some of his friends, most of them defenders of the homosexuality (chiefly between boys and men, not between grown men) now more or less tolerated by some of Athens' upper class (Marrou, 1956).

Plato puts in Socrates' company the playwright Aristophanes, who tells a story to explain the insistent, magical quality of passionate love. He says that originally there were three sexes, male, female, and hermaphrodite. Zeus severed them all in half, and from those halves all humans are descended. People descended from halves of the original male are male homosexuals; those from halves of the original female are female homosexuals; those from halves of the hermaphrodite are heterosexual

---

Passionate Love

. . . as I look at you my voice fails,
my tongue is broken and thin fire
runs like a thief through my body.
My eyes are dead to light, my ears
pound, and sweat pours down over me.
I shudder, I am paler than grass
and I am intimate with dying—but
I must suffer everything, being poor.

—Sappho, Lyrics (Seventh century B.C.)
trans. by Willis Barnstone

---

men and women. All people go through life seeking their original other halves, to feel complete again. "Love," says Aristophanes, "is simply the name for the desire and pursuit of the whole."*

Socrates (or Plato) then gives his own view of love. Essentially, it is this: what is beautiful is good; we love the good-and-beautiful; men are better and more beautiful than women; therefore the highest love is male homosexual love. It is obviously not Plato's downgrading of women and his homosexuality that make him the West's most influential philosopher of love, but this mystical vision of *ideal love,* or *agape,* a transcendence of eros and the flesh by love of an ideal or idea. Socrates says that now, in middle age, he is free at last from sensual passion, "a mad and furious master," and can seek the beauty of moral perfection rather than of pretty boys.

Mechanistic and Tactical Love

Greece was conquered and became part of the diverse, cosmopolitan Roman empire. The passionate voice of Sappho was taken up in the first century B.C. by the Latin poet Catullus (1956). His poems have Sappho's tortured lyricism, but most are about heterosexual love. Catullus invented the classic phrase of passionate ambivalence, *"odi et amo,"* "I hate and I love." Most modern marriage counselors

would deplore Catullan love as adolescent infatuation, but his poetry movingly portrays a recurrent human experience, whether psychologists approve or not.

The Stoic philosophers and poets had a quite different view of love and sex, one we will call *mechanistic* or *utilitarian,* because it minimizes emotion and stresses the satisfaction of needs. Such poets as Lucretius and Horace considered sex a hygienic necessity, passionate love a degrading disorder that destroys judgment and dignity; it should not disturb one's sleep or digestion, let alone one's mind. Pragmatic and cool, they called for decency, moral courage, and self-sufficiency, not for passion or intimacy (Brinton, 1959; Karlen, 1971).

Another attitude came from the Roman poet Ovid. His *Art of Love* (1957) is an urbane guide to the politics of love, sex, and seduction. Detached, graceful, shrewd, Ovid instructed readers to see love as a social and psychological game in which, by winning, one gives pleasure to oneself and often to others. Ovidian love is not intimate or passionate but *tactical.* To some people it seems not love at all. Yet there were and are Ovids, who feel that if each person practiced sensible pleasure-seeking, the world would be happier than if run by earnest moralists. Only their partners, and those of moralists, can fairly judge.

In the Greco-Roman world, then, there already existed many of the views of love we know today: earnest, devoted, companionate love; the ecstasy and anguish of passionate love; the transcendent flight above *eros* to altruistic *agape,* the love of soul for soul; the tactical view of love as zestful manipulation; the utilitarian view that says one should seek pleasure, keep a cool head, need no one, and live in rational, reserved dignity.

---

* The real Aristophanes poked fun at Plato's disciples, calling them hypocrites who used philosophy as a front for seducing boys. He, rather than Plato, apparently spoke for the mainstream of their society (Karlen, in press).

Courtly Love

In the fourth century, Saint Augustine (1957) developed an ascetic Christian platonism—the view that *eros* is spiritually inferior to asexual *agape*. This tinged views of love all over Europe as the church's influence spread. Then in the eleventh century, a new idea of love appeared, from which modern romantic love is descended.

There arose in the castles and courts of southern France poets called *troubadours,* whose songs and tales in verse (called romances) described *courtly love* (De Rougemont, 1966). A lover entered a noble lady's service, as one swore fealty to a feudal lord. The lady was often described as a distant and angelic figure, but she could not be the man's wife; courtly love was voluntary, not a marital obligation. The man was to ennoble himself for her through trials of his bravery, sacrifice, and virtue. His reward was not sex, a mere physical satisfaction and marital right, but to receive a kiss or perhaps even to lie beside her and caress her naked body chastely. In practice, this may or may not have been the case.

This *amor puris* (pure love), as it was also called, resembled the transcendent love of Plato, but it was also erotic, heterosexual, and adulterous. It was passionate yet spurned physical fulfillment. In fact, it fed on frustration rather than consummation (De Rougemont, 1966). For the first time, people seemed in love with love itself; they welcomed it as an irresistible force that swept one away on wings of suffering. Romantic love was born.

Courtly love soon traveled to most of Europe's upper class. Everywhere it taught that romantic yearning—chaste and spiritual yet passionate and adulterous—was a law unto itself, perhaps life's purpose. It found some of its greatest expression in the poetry of Petrarch and Dante, and its best satirist in Cervantes. The theme still shows no signs of exhaustion.

Platonic and Puritan Love

During the Renaissance, a new form of platonic love swept through Europe. Courtiers and urban gentlemen wrote of attaining the divine through chaste contemplation of the beautiful and good in those they loved. Some hard-headed satirists considered the new platonic love a veneer for cynical seduction, but it

---

The Triumph of Romance

[The myth of courtly love] operates wherever passion is dreamed of as an ideal instead of being feared like a malignant fever; wherever its fatal character is welcomed, invoked, or imagined as a magnificent and desirable disaster instead of as simply a disaster. It lives upon the lives of people who think that love is their fate . . . that it swoops upon powerless and ravished men and women in order to consume them in a pure flame; or that it is stronger and more real than happiness, society, or morality. It lives upon the very life of the romanticism within us.

—Denis De Rougemont, *Love in the Western World* (1966)

---

moved such poets as Shakespeare and John Donne to create marvels of poetry about love for women, for male friends, for ideas, for love itself, and for God.

In the sixteenth and seventeenth centuries, the Puritan view of love and marriage emerged. Modern cliché associates the Puritans with sexual and emotional restrictions, but in this they were no different from many of their Catholic forebears and Protestant contemporaries. The real Puritan revolution was to move the passions of love and sex from adulterous romances into the marriage bed.

The growing urban middle class built its life not around crusades or court intrigue but the family. Books on love, women, and marriage became a thriving industry. Some of these seriously discussed marrying for love (many or most middle-class marriages were still arranged, for practical reasons). Martin Luther, John Calvin, John Knox, and other reformers insisted on the novel idea that love, marriage, and sex were inseparable. Puritan Daniel Rogers wrote (Hunt, 1959) that "husbands and wives should be as two sweet friends," their love a "sweet compound" of the spiritual and physical. The greatest Puritan poet, John Milton (1953–62), urged in vain that Parliament legalize divorce on grounds of "contrariety of mind," since there is true marriage "not in forced cohabitation, and counterfeit performance of duties, but in unfeigned love and

---

Love: Platonic and Not So Platonic

Let me not to the marriage of true minds
Admit impediments, love is not love
Which alters when it alteration finds,
Or bends with the remover to remove.
O no, it is an ever-fixed mark
That looks on tempests and is never shaken;
It is the star to every wand'ring bark,
Whose worth's unknown, although his height be
   taken.
Love's not Time's fool, though rosy lips and cheeks
Within his bending sickle's compass come,
Love alters not with his brief hours and weeks,
But bears it out even to the edge of doom.
If this be error and upon me proved,
I never writ, nor no man ever loved.

           —William Shakespeare,
             Sonnet CXVI (1609)

Tell me no more of minds embracing minds,
   And hearts exchang'd for hearts;
That spirits spirits meet, as winds do winds,
   And mix their subtlest parts;
That two unbodi'd essences may kiss,
And then like angels, twist and feel one bliss. . . .

I was that silly thing that once was wrought
   To practise this thin love;
I climb'd from sex to soul, from soul to thought;
   But thinking there to move,
Headlong I rolled from thought to soul, and then
From soul I lighted at the sex again.

As some strict down-look'd men pretend to fast,
   Who yet in closets eat;
So lovers who profess they spirits taste,
   Feed yet on grosser meat;
I know they boast they souls to souls convey,
Howe'r they meet, the body is the way.

           —William Cartwright
            (1611–1643)

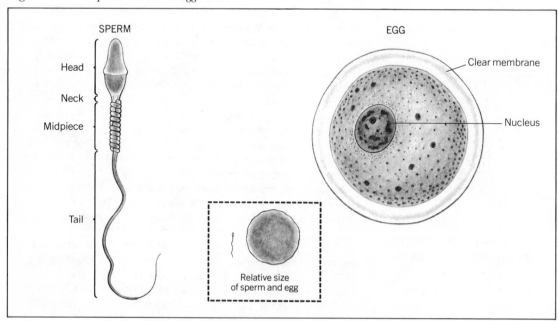

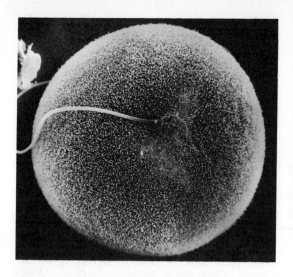

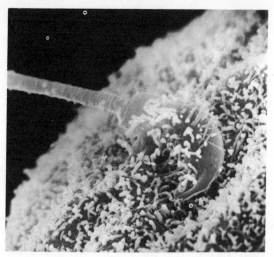

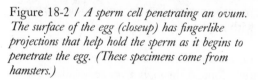

sexual play, people are physically and emotionally vulnerable; if unable to trust, one does not relax and fully respond. Especially when a relationship is new or when an established one seems insecure, it can be difficult to trust, admit need, and risk rejection and hurt. Some people need verbal reassurance; others depend more on touch. However expressed, trust opens the door to emotion and physical response.

Trust and vulnerability make sex a serious matter for some people; to others, sex can be a game played for its own sake. These differences in attitude can lead to misunderstanding or conflict. Perhaps some people resist factual or playful talk about sex because it seems to lack emotional seriousness. They may even suspect that those who can be playful about sex have no capacity for intimacy. Conversely, people who are playful about sex may assume that the more earnest are merely inhibited. Partners should be aware of each other's degree of seriousness and of play, generally and at any given time.

Communicate. People communicate many subtle messages during sexual play—a sigh, a facial expression, speaking or not speaking. Unfortunately, many messages are not given clearly or interpreted correctly. It is always good to clarify one's feeling, action, or inaction, whether directly or indirectly. And it never hurts to tell one's partner that something feels good or that one is satisfied. Asking a person to do something may be more difficult; it requires trust and confidence. It can be harder still to say that an act is unappealing. However, this can usually be done with a tactful explanation that creates no shame, guilt, or feeling of rejection. Certainly *not* talking also expresses thoughts, feelings, and attitudes. To keep communication

open and clear, it helps to keep these points in mind:

1. Don't hold back from expressing likes, dislikes, fantasies, and desires ("I wish you'd do more of what you did last night.").
2. When turning down an invitation, say what you would rather do instead ("I'd rather sleep now so I can wake up refreshed and be better company then.").
3. Acknowledge what you enjoy and give your partner credit for it; adding a compliment never hurts.
4. Don't dwell on past grievances. Instead, put pleasure in their place ("I'd like you to make the first move next time, because it excites me to feel wanted.").
5. When in doubt about a partner's wishes, ask instead of guessing.

Some experiences are memorable for their spontaneity, and the best techniques can be frustrating failures if each partner's feelings and the situation are ignored. If these are kept in mind, all but the most inept encounters can be satisfying.

Erotic Techniques

Flirting, Courtship, and Seduction

Every sexual encounter starts with an invitation. Sometimes *flirting,* the give and take of invitations, is a game played for its own sake. Whether this is the case or whether it leads to coitus, it tends in societies all around the world to follow the courtship pattern of most higher animals: the male makes ritualized gestures of preening and aggression, the female ritualized gestures of submission or flight (Eibl-Eibes-

311

feldt, 1974). People do this through words and movements of the eyes and body.

The man usually begins with a strong, perhaps challenging glance. He stands straight and draws close to the woman (*proceptive,* or mate-seeking, behavior). He may make sexual jokes or innuendos, softening them with a smile or a laugh. In some ethnic groups and subcultures, there is obvious, aggressive display, like that of the courting peacock or lion. A woman usually responds with coyness, a ritualized flight gesture that is actually an invitation to pursuit; she returns the man's glance for a moment and then turns away or lowers her head or eyelids. She may smile and cover her mouth with her hand, even while she sits straighter, holds her head high, and straightens her back. Sometimes the woman begins the exchange, by looking at the man in the eyes, with a smile, or as if responding to a male approach (though none was made). This may sound like a caricature, but film studies of body language show that these patterns are carried out with surprising regularity (Eibl-Eibesfeldt, 1974; Scheflen, 1974). Scheflen (1974) says that "the men and women of the new [youth] culture . . . seem to stand closer, touch more, and display less flirting, dominance, and metaphorical kinesics," but the basic pattern persists.

When many people flirt, they make the sexual invitation so that it can be taken innocently or as a joke. Showing desire and exposing need mean vulnerability; a joking approach shields one from the hurt or humiliation of rejection. One can turn away as if no serious message was sent or received. For the same reason, a joking sexual invitation may be accepted indirectly.

Sometimes flirting is so indirect that it doesn't come across. Or because of personal or cultural differences, what one person considers mere flirting seems offensive to another or what one thinks a direct advance seems mild to the other. The subtleties of effective flirting are among the last social skills many people learn, and some never learn at all.

Often flirting is done unconsciously. And even when deliberate, it is often meant to go nowhere. If both people understand the nature of the game, and neither has serious intent, no one gets hurt. Otherwise one or both may end up feeling challenged or hurt. One must learn by trial and error what an individual considers flirtation and what meaning he or she gives it.

When flirting is exploratory or serious, it is testing for *seduction,* an attempt to persuade another to engage in sexual activity. The word often implies doing so against the other's full or initial desire, and perhaps with an element of deceit or of taking advantage of limited knowledge. In some states, seduction is a crime if coitus results from a false promise. If one person is under a certain age, seduction may be assumed even though both partners were willing; the law doesn't accept that a minor can fully understand the implications of flirting or coitus (see chapter 22).

Seduction involves power games and can be very satisfying for the seducer; many men and women relish having conquered prestigious, difficult, or reluctant partners. This doesn't necessarily mean that both partners won't enjoy the result. Some people like being thought worth the effort and expense of seduction. For some, not having been easy prevents guilt. And some enjoy the dance—the teasing, the ritualized approach and drawing away, the final meeting.

If both partners enjoy seducing and being seduced, no one else can object. However, being seduced can leave a person feeling be-

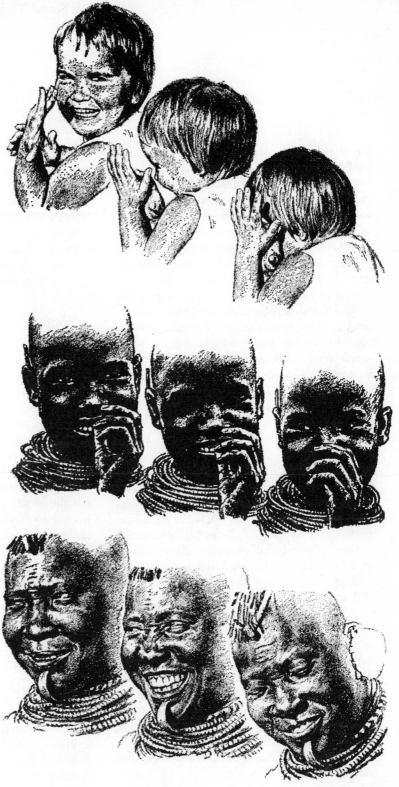

Figure 15-1 / *Virtually all higher social species use innate, ritualized behavior in courtship: the male's ritualized aggression (strutting, approach) is answered by the female's ritualized flight (avoidance). A Western child (top) and a Samburu girl (middle) and Turkana woman (bottom) of East Africa all flirt or respond to compliments by averting the eyes, lowering or turning the head, or covering the face. Such gestures can hardly be learned, since they have been observed in very young children who were born blind.*

trayed or foolish, and less willing or able to trust in the future. If so, the seducer may feel that he or she has won a hollow victory. The game of seduction remains fun only as long as both people see it the same way.

There have been many guides to seduction, from Ovid's *Art of Love* to innumerable recent books and magazine articles. Some contain shrewd and useful advice. These books will remain useful as long as many people are turned on by others' real or pretended unavailability and by efforts to challenge, persuade, and entice—that is, for the indefinite future. Some people feel, to the contrary, that the greatest excitement and most satisfying experiences occur when two people are open and warm. For them, that often turns out to be true.

Touching

Touching and being touched, holding and being held, are among life's greatest pleasures. Touching is vital to children's psychological and physical development (Spitz, 1965; Prescott, 1977); in fact, its absence is devastating to their physical and emotional development (Bowlby, 1969). The need for touching and holding remains very strong in many adults.

A touch may be a way of saying one desires and cares. It may be part of flirtation or one of the most sensuous parts of coitus, from tender stroking to passionate embrace. Yet touching means entering another person's "body space," and doing so without direct or implied permission violates rules of conduct in every culture (E. Hall, 1966). Obviously much depends on the social context and how and where one touches. As in flirting, there is much room for misunderstanding, and a need to learn fine social and emotional cues.

The most extensive and potentially erotic touching is massage. The word massage has taken on sleazy overtones because of its association with prostitution. But in its many traditional forms, massage is relaxing, involves mutual trust, and can be erotic even if the massager does not touch the sexualia. Mutual full-body massage is now widely recommended to develop a couple's trust and erotic response.

Kissing

A kiss can show anything from formal respect to nonsexual tenderness to erotic passion. Usually the sexual kiss is long and directly on the mouth. It may be delicate, gentle, or forceful, and may involve nibbling or sucking the lips or any part of the face or body. In the deep kiss ("soul kiss," or "French kiss"), the tongue penetrates the partner's mouth, sometimes suggesting or accompanying genital penetration. Some societies (see chapter 11) practice not the mouth-to-mouth kiss but a rubbing or nuzzling of nose and mouth, often while exchanging breath.

In our society, few acts convey intimacy and care as well as a kiss. This realization starts in early life; with time, sensuality is added to intimacy and care. Books on love and sex have long described many intricate varieties of kissing. For instance, the fourteenth-century Persian book *The Perfumed Garden* (Nefzaoui, 1964) says:

The best kiss is the one impressed on humid lips combined with the suction of the lips and tongue, which latter particularly provokes the flow of sweet and fresh saliva. It is for the man to bring this about by slightly and softly nibbling her tongue, when her saliva will flow sweet and exquisite, more pleasant than refined honey. . . . This maneuver will give the man a trembling emotion, which will run all through his body, and is more intoxicating than wine drunk to excess. . . . A humid kiss is better than hurried coitus.

The ancient Indian *Koka Shastra* (1965) catalogues the formal kiss, the suction kiss, the thrusting kiss, and others. In reality, most people learn to kiss not from books but from their own spontaneous actions and from the people they kiss.

Intensely passionate kissing may lead to playful or even rather severe biting. If this is done with strong suction, it raises bruises on the skin, known in slang as "hickies." To some people, particularly some teenagers, hickies are badges of sexual experience. These love bites are signs of sexual interest to some people, physical testimonials to passion. To others they are distracting or annoying. Scratches on the back or other parts of the body have the same variety of meanings and effects.

Petting

Petting is caressing or stimulating any part of the body (see chapter 11). It may be a prelude to coitus or an end in itself, and may involve mutual masturbation or other noncoital acts leading to orgasm.

Petting commonly involves the breasts, buttocks, and genitals, but for some people, stroking almost any part of the body—the ears or hairline or anus—can be highly erotic. Individual preferences vary enormously; partners have to discover by experimentation what most pleases themselves and each partner. Masters and Johnson (1966) have coined the phrase *sensate focus* to describe concentrating on areas and stimuli one finds erotically exciting.

Some men like soft stroking of the penile shaft or a spidery walking of fingers on the lower belly or thigh. Others like strong strokes and more pressure. Some women like sustained movement and pressure on the clitoris. Others prefer stimulation of the labia or vaginal probing. Some men and women like anal stimulation, others are indifferent to or dislike it. Both men and women may enjoy stroking of the back, chest, feet, fingers, toes, neck, or other nongenital regions. Sometimes people stimulate their own genitals as well as their partners' while petting.

A person's sexual tastes may not be predictable or consistent. Therefore good communication between partners increases the chances of giving and obtaining the most possible pleasure. It also helps overcome differences in likes and dislikes. For example, many women object to men making too rapid a transition from kissing to genital stimulation—the "dive to the pelvis." Many men, to the contrary, object to women's hesitance in doing so. People should communicate about such things verbally or nonverbally; a gentle guiding of the hand, leg, or body, a smile or a sigh, can tell a great deal.

Two things often interfere with satisfactory petting. One is the tendency to assume that people of the other sex are excited by the same things as oneself. Sometimes this is true, sometimes not. Both sexes tend to assume that the other is excited by stimulation of the nipples; but some women are not, and only one man in five is (Kinsey et al., 1948). Such differences are best worked out with each partner by open communication.

The other common problem is disagreement, often silent, about who should initiate petting. Many men wish women would do so more often; some women would like to but

315

Figure 15-2 / *"Nondemand" sexual stimulation is giving pleasure without expecting immediate return. Receiving nondemand pleasure helps some people become comfortable with their erotic responses; it is therefore used in some forms of sex therapy.*

aren't comfortable doing so. We suggest that partners set no rule about who starts erotic activity or how. Again, open discussion may prevent dissatisfaction or resentment.

Oral-Genital Activity

For more than a half century, an increasing number of people have been accepting oral-genital intercourse as foreplay or as a sexual pleasure in itself (see chapter 11). Some consider it especially intimate and permit or perform it only in a close relationship. Others are reluctant to engage in it at all, considering it perverted or just unappealing. Many people lose such feelings after a bit of experience.

Oral-genital play can add novelty and pleasure to eroticism. The sensations of wetness, sucking, warm breath, nibbling, and licking can be exquisite. The orgasm brought on by oral

sex is usually psychologically different from those caused by coitus or masturbation.

Almost any oral technique can be pleasant; some people even enjoy gentle biting of the penis or clitoris. Caressing the sexualia with the hands and making body movements usually enhance the effect of oral sex. Like kissing, fellatio and cunnilingus probably are taught less well by books than by sensitivity to another person's reactions and by frank discussion of the most pleasurable ways to do them.

Some men avoid cunnilingus because of aversion to the idea or because they find the taste or odor of the vulva unappealing. If this is the case, the best time to experiment is after a relaxing warm bath or shower together. Many men find the odor of the female genitals pleasant and stimulating—if not at first, then after some experience.

Similarly, some women avoid fellatio but accept relaxed, post-bath experimentation. They may dislike the taste and smell of semen; this, too, often changes with experience. A woman may accept fellatio but not want the man to reach orgasm in her mouth, fearing that the ejaculate or the penis itself will make her gag. This may be realistic, for some men make reflex pelvic thrusts during orgasm. To avoid gagging, the woman should find out how much of the erect penis she can comfortably accommodate and grip the shaft in a way that prevents further penetration.

A number of people enjoy simultaneous fellatio and cunnilingus (popularly known as "69"); the partners lie head to toe on their sides or one rests on hands and knees above the other. Others prefer to take turns at oral sex, so that each can fully concentrate on his or her own response. Many people also enjoy other kinds of oral activity, such as sucking the breast, nipple, neck, or toes. Some also enjoy licking the anus (*anilingus,* or a "rim job").

Coitus

The majority of modern sex manuals have recommended prolonged foreplay, extended coitus, and simultaneous orgasm; recently, though, some have suggested avoiding simultaneous orgasm. Some of these recommendations reflect attitudes as much as they do scientific fact. Satisfying coitus can be vigorous, passionate, and brief, and many recent works on sexual techniques ignore how infectious excitement can be (Karlen, 1979a). We suggest experimenting with different kinds of coitus, trying to enjoy it in different ways at different times, without taking any one style as a model.

It is true that in our society many people have rapid, straightforward coitus only because of inhibition or ignorance of other ways. Some, for instance, still feel that varying coital position and techniques reflects immorality or perversion; others fear being rejected or laughed at. Humans are probably the only land animals that usually copulate face to face. Many other positions are possible, and some cultures commonly use the *ventral-dorsal* rear approach (*coitus a tergo,* or "doggy style") used by most land mammals. Others prefer coitus face to face while lying on their sides. Certainly the most common coital position in the United States is *prone-supine,* with the man on top ("missionary position"). One probable reason is that it allows the kissing, talking, and face-to-face contact which help create a feeling of intimacy.

Conflicts over coital positions are common complaints in counselors' offices. The matter is often emotionally loaded for one or both partners. Many individuals and some societies are averse to the woman being on top, feeling that it makes her inappropriately assertive or dominant, and hence unnatural. Others find this position particularly satisfying. Many men and some women enjoy kneeling ventral-dorsal (rear-entry) positions, but some women are, at least at first, reluctant to use them. One researcher (Beigel, 1953) found that many women felt the position impersonal and dehumanizing. The lack of face-to-face contact made them feel that they were not making love but "fucking," doing only what animals do. It may be that the more distance there is between partners' faces and upper bodies, the more difficult it is for some people to accept a coital position. Some people are embarrassed about having their bodies or faces seen during coitus, especially during orgasm (Karlen, in press, b).

Furthermore, some people find coitus more acceptable if they feel they have glided from kissing and petting into lovemaking without decision. The woman-superior and ventral-dorsal positions don't allow one to think that coitus just happened. A similar reluctance to admit having chosen coitus may account for the objection that stopping for contraceptive precautions breaks the mood (see chapter 19).

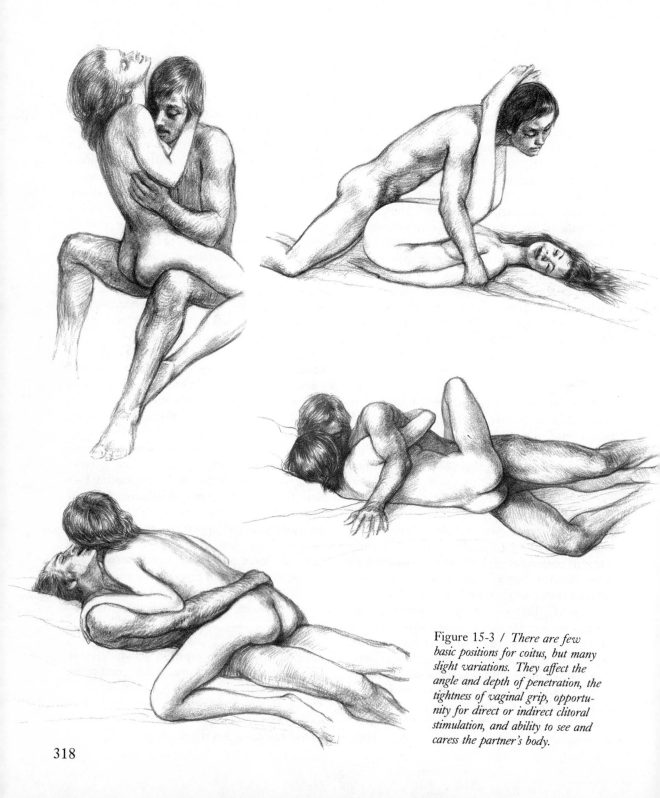

Figure 15-3 / *There are few basic positions for coitus, but many slight variations. They affect the angle and depth of penetration, the tightness of vaginal grip, opportunity for direct or indirect clitoral stimulation, and ability to see and caress the partner's body.*

A number of Western and non-Western books on sexual techniques list a great variety of coital positions. In fact, the number of positions is limited only by the farthest limits of imagination and physical comfort. However, complicated positions are usually used only during the arousal and plateau phases or during a second, slower coitus; it is often difficult to maintain complicated positions as orgasm approaches and occurs. Probably most unusual positions are used rarely.

How well any coital position works for each couple depends on how they are built, generally and genitally, and on their attitudes and individual responses. We suggest the following, though, as generalizations. When a woman lying on her back raises her knees or legs, it usually allows deeper penetration. Resting her legs on the man's shoulders may increase or decrease this effect. The farther apart the woman's legs are, the deeper penetration is likely to be, and the looser the grip on the penis. If the legs are closer together, the opposite is true. When the woman is sitting or kneeling on top of the man, she has greater control of the depth and angle of penetration as well as of coital movement. Some women can reach orgasm only in this position.

Each sexual position has its own benefits and drawbacks for each person. Some women have orgasm more easily or only when on top, some when on the bottom or in other positions. A man may find that entry from behind gives greater penile friction and allows him or the woman to stimulate her clitoris. It also allows full containment without too much vaginal penetration, which is helpful if a woman has a short vagina or a man a long penis.

Some unusual positions can be tried by people with physical flexibility, a willing partner,

and the desire to experiment. *The Perfumed Garden* describes about forty coital positions. One is called "piercing with the lance":

You suspend the woman from the ceiling by the means of four cords attached to her hands and feet; the middle of her body is supported by a fifth cord, arranged so as not to hurt her back. Her position should be so that you stand upright before her, her vagina should just face your member which you introduce into her. You then communicate to the apparatus a swinging motion, first pushing it slightly from you and then drawing it towards you again; in this way your weapon will alternately enter and return from its sheath, you taking care to hit the entrance on her approach.

This position has probably always been more common in sex manuals than in life, but it does appear in the erotic art of Japan and China and is jokingly known in American folklore as a "Chinese Basket Job."

Just as important as coital positions is coital movement. In this, too, there is great variation among individuals and occasions. Some people prefer, usually or at a given time, that the man's strokes are slow, gentle, and deep; others prefer strong thrusting. The woman can move her pelvis vigorously or relatively gently—up and down, laterally, or in circles. Both partners can thrust and withdraw the pelvis at the same time or they can take turns thrusting. The man can make teasing strokes—quick short motions that engage only the head of the penis in the vagina—and then plunge in fully. The woman can produce the same effect. The man can make rotating strokes, thrusting deeply in and out and also from side to side. Partners can alternate in taking the lead, each resting when the other is more active; this is often good for prolonging coitus.

We emphasize again that no coital position or movement is best. Furthermore, coitus can be enhanced by many kinds of sexual play; one can stroke the testicles and clitoris, caress the entire body, kiss, and whisper words of endearment or of obscenity, or do none of these things. We suggest only that what is done on one occasion may encourage experimentation later, with the discovery of still other pleasurable techniques.

Two Popular Views

The Total Woman, by Marabel Morgan (1973), provides specific recipes for marital sexual happiness. It has appealed to many women and angered others. The anger was over its position that marital fulfillment requires women to anticipate and satisfy men's erotic preferences. But many women apparently have found that doing so improved their marital and erotic lives. Among its recommendations:

"Sex is an hour in bed at ten o'clock; super sex is the climax of an atmosphere that has been carefully set all day. Your attitude during your husband's first four waking minutes in the morning sets the tone for his entire day. . . . Give him a kiss first thing tomorrow morning. Rub his back as he's waking up. Whisper in his ear. . . .

Make up your mind to be available for him. Schedule your day so you won't start projects at nine o'clock. The number-one killer of love is fatigue. . . . You'll have the energy to be a passionate lover. . . .

"Sexual intercourse is an act of love. Express your love by giving him all you can give. A woman's hands should never be still when she is making love. By caressing tenderly, you assure him that he's touchable. Tell him 'I love you' with your hands."

Morgan prescribes homework assignments:

"Once this week call him at work an hour before quitting time, to say, 'I wanted you to know that I just crave your body!' or some other appropriate tender term. Then take your bubble bath shortly before he comes home. . . .

"Be prepared mentally and physically for intercourse every night this week. Be sure your attitude matches your costume. Be the seducer, rather than the seducee."

These recommendations, of course, could apply to men as well as women. The important point is that sexual activity should be planned, looked forward to, done creatively, and enjoyed by both partners.

Another book with essentially the same theme and applicable to both men and women is The Sensuous Woman, by J. (1969). It offers four keys to sensuality:

1. Heightened sensitivity. Practice being aware of all your senses with a pleasure-seeking attitude. Develop appreciation of touches, strokes, and textures, of odors, sounds, tastes, and muscle tensions in your body. Practice your sexual response by masturbating.
2. Sexual appetite. This stimulates exploration of your partner's body and your own. It excites both of you and sparks a reaching for physical pleasure.
3. The desire to give. Give yourself and your lover as much pleasure as possible. One way to get pleasure is to give it, for it will be repaid in kind.
4. Sexual skills. The art of sexual pleasure doesn't always come naturally. Practice and experiment are needed. These skills are psychological as well as physical, and few details are too small to deserve attention; kissing as well as coital techniques can benefit from thought and practice. Stay innovative.

After Coitus

Some couples find their greatest satisfaction after erotic play or coitus. Having exchanged trust and pleasure, they feel relaxed, secure, close, and warm. They may continue kissing, petting, and oral-genital play, and eventually resume coitus. Or they may relax in each other's arms, holding and stroking one another. Some people prefer not to talk a great deal. For others, this is an excellent time to communicate their good feelings by words or by touch. Some people, far more men than women, experience a deep and rapid resolution phase (see chapter 3) and may rest or sleep soon after orgasm. This should not be automatically interpreted as lack of interest or pleasure, selfishness, or taking the partner for granted.

Many people feel especially vulnerable before coitus and after orgasm. They are especially receptive then to both compliments and rejection. These times call for gentleness, care, and warmth. The promise of sexual satisfaction and emotional fulfillment also colors perceptions and values, and lowers resistance to many ideas. It is shortly before and after coitus that one often hears, "I love you," and "Let's run away and get married," and "I want to have your child, let's not use a contraceptive," and "I'll give you whatever you want." Sometimes this is a revelation of truth, sometimes a misleading light. A novelty firm sells cards for posting over beds: "All promises made between one hour before orgasm and one hour afterward are hereby declared null and void."

Increasing Satisfaction

In all sexual encounters, some things decrease or increase sexual arousal and pleasure.

1. *Privacy and security.* Sometimes sex is made more exciting by risk or the possibility of discovery, but most people usually enjoy sex more when they feel physically and emotionally secure, unworried about interruption, pregnancy, or venereal disease.
2. *Warmth and communicativeness.* It always helps to be pleasant, concerned, and interested in one's partner, both sexually and nonsexually. Many people think it essential.
3. *Preoccupation.* Thinking about other matters almost always hinders sexual satisfaction.
4. *Fatigue.* Fatigue is one of the worst dampeners of eroticism. It hinders both physiological and psychological responses.
5. *Guilt.* To anticipate feeling regret or self-blame tomorrow inhibits openness and pleasure today.
6. *Attractiveness.* Some people appreciate earthiness, others don't. One should be aware of body odor, mouth odor, and cleanliness. Having soft hands never hurts; rough hands can be helped by lotions.

Disparity in Erotic Interest or Arousal

Among the commonest sources of discontent between sexual partners are differences in the preferred time, frequency, duration, and intensity of sex activity. Obviously no amount of interest is right. Twice a week is no more correct than twice a day or twice a year. Differences must be worked out by each couple through change, acceptance, or compromise—if possible, without resentment or blame.

There are common terms for a woman who is sexually unresponsive (*frigid*) and for one

321

who is exceedingly active *(nymphomaniac)*, and for an exceedingly active man *(satyr)*. We mention them only to discourage their use; at best they are relative. People respond differently, and differently to each partner. One man's frigid partner may be another's nymphomaniac; one woman's stud may be another woman's dud. We suggest the term *anarousmia* for the inability to be sexually aroused. In one study (E. Frank, Anderson, and Rubinstein, 1978) this was the most common complaint of women about their own sexual functioning. Sometimes this rises from *sex phobia*, or fear of any sexual arousal or contact (H. Kaplan, 1974; Masters, Johnson, and Kolodny, unpublished), a condition that requires professional consultation and therapy. Sometimes anarousmia has complex sources. It may rise gradually or

abruptly in a relationship, and often creates ill will, complaints, and accusations.

More often, but not always, it is the man who says, "You're never interested . . . I love sex . . . I don't want to be ignored . . . I want your real interest . . . you never want my body." More often one hears from the woman, "All you ever want is sex . . . I don't enjoy sex . . . I don't want to be used . . . I don't get satisfied . . . I can't pretend to be interested . . . all you want is my body." These statements may be genuine or may reflect nonsexual conflicts. A couple must seek the sources of their feelings and see whether they can compromise for the sake of the relationship. It is a common professional opinion that a couple can move more easily toward more rather than less sexual activity.

Aids to Sexual Stimulation

Dildos (artificial penises), "French ticklers," exotic condoms, vibrators, and other devices meant to increase stimulation of the sexualia have long been available (see page 155).

Some women learn sexual responsiveness most easily in privacy, through masturbation, before trying it with a partner. Many find that vibrators are convenient, pleasurable, and tireless. Fantasy, games, erotic conversation, pornography, and play acting can also be stimulating. Fantasy may help speed orgasm in anorgasmic women and in men with retarded ejaculation. After trying some of the things suggested above, a woman can try for coital orgasm by relaxation and sensate focus. It may help her to direct activities, and even to think of the contained penis as hers to play with, and of her partner's actions as devoted to her pleasure.

Many anorgasmic women and impotent men say that their response shuts off at a certain point or that they find themselves thinking about other things. Often shame, guilt, or fear of losing control is the reason. For some, response comes most easily with a loving partner, without concentrating on reaching orgasm.

Renewing Interest, Excitement, and Pleasure

A commonly asked question is whether time brings sexual boredom, and if so, how to rekindle excitement. As some couples stay together, their sexual relationship improves; others cool or begin to take each other for granted. Furthermore, school, work, children, and home responsibilities all take time and attention away from a sexual relationship. In sex as in other matters, a good relationship demands time and effort. It helps many couples to set aside time for returning to giving each other attention. They should set aside periods for talk and play, make a date, have special evenings together—almost as if planning an affair together. Partners can ask what new things can be brought into the relationship, both in and out of bed. It also helps to avoid falling into a sexual routine, allow sexual spontaneity, and try sex in new ways, times, and places.

Overview

We have tried to provide less a how-to chapter than a how-with chapter. To us, the relationship or interaction between partners is inseparable from sexual techniques. Improving a relationship may help improve techniques, and good sexual interaction often enhances the relationship.

A great deal of writing, counseling, and individual effort has gone into trying to improve erotic techniques over the past half century. Sex-behavior data show that during this period, more people have indeed expanded their erotic repertoires and sexual responsiveness. However, many find that their satisfaction increases most when they lose inhibitions and habits of overcontrol. The greatest aphrodisiac is often passion itself. The benefit of many attempts to expand erotic technique may rise as much from the search to leave behind inhibiting patterns as from acquiring exquisite secrets of technique.

We must add that we think no one physical state or emotional tone should be made a general prescription. Sexual activity becomes a vehicle for every emotion—tenderness, anger, reverence, revenge, playfulness, whatever. And sometimes it is routine, a sedative, or serves nonsexual needs. To expect it to fit one formula all the time is, we think, not only tyrannical but unrealistic. The only suggestion that approaches universal applicability is to have enough flexibility to find the things that most genuinely express one's feelings and desires and bring the widest range of satisfactions. It should go without saying—but unfortunately cannot—that a pleased partner is one of the deepest pleasures.

Review, Discuss, Decide

1. What parts of the sexual response cycle and of a sexual encounter do some people find most pleasurable? Which do you enjoy most? Has this changed?

2. Does the idea of exploring sexual techniques seem appealing or unappealing? Why?
3. What are some of the things people enjoy most or least about a partner's sexual technique? How can one try to modify a partner's technique?
4. Why are there advantages for some individuals in one coital position rather than another?
5. What sexual techniques have you tried or heard of that are not discussed in this chapter?
6. Does one get more pleasure from receiving erotic attention or giving it?

16

Psychosexual Health and Dysfunction

Are most sex problems physical or psychological?

Does having a dysfunction mean a person is sick?

How does society affect ideas of sexual performance?

How can I try to solve the sexual problems my partner and I are having?

How do I know if sex counseling can help me?

If I need help, who can help me?

In chapter 8 we discussed physical health. But the majority of sexual problems are not physical, they are psychological. Furthermore, many people without problems wonder whether some of their sex behavior and feelings are healthy or normal, and many are too embarrassed to ask anyone. Some read books, talk to friends, or ask health professionals, especially when their preferences conflict with their partners'. But even professionals may give a confusing variety of opinions.

Defining Health and Dysfunction

Sexual Health

Harold Lief has said (in press) that there are three common definitions of sexual health. One is normative: it makes what the majority of

people do a standard of health. Another is subjective and relativistic: it says that whatever any person does and enjoys is healthy. A third is medical and ideal: it holds up a theoretical ideal of perfect physical and mental well-being. Each definition contains an element of truth but is, by itself, inadequate.

To say that what the majority do is healthy ignores the great physical and emotional variety among individuals. And in our pluralistic society, it ignores subcultural variety. Furthermore, the norms of some locales or groups may be abnormal in others. Enshrining majority behavior may label people unhealthy merely for being more or less vigorous or imaginative than average. And some degree of sexual dysfunction is the norm in some societies; Masters and Johnson (1970) believe this is true of ours, and they aren't alone in this view. A survey of 2,500 psychiatrists *(Medical Aspects of Human Sexuality,* 1977) showed that 70 percent believe that half or more of American couples live with impaired sexual function.

It is humane to go to the other extreme and say that anything anyone likes to do is healthy. However, this view ignores important realities. Self-evaluation is not a reliable standard of health; some people who are impotent or anarousmic rationalize their conditions as natural, at least for them. And relativism has limits as a standard for cultures and individuals: virtually all societies discourage certain sex behaviors even though they are not physically unhealthful (see chapter 20).

As for the medical definition, perfect vigor and function can't be defined or reached physically, let alone psychosexually. Is a star quarterback with battered knees sick? How healthy, by comparison, is a frail, poorly coordinated person with sound knees? How about someone who is occasionally impotent or anorgasmic? Obviously one can be healthy over-all despite a sexual dysfunction; and not having a specific dysfunction doesn't mean having optimal health.

A definition of sexual health, Lief suggests, should borrow from all three views, the normative, relativistic, and medically ideal, but ultimately sexual health is best defined in terms of its hoped-for results—the enhancement of personality, relationships, and the capacity for intimacy and love. We agree, but add to the definition erotic pleasure and sensuality, which for many apparently healthy people occur outside as well as within intimate relationships. A simple definition of psychosexual health is the relatively full expression of one's sexual potential without dis-ease in self, partner, or society.

Sexual Dysfunction

In defining psychosexual health, we distinguish dysfunction from sickness. We call dysfunctional any sexual behavior that does not bring a person as much satisfaction as he or she wishes or could realistically attain with a responsive partner. For example, if a man is impotent and he or a desired partner doesn't accept it, he has a dysfunction. And even if he accepts it, he is missing common pleasures and

opportunities for rich personal experiences, so it might be considered dysfunctional.

There are also social considerations. Virtually all societies (Ford and Beach, 1951; Gebhard, 1971; Karlen, 1971; Murdock, 1949b) consider it dysfunctional for adults to engage predominantly in any sexual behavior except coitus. Many societies do have high rates of other behaviors, but when an adult's preferred sex object most or all of the time is a shoe, a small child, or someone of the same sex, society almost invariably regards it as a dysfunction (see chapter 20). Usually included among sexual dysfunctions are failures of sexual mechanisms (impotence and many cases of anorgasmia), some cases of anarousmia and of total abstinence, and the paraphilias—predominant or exclusive adult homosexuality, transvestism, fetishism, voyeurism, sadomasochism, preference for immature partners, and exclusive adult use of masturbation, oral-genital or anal-genital intercourse, and other noncoital acts. Society may define behaviors as dysfunctional even though the participants concerned are satisfied with the situation.

Some people say that any activity a person prefers should be considered a choice, never a dysfunction. We believe that few people choose dysfunctional acts as one would choose chocolate or vanilla ice cream; there is usually a strong element of compulsion. Some psychological theories say that all emotional problems have sexual symptoms and that all sexual dysfunctions reflect emotional conflict. In many cases, sexual and nonsexual conflicts are indeed intertwined. But there is increasing belief that some people's sexual function isn't grossly impaired by emotional conflict, neurosis, or sometimes even severe mental disorders, and that the ability to cope well with life isn't necessarily impaired by sexual dysfunction (Kupfer, Rosenbaum, and Detre, 1977).

A sexual dysfunction, then, does not in itself make a person sick. Recall the example of the athlete with creaky knees. Most of us have some dysfunctions—exaggerated fears or angers or guilts, problems in love or friendship or work. Someone with a sexual dysfunction may cope well and rewardingly with most of life—as do many people without such dysfunctions or with nonsexual dysfunctions. A dysfunction leads to sickness if it becomes physically or emotionally painful or if it prevents one from functioning well in work, home, play, and relationships.

Any definition of dysfunction will seem too broad to some people, too narrow to others. One of us (Karlen) considers dysfunctional any sex behavior that largely or completely displaces coitus in adults or that, in children, leads to such a pattern. The other (Diamond) considers dysfunctional only behaviors that are not voluntary or that are destructive to partners.

Types and Causes of Common Dysfunctions

Types of Problems

Some elements of coitus, such as arousal, potency, orgasm, and orgasmic timing are sometimes under less control than either partner desires (see chapter 8). In fact, dysfunctions involving sexual mechanisms occur now and then in many or most people's lives—inability to have an erection or to vaginally lubricate, reaching ejaculation too quickly to satisfy oneself or a responsive partner, or inability to reach orgasm. For instance, a study of 100 middle-class couples showed that almost half the women felt they had "difficulty getting excited," and one-third said they had difficulty maintaining excitement (E. Frank, Anderson, and Rubinstein, 1978). Here we will discuss such mechanism problems (the paraphilias are discussed in chapter 12).

The ability to reach and maintain erection long enough for coitus is called *potency*, its ab-

---

"To Love and To Work"

Freud was once asked what he thought a normal person should be able to do well. The questioner probably expected a complicated, "deep" answer. But Freud simply said, *Lieben und arbeiten* ("to love and to work"). It pays to ponder on this simple formula; it grows deeper as you think about it. For when Freud said "love," he meant the generosity of intimacy as well as genital love; when he said love and work, he meant a general work productiveness which would not preoccupy the individual to the extent that he might lose his right or capacity to be a sexual and loving being.

—Erik Erikson, *Identity: Youth and Crisis* (1968)

---

sence *impotence*. No man can simply will an erection. Neither can every woman stimulate erection in every man, nor in any man all the time. A man who has never attained an erection has *primary impotence*; this is relatively rare. Far more common is impotence that occurs occasionally or in certain circumstances; this is *secondary (situational) impotence*. It may happen with a new partner or during a period of depression, anxiety, or preoccupation.

Almost all men and most women can reach orgasm; inability to do so is *anorgasmia*. It may be *primary* (orgasm has always been absent) or *secondary*. Only a minority of people can have orgasm whenever they like. Men's most common concern is orgasm occurring too soon for either or both partners' satisfaction—*premature ejaculation*. Sometimes it takes longer to arrive at orgasm than one desires—*retarded ejaculation* in men and *delayed* or *retarded orgasm* in women. These terms beg the question, "How long should it take?" Every answer is somewhat arbitrary. Prematureness has been variously defined as orgasm occurring thirty to sixty seconds after intromission (cited by Marmor, 1976), before the man desires it (Hastings, 1966a), or so that the partner isn't satisfied at least half the time (Masters and Johnson, 1970). Retarded ejaculation and orgasm are also difficult to define except in the extreme—

Ejaculation: Premature for Whom?

Standards of sexual health are influenced by social traditions and by the best available knowledge—which sometimes isn't very accurate or complete. A century ago, dominant medical opinion held that female orgasm was unhealthful; today, anorgasmia has become an equally tyrannical measure of sexual health to some people. Early in this century, as the expectation grew that women could (or should or must) reach coital orgasm, premature ejaculation received extensive attention for the first time. The amount of time that defined prematureness kept growing. By the 1930s, some writers claimed that if a man reached orgasm after thirty minutes of coitus but the woman had not, ejaculation was premature (Karlen, 1979). One must ask, premature for whom? Still, it became standard marriage manual advice that men should slow down, not that women should hurry up. This seems to have been part of the struggle to justify and encourage female responsiveness, though not always a successful one.

No definition of premature ejaculation has universal clinical acceptance. There is a reproductive problem if a man usually reaches orgasm before penetration, and perhaps an orgasmic one for his partner if he does so seconds after penetration (a problem now often treated successfully). But some men's anxiety about being too quick is a product of social lore and attitudes rather than of dysfunction.

---

after coitus, not at all, or much later than a person or couple wish. Some women have another condition that can be distressing, *vaginismus*—constriction of the vaginal outlet that prevents penetration.

Not all mechanism failures are clearly dysfunctions. For instance, anorgasmia is almost always a sign of physical or emotional difficulties in men, but women's orgasmic responses vary from person to person, partner to partner, and time to time. We have noted that there are women who sometimes or often feel satisfied without climax (Gebhard, 1970; Wallin and Clark, 1963). Female anorgasmia becomes a dysfunction if the woman or her partner finds it a source of distress.

Mechanism problems may reflect a number of sexual and nonsexual difficulties, which we will now discuss.

Situational Stress

Sometimes sexual dysfunction rises from the stress of a special situation, such as fear of discovery, fear of "not doing well," or, if no contraceptive is available, fear of pregnancy. Coitus may then be unpleasant, even impossible. Anxious preoccupation with a situational failure can cause difficulty the next time, starting a vicious circle of failure, anticipation, becoming a mental spectator rather than a participant, and further failure (Masters and Johnson, 1970). This is one of the commonest causes of secondary impotence and anorgasmia. Becoming conscious of this and not imposing the ghost of past experiences on the present may be enough to solve the problem. If not, counseling or sex therapy often does.

Misinformation and Unrealistic Expectations

One can be disturbed about one's sexual behavior and feelings because of misinformation or unrealistic expectations of oneself or a partner. Some people, distracted by erotic thoughts in nonerotic situations, do not know that others have the same experience and fear they are abnormal. Many people do not know how common it is to occasionally fail to maintain erection, experience vaginal wetting, or reach orgasm. Realistic information and reassurance (a few educational or counseling sessions) often resolve such problems.

Unfortunately, some unrealistic expectations come from sexologists, both qualified and self-styled. For several decades, many marriage manuals made people feel sexually deficient for not achieving simultaneous orgasm (Karlen, 1979). Today some sexologists recommend against it. Now some men and women feel there is a problem if the woman doesn't reach multiple orgasm. These matters are still open to debate. We can only say that there are fashions and fads in medicine, in psychology, and even in the so-called hard sciences. As in the rest of life, one must try to distinguish real from theoretical dissatisfactions.

This is not always easy, for others' attitudes and experiences can affect one's own expectations. Some women think, "If other women are orgasmic (or multiorgasmic), why not I?" Men who learn that some other men can maintain an erection for half an hour or can have coitus and reach orgasm several times in one night wonder, "Why can't I?" They should remember that there is a great range of normal sexual desires and capacities. The real problem may

329

be competitiveness or lack of security and self-acceptance. Is one dissatisfied about missing something or driven to match or outdo others? One gains no satisfaction from glaring at what is on others' plates instead of enjoying what is on one's own.

Nonsexual Stress and Conflict

Pressures and conflicts involving school, work, family, and close relationships can easily produce anxiety or depression. Fatigue and depression tend to make people feel sluggish and have difficulty concentrating and sustaining effort; they similarly affect sexual function. Anxiety can have the same (or a contrary) effect. Often one isn't aware that such things are happening. In fact, anarousmia, impotence, dyspareunia, or anorgasmia may be the first dramatic sign of nonsexual stress or conflicts. Any sudden change in one's frequency or type of sexual activity may signal nonsexual distress.

Intrapsychic Conflict

Intrapsychic problems seem to more often decrease than increase sexual activity. However, some people use sex as an outlet for anxiety, angry rebellion, a need to dominate, or a need to feel humiliated by doing something forbidden or dirty. Often a depressed person accepts reduced sexuality; an anxious one may do the same or may find temporary relief in increased sexual activity. They may not identify their sex behavior as dysfunctional. Often it is a partner who insists that there is a problem and that help be sought. This is especially common when events at work or school spark conscious or unconscious fear of competitive failure or success (Ovesey, 1969).

One of the most common and sometimes severe intrapsychic sexual conflicts is having both a mental red light and green light about sex. Having been raped, exaggerated fear of pregnancy, fear of going crazy through unrestrained sexuality, and rigidly antisexual upbringing all conflict with desires for erotic intimacy and pleasure. The conflict may be so troubling that it is pushed from consciousness. One of the more common barriers to female orgasm is buried conflict about losing emotional control during orgasm (Gadpaille, 1975).

A sexual dysfunction can cause depression, guilt, shame, fear, and loss of self-esteem. It is often difficult or impossible to determine whether the sexual dysfunction is a cause of emotional conflict, a result, or both. Logic and intelligence may not tell, for deep and irrational reactions are often involved. One of the most important parts of counseling and therapy is to find the right handle on such problems.

Interpersonal Conflict

Sometimes people enter sexual situations even though they don't know or like each other, let alone feel love or the desire to please and be pleased. Mild or severe dysfunction may temporarily appear. Conflicts can also arise for short or long periods between people with basically satisfying relationships. The results may be guardedness, hostility, or sexual dysfunction. Also, many people use sex to bribe or punish a partner over nonsexual matters; this is almost sure to increase conflict.

Some people's intrapsychic problems and character traits create conflict with some or all partners. Some incorrectly learned as children, by interpreting or misinterpreting their parents' behavior, that sexual intimacy is a kind of domination or slavery (Hendin, 1977). Without being aware of it, they generalize from the past to the present. Their behavior triggers defensive reactions in partners, setting off a vicious circle of mutual hostility and withdrawal.The final result can be sexual dysfunction in one or both partners. This is one of the commonest problems sex counselors deal with.

Problem Solving

Self-Help

We can provide here only a few suggestions for helping problems of potency, orgasmic timing, and orgasmic ability. We assume that a person with such a problem has had a physical examination and no physical causes were found, which indicates that the reasons are not organic but psychological.

All such problems involve the autonomic nervous system (see chapter 4). Fear, stress, the fight-or-flight reaction, all can arise inappropriately in a sexual context. The first step in self-help, and part of most therapies, is to replace fear and stress with relaxation.

Two concepts of Masters and Johnson (1968, 1970) can be helpful. One is the *sexual unit:* both partners must be considered, for what one does or doesn't do affects the other. As Masters and Johnson (1968) put it, "There is no such thing as an uninvolved partner." If both people are involved in an undesirable sexual situation, it is best if both are involved in changing it. This attitude makes partners mutually supportive rather than accusatory and antagonistic. Too often a sexual difficulty is seen by both partners as inadequacy; this only leads to resentment and loss of self-esteem.

The idea of the *spectator role* is also helpful. Many people, instead of acting spontaneously, become spectators of their own sexual performance. They mentally step back to watch and evaluate themselves. But as we have said, one cannot fully feel and perform at the same time.

The first step in removing any sexual dysfunction is finding the nature of the difficulty. A couple should try to see if the sexual situation involves such common impediments as depression, anxiety, preoccupation, or fatigue. These feelings may have such nonsexual sources as job, school, or home. Fear of pregnancy, of venereal disease, or of discovery can also induce problems, from secondary impotence to anorgasmia.

The simplest problem to understand and deal with is *fatigue.* If realistic *fear* is the problem, one should identify its source and act to remove it—for instance, using adequate contraceptives, checking for STD, or ensuring privacy. Irrational fears, such as fear of "going crazy" during the excitement of orgasm, may yield to discussion or brief counseling. If depression, anxiety, and preoccupation have nonsexual sources, dealing with the sources may remove the sexual difficulty.

Anxiety over the sexual situation is often caused by overconcern about performance *(performance anxiety).* Impotence or anorgasmia may reflect a kind of stage fright in the bedroom. Ceasing to see coitus as a test of love, prowess, or gender role may resolve this. It also takes partners out of spectator roles, making room for desire, spontaneity, and pleasure.

It is easy to talk about removing performance anxiety and substituting relaxed mutual pleasuring—to be *nondemanding*—but doing so may be very difficult, even become another performance demand. It helps some people to

(a) not make coitus or orgasm a goal for several evenings or a week or even to avoid it; (b) spend that time finding out what noncoital play, such as stroking and petting, pleases them and their partners; and (c) concentrate on relaxed, unhurried pleasuring. If both partners focus on giving and receiving pleasure all over the body rather than on getting an erection or relaxing the vagina, impotence or vaginismus may disappear. Also, the following suggestions have a fairly good history of success.

Potency. Most cases of impotence are situational and reflect the man's feelings of insecurity, conflict, or distraction. Such impotence usually fades when self-confidence and relaxation return. The woman should do nothing to lower the man's self-esteem and feeling of masculine competence; she should continue to show affection and respect and exercise patience. In a relaxed situation, she should stimulate him manually, orally, or however he finds arousing. If impotence has occurred more than once, several days of pleasuring sessions may be needed to try to dispel it. The woman should stimulate the man until erection occurs and then maintain the stimulation but postpone coitus. They should repeat these stimulation sessions for a couple of days or until erection develops with ease. Then they should go on to coitus.

Vaginismus. This spasmodic tightening of the vagina usually rises from cultural learning and individual experience (H. Kaplan, 1974). It can result from a woman being brought up to believe that sex was dirty or sinful or from having suffered a sexual assault. There are many other, more subtle reasons rising from interpersonal

and intrapsychic conflicts. Some women with this problem require counseling or therapy, but some can help themselves.

First, a woman can test her own reaction to the insertion of a tampon. If she can relax enough to accommodate one, she can then, over several days, gradually insert tampons of larger diameter. When the vagina comfortably accommodates her finger, she can use it to continue trying to relax and dilate the vagina and then use two fingers. Next, she can have her partner insert one and then two fingers as part of relaxed sexual play. She should tell him what she finds pleasurable. They should continue these exercises until penetration and, finally, mutually satisfying coitus is possible. Her partner will have to be patient and let her proceed at her own pace. He must follow her directions, support her efforts, accept her as a person, not lower her esteem as a woman, and be willing to help her as she wishes. She can take confidence from knowing that this problem is very often resolved.

Dysparunia. This is pain in or around the vagina caused by coitus. It may result from penile penetration, or from other deep probing. The cause may be physical or psychological, but the problem can almost always be helped (Abarbanel, 1978).

Premature Ejaculation. A man can gradually learn to delay his ejaculation for longer periods, especially if he and his partner devote time to practice sessions in a relaxed setting. Her help is needed, and she must be tolerant and affectionate as he learns to control ejaculation first with manual stimulation and then in coitus.

First the man should lie on his back, the

Figure 16-1 / *The "squeeze technique" is often used successfully in treating premature ejaculation; usually it is part of a program of sexual counseling.*

woman sit or kneel between his legs. She manually stimulates his penis slowly until he feels orgasm approaching *(ejaculatory inevitability)*. He immediately tells her or signals her to stop; she removes her hand from his penis till the sensation disappears. When he is ready, she begins again, and they repeat the exercise, stopping whenever he anticipates ejaculation.

If the feeling of pending ejaculation comes only immediately before orgasm, they can try the *squeeze technique*. When he signals that he is about to ejaculate, she quickly and firmly grasps the penis and applies strong pressure at and below the corona. He will immediately lose the urge to ejaculate, and his erection will diminish. After fifteen to thirty seconds, they repeat the exercise. This should be done four or five times at each practice session. If the man ejaculates accidentally, further efforts must wait till he can reach erection again. Meanwhile he can fondle and pet with his partner for their satisfaction.

When both partners feel that he is reaching ejaculatory control, ejaculation should be allowed without coitus. The man can satisfy his partner manually or orally. After two to four

days of practice, if the couple feel relatively secure about the man's ejaculatory control, they can proceed to intromission in a nondemanding way. The woman mounts the man, who is lying on his back, and stays motionless. Her best approach is not directly down on the penis but at an angle; this allows her to dismount quickly and apply the squeeze technique when he signals ejaculatory inevitability. After his urge to ejaculate subsides, she remounts and again remains motionless. They repeat this until the man has regained ejaculatory control.

After several days of this, coital movement can be started slowly, the man signalling the woman to stop moving till he can control the timing of his ejaculation. Finally, he can take the superior position, and the couple proceed as before until both can move comfortably without fear of premature ejaculation.

What we have described is a modification of techniques perfected by Semans (1956) and Masters and Johnson (1970). By itself or with professional guidance, it has often succeeded in eliminating premature ejaculation, greatly improves sexual (and often nonsexual) communication, and gives each partner greater understanding of the other's erotic preferences. Such exercises also sometimes help women who have never or rarely reached orgasm to do so, since time is reserved for both partners to concen-

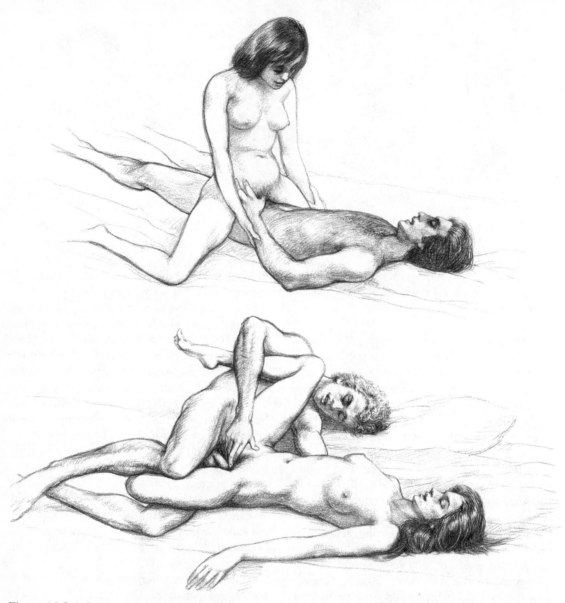

Figure 16-2 / *Some coital positions are helpful in treating certain sexual dysfunctions. Woman-superior positions allow the woman to receive or give herself direct clitoral stimulation, and they are sometimes used in certain stages of treating impotence and premature ejaculation. Male-superior and side-by-side positions also allow direct clitoral stimulation.*

trate on her pleasure. We suspect that the sharing and tenderness expressed by the couple in these exercises is a major part of the therapy (see also Valsalva maneuver, page 350).

Anorgasmia. Men rarely have this problem for an extended period of time until they are quite old. In women it is more common, but

334

can often be dealt with by a combination of the techniques given above, in sessions devoted primarily to giving the woman pleasure. In fact, it often helps to treat anorgasmia as one does impotence. With her partner, she should explore her responses to discover which erotic acts she is most aroused by. A couple can begin by caressing nongenital erotic areas and, at the woman's direction, proceed to the sexualia.

As the woman learns more about her desires, anxieties, dislikes, and responses, she should tell her partner what she has learned and, in the security of her bedroom, try to let herself be uninhibited. She should not have to fear censure, ridicule, or punishment; rather she needs approval, praise, and appreciation. She may be feeling low or inadequate, so her partner should do nothing to lower her self-esteem or feeling of femininity. He must be patient and nondemanding.

After the couple become comfortable with this exploration and pleasuring, they can continue until she achieves a satisfying level of sexual excitement. It usually takes a number of trials before they can go on to try ways of increasing sexual tension until orgasm occurs. This may be manually, orally, through coitus, or with the aid of mechanical devices.

General Suggestions. Jack Annon (1976) has created the acronym PLISST for things therapists should attempt with patients with sexual problems. They are a good guide for examining and trying to solve one's own problems.

Orgasm Control

Often men try to delay orgasm by mentally removing themselves from the situation, and occasionally they succeed. They count or think about baseball scores, homework, a job. Henry Miller described this in his novel *Tropic of Capricorn* (1961):

"Whenever I felt in danger of going off I would stop moving and think—think for example of where I would like to spend my vacation, if I got one, or think of the shirts lying in the bureau drawer, or the patch on the bedroom carpet just at the foot of the bed . . . I didn't care to think what she might be thinking or I'd come immediately. Sometimes I skirted dangerously close to it, but the saving trick was always . . . the corpse at Grand Central Station. The thought of that, the humorousness of it, I mean, acted like a cold douche."

Unfortunately, such efforts often fail, and they decrease erotic pleasure—coitus, after all, is usually done for pleasure, not to avoid thinking about it. The same can be said about ointments and salves that decrease penile sensitivity. The most basic way to delay orgasm is simply to stop coitus briefly and exhale forcefully.

P = Permission: Do you and your partner let yourselves feel free to do what you want sexually?

LI = Limited Information: Know as much as possible about sexuality and your sexual concerns. There are many misleading books, so seek knowledgeable sources.

SS = Specific Suggestions: Make specific suggestions to your partner and ask for them in return. Give and take them without hostility or defensiveness.

T = Therapy: If you cannot solve a problem, seek professional help. Brief counseling may be enough; severe or long-standing problems may require intensive or extended therapy.

Professional Help

Sometimes dysfunctions are not solved quickly or easily, especially if they are severe, long-lasting, or entwined with other problems. Then it is best to seek help from a counselor, psychologist, or sex therapist.

Finding a Therapist. Sexual dysfunctions, problems with relationships, and emotional conflicts are treated by many kinds of professionals. Some states allow certain titles to be used less strictly than others; here we give the commonest ones and the training they usually require.

Physicians (M.D., D.O.) have doctoral de-

How-To Books

Some books on sex may dispel misinformation and groundless fears, but they don't necessarily help certain problems. A karate manual doesn't enable a timid person to leap effectively into a brawl; similarly, reading a sex manual may not bring instant joy to those with dysfunctions, inhibitions, or fears of inadequacy. Many people bought Masters and Johnson's *Human Sexual Inadequacy* (1970) in hopes of improving their sexual performance or response, though the book wasn't meant to be used that way. Many books promise to solve dysfunctions and interpersonal problems by simplistic formulas and mechanical programs—not usually a promising approach. Some books that offer more human self-help programs, especially for anorgasmic women (Barbach, 1975; Heiman, LoPicollo, and LoPicollo, 1976), may aid some disciplined and persistent people.

Many sexual how-to programs make sex a laborious project with demanding standards—hardly an invitation to spontaneity, passion, or pleasure.

Sex becomes exercise, then work (L. Lewis and Brissett, 1967), and finally no fun at all. As Sayre (1973) put it:

"As the couple reads, one person may be charmed and the other dejected by the prospects—which could lead to one of those fights which the book was supposed to prevent. Being strapped wrist over wrist to the shower nozzle, in a rotten temper, might only intensify their battles over the expense of next year's roof repairs. The example may be extreme, but sex manuals do stimulate that kind of imagined scenario, complete with dialogue: "Oops, sorry." "You're not sorry." "I am." "Get off my corn!" "I can't breathe." "Where are the grapes?" "Down here, by the feathers . . ." "Look out!" "Ow! I think I'm in the wrong place." "This was your idea, not mine." "Oh, no it wasn't." "Shut up, I have to sneeze." "Listen! The guests are downstairs." "Oh, God, they're early. . . . That's your fault." "What'll we do? We're all wet." "Untie me!" "I'm trying . . . I can't."

grees in medicine and are the only people licensed to diagnose and treat organic disorders. But only in the past dozen years have more than a handful been trained to recognize and treat sexual difficulties (Lief and Karlen, 1976). For physical problems with their sexualia, reproduction, and fertility, women should consult specialists in obstetrics-gynecology. Men with such concerns should see urologists. Some of these specialists are trained to handle psychosexual problems and dysfunctions; far more are not. Concerns about STD are best taken to a dermatologist or public-health clinic. The sexual effects of illnesses should be discussed with internists. The physically handicapped should seek specialists in physical medicine or physical therapy; the latter may be a nurse or have a degree other than an M.D.

Psychiatrists (M.D.) are physicians with additional training in mental health, dysfunction, and illness. As a group, they are probably the physicians who know most about psychosexual problems, but even many of them lack specific training in this area.

Psychologists and sexologists. (M.A., M.S., Ph.D.). Some but not all psychologists are trained to deal with intrapsychic, interpersonal, and sexual problems. *Clinical psychologists* are most likely to have had supervised training in counseling and psychotherapy. The majority of psychologists and sexologists are not trained in sex therapy.

Psychoanalysts are psychotherapists who adhere to particular schools of theory and therapy (Freudian and neo-Freudian). Many are physicians trained in psychiatry. Those without medical degrees, called *lay analysts,* have been certified by psychoanalytic schools and may have other advanced nonmedical training. Psychoanalysts treat the problems of individuals and sometimes of couples. Some are specifically trained in treating sexual dysfunctions; probably the majority are not.

Psychiatric social workers (M.S.W.) are likely to have had some supervised training in psychological counseling and perhaps marriage counseling. Many work in public clinics, religious and community agencies, and hospitals, giving both practical and psychological help, sometimes in conjunction with a physician or a psychologist (Gochros and Schultz, 1977).

Clerics of many faiths have been trained in recent years in pastoral counseling—psychology, marriage counseling, and sometimes human sexuality. Some such training is thorough, some leaves much to be desired.

Sex therapists constitute a speciality that has developed during the past decade. Practitioners, from physicians to self-appointed experts, range from highly trained and qualified to fraudulent. Some have been very effective in helping with mechanism dysfunctions (impotence, anorgasmia, etc.).

Marriage counselors, nurses, and others can also be consulted. Many counselors, nurses, teachers, and people with other degrees and titles offer marriage counseling and sex therapy. Some are highly competent, others incompetent. A small but increasing number receive at least some training in sexuality and sex therapy.

Most sexual dysfunctions, we have said, have psychological roots and require no organic treatment, though a physical examination should be done to eliminate the possibility of organic causes. And clearly the majority of health-care professionals have had little or no training in diagnosing and treating sexual dysfunctions, though the number who have in most of these fields is now growing. Some who claim training have had only a few weekend seminars.

A professional's personality and training in sexuality are probably more important than his or her specialty. A nurse trained to deal with sex problems may be more helpful than a urologist or psychiatrist who isn't. Clerics sensitive to sexual concerns may help more than psychologists who aren't. Amplifying some suggestions by LoPicollo and LoPicollo (1978), we offer these guidelines for selecting a therapist or counselor.

1. Try to get a referral from someone you know and trust—if possible, someone who had a similar problem and was helped by the therapist. Learn more about people recommended by doctors and local medical societies, and ask how they were chosen for referrals; they may be good, but they may just be the doctor's friends or names on a rotating list of the society's members.
2. If you can't get a personal referral, try institutions you trust, such as medical schools, universities, or religious or civic agencies. Many of these monitor the quality of their services. If they don't offer such services, they may make knowledgeable recommendations.
3. Be wary of inappropriate advertising. Most qualified professionals gain patients through personal recommendations and medical speciality organizations. In some states, anyone may advertise and practice as a sex therapist, psychologist, or marriage counselor; some who do so are competent, others charlatans.
4. Try to learn what a therapist's peers think of him. Is he considered competent? If his state licenses his type of therapist, is he licensed? Is he certified by a medical or other specialty board? Is he trained as a sex therapist? The American Association of Sex Educators, Counselors, and Therapists (AASECT) certifies people who meet certain *minimum* requirements.
5. Consider your first meeting with a therapist a trial session. He must gain your respect, communicate easily, and listen with empathy yet with objectivity. Can you accept his manner, treatment method, and fee? Does his approach meet your personality and needs? Are you most comfortable with a therapist of the same or the opposite sex? If not, try another therapist.

Man-woman teams, such as Masters and Johnson (1970) and Hartman and Fithian (1972), are often effective, but so are single practitioners of both sexes, regardless of the problem (Fordney-Settlage, 1975; H. Kaplan, 1974; LoPicollo, 1979; M.-J. Rosenbaum, 1979; Vincent, 1973).

Following these guidelines does not guarantee satisfaction, but it does raise the chances of finding a qualified therapist or counselor who will meet your needs.

Kinds of Therapy. Therapy for sexual dysfunctions and problems with relationships ranges from long-term psychoanalysis to short-term behavior modification to brief, intense group marathons. Here are capsule descriptions of some common therapies.

Classical psychoanalysis is practiced little in the United States today except as a training method for future analysts. It has been gradually replaced, even among many analysts, by various forms of *psychodynamic therapy*. This is shorter and more problem-oriented but uses some basic psychoanalytic concepts and methods—especially a belief in the importance of unconscious thoughts and feelings and a search for insight into the motives (not always the origins) of present behavior. It now often includes some techniques of behavior modification. It is widely called *psychotherapy* and is practiced by many psychiatrists, clinical psychologists, marriage counselors, and psychiatric social workers. It has had varying degrees of success with such dysfunctions of mechanism and orientation as impotence, anorgasmia, transvestism, and homosexuality. Most psychodynamic therapists offer brief or extended therapy for individuals, and many for couples and groups as well.

Behavior therapy concentrates on unlearning (or deconditioning) old behaviors and learning (or conditioning) new ones (Bancroft, 1977). Most of the theorists and practitioners are psychologists. They may give little or no attention to the motives or symbolic meanings of behavior or to the unconscious mind. Behavior therapy has been tried extensively on sexual problems from transvestism to impotence for many decades, with varying success. Behaviorists have used electric shocks, nauseating drugs, and verbal retraining to remove unwanted behavior, and positive incentive therapies and reward to encourage desired behaviors.

In the 1970s there was growing acceptance of the so-called Masters and Johnson method of treating such sex dysfunctions as impotence and anorgasmia. This basically behavioral method calls for intensive treatment of both partners by a male-female team *(conjoint therapy)*. Follow-ups have shown a high success rate for carefully selected patients with severe problems (Masters and Johnson, 1970).

There are many other theories and techniques of therapy. One is treating people in *groups,* either exclusively or in addition to individual or joint therapy (e.g., Golden et al., 1978; Sotile and Kilmann, 1978). This allows each member of the group to receive insight and support from other members. Some groups consist of people with a variety of problems. Others are composed entirely of people with one problem, such as nonorgasmic women (or preorgasmic women, as they are sometimes euphemistically called) or homosexuals. Some groups have used nudity as part of therapy, trying to increase sensuality, trust, and acceptance of one's own and others' bodies. This has been misused in some "T groups," sensitivity sessions, and consciousness-raising groups.

There are many other therapies, such as hypnotherapy, gestalt therapy, existentialist therapy, transactional therapy, and family therapy. Some are new and perhaps more read or heard about than used. Most therapists one is likely to encounter fit one of the major categories above.

Effectiveness of Therapy. Every therapy has supporters and detractors. Paradoxically, as the theoretical differences are argued more and more sharply, the major therapies go on borrowing from each other. Many psychodynamic therapists have long used behavior-modification techniques, and many behavior therapists offer the concern and support that psychodynamic clinicians recommend (Karlen, 1971).

We believe that there is no single correct therapy, and that treating sexual and emotional problems remains as much an art as a science.

Some people use rigorously scientific techniques with poor results; others depend more on experience, intuition, and insight, and help many people. Different therapies probably work better for people with various personalities and problems. For instance, people who volunteer for intensive, rigorous and directive behavior therapy may have different personalities and motives than those who seek less directive, long-term treatment that provides emotional support and insight. This is necessarily only an impression; there are few long-term follow-up studies. The few follow-ups done on therapy for orientation dysfunctions (homosexuality) show the same moderate success rate for behavioral therapy as for psychodynamic therapy (Bieber et al., 1962; Feldman, 1966; Karlen, 1971)—about one-third changed and one-third partly changed. The success rates of therapy for mechanism dysfunctions—impotence, anorgasmia, premature ejaculation—is higher for some behavior therapists (Hartman and Fithian, 1972; Masters and Johnson, 1970) than for some psychodynamic therapists. However, some psychodynamic therapists have been effective with transvestites, exhibitionists, or others whom many behaviorists handle less well (Beigel, 1967; Green and Money, 1969). Many marriage counselors are quite good at dealing with relationship problems that interfere with sexual performance.

Psychotherapy, behavior modification, and sex therapy are among the newest kinds of treatment. Like heart surgery, orthopedics, and other types of treatment, they don't always work, but they help more people now than in the past. In the future they will probably become still more effective. The person who feels in need of help for problems with sex and relationships should seek the therapy and therapist who seem most helpful.

Adjuncts to Therapy

Several controversial techniques—not therapies by themselves, but adjuncts to therapy—have attracted wide attention. They are often opposed for many reasons, not the least of which is that some think they cheapen the health-care professions.

Surrogates. Many sex therapies require a willing and sympathetic partner, but some patients lack one. Therefore some therapists use paid assistants, male and female, as stand-ins, or *surrogates.* Surrogates have a wide range of training and expertise, from almost none to a great deal.

Surrogates can be trained to respond to the therapeutic situation; they are more objective than a regular partner about the patient's problem and have fewer needs and demands; they ensure that retraining exercises are done. Success in treatment with surrogates is reported to be high (Masters and Johnson, 1970). However, using surrogates has been criticized for several reasons. Sometimes it raises legal and ethical problems; some patients have difficulty carrying over the results of treatment to other partners; the surrogate and the patient may become emotionally attached; control passes from the therapist, who is trained and possibly licensed, to the surrogate, who is unlicensed and less trained (Apfelbaum, 1977). Poorly trained and perhaps therapeutically destructive surrogates are apparently used in some of the store-front sex-therapy clinics now proliferating.

Sexually Explicit Material. Many therapists try to desensitize people to sex—that is, make them stop reacting with automatic discomfort to the thought or sight of a variety of sex behaviors. This is done by showing sexually explicit films or pictures. It has become a standard part of eduation in human sexuality in some college and medical and other professional schools. After having seen the films, people examine and express their reactions in small-group discussions. Many leading educators consider this a very effective, even indispensable, teaching technique (Lief and Karlen, 1976; Vandervoort and McIlvenna, 1979).

Explicit material has also been used by some psychologists and marriage counselors to get couples to communicate freely about sex. This has been criticized by some as likely to increase certain patients' anxieties and resistance to treatment, and as presenting misleading educational material (see chapter 22), but its advantages are believed to outweigh its disadvantages (W. Wilson, 1978).

Overt Transference. This phrase is sometimes used for sexual contact between therapist and patient. McCartney (1966) and Shephard (1971) have said that in some cases it may be therapeutic; McCartney claims to have had intercourse with many of his patients, with beneficial results. Masters and Johnson (1970) reported that many such encounters reported by their patients seemed nontherapeutic and exploitive. They occur often enough to be a real issue.

There are no extensive, reliable data on the effectiveness of any of these controversial adjuncts to sex therapy and sex education. The recent informal consensus of the Committee on Sexuality of the American Medical Association was that specially produced explicit films are useful in training and therapy; that surrogates may be helpful, but their use is open to abuse and legal problems; and that sex relations between therapist and patient can never be recommended or condoned. Codes of ethics stating the latter have been proposed for acceptance by the AMA and AASECT (American Association of Sex Educators, Counselors, and Therapists, 1978; Kolodny et al., 1978). They have won widespread but not unanimous approval by the memberships.

Overview

There is no simple or universally accepted definition of psychosexual health and dysfunction. Still, there is broad agreement that a number of sexual behaviors and inabilities are dysfunctional, because they reduce the ability to receive and give sexual satisfaction without emotional or social conflict. Some people feel troubled and think they suffer from a sexual problem because of guilt or lack of knowledge. Some with apparent problems claim they have no problem because of ignorance, rationalization, or resignation.

Shame, secrecy, and pessimism prevent many people with dysfunctions from trying to improve their situations or from seeking professional help. Every decade a larger proportion of people with dysfunctions, from mild to severe, can be helped by short- and long-term counseling or other treatment. There is more room than ever for therapeutic optimism, and every reason to believe further gains will be made. This is very important to know, for sexual dysfunction occurs, if only briefly, at some time in many people's lives, and unless it is successfully dealt with, it can severely damage self-confidence, self-esteem, and relationships.

Review, Discuss, Decide

1. Do the various definitions of psychosexual health rise from experience, evidence, moral convictions, or something else?
2. Does your idea of sexual health differ from what it was a few years ago?
3. What is the difference between being sick and having a dysfunction?
4. What psychological and interpersonal factors can lead to difficulties in sexual function? Can you think of any not mentioned in the chapter?
5. How might you first try to help yourself or a relationship if you feel there is a sexual problem?
6. How should one choose a professional to help with sexual problems?
7. How can male orgasm be delayed? How can a woman learn to reach orgasm or to reach it more often or more quickly?
8. What are sensate focus, spectatoring, and nondemand?
9. What major types of therapy are available? What might be the advantage of each?

Part V   Reproduction

Reproduction is only one function of sex, but it is a very important one. Reproduction involves some of the most important decisions individuals and couples have to make, and more factual questions are asked about it in sexuality classes than about any other aspect of the subject. People are aware that sexual behavior is for now, but that reproduction is forever. And even though biology has arranged it so, one can to some extent decide how to live with it.

Reproduction raises questions about such matters as individual health, love and sex relationships, and world health. Every sexually active person must deal with conception or conception control, and most must deal with pregnancy, childbirth, and childrearing. Everyone must also deal with ego-involvement in his or her reproductive system and ability to reproduce; it is difficult to enjoy one's self and life when troubled about something so central to one's self-concept as reproductive capacity. Also, health problems can arise: about one-third of all women will have a hysterectomy, more than one man in twenty cannot father children, and both members of a couple must cope with menstruation, pregnancy, and menopause.

There are also emotional, social, and ethical aspects of parenthood and family life, and positive, negative, or ambivalent ties to spouses and children. Our society, like virtually all others, passes on strong values and attitudes about menstruation, marriage, fertility, childbirth, and childrearing that have strong personal repercussions. And finally, our species faces a crisis of survival because of overpopulation; we need solutions other than famine, war, and pestilence.

We begin this part of the book with a description of the reproductive system. Then we go on to reproduction (conception, pregnancy, and birth) and to reproduction control.

17

The Reproductive System

What happens to sperm if there is no ejaculation?

What does the prostate gland do? The ovaries?

Why are women's reproductive systems cyclic and men's not?

What is involved in menstruation, physically and mentally?

Is coitus during menses unhealthful?

The relationship between sexual behavior and reproduction goes beyond the obvious one that coitus may lead to pregnancy. One's self-image and perhaps one's self-regard are involved in reproductive capacity and ability, and sexual activity is often a result of this ego involvement.

While discussing the reproductive system, we will present some common sexual concerns. The anatomy material needs few references—there is no debate on it—and those who want further information can consult any standard text on anatomy, gynecology, or urology.

The Male System

The Male Gonads, or Testes

The gonads are a person's biological *primary sex characteristic*. The presence of *testes*, or *testicles*, makes a person male; the presence of

ovaries makes a person female. The other physical characteristics that distinguish males and females are called *secondary sex characteristics*. These may vary, but they do not affect biological sex—for instance, in very rare cases a male is born without a penis, but the presence of testes defines him as a biological male. The testes have two major reproductive functions; they produce *spermatozoa*, or *sperm cells* (male gametes), and *androgens* (male hormones). (See Figure 17-1).

The Tubules. The sperm-producing portions of the testes can be visualized as spaghettilike tubes, the *seminiferous tubules*, packed in compartments that resemble the sections of an orange. Each compartment contains hundreds of feet of these microscopically thin tubules.

The tubes are lined with cells called *spermatogonia*. Like all cells in a male's body, they contain forty-six chromosomes arranged in pairs—twenty-two pairs of similar chromosomes *(autosomes)* and one pair of different (X and Y) *sex chromosomes*. The sex chromosomes determine, among other things, an offspring's sex. At puberty spermatogonia begin to divide. The first appearance of sperm during the period of puberty is termed *spermarche*, or *thelarche*. It is comparable to *menarche*, the onset of menses in females.

In a process called *spermatogenesis* (Figure

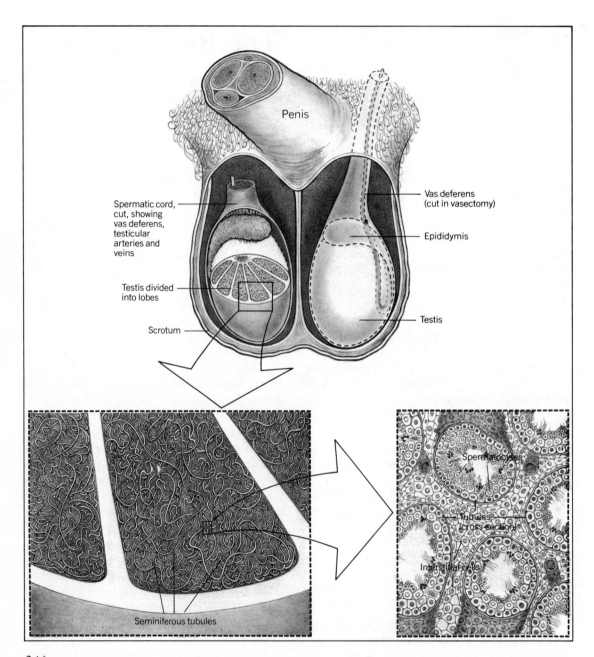

Penis

Spermatic cord, cut, showing vas deferens, testicular arteries and veins

Vas deferens (cut in vasectomy)

Epididymis

Testis divided into lobes

Scrotum

Testis

Seminiferous tubules

Spermatocytes

Tubules (cross-section)

Interstitial cells

Figure 17-1 / *The scrotum contains the testes (one seen here in cross-section) and epididymides. Within each of a testicle's many compartments are seminiferous tubules, where sperm cells develop. The interstitial cells that lie between the tubules produce androgens.*

17-2), spermatogonia undergo several complex divisions from which result cells called spermatocytes, each containing twenty-two unpaired autosomes. Each of the millions of spermatogonia "parent cells" continually gives rise to four spermatozoa (sperm), any of which is capable of fertilizing an egg (see page 369) for egg development). Half of these cells contain one X chromosome, and half contain one Y chromosome. All female egg cells contain one X chromosome, so an egg's union with an X-chromosome sperm produces a female (XX); its union with a Y-chromosome sperm produces a male (XY).

A spermatocyte takes about sixty-five days to become a mature sperm cell. As many as 100 to 500 million may mature each day. Sperm development proceeds best at a few degrees below normal body temperature, so the testes are suspended outside the body cavity, within the scrotum. Long periods of high temperature, such as during extreme fevers caused by disease (e.g., mumps), can cause temporary or permanent sterility. A temporary decline in sperm production may follow a very long hot bath, but cannot be counted on as a contraceptive measure.

Interstitial Tissue. Between and around the seminiferous tubules is *interstitial tissue.* This tissue contains *Leydig cells (interstitial cells),* which produce testosterone (see chapter 6), the androgen that maintains all male reproductive and sexual tissues. Castration, or removal of the gonads, makes men not only sterile but less aggressive sexually and in general.

The Epididymus, Ducts, and Accessory Organs

The Epididymus. The *epididymus* (pl. *epididymides*), a long mass attached to each testicle, can be felt through the skin of the scrotum. It consists mostly of twenty feet of coiled tubes. Sperm pass from the testis into the epididymus and then to the *vas deferens* (outward duct), which leads to the penis. The vas deferens and the testicular artery, vein, and nerves are contained in the *spermatic cord,* which can be felt inside the scrotum.

The Duct System. Sperm cells mass for days or months in the epididymus and *proximal* (near part) *vas.* Some older sperm are normally resorbed here, and some pass to the bladder for excretion with urine. Accumulated sperm may also leave the body in nocturnal emissions. Ejaculation during sexual contact, then, is not necessary to remove sperm for health reasons. The amount of stored sperm does not affect sex drive; the time lapse after previous ejaculation does so, along with other factors.

Each vas deferens joins one of the two *seminal vesicles* to form an *ejaculatory duct.* The seminal vesicles, which constitute one of three *accessory organs,* do not, as their name suggests, store sperm or semen. These specialized glands produce fluids, sugars, and prostaglandins, all of which nourish sperm and promote their survival after ejaculation. The ejaculatory ducts are also misleadingly named, for they are no

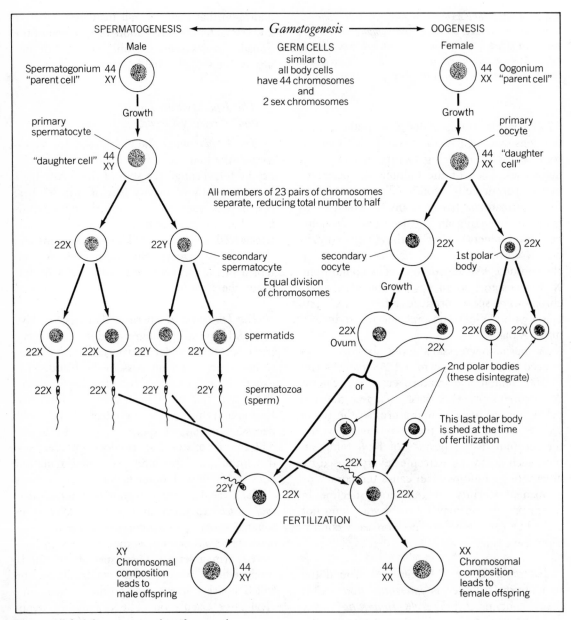

Figure 17-2 / *Spermatogenesis and oogenesis.*

more responsible for ejaculation than any other part of the duct system. These short tubes pass through the prostate gland, linking the vas deferens and seminal vesicles with the urethra.

The *urethra* is the thin, flexible tube that carries both urine and semen. It begins at the base of the bladder and travels a long, curving course through the prostate and the *pelvic diaphragm* (a muscular sling supporting the bladder, prostate, and abdominal organs) to the penile meatus. If a man has difficulty urinating as a result of venereal disease or other physical problems, a flexible rubber tube (catheter) must be passed through the urethra, from the meatus to the bladder. It is at best uncomfortable. For a woman, with her shorter, less tortuous urethra, this is less difficult.

Figure 17-3 / *Castration was practiced rather commonly in some parts of the world well into this century. This old eunuch, who had served in the late days of the Chinese imperial court, was photographed in Peking only a few decades ago.*

The Castrati

Accounts and pictures of castration go back thousands of years. In many societies it was inflicted on prisoners of war. In the ancient West and Near East, and more recently in China and parts of the Arab world, some men were made *eunuchs* (castrated) to be safe servants of women and overseers of harems. The penis might be amputated along with the testicles; otherwise safety was far from guaranteed (Humana, 1973). A male castrated before puberty will not develop typical male physique and has little or no sex drive; but a male castrated after puberty, though sterile, may show only a gradual decline in desire and erectile ability, over a period of many years. Today administering testosterone offers recovery from this decline.

In recent centuries, some religious zealots have castrated themselves, as did some of the early Christian fathers, to destroy any chance of sexual sin. Castration has also been used during this century as a legal preventive measure or punishment for some sex offenders in the United States and Europe. This has almost ceased, partly because castration is now considered cruel and unusual punishment. However, chemical castration by antiandrogenic drugs has come into use (see chapter 6).

Boys have been castrated, probably as recently as the nineteenth century, to produce operatic *castrati*. If a boy is castrated shortly before his voice changes, the eventual result is a voice with a boy-tenor quality supported by an adult chest and diaphragm—quite different from any other adult voice, male or female. Händel, among other composers, wrote parts for castrati, and some castrati were among the great opera stars of their time.

By using the muscles of the pelvic diaphragm, a man can sometimes control ejaculation and orgasm. Before ejaculation seems inevitable, he simultaneously flexes this diaphragm (by bearing down as if to stop urine flow) and holds his breath *(Valsalva maneuver)*. This raises blood pressure in the vessels supplying the penis and reduces sensations conducive to orgasm and ejaculation (Marcott and Weiss, 1976).

The Prostate Gland. This gland surrounds part of the urethra and empties into it, and provides much of the fluid that makes up semen. It also produces *prostaglandins,* hormones that stimulate smooth-muscle activity in the male and female reproductive systems, increasing the contractions of orgasm and thus aiding the travel of sperm and egg. Prostaglandins are used medically in high doses to induce abortion.

The Bulbourethral Glands. These pea-sized glands (also called *Cowper's glands*) lie within the pelvic diaphragm and empty into the urethra at the base of the penis. They produce a clear, sticky secretion, sometimes called "love drops," that appears at the meatus early in sexual excitement. This fluid helps prolong the life and activity of sperm. It can also carry enough sperm to cause pregnancy, making *coitus interruptus* (withdrawal before ejaculation) a risky contraceptive practice.

Figure 17-4 / *The male reproductive system, seen in cross-section.*

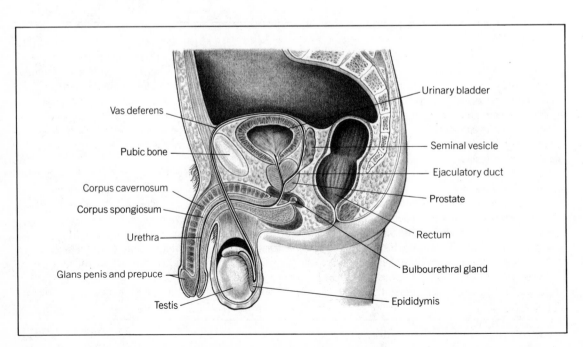

The Female System

A woman's reproductive system (Figure 17-5) commands more of her attention than a man's does of him. She is periodically reminded of it from puberty until menopause, and it demands physical and psychological involvement during pregnancy, labor, and nursing.

Even routine reproductive functions often cause healthy women physical and emotional discomfort—painful menstruation *(dysmenorrhea)*, painful ovulation (*mittelschmerz* = middle pain), and difficult labor and nursing. Such problems may have biological, cultural, or individual sources. They may also produce very different reactions among women. For instance, mittelschmerz is a welcome sign to a woman trying to conceive, since it signals ovulation; to women who don't want to be pregnant, even painful menses can be a relief.

Men and those women who feel no routine reproductive discomfort may find it difficult to accept, understand, and be sympathetic to such problems. But a woman with dysmenorrhea or mittelschmerz feels real pain, and it may color her view of being female, of reproduction, or of genital activity. Rarely do men have comparable problems.

The Female Gonads, or Ovaries

The ovaries are a female's gonads, her primary biological sex characteristic. They have the same chief functions as the testes—to produce gametes and secrete hormones that influence reproduction, sexual development, and sexual activity. The other parts of the female reproductive system are the oviducts (Fallopian tubes), uterus, vagina, and breasts (the vagina and breasts are discussed in chapter 3).

The ovary is an oval organ about the size of an adult's first thumb joint. One lies on either side of the abdominal cavity, near the floor of the pelvis. In a pelvic examination, the ovaries can be felt through the vaginal wall. Pressure on the ovary, as on the testis, can be quite painful. Each ovary contains follicles, corpora, and a stroma.

The *stroma (interstitium),* the large body of the ovary, contains the developing follicles and corpus luteum. The *ovarian follicles* are egg-bearing structures within the ovary. After ovulation, the cells of a mature follicle *(Graafian follicle)* collapse and develop into a *corpus luteum* (yellow body). The corpus luteum's main function is producing progesterone; this hormone prepares the uterus to support a pregnancy. In a normal menstrual cycle, a corpus luteum functions for about six to ten days. If the woman becomes pregnant, it remains functional for three to nine months, depending on how much the placenta takes over its support of the pregnancy.

The ovaries produce progesterone, estrogens, and androgens in amounts that vary with the reproductive cycle. As follicles develop, their cells and the interstitial cells create and release estrogens. The stroma produces small amounts of androgens, which in both sexes are the chief libidinal hormones, but women's main source of androgens is the adrenal glands.

The Oviducts, or Fallopian Tubes

The *oviducts (Fallopian tubes,* or *ovarian tubes)* carry eggs from the ovary to the uterus slowly (in about three days) and conduct sperm toward the ovary quickly (in minutes). The oviduct has several portions. Its fingerlike projections, called *fimbriae,* pass over the ovary,

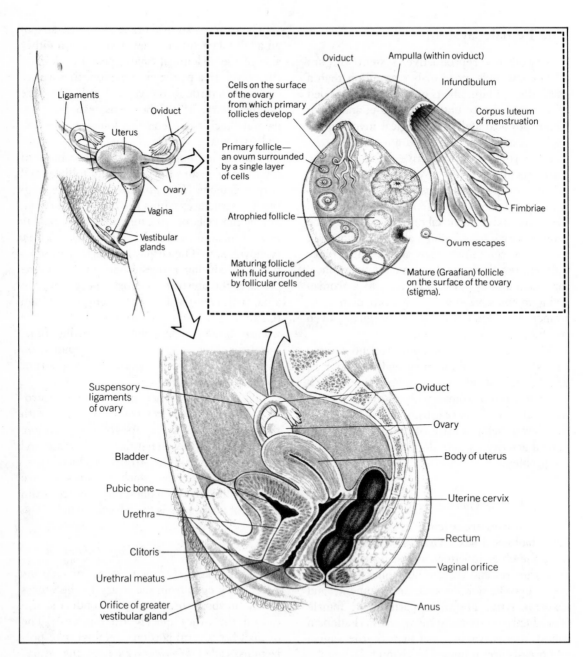

Ligaments

Oviduct

Uterus

Ovary

Vagina

Vestibular glands

Oviduct

Ampulla (within oviduct)

Cells on the surface of the ovary from which primary follicles develop

Infundibulum

Corpus luteum of menstruation

Primary follicle— an ovum surrounded by a single layer of cells

Atrophied follicle

Fimbriae

Ovum escapes

Maturing follicle with fluid surrounded by follicular cells

Mature (Graafian) follicle on the surface of the ovary (stigma).

Suspensory ligaments of ovary

Oviduct

Ovary

Bladder

Body of uterus

Pubic bone

Urethra

Uterine cervix

Clitoris

Rectum

Urethral meatus

Vaginal orifice

Orifice of greater vestibular gland

Anus

Figure 17-5 / *The female reproductive system, seen in cross-section.*

sweeping *ova* (eggs) into the *infundibulum*. This funnel-shaped structure leads to the *ampulla.* There fertilization usually occurs, often with sperm from coitus that occurred a day or two before ovulation. The ampulla leads to the remainder of the oviduct, which joins the uterus.

Sometimes poor ovum transport, blocked oviducts, or some other problem allows a fertilized egg to implant in the oviduct. Such *ectopic* (out of place) *pregnancy* eventually produces sharp abdominal pain and requires immediate medical action to remove the embryo, for it threatens the mother's life.

The Uterus, or Womb

The *uterus*, or *womb*, is the chamber in which an embryo develops until birth. In a mature, nonpregnant woman, it is about the size and shape of a pear. It is very muscular and expands at least threefold during pregnancy.

The uterus has four main parts. The *fundus,* the upmost part, lies above the entrance of the oviducts. The *body*, within which the fetus normally attaches, is quite thick. The *isthmus* is the narrow region between the body and the *cervix,* which leads to the vagina.

The uterus usually lies at a right angle to the vagina, with the fundus forward and the cervix projecting into the vagina, where it can be felt by an inserted finger. The sharp angle between the vagina and uterus makes nonprofessional

Hysteria: The Wandering Womb

The word hysteria comes from the Greek *hysteron*, or womb (see Vieth, 1965). This emotional disorder, more common in women than men, can appear as convulsions, inability to swallow or breathe, temporary blindness or paralysis—almost any psychosomatic symptom—or may be a pervasive personality trait. The ancient Greeks thought these symptoms resulted from the womb wandering about in the body, causing discomfort wherever it went. Consider this tenth century incantation: ''I conjure thee, O womb, not to harm that maid, not to occupy her head, throat, neck, chest, ears, teeth, eyes, nostrils, shoulderblades, arms, hands, heart, stomach, spleen, kidneys, back, sides, joints, navel, intestines, bladder, thighs, shins, heels, nails, but to lie down quietly in the place God chose for thee.'' This view of hysteria had few opponents till almost the turn of this century, when Freud (1938) concluded from his first experiments in psychoanalysis that hysteria is caused by emotional conflict, often involving unconscious sexual impulses.

abortions potentially disastrous; the uterine wall can be accidentally perforated.

As pregnancy advances, the angle between the vagina and the uterus decreases. The growing weight of the fetus then bears more directly on the cervix. (Pressure from the enlarged uterus on the bladder makes urination more frequent during pregnancy). The uterus is supported not only at the cervix but by several ligaments, especially the *broad ligament.* Sometimes the broad ligament is torn during pregnancy or birth; this causes pain during deep penile penetration and requires surgery.

The uterus consists mostly of thick bands of entwined muscle, the *myometrium* (*myo* = muscle, *metra* = womb). It is lined with a layer of changeable tissue called the *endometrium* (*endo* = inner). Each month, the endometrium becomes more thick, glandular, and receptive to implantation. If a fertilized egg does implant, the endometrium keeps growing to support the pregnancy. If none is implanted, the endometrium sheds through the vagina, a process called *menstruation.*

Menstruation, or Menses

The Process. Menstruation is the periodic breakdown and elimination of the *decidua* (shedding portion) of the endometrium. The decidua grows each month in response to ovarian hormones. Its breakdown is signalled by bleeding caused by the rupture of the endometrium's many small blood vessels. This cyclic bleeding is called *menses* (monthly) or *period* (since it is periodic). There are many slang terms for it, such as "the curse" and the "red flag."

Figure 17-6 / *Use of the tampon and the sanitary napkin during menses.*

A girl's first menses, called *menarche* (pronounced meh-nař-ky), most commonly occurs at age eleven to thirteen, but it may normally happen as early as nine or as late as fifteen. Menstruation lasts for three to seven days, usually four to five. The time varies for several reasons, but chiefly because only part of the endometrium is shed on a given day. Since some parts are always intact, implantation and thus pregnancy can occur during menses.

As ovarian follicles develop, they produce estrogens, which spur regrowth of the endometrium and its blood vessels. This growth begins with menses and continues for about two weeks till ovulation has occured. Then the progesterone produced by the corpus luteum continues to enhance endometrial growth. Thus the uterus is usually changed in synchrony with the development of ova.

During menses, a woman releases four to sixteen tablespoons or more of blood, along with endometrial cells and mucous from the uterus. Menstrual flow varies among women, and over time for each woman. The amount and duration are usually decreased by oral contraceptives and increased by intrauterine devices (IUDs). Women should be sure their diets contain sufficient iron, which the body needs to produce blood. Unlike blood from other parts of the body, menstrual blood does not readily clot.

In most nontechnological societies, women place dried fiber, dried moss, or cloth against the vulva to absorb menstrual discharge. Cloth,

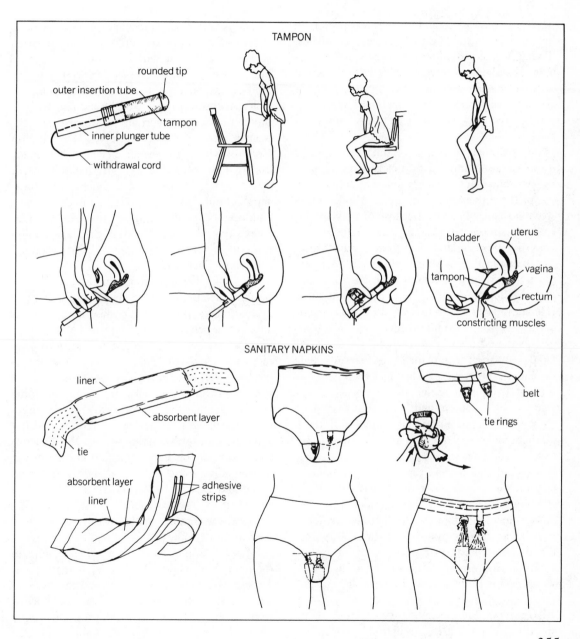

TAMPON

rounded tip

outer insertion tube

tampon

inner plunger tube

withdrawal cord

bladder

uterus

tampon

vagina

rectum

constricting muscles

SANITARY NAPKINS

liner

absorbent layer

tie

belt

tie rings

absorbent layer

adhesive strips

liner

which can be washed and reused, was preferred in much of the West in recent centuries. Today, women in affluent societies use disposable absorbent products, especially external *sanitary napkins* and internal *vaginal tampons.* An internal plastic cup or rubber diaphragm can be used by a woman with heavy menstrual flow.

Most women have at some time experienced *dysmenorrhea.* Menstruation causes severe pain in one woman out of nine, moderate pain in one out of three (Kessel and Coppen, 1963). Some women require bed rest because of pelvic pain, cramps, nausea, headaches, and general discomfort. Prostaglandins in menstrual fluid (produced in the endometrium) have been implicated in menstrual cramps. However, social and psychological forces may also be involved (Delaney, Lupton, and Toth, 1976). Dysmenorrhea is more common in some religious groups than in society as a whole; psychosocial factors apparently influence the women's feelings about menstruation or affect their perception of pain. One clinician (Shainess, 1962) studied 103 women and reported that only those who had felt emotional conflict with their mothers and were not prepared for menarche experienced menstrual pain. Most scientists, however, do not believe that such psychological factors cause all or most menstrual pain. This common problem still awaits clarification.

Dysmenorrhea can usually be eased by aspirin, rest, or alcohol. Sometimes orgasm, through masturbation or coitus, brings relief from uterine cramps and shortens the menstrual period (Masters and Johnson, 1975).

Menstrual Taboos. In many societies, menstruating women are considered unclean or taboo, as sexual partners and otherwise. Among Polynesians, as in many cultures, menstruating women used to spend the menses in special huts, isolated from males and barred from sacred events. In a number of social and religious codes, menses are followed by a ritual bath or other purification ceremony to prepare the woman for return to society. The Hindu's Code of Manu, for instance, says, "A woman, during her menstrual period, shall retire for three days to a place apart. During this time, she shall not look at anybody, not even her own children, or at the light of the sun. On the fourth day, she shall bathe." Similar prohibitions exist among Moslems, Orthodox Jews, and many Christians.

Negative feelings about menstruation may be mild, as among many people in the United States today; these feelings may be severe, as among the people of the Mangareve Islands, in the Pacific, who believed that coitus during menses made a man blind. The commonest fear has been that contact with menstruating women is unhealthful or unlucky to men, but some peoples, such as the Chukehee of Siberia, think it can harm women, perhaps make them sickly and sterile. A few societies, such as the Trukese and Maori of the Pacific, permit coitus during menses, and some believe it aids conception (Ford and Beach, 1951). This was believed as late as the 1930s by some Westerners, who thought conception analogous to planting a seed in moist soil.

Many attempts have been made to explain the menstrual taboo. One theory is that by enforcing abstinence, it renews sexual interest and vigor; another is that it gives overworked women respite from labor. Menses is the time of least frequent coitus in nonhuman primates—logically, in biological terms, for then conception is least likely. However, strong psychological forces underlie the intense anxiety about menstrual blood in many societies. Probably one reason is fear of contagion—that any apparent illness or injury can be transmitted. Certainly many people are upset by the sight of blood, especially when it flows from the genitals—evoking, some clinicians believe, fantasies of genital mutilation (Gadpaille, 1975).

Medical, Hygienic, and Esthetic Concerns. There is no medical or hygienic reason to abstain from genital activity during menses. Some couples find coitus at this time distasteful, others find it especially exciting; many find that over time, initial distaste and embarrassment fade. Many who use the rhythm method of contraception favor menses as a time for coitus. Women who use a tampon may find it helpful to use an artificial lubricant for coitus soon after removing a tampon. The tampon absorbs not only menstrual flow but normal vaginal fluids.

The age of menarche appears to have decreased along with an increase in better nutrition; the age of menopause, however, is remaining about the same (Goodman, Grove, and Gilbert, 1978). We have presumably reached the lower limits to normal menarche.

The HPG Axis and Sexual Cyclicity

The Female HPG Axis

Menstruation is a process of the uterus, ovulation a process of the ovary. Both are stages of a complex cycle that must proceed smoothly for reproduction to occur. The ovary and uterus are kept more or less in concert by hormonal signals traveling in mutual feedback between these two organs and the *hypothalamus* and *pituitary gland.* The hypothalamus is a part of the brain that governs many emotional and physical responses. It and the pituitary, a small gland attached to it, affect growth, sexuality, reproduction, and the interaction of other endocrine organs. One such set of interactions is the *hypothalamic-pituitary-gonadal (HPG) axis.* The following simplified description shows how this axis regulates the reproductive cycle (see Figure 17-7).

The hypothalamus and pituitary release into the bloodstream *gonadotropic* (gonad-stimulating) *hormones.* Two are *FSH* (follicle stimulating hormone), which stimulates the growth of ovarian follicles, and *LH* (luteinizing hormone), which helps form and maintain the corpus luteum. Stimulated by FSH and LH, ovarian follicles develop into larger, more mature *Graafian follicles.* These produce estrogens, which circulate in the blood back to the hypothalamus and pituitary. As a thermostat signals a furnace to vary its output, the estrogens signal the hypothalamus and pituitary to produce more LH. That LH flows to the ovaries and helps the follicles to mature and ovulation to occur. A third gonadotropin, prolactin, comes into play for pregnancy and lactation.

In no woman is the menstrual cycle consistent in frequency. The average length is 28 days, but normal cycles vary from 20 to 40 days (Vollman, 1956). A follicle may take ten to fourteen days to mature, but sometimes it takes as many as forty; this variation chiefly determines the length of a menstrual cycle, for unless pregnancy occurs, the corpus luteum regularly lasts some six to ten days after ovulation, and menstruation follows.

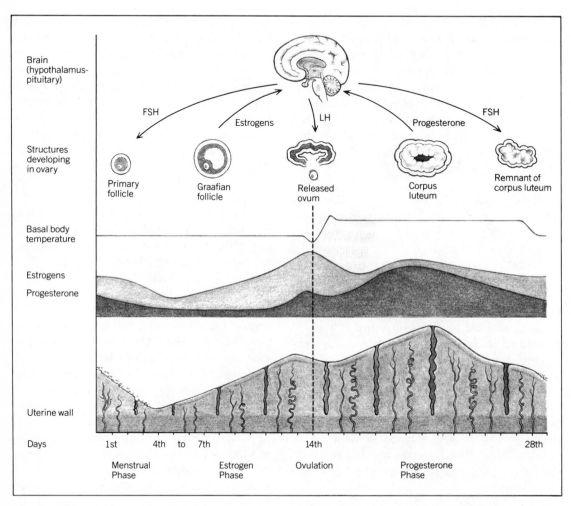

Figure 17-7 / *The female HPG cycle.*

Ovulation is followed by formation of the corpus luteum, a rich source of progesterone. The high progesterone level signals the hypothalamus and pituitary to reduce FSH and LH production. While estrogens and progesterone from the ovary feed signals to the hypothalamus and pituitary, they also nourish the oviducts and the endometrium. These hormones bring the endometrium to its greatest thickness and readiness for implantation. If implantation does not occur, the gonadotropins rapidly decline, as do progesterone and estrogens. It is hypothesized that if no fertilized egg is implanted, a substance from the endometrium called *luteolysin* feeds back to the ovary and makes the corpus luteum regress.

As ovarian hormones decline, the endometrium begins to slough, and menstruation begins. This decline also stimulates the hypothalamus and pituitary to renew first FSH and LH production, and another menstrual cycle begins. If implantation occurs, the endometrium is not sloughed, the prolactin and ovarian hormone levels remain high, and pregnancy begins. After pregnancy, the menstrual cycle resumes.

The Male HPG Axis

The male does not have a reproductive cycle. This difference is set during fetal development by the presence or absence of adrogens, which acts on the nervous system to determine cyclicity (Barraclough and Gorski, 1961; Whalen, 1968). In both sexes, however, the same HPG hormones and feedback system exist, and the gonads depend on the hypothalamus and pituitary to function healthily.

In males, LH has the alternate name *ICSH* (interstitial cell stimulating hormone). It stimulates testosterone and sperm production; then in thermostat fashion, rising blood levels of testosterone make the hypothalamus and pituitary release less FSH and LH, re-establishing homeostasis, or balance, in the HPG axis. (Sperm production may create a substance, tentatively called *inhibin,* that reduces FSH output.) As we have noted, this HPG axis activity is not cyclic, as in females, but *tonic,* or continuous.

Psychological Aspects of Cyclicity

The HPG axis alone does not fully explain the reproductive cycle. The hypothalamus probably has its own biological clock, regulating components of reproduction and sexual drive. This clock also initiates menarche and menopause. Furthermore, emotions, thoughts, social learning, and external events influence behavior and endocrine function, ultimately by sending messages to the hypothalamus and pituitary. For instance, a significant event, such as a wedding or school examination, can cause early or late ovulation or menstruation.

We have mentioned the debate on whether or how the emotions and social attitudes affect the likelihood of menstrual pain. Psychological and social influences have been implicated in some cases of sterility and chronic miscarriage (Gadpaille, 1975; Noyes, 1968). Clinical observations and animal experiments suggest that there are many other relationships between the psyche, the reproductive cycle, and behavior.

The only animals besides humans that menstruate are monkeys and apes, but in all nonhuman mammals, females' sexual activity changes with hormonal rhythms. Females appear more attractive to males at certain times *(attractivity).* They copulate only or most often when the chance of fertilization is highest. A female monkey places herself closer to males as the follicular phase proceeds and ovulation nears *(proceptivity).* She shows lordosis more often, and less often rejects males' attempts to touch and mount her *(receptivity).* She is least likely to do all thse things when menstruating, and males are less likely then to approach her sexually (Beach, 1977a; Ford and Beach, 1951).

A human female's behavior does not follow her reproductive cycle that rigidly; it also responds to many individual and social influences. But some tendencies do become apparent in studies of large populations. The ovulatory phase tends to bring feelings of self-satisfaction and of ability to cope well with life (Bardwick, 1971; Silbergeld, Brast, and Noble, 1971). Many women say that at this time, their moods range from pleasant (Moos et al., 1969) to elated (Altmann, Knowles, and Bull, 1941). It seems significant that college women are more likely to volunteer for immediate or future tasks when ovulating than when menstruating (Doty and Silverthorne, 1975).

Premenses and menses tend to bring irritability, depression, anxiety, negativity, fatigue, or low self-esteem to 30 to 65 percent of women (S. L. Smith, 1975). These symptoms were recognized as a medical entity, *premenstrual tension*, some fifty years ago (R. Frank, 1931). Subsequent research has shown that premenstrual tension affects almost all women at some time, and some women always. Such tension is not always present and does not necessarily influence a woman's job or other activities, but the menstrual and premenstrual periods have been statistically correlated with increases in women's violence, suicide, admissions for psychiatric care, acute medical and emergency treatment, and relatively poor performance on examinations and in athletics (S. L. Smith, 1975; Dalton, 1964). However, one study (Sommer, 1973) found a discrepancy between women's reports of their behaviors and their performance according to objective measures, and another (Parlee, 1973) has called some research in this area questionable. The subject, which has many social implications, still requires more research.

Many women desire sexual activity more often during ovulation than before or after. For reasons less well understood, sexual arousal is often relatively high just before and after menses; perhaps this is because androgen levels are higher then. Not surprisingly, masturbation and coitus occur more often around ovulation, and women are more likely to reach orgasm then (D. Adams, Gold and Burt, 1978; McCance, Luff and Widdowson, 1937; Udry and Morris, 1968). More research is needed to clarify this matter, for it is difficult to know when ovulation occurs (Udry and Morris, 1978).

Men may be influenced by the cyclic changes in the women with whom they live. A study (Persky et al., 1978) of both partners' behavior and hormone levels showed that the men's testosterone levels reached their peak soon after the women's ovulation. The reason is not yet known, but visual, behavioral, and especially olfactory cues may be involved. Such mutual feedback of cues occurs in many higher species.*

These parallels between humans' and other mammals' behavior suggest evolutionary continuity. Estrogens, which are highest during ovulation, are related to sexual receptiveness. Low levels of progesterone at ovulation seems to precipitate sexual activity. The higher progesterone levels after ovulation correlate with lower sexual activity. Estrogens also decrease at this luteal period; this combination of low estrogen and high progesterone levels is the one least likely to encourage sexual activity.

---

* Vaginal odors vary during the menstrual cycle. At ovulation, odor is lowest and is reported as least unpleasant (Doty et al., 1975). However, reactions to body and vaginal odors are subjective and strongly influenced by individual and social factors. Many men find vaginal odors arousing.

The interaction of hormones, behavior, and nervous system is also influenced by the senses. Women see, hear, smell, and taste with greater sensitivity around ovulation, less acutely at menses. Their pain reactions work the opposite way; they feel pain the least at ovulation, most during menstruation. Such sensory changes seem conducive to coitus during ovulation, the time of greatest fertility (Diamond, Diamond, and Mast, 1972). In men there is no link between sensory perception and spermatogenesis.

Other evidence relates women's moods and behavior to their reproductive cycle. Those who take oral contraceptives do not experience the full swings in mood and arousal felt during natural cycles. Contraceptive pills with various amounts of progesterone and estrogens have effects on moods consistent with the hormone influences described.

Obviously a woman's sexual activity is not based on her neuroendocrine functions alone. Women don't jump into bed because they are ovulating or jump out because they are menstruating. The right person, time, and place are important enough to override the patterns seen more rigidly in our primate ancestors. But the right person, time, and place do seem to appear most often during ovulation (D. Adams, Gold and Burt, 1978; McCance, Luff, and Widdowson, 1937; Udry and Morris, 1968).

Absence of the Menstrual Cycle

Women do not experience the reproductive cycle before puberty, when taking oral contraceptives, after menopause, or after removal of the ovaries. Without the cycle, they respond to their own hormones in quite individual ways.

Some women are *amenorrheic* (without menses), *anovulatory* (without ovulation), or both. These conditions are not uncommon in female athletes or severely underweight women, those with little body fat (Frisch and McArthur, 1974). Prolonged amenorrhea in otherwise normal women usually indicates pregnancy. It should always be checked. Neither amenorrhea nor anovulation is associated with any particular pattern of sex behavior.

Several conditions can make a woman anovulatory; she probably won't be aware of them unless she is trying to become pregnant. A common one is the presence of a tough membrane around the ovary, preventing the ovum from leaving (Stein-Leventhal syndrome); often part of this membrane can be surgically removed. Another common cause is malfunction of the HPG axis (usually insufficient production of FSH and LH); in such cases, ovulation may be induced by drugs. These drugs cause the high incidence of multiple births in previously infertile women. There is help for many women who have difficulty in gamete production, but for few men with this problem. Knowledge of female reproductive processes seems greater than that of male processes. This allows for greater medical aid for females in cases of infertility and less for males in need of contraception.

Certain medical conditions, especially in middle and later life, require *hysterectomy* (removal of the uterus) or *radical hysterectomy* (removal of the uterus and ovaries). This is the third most common surgical procedure for women, after abortion and appendectomy. The uterus is not part of the HPG axis; if it alone is removed, conception and menstruation are, of course, impossible, but the other cyclic functions of the HPG axis continue. Removing the ovaries *(castration)* does break the HPG cycle and may gradually have other effects as well; loss of desire for physical reasons is not one of them, for as we have seen, women's chief source of libidinal hormones is the adrenal glands. Hormone-replacement therapy can prevent or reduce many unwanted results of castration. After recovery from surgery, and with hormone therapy, even radical hysterectomy does not seem to physically diminish a woman's sexual desire or responsiveness.

Overview

Men are capable of reproduction for up to seventy years, from about ages ten to eighty. Women are fertile for about half as long, from about ten to forty-five or fifty. Understanding the basic anatomy and processes involved is important through most of life.

Of the major cyclic biological events, menarche and menstruation are among the most important, not only physically but psychologically and socially. They remind women of their reproductive potential, regardless of whether the women are sexually active. Despite some fear or embarrassment, most women greet menarche with a degree of satisfaction. One of the authors (Diamond) has four daughters and has instituted a family celebration—a night on the town—for each daughter's menarche, to foster positive acceptance of menstruation and affirm it as a symbol of adulthood.

Over the years, most women have varying or mixed feelings about menses, but very rarely does a woman miss a period with equanimity. If she wants a pregnancy, she is delighted. If she doesn't desire pregnancy and has been having coitus, she is distressed. If she hasn't been having coitus, she is justifiably concerned about her health.

For men, the only event comparable to menarche is first ejaculation. Subsequent ejaculations are primarily associated with sexual pleasure, not reproduction. This, we believe, is one of the major reasons men and women view coitus differently. Most men think primarily of the pleasure of ejaculation first, the responsibility of reproduction second. Many women think of reproduction and its responsibilities first, the pleasure of coitus second (Bernard, 1966). Modern contraception has somewhat altered this (see chapter 19).

In the next chapter we will discuss pregnancy, which affects the great majority of people and is a highly significant event in their lives. We will also discuss the unwanted absence of pregnancy, which is a problem for many people.

Review, Discuss, Decide

1. How do the gonads contribute to reproduction? What changes in behavior are likely to follow castration in men? In women?
2. How do hormones affect mood and behavior in both sexes?

Have you been aware of these effects in yourself or a partner? How can they affect decisions about sex behavior?

3. What accounts for the HPG activity of women being cyclic and that of men not being cyclic?

4. What do you think are the most common attitudes toward menstruation in our society? What are yours? Have they changed during your life? Do they affect your decisions about coitus or genital play?

5. It has been suggested that periodic mood shifts may make women unsuitable for certain jobs. What do you think of that suggestion? Might there be positive aspects of cyclic mood change? If so, what are they?

6. For people who live a full life span, men are fertile far longer than women. What are some of the implications and possible results of this for individuals and for society?

18

Reproduction

How easy is it to conceive?

Do I want a child?

How do I know whether I'm fertile? Pregnant?

Can I plan to have a boy or a girl?

Should I have natural childbirth? Should I nurse my child?

How will children affect our relationship?

How to have children or avoid having them occupies almost everyone's thoughts at some time. Men are fertile from early adolescence until advanced old age. In many parts of the world, women are either pregnant or briefly between pregnancies much of their adult lives; this was true in our society until about a century ago. Even today, most American women spend some three decades of their lives having and rearing children. Modern contraception has started a vast biosocial change: for the first time, women can choose sexually active lives without pregnancy. The social and emotional implications are enormous (see chapter 21).

Deciding on Reproduction

At some time during their lives, most people see themselves as becoming parents. In one study, fewer than 5 percent said they had never wanted children (Pohlman, 1969). A majority of college students say they would hesitate to marry someone who did not want children, and that they expect family relationships to provide their greatest satisfaction (Goldsen et al., 1960).

People decide to have children for many reasons (Fawcett, 1970; Pohlman, 1969).

1. *To give love.* A baby is someone one can love, and a way to share loving a mutual creation.

2. *As proof of sexual maturity or capability.* This motive may be strong in the young or elderly. Many men see a child as proof of virility. Efforts to expand women's lives beyond the maternal role must contend with the fact that many women consider motherhood a primary confirmation of their femaleness. This is stronger in lower socioeconomic groups (Rainwater, 1960), but is true at all levels.

3. *To meet or reject others' expectations.* Some people want to satisfy their parents' desire for grandchildren. Some try to prove they can have as many or more children than others. And often, people refuse to meet others' expectations out of defiance.

4. *To create an extension of oneself or add to a family.* The desire to extend oneself in time, build a clan or dynasty, or perpetuate an ethnic or social group seems to concern

more men than women. It may be one reason that most families in the United States, as in many other countries, want a son first, then a daughter.

5. *To conform to social norms.* Waller and Hill (1951) write of two conspiracies, to get the unmarried married and then to get the childless children.

6. *As an expression of a parental instinct.* Such an instinct may exist or, more likely, a number of drives, biosocial tendencies, and personal desires may give the impression that it does. People more often think of maternal than paternal instinct, but both are widely thought to exist.

7. *Because children provide enjoyment.* One of the commonest reasons people give for having children is that they like them. There is probably a biosocial basis for this.

8. *Because children are thought necessary for a happy marriage* (Christopherson and Walters, 1958). Perhaps the presence of children confirms expectations of family life. Some people hope that having a child will create a common bond in a troubled marriage.

9. *To change the parents' status.* In some cultures, people are viewed as adults only after they have a child. This seems true to some degree in ours. Some teenagers use pregnancy to assert their adulthood and independence ("You can't treat me like a child any more").

10. *Out of compensatory and neurotic motives.* These lie behind many pregnancies. Some people hope to live vicariously through their children. Some men and women actually desire not a child but a pregnancy, to confirm their fertility or sexuality. Preg-

nancy brings attention and support, which some women feel they don't get enough of. And some women see having a child as the most or even the only creative thing they can do.

11. *For religious reasons.* Some religions strongly discourage limiting reproduction. Mormons, Hindus, Orthodox Jews (with some prescribed exceptions), and Roman Catholics all forbid contraceptive devices.

12. *As justification for coitus.* Some people say, "If I have sex, I'm willing to care for the baby if that's the result."

Many children arrive after less planning than goes into buying a car—some even more from carelessness than a decision. Half or more of pregnancies in the United States between 1970 and 1977 were unplanned; about 30 to 40 percent of these were aborted (Diamond et al., 1973a,b; Jaffe, 1971; Forrest, Tietze, and Sullivan, 1978).

Children, we believe, are too important to be left to chance; each person should carefully consider his or her reasons for choosing them. One should also consider one's desire and ability—emotional, financial, medical, and social—to rear them. A child requires love, time, money, energy, and willingness to share one's partner's attention without jealousy. Routines, free time, social life, responsibilities, all change with parenthood. One should ask oneself about accepting such changes without resentment. And will there be parents, friends, or others to share the experiences of childrearing and give psychological or practical support?

One should be medically fit to reproduce. Past or current illnesses may make childbirth or childrearing difficult, even dangerous. Blood disorders (for example, Rh sensitivity) and diabetes can affect both mother and child. Either parent may have a family history suggesting a high risk of genetic disease or abnormality in the child. If there is any doubt about this, it is advisable to consult a genetic counselor.

About 80 to 85 percent of couples in this nation can have children without much physical difficulty. For 15 to 20 percent, parenthood must come through artificial insemination or adoption. This figure is surprisingly high to most people. These practices still cause much ambivalence, secrecy, and fear that they reflect on one's masculinity or femininity.

Genetic Screening

There are many conditions that couples may not want to pass on to children. Some can be detected during pregnancy (see page 380 on amniocentesis). Others cannot be found till the child is born, but sometimes genetic counseling can tell parents the odds that a child will inherit the disease. With that knowledge, they can decide to take the risk, abort, attempt artificial insemination, or adopt.

Some genetic diseases occur predominantly in certain ethnic groups. This is true of three conditions for which screening is possible: Tay-Sachs disease, a fatal illness limited almost entirely to Jews of East European ancestry; sickle-cell anemia, a debilitating, sometimes fatal disease common in parts of Africa and among black Americans (though not limited to them); and cystic fibrosis, a fatal illness most common in Caucasians.

Some blacks object to genetic screening for sickle-cell anemia as a kind of genocide (though Jews, much fewer in number, apparently don't feel that way about Tay-Sachs disease). Some also argue that treatment for anemia may soon improve. What odds, they ask, should discourage reproducing, especially for a minority?

It is true that totalitarian governments and even well-meaning democracies have misused genetic planning. In Hitler's Germany, millions of people were sterilized for alleged genetic reasons. Early in this century, the United States and many European nations forcibly sterilized people for such signs of alleged hereditary taint as having illegitimate children, antisocial behavior, and masturbation (Karlen, 1971). Such practices have decreased but not stopped entirely. Voluntary screening, however, rouses little opposition, can help avert mental and physical suffering, and allows more informed decisions about reproduction.

How Reproduction Begins

Sperm and Semen

Sperm. Pregnancy results from the fusion of a sperm cell *(spermatozoan)* with an egg, usually after coital ejaculation. At puberty, sperm and semen develop sufficiently in quantity and quality to allow fertilization. A mature sperm cell consists of a *head, neck, midpiece,* and *tail* (Figure 18-1). The head is packed with chromosomes. The cylindrical neck probably provides the driving force for the whiplike tail that keeps the sperm active. Sperm become *motile* (mobile) only when they leave the testes.

Semen. Semen *(seminal fluid)* is the fluid in which sperm are carried from the testes through the penis and into the vagina. This milk-colored liquid is composed of secretions from the male accessory organs—the prostate, seminal vesicles, and bulbourethral glands. The prostate (not prostrate!) is responsible for most of semen's color and odor, but for only about one-third of its volume. The seminal vesicles provide about 60 percent. Seminal fluids nourish the sperm, reduce coagulation of the ejaculate, and stimulate sperm motility. The prostate also produces *acid phosphatase,* which nourishes sperm. In rape cases, the presence of acid phosphatase in the vagina is taken as evidence that coitus occurred. Sperm and semen consist mostly of proteins and carbohydrates,

Figure 18-1 / *A sperm cell and an egg cell.*

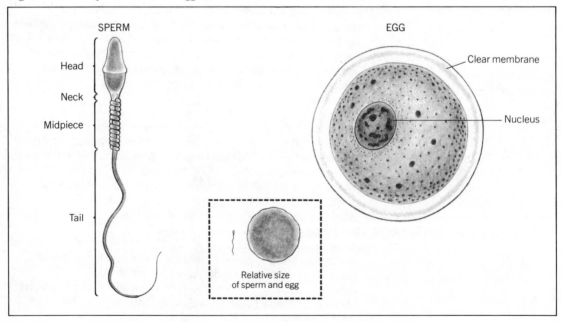

SPERM
EGG
Head
Neck
Midpiece
Tail
Clear membrane
Nucleus
Relative size of sperm and egg

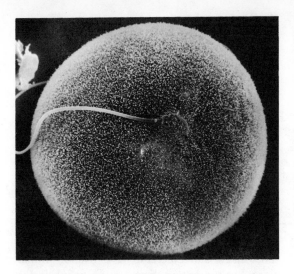 

Figure 18-2 / *A sperm cell penetrating an ovum. The surface of the egg (closeup) has fingerlike projections that help hold the sperm as it begins to penetrate the egg. (These specimens come from hamsters.)*

and there is no harm in swallowing ejaculate.

A small amount of clear fluid from the bulbourethral glands is released before ejaculation. Being alkaline, it neutralizes the urethra's normal acidity, promoting sperm survival. Because it washes the male duct system, it can pick up sperm in sufficient quantity to cause pregnancy. This is one reason couples who use penile withdrawal before ejaculation (coitus interruptus) as contraception risk pregnancy.

Sperm Transport. After entering the vagina, sperm cells begin a long journey that few complete. A typical ejaculation contains 150 to 500 million sperm cells, but most do not get beyond the vagina. Depending on the woman's position (on her back, kneeling, or upright), sperm pass more or less easily to the uterus. The seminal fluid remains behind.

Some sperm reach the ovary two to twenty minutes after ejaculation; within thirty minutes, most that will reach the oviduct have done so. Since sperm probably swim only one inch an hour, their own motion accounts for little of their progress. They are probably helped by *peristalsis* (spontaneous muscle contractions) of the female reproductive system. Coitus probably increases peristalsis; orgasm involves contractions of the vagina and uterus, so it may raise the probability of conception (Fox, 1977). While the oviduct moves sperm upward, it moves the ovum downward by a complex interplay of movements, fluid currents, and other mechanisms.

Few spermatozoa succeed in reaching the ampulla for fertilization; the fate of the other sperm cells is still unknown. Sperm probably survive only one or perhaps a few days in the oviduct. A sperm must meet an egg when both are capable of union; this period is short, perhaps a matter of hours. Reproduction usually results from coitus happening often enough to create a rather steady supply of sperm in the oviduct, ready when an egg arrives. Nevertheless, if the timing is right in relation to ovulation, one ejaculation can be enough.

Egg (Ovum)

In considering a man's part in reproduction, we can concentrate on the sexualia and accessory glands and ignore most body functions not involved in coitus. This is not true of a woman. Reproduction involves more of her body and her time, as we will see in discussing egg production and transport, fertilization, pregnancy, birth, and nursing.

Egg Production. A human egg *(ovum-female gamete)* has a large, round nucleus that bears chromosomes (Figure 18-1). Egg production differs from sperm production in many ways. Sperm production doesn't swing into high gear until puberty (see chapter 17), but *ovogenesis* starts before birth. Of some 400,000 *oogonia* (primitive eggs) in a female fetus's ovaries, fewer than 400 will eventually mature—why certain ones and not others we do not know. When oogonia become surrounded by protective and nourishing *granulosa cells,* they are called *primary follicles.*

Before a female is born, her oogonia, in a process called oogenesis, begin to divide (as spermatocytes do at puberty). Within the primary follicles, however, eggs remain dormant until some time after puberty (for any given egg, dormancy lasts from ten to fifty years). At puberty, prodded by hormones from the hypothalamus and pituitary gland, each egg destined to develop begins a series of divisions so that a *mature secondary oocyte* forms within a fluid-filled *antral* (lake) *follicle.* Each oogonia "parent cell" gives rise to four more cells, but only one, the *ovum,* is capable of being fertilized. The other three cells are called *polar bodies;* these disintegrate. The last polar body separates from the maturing ovum after ovulation only if fertilization occurs. (See pages 345–347 for sperm development.)

As ovum development proceeds, fluids keep accumulating in the follicle, which becomes large enough to distend the surface of the ovary; it is then a *mature follicle,* or *Graafian*

follicle. This follicle can be seen and felt on the surface of an exposed ovary when the egg inside it is still smaller than the dot of an *i.* All mammals' eggs are rather similar in size, but follicle size is roughly proportional to ovary size, which depends on the size of the animal. The shrew and elephant have ova of similar sizes, but the entire shrew might fit inside the elephant's mature follicle, and would certainly fit within its ovary.

Ovulation. The ovum is released from the mature follicle through a process called *ovulation.* Humans ovulate with some regularity despite environmental events; however, a woman's ovulation, menstruation, and other reproductive functions are somewhat influenced by life experiences and anxieties (Jöchle, 1975). A few researchers (Zarrow and Clarke, 1968; Jöchle, 1975; Diamond) believe ovulation may be induced by the physical and emotional stimulation of coitus.

Ovulation begins with an increase of follicular fluid. Simultaneously, the follicle walls weaken, thin, and finally rupture. The fluid oozes from the follicle, taking the ovum with it. Some women often know when they are ovulating, and a few almost always know. Their clue is *mittelschmerz* (German: middle pain), an aching discomfort below the navel and to one side. This is sometimes accompanied by *spotting,* or brief bleeding.* Rest, mild pain killers such as aspirin, and locally applied heat usually help.

* In some animals, such as dogs, the blood flow associated with ovulation may be quite heavy. This is not menstruation; the blood comes as a transudate from the uterus. Such bleeding and the behavioral signs of estrus indicate that the animal is ready for copulation and reproduction.

Egg Transport. After ovulation, the egg is moved by fluid currents and the fimbriae toward the oviduct's mouth. The fimbriae sweep across the ovary, guiding the ovum to the ampulla. If the egg is fertilized, it takes about three days to pass through the oviduct to the uterus. If not fertilized, the egg disintegrates during its passage through the ovarian tube. Menstruation, then, is not getting rid of an unfertilized egg, as some people believe (see chapter 17).

Fertilization, The Child's Sex, and Fertility

Fertilization and Implantation

Fertilization is the union of a sperm and an egg to form a *zygote.* The zygote develops into an embryo and then a fetus; at birth it is called a baby.

The sperm penetrates the egg and is incorporated by it within three hours after contact. About twelve hours after penetration, the zygote begins *cleavage,* or splitting (into two cells then four, eight, etc.), which continues during passage through the oviduct. After about three days, the developing organism reaches the uterus. Now a ball of cells, it remains unattached within the uterus for about three days more. Then the *embryo,* as it is now called, begins to attach to the endometrial layer of the uterus; this is called *implantation.* For many reasons, perhaps half or fewer of fertilized ova complete implantation (Hertig et al., 1959; Vesterdahl-Jørgensen, 1970). Where the embryo contacts the uterus, it forms a placenta and other tissues that support the embryo's life.

The Child's Sex

The sex of a zygote is established at fertilization. Every ovum carries an X sex chromosome; union with an X-bearing sperm produces a female (XX), union with a Y-bearing sperm a male (XY). From 120 to 150 XY zygotes form for every 100 XX zygotes; this is the *primary sex ratio.* The reason for this is not known, but one theory is that Y-bearing sperm, being lighter, reach the egg more swiftly. An erroneous theory is that because more females survive the prenatal period and infancy, more males must be conceived if the sexes are to be of roughly equal number by adulthood.

Some couples strongly desire a boy or girl, especially as a first child. The reasons are many, complex, and not fully understood. About one-third of women have no preference (Dinitz, Dynes, and Clarke, 1954; Westoff and Rindfuss, 1974). Of people who do have a preference, more of both men and women want a boy, especially as the first child. This preference has been decreasing for twenty years among men, but less among women. Some recent attempts to control the baby's sex have concentrated on the environments supposedly preferred by Y sperm (alkaline) and X sperm (acidic) (Shettles, 1972). However, this work has been challenged, and no sure method for having a girl or a boy has been found (Guerro, 1975).

Attempts to control the baby's sex have gone on for millenia and have ranged from folklore to ingenious experiment. Aristotle suggested coitus in a north wind for having boys, in a south wind for girls. One European folk prescription has the woman lie on her right side during coitus to produce a boy, on the left side for a girl. Another old piece of lore—that the baby is likelier to be a boy if the woman reaches orgasm during coitus—has been revived recently. It is argued that orgasm, by enhancing sperm transport, may help the presumably lighter Y sperm to reach the egg faster than the X sperm. This remains to be proven.

Fertility

A man is likely to be more secretive or embarrassed about seeing a physician for a fertility problem than for venereal disease. The feelings are reversed for women. But both sexes strongly tend to see infertility as a personal failure. Most people take for granted their ability to reproduce and plan to have children; learning they cannot do so may wound their self-esteem badly.

Usually the woman seeks help first; tradition says infertility is her problem, and it is indeed she who does or doesn't become pregnant. Men find it difficult to accept even partial responsibility, but infertility is as often a problem of the man or of both partners, and treatment usually involves both.

When a woman reaches a physician's office, the couple has probably been trying to produce a pregnancy for a long time. If the couple has had coitus close to the time of ovulation for about a year or more, the physician will examine the woman and ask to see the husband. This is only a rule of thumb; 20 percent of all couples take more than six months to produce a pregnancy, and many more than a year.

Male Fertility. For a man, as for a woman, laboratory measurements of fertility are few and imprecise. Tests can rule out certain problems, but some people with poorly functioning reproductive systems have many children, while many apparently normal ones produce none (Noyes, 1968). Men are evaluated primarily by tests of their semen and sperm. About 50 to 100 million sperm per milliliter, and three to five milliliters of semen per ejaculation, is usually considered normal, but the figures vary for most men. Too few sperm, too many sperm, or too dense an ejaculation may be associated with low fertility or sterility, but low sperm motility has been considered most important (MacLeod, 1971). Sperm shape and abililty to penetrate an egg are also important (J. Rogers et al., in press). Other, still unknown factors affect male fertility.

Female Fertility. A woman's fertility is evaluated primarily by her ability to ovulate and the functioning of her reproductive and endocrine systems. Ovulation is not easily detected. The commonest method is charting her *basal body temperature* (BBT) over the course of several menstrual cycles (Figure 18-3). This does not enable one to predict ovulation, only to know that it probably has occurred. More accurate and reliable tests for ovulation exist, but they do not lend themselves to the daily use necessary for fertility evaluation.

The *Rubin test* reveals whether an obstruction prevents passage of eggs to the uterus. Harmless gas (CO_2) is passed into the uterus; resistance to passage of the gas into the oviducts reveals an obstruction. Occasionally the gas removes the obstruction. A common cause of tubal blockage is scarring caused by gonorrhea or other pelvic infection.

Treating Fertility Problems

Of couples who seek medical help for fertility problems, about 40 percent conceive with or without treatment or counseling. In another 40 percent, the cause of sterility is found but cannot be reversed. In the remaining 20 percent, no cause is found and no pregnancy occurs (T. Evans, 1971).

If general health is poor, it must be restored. The frequency or timing of coitus may need to

be changed. If ovulation is a problem, it can sometimes be induced by administering gonadotropic hormones. There are also nonhormonal drugs (such as clomiphene citrate) that induce ovulation. Ovulation-inducing drugs are powerful, cannot always be adequately controlled, and may cause the development of twins, triplets, or quadruplets.

Obstructions or cysts in the vas deferens, which account for 40 to 50 percent of male fertility problems, can be treated surgically. Little can now be done in cases of inadequate sperm characteristics (abnormal shape, poor viability, etc.) except artificial insemination.

Figure 18-3 / *The relation of BBT (basal body temperature) to the menstrual cycle and ovulation. BBT patterns vary among women, but the most reliable sign of ovulation is a relatively large drop in temperature followed by a larger rise.*

Artificial Insemination

It has been estimated that at least one out of fifty babies now born in the United States re-

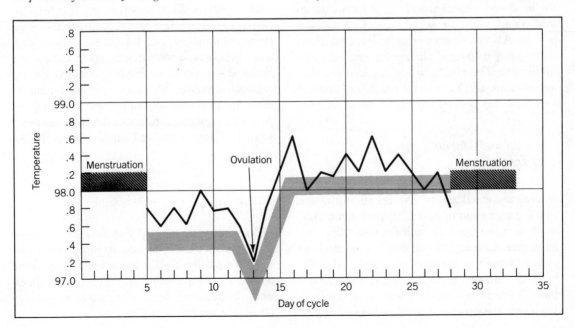

sults from *artificial insemination* (AI)—introducing sperm from the husband (AIH) or another male (AI Donor) without coitus. The practice has been used by animal breeders since Biblical times; its effective use among people is relatively recent. The sperm is usually obtained by having the man masturbate into a glass vial containing a preservative. It is then deposited in the woman's vagina when she is thought to be ovulating. Sometimes the husband's semen is mixed with a donor's; this doesn't make the semen more effective and may even harm it, but it helps many couples psychologically by offering the possibility that the husband's sperm fertilized the egg.

Using a donor's semen can touch off strong feelings about "infidelity," even if the donor is anonymous. Sometimes this may be more a psychological than an ethical problem. In fact, the legal and ethical aspects of AI provide an interesting study of social values. To some people, AI seems adulterous and unethical; to others, it is a coveted chance for reproductive fulfillment. The emotional, social, and political implications of AI are far-reaching, and no view of it has been accepted by all of society.

Sexual and Marital Effects of Infertility

There is no known relationship between fertility and coital ability. Doubts about this are in the imagination or ego of the beholder. And most often, no one is at fault for infertility, any more than for being tall or short or having blue eyes. However, many sterile couples find it difficult or impossible to accept their state, and their desire to reproduce grows more intense. Each sexual encounter may then become a des-

perate attempt at pregnancy, each failure another blow to their self-esteem. Coitus can become mechanical, disappointing, and emotionally painful, and often the frustration turns to anger and mutual blame. Occasionally men and women enter extramarital affairs to try to conceive with another partner, to prove they aren't at fault, or for spontaneity and romance after laboring at coitus for reproduction.

The commonest male sexual problem in sterile marriages is seeing infertility as failed manhood. This may cause difficulty in maintaining erection or ejaculating. The commonest female problems are decreased arousal, enjoyment, orgasm, and frequency of coitus. However, some infertile women initiate coitus more often. Their partners may respond with impotence or anorgasmia (Debrouner and Shubin-Stein, 1975), probably because they feel the women are seeking procreation, not love or recreation. They feel like reproductive objects rather than objects of love, desire, and pleasure. Similarly, a woman may come to resent a husband's imposed or implied demand for reproductive coitus. These interpersonal conflicts may make coitus so unpleasant that even if pregnancy occurs, the marriage is severely strained (Debrouner and Shubin-Stein, 1975).

Pregnancy

Pregnancy is usually signalled by a missed menstrual period. This may frighten or depress people who don't want a child and elate those who do. Contradictory feelings—joy, depression, pride, and fear of responsibility—may occur in turn or together.

In biological terms, conception begins development from zygote to embryo to fetus. However, most people think "baby" from the start, and this is the crux of many emotion-laden theological, intellectual, and political debates about contraception, abortion, and reproduction experiments (Steinhoff and Diamond, 1977). The organism has a humanoid appearance after about two months, but without aid it usually cannot survive outside the womb until the eighth month.

Gestation, or development within the uterus, takes about 266 days (thirty-eight weeks, or nine months). It is usually discussed in terms of three trimesters of three months each.

First Trimester

During the first three months, the embryo increases more than 300 times in length, from less than 0.2 millimeters to about 70 millimeters in total length. The growth in weight is even greater, from a single cell to about 20 grams. The *placenta,* other supporting tissues, and amniotic fluids grow correspondingly. The placenta exchanges nutrients and waste products between embryo and mother and acts as a selective screen for many other substances. It is connected to the embryo by the *umbilical cord,* at what will be the child's navel.

At two weeks of age (postfertilization),* the embryo is just visible to the naked eye. It begins to develop a nervous system and a head;

* The embryo's age can be calculated from the time of last menses (menstrual age) or from the time of fertilization (fertilization age), two weeks later. However, most embryology studies determine age by measuring embryos and fetuses in length, from the crown of the head to the bottom of the rump.

the latter is disproportionately large and will remain so till after birth. At age eight to twelve weeks, the embryo's head is about 40 percent of its body length, at birth 35 percent; in adulthood it is 15 percent.

The limbs start taking shape during the seventh to twelfth weeks, but remain relatively small. A tail appears around the fourth week, but it is almost gone by the eighth. The most significant changes of the sexualia and reproductive system occur during the seventh to twelfth weeks (see chapter 7). From the ninth to twelfth week, the embryo acquires a human appearance. After this occurs—strictly speaking, from the ninth week until delivery—it is called a *fetus.*

Until the end of the first trimester, ovarian hormones nourish and support the uterine tissues that support the embryo. By the end of the trimester, the placenta has gradually taken over this function. If this does not proceed properly, there may be a *miscarriage,* or spontaneous abortion. One cannot accurately estimate the rate of miscarriage, for often a woman does not know that she was pregnant and that miscarriage occurred. Estimates range from 10 to 30 percent of pregnancies. Miscarriages may be unpleasant but fortunate; in very many cases, the fetus was defective (Goodlin, 1971).

The first trimester brings important changes in the mother, almost all associated with changes in her hormone balance. The most obvious one is the end of menstruation. Although this can be caused by things other than conception, pregnancy is the commonest reason in healthy women. About one woman in five continues to have some cyclic bleeding for several months after conception; it is usually lighter than menstrual flow, but it can mask pregnancy

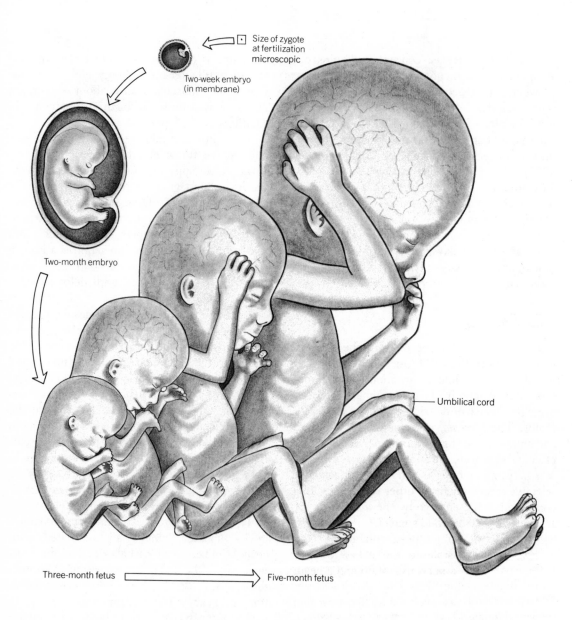

Size of zygote
at fertilization
microscopic

Two-week embryo
(in membrane)

Two-month embryo

Umbilical cord

Three-month fetus ⟶ Five-month fetus

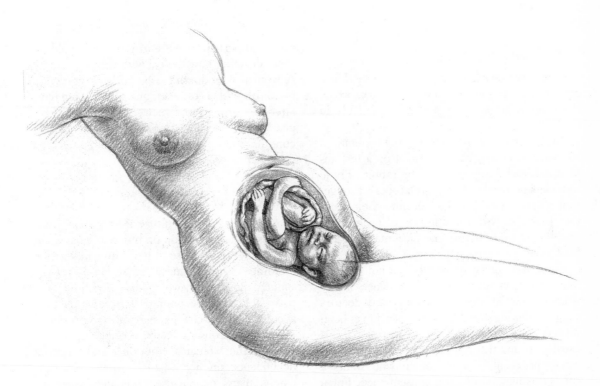

Figure 18-4 / *By two weeks after fertilization, the microscopic zygote has become an embryo of barely visible size; by three months it has a humanoid appearance and is called a fetus. It grows more slowly the last few months, then quickly again the last few weeks (above), as it turns head downward.*

for a while. Spotting may indicate spontaneous abortion or may have no significance. If it occurs, a physician should be consulted.

Enlargement, tenderness, and fullness of the breasts begin early in pregnancy. Women may or may not find this pleasant. Sometimes the areolae deepen in color and develop small bumps, and the nipples may become very sensitive to touch.

The physiology of *morning sickness* is poorly understood, and the only remedies are simple and rather unreliable. This nausea is felt on awakening or at night by three out of four pregnant women at some time in the first trimester. There may be short or long periods of vomiting and dizziness. In some women, it is associated with motion (car sickness), in others with certain foods or odors. It has been suggested that morning sickness indicates unwanted pregnancy or rejection of the female or maternal roles; there is no experimental evidence to support this clinical impression (Pion and Cox, unpublished study).

A woman may or may not have any of these signs of pregnancy. For many, only a home or commercial laboratory test can accurately show early in gestation whether they are pregnant.

Diagnosing Pregnancy

There are several tests for pregnancy. Until recently, all required some laboratory procedure, but a home method is now available in drug stores.

In the past, a physician would obtain a woman's urine and note its effect on a test animal, such as a mouse, frog, or rabbit. These tests depend on the growing placenta's production of hormones (HCG); therefore their accuracy increases with the duration of pregnancy. Such a test made before the placenta produces HCG may give false negative results.

Since false negative results are not uncommon early in pregnancy, and since many women sometimes miss a period, many doctors suggest waiting until two periods have been missed before having a pregnancy test. This usually means that the woman is at least six weeks pregnant. For a woman who wants a child, this may be of little consequence. For a woman who does not, it can be an agonizing wait, and perhaps a waste of time that could be spent deciding how to deal with the pregnancy. A woman who doesn't want to be pregnant is better off with a test even one week to ten days after her first missed menses; this can be repeated a week later if necessary. She can also consider the option of having menses induced (see chapter 19).

Psychosocial Changes

A woman and her culture see pregnancy not only as a physical condition but as a social state, for her and those close to her. She will become a mother, her husband a father. They are assuming the roles in which they saw their own parents, and are becoming a family rather than a couple. This change may bring emotional growth or arouse anxiety (Gadpaille, 1975). Usually the woman's emotional and material dependence on her partner grows. Unfortunately, many people use pregnancy as an attempt to shore up a shaky marriage or to pres-

False Pregnancy

Sometimes a nonpregnant woman becomes convinced that she has conceived. Her menses may end, her breasts become tender; she may gain weight and girth, develop nausea, and have contractions that seem like fetal movements. Such *pseudocyesis*, or false pregnancy, is often associated with intense desire to be pregnant and usually occurs in young women (even in virgins) or around menopause. In some cases, the women believe they are pregnant as punishment for coitus. Sometimes false pregnancy goes away after a few months or is dispelled by psychotherapy. In extreme cases, however, the delusion lasts for years; or on the "delivery date" fluid and air may be expelled (McCary, 1973). False pregnancy occurred among some nuns in the Middle Ages, who believed they had been impregnated by Christ (Cleugh, 1964; G. Taylor, 1954).

sure a reluctant partner into marriage. Such motives are bound to affect both partners' feelings about the pregnancy, and the results may not be those hoped for.

Prenatal Care

For most women, pregnancy goes well, but for a few it is uncomfortable, difficult, or even dangerous. A pregnant woman should see a doctor who can respond to any problems or questions objectively and with skill. She should not hesitate to ask questions, and if she cannot talk comfortably with her doctor, she should consider finding another.

A *prenatal examination* is necessary for the safety of both the pregnant woman and the fetus. This includes a general physical examination, with special attention to the condition of bones, teeth, and mouth; a pelvic examination; a blood test for syphilis; urinalysis, which may reveal infection, kidney problems, or diabetes brought on by pregnancy; and tests for anemia and blood type. Both parents should have their blood tested for Rh type.

Most subsequent examinations are similar, with particular attention to weight, diet, blood pressure, and urine contents. Excessive weight gain and diet deficiencies should be avoided. Examinations should be more frequent as gestation advances; in the final month, weekly visits are usual.

Many medications and drugs can pass to the fetus; therefore the mother must be careful about what she takes into her body. Once pregnant, she should not take birth-control pills or any medication not approved by a doctor who knows of the pregnancy. If she is addicted to heroin during pregnancy, the fetus also will be addicted and will have to undergo painful detoxification. Smoking and drinking—even routine social drinking—may also be bad for the fetus (Streissguth, 1977).

Second Trimester

In the second trimester, the fetus may reach a weight of 850 grams, or two pounds. The mother begins to feel fetal movements *(quickening)*, and the fetal heartbeat can be detected. These two developments occur around the seventeenth to twentieth weeks—usually earlier in *multigravida* (women with previous pregnancies) and later in *primagravida* (women in their first pregnancy).

The mother's abdomen and breasts enlarge more; she now looks and feels pregnant. There often comes a blooming in pregnancy, an appearance of physical health and ripeness, and an emotional contentment. Some women develop skin discoloration on their faces and abdomens, and particularly on the areolae. A clear yellow secretion *(colostrum)* may seep from the nipples.

To the couple, the fetus becomes real. They can share feeling its movements and listening to its heartbeat. They both may start to have ambivalent feelings—distressed at the wife's loss of shape but delighted by the prospect of the birth.

Even during the smoothest pregnancies, the couple may sometimes feel inadequate and depressed. Future responsibilities, life changes, and uncertainties loom large. Many of their fears may be realistic, others unnecessary or easily resolved. Now that it is time to plan for the future, the couple may benefit from calling on family and friends for help.

If a couple suspects a fetal problem, and feels

it is worth the physical, emotional, and financial expense, after the sixteenth week of gestation they can ask for *amniocentesis*, the removal of fluids surrounding the fetus, for analysis. This is not a routine procedure, so the risk must justify the effort. If amniocentesis reveals that the fetus has inherited or developed a serious problem, abortion or other arrangements can be made.

Third Trimester

During the last trimester, the fetus grows more slowly till the last several weeks, when it gains about a pound a week; at *term*, the end of fetal growth, it weighs about seven pounds (3,300 grams) and is about twenty inches (about fifty centimeters) long. It moves often and sometimes violently. During the last weeks, it assumes a head-down position, and the head descends into the pelvis, where it is supported by the pelvic muscles and cervix. This support can be felt and is called *lightening* (*dropping* or *engagement*). The cervix begins to soften as the fetus drops and becomes thinner *(effaces)* as childbirth nears.

By this time, some sitting and lying positions are no longer possible, unaccustomed aches appear, fatigue comes easily, and breathing is occasionally labored. The pelvis begins widening *(relaxing)* to accommodate the fetus and prepare for birth; this makes walking awkward, sometimes painful. The uterus bulges against the bladder, so urination is more frequent.

Most physicians want to see a pregnant woman at least once a week during the last month. They check how lightening, effacement, and dilation are progressing. *Dilation,* the widening of the cervical opening, is usually measured in centimeters or "fingers" (1 finger

---

Danger Signs During Pregnancy

If certain symptoms occur at any stage of pregnancy, a physician should be contacted immediately.

1. Vaginal bleeding, except at the time of expected menses, may mean placental rupture, hemorrhage, or spontaneous abortion.
2. A sudden rush of clear fluid (breaking water) from the vagina may mean premature delivery.
3. Reduced amount and frequency of urination may signal kidney failure.
4. Headaches that don't respond to aspirin or rest, dizziness, and swelling of the hands and feet may all indicate toxemia, a kidney disorder. Toxemia afflicts only 2 to 3 percent of all pregnant women, but affects 8 to 20 percent of those who receive no prenatal care (Dennis and Hester, 1971).
5. Recurrent and prolonged cramps may signal miscarriage or premature labor.

---

is approximately 2 centimeters). When dilation approaches five fingers and effacement progresses, childbirth is near.

Sexual Activity During Pregnancy

Many people have physical fears and emotional inhibitions about coitus and other sexual activities during pregnancy. Not long ago, many doctors routinely warned against coitus anywhere from six weeks to three months before and after childbirth. Today it is widely believed that any genital acts are safe as long as there is no vaginal bleeding, ruptured membranes (shown by "broken water"), or history of premature deliveries. Cunnilingus accompanied by blowing into the vagina has been discouraged late in pregnancy because of rare but fatal cases of air entering the uterus and causing an air embolism (Goodlin, 1975). No sex act is known to affect the baby's health.

During the first several months of pregnancy, most women's sexual activity decreases slightly or not at all. As more time passes, sexual frequency declines, and in advanced pregnancy, women's sexual interest and orgasmic response drop as well. Many couples abstain from sexual activity completely (N. Morris, 1975; Solberg, Butler, and Wagner, 1973). But as in most aspects of sexuality, there is much individual variation; some women's sexual activity increases during pregnancy.

These changes are not caused only by conservative medical advice; relatively few women receive any medical advice on the subject. Reports on sixty preliterate societies (Ford and Beach, 1951) parallel these findings in the United States; during the ninth month, coitus occurs in only 25 percent of them. The reason usually given is to avoid injuring the fetus.

American women give many reasons for this reduced sexual interest and activity. About half mention physical discomfort; a quarter express fear of injuring the baby or loss of interest; only 4 percent say they feel less attractive. Preoccupation and fatigue depress genital activity, and both are increasingly common as pregnancy advances. Furthermore, the increasing levels of progesterone may reduce sexual interest. And some men say that they become sexually less interested in their pregnant wives.

The man-superior coital position is preferred by some 80 percent of couples in our society before pregnancy and into the second trimester. As pregnancy proceeds, couples increasingly use woman-superior, side-by-side, and rear-entry positions. During the last month, side-by-side is most preferred (Butler, Reisner, and Wagner, 1979).

Some men feel frustrated or anxious about the decline in sexual activity during pregnancy. They should remember that it does not necessarily reflect loss of love in the woman, nor does it reduce her need for love, tenderness, and care. Such love and care affirm that she is valued for herself, not only as a sexual partner and a mother. Although pregnancy usually confirms a woman's sense of being female and deepens her attachment to her partner, it may also create uncertainty and self-doubt. It helps both partners if the man keeps this in mind when, toward the end of pregnancy, she gives increasing attention to preparing for the baby's arrival and seems preoccupied with "nest building."

Birth

In the past, many women experienced child-birth *(parturition)* attended by female relatives, friends, and perhaps a midwife and the father. But in our mobile society, family and friends are often distant. In many hospitals, the father is kept at a distance, and birth often seems a production-line affair. Both mother and infant may be drugged, their senses dulled. Since giving birth is one of life's most important events, some people want to consciously participate and take pleasure in it.

There are many methods of childbirth. None is best for all people, but it is usually possible to combine health safeguards with conscious participation by the woman and emotional support from her partner.

Labor

Labor is the passage of the fetus from the uterus outside the body (Figure 18-5). It has three stages. The three signals of the first stage may occur separately or simultaneously. One is recurrent cramping *contractions* (labor pains) in the lower back, lower abdomen, or both. These are not necessarily painful; they may feel like forceful bowel movements. When they happen at intervals of ten to twenty minutes or less, the woman should head for the hospital. She should phone the hospital staff that she is coming and ask them to contact her physician. The first contractions usually dislodge from the cervix a mucous plug that shows specks of blood *(bloody show)*. This may be followed by a third sign, a sudden gush of clear (amniotic) fluid, called the breaking of the water.

The uterine contractions of labor push the fetus downward and dilate the cervix. They can be distinguished from ordinary muscle cramps by the relaxation that follows them. As labor progresses, contractions become longer and more frequent. Their force depends on the fetus's size and position, the mother's physical condition, and other factors.

Couvade: "Male Labor"

Many men show some of the symptoms experienced by their pregnant wives, such as nausea, backache, mild depression, constipation, even the baby blues that often follow delivery (Trethowan and Conlon, 1965). This pregnant-husband syndrome is variously estimated to affect 10 to 65 percent of men to some degree. Some societies in South America, Africa, and other parts of the world have made it a custom for the husband to go to bed during his wife's delivery, receive medications, take part in rituals, and perhaps simulate delivery (Davenport, 1977). This custom, called *couvade* (French: hatching), is believed in some cultures to decoy evil spirits away from the mother and baby. The men of the Hua people of New Guinea not only perform *couvade* but imitate menstruation (Meigs, 1976).

The first stage is complete when cervical dilation reaches ten centimeters. This usually takes from two to twenty-four hours; the average is twelve to fifteen hours in first deliveries, about half that in subsequent births. When labor seems too long or if for some reason delivery should be speeded up, the mother is given the hormone oxytocin.

During the second stage, contractions occur every three to five minutes. The fetus leaves the uterus and passes through the vagina; its arrival outside the vagina is called *delivery*. This takes from about thirty minutes to two hours. When it is over, the most difficult and painful part of childbirth is past.

During the third stage of labor, the placenta and fetal membranes *(afterbirth)* separate from the uterus and are delivered. This takes about thirty minutes to an hour and brings pregnancy to an end.

In about one of fifteen pregnancies, labor starts *prematurely,* defined as any time before the fetus weighs 2,500 grams, regardless of its age. After ten months of pregnancy, labor is usually induced.

Methods of Delivery

The method of delivery used depends on a woman's feelings about birth, her physician's advice and preferences, and local facilities. The great majority of women have their babies delivered in hospitals by routine procedures. The most common methods are the standard, natural (Dick-Read), Lamaze, and Leboyer. Women should consider the advantages and disadvantages of each in order to make the most satisfying choice.

Standard Childbirth. The most widely used method we call the *standard* method. When labor begins, the woman goes to the hospital. There, in a labor room, she receives a mild painkiller and an enema, and her pubic region is washed and shaved. In many but not all hospitals, her husband may stay with her during the first stage of labor. Obstetrical nurses periodically check the extent of dilation, and her physician will probably arrive and check her progress. If the woman desires or requires it, a local (saddle-block) or spinal anesthetic is given.

When the second stage begins, the woman is wheeled to a delivery room containing obstetrical and medical-emergency equipment, and transferred to a delivery table. In most hospitals, her husband must now leave her. The physician and one or two nurses watch the second stage of labor progress. When the baby seems ready to descend from the vagina, the woman's legs are put up on rests, to allow the baby more room to maneuver and to give the doctor a good view of its progress.

As the baby begins to emerge, the physician helps in every way possible. If the doctor or the woman thinks it necessary, she is given an anesthetic, such as nitrous oxide (laughing gas). Especially during a first birth, an *episiotomy* is made; this surgical incision enlarges the vagina, protecting it from being torn by the emerging baby. Forceps are used in a small number of deliveries to widen the cervix and vagina and rotate the baby to facilitate descent, but only rarely to pull it.

After the baby has been delivered, it is examined, its air passages and throat are cleared, and eye drops are administered to prevent eye

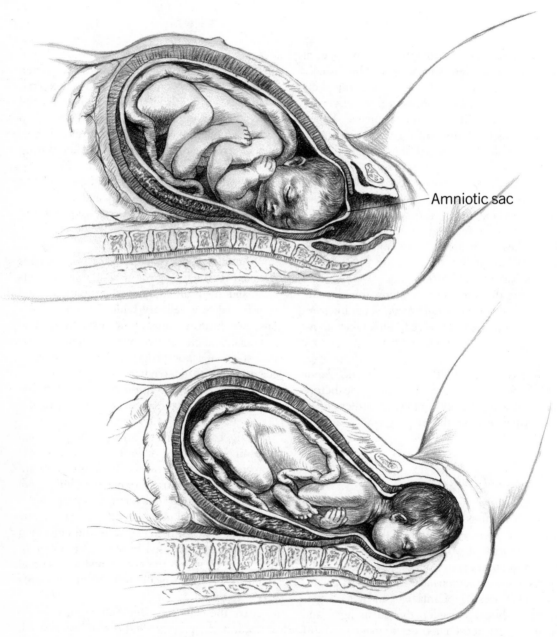

Amniotic sac

Figure 18-5 / *The process of birth: (top left) the first stage of labor starts, the cervix dilates, and contractions begin; (bottom left) in the second stage of labor, the baby makes its passage through the vagina; (top right)*

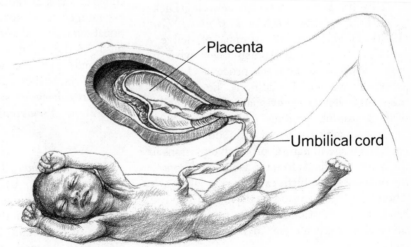

Placenta

Umbilical cord

the second stage of labor is completed with the delivery of the baby; (bottom left) in the third stage of labor the *placenta and fetal membranes are delivered.*

infection. The baby now is breathing by itself, stimulated by the birth process or aided by the physician's slap. When pulsations in the umbilical cord stop, it is cut.

The baby is given to the mother to hold, if she feels up to it. The sight, odor, and sounds of the baby act through her neuroendocrine system to make her uterus contract. This helps dislodge the placenta. The episiotomy is repaired, and the mother is wheeled to the maternity ward for a rest: for most women, giving birth is deeply rewarding but physically and emotionally exhausting. The baby is taken to the hospital's newborn ward, where the father may see it. Usually he does not get to touch the baby for a day or two, so that he will not infect it.

Natural Childbirth. The term *natural childbirth* is used for a method first advocated in 1932 by the British physician Grantley Dick-Read in his book *Childbirth Without Fear* (1944). He believed the trauma of delivery could be decreased if women knew what to expect and how to help the process. Only superstition and social traditions, he felt, had made them and their physicians consider childbirth a painful, perilous ordeal. He wrote: "Fear and anticipation of pain during labor have given rise to natural protective tensions in the body . . . which close the womb and oppose the dilation of the birth canal during labor. . . . Therefore, fear, tension, and pain go hand in hand, then it must be necessary to relieve tension and to overcome fear in order to eliminate pain."

Dick-Read began teaching women what to

386

expect of pregnancy and birth, and training them to relax physically and mentally, so that they could help rather than fight labor. Aside from the preparation and training of this method, delivery is standard and occurs in a regular delivery room. However, anesthesia is used sparingly or, if possible, not at all, so the woman can voluntarily relax her pelvic muscles and help the contractions.

Lamaze Method. The method of the French physician Fernand Lamaze (1970) is now perhaps the most popular alternative to standard delivery. The wife and husband both attend classes to learn what to expect during delivery and how to help it along. The woman is trained to consider birth normal, not painful; most important, she does exercises to enable her to relax and breathe in ways that help control contractions and reduce pain. The husband is encouraged to be at the delivery to give emotional support and remind her to relax and to push at the right times. Anesthesia is discouraged, but the woman receives nitrous oxide if she wishes it. Since she has been exercising regularly to stretch her perineum, an episiotomy is not routine.

Leboyer Method. The book *Birth Without Violence* (1975), by the French physician Frederick Leboyer, presented the idea that delivery should take into consideration the sensitivities of the infant. Labor and delivery take place in a hospital, so medical equipment is available if needed, and a modified standard de-

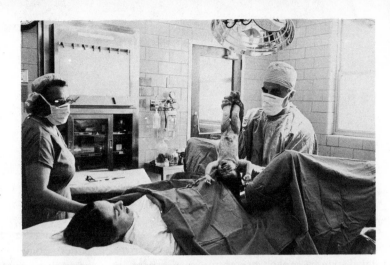

Figure 18-6 / *The standard method of delivery (top); a class (bottom left) for couples learning the Lamaze method of childbirth; (bottom right) bathing of the newborn following the Leboyer method of delivery.*

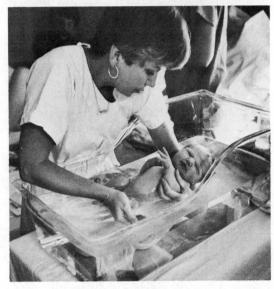

livery occurs. But instead of entering the world with a shock, the baby is delivered into a warm, gentle, secure environment as much like the womb as possible. The delivery room is warm, the lights are kept low. People speak in hushed tones. After delivery, the baby is gently washed in warm water, rocked, and given to the mother to be held and given love. Although Leboyer puts the newborn's comfort and serenity first, he likens giving birth to an erotic experience: "Childbirth is also passion. [It] should be an ecstatic experience."

Caesarean Delivery. About 5 percent of pregnant women in the United States have their babies delivered by *caesarean section.* The baby is removed through an incision made through the walls of the abdomen and uterus. This is done if the baby is too large or improperly positioned for passage through the vagina. Women need not necessarily have subsequent deliveries by this method, nor is the number of such deliveries limited to one. However, the chance of complications increases with subsequent pregnancies.

Delivery at Home. Women can have babies at home if they are informed, trained, and have certain equipment available. When supervised by midwives, home delivery may be quite effective, satisfying, and relatively cheap. However, about one delivery in twenty has a problem, such as breech presentation (the baby is positioned sideward), that requires a physician's help. Other unpredictable problems can threaten the life of the baby or mother. Therefore delivery in a hospital, with its emergency equipment and trained personnel, is widely preferred.

Comparison of Delivery Methods

No method of delivery is best for everyone, and probably few laymen or physicians accept them all equally. Furthermore, all methods are not available everywhere. The woman and her husband should discuss with her physician which method best meets their needs and desires, comparing them in terms of pain, anxiety, training required, the husband's involvement, effects on the baby, feelings of emotional responsibility, and cost.

Compare, for example, the standard and Lamaze methods. In the standard method, anesthetics minimize the mother's discomfort, but she sacrifices awareness of the birth. The physician is responsible for the delivery; this may relieve her of anxiety before and during delivery, and of guilt afterward if anything goes wrong. However, she may feel guilty for not participating more. The husband is not in the delivery room, so he doesn't get in the way or distract the mother and physician, and his wife needn't worry about performing well for him. Of course, he cannot offer emotional support or share the experience. Since no training and little preparation are required, there are few demands on the mother and almost none on the father. Some people are concerned about reports that anesthesia may have long-lasting effects on the baby.

In the Lamaze method, the woman is aware of labor and delivery; she has been taught to think of them as effort and discomfort, but not as pain. Nevertheless, in some cases there is pain. She shares responsibility with the physician and aids the birth process. She usually feels less anxiety about delivery, because she understands and participates in it, but she may fear performing poorly and feel guilty if things go wrong. Also, the Lamaze method requires training and commitment, often of the father as well as the mother. Since all nonstandard methods require training, they are often more expensive.

Multiple Births

Multiple births occur about once in eighty-five deliveries. For genetic reasons, they happen more often in certain families, more among blacks than whites, and more among whites than Orientals. They are also more common among women in their thirties than those in their twenties. The gestation of twins is usually about three weeks shorter than that of single infants (Scheinfeld, 1973).

Twins are of two types, *identical (monozygotic,* or one-egg) and *fraternal (dizygotic,* or two-egg). Monozygotic twins develop from the splitting of a single fertilized egg. They have exactly the same genetic makeup, are of the same sex, and usually look much alike. So-called Siamese twins are monozygotic twins who remain joined because the original zygote did not split completely.

Dizygotic twins develop from two eggs, each fertilized by a separate sperm cell. They may be of the same or opposite sexes, have genetic inheritances like those of any other separately conceived siblings, and look as little or as much alike as other brothers or sisters.

Triplets arrive only once in 5,000 to 6,000 births, quadruplets once in a half million. Usually only some infants of a large multiple birth survive early life. The Dionne quintuplets, all girls, born in 1934, were the first set of quints who all survived infancy.

After Delivery

After delivery, the mother undergoes a host of physical, psychological, and social changes. As we noted, the mother seeing, hearing, and smelling the baby induces the uterus to shrink back to normal size. The primary cause is the release of the pituitary hormone oxytocin, which produces muscle contractions — not only in the uterus but in the breasts, aiding milk production.

Nursing

About 20 percent of American women now choose to *nurse* (breast-feed) their children. Nursing can continue for years, but most mothers stop within three months, because they

---

Twins: Fact and Magic

The birth of twins has been thought amazing or unnatural by many peoples around the world, and twins abound in myth and folklore (Scheinfeld, 1973). Some Indians of the American Southwest scorned multiple births, viewing the infants as if they were litters of animals, and in parts of West Africa twins are considered products of evil spirits, the mothers accursed. The Kaffirs of Africa traditionally assumed that twins were children of different fathers, their mothers adultresses.

According to some folklore and legends, one twin is good, the other destructive, like Jacob and Esau in the Old Testament. Therefore one or both were killed by the Ainu of Japan, the Australian aborigines, and many tribes of Africa and the Americas. The Peruvian Incas considered twins a perfect sacrifice to ward off plague and famine.

Twins have also been considered gifted, heroic, and bringers of good luck, as were Romulus and Remus, the legendary founders of Rome, and the Greek demigods Castor and Pollux, who formed the twin constellation Gemini. In some parts of West Africa, parents of twins are thought to have magical powers of fecundity and are called on to perform fertility rituals over fields and domestic animals. The Yoruba tribe of Nigeria (from whom many American blacks are descended) have the highest twin rate in the world, one of every twenty-five pregnancies. They consider twins good omens. When twins are born, the parents have wood figures carved called *Ibeji*, which symbolize the twins. If one twin dies, the other carries about his or her figurine and washes, dresses, feeds, and devotedly cares for it. (Eibl–Eibesfeldt, 1974.)

Figure 18-7 / *The young woman on the left has never nursed a child. Nursing makes the breasts fuller, the areolae darker, and the nipple more prominent. The extent of change varies greatly among women.*

must work or because they lose interest. Since the baby sucks instinctively soon after birth, the mother can start immediately. The breast may first produce clear fluids called *colostrum;* and *lactation* (milk production) usually goes into full swing only two or three days after birth. To a mother anxious to nurse, the first few days may be frustrating, but most women are physically able to nurse. If a mother decides to do so, the sooner she starts the better. If she decides not to, she should interrupt the nursing mechanism quickly. Hormones can be administered to end lactation.

Whether to nurse is a decision with psychological and social elements. Some people consider nursing degrading, old-fashioned, and primitive; others see it as natural, virtuous, or chic. Nursing has gone in and out of fashion at

various levels of society. During the 1920s and 1930s, it was considered a mark of education and being modern to bottle-feed. Today, the higher a woman's level of education, the more likely she is to nurse her baby.

Certainly mother's milk contains the proper nutrients for most babies; it also has antibodies that protect the baby from many diseases. It is free and doesn't have to be prepared in the middle of the night or while riding on a turnpike. Also, the bowel movements of breast-fed babies usually have far less odor than those of bottle-fed babies. More important, many researchers believe that the body contact and physical intimacy of breast-feeding are physically and emotionally beneficial to the baby (Bowlby, 1969; Klaus et al., 1970).

Nursing enlarges the breasts and, if they are already large, increases sagging, though a good nursing brassiere provides support and lessens this problem. A painful difficulty sometimes associated with nursing is cracked nipples, which can usually be cured by applying cocoa butter.

Sometimes fathers become jealous of the nursing baby. There is no harm in baby and father both enjoying the mother's breasts. A number of women find nursing highly erotic; some even reach orgasm as a result. Conversely, coital orgasm often triggers milk ejection; the mother need feel no discomfort or guilt about this.

Sexual and Marital Readjustment

The mother will probably leave the hospital a few days after delivery. Her return home brings new situations that can strain sexual and social relationships. She and her husband have new responsibilities to each other and the child, and the strains this transition can cause may show in many ways. Very many women undergo some degree of *postpartum depression* (Deutsch, 1945; Oliven, 1974). They may be moody, listless, and tearful, and feel overwhelmed by responsibility and by having someone utterly dependent on them. At this time they need extra emotional support. Some become cool or even resentful toward their husbands, and some show their children more affection than they ever have their partners; the husband may become resentful, withdrawn, and competitive. Fortunately, this depression is usually transitory; when it is not, counseling or therapy is often helpful.

Before leaving the hospital, the woman should receive instructions on douching and care of the perineum, which normally should be kept clean and dry. Coitus may be resumed as soon as there is no discomfort and no more concern with healing and repair of the perineum (especially the area of the episiotomy). Most women produce a vaginal discharge (lochia) for about four weeks after childbirth, but it need not prevent coitus.

Overview

The great majority of people must deal throughout life with the fact that their sexuality involves the capacity for reproduction. Many who lack that capacity or have difficulty realizing it are even more preoccupied by it. It is often difficult to decide whether to have children, when, with whom, or how many times. By knowing the physical facts and understanding the options, one has a greater chance of deciding about one's reproductive life rather than letting it be decided by default.

One must also make decisions about how to have a child delivered and how to safeguard the health of mother and child. These decisions, like those on having children, are often rooted in ignorance and folklore as much as in knowledge. This is unfortunate, for in few areas of sexuality are those who possess the facts so likely to benefit directly. And in few things are the consequences so long-lasting for oneself and others.

Review, Discuss, Decide

1. Why do people have children? What do you think were the reasons of people you have known?
2. What are signs that pregnancy has begun? Signs of possible

miscarriage? Danger signs of pregnancy? Signs of the onset of labor?

3. Should people need licenses to reproduce, as they do to marry? Give reasons pro and con.
4. What genital activities are safe during pregnancy?
5. How is reproduction a family, social, and psychological situation as well as a biological one?
6. Do you think you should or should not have children? Why?
7. How would you respond to a friend who said. "I don't want to bring children into a world like ours"?
8. Why do you think 80 percent of women choose not to nurse?
9. How might you react if you found you had a fertility problem or were sterile? If your spouse were sterile? Might your sex behavior change?

19

Sex Without Reproduction

Does using contraceptives lead to promiscuity?

Is there really a population explosion?

Which contraceptive is best for me?

How safe is the pill?

Does my religion approve of my using contraception?

Will abortion cause me lifelong regrets?

Would sterilization affect my sex drive?

In all societies, one expectation of marriage, or even justification of it, is having and rearing children. Although most couples do plan to have or adopt children, very few want the thirty to forty a woman may be biologically able to produce. This chapter will discuss reasons for wanting to limit family size and ways to be sexually active without reproduction. The pros and cons of various options are presented as background for making informed decisions.

The words birth control, contraception, family planning, abortion, sterilization, and infanticide are neutral to few people. All represent different approaches and attitudes toward limiting reproduction, before or after conception, before or after birth. For a given person, any of these may be a realistic alternative or may touch special sensitivities. The phrase birth control in a government program may be

seen as a ploy to limit racial minorities, the words abortion and sterilization as antireligious or unnatural, the phrase family planning as ignoring the single and childless. To other people, these terms seem a recognition of their right to make independent and very personal decisions.

Limiting Reproduction

Personal Reasons for Reproduction Control

People give many reasons for controlling conception. Some of the commonest are:

"I'm not ready to start a family yet."

"My family is big enough; I want more time with the children I already have."

"I can't afford a (or another) child."

"I can't cope with a (or another) child emotionally."

"I want more time for myself."

"The world is already overpopulated."

"My spouse doesn't want any (or more) children."

The decision to limit reproduction is being made earlier and more often than in the past. A generation ago, many women in developed nations had four or more children; fewer than 6 percent now do so *(Population Reports,* J-8, 1975). Since 1960 the *birthrate* (number of births per 1,000 women) has decreased in the United States by about 50 percent. Compare how many children your grandparents had with the number your parents had and the number you would like.

One reason for this change is the dramatic drop in infant mortality brought about by modern medicine and hygiene. A century ago, it was still common for half of a couple's offspring to die in infancy or early childhood; a large crop of babies did not ensure having many grown children. Also, many children used to begin contributing at an early age to the family's subsistence. Now many couples are free of such problems and do not want the economic, social, and emotional demands of large families. Some say they see overpopulation as a direct, personal issue rather than an abstract problem. If these couples don't want to give up coitus, their only solution is conception control.

The implications of a woman having control of her reproductive life are enormous for her, her family, and society. She is no longer tied to the concerns of pregnancy, childbirth, and childrearing unless she so chooses. She and her husband can plan if or when they would like a family and how large it will be. They can follow their erotic desires without worrying about pregnancy. The woman's occupational possibilities change; she can make long-term career plans without fear that unwanted pregnancies will interrupt them. The implications for her husband's career plans and life-style are also great. Therefore the decisions whether, how, and when to use contraception are among the most important ones people make.

394

Social Reasons for Reproduction Control

Overpopulation is not a number but a concept, a ratio between the number of people in an area and its ability to provide food, shelter, and a desired quality of life. Not everyone believes the world is or will be overpopulated; some say we only need better ways to use and distribute resources. Theirs is increasingly a minority view. If the present birthrate continues, the world's population of four billion will double in thirty years; many world leaders see this as the most serious threat to human life.

One way of limiting births is limiting coitus to the married and controlling who can marry whom and at what age. Such controls are weaker in our society than they were a few generations ago, but they are not gone. Another way is using contraceptives, yet ever since reliable contraceptives became available, many people and groups have tried to prevent or restrict their use. Even physicians were restrained from distributing contraceptives in many states until a 1965 Supreme Court decision *(Griswold* v. *Connecticut, 1965).*

Means of Reproduction Control

Reproduction can be controlled by intervention at any stage of the reproductive process. One extreme is abstaining from coitus. Another is using no contraception and inducing menstruation if a period is late or aborting an embryo that develops. Another is infanticide, which has been used selectively by many societies around the world, including parts of ancient Greece and medieval Europe (Ellis and Abarbanel, 1973).

People have tried many methods (Finch and Green, 1963). In ancient India and Asia, women placed feathers in the vagina to prevent conception; in the ancient Middle East, the rabbis advised small fiber sponges. The great seducer Giovanni Casanova claimed to have used a gold ball. Others have used a hollowed-out half lemon cupped over the cervix, which would inhibit sperm passage and kill sperm by creating an acid environment. Probably most women through history just hoped and prayed. In our own society, many women still do just that. The result, sooner or later, is usually pregnancy, and the woman must decide to add an unwanted child to her family, abort, or otherwise deal with the situation. Of course many unplanned pregnancies lead to children that are wanted, but we have seen (chapter 14) that such a choice has relatively low odds in terms of the happiness and health of child, mother, and others.

In the 1840s, the vulcanizing process made available strong yet pliable rubber goods, and thus the first cheap, effective contraceptives. The *condom* ("sheath," "safe," "rubber," "prophylactic," "French letter") had been made on and off for millenia of material other than rubber, such as animal gut, and used by people who could afford it. The rubber condom and the rubber *vaginal diaphragm*, also perfected in the late nineteenth century, began to rise in popularity.

In the 1960s, two more effective contraceptives became widely available, the *oral contraceptive* ("the pill") and the *IUD* (intrauterine device), a small device inserted in the uterus. Unlike the condom and diaphragm, the pill and IUD don't have to be applied just before coitus; women can use them without seeming to themselves or their partners to want coitus at a given moment. This makes contraception more acceptable to many women. Other methods, described below, have further increased contraceptive choices.

Malthus and After

Thomas Malthus (1766–1834), a clergyman and economist, argued in 1798, in *An Essay on the Principle of Population* (1929), that unchecked population growth increases geometrically (twofold, fourfold, eightfold, etc.), outstripping the means of subsistence, which tend to increase in linear fashion (onefold, twofold, threefold, etc.). By not stemming the birth rate, he said, the world was paving the way for poverty, disease, war, and vice. Malthus advised sexual abstinence and late marriage; he set an example by marrying at age forty, still a virgin. From his work sprang the Malthusian movement and later the Neo-Malthusians, who denied that sex is meant only for reproduction and advocated contraception rather than abstinence. From the Neo-Malthusians grew the modern birth-control movement. The phrase birth control was coined in 1914 by Margaret Sanger, perhaps the greatest single pioneer of the movement.

Personal Obstacles to Reproduction Control

Contraceptives, though widely available, are often used ineffectively or not at all. About half of all pregnancies in the United States are unplanned* (Munson, 1977; Diamond et al., 1973b). This doesn't mean that half of sexually active, fertile women shun contraception; in any year, some 90 percent try to avoid unwanted pregnancy, and they usually do. Of the remaining 10 percent, fewer than half plan to become pregnant, but they do, some more than once. Why do some control conception well and others poorly? First, no contraceptive is perfect. Also age and marital status are factors, as are individuals' fantasies and associations about certain contraceptive devices (Devereaux, 1965). But most important is accepting both one's own sexual activity and the reality of pregnancy.

The study of unwanted pregnancy has concentrated largely on women, because it is they who have the ultimate responsibility and decisions; they can become pregnant and men cannot. Not surprisingly, many males do not associate sexuality with reproductive capacity as deeply or automatically as many females. Therefore it is especially striking that many unmarried pregnant teenagers, asked why they didn't use contraceptives, reply, "I didn't want sex to seem planned." Many older women give a similar answer: "Sex was unexpected." Both answers can be interpreted as, "I won't say to

myself in advance that I might have coitus." Many women want to avoid seeming sexually easy or aggressive, to themselves or their partners, even when they think coitus likely. Consistent use of contraceptives may cause "prostitution anxiety" (Bardwick, 1973). The younger woman may imagine coitus, if at all, only with a certain person or only happening spontaneously, because the man or the situation swept her away. The result is that very many sexually active adolescent girls use contraception improperly or not at all, and may become pregnant (Diamond et al., 1973a; Zelnick and Kantner, 1972, 1977).

The older single woman says essentially the same thing: "I'm not married or involved with anyone permanently; what sort of woman would I be if I kept contraceptives available?" She cannot let herself think that she would have coitus with forethought or with a new partner, though she may indeed do so. Even many older married women like at least the appearance of being swept away by emotion; they complain that some kinds of contraception ruin the mood or are messy. For many women of all ages, then, the real problem seems to be saying even to themselves, "I am choosing coitus now."

Most young people use birth control to postpone pregnancy, not because they don't ever want children. This is increasingly true as more people begin coitus younger and marry later (Diamond et al., 1973a, b; Zelnick and Kantner, 1972, 1977). Many use contraception inconsistently at best. They may give such reasons as, "My church wouldn't approve," "My partner wouldn't approve," "I thought I was in a safe period," or "I thought there wasn't much chance of getting pregnant."

---

* Unplanned pregnancies do not necessarily lead to unwanted children; fewer than half of unplanned pregnancies are aborted (Diamond et al., 1973b).

Obviously feelings, attitudes, and misinformation are more responsible for failing to control conception than is inability to get and use contraceptives. Some mistaken beliefs are quite common.

Belief: A large majority of teenagers don't believe they can easily become pregnant. They think they are too young, that conception can happen only at certain times, or that it takes more than once. These reasons, among others, are given by a majority of unmarried teenage women for not using contraception regularly (J. Evans, Selsted, and Welcher, 1976; Zelnick and Kantner, 1972).

Fact: Conception is most likely to happen at ovulation but ovulation can occur on any day, even during menses, and pregnancy can result from a single coition. Even heavy petting can start pregnancy if sperm travels from hand to vagina.

Belief: If contraceptives are available, sex will seem planned. The man will think his partner promiscuous or she will think that he is presumptuous.

Fact: Sometimes this is true, but raising the matter of contraception honestly yet tactfully can be seen as trustworthy and responsible. And it can be pointed out that contraception being available doesn't mean it's necessarily in frequent use.

Belief: Making contraception available encourages promiscuity, so contraceptive advice or devices should be limited to the married or legally adult. Teenagers seeking them will be treated rudely or made to feel embarrassed.

Fact: By the time most people seek contraception, they are already sexually active (Ford-ney-Settlage, Baroff, and Cooper, 1973); only a minority of people avoid coitus for long from fear of pregnancy (S. Brown, Lieberman, and Miller, unpublished). Using contraception does tend to increase the frequency of coitus somewhat, but not its incidence or the number of partners (R. Freedman, in press; Garris, Steckler, and McIntire, 1976). All states now allow the unmarried to request or obtain contraceptives without parental consent. Although condoms and vaginal contraceptives are not available everywhere, they are sold by mail and in most drugstores and in many discount and department stores. Most large communities have at least one hospital, clinic, Planned Parenthood office, or women's group that offers advice and devices—in many places free or at low cost. (One can check a phone book under Pregnancy Testing or Planned Parenthood or ask telephone information.) The local medical society may also help. In the past, most physicians were reluctant to help young people obtain contraceptives, but today the majority will probably do so with confidentiality.

Belief: Contraceptives ruin the mood or are messy and unappealing.

Fact: This is true for some people, but it need not be, and the absence of contraception can ruin the mood as badly (Hawkins, 1970). Some people incorporate the use of contraception in sexual play. Women can sensuously place condoms on their partners, and men can erotically insert foam or other vaginal contraceptives in their partners—if they are shown how to do so properly. The added sense of security and mutuality can help the mood.

Types of Contraception

Contraceptive techniques may be used by men or women, be dependent on or independent of coitus, temporary or permanent, behavioral or nonbehavioral, mechanical or chemical. Obviously most methods fall in more than one pair of categories (Diamond, 1979b). All should be evaluated for effectiveness, ease of use, availability, and cost.

Used by Men and Women

Contraception can be used by the man (the condom and withdrawal) or by the woman (the diaphragm, pill, IUD, and douching). Both men and women, as regular or irregular partners, can always be ready to take the responsibility for contraception.

Some people object to certain contraceptives because they are completely one's own respon-

---

The Costs of Contraception and Childrearing

Some people think it callous to even talk about comparing the costs of contraception to those of having and raising a child. Nevertheless, common reasons for contraception are, "We just can't afford a (another) child" and "We couldn't give a child the upbringing it deserves." The cost (in 1977 dollars) of raising a child is about 15 percent of family income (about $53,000 for a moderate-income family), and the amount increases as the child grows older; and if a college-educated woman remains at home until her oldest child is fifteen, her loss of income might be at least $100,000 (Espenshade, 1977). The Health Insurance Institute has estimated that routine hospital delivery costs more than $1,200, and a typical layette another $1,000 (Changing Times, 1976). Few contraceptive methods are beyond many people's means, as the following chart shows.

Birth control costs*

Method	Approximate 1980 costs	Estimated 30-year costs
Condom and foam	$50–75	$1500–2250
Diaphragm (with jelly)	50–75	750–1000
IUD	50–150	500–750
Pill	25–50	750–1500
Sterilization (male)	50–150	50–150
Sterilization (female)	350–750	350–750

* Includes initial and thirty-year replacement costs and professional services. These are estimated by the authors on the basis of present figures.

---

sibility or fully out of one's control. Responsibility, of course, serves both partners. They can agree on which method is most pleasing, available, and dependable. Some women ask with curiosity or anger, "Why isn't there a male pill?" The answer is that researchers have not yet been able to find a suitable one. The reality remains that women become pregnant and men don't, so women must consider their vulnerability. Responsible men share that emotional concern, but even if a woman could give the responsibility to her partner, she would be unwise to do so when a relationship is new or unstable.

Coitus-Dependent or Coitus-Independent

The condom and diaphragm are coitus-dependent; they are effective only if applied before each coition. The oral contraceptive is coitus-independent; if taken regularly, it is in effect whether one has coitus or not. Coitus-dependent methods appeal to many who need them only occasionally. They are also relatively inexpensive and more easily available to the young. Side effects are few.

Such coitus-independent methods as the pill and IUD are very popular in the United States. They allow freedom in time and place of coitus and give protection regardless of the partner's actions. Therefore they encourage many people to think of coitus as separate from reproduction; this offends some and is welcomed by many.

Temporary or Permanent

For the large number of people who want to postpone or space the births of their children, a temporary contraceptive is ideal. It works when used, has no effect when unused, and use can always be resumed. People who decide never to have children and those who have reached the family size they desire can seek permanent birth control through *sterilization*. One must be certain of this decision, for reversibility cannot be assured. Of course the birth of an unwanted child is also irreversible.

Behavioral or Nonbehavioral

Behavioral methods depend on how people act or do not act sexually; nonbehavioral methods do not. For a long time, only behavioral controls, such as abstinence and rhythm, were widely available. To some religious groups, especially Roman Catholics, behavioral methods are the only ones permitted. However, not all behavioral means are approved by all religious groups. Anal intercourse, fellatio, cunningus, withdrawal, or any other genital activity, when used to prevent pregnancy, can be considered behavioral contraception, but many are disapproved or discouraged for that purpose by religious traditions.

Some of these methods are among the less effective ones, and most tend to be used inconsistently. Their chief advantage is that nothing mechanical or chemical is taken into the body, which for some people is a major concern. They are also without cost.

Mechanical or Chemical

Mechanical-barrier contraceptives, such as the condom and diaphragm, work by preventing sperm and egg from meeting. Foams and jellies act both as barriers and as chemical spermicides (sperm killers). The IUD, contrary to common belief, doesn't act as a barrier. Many barrier methods are quite effective, but some people find them distasteful and therefore use them inconsistently.

Chemical methods alter a person physiologically or change the environment of the sperm, egg, or zygote. The oral contraceptive pill is the best known chemical method. Others are placed in the vagina, injected, or implanted under the skin. These are relatively inexpensive and, when used properly, quite effective. However, some people use them inconsistently, fearing that putting foreign substances in their bodies may have still unknown effects.

Effectiveness

No contraceptive technique except castration and hysterectomy works 100 percent of the time. Two main evaluations are used, *method effectiveness* and *user effectiveness*. For example, abstinence has better method effectiveness than the pill, for it is 100 percent effective. However, abstinence is not often used well for long periods, while the pill is.

The Pearl Index and life-table analysis rate both types of effectiveness. The *Pearl Index* counts the pregnancies in a population of women, computed as if they used the method for 100 years and could conceive twelve times a year. A Pearl Index of 2 means that two women out of 100 would become pregnant in a year if using this method. *Life-table analysis* is similar, but also considers how often the method is begun, discontinued, or resumed. This more sophisticated rating is gaining wider use.

A comparison of the effectiveness of various methods is given in Table 19.1. Most studies show that less depends on the method than on how well it is used. The more a method depends on motivation, ease and consistency of use, and comfort, the more failures occur. The IUD, over which a couple has little control, is the only temporary technique free from user error. Motivation is crucial: regardless of method, people who try to prevent pregnancy entirely rather than delay it are more successful (Ryder, 1973).

Rules for Contraception

1. Any method is better than none.
2. Two methods combined are better than one.
3. No method is perfect; all have failures or side effects.

The first two rules are obvious; the third needs explanation. The ideal contraceptive would be perfectly effective, coitus-independent, temporary, usable by both men and women, cheap, esthetically pleasing, socially and ethically acceptable, and without side effects. But this hasn't been developed, and it isn't likely to come along in the near future. Trade-offs must be made. Some women tolerate the immediate or potential side effects of the pill or IUD because they desire the ease of use, high efficiency, and independence of coitus. Others prefer the combination of diaphragm and jelly or the visible, easy-to-use condom.

Most studies show that the unmarried and teenagers, whether college students or not, use contraceptives inconsistently and unreliably. Many young people are in conflict about being moral and being pragmatic; this contributes to

Table 19.1 / *Birth control methods compared*

Control method	Male	Female	Coitus-dependent	Coitus-independent	Temporary	Permanent	Behavioral	Nonbehavioral	Mechanical	Chemical	Vaginal	Nonvaginal	Effectiveness index (pregnancies per 100 women years)*
Abstinence	■	■	□		■		□						0
Breast feeding		■		□	■		□					□	Causes average of 6 months of amenorrhea
Condom	■		□		■			□	■			□	2–5
Diaphragm		■	□		■			□	■			□	5–12
Douching		■	□		■		□					□	30–40
Foam, jelly, film		■	□		■			□		■		□	3–10
Hysterectomy		■		□		■		□	■			□	0
Injectables and implants	■	■		□	■			□		■		□	.01–1
Intrauterine devices		■		□	■			□	■			□	.1–5
Pill		■		□	■			□		■		□	0–4
Rhythm		■		□	■		□					□	20–40
Sexual behavior technique (nonvaginal intercourse)	■	■	□				□					□	No data (< 5?)
Suppository		■	□		■			□		■	□		2–5
Tubal ligation		■		□		■		□	■			□	.01–.5
Vasectomy	■			□		■		□	■			□	.01–.5
Withdrawal	■		□		■		□						No data (> 20?)
No control													65–80

* Composite of Pearl Index and Life Table data. These figures, derived from many studies, provide relative rather than absolute comparisons.

ineffective and sporadic contraceptive use. For most, first coitus is without contraception. We suggest that people accept the fact that a majority of people will engage in premarital coitus, and that there will be a risk of pregnancy. If sexually active, they should keep contraceptives handy. Decisions about such precautions should be made before the day arrives, not left until the heat of passion. Having contraceptives available is responsible behavior.

Contraceptive Methods

Abstinence

Abstinence has been a birth control method for as long as people have linked coitus with reproduction. Though difficult for most people, it has been recommended by many religious and social institutions, either outside marriage or periodically for married laymen, and for life for some clerics. Complete abstinence was advocated for everyone by the Shakers—who, not surprisingly, no longer exist.

The Roman Catholic church advocates periodic abstinence (the *rhythm* method) to limit conception. This has been possible only since the 1930s, when Ogino (1930) and Knaus (1933) discovered that ovulation usually occurs between menses and that this is the most likely time for conception. The term rhythm method was apparently first used in 1932 by L. J. Lätz in his book *The Rhythm of Sterility and Fertility in Women*. The papal encyclical *Casti Connubii* by Pope Pius XI in 1930 (Pius XI, 1930) denounced artificial methods, but not periodic abstinence. The church first publicly approved rhythm in 1951. Since then papal authority has continued to ban nonrhythm methods as unnatural and to approve periodic abstinence.

The rhythm method depends on avoiding coitus when ovulation is likely. The two chief techniques for this are the calendar method and temperature method. The two methods can be used together.

The Calendar Method. This method assumes that ovulation will occur between the twelfth and sixteenth days before the start of menses, and that sperm may live for three days inside a female; both are true often, but not always. The woman is to abstain during these eight days of peak risk. To know when menses are due, she must have charted her cycles for the previous six to twelve months. This method has many difficulties; most important is that no woman's cycle is fully regular or predictable.

The Temperature Method. This depends on identifying the rise in *basal body temperature* (BBT) that normally occurs when progesterone is released by the ovary after ovulation. Readings must be taken orally or rectally at the same time each morning while still in bed, after five hours of uninterrupted sleep. A special thermometer is used which is especially sensitive in the normal ranges. A woman must accurately plot her BBT for at least six months to discover her temperature curve and calculate her "safe period."

Since one cannot always predict when ovulation will occur, one must limit coitus from the late post-ovulatory phase until the next menses. An anovulatory (no ovulation) cycle occurs occasionally in all women; then they may have to avoid coitus for sixty days or more. For many couples, this is difficult at best.

In the United States, the use of rhythm has declined from about 20 percent of those practicing birth control in 1955 to less than 5 percent even among Roman Catholics two decades later, and seems "destined to be of historic interest only" (Westoff and Jones, 1977b). Even for highly motivated and well instructed people, it is extremely unreliable and inefficient (World Health Organization, 1978).

Side Effects. There is a higher probability of a malformed child developed from an aged ovum fertilized by postovulatory coitus (Thibault, 1970). Therefore couples who limit coitus to the postovulatory phase have more abnormal pregnancies and children (Jongbloet, 1971). Certainly not all gestations following late conception are abnormal, but people practicing rhythm should be aware of the possibility (Orgebin-Christ, 1973).

Anxiety over possible failure of the method can cause many psychological problems. More than 40 percent of highly motivated couples using rhythm for more than two years have reported anxiety over pregnancy and a dampening effect on coitus. More than half found abstinence difficult sometimes, 31 percent often. Women were more distressed by fear of pregnancy, men by abstinence (J. Marshall and Rowe, 1970, 1972).

Figure 19-1 / *The calendar method for predicting ovulation presumes an 8-day "unsafe" period in a 25- to 35-day menstrual cycle (top). For a woman whose cycles have varied from 26 to 31 days over the preceding year (bottom), the ovulation calendar shows a "safe" period of 4 preovulatory days (not counting the 4 days of menses) and 4 to 10 postovulatory days, depending on the length of the current cycle.*

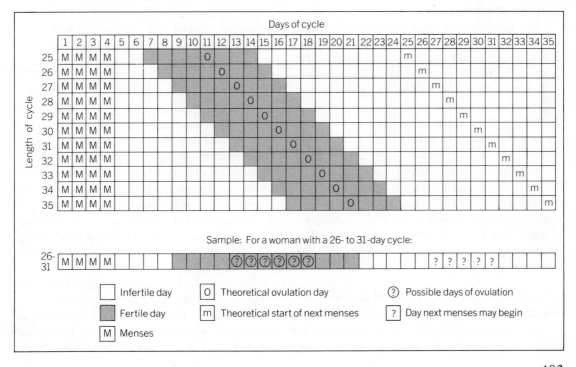

Barriers

Vaginal Contraceptives. These are among the oldest forms of birth control. Some are still widely used, without any need for professional help and only rarely with serious side effects. All have a twofold action: they create a barrier to sperm passage and kill sperm. Among them are *foams, creams, pastes, jellies,* and *suppositories* inserted in the vagina.

Most jellies and foams are taken from a tube or aerosol container into an applicator that allows placement near the cervix. The applicator has the psychological advantage of making it unnecessary to use the fingers, which some people find unpleasant. Creams, pastes, and suppositories are inserted by hand.

Any vaginal contraceptive should be applied just before coitus, for the material has peak effectiveness for about an hour; more should be added after that time. If it is used before coitus at night, and coitus is desired again in the morning, more should be applied then. The chief drawbacks of vaginal contraceptives are this need for application before each coition and inconsistent use. Some people, we have noted, consider them messy and an interruption of mood, and their taste tends to discourage oral-genital play. Their major advantages are lack of serious side effects and a small but significant degree of protection against venereal disease (*Population Reports,* H–3, 1975). They also aid some people by providing vaginal lubrication.

Condoms. The condom is still in wide use and seems to be gaining in popularity. Oddly, physicians rarely recommend it. Many family-planning programs and health facilities do rec-

ommend it highly for its portability, ease of use, and protection against venereal disease (*Population Reports,* H–2, 1974).

Most condoms are made of rubber latex. Originally they were made of "skin," which was actually a pouch-like portion of animal intestine. Recently plastic condoms have come into use. There are many designs; various brands offer prelubrication, added space for the ejaculate, color for novelty, and ribs or attachments for (supposed) erotic stimulation.

Condoms are usually packaged rolled. They are unrolled onto the erect penis shortly before vaginal entry (see Figure 19-3). For most effective use, a little extra space should be allowed at the tip. After ejaculation, the condom should be grasped at the base of the penis during withdrawal from the vagina, so that it does not slip off and sperm doesn't leak out.

Condoms are inexpensive and without side effects, but they reduce sensitivity to touch, temperature, and lubrication. Some people complain of the decreased penile and vaginal sensitivity; others prefer condoms because they may increase the time it takes to reach orgasm. Skin condoms allow more sensation than rubber ones, and many are lubricated; they are at least twice as expensive. For many years the most advertised benefit of the condom was its protection against venereal disease; this is still one of its major advantages. Its major disadvantage is inconsistent and careless use (Tietze, 1960).

Diaphragms. This inexpensive device has been recommended by physicians and clinics alike. Slightly effective as a sperm barrier, the diaphragm is usually used with a spermicidal vaginal jelly. Before coitus, jelly is applied to

404

the diaphragm, which is inserted in the vagina to cover the cervix. It should remain in place for at least six hours after coitus to ensure

spermicidal action; a woman should not douche to help the process. It may remain in place up to twenty-four hours; longer is not advisable. If coitus occurs more than six to eight hours after insertion, additional contraceptive jelly should be placed in the vagina (*Population Reports,* H–4, 1976).

Figure 19-2 / *Insertion of contraceptive vaginal foam or jelly (left) and of a contraceptive tablet or suppository (right).*

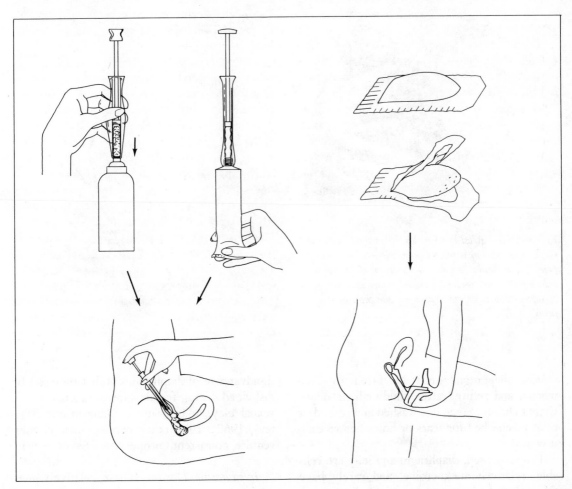

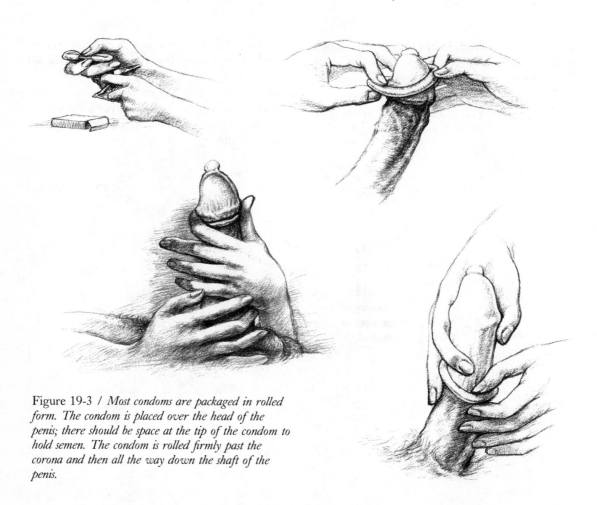

Figure 19-3 / *Most condoms are packaged in rolled form. The condom is placed over the head of the penis; there should be space at the tip of the condom to hold semen. The condom is rolled firmly past the corona and then all the way down the shaft of the penis.*

The diaphragm must be fitted to each woman and refitted after childbirth or major weight change. Since it is washed and reused, it must be checked for tears or holes before each use.

Properly used, diaphragm and jelly are reliable, relatively inexpensive, and rarely have side effects. Some women use their diaphragms during menses to retain menstrual fluids. One disadvantage of diaphragms is that they can be dislodged during female-superior coitus, active sexual play, or orgasm (V. Johnson and Masters, 1962). Like other barrier devices, they require consistent, proper use (Savel, 1971).

Intrauterine Devices. These relatively new devices are now the leading birth control method in at least ten countries (*Population Re-*

Figure 19-4 / *A contraceptive vaginal diaphragm must be prescribed in the correct size by a physician. Contraceptive cream or jelly is placed in the bowl or on the dome, and a little around the rim. Then the diaphragm is inserted while the woman stands, squats, or lies on her back. Properly placed, the diaphragm completely covers the cervix, and the cream or jelly acts as a chemical barrier that kills sperm cells.*

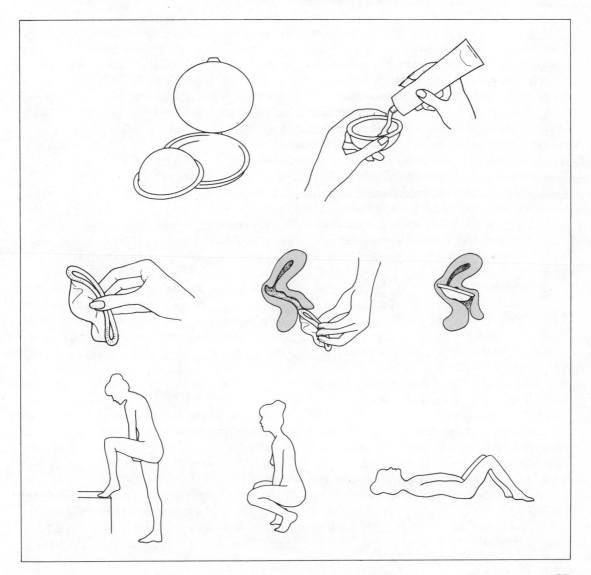

ports, B–2, 1975). In the United States they are increasingly popular and are used by five to eight million women. IUDs are highly effective, coitus-independent, and do not need daily attention. Furthermore, most don't affect the body chemistry.

Why don't more women use them? Some fear placing the object in their bodies; some want a contraceptive that doesn't require medical insertion and removal. Others have experienced or heard of such side effects as uterine pain and trauma, infections, and longer and heavier periods; some fear the device being expelled without their knowledge. All of these can occur, but most women do not experience these problems (Population Reports, B–2, 1975). Infection used to be the most common major complication, but with newer models and proper insertion, this is rare. All common IUDs now have one–thread filaments that protrude from the uterus into (not out of) the vagina, so that one can check to be sure the device is in place.

There are many types of IUDs, such as the Lippes loop, shield, spiral, copper T, copper 7, bow, and progestcert. This variety allows for differences among women in uterine shape and size, parity, age, and physiology. All are designed to be easily inserted and removed, cause minimal side effects, and have maximal effectiveness. None meets all the criteria equally well; each compromises in some way. The most widely used IUDs are made of inert plastic and come in various sizes. The plastic has "memory"; it deforms for placement within the uterus by a strawlike instrument called an introducer and then returns to its original shape.

No data exist to show that any type is better than any other for all women (Goldsmith,

Figure 19-5 / *There are many kinds of intrauterine devices (IUDs), which are inserted through the cervix into the uterus. (Life size.)*

Brenner, and Edelman, 1974). Evidence is accumulating, however, that the addition of copper and release of progesterone offered by some "active" IUDs helps prevent expulsion (Population Reports, B–2, 1975). The IUD probably has several modes of action. It seems to affect uterine prostaglandins, which change the rate of gametes' and zygotes' travel, thwarting proper timing for fertilization and implantation. It seems by itself to make implantation difficult. It also stimulates white blood cells to accumulate in the uterus and destroy sperm or the zygote.

If pregnancy should occur while an IUD is in place, the device does not deform the fetus. Whether the device should be removed depends on several factors, including the type of device and its location relative to the fetus. It may remain in place until delivery without harm to the fetus or woman. A physician should be consulted to determine the best course of action.

Oral Contraceptives

No contraceptive has been accepted so quickly by so many people as the oral contraceptive (OC), or "the pill," a combination of synthetic chemicals that prevents ovulation. More than fifty million women around the world use this method (Population Reports, A–5, 1979). For many young women, going on the pill has become a mark of status (as getting a diaphragm used to be). Like the IUD, the pill

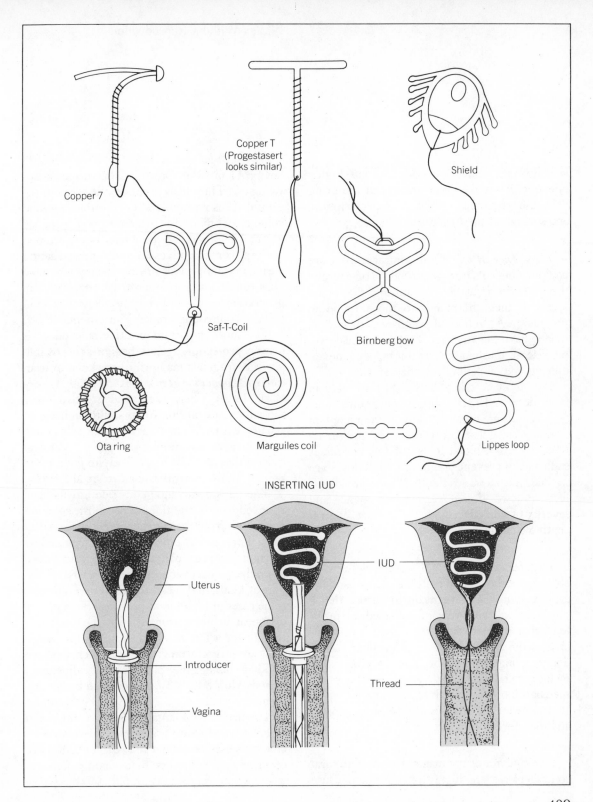

Copper 7

Copper T
(Progestasert
looks similar)

Shield

Saf-T-Coil

Birnberg bow

Ota ring

Marguiles coil

Lippes loop

INSERTING IUD

Uterus

IUD

Introducer

Thread

Vagina

is coitus-independent, temporary, and highly effective. It has the disadvantages of requiring daily use, requiring a physician's prescription, and sometimes producing side effects.

How They Work. Oral contraceptives are combinations of estrogens and progesterone that prevent ovulation by raising the blood levels of these hormones to those found in pregnancy. As in normal pregnancy, these hormones have negative feedback on gonadotropin-release mechanisms, inhibiting egg development and ovulation (see chapter 18).

OCs must be taken daily, and they vary in type, dose, and packaging. Some brands must be taken during menses; many of these contain iron to restore that lost from normal menstruation. To make blood levels of the hormones sufficient to prevent pregnancy, high doses are needed; this increases the likelihood of side effects. A lower dosage reduces the chance and severity of side effects, but also reduces contraceptive efficiency.

Distribution and Use. OCs are widely available, but in the United States, a user must have a prescription. This is meant to ensure that a physician will be aware of any medical problems that develop from their use. It also increases the cost and limits sale to pharmacies. Some young women, because of embarrassment, obtain OCs from their friends; this raises the chance of a mismatch of user and pill type. It also lowers the chances of a constant supply, and therefore of efficient use.

Side Effects. For the majority of women, oral contraceptives are highly effective and cause few problems. For some, OCs have special advantages. They may relieve the cramps of painful menstruation, reduce the duration and volume of monthly bleeding, and produce greater regularity of the cycle. Some women use oral contraceptives to avoid menstruating during certain periods of time. Many who take OCs report lower premenstrual tension and a general sense of well-being. OCs lessen acne in certain women but worsen it in others.

The most important positive side effect is proven protection against benign and possible protection against malignant breast and ovarian tumors (*Population Reports,* A–5, 1979; Vessey et al., 1976). There is no evidence that using the pill causes uterine tumors, although a correlation exists. Women who are sexually active at early ages are more likely to get cervical cancer; they are also more likely to choose the pill for birth control (Melamed et al., 1969).

The pill's disadvantageous side effects have received wide attention. The most common ones result from the chemical pseudopregnancy the pill produces. Some women are troubled by morning sickness, nausea, vomiting, dizziness, headaches, depression, tender breasts, retention of fluids, and weight gain. There are also some cases of high blood pressure. Such effects disappear in many women after they've taken the pill for a few months, so unless the symptoms are severe, women are usually encouraged to keep taking the pill for this adjustment period. Most effects can be reversed by ceasing to take the pill.

The major disadvantage of OCs is the possibility of blood clotting *(thromboembolism).* Several studies have shown that this occurs more often among pill users than among nonusers who are not pregnant. With pill use, the chance of a clot in a superficial blood vessel of the leg rises from about two per 1,000 women a year to three; the condition is uncomfortable but not dangerous. Deep blood clots are dangerous, and pill use increases the risk of those five times, from two per 10,000 women a year to ten. Pill use raises the risk of the more serious

and rare problem of a brain clot *(cerebral thrombosis)* from one per 10,000 to about four (Vessey et al., 1976; *Population Reports,* A-5, 1979). The risk of clotting is greater for women over forty, so the pill is not recommended after that age. For women who smoke, the risk is greater, and the pill is not recommended for smokers over thirty-five.

It must be emphasized that these problems have been compared in pill users and in non-users who were not pregnant. Pregnancy increases the same clotting risks associated with the pill. Most studies conclude that the health risks of using OCs are less than those of normal

Figure 19-6 / *Beneficial and adverse side effects of oral contraceptives. compared to those of the diaphragm and IUDs. (Figures adjusted for age, parity, social class, and smoking.)*

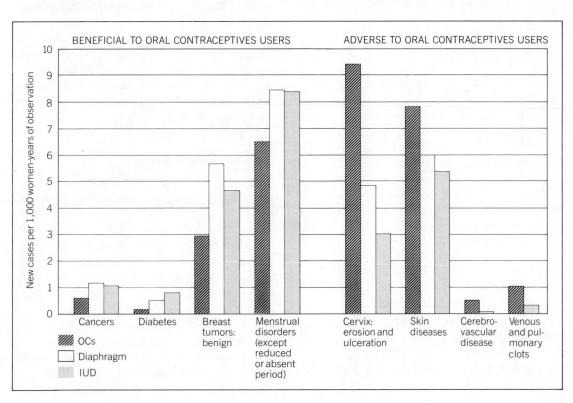

pregnancy and delivery at all ages for non-smokers, and until age forty for smokers (Tietze, 1977a,b). High blood pressure and diabetes can be worsened by pill use, but less than by pregnancy. That is, pregnancy and smoking are more dangerous than pill use.

Vulnerability to venereal diseases and to vaginal problems was once thought to be a side effect of OCs. Using OCs can change the vaginal environment, encouraging the growth of microorganisms, but evidence now suggests that women on the pill are not more likely than nonusers to contract gonorrhea and urinary-tract infections (Darrow, 1975). Vaginal discharges, however, are more prevalent in pill users.

The Pill and Sexual Responsiveness. There has been a good deal of controversy over the effects of OCs on sexual response and behavior. Masters and Johnson (1968) have reported a decreased sex drive and difficulty reaching orgasm in some women after using OCs for eighteen to thirty-six months. Other investigators report unchanged or even increased sexual activity in some women (Westoff, Bumpass, and Ryder, 1969). The issue remains unresolved; results probably depend on the type of pill (there are about a dozen varieties) and the individual woman.

Behavioral Methods

Behavioral methods differ in acceptability to couples and in the sexual satisfaction they offer. Oral-genital and anal-genital intercourse are sometimes used to prevent conception, but in very few cases for a long time. Relying on the fact that conception is somewhat less likely when a woman is nursing is relatively unsafe.

Pregnancy can and often does occur during lactation; ovulation resumes within a year of parturition (*Population Reports,* J-4, 1975).

Withdrawal, or *coitus interruptus,* is withdrawing the penis before orgasm, so that ejaculation occurs outside the vagina. Most men know when ejaculation is about to happen, but most couples prefer orgasm inside the woman and find routine withdrawal frustrating. If the woman is also reaching orgasm, the excitement affects them both; this is not an easy time to withdraw, and last-second failures occur. And there are often enough sperm in the fluids released from the penis before ejaculation to cause fertilization. The only advantage of withdrawal is that it is better than nothing.

Coitus reservatus is coitus without ejaculation. With training, a man can learn to reach orgasm or a feeling of satisfaction without ejaculation. There is risk of sperm leakage, and for women who like to feel the man's ejaculation, this may not be satisfactory.

Injectables and Implants

Among the newer contraceptives are drugs, especially synthetic progesterones, that are injected or implanted under a woman's skin. These are effective for three to six months. Though still being tested in the United States, they are in use in many countries. Since they don't affect lactation, women can take them immediately after delivery, when motivation for contraception is high and the woman is in a health facility (*Population Reports,* K-1, 1975).

These implants are very efficient and give freedom from daily pill taking. They will be available in this country if they pass federal tests for safety and the reversibility of effects.

Injectables and implants for men have been

tested. They are effective, but so far such side effects as lower sex drive and occasional impotence have made them unacceptable. No comparable effect has been noticed in women. Research on injectables for men is continuing.

Postconception Birth Control

No contraceptives are foolproof, and what can be done about unwanted conception is a matter of passionate private and public debate. It is usually argued along religious, philosophical, or moral lines, but for most women the decision is quite personal and emotion-laden. No woman becomes pregnant in order to have an abortion, and few make the decision to abort lightly. The great majority feel that the decision should be theirs alone.

Of women who do not want to remain pregnant, about three to four in ten choose to abort; the others maintain the pregnancy. Women choose to end pregnancies for many reasons. Rape and incest are commonly used to justify abortion, but they prompt less than 1 percent of abortions. Medical reasons account for less than 2 percent. The vast majority of women who have abortions give social and personal reasons (Diamond et al., 1973a). (See Table 19.2.) Even in the 1930s and 1940s, when abortion was illegal, about one married woman

---

Abortion: Pro and Con

The following is testimony from 1970 about the repeal of antiabortion laws in Hawaii, which was the first state to legalize abortion upon a woman's request (Steinhoff and Diamond, 1977).

The child resulting from compulsory pregnancy is by such laws guaranteed the right to existence and nothing more. Compulsory pregnancy laws have never been concerned with whether this child will . . . develop into normal adulthood with a chance at what we call "the good life."

Supporters of [anti-abortion] laws go to great length to protect the right of existence of the fertilized egg, a *potential* human being, while disregarding completely the right of an *actual* human being, the pregnant woman, to determine the course of her own life.

—Laurel Kasaoka, representative,
Democratic Action Group

The church has consistently and without hesitation supported the position that once human life exists, it has a right to be born. We are not speaking of a spiritual soul but of human life.

—Monsignor Francis A. Marzen

There is ample evidence that unwanted children produce an increase in mental illness, an increase in functional and cultural mental retardation, an increase in juvenile delinquency, crime and various social ills.

—Pediatrician Roy Smith

As women we have been granted the exalted role of cradling this new life within ourselves for nine months. . . . This life is the blessing of a cooperative act by man and by woman . . . the man has as much right over this new life as the woman . . . a woman cannot indiscriminately dispose of this life without the man's consent and both must share in the guilt of such an act of murder as is the case in abortion.

—Mrs. Edward S. Ehlen,
Catholic Women's Guild

Table 19.2 / *Reasons women give for having an abortion*

Reason	Percent*
I am not married.	34.3
I cannot afford a child now.	31.5
A child would interfere with my education.	22.0
I feel unable to cope with a child now.	22.0
I have enough children already.	16.3
I think I'm too young to have a child.	14.3

* Percentages total more than 100 because most women gave more than one reason.
  Source: Diamond et al., 1973a.

out of four or five had an induced abortion (Gebhard et al., 1958). Perhaps as many as half of all women voluntarily abort a child during the course of their lives (Pakter, Nelson, and Svigir, 1975).

There are two common ways to interrupt early pregnancy. One prevents implantation; the other dislodges the implanted embryo or removes the fetus. The first method is easier and employs the so-called day-after pill. The second employs menstrual extraction or one of several types of abortion.

Day-After Pill

This is actually a series of pills containing high levels of estrogens; they are taken for three to seven days, starting the day after coitus. They make the zygote travel faster than usual, so it arrives in the uterus before the endometrium is ready for implantation, and change the endocrine balance needed to support the zygote in the uterus. This is highly effective, but the high intake of hormones nauseates some women. Most women prefer con-

traception to day-after pills, to avoid both the side effects and the ethical conflict.

Menstrual Extraction

By the time a woman realizes her period is late, she may be two or more weeks pregnant. The embryo is still much smaller than the nail of an adult's small finger, so it is simple to insert a thin, flexible plastic tube *(cannula)* through the vagina and into the uterus and, with slight suction, remove the endometrial lining—and with it an embryo, if one is present. This takes from two to ten minutes, depending on how advanced gestation is and how skilled the physician. The woman usually receives only a local anesthetic and can resume normal activities after a brief rest. She is advised to abstain from coitus for a week or ten days and then return for a check-up. Usually a menstrual period of normal or somewhat shorter duration follows extraction. Early menstrual extraction (also called *menstrual induction* and *menstrual aspiration*) is quite safe (Center for Disease Control, 1976). It is generally used only during the first four or five weeks of pregnancy, but with modifications can be used until the twelfth week or even later.

Prostaglandins

These substances (see chapter 17) are now being improved for fertility control by inducing menstruation. Taken in vaginal suppositories, they have proved highly successful, but there are such side effects as uterine pain, vomiting, and diarrhea. These drugs are used in clinics (see below); whether they will become safe enough for routine home use remains to be seen.

Abortion

Abortion is the deliberate termination of pregnancy at any time. It is now the most common surgical procedure in the United States. Voluntary abortion is usually done during the first twelve weeks of gestation, but it is not uncommon up to the twentieth week. Modern techniques involve less health risk to the woman than does full-term delivery of a baby (*Population Reports,* F–3, 1973), and done properly, abortion affects neither sexual nor reproductive ability.

Usual Techniques. Abortion methods are fairly standardized. During the sixth to twelfth weeks of gestation, the most commonly used technique is similar to menstrual extraction and is called *vacuum aspiration.* It usually takes less than fifteen minutes. At the eight-to-twelve-week stage, a *dilation and curettage* (D and C) may be performed. The cervix is dilated, a curved *curette* (scraper) is passed into the uterus, and the endometrium is removed. This was once the preferred method of abortion. Now it is used less than aspiration.

After the twelfth week of pregnancy, the fetus has grown too large for aspiration, and curettage is no longer safe; the wall of the uterus has become quite thin and can be perforated. Now the best method of abortion is dilating the cervix and placing prostaglandins in the vagina. Late in pregnancy, some clinics use a *saline* or prostaglandins abortion. A hypodermic needle is used to remove some amniotic

Figure 19-7 / *Menstrual extraction.*

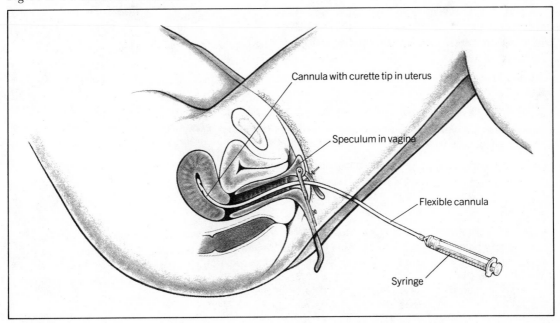

Cannula with curette tip in uterus

Speculum in vagina

Flexible cannula

Syringe

415

fluids surrounding the fetus and replace them with a saline (salt) solution. Usually within a day, the tissues react to the saline or prostaglandins, and abortion occurs. The woman then rests for a day or two in the hospital. Prostaglandins and saline can be used to induce abortion until at least the twenty-sixth week of pregnancy (*Population Reports,* F-5, 1976).

In many East European and Asian nations, the abortion rate is considerably higher than the birthrate (Tietze, 1977a,b). In recent decades, women in Poland, Romania, and Hungary preferred abortion to contraception as the primary method of birth control; some have had twenty or more abortions without known ill effects. Recently contraception has become more accepted and prevalent.

Do-It-Yourself Abortion. There are no simple, safe abortion techniques that can be used at home. No exercise, pill, douche, diet, sexual activity, or other method will work. If the home use of such drugs as prostaglandins becomes safe, they will almost surely require a prescription.

Psychological and Social Factors. The number of women obtaining abortions seems to be increasing slowly but steadily (Steinhoff and Diamond, 1977). We have said that now perhaps one woman in two experiences abortion; about 15 percent of these do so twice or more. Actually, this is no larger a figure than would be anticipated statistically in the light of contraception failure alone (Steinhoff et al., 1979). To some, these figures all seem high; it must be noted that when women have been denied abortions, the resulting children have suffered relatively more sickness, handicaps, and childhood deaths, were more often in trouble with the law, and were more dissatisfied with life (David et al., 1977; Forssman and Thuwe, 1976; Dytrych et al., 1975; Matějcěk, Dytrych, and Schüller, 1978).

Abortion and the Law

Under continual pressure by groups wanting to liberalize or restrict abortion, the U.S. Supreme Court ruled in 1973 (*Roe* v. *Wade; Doe* v. *Bolton*) and subsequently that:

1. Abortion is the decision of only a woman and her physician.
2. Abortion must be done by physicians in approved health facilities.
3. Neither the woman's partner nor parents need be consulted, regardless of her age.

Some local laws and hospital procedures have been set up to get around these rulings, but they have not held up in court. Many public or private social agencies will pay for the abortion of a woman who can't afford it, and many insurance companies cover abortion in their policies. However, psychological and social help are not available everywhere. Continuing efforts to make abortion more or less available are still being challenged in courts.

Women who have abortions come from all social classes, religions, and ethnic backgrounds, and they have a variety of life-styles and marital situations. Statistically, the typical woman who has an abortion is twenty-four years old, white, Protestant, single, wants to postpone motherhood rather than avoid it, and is going steady or living with a man. It is more likely than not that she had had some college education. She may or may not have been using some contraceptive technique. Economic level is hard to judge, since many young women are students or living at home, and still dependent on their parents (Steinhoff, 1973; Steinhoff, Smith, and Diamond, 1972). Older studies, done when abortions were illegal, showed the majority of women who had abortions were married and older (Gebhard et al., 1958).

About two-thirds of women who choose abortion make the decisions as soon as they know they are pregnant. One study found that about 8 percent of women who aborted had decided they would do so before they became pregnant (Diamond et al., 1973b). Women who have abortions after the sixteenth week are likely to be younger, living at home, and less independent financially and emotionally—characteristics that tend to make them take longer to decide on and carry out abortion.

Despite the church's opposition, between one-quarter and one-third of all women having abortions are Roman Catholic—about the proportion of Catholics in the total population (Diamond et al., 1973b). However, a study in a region where 25 to 30 percent of the women are Roman Catholic found that about half the women who are pregnant at any given time are Catholics, probably a reflection of church attitudes toward contraception (Leon and Steinhoff, 1975).

Most women feel that they are making the best decision under the circumstances, despite any regret, grief, or guilt. Follow-up studies have consistently shown that after several years, "no regrets" is the commonest response (Osofsky, Osofsky, and Rajan, 1973). It should be mentioned that many women who have unplanned children regret not having had an abortion. Much seems to depend on how the decision was made to deal with the unwanted pregnancy; this decision was related to the women's age, marital status, social background, and other factors (Steinhoff, 1978).

Sterilization

Many people who feel they have all the children they will ever want choose to undergo sterilization, which permanently prevents conception. Until recently this choice was influenced less by medical technology or law than by age, marital status, number of children, religion, place of residence, the person asked for help, and coital activities. In some parts of our country, social pressures still make it difficult or impossible for an unmarried person under twenty-five to be voluntarily sterilized—or, for that matter, for any married person without children, a Roman Catholic, or a Mormon without at least two children. Nevertheless these restrictions placed by medical and religious groups have been successfully challenged in many courts, and the procedures are now widely available and increasingly used (Westoff and Jones, 1977a).

Sterilization is usually a rather brief and simple surgical procedure for both men and women. The tubes which carry the sperm or eggs are cut and tied (tying the tubes), thus preventing conception. Sterilization is being

417

chosen by an increasing number of the world's people. In 1975 an estimated 15 percent of adult women and 11 percent of adult men in the United States had been sterilized. Sterilization is now the most popular method of contraception for people married ten years or more, and its use is steadily increasing (Westoff and Jones, 1977a).

Male Sterilization. To perform a *vasectomy,* the physician locates the tubes (vas deferens) through the scrotum. A local anesthetic is applied, and a small slit is made in each side of the scrotum. Each spermatic cord is pulled through the skin, and the vas deferens is tied or clipped in two places and burned or cut between the ties. The severed ends of the tubes are then put back in the scrotum and the incision closed.

After resting fifteen minutes to a few hours, the man is ready to leave the physician's office. He is advised to avoid physical exertion for a day or two. If he doesn't do strenuous labor, he may return to work the same day or soon after (*Population Reports,* D–1, 1973). Some men have no postoperative problems; others experience temporary swelling, discoloration, and pain. Ice packs and aspirin usually relieve the discomfort. Since live sperm remain in the vas deferens for a while after vasectomy, contra-

ception is required until a sample of ejaculate appears clean on microscopic examination (usually after some fifteen ejaculations). Vasectomy does not affect testosterone production, and in most men, sexual response remains the same or is improved (see Table 19.3). In a small percentage, for reasons apparently not associated with the surgery, sexual activity decreases (*Population Reports,* D–2, 1975). No other side effects are known.

Female Sterilization. Since a woman's oviducts are less accessible than a man's tubes, female sterilization is more difficult. It is usually done in a hospital, whereas vasectomy is a simple office procedure. Three techniques are used, though once the ducts are accessible, the procedures are quite similar.

A *minilaparotomy* most resembles vasectomy. The woman receives a local anesthetic, and two small incisions are made along the pubic hairline. The tubes are brought out through the incisions, tied, and cut. Closing the incision is not as simple as in men, since more layers of tissue are involved. Sutures must be used, and certain kinds must be removed about ten days later.

Today most physicians prefer to use a tube-like instrument, the *laparoscope,* which punc-

Table 19.3 / *Sexual response after vasectomy*

	Sexual pleasure	Desire	Frequency of coitus	Erection	Marital harmony
Unchanged	46%	64%	64%	67%	61%
Increased	45	17	24	7	43
Decreased	4	14	27	9	2

Source: From *Population Reports*, Series D, No. 2, January 1975.
Note: Some multiple answers were given, and some were omitted, so the total is not always 100 percent.

tures the abdominal wall and allows the physician to see into the pelvis and perform the procedure internally. The tubes are found and cut, and the instrument withdrawn. Often this can be done through the navel so that no visible scar results. Sometimes a similar but slightly thicker instrument is used to approach the tubes through the vagina. This is simpler and less expensive; few complications have been reported, and there are no external scars.

Recovery from a minilaparotomy is rapid. The woman is advised to rest for several hours; aspirin seems enough for postoperative pain. She can resume coitus as soon as she wishes; usually this is not for at least several days. Recovery after vaginal sterilization is also usually rapid; the woman may leave the hospital as soon as two to four hours later, and most leave within twenty-four. After vaginal sterilization, coitus is discouraged for two to three weeks. Most women report no side effects and no change in sexual desire or functioning after sterilization by any method. These procedures are usually effective, but some women's recuperative powers and the poor techniques of some surgeons lead to reconnection of a severed tube, and occasionally pregnancies occur (*Population Reports,* C–7, 1976).

Many women are sterilized as a result of *hysterectomy* (removal of the uterus). Almost 30 to 40 percent of women will have a hysterectomy by age sixty-five because of a uterine problem such as a tumor or bleeding. It is the third most common female operation. Simple hysterectomy has no significant effect on levels of gonadal hormones or on sexual desire and response.

For many people, the emotional and financial freedom from unwanted pregnancies outweighs concerns about sterilization. However,

a person who doubts his or her reaction to the procedure should not seek it. The association of fertility with masculinity or femininity is firmly, almost irreversibly, established in many people's minds. One must be thoroughly convinced and comfortable with this choice. Neither should anyone seek sterilization who has any doubt about closing the door permanently on having children. Efforts are continuing to perfect reversible sterilization techniques (*Population Reports,* D–3, 1976).

Overview

Reproduction control of some kind has been used by virtually all societies and religious groups. The reasons for using contraception vary, and so do the methods. Unfortunately, no method is without physical, practical, or psychological disadvantages. Nevertheless, any individual and couple should be able to choose a method that meets their needs. One should bear in mind that contraceptive choices need not be permanent; most women do change their contraceptive techniques. One method may be best at one time in life, others preferable later.

Contraception, abortion, and sterilization involve complex ethical issues; so does giving birth to an unplanned or unwanted child. Accepting oneself as a sexual being includes accepting responsibility for reproductive potential and awareness of these issues. We agree with Father Robert Drinan (1967), former dean of the Law School at Boston College and congressman from Massachusetts, that the law "should withdraw from the area of regulating abortion" and leave the decision to individual conscience. We believe that everyone should have access to every means of pre- and post-conception control, with support by society.

Review, Discuss, Decide

1. Which contraceptive, if any, would be best for you at this time in your life? Why?
2. Whom might you ask for information on contraception?
3. How much say in this matter should you give to your partner, church, parents, physician, friends?
4. What are your feelings about abortion? How are they colored by your ethical and religious convictions? How by your marital and personal situation?
5. Imagine that you are twenty-five to thirty years old, happily married for more than five years, have two children, and want no more. What might you decide about the following options for yourself or spouse? Why or why not?
   a. Using oral contraceptives until after menopause.
   b. Using oral contraceptives for a trial or limited period (say, five years) and then changing to another method.
   c. Using an IUD, with abortion as a backup if necessary.
   d. Using a diaphragm, foam, or condom, with abortion as a backup if necessary. (Note: The chance of pregnancy in the twenty-five or so years remaining until menopause while using these contraceptives approaches 100 percent.)
   e. Using a preferred method of contraception and accepting a pregnancy if it comes.
   f. Sterilization for you or your spouse.
   g. Having an unplanned and unwanted child.
6. What are the possible sexual effects of these decisions?
7. How might our society encourage more men to be concerned with conception?

Part VI   Society

So far in this book, we have often considered society's influence on sexuality by discussing attitudes, sociological data and theory, cross-cultural comparisons, and historical continuity and change. In Part VI we will look in detail at some aspects of culture that can be the predominant influences on the organization, control, and expression of sexuality.

The chapter "What Societies Say" gives an overview of other societies and our own, to point out their diversity and similarities. We then examine some societies' sexual customs and practices from a functional viewpoint, asking how they are adaptive and how well they serve people's needs. Finally, we discuss which options societies suggest about sexual matters.

The chapter "Gender Roles" reviews a subject that often raises deep emotion. People have choices in whether or how to follow some aspects of socially established gender roles; in other aspects, choices are relatively limited. Are stereotyped gender roles helpful or harmful? What functions do they serve? If society can alter them, how?

These issues lead to the concerns of the last chapter, "The Law, Morality, and Ethics."

We have touched these subjects in many chapters, for there is almost no fact or decision about sex without moral or ethical implications. We have chosen as examples some issues involving values and the law that have recently been subjects of widespread debate.

20

What Societies Say

Why can't anyone I like be a sexual partner?
Is our society stricter about sex than most others?
Which ideas about sex are just our society's traditions? Which are believed elsewhere? Everywhere?
How much of a conformist or nonconformist am I in my sexual acts and attitudes?

A chief reason for curiosity about other cultures' sexuality is the wish to assess one's own normality in both popular senses of the word—average and healthy. Is one impoverished or enriched by inherited ideas of how men and women should act? By laws and customs governing who may be a sexual partner and what partners may do together or separately? Lurking in much cross-cultural sex research are these questions, "If my sexual wishes or beliefs differ from my society's, which should I follow? Do other cultures offer clues?"

Therefore the social sciences abound with emotional debates about permissiveness and restrictiveness, monogamy and polygamy, gender roles, norms, deviance, and childrearing. These issues all hinge on a larger one: if certain behaviors, customs, and values occur in virtually all societies, they may be part of human nature—our biosocial inheritance.

A Search for Standards

Reporting other cultures' sexuality is almost as old as history. The ancient Hebrews and Greeks wrote about sex among their neighbors. The Roman historian Tacitus (1948) used accounts of Teutonic tribal life to argue against his society's growing permissiveness. During the great voyages of discovery in the sixteenth and seventeenth centuries, explorers and missionaries brought back from all over the world tales, true and untrue, that variously delighted and horrified their listeners—of nudity, polygamy, violent repression, harems, homosexuality, transvestism. Until the twentieth century, colonial expansion increased the flow of "missionary" (amateur) anthropology—sometimes accurate, but often inexact, fragmentary, and moralizing.

From such reports it became easy to make a case for mankind's startling sexual diversity. There were (and still are) societies where women could not reveal even their faces, others where they wore only tiny pubic aprons; where widows perished with their husbands' bodies, and where women had several husbands; where girls' labia were sewn together to ensure virginity, and where they began coitus at ten and eleven; where one homosexual act brought the death penalty, and where most men had had

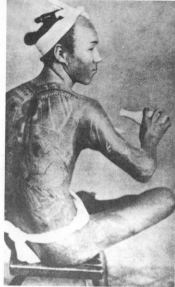
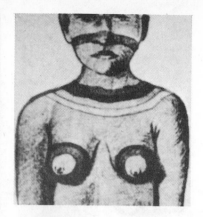

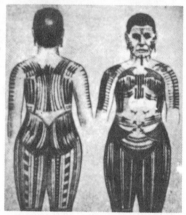

Figure 20-1 / *Some nineteenth-century founders of anthropology studied sex, marriage, and kinship as keys to social organization but many early efforts were grab-bags of non-Western sexual life that seemed shocking, even bizarre, to Victorian readers. If nothing else, they helped introduce people to the concept of cultural relativity. These are illustrations from* The Sexual Relations of Mankind, *by the pioneering Italian sexologist Paolo Mantegazza.*

homosexual experience; where few women masturbated, and where many did, sometimes with such aids as an ivory phallus or a live mink with its jaws tied shut (Ford and Beach, 1951).

In the later nineteenth century, such men as the English writer and adventurer Richard Burton (1967), pioneer sexologist Havelock Ellis (1936), and the Italian anthropologist Paolo Mantegazza (1966) collected cross-cultural sexual reports not as grab bags of anecdotes but to make a point. By showing humanity's sexual diversity, they hoped to liberalize their own society. Tacit or open envy showed in many descriptions of permissive societies, which seemed to have realized a sexual utopia.

However, those who looked beyond the West for models of sexual freedom remained a minority; most people still thought of non-Westerners as backward and promiscuous. But

scientific anthropology was developing, largely through study of sex, marriage, incest, and the family. These origins deserve a brief survey, for many of the controversies aroused then are still with us, affecting everyday behaviors and decisions.

The First Findings: Promiscuity and the Family

In the eighteenth century, a number of people theorized that through human history, sex had led to love, love to marriage, and marriage to a spirit of mutual protection and thus to civilization (Brinton, 1959). During the nineteenth century, many similar theories appeared, assuming social evolution by predict-

424

able stages, up from animalistic greed, lust, and violence. Evolutionary ideas also arose in geology (by Charles Lyell), biology (by Charles Darwin), economic history (by Karl Marx), and other fields. Some such theories are still accepted in the physical and biological sciences, but schemes of social evolution rested on two now discredited ideas: first, that animals and early man were full of unlimited aggression and lust; second, that preliterate societies were arrested at low stages of social evolution and reflected the West's past. Apparently science's job was to show how Christian Europe had risen above them, to the moral heights of the monogamous Victorian middle and upper classes (Kardiner and Preble, 1965).

Some social-evolution theories, long dead among social scientists, remain popular with laymen. For instance, in the mid-nineteenth century there appeared the theory (Bachofen, 1967) that humans had progressed from a "promiscuous horde" to a golden age of *matriarchy* (rule by women) and then fallen into dismal *patriarchy* (rule by men). Soon afterward, the Scots scholar John McLennan (1970) proposed that all societies pass through a stage of marriage by capture. In the 1870s, the American pioneer in anthropology Henry Lewis Morgan (1963) sometimes seemed to equate social progress with monogamy. All three of these notions perished among anthropologists but still have believers, even among scholars from other fields who dabble in anthropology.

The Myth of Marriage by Capture

In 1865, John McLennan's *Primitive Marriage* (1970) introduced the important and lasting concept of *exogamy,* the tendency to marry outside one's social group (family, clan, tribe). McLennan also theorized that all societies go through a period when men violently capture or abduct their mates. There have indeed been societies where some brides are abducted, in earnest or in ritual fashion, but McLennan's theory was soon demolished. Nevertheless, it appealed to the popular imagination. It is the source, a century later, of cartoons in which men in fur suits club their beloveds and drag them off by the hair to bridal lairs. This isn't the only anthropologist's fantasy to survive a thousand intellectual deaths.

Reproduced by Special Permission of PLAYBOY Magazine, copyright © 1973 by Playboy.

Morgan (1963) was correct, though, in saying that societies everywhere have kinship systems, incest taboos, and other rules about sex and marriage, and that these may be enormously complex in "primitive" (nontechnological) cultures. From the late nineteenth to mid-twentieth century, the foundation of modern cross-cultural sex research was built by such innovators as Tylor, Westermarck, Boas, Malinowski, Freud, Mead, and Kinsey.

The Englishman Edward Tylor (1832–1917) is widely considered the founder of modern anthropology. He set new high standards (1963) of evidence and emphasized *cultural relativity*, the idea that societies' values vary, and one should not judge other cultures by the standards of one's own.

Edward Westermarck (1862–1939) produced many major studies (1922) of sex and marriage. Unlike most nineteenth-century theorists, he did not see marriage as a cage for early man's presumed animal lust. Early societies, he believed, had consisted of families and groups of families; marriage had always bound people together so that they could protect their offspring during nature's longest childhood. Society had developed not through unwelcomed restraints but by the process of natural selection that shapes all biosocial life. Westermarck thus anticipated contemporary views. He also gave the definitive argument against evolutionary matriarchy theories—not the least evidence being that no matriarchical society has been found to exist in the past or present (Kardiner and Preble, 1965).

Franz Boas (1858–1942), a tough-minded skeptic, shunned emotionally attractive theories based on second-hand reports. He insisted on direct observation and precise data and set

an example as a *participant-observer*, living among a people, speaking their language, and learning to see the world through their eyes.

Bronislaw Malinowski (1884–1942) stressed *functionalism*, an idea already accepted in many other fields. Darwin had said that seals' flippers were not decorative curiosities but modifications that allowed adaptation to sea life. Malinowski argued that social customs and institutions also evolve for adaptive reasons, through the interplay of environmental, social, and psychological forces. No sexual custom should be considered merely an oddity; studying it outside its social context will produce a distorted view of it.

Malinowski was also one of the first anthropologists to try using psychodynamic ideas in cross-cultural sex research. In 1913, in *Totem and Taboo*, Freud (1952) had suggested correspondences between mental and social processes: for instance, he said people's feelings toward chiefs and gods echoed those of children toward their fathers (hence the phrase "father figures"), and that laws of exogamy resembled incest taboos. He also felt that preliterate societies showed the same mental processes and sexual-development patterns found in the West, including the Oedipus complex (see chapter 7). If this was true, he had found a way to link biological man (instinct), social man (institutions), and inner man (emotion and personality).

Malinowski (1929, 1955) went to the Trobriand Islands to learn whether "the conflicts, passions and attachments within the family vary [or] remain the same throughout humanity." He had picked a society very different from the West, one that was both *matrilineal* (descent follows the mother's family line) and *matrilocal* (married couples live with the bride's family). He studied and reported on behavior, institutions, feelings, dreams, and, in frank detail, sexuality. He found that Freud had been wrong in detail but right in principle: intense, erotically-tinged relationships pervaded the nuclear family and were crucial to individual development and to socialization—teaching society's values so that they seem second nature. A recent study using the Standard Cross Cultural Sample of world societies offers correlations confirming this view (Carroll, 1978).

Margaret Mead (1901–1978) also worked outside the West, testing the assumption that adolescence is inevitably a time of stress and conflict. She studied psychosexual development in Samoa and reported (1928) that customs and institutions there made female adolescence a period of easy transition to adulthood. Later (1935) she compared gender roles in three non-Western cultures, stressing their variety (see chapter 21). She called for greater permissiveness and gender-role flexibility in the West, ideas which more and more people were welcoming. Probably more than any other recent American, Mead popularized cultural relativism in viewing gender roles.

During the Twenties, Thirties, and Forties, many researchers studied sexual development and behavior in non-Western societies (among others, Claude Lévi-Strauss, George Devereaux, and Erik Erikson). Some, such as Robert and Helen Lynd (1959, 1963), John Dollard (1937), and Hortense Powdermaker (1971, 1966), turned anthropological techniques on their own society, and found many Westerners just as irrational in their sexual beliefs and customs as any preliterate tribe. It all depends on one's point of view.

Counting Among Strangers

An old problem in cross-cultural sex research became glaring when the studies of Kinsey et al. appeared. They upset many scientific and popular truisms and showed that common knowledge must be verified or disproven. Even many famous, influential studies by anthropologists are *impressionistic* rather than *quantified*—giving the researcher's or his informants' impressions rather than quantified frequencies and incidences of behaviors. If Kinsey et al. found it difficult to gather sex-behavior data in their own society, it is no surprise that anthropologists have greater problems in other cultures. There is still surprisingly little firm information on such basic matters as age of menarche and coital frequency outside the West. Some impressionistic studies are no doubt accurate, but deciding which ones remains a matter of individual judgment, for they lack the procedures, data, and rules of evidence usually demanded today in behavioral science.

Ford and Beach (1951) examined reports on sex behavior in almost 200 preliterate societies; their survey remains the best of its kind. But they warn that much of the information they used was impressionistic, and there are still very few quantified cross-cultural studies (Gebhard, 1968, 1971; Karlen, 1971). Moreover, even a skilled observer can be hampered or misled by a society's taboos and sexual etiquette. For instance, a society may be either permissive or restrictive about sex behavior, but quite the opposite about sexual talk (Karlen, 1971). And finally, researchers' interests and personalities affect their reports. For instance, anthropologist Ralph Linton and psychoanalyst Abram Kardiner produced a

427

thoughtful interpretation of Marquesan culture and sexuality (*The Individual and His Society*, 1939), but anthropologist Robert Suggs's more Kinseyan study produced contradictory results (*Marquesan Sexual Behavior*, 1966). When credible experts collide, bystanders can only scratch their heads. In reading cross-cultural studies, one must be both critical and open-minded.

The Social Control of Sexual Behavior

Every society has formal and informal ways of influencing and controlling sex behavior, from laws to customs to folklore. Davenport (1977) has said, "Those aspects [of sex] that are tied closely to biological foundations are conservative; those tied to the internal logic and consistency of the rest of culture are easier to alter." Some sexual and sex-related behaviors, such as menstruation and nocturnal emission, can't be socially controlled; what can be influenced is how they are viewed, experienced,

and dealt with. Other behaviors are more easily controlled. For instance, some societies allow coitus during lactation and pregnancy, while others forbid it strictly and believe that the moral, physical, or magical results are severe.

Our first step in seeing how society controls sexuality will be to look at certain acts virtually all societies discourage, to see the social limits of sexuality.

Incest: A Model of Deviance and Control

The family and the incest taboo are among the few universals of human society, and they offer a good model of the social control of sex.

We have defined incest (see chapter 12) as sexual activity between people considered too closely related by blood to marry and between certain other kin. The prohibition seems as much social as biological; everywhere it includes not only all members of the nuclear family except one's spouse but other kin, both consanguine (blood) and socially designated (Murdock, 1949b). In only a handful of soci-

---

The Beholder's Bias

The story is often told among social scientists that a famous anthropologist, whom we will call X, studied a village and found its people prudish and repressive. Later Y, equally eminent, studied the same village and reported that sex was the major local sport. X revisited the village and asked with alarm, "Why didn't you tell me all the things you told Y?" The villagers said, "Well, you didn't seem very comfortable talking about sex." They hinted, however, that they had exaggerated to Y. But why, X asked, had they exaggerated in the other direction with him? They replied, "Sex was all he wanted to talk about!"

---

eties are aunts and uncles potential sexual partners, and almost all cultures ban at least one kind of cousin.

Western societies forbid or discourage sex and marriage not only within the consanguine nuclear family but with adopted children, stepchildren, stepsiblings, uncles, aunts, and to some extent with cousins. (First-cousin marriage is forbidden by the Roman Catholic and Greek Orthodox churches and by many states' laws, but not by some states nor by the codes of Jews, Muslims, and many Protestants.) We are not among the most restrictive societies in regard to incest. Of the cultures surveyed by Ford and Beach (1951), almost three-quarters extend the taboo much further.

Incest bears a unique burden of aversion. In Shakespeare's tragedy, Hamlet raged over his mother's hasty remarriage to her dead husband's brother, "O, most wicked speed to post / With such dexterity to incestuous sheets."

Many people consider incest unthinkable and attribute it to the insane, feebleminded, and socially and morally outcast (K. Weinberg, 1976). Trobrianders, said Malinowski (1929), consider sibling incest "the prototype of all that is ethically wrong and horrible," and social pressure would probably drive offenders to commit suicide.

All over the world, incest is punished by death, imprisonment, exile, or deep scorn. Even the accidental incest of Oedipus brought him disaster (see chapter 7). In more recent literature as well, doom awaits those whose love is implicitly incestuous (Poe's "Fall of the House of Usher," 1975) or openly so (Nabokov's *Lolita*, 1972). In a lighter vein, a story by science-fiction writer Theodore Sturgeon (1967), "If All Men Were Brothers, Would You Let Your Sister Marry One?" describes a planet where incest is credited with making society and individual life perfectly happy. But

Permitted Incest

Exceptions don't prove a rule, but sometimes they clarify it. The chiefs of the Azande of Africa once allowed parent-child marriages in their royal families. In ancient Egypt, incestuous marriages occurred through ten generations of the Ptolemaic dynasty; Cleopatra was the offspring of an incestuous union and entered one herself. The royal families of ancient Hawaii, Ireland, Siam, and a few other societies have also allowed such marriages. In such cases, a few people apparently were permitted incest to perpetuate a society's ruling group and ensure political stability or as a privilege of their status (K. Weinberg, 1976). In Biblical history, it was to perpetuate their family that Lot's daughters, isolated survivors of the fall of Sodom and

Gomorrah, conspired to have coitus with their father to provide him with heirs, considering an incestuous family better than none. So the incest taboo, apparently meant to preserve the integrity of the family, has sometimes been suspended during even greater threats to the family and society. The Mormons, perhaps alone in history, once approved incest for all their community (Muncy, 1974), on the grounds that all people are descended from Adam and Eve and are therefore related anyway. In fact, the early Mormons were polygamous, so a man might marry several female relatives. The Utah legislature outlawed the Mormon marriage code in 1892, but polygamy continues among some of the devout.

the interplanetary travelers who discovered the place conspire to keep its existence secret, fearing that importing the system to earth would disrupt human life irrevocably.

Incest aversion, Freud thought (1962), occurs because eroticism tinges family relationships from early life on, so both parents and children must curb it for the sake of family cohesion. As Alex Comfort (1966) has put it, "The family is a [social] uterus from which the child must not be expelled until gestation is over." Incest can disrupt a family in ways far beyond sexual competition, causing abuse of parental authority, favoritism, competition, and jealousy (K. Weinberg, 1976).

The family fills many needs—physical protection, economic support, emotional nurture, education, socialization. And throughout history, most people have probably depended to some degree on secondary kin as well for support, even survival. The rivalries and role confusions of incest can disrupt the extended as well as the nuclear family; therefore incest taboos universally extend beyond the nuclear family, though with less intensity. Apparently societies everywhere have felt that limiting sexuality seems a small price to pay for supporting the family's integrity.

Moreover, marrying into other families has social benefits. First, a family has its own miniature culture; in marriage, the partners bring their family cultures together and pass on some of both, in a kind of social cross-fertilization. Second, marriages linking families and social groups create a wide network of bonds for defense and survival, through family feeling and kinship obligations. For these reasons, rules governing incest and exogamy may well have developed very early in human history as means of social survival.

There have been several efforts in recent times to encourage incest, relax its definition, or at least remove some of the stigma attached to it. The Guyon Society, named after a nineteenth-century judge of France's supreme court (Guyon, 1934, 1950), advocates childhood sexuality and doesn't discourage incest; one of their sayings is: "Sex before eight, otherwise too late." In 1977 a government committee in Sweden recommended abolishing all laws forbidding incest except where minors are involved (MacNamara and Sagarin, 1977). Actually, the Swedish proposal does not erase the incest taboo but puts an age limit on it. If the law changes, time will show whether custom follows.

The study of incest shows that while human sexuality has astounding variety, it also has some universal rules, learned and internalized early, in the intimacy of the family. Culture-bound moralizing distorts the picture of human sexuality, but so does extreme relativism, the belief that all sexual limits are arbitrary and changeable. Anthropologist Lévi-Strauss, in an instructive overstatement, has said that people live in culture as animals live in nature, and society's lasting law is that when it comes to sex, one may not do exactly as one pleases. People's first, crucial lesson in this is that we may love our close relatives, but not as sexual partners and mates.

Other Universal Deviances

Defining Deviance. Many sexual behaviors besides incest are forbidden or discouraged virtually everywhere (see chapter 12). They are, in the strict sense of the word, *deviant*—never the most frequent acts of the majority. Some are also deviant in the looser sense of being

430

looked down on or merely tolerated. Almost all exceptions to the universal deviances (in the stricter sense), such as permitted incest, involve special situations.

What societies call deviant often depends on the sex, age, social class, and marital state of the person who performs an act. In fact, many non-Western customs and practices are thought strange and shocking in the West because they rise from unfamiliar linkages of sexual activity with age, defined maturity, and other social factors. For instance, virtually all societies expect men to show more overt sexual desire and initiative than women; some societies expect greater female eroticism and initiative than ours, but they expect even more from males (Gebhard, 1971). The norm of greater male aggression often extends beyond sex acts to many gender-role behaviors. In some societies, the male-female differences are great in number and scope, in others relatively small (Broude and Greene, 1976).

Concepts of Modesty. The concept of modesty is virtually universal (H. Ellis, 1936). Almost everywhere, people are expected to cover parts of their bodies, especially the genitals and particularly after reaching sexual maturity. For a woman not to do so is considered a sexual invitation (Ford and Beach, 1951). Our society legally forbids exhibiting some parts of the body, though changing customs have altered the definition through history, except for exposing the genitals, which has always been forbidden. There is also a universal tendency for couples to seek total or partial privacy during sex acts.

Age-Related Deviance. Age is a major factor in defining sexual norms and deviance. In most societies, each generation tends to seek sex and marriage partners within its own ranks. Not every person does so, but many of the exceptions follow a pattern. Young men may be initiated by older women, and young women by older men; but where there is a great age difference between partners, the older one is usually the man, often one with great power or prestige (Goode, 1964; Murdock, 1949b). One reason may be that females mature earlier than males. Another may be the tendency in many higher species for the highest-ranking males to have the widest choice of sexual partners; men who are older and better able to support partners may have an advantage in choice. In our society and probably most others, as men age, their pool of available partners expands. Men of thirty may date or marry women from eighteen to thirty; men of forty may find partners from eighteen to forty. But with time, women's pool of potential partners decreases. People who do find partners outside the socially expected age cohorts may well be considered deviant to some degree.

Our society, like many others, tends to consider overt or even private sexual activity by older people inappropriate, unnatural, immoral, or sick; this feeling may be stronger in restrictive societies. Children or even adults may think, "My mommy and daddy don't do that thing." Many people in their twenties think old starts at forty; typically they don't think of their parents as sexual, and certainly don't see their grandparents that way (Pocs et al., 1977). The joking stereotype of the dirty old man is usually at best a left-handed compliment. The phrase dirty old lady also exists, but is used far less commonly, since society tends to see females as sexually less driven and less active than males.

The West has historically considered the

very young, like the old, relatively nonsexual. The innocence of childhood was so deeply believed in a century ago that sexually active children were thought the victims of genetic taint. In restrictive societies many children are indeed relatively unknowing and inexperienced, but many are so out of fear, guilt, or lack of opportunity rather than lack of interest or unresponsiveness (Martinson, 1973).

Sociosexual maturity, however defined, is important everywhere, but it doesn't necessarily or even usually coincide with physical maturity. In traditional Marquesan society (Davenport, 1965; Suggs, 1966), coitus probably began at eight or nine for girls, perhaps earlier for boys. Many people in our society feel that marriage, not puberty, means a person is sexually of age. In many states, coitus with a willing "child" in her middle teens is statutory (legal) rape, though she may be legally allowed to marry. In maturity, again, there is a sex difference. A young female who experiences coitus may be considered a victim, a young male lucky.

The very young are everywhere protected from the full impact of adult sexuality. Even very permissive societies forbid coitus between adults and quite small children. In our society, an adult who has even minimal erotic contact (touching) with a child is commonly the object of rage, contempt, and, if prosecuted and convicted, severe punishment (see chapter 12). The child molester is despised even by other imprisoned sex offenders (Gebhard et al., 1965).

Choosing Mates and Marrying. Some sex-related events define norms and deviance in ways that surprise Westerners. We think of betrothal and marriage as events that follow or

even confirm maturity. In some societies and in the Western past, people have been betrothed or married in childhood, even before birth. Of course these marriages are family and social alliances, meant to be consummated after childhood. Americans have traditionally assumed that marriage permits active sexuality. But until rather recently in some parts of the West, such as certain areas in rural Sweden, a betrothed couple would wait until the girl was pregnant—ensuring a fertile match—before marrying (Linnér, personal communication).

Class and caste also affect people's choice of sex and marriage partners. Rules of exogamy require marriage outside certain social groups; in some societies (especially larger ones), there are also rules of *endogamy* (*endo* = within), which encourage marrying within one's caste, class, or clan. Geographical location often plays a part; people may be encouraged to marry within or outside their village, neighborhood, or town.

In the West, people tend not to cross lines of social class in finding sexual partners. Still fewer do so when they marry. A lawyer and a waitress, a debutante and a mechanic, are less rather than more likely to have a sexual relationship; they are still less likely to wed.*

Racial, ethnic, and religious identity also influence choices in sex and marriage. This results partly from formal or informal sanctions, partly from lack of social contact between groups, and partly from social customs and differences that tend to push individuals apart

---

* This excludes considering work-related sexual involvements where employer-employee erotic relations exist. These may be exploitive or volitional; they are not typically socially approved.

rather than together (see chapter 16). A stigma still falls on many who marry outside their groups.

Marital status strongly affects who may be a sexual partner. All societies have some form of marriage, and it always involves sexual access and sexual obligations. Our society, like many others, has traditionally forbidden premarital and extramarital coitus. These rules have steadily relaxed in many parts of the world during this century (Goode, 1964); nevertheless, such acts are still widely forbidden by law and frowned on by society. As with other sexual behaviors, some exceptions are allowed or tolerated, formally or informally—for instance, if a spouse is sexually inactive or if the non-marital partner is a prostitute. Some societies approve of coitus by the still-unmarried and the formerly married, and even of extramarital coitus with certain people under certain circumstances (Broude and Greene, 1976). But the vast majority of people around the world assume that adult sexuality should center on marriage, and that spouses should turn to each other first for sexual satisfaction. That is indeed what usually happens (Kinsey et al., 1948, 1953).

Other Sex Behaviors. Unlimited sexual activity is forbidden everywhere (Ford and Beach, 1951; Murdock, 1949b). With one or two pos-

---

Who Is a Potential Partner?

If you are looking for a sexual partner or mate, you theoretically have your entire social world to choose from. However, society forbids—and discourages you from even wanting—a large part of it. Your choices diminish something like this:

1. All possible partners.

2. Exclude those of same sex.

3. Exclude those of inappropriate age.

4. Exclude those of inappropriate family, caste, religion, nationality, or race.

5. Exclude those of very different educational level, social background, or life-style.

6. Now select someone you find attractive, interesting, and compatible.

It now seems that you might be lucky to find a partner.

sible exceptions, even very permissive societies have some definition of what the West calls promiscuity. Some definitions are far stricter than ours, some much looser. But in most societies, any individual has relatively few potential sexual partners (see page 433). The list of possible partners is further narrowed by customs, opportunity, and personal preference. The prostitute, who goes far beyond the usual limits in accepting partners, is probably universally deviant.

Rape seems to be almost everywhere condemned and punished (Henslin and Sagarin, 1977); obviously society is not served by sexual violence and its consequences. Many incidents of rape involve real or perceived deviance on the part of victim or perpetrator (the victim is known or thought to be sexually deviant or "promiscuous" or the rapist is a criminal in other ways). Some societies more or less tolerate rape if the woman belongs to an enemy people; that is, violence against enemy women, as against enemy men, may be condoned. People often seem to treat the enemy and outsiders like a hostile species, not protected by the usual social or biosocial limits (Brownmiller, 1975). Many rape victims are, of course, simply unfortunate, and in some societies being raped stigmatizes a woman.

Chastity is nowhere an accepted way of life for most adults. Our society and others have accepted or even required chastity of some people, especially those with a religious calling or ritual tasks. Chastity may also be expected during menstruation, pregnancy, or lactation, before combat, and on other occasions. But lifelong chastity is rare everywhere. The West has linked chastity with not being married and made the usual male-female distinction *(double*

standard) in sexual expectations. It has a social role and a term ("spinster" or "old maid") for an unmarried woman, who is assumed to be chaste; she is thought a bit odd but tolerable. The lifelong bachelor may be thought a bit odd, but he is not necessarily assumed to be chaste (D. Abramowitz, personal communication).

Sexual Identity and Gender Role. Some societies have special social niches for transvestites, effeminate male homosexuals, and masculine female homosexuals. Except perhaps in some cases of transvestites filling religious roles (as in some Siberian and American Indian cultures), such people are often looked down on or, at best, viewed with ambivalence (Karlen, 1971). No society encourages denial of one's biological sex and the gender role and orientation that usually go with it. Nowhere, apparently, do parents say, "It's just the same to me if my child dresses, acts, and lives like the opposite sex."

Noncoital Acts. As preferred adult practices, noncoital sex acts are apparently frowned on everywhere. This doesn't mean that such acts are necessarily forbidden or even disapproved of, but that an adult is considered deviant if the act becomes his major or exclusive sexual outlet (Davenport, 1977; Ford and Beach, 1951; Karlen, 1971; Kinsey et al., 1948, 1953; Marshall and Suggs, 1971).

Homosexual acts are utterly forbidden in some societies. This has been true in the West throughout much of its history. Many cultures, however, allow or even accept homosexual acts at certain ages and with certain partners—as long as they do not, in the long run, interfere with coitus, marriage, and family life. Also, some conditions lessen or remove the stigma from homosexual acts. For instance, such acts may be tolerated among people deprived of heterosexual partners (in harems or jails). Some cultures categorize people as either men or nonmen, including among the latter both women and boys; these cultures more or less accept a man having genital relations with women or boys, but not with other mature men (Karlen, 1971).

Oral and anal intercourse are common or encouraged in some societies, forbidden or virtually unknown in others (Ford and Beach, 1951; Gebhard, 1971). Oral sex seems more widely accepted and practiced than anal sex. Attitudes toward both have fluctuated through Western history. Today probably a majority of Americans have practiced fellatio or cunnilingus at some time. This is a great change from the behavior patterns at the turn of this century (Kinsey et al., 1948, 1953). But probably in no culture does a person escape negative comment if oral or anal sex becomes a predominant or exclusive sexual practice.

Masturbation is forbidden or scorned in some societies, approved in others if done by children or occasionally by adults. But probably in all societies, adults who make masturbation their chief outlet are both uncommon and looked down on (Kinsey et al., 1948, 1953). The same is true of bestiality, sadomasochism, and many other uncommon sex behaviors (Ford and Beach, 1951).

Universal Norms

After all these universal deviances, the list of universal norms seems short. These are things done by the majority of people the majority of the time, and everywhere approved.

Heterosexual coitus is everywhere the commonest, most sought-after, and most approved adult sex behavior (Ford and Beach, 1951; Gebhard, 1971). Except perhaps in a few very permissive societies, the majority of adult coitus probably occurs within marriage. Morton Hunt (1959) has said that "when the wishful thinking of the young and the envious reminiscence of the old are put aside, the unglamorous truth is that . . . nonvirgins under twenty have intercourse only once every five to ten weeks, and those over twenty only once every three weeks or so. In comparison, the stodgily married live in riotous debauchery." The figures have changed since these words were written, but the basic comparison still holds.

A majority of the world's societies formally allow a man to have more than one wife at a time (Ford and Beach, 1951). Few men, though, can afford to meet family obligations with more than one wife; plural marriage is limited largely to the affluent and privileged and to special situations (Mair, 1971). Concubines and other secondary sexual partners are allowed to men in many societies when the wife is pregnant or when the husband must be away from home for long periods. Only a few societies allow women more than one husband.

To some people, all these facts about social limits on sexuality are reassuring, to others a promise of sexual limitation or dullness. The exceptions and rule-breaking that do exist may seem either threatening or a hope of sexual liberation.

There is no apparent harm to an individual or society in many universally deviant acts. But heterosexual coitus and the family have obvious advantages to the species whose young must survive the longest, most dependent childhood

435

Figure 20-2 / *The "children's hour" at the Oneida community. This nineteenth-century American experiment in communal living—including the sharing of sexual partners—survived for several generations, perhaps partly because it had social structures minimizing competition and conflicts about labor, money, and sex.*

in nature, and whose females are sometimes vulnerable or physically limited by bearing and rearing those children. The family has provided physical and social protection, and many sexual sanctions have probably developed to promote its formation and integrity (Goode, 1970; Murdock, 1949b). It has been argued that engaging in nonreproductive sex might now benefit our species as a means of population control, and that some traditional functions of the family are no longer as important as they once were. But millions of years of evolution have encouraged reproductive sexual patterns and the behaviors and social institutions that support them. They probably will not be easily reversed, regardless of what anyone thinks could be or should be.

Sanctions: Keeping and Breaking the Rules

Freedom and Limits

Some people view any sexual expression as natural, and sex behavior ideally a matter entirely of personal choice. Others feel that sexual expression, by its nature, threatens social order. Still others believe that only within society's limits are people truly human; social

guidelines help them develop and satisfy needs. Our own view is that the individual and society develop by interaction, each depending and drawing on the other. Customs and laws, we believe, channel and limit sexual desires but can also offer ways to fulfill them without extreme social and interpersonal conflict (Petras, 1973).

Certain social institutions and experiments have been pointed to in support of all these views. For instance, many sexual communes of the past decade were based on the assumption that society so restricts sexuality that special communities must be created to free people from them (few saw these assumptions borne out). At another extreme, the custom of the chaperone arose from the view that human sex drive is so strong that only powerful social controls can restrain it.

Of course, some young couples evade chaperones, and only in fantasy is there a place where anything goes. Even among swingers there are explicit or unspoken rules about who may do what to whom (Bartell, 1971). In the United States today, few people believe that such direct external control as chaperonage is necessary; they count on internal controls (conscience, shame, and the wish for approval) to keep sex from disrupting social institutions.

Obviously there are sexual rules everywhere, and everywhere they are sometimes broken. People do commit incest and rape, take unapproved partners, engage in nonmarital and adult-child relations. It may seem logical that the more restrictive the rules, the greater the desire to violate them, but this isn't necessarily true (Karlen, 1971); society not only punishes deviance, it rewards compliance. And nowhere are starkly deviant acts, however defined, widespread, and nowhere are they common or accepted models for behavior or the aims of childrearing.

Sanctions

The forces that maintain the social controls of sex are *sanctions*. A sanction can be positive (encouragement, esteem, or material reward) or negative (shame, ridicule, isolation, or punishment). Positive and negative sanctions and deviance are abstract ideas of social science. In daily life, these words stand for cherished values, compulsions, shame, and defiance—the private and public dramas of doing or refusing to do what others expect. They can mean being proud and admired, being laughed at, having a bad reputation, or being refused courtesy, housing, a job, citizenship, or physical freedom.

Civil law is only one of society's sanctions, and not always the strongest one. There are also religious laws, ethical values, mores (customs), folkways, humor, spoken and unspoken beliefs and attitudes. These all affect a person from infancy till old age, in myriad direct and indirect ways. The social controls of sex are an integral part of a culture, absorbed through daily socialization till most people think of

---

The Weapon of Laughter

Konrad Lorenz stressed that animals are more afraid of, and more aggressive toward, a deviant of their own species than toward a member of another species. You can observe gulls attack *en masse* an individual that acts or looks abnormal—say, one that was beaten so badly in a fight that it no longer walks or flies normally. It's what Lorenz called a spook reaction. Ask a person to draw a spook, and he draws a distorted human. I believe that our rejection of [effeminate] homosexuals, while in part a cultural phenomenon, may have such a deep root. Look at the reaction to stammerers, who distort normal speech behavior. I can always predict when people will laugh while watching films of animals; it happens when they're embarrassed at seeing themselves in distorted forms.

Laughter is one of the many means that humans use, as social animals, to control deviance, and it may be a signal system with biological roots. When one's behavior elicits contemptuous laughter, one tries to conform.

—Niko Tinbergen (condensed from Karlen, *Sexuality and Homosexuality*, 1971)

them as natural or even as part of themselves; sanctions are then said to be *internalized*.

In fact, there is sometimes a great gap between laws and informal sexual codes. Kinsey et al. (1948) said that if all existing sex laws were enforced, 95 percent of American men would go to jail. These men and many women have broken laws against fornication, adultery, oral-genital intercourse, homosexual acts, etc. In many states, husbands and wives can be sent to jail for performing oral-genital or anal-genital intercourse in their own bedrooms, but very few people seem eager to enforce such statutes. In fact, the enforcement of many sex-control laws seems a rarity. Estimates of how many homosexual acts end in court convictions range from one in 30,000 (Kinsey et al., 1948) to one in 6,000,000 (Schur, 1965).

Our restrictive formal tradition has left some very stringent sexual rules in the law books. But we also have a strong informal tradition of tolerating private behavior. Queen Victoria is said to have declared that she didn't care what people did as long as they didn't do it in the streets and frighten the horses. It should hardly surprise us that out of sight usually means out of court. Our pluralistic society seems to satisfy the conservative by keeping restrictive laws on the books and to satisfy the permissive by usually punishing only flagrant lawbreakers. This can be viewed as hypocrisy, as tact, or as social efficiency.

The punishments for performing forbidden sex acts are very severe; often this is because more than one norm has been violated (Karlen, 1971). In our society, a homosexual act is a no; so is a public sex act. A public homosexual act is a double no. Rape is a big no, sex relations with children is a very big no; raping a child is an enormous no.

A yes may almost cancel out a no. Consider the adolescent boy who has sexual relations with an older woman. The alleged asexuality of youth has been violated, but the expectation that males be sexually arousable, active, and experienced has been fulfilled. The reaction may be dismissing the matter with a nod—although, in some people, an ambivalent one.

There have been sexual sanctions involving ethnic, racial, religious, and social-class groups. A pregnant, unmarried, middle-class girl may be sympathized with as emotionally disturbed, a pregnant, unmarried, poor girl punished as delinquent. Alleged or actual coitus between black men and white women has led to many atrocities, and only in recent years have interracial coitus and marriage become legal in much of the United States.

Many inconsistencies result from a gap or even a clash between *overt* (open) *mores* and *covert* (hidden) *mores*. What a person thinks wrong in principle when speaking in public he may shrug at in private practice. Consider adultery by a woman whose husband is alcoholic, abusive, and irresponsible. A neighbor, asked in a questionnaire about adultery, may say it destroys families and society and call for a deterrent law against it. But asked about her neighbor's adultery, she may say, "With a husband like that, I don't really blame her."

Our society, in its transition to greater permissiveness, often shows such contradictions. A woman may condemn nonmarital coitus to her teenage daughter, approve it for a younger but married teenager, accept it for the widowed, be mildly accusatory of it by the divorced, yet expect it in most adults on the grounds that it is natural or for the sake of mental health.

As we saw in examining sex behaviors (chapter 11), the United States contains many subcultures, and sexual attitudes and behavior vary among religions and ethnic groups, urban and rural people, and socioeconomic classes. Early attitudes and behavior sometimes outlast changes in life-style. For instance, a man from a blue-collar family (Kinsey et al., 1948) may become a judge but retain his early belief that coitus is more normal than masturbation for a boy of fourteen. His colleague in the next courtroom, who comes from a college-educated, middle-class home, may hold the opposite view.

Attitudes tend to change with age and marital status. A single young person may think laws against adultery are pointless laws of sexual property. After ten years as a spouse, he may feel more in tune with traditional restraints. Ten years later, after experiencing harsh marital strains, he may accept adultery as an unfortunate necessity or even a personal liberation. On the other hand, a schoolmate of his may have always been against legally controlling private adult sex behavior—yet never have broken one traditional stricture himself. And although the "generation gap" in sexual attitudes is probably smaller than adolescents and young adults think it is (Walsh, 1970), being a spouse and a parent (and thus being responsible for the consequences of children's sexual activity) seems in itself to reduce overt permissiveness (R. Bell and Buerkle, 1961).

Overview

Sexual regulation is basic to all societies. Some regulations seem to be universal, and they can be explained as adaptations that promote lasting sexual, marital, and childrearing bonds. If one makes a continuum of world cultures, from restrictive to permissive, our society is now probably somewhere around the middle (Ford and Beach, 1951). Most Western nations have, like us, been taking a more permissive stance in this century. Right now there are pressures in both directions about coitus, cohabitation, abortion, divorce, childrearing, gender roles, pornography, prostitution—almost every aspect of sexuality.

One reason for looking at other societies is to see whether any set of customs and values allows a more happy, healthful, and productive life. But there is no proof that any particular sexual way of life produces greater individual satisfaction or social advantage. There are only more or less informed opinions. Before giving ours, we should like to present two short reminders from history.

Almost two centuries ago, France dropped its old legal system and began living under Napoleon's Civil Code, which allowed divorce and consenting private homosexual acts by adults. Many people expected the breakup of families and a rampage of deviance. But relatively few people applied for divorce, and most homosexuals kept their orientation secret, and they were still harrassed by police and other citizens (Karlen, 1971).

A similar anticlimax followed both the passage of the first United States law permitting abortion, in Hawaii in 1970, and the 1973 U.S. Supreme Court ruling that left the decision to abort to the woman. Some people predicted the collapse of all sexual restraints. But the only significant change was that abortions were done legally and safely rather than illegally and dangerously (Diamond et al., 1972; Steinhoff and Diamond, 1977).

Both cases show that laws do not order society about; rather, they interact with other

439

sanctions, formal and informal. Many unpopular laws lie unenforced, and we doubt that laws alone prompt or prevent much sex behavior. This century's trend toward permissiveness has not been caused by legal changes. Ovid accurately said that one custom is worth a thousand laws.

We do not mean that laws are unimportant. Four centuries ago, certain acts, now legal in some states, were punished by burning at the stake. We mean that law is only one agent of sexual regulation. Recently some archaic laws have been repealed, but conservative movements have also risen in reaction, and there are still strong social pressures against sexual victimless crimes—violations of sex-control laws by consenting adults (Coleman, 1978).

Some experts and laymen fiercely oppose relaxing sexual regulations; some others are uncertain. Even small relaxations of sex-control laws bring cries about degeneracy, the derogation of love, and the decay of civilization. However, many experts in psychiatry, psychology, law, sociology, penology, and related fields have for several decades recommended relaxing our formal sanctions (*U.C.L.A. Law Review,* 1966). They suggest that since socialization and informal sanctions remain strong, changing certain harsh laws is a necessary humane step. We agree with the increasingly popular idea that sexual behavior between consenting adults should be guided by conscience rather than law.

Our society's strong informal limits on many sex behaviors are still so powerful that we may be living with some legal overkill. We believe, in fact, that society has far to go to make sex the source of joy and fulfillment it can be. It is possible, of course, that continuing to transfer sex control from law to choice will cause social damage we cannot foresee. But long-standing problems with divorce, illegitimacy, and lack of fulfillment in eroticism and relationships suggest that we need not more sanctions but greater knowledge about sexuality and more emotional comfort with the subject.

Review, Discuss, Decide

1. Are you surprised at how much control society tends to exert on your sexual behavior? Need it do so? How strictly? Why?
2. What formal and informal sanctions do or could affect your sex behavior? How?
3. Which of society's prohibitions do you believe are justified? Which are not?
4. Do you feel there have been times when social rules about sex unnecessarily limited your life? When they helped and guided it?
5. Are there any social attitudes or laws you would like to see changed? Which ones, and why?
6. Do you recall any conflict about sexuality between yourself and another person that seemed to result from differences in cultural backgrounds?

21 Gender Roles

Why are some things considered masculine, feminine, or neutral?

Why do men have greater power and prestige than women?

Which role behaviors are or aren't easily changed by the way children are raised?

How are gender roles related to sex behaviors?

In the past two decades, debate has revived and intensified on a major issue of our era—the expectations, training, and opportunities offered to men and women. Women's rights and opportunities now receive more attention, but since the sexes are interdependent, complementary issues are raised for men.

The fundamental question is the degree to which we are persons or are female persons and male persons. This has been taken up by women's groups, professional organizations, and scientific societies. Some very important social issues are at stake. What people decide is appropriate for each sex will deeply affect their lives and their childrens'—how they live and work, how they educate and are educated, and how they conduct relationships. It is not within the province of this book to explore in detail the social and political aspects of these matters. We will, however, examine basic questions and information about gender roles.

Definitions

A *role* is a part played by an actor; the word is often used by sociologists for the behavior expected of an individual in a given social situation (Gross et al., 1958). One may play a role in one's own eyes, in others' eyes, in action, or in any combination of these. Some sociologists believe that roles clarify and simplify communication; being able to predict another's behavior and knowing what is expected of oneself can ease social intercourse.

Some roles, such as those conferring class or prestige, are *achieved*. Others, such as sex and race, are *ascribed;* they result automatically from unchangeable, visible characteristics (Dahlström and Liljeström, 1971). Those for males and females are called *gender roles* (see chapter 7), their content *masculine* or *feminine.* The term *sex role* is also often used, but we prefer to use the word gender for the social aspects of being biologically male or female.

The word role is sometimes used very loosely today. It is a metaphor suggesting that much of life is performed (rather than genuine), and that society is a stage for learned behavior. But gender roles and other social roles often are not felt as performances. People internalize much socially learned behavior and see it as natural or even necessary. And much so-called role behavior actually rises from the interaction of biological, social, and psychological development.

There is still uncertainty and argument about the degree to which many behaviors reflect inherent sex differences, social and individual learning, or combinations of these. Exploring the subject calls for as much clarity in terms as possible (see chapter 7). Several terms are now used so loosely that they have different meanings to many people.

One of these words is *stereotyped*. Biologists use the word for genetically programmed behavior; social scientists use it for socially learned behavior. Originally a stereotype was a picture viewed in a stereopticon, a nineteenth-century viewing machine; many stereotypes were idealized rather than realistic renderings of famous sights. The term took on a vaguely pejorative ring, but all societies pass on attitudes and behavior patterns. Stereotypes are not all harmful or arbitrary, and each should be viewed independently. For instance, the American stereotype of tea drinking as feminine or genteel has no serious social implications. Another social stereotype, that women are incompetent at mathematics and business, has serious consequences.

The terms machismo, sexism, chauvinism, and feminism are often used in discussing gender roles. *Machismo* is a complex of masculine attitudes and behaviors originally observed in certain Latin American and Mediterranean cultures. It includes courage, bravado, pride in being male, and protectiveness of females. It is now often used for almost anything proudly or exclusively male or masculine, and can be either positive or derogatory. Such indiscriminate and imprecise usage often obscures whether a behavior is a sex difference or part of

a gender role. We prefer to use the word only in its original, more precise sense, in the context of a particular culture area.

The word *sexist* parallels the word *racist*. *Chauvinism* means excessive pride in one's own country and hostility to other places and peoples; recently the word has been extended to attitudes toward the opposite sex. Perhaps some people do regard the opposite sex as they do people of other nationalities and races, but there may also be differences between the ways people view these "others"; there are no precise studies to prove either belief. We would rather know and understand any differences than lump them together under umbrella terms.

Feminism is a theory and social movement aimed at changing or eliminating feminine stereotypes and equalizing females' and males' rights and opportunities. It tends to see all feminine stereotypes as detrimental. As with the term machismo, the tone of voice or the context may make the word or its adjectival form, *feminist*, derogatory, complimentary, or neutral.

Gender Roles and Expectations

Biology, Society, and Interaction

We must briefly review some points covered earlier (chapter 7). Since the Twenties, a number of people have said that most or even all sex differences except those which medical schools call "the plumbing" are socially learned. These people are significant in number among both scholars and society at large. Another group of scholars and laymen sees direct biological causes for many or most sex differences. The dispute over these views has become widespread and heated. Unfortunately, many of the basic issues in such arguments remain unspoken.

Many people feel that admitting there are any inherent sex differences other than the sexualia amounts to *biological determinism*. It arouses feelings about innate weaknesses or superiority, unalterable defects or powers. It creates fears that people cannot make free choices and direct their own lives. There is also fear that proof of traits being innate may be socially and politically abused. For instance, sociologist Alice Rossi said in 1973 that most feminists were calling for "a rejection of any physiological as opposed to a culturally conditioned basis to sex differences [out of concern that] any evidence of physiological influences will be taken as grounds for the perpetuation of sexual inequalities in family, political, and occupational roles." She herself cautioned this rejection might be premature, and more recently conceded (Rossi, 1977) that sexual development elaborates on some given sex differences.

The belief that social convention and tradition alone determine males' and females' behavior is *social determinism*. Some people fear this viewpoint as well, for it implies that there are no limits to the ways and degree to which society can manipulate people. Furthermore, if there actually is a core of biological human nature, attempts to override it with social conditioning may cause conflict and suffering to individuals and society.

Therefore discussions about sex differences and sex roles often arouse passionate arguments

that give evidence a low priority. Extreme views offer a choice between the tyranny of the genes and the tyranny of social and political engineers. As we said in chapter 7, we do not think one need choose between these extremes. We believe that biology predisposes a person to act in certain ways; it sets ranges of potential development that may or may not be realized, depending on the environment (Diamond, 1965, 1977b, 1979a). As Tiger and Shepher (1975) have said, "Biology is not destiny, it is a statistical probability." Genetic codes determine some phenomena firmly, others loosely; all people die, but when and of what varies enormously, and depends in part on the individual's interaction with his environment.

To put it another way, behaviors and traits can be described as falling on bell-shaped curves (Figure 21-1). The curves for males and females will overlap not at all for some things (ejaculation, breast feeding), somewhat for others (body weight, nurturing behavior), and virtually completely for others (memory ability). Most behaviors and traits probably are not polar opposites, exclusive to men or to women, but tendencies greater in one sex or another (Diamond, 1977b).

Many views on gender roles are held on emotional grounds, argued on ideological grounds, and defended with selected research that supports the ideology. We repeat that there is a need for definitive research. In fact, debates are often based on inadequate reports in the mass media and on impassioned personal testimonies. Some arguments rise from disagreement over facts, others from disagreement over values—but these go together, since there is virtually no fact on this subject to which people do not attach a value or attitude.

Symbolic Role Differences

To determine that something is masculine or feminine (socially learned as part of a gender role) one must determine that it is not biologically given. One way to do this is to observe whether it varies or is consistent among individuals, among societies, and throughout history. Many differences between males' and females' behavior, however passionately adhered to, change over time, so they are clearly aspects of gender roles. A couple of centuries ago, a fashionable Don Juan might have worn face makeup and ruffles; a century ago, the wives of ranchers and sodbusters wore cumbersome skirts. Clearly much gender-role behavior is functional chiefly as social communication; it is symbolic of sex differences and closely sex-linked differences.

When one looks back through time and at other societies, the variety of some gender-role behaviors is striking. Yet some gender-role differences are the same in most or all societies. This is evident in the division of labor. In societies everywhere, many tasks are sex-typed (assigned either to males or to females). There are obvious physical reasons for some of this sex-typing. Women everywhere feed the young; humans are mammals, there has been no substitute for mother's milk till recently, and in any case, females everywhere tend to spontaneously feed and nurture the young (Maccoby and Jacklin, 1974). Men virtually everywhere do the mining and smelting, which demand great muscular strength and muscular endurance. However, not all tasks are sex-typed because of physical sex differences; many ap-

Figure 21-1 / *Many traits can be thought of as falling along a bell-shaped curve in distribution. Some traits, such as ejaculation and breast feeding, occur only in people of one sex. Some, such as relatively high body weight and nurturing behavior, occur more often or more strongly in one sex, but also appear in the other. And some traits, such as memory ability, seem to occur equally in both sexes.*

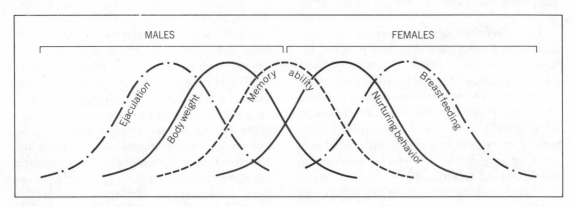

parently are sex-typed because they are related to other tasks that do involve sex differences. For instance, in most societies, fine metal work is done by men, and women usually make cooking fires and preserve food. These sex-typings seem to be symbolic extensions of the more fundamental sex-typing of mining and child-feeding (Murdock and Provost, 1973).

There has been a growing movement in Western society for about a century to allow both sexes access to most or all activities. The traditional, symbolic sex-typing of certain tasks—and the differences in pay and prestige that go with them—have caused some individuals to suffer emotional, social, and economic hardship. There is still dispute about whether certain tasks are performed better by some or many members of either sex.

Social Expectations

Every society ascribes different roles to males and females. These gender roles permeate almost all human interactions. Both males and females have many expectations of their own and the other sex, and these are crucial in forming and developing an identity, self-image, and sexual and nonsexual relationships. They also affect how one perceives and lives such roles as friend, lover, spouse, and parent.

Gender roles, like other roles, are socially functional. They allow one to know how to act and what to expect from people; every social encounter need not be explored from scratch. Just as one expects different things from a general and a private, a stranger or a friend, one has different expectations of a male and a fe-

The Types of Gender Roles

Experts and laymen have taken various ideological positions on gender roles, basing their stands on evidence, conviction, or both. Views on gender roles can be seen as belonging to any of six categories (Dahlström, 1971).

1. *Traditional.* Men and women are in many ways different kinds of beings. Their different strengths and weaknesses are reflected by their different status, rights, and duties.
2. *Early Liberal.* All individuals are unique, of equal value, and have the same rights. However, the sexes have different obligations and duties.
3. *Romantic.* Men and women differ in their capabilities and roles, but these have equal social value.
4. *Communistic.* This is like early liberal, but proposes to achieve full equality of value between the sexes.
5. *Radical.* There should be absolute legal, social, and sexual equality of the sexes in every sphere of life.
6. *Moderate.* Two social functions must be performed by both men and women. They must forego or maintain a family, and they must pursue individual careers. Each person, however, may do this as he or she thinks best. Dual careers (in and out of the home) are options, not requirements, and one may make different decisions about this at different times of life or of family development.

445

male. Fulfilling role expectations can give a feeling of competence and success, and often it brings rewards from others.

For the same reasons, roles have disadvantages. They can be barriers to forming and expanding one's personality, activities, and relationships. They can thus be psychological and social pigeonholes into which people feel forced. A general may sometimes envy the private's lesser responsibility, a woman prefer activities considered masculine. Many people sometimes wish they could choose their roles or act and be judged independent of them. However, in other situations, the same person might be content to benefit from a role—for instance, "She's very efficient in business, but since she's a woman, we can probably count on her being warm and sensitive to clients." Or, "He doesn't seem very forceful, but he'll probably feel he has to meet the challenge of the new work."

Some expectations are similar for both sexes; both mothers and fathers are expected to be nurturing, if in different ways and degrees. Other expectations differ; men are widely expected to be independent, assertive, strong, tenacious, and decisive, women to be dependent, accommodating, emotionally expressive, vulnerable, and flexible. Some people don't fit their roles; they and their partners must work out agreements and accommodations if they are to avoid conflict.

Sometimes people prefer deviance from roles in a partner, sometimes not. A man may welcome his wife taking greater financial responsibility and sexual initiative; he may nevertheless discourage her departure from housework. Similarly, a woman may welcome her husband taking greater domestic responsibility and being less sexually assertive, yet discourage his leaving a high-paying or high-status job or dislike having to rouse his sexual desire.

As a relationship continues, following or departing from role expectations can be crucial to its success. Some individuals and relationships are more flexible than others. Sometimes social background has an influence; lower-class people tend to tolerate deviations from anticipated roles less than middle-class people (recall the discussion of masturbation and coitus in chapters 9 and 11).

In sexual situations, many people act on unspoken expectations; until a couple know each other well, they have no choice. In a pick-up or date situation or early in a relationship, they ask themselves, "What should I do now?" and "What does he or she think I should do?" and "If I do X, will he or she do Y?" Often both people are victimized by their assumptions and expectations, but such strategy seems inevitable (Balswick and Anderson, 1969). One study (M. Rosenbaum, 1976) implies that seduction involves interpreting adherence to gender-role expectations ("pass makers" versus "pass receivers"). Confusion arises if the setting is unusual, the pass maker acts out of role, or the pass or response is too ambiguous.

In sexual relationships, gender roles influence (but do not solely determine) who asks whom for a date or sexual contact, who agrees to it, and under what conditions, what coital position is used (especially who is on top), and who reaches orgasm first. As in nonsexual matters, traditional expectations bring pleasure and reassurance to some, frustration and conflict to others. Jessie Bernard (1972) has described "his" marriage and "her" marriage—two different views of reality that people bring to a marriage and do not verbalize. Men and women, she says, often see a relationship differently, experience it differently, and act in it differently, all in ways (economic support, child care, etc.) predictably linked to gender roles in all societies.

Some social psychologists studying social roles use the concept of *symbolic interaction,* formulated by sociologist George Herbert Mead (1934) and developed by Schvaneveldt (1966), Singelmann (1972), and others. They believe that gender roles are entirely social creations. The theory has implications for understanding gender roles and sexual behavior. The theory states:

1. The basis of all decisions involving changing situations is socially learned.
2. A person makes decisions that will preserve a positive self-concept.
3. In any sexual situation, one tries to maximize one's status or situation. Ego needs, social pressures, and personal desires interact to produce a decision.
4. Interaction with others requires finding out how they perceive an act or situation.
5. Decisions involve memory of past events; the present is constantly reevaluated in the light of previous experiences and is often seen ambivalently.

These last two points imply that in making any decision, one considers how a behavior will be evaluated by oneself, by one's partner, and by society.

According to this theory, if women perceive men's roles as better than their own, they will act to attain them. If they see their own as better, they will act to preserve them. The same would be true for men. Of course one doesn't have to change the entire role. One can choose to alter only certain components of it, such as those involved in emotional and sexual relationships (Libby, 1978).

Sexual, Marital, and Parental Roles

Roles and Equality

In our society, men have traditionally been seen as aggressive, independent, sexually excitable (and orgasmic), and financially responsible for the family, yet less concerned with family than career. Women have been seen as more passive and dependent, less sexually arousable (and less regularly orgasmic), responsible for the children and home, and more concerned with family than career. It is often asked how many of these qualities are purely social and variable, and what effects they have on social equality and opportunity.

It is fact, not social stereotype, that men virtually everywhere are sexually more active and aggressive than women, and that if either sex is to have more than one sexual partner, it is likely to be men (Gebhard, 1971). And in all known societies, men have greater authority than women both inside and outside the home (Romney, 1965; Stephens, 1963). Images of power and success as masculine seem deeply rooted in the minds of both men and women, in our society and probably in virtually all others (Maccoby and Jacklin, 1974; Ovesey, 1969).

It is also fact that in most animal species, including most primates, the male must be more dominant than the female before she will

447

allow copulation. We noted in chapter 12 that this is one possible reason for the rarity of mother-son incest in any species; a male rarely dominates an older female who was long dominant over him. This relationship of male aggressiveness with sexuality may well exist to some extent in humans (Harlow, 1974); the matter is now emotionally debated.

The onset of a popular resurgence of the movement to expand women's opportunities and to assail sex roles stereotypes has often been associated with the publication in 1963 of Betty Friedan's *The Feminine Mystique.* In an effort to end traditional gender roles, some feminists have called for an end to marriage and the family (Leacock, 1972; Figes, 1971; McCracken, 1972). For instance, Germaine Greer says (1972):

I'm passionately opposed to the nuclear family, with its mom and dad and 2.4 children. I think it's the most neurotic life style ever developed. There's just no space between the mother and the children. And the husband on the other hand, is an extraneous element in the household. . . . The nuclear family is just too small, too introspective and incestuous as a unit.

Robin Morgan (1970) says:

The nuclear family unit is oppressive to women (*and* children *and* men). The woman is forced into a totally dependent position, paying for her keep with an enormous amount of emotional and physical labor which is not even considered work.

Many radical feminists have seemed hostile toward men, marriage, maternity, nurture, and sexuality (or at least to heterosexuality). Mary Wollstonecraft, the founding feminist theorist, wrote in *The Rights of Women* (1929) that man

is a "lustful prowler" and that "all female failings branch out of one great cause—want of chastity in men." Marriage has been called a result of "laws of sexual property," especially by Marxist theorists (Engels, 1972). For almost two centuries, a chief aim of the women's movement has been to relieve women of exclusive or nearly exclusive responsibility for child care and domestic tasks, to free them to pursue the same tasks and goals as men. Some feminists have also urged that women not only accept their own sexual responsiveness but make it independent of men, through masturbation and lesbian relationships.

Perhaps one reason many efforts at female equality have made slow headway in our society is such extreme positions. Probably most people do not feel so strongly that sexual interdependence, marriage, parenthood, and nurture are necessarily destructive either to women's or to men's civil rights, individuality, and feelings of fulfillment. A large majority of women seem to want to increase their rights and privileges within traditional family and marriage structures. The conditions of these activities have sometimes limited women severely and men less; what is open to question is how, how much, and why.

There have historically been greater restrictions on women's marital rights than on men's. Neither decision making nor division of labor in the family is egalitarian, even among middle-class spouses. Safilios-Rothschild (1972), studying equality within and outside the family, found that feelings of equality seem to depend on whether the wife has a job that supports the family as much as or more than her husband's. Nevertheless, such a position is not most women's goal; they still put chief value on personal fulfillment as wives and mothers. Wives therefore, she writes,

tend to keep exclusive rights to housework and children, including decisions concerning home and children. Such an exclusivity precludes the husband's effective participation in housework and child-related tasks, since a more equalitarian division of labor would tend to diminish the wives' self-esteem.

There could be even greater loss of self-esteem if the husband participates and does the work better—comparable to what can happen if the wife's job pays more than the husband's.

A *Psychology Today* questionnaire survey of 23,000 men and women (Renwick and Lawler, 1978) found that more than 90 percent of the women had full-time jobs. However, 64 percent of the women, and only 19 percent of the men, said they would move if the spouse were offered a better job in another city. The size of the wife's income "had absolutely nothing to do with what the husband said he would do. It seems that reports of the death of traditional sex roles are greatly exaggerated" (Renwick and Lawler, 1978). Both sexes equally opposed (82 percent) giving hiring preference to women or other minority groups. This is striking, since most of the respondents were working women, the majority of whom consider themselves liberal, and 43 percent of whom said they had been victims of job discrimination within the past five years. Perhaps they felt they had finally worked their way up by merit and others should do the same.

Society has, while denying women certain rights, offered some protections, and we doubt that the concepts of paternalism and sexual property sufficiently explain why. For instance, the customs of dowries and bride prices are often mentioned as evidence that marriage is essentially an exercise of male domination and sexual ownership. However, economic gain is usually not the main motive for bride price (Davenport, 1977) or even a motive at all. Often the goods or money received for a daughter are given to a son to provide the bride price he will need to get married. Such exchanges create indebtedness and cooperation between families and act as deposits to guarantee good treatment of the bride—a bride price may have to be returned if a wife is mistreated by her husband or his family. In modern Greece, as in many other societies, the dowry is a method of transferring wealth to a daughter when it would otherwise go to a son (Lambiri-Dimaki, 1972). That is, sons acquire their share of family wealth mainly through inheritance; daughters acquire it sooner as dowries.*

Desire for Role Change

John Stuart Mill (1929) wrote more than a century ago, "Women are what we have required them to be." Some have gone farther and suggested there has been a male conspiracy to limit women's rights. We suspect other forces are at work.

Throughout most of history, women have spent a great deal of their adult lives bearing and raising children. A century ago, in the name of science, many authorities praised as mental and social health the restriction of women to maternal and domestic tasks (Fee, 1976). In our day, some authorities have swung

---

* This discussion does not negate the fact that in some cultures dowries are used to insure acceptance of a spouse and families may go into debt to provide them.

449

to the other extreme and claimed that being a mother and housewife inevitably leads to frustration and increased mental illness (Gove and Tudor, 1973).

We do not know how many women desire to change traditional marital roles. Most research on this has been done with white, middle-class women (Hochschilde, 1973). Very different views about changing roles and goals have been heard from other women.

We suspect that less rigid expectations of sexual, marital, and domestic behavior may bring greater happiness to many people in our society. We also believe that equal opportunities should be open to all. But these are only opinions. Little is known of the long-term effects of gender-role changes on individuals, families, and children. Studies of children raised

in one-parent households and in day-care centers and nurseries are still inconclusive.

Also, gender-role research has concentrated on women and children. Too little is known of the roles of husband and father. Permanent male mates are not common in the animal kingdom. The human family as we know it results from adding an adult male to the ancient mother-child bond (Lancaster, 1976). There is obvious survival value in this, but probably most men feel the bond as an emotional rather than an economic or a biological need. Tiger and Shepher (1975) say, "The broadest question in the study of human kinship systems is also very incompletely answered: Why do men, to the extent that they do, support children and women?"

We believe that society has a stake in rela-

A Black Woman Speaks on Feminism

The majority of black women essentially view the new feminism as a dialogue between white women and white men. . . . [feminism] does not touch the fundamental issue of the powerlessness of the lower-class black male to protect his family according to the value system of the larger society in which he lives. Equal pay for equal work and proportional representation [means] the right to compete with black men for the new jobs of janitor, custodian, stock clerk, sanitation engineer, and similar lower-class jobs. . . . Freedom from suburbia, kitchen gadgets, babysitting, and bras: Most black women dream of the day when they can escape the rat-infested, treeless, cement jungle. . . . As for taking off the bra, for many a black woman it has been only recently that she has been able to afford to put one on . . . and it is an achievement and a

status symbol to be able to remain home and care for one's own children. . . . Black women, today, recognize that without liberation for the black male there can be no real freedom for anyone. . . . Lower-class black women are tired of being forced to make decisions. They are tired of the exclusive right of self-determination and long for the right of shared destiny and mutual participation in family matters. . . . So long as black women have black sons they will remain skeptical of an alliance with women to achieve the dubious equality which guarantees less than full manhood for him for whom she has labored and given birth. For the black woman, maternalism, sexuality, and the new feminism come full circle back to the black male.

—Julia Mayo, "The New Black Feminism: A Minority Report" 1973

tive harmony between the sexes. If the father-husband role is indeed a new, relatively fragile development, perhaps it should be understood before it is discouraged—for the sake of women, men, and children. We doubt that society as a whole will act as a parent to all children, replacing individual parental bonds. First, it may not want to. Second, many women do not want it to. Gadpaille (1975) says that

fully nine-tenths of all women, including those with the best and most liberated education, opt willingly for home and family and the nurturant activities inherent in the traditional division of labor. The valid social goals of feminism notwithstanding, there is little evidence that this will cease to be the dominant pattern in the foreseeable evolutionary future.

Changing Roles, Sex Behavior, and Satisfaction

There are now some reports that greater female sexual assertiveness is resulting in impotence (Ginsberg, Frosch, and Shapiro, 1972). This alleged increase in impotence has also been attributed to feminization of males (Rader, 1970). A recent survey of 500 psychiatrists revealed that 62 percent thought married couples with traditional values were more content with their sexual relationships than less traditional couples (M. Goldberg, 1978); 10 percent felt that more than half of men object to women initiating sexual relations. But it remains to be proven that these impressionistic reports about impotence, assertiveness, and role changes are true of society at large. And if they are true of even part of society, it remains to be learned whether they are caused by other gender-role changes or have different sources, such as social or child-rearing influences.

In Sweden, where the government has been trying to remove gender-role distinctions since the 1930s, researchers have been trying to assess the effects on marital and sexual happiness (Dahlström, 1971). After reviewing the evidence from Europe and the United States, Dahlström and Liljeström (1971) found a "confusing and controversial array of data and assumptions." Some researchers say egalitarian couples are more compatible and more likely to stay together; others say that traditional couples are more compatible and stable. In any case, Dahlström and Liljeström concluded that often the new equality is more apparent or formal than real. Swedish wives have the same legal and social rights as their husbands, but more power is still exercised by husbands.

Bernard (1966) cautions that sexual equality for women probably will not solve problems in the relations of the sexes. She agrees with Ira Reiss (1960) that men and women may come to better understand and live with each other, but that no general pattern for relationships will evolve. She warns,

There must, perhaps, always be the seeds of potential hostility between men and women, intrinsic to the relationship . . . and no matter what we may say or do, the sexes are dependent on one another; they need one another. But they are different. Some normative patterns of relationships between the sexes favor men, some favor women.

Sex, Labor, and Power

There is firmer evidence about some other aspects of gender roles, such as work and social power. We have said that societies assign many tasks primarily to men or to women. Conditions of life and work in the United States today are unlike those in much of the world, and quite unlike those anywhere until recent times.

Throughout most of human existence, survival depended on hunting and gathering. In virtually all societies, men are the hunters, deep-sea fishers, trappers, and fighters; women care for children and do the gathering, preparing, and cooking of food, although men in some societies help in preparing food (Friedl, 1975). Jane Lancaster (1976) points out that

child-care responsibilities are only compatible with activities that do not demand long trips from home; with tasks that do not require rapt concentration; and with work that is not dangerous, can be performed in spite of interruptions, and is easily resumed once interrupted.

Obviously hunters and fighters cannot take infants and small children along with them.

In every known society, past and present, men have had greater authority than women inside and outside the home and have received greater deference than women. And almost everywhere, men have contributed more to subsistence, unless military duties demand their chief energies (J. K. Brown, 1976; Ember and Ember, 1971). During the past 10,000 years, since the development of agriculture, women have probably contributed more to subsistence, and a greater variety of labor patterns may have developed, producing greater variety in gender roles (Friedl, 1975). Women's increasing employment and financial emancipation may continue to have such an effect.

Much has been written about supposed *matriarchal* societies (where women exercise most authority), *matrilinear* societies (where descent is traced through the mother and her family) and *matrilocal* societies (where a married couple

---

Laws, Social Change, and Women

Laws and social change notwithstanding, most women would continue to use their sexuality to get them what they wanted, would continue to rely upon being sexual objects, because deep in our personal and historic past lies the belief that that's what we *are*. Learning to be something else is a long process; learning that it serves a *purpose* to be something else, that it will get you to the same place or further, is perhaps an even longer process. . . . For most women, including myself, being sexy is both a tool, a weapon, and a source of pleasure. It has always guaranteed my survival in situations that were inimical to survival . . . could I easily surrender that mechanism of survival . . .? Yes I could, but with difficulty, and *only* if I thought more human behavior could achieve the same results. . . . It is, in addition, I think, one of the prime sources of female ambivalence: astonishment that men can be so easily seduced and contempt for the fact that it requires such a second-rate skill, which in its "natural" state would not be a skill at all, but an expression of deep feelings.

—Ingrid Bengis, *Combat in the Erogenous Zone* (1972)

live with or near the bride's family). But no matriarchy has been discovered anywhere in the world, and there is no evidence that any has ever existed (Friedl, 1975). A small number of matrilinear and matrilocal systems do exist; Murdock (1949b) has suggested that they develop in agriculture-without-cattle economies, where women do all or most of the food gathering and most of the subsistence labor. But even in matrilinear and matrilocal societies, greater authority is exercised by the mother's male kin than by the mother (Romney, 1965).

Exceptions do exist. In some societies, women do more subsistence work than men; this usually happens when warfare and defense constantly prevent men from doing so regularly (Ember and Ember, 1971). Women have been known to enter combat, but usually only in defense of home territory (Tiger and Shepher, 1975). In our society, a woman acts as the head of about one household in seven, but many of them do not do so because they wish to (as is true of many men). There are societies where women trade, travel, and do arduous labor, but usually it is young and older women—those who have not yet had children or whose children are grown up (J. K. Brown, 1976). In some societies, women hold political office and have great social authority; several have recently been leaders of nations. And in some societies, such as the Iroquois, they do not hold high offices but greatly influence the selection of men who do (J. K. Brown, 1970).

The fact remains that in all societies, men as a group have higher status and more power at home, at work, and in society at large. Economic explanations have logic and are supported by some evidence, but where women have gained greater economic and social positions, the most prestigious work and jobs still tend to go to men (Hutt, 1972). And since men's role and work have more prestige, women are more often eager than men to change role traditions. In Russia and China, which have tried to modify traditional gender roles, women have moved into traditionally male categories far more than men have moved into women's. Women are now easily accepted in Russia as physicians; men are not as easily accepted as homemakers, nor do they accept the role. Furthermore, woman physicians generally return to their families in the evening to prepare the meals and do the dishes or have other women do it for them (Rosenthal, 1977).

Several explanations have been offered. One is that the status of a task is determined by who does it: it isn't that men get the high-status jobs, but that tasks have more prestige if men do them. When women entered clerical work and teaching, which had previously been predominantly men's jobs, the prestige of these jobs declined (Sullerot, 1971). One must note, of course, that most men do not do prestigious work. Far more are janitors, postal clerks, and garbage collectors than are presidents of universities, corporations, and nations.

Another explanation (Millett, 1970) is differential socialization (see chapter 7). Children grow up seeing women cook, clean, nurse, comfort—or, if they have jobs, doing work that is more nurturing and less prestigious than men's. Children also see that men are bigger, stronger, more aggressive, and, in most homes, the chief economic supporters of families. Differential socialization obviously takes place, but it may not affect role differences more than greater male aggressiveness and greater female nurturance and compliance. If one is to say that such differences are socially created, one must explain why they are created in all societies.

Psychologists Eleanor Maccoby and Carol Jacklin (1974) conclude that "socialization pressures whether by parents or others do not by any means tell the whole story of the origins of sex differences."

A few people, we noted, have argued that a male power conspiracy keeps women from independence and prestigious work. In a small number of situations, men's shared attitudes may make this seem true. But as Tiger and Shepher (1975) say, "It is paradoxical to argue that there are no important differences between the sexes, but that men alone are both greedy for power and effective in retaining it, and that women are painfully susceptible to the duress of men."

We must, then, account for two contradictory facts. First, men everywhere have, and probably always have had, more power and prestige than women. Second, this difference has not been absolute; in various periods and societies women have had very much more or less freedom, opportunity, power, and prestige than in our society today. This has been shown by two very different and significant cross-cultural studies of sex roles. We will look at them and then compare them to studies done recently in the United States and elsewhere.

A Cross-Cultural View

Two Cross-Cultural Studies

Mead: Relativism. In the Twenties, more and more women were accepting an attitude of greater sexual permissiveness, obtaining higher educations, and entering professions. Anthropologist Margaret Mead began several decades of work that still introduces many people to the cross-cultural study of gender roles. Her books *Coming of Age in Samoa* (1928), *Sex and Temperament in Three Primitive Societies* (1935), and *Male and Female* (1949) reinforced the increasingly popular view that traditional Western gender roles create inner suffering and social conflict.

In *Sex and Temperament,* Mead reported her efforts to find whether men and women are inherently suited for different ways of life or whether tradition alone dictates such differences. She studied three very different cultures in New Guinea. Among the Arapesh, she said, both men and women had the nurturing, tender qualities our society considers feminine. The Mundugumor, who were headhunters and cannibals, expected of both sexes the violent, competitive behavior our society associates with men. The Tchambuli, like Westerners, viewed the sexes as temperamentally different but complementary, but in the opposite way; they saw men as emotional, dependent, and vain, women as efficient and cooperative.

Mead showed that many aspects of gender role vary from society to society, and that male and female roles are not necessarily polar opposites. She also claimed that rigid gender roles take a psychological and social toll. The "feminine" Arapesh tended to fall apart when events called for aggression and resourcefulness. The "masculine" Mundugamor barely held their aggressive, competitive society together. The Tchambuli produced unhappy men but contented women—the reverse, said Mead, of what happens in our society. In all three societies, said Mead, people who failed to meet gender-role expectations because of their temperaments paid a price, and society lost the benefits of their individual qualities.

Sharply defined and demanding gender roles, Mead concluded, are inevitably destructive, because in every society there is an equally wide genetic range of temperaments among both men and women. She said that

every time the point of sex-conformity is made, every time the child's sex is invoked as the reason why he should prefer trousers to petticoats, baseball bats to dolls, fisticuffs to tears, there is implanted in the child's mind a fear that, indeed, in spite of anatomical evidence to the contrary, it may not really belong to its own sex at all.

Those who suffer in our society, she said, are dominant, aggressive women and emotional, nurturing men. As an example, Mead pointed to the institution of the *berdache*, the transvestite and/or homosexual role taken by some men in certain Siberian, American Indian, and other societies. The *berdache*, she said, was a warning to every father who found that his son did not adequately fill his society's masculine role, making him redouble "the very pressure which helped to drive a boy to that choice."

Despite its worth and influence, Mead's work has some weak points, which have been widely criticized. First, there is no proof that genes set the same range of temperaments in all people of both sexes the world over; in fact, there is evidence to the contrary (see chapter 7). Second, Mead avoided basic biological differences, saying it is merely more convenient for women than men to raise children. Third, there is no proof that contrasting or rigid roles necessarily create unhappiness, neuroticism, or deviance. The Plains Indians, with their very rigorous masculine role, apparently had proportionately fewer *berdaches* than there are homosexuals and transvestites in the contemporary West (Karlen, 1971). Last, Mead was not discussing societies as we typically think of them. The Arapesh, Tchambuli, and Mundugumor are more correctly considered villages of 200 to 300 people.

Mead failed to point out that when a society sets a standard or makes a demand, it not only punishes those who fail it but rewards and supports those who live up to it—as the majority of people do. It is true that a society such as ours often frustrates gifted and aggressive women and uncompetitive, passive men, but that does not justify generalizations about all people or all societies. Later, Mead did moderate her position and say that males and females, as groups, have somewhat different gifts to cultivate.

Tiger and Shepher: "Biogrammar." Another cross-cultural study, *Women in the Kibbutz* (1975), by sociologists Lionel Tiger and Joseph Shepher, reported very different findings about roles. Their work was done in the *kibbutzim*, or communal settlements, that have existed in Israel since the beginning of this century. Their massive study used data, observations, and interviews involving about 100,000 women over three generations.

The authors point out that nowhere in the world have so many people made so radical and prolonged an effort to destroy traditional gender-role distinctions in work, power, prestige, and life-style. For several generations in hundreds of kibbutzim, people have made a voluntary, idealistic effort to end private property, sustain direct democracy, dissolve traditional family roles through communal child-rearing, erase sex-typing of labor, and avoid distinctions between the sexes by socializing children the same way.

455

Figure 21-2 / *For three generations, the kibbutzim of Israel have tried to erase gender roles. Much change occurred in the kibbutzim and the rest of Israeli society (top). But some sex-typing of tasks and gender-role distinctions reappeared, chiefly because of women's eagerness to be involved in childrearing (center), and finally their insistence on keeping close personal ties with their own children rather than allowing completely communal childrearing (bottom).*

The kibbutzim succeeded in most of these things. They are direct democracies, and there has been very limited return to private property. Boys and girls are socialized perhaps more equally than anywhere else in the world, and more women are politically active in kibbutzim than anywhere else. Only one goal has not been sustained—the abolition of gender roles.

Even in these equalitarian agricultural communes, pregnant women were not expected to drive tractors or enter combat. But this does not fully account for the gradual return to traditional division of labor and gender roles, with the most arduous tasks going to men and many of those connected with nurture going to women. Preference has played a large part.

Tiger and Shepher observed that wherever single-sex work groups exist, men seem to work more easily as teams with leaders, but in female work groups, there is reluctance to take positions of command. Women often prefer mixed-sex work groups or male leadership to all-female work groups. This corresponds with findings in the United States (Maccoby and Jacklin, 1974) that males in groups seem both more competitive and more cooperative than females, as the situation demands.

Despite continued urgings by kibbutz men to enter political debate and decision making, women participate less. Most of those who become politically active are in or near middle age, when most of childrearing is behind them.

Most important, women were willing to put their children in communal nurseries early in the kibbutz movement, but in the long run they didn't want to be separated from them. First they took short breaks from work to visit the nurseries—periods which became known as "happy hours." Many women enjoyed spending time with their own and other women's children by working in nurseries and primary schools (few men did). Although men take part in domestic tasks, women do so more, and because of this have greater decision-making voice in domestic matters. Women's desire to retain the mother-infant connection was crucial to the failure to sustain the early kibbutz ideal of erasing gender roles.

Some critics might speculate that the socialization of kibbutz women never changed sufficiently or that the values of nonkibbutz culture subverted communal efforts to change. Yet even though the kibbutzim contain only a small part of Israel's population, they represent its national ideals and are strongly supported. And gender roles are the only aspect of kibbutz life that persistently—even increasingly—resisted change. Why should all other kibbutz values be accepted and all other values of the larger culture be rejected?

Tiger and Shepher say that the overwhelming majority of kibbutz women

not only accept their situations but have sought them. They have acted against the principles of their socialization and ideology and against the wishes of the men of their communities, against the economic interest of the kibbutzim, in order to be able to devote more time and energy to private maternal activities rather than to economic and political public ones. Obviously these women have minds of their own; despite obstacles, they are trying to accomplish what women elsewhere have been periodically urged to reject by critics of traditional females roles.

This Tiger and Shepher attribute to a biosocial tendency, the elements of which they call the "biogrammar" of human social life.

Contemporary Sweden

To these two bodies of observation we must add a third. On a scale unmatched by any other

European country, Sweden has been attempting for about half a century to change gender roles by legal reform and changing education (Dahlström, 1971). The intention was not only to offer women more career opportunities but to increase men's participation in the home. Before this movement began, Sweden had a very restrictive sexual code and traditional gender roles, though some Swedish intellectuals strongly supported the rights of women.

In the 1930s, the Swedish government declared that women could not be discriminated against at work or in other aspects of life because of marriage or pregnancy. Steps were taken to reduce men's work day so that they could participate more in domestic life (Myrdal, 1971). Since then, many women have taken jobs and built careers, contributing income to their families and satisfying personal desires. About 15 percent of the Swedish legislature are women.

The government has continued to encourage a break with traditional gender roles, but with quite limited success. In many homes where the woman is fully occupied outside the house, she hires another woman to do the domestic chores. Although men contribute more at home than they used to, their roles have changed less than women's. Only about 10 percent (most of them middle- or upper-middle class) take time from their jobs for domestic tasks, and few of them extensively or for extended periods.

In short, traditional domestic and family roles still seem entrenched in Swedish life. Men still occupy most positions of prestige, and women remain the primary caretakers of children and homes. The government has been able to remove formal obstacles to change, but as in the kibbutzim, change is not always adopted or even desired. And in Sweden, as in Israel, the greatest resistance is often by women (Dahlström, 1971), who want to retain the status, social rewards, and personal satisfactions of being wives and mothers.

Dahlström concludes that the majority of men and women may desire the status quo. Efforts to further change roles or to return to more traditional ones don't muster much support. Some critics have said Sweden did not go far enough in breaking with old roles. But a question arises: in a democratic society, how far should one take a social experiment when it conflicts with the will of the majority it is supposed to benefit?

Comparison with the United States

Mead and others established that many behaviors and traits which the West has considered inherently masculine and feminine reflect only one society's gender roles. The work of Tiger and Shepher and others shows that there are limits to cultural relativism, and that some aspects of gender roles may well rise from inherent tendencies—a "biogrammar" underlying some human behavior. Studies in Israel and Sweden show both change and limits in altering gender roles, and arguments about the need or desire for such change are still unresolved.

For instance, the relatively high degree of female political participation in those nations shows that many women can be effective social leaders. Yet even there, fewer women than men do so or want to do so, and they are most likely to do so when the years of intensive childrearing are past. Studies of career women (Gavron, 1966; R. Rapoport and Rapoport,

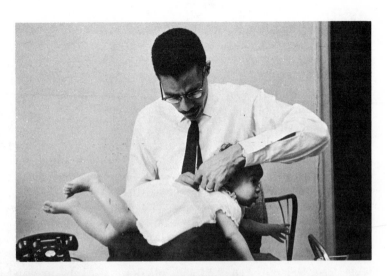

Figure 21-3 / *In the United States, Sweden, and some other Western nations, the sex-typing of tasks is somewhat diminished. More men participate in domestic work, and more women have jobs once held mostly or entirely by men. So far, such change seems to have deeply changed the lives of relatively few people, but the process is continuing.*

1972) showed that although they were highly motivated and involved in their work, they felt that if a conflict arose between work and family, the family should come first. They were also less likely than men to be interested in empire-building and administration, and were less competitive at their jobs and in promoting their careers. We have mentioned comparable findings in the survey by Renwick and Lawler. Corinne Hutt (1972) says it should not be surprising that distinguished career women have "characteristically female cognitive styles and orientations."

In the United States today, some impediments to women entering certain jobs and lifestyles have been removed. And some men seem to spend more time at home and share domestic tasks. Our society is probably seeing what has been found in other times and societies: women modify their roles more readily than men, but they resist relinquishing certain ones just as strongly as men. Each sex seems to have an affinity for certain aspects of gender roles, particularly those most tied to reproductive functions and basic survival mechanisms. Whether roles will soon change more in our society than in Israel or Sweden remains to be seen. Present evidence is against it.

Overview

We have viewed gender roles from many viewpoints, real and symbolic, social and emotional and cross-cultural. Many writings, from the popular and polemical (Millett, 1970; Greer, 1971) to the academic (Bernard, 1972) call for continued reevaluation of gender roles, an end to labeling behaviors masculine and feminine, and greater social and sexual opportunities for both sexes, but especially for women. Some have even called for *androgyny* (Bem, 1975; Kaplan and Bean, 1976), a melding of characteristics associated with males and females. Others have argued (S. Goldberg, 1973) that where there is a biosocial basis for behavioral tendencies, societies should socialize children in ways that are consonant with them. Since most women (and only women) will be mothers, they say, and most men will have to cope with male aggression, society should prepare the young appropriately.

It has been argued that we no longer live under the conditions in which many biosocial tendencies developed—that many gender-role behaviors and even sex differences are anachronisms in a technological age. Many ethologists agree. In fact, they consider the conflict between many inherited patterns with the conditions of modern life the greatest human problem today. But if we are to attain greater social equity and individual satisfaction, it will not be done by ignoring reality, but with awareness of both our inheritance and our adaptive powers.

Considering how slowly a society's basic values are likely to change, there has been striking response to new attitudes and demands during the past decade. Academia and the mass media are becoming very conscious of gender-role stereotypes and of real or possible restrictions on men's and women's opportunities, obligations, and rights. Many companies, crafts, and professions have made efforts to correct possible inequities, although a great many legal, social, and economic issues remain.

One of the chief barriers to change is fear that any revision of gender roles threatens the family and society. In the late nineteenth and early twentieth centuries, as the "new woman" emerged, a number of scientists (Fee, 1976) saw woman's shift from domesticity to jobs and professions as a threat that all gender distinctions would disappear, to the detriment of society. For many people, this fear remains.

We suggest that there is nothing to fear if women wear pants, if men go back to makeup, or if any other obviously symbolic aspects of gender roles change. People will still know and maintain their sexual identities. Some role patterns may change, but males will probably still have the more prestigious roles. Whether this is because they take them or because they are given them remains unsettled. The point is that so far, concerted efforts to change this situation have had real but distinctly limited success.

Consider, for example, that the unisex movement of the Sixties and Seventies meant primarily that women might cut their hair short and wear slacks. Men wore their hair long but stopped short of putting on skirts (Friedl, 1975). When a male seems to reject his gender role, he is rejecting some of society's most deeply held values. When a female strives for the masculine role, it is considered understandable, for it is the preferred role (Karlen, 1971).

Probably the easiest gender-role changes will be those that do not threaten sex-fixedness.

We see no reason why a woman cannot or should not be a stockbroker, the head of a corporation or nation, a physician, or a professor. We feel that it is unjust to make it more difficult for a woman to do so or to fail to encourage a woman who wants to. But there may always be more men who want to do so than women. It is also possible that when women do so, many will not follow quite the same style or timetable as the majority of men. We also feel that anyone should be free to choose child care or domestic work and derive pride and satisfaction from them.

We believe that in our society, people may benefit more from choice than from coercion in gender-role development. One of us has written elsewhere (Diamond, 1978):

The healthiest environment for sexual growth is one that provides the richest possible banquet of experiences and models from which the individual can learn without fear of social censure. If each individual is free to act according to his or her sense of sexual identity, preference, and role, then men and women will be truly able to express who they are.

Review, Discuss, Decide

1. What are roles and stereotypes? What are their possible advantages and disadvantages?
2. What do you feel about the implications of biological determinism and social determinism? Can you suggest examples of how each position translates into social goals and policies?
3. If evidence about sex differences and gender roles could be used or misused politically, what should researchers and

citizens do?

4. What are some symbolic masculine and feminine traits and behaviors, in our society or others? Are any of them related to biological sex differences?

5. Which tasks are traditionally masculine in our society and which feminine? Which divisions of labor are worldwide and which peculiar to our society or our time in history?

6. Why do men want to be husbands and fathers? Why do women want to be wives and mothers?

7. What are the major points made by the cross-cultural studies discussed in this chapter?

8. What position do you think our society should take in regard to gender roles and stereotypes? Remove them? Reinforce them? Be neutral?

9. How would you raise children and conduct your own life?

10. How will you want those close to you to act?

22

The Law, Morality, and Ethics

Why are some sexual behaviors controlled by law and others not?

How much do laws really affect what people do sexually?

How do federal and state laws deal with sexual issues?

What moral and ethical issues rise from rape, prostitution, and pornography? From laws controlling them?

Is there a sexual ethic that applies to everyone? Or can everyone create his own standards?

Morality is often defined as a sense of right and wrong, *ethics* as formalized beliefs about right and wrong. Some people hold that morality is a religious study, ethics a philosophical one; others say that morality and ethics are really the same thing. In any case, it is generally agreed that morality and ethics are part of a culture's fabric, inseparable from laws, attitudes, and customs. In our pluralistic society, several complex codes of sexual conduct coexist with a variety of public and private attitudes and behaviors. This often makes decision making complex, difficult, and conflict-laden.

To review all religious and philosophical views of sexuality and all laws bearing on sex would demand another volume. We have cho-

sen some principles and public issues that have recently raised controversy, to use them as examples of the moral, religious, legal, and ethical aspects of decision making.

Absolute and Relative Morality

Moral standards are absolute or relative. *Absolute standards* of right or wrong remain the same in all situations; people who hold them think certain choices should be made and others shunned by everyone, regardless of the circumstances. For some Jews and Christians, belief in the Ten Commandments places certain aspects of life beyond debate; they feel adultery is immoral and subject to punishment in the spiritual and physical worlds. Some people continue to believe in absolute standards even though they sometimes bend or break them, and neither they nor their beliefs can be dismissed on charges of hypocrisy, for the belief, the intention, and the moral guilt are genuine.

Under a *relative standard,* adultery may be good or bad, depending on the circumstances. Extreme relative morality shows in the popular expressions "do your own thing" and "different strokes for different folks." In other words, one should not necessarily comply with others' values; in fact, one's ethical obligation is

463

largely to oneself. Less extreme relativism says that when faced with the complexities of life, one should base a decision on the context and the effects. Whether adultery is ethical depends on the relationships between the spouses and between the adulterous partners, the act's acceptability to all concerned, the motives for the action, and the results. This sort of relativism is not foreign to the Jewish tradition, and it appears in the writings of Martin Luther and other Christian leaders (W. Cole, 1966). In recent decades, Joseph Fletcher (1966, 1967), a Methodist minister, simplified and formalized these complex issues of moral relativism as "situation ethics." He said one should base moral decisions on what is most loving in a given situation, and defined love as *agape*, or spiritual love.

Western religious tradition has shown both continuity and change in its views of sex behavior. In the Old Testament and in written and oral Jewish tradition, almost every aspect of sexuality is dealt with—coitus, marriage, family life, divorce, procreation, adultery, homosexuality, bestiality, rape, and transvestism. The values have been believed to be those of God, or at least to be divinely inspired. Judaism has held that sexual relations are God-given, and through them one can serve God's plan. Not only Orthodox Jews but also many fundamentalist Protestant sects have continued to limit sex largely to marital coitus but to give it positive value. The Mormons believe that almost any sexual practice is acceptable between husband and wife, but that sex must be limited to marriage.

In early and medieval Christianity, some new attitudes and emphases became promi-

---

Situation Ethics

The situationist enters into every decision-making situation fully armed with the ethical maxims of his community and its heritage and he treats these with respect as illuminators of his problems. Just the same he is prepared in any situation to compromise them or put them aside in the situation if love seems better served by doing so. . . .

The situational factors are so primary that we may even say 'circumstances alter rules and principles.' . . . [Situationalism] is antimoralistic as well as antilegalistic, for it is sensitive to variety and complexity. It is neither simplistic nor perfectionist . . . situationalism is a method that proceeds, so to speak, from (1) its one and only law, *agape* (love), to (2) the *sophia* (wisdom) of the church and culture, containing many 'general rules' of more or less reliability, to (3) the *kairos* (moment of decision, the fullness of time) in which the responsible self in the situation decides whether the *sophia* can serve love there or not. This is the situational strategy in capsule form.

—Joseph Fletcher (1966)

---

nent—for instance, the view of Saint Paul, Saint Augustine, and Thomas Aquinas that sexual activity, even in marriage, is less desirable than abstinence (W. Cole, 1966). This has remained Roman Catholic doctrine and is believed by some ascetic Protestants.

In our society today, there is often conflict between absolute and relative values; observing God's law or man's may break the other. For instance, the contemporary argument that a woman should have control over her own body could be used to justify abortion, denying coitus to a husband, or becoming a prostitute—all of which violate Jewish and Christian absolute religious values.

The Nature of Sex-Control Laws

All societies have resort to some final authority for resolving conflict, be it a religious code, a legal system, or customs. In the Christian era, the church and civil law shared authority over sex behavior until the late Middle Ages and early Renaissance, when civil law largely took control.

Law is a changing code by which society institutionalizes its ideas of morality, correct behavior, and social order. In our pluralistic society, many different groups have unwritten codes, which may be more influential than the written law. For example, there is a widespread unwritten (and illegal) "law" that a deceived love partner or a rape victim can take vengeance. Sometimes formal and informal codes conflict, but in a given case, either may bend somewhat to acommodate the other.

Laws in the United States apply to various jurisdictions—federal, state, county, and city.

According to the Constitution, all law is legitimized by the consent of the governed rather than by any religious code. Of course, the majority of those who wrote the Constitution came from similar religious and cultural backgrounds, and this precluded certain choices in our laws. Laws are subject to judicial review. The final review, by the highest court in a state or the nation, establishes whether the law and its various applications are in accord with the Constitution. Some laws governing sexuality are part of the *criminal codes,* which deal with acts thought to harm society, such as rape. Others are part of the *civil codes,* which deal with the rights and obligations of individuals and groups, such as laws prohibiting sex discrimination. *Family law,* a branch of civil law, deals with such matters as parent-child conflicts, and it leaves much to a court's view of the unique circumstances of each case. For example, whether to return home a girl of seventeen who is living with a lover may be left completely to a judge's discretion.

Most statutes governing sex behaviors are in state criminal codes. They vary a great deal from state to state. For instance, in some states homosexual behavior is legal, in others not. Prostitution is legal in some counties of Nevada, illegal in all other counties and states. From state to state, oral-genital and anal-genital intercourse, adultery, fornication, and seduction vary from minor crimes (misdemeanors) to major crimes (felonies). The age at which one may engage in sexual activity or obtain contraceptives or assistance for STD also varies, in most states from twelve to eighteen. Laws regulating sex behavior have changed through history, becoming more restrictive or permissive by turn.

465

Federal Laws and Policies

Extent of the Law

Most people aren't aware of the extent of the federal government's concern with sexual matters unless they enter military service, seek certain government jobs or health-care benefits, or apply for a passport and are openly deviant. However, federal guidelines are extremely powerful and affect many people. And while the federal government has enacted few laws about sexual matters, those that exist serve as models for many state laws. There are federal statutes, policies, and court rulings about:

1. Reproduction control (contraception, abortion, and family planning).
2. Pornography and obscenity.
3. Prostitution: The Mann Act makes it illegal to transport a person across a state line for immoral purposes. From its passage in 1910 till 1978, this applied only to women; now it applies to men as well.

Many federal laws and policies relating to reproduction control and pornography reflect the traditional view that "sex is for procreation, not recreation." This is seen in the Uniform Code of Military Justice and the rules of the Immigration and Naturalization Service. Homosexual orientation (not necessarily committing homosexual acts) or committing what the government may consider deviant heterosexual acts (for example, oral-genital intercourse) can be cause for removal from the military service, extradition from the country, or denial of a passport or entry visa. Even tourists may be, and have been, barred from visiting the United States if they admit to homosexual orientation. The Federal Communication Commission

(FCC) sets radio and television standards—no obscenity, pornography, or gratuitous nudity. There is little overt sex behavior on television and radio. Coitus, adultery, homosexuality, and other behaviors are mentioned or discussed, but rarely seen (Franzblau, Sprafkin, and Rubinstein, 1977).

There are also sex-behavior guidelines for government employees, and the federal government is the nation's largest employer. It may dismiss those who perform any sexual act except marital coitus, and it has done so. The government has also discriminated against women, and some say it also discriminates on the basis of marital status, preferring to hire the married (Barnett, 1973).

Federal law and policy are established in several ways. One is legislation. This happens infrequently in sex-related matters and usually reflects immediate national concerns. For example, the Mann Act was prompted by allegations (unproven) that a nationwide prostitution ring abducted women and sent them to brothels all over the country as "white slaves." In 1978, an antipornography law went into effect in response to rising concern over "kiddy porn." More commonly, federal legal guidelines are established by Supreme Court rulings on the constitutionality of decisions by state courts or lower federal courts. Most rare are constitutional amendments, such as the proposed Equal Rights Amendment.

Some historians trace extensive direct federal legal involvement in sex to the so-called Comstock laws. The first was enacted in 1872 under the influence of Anthony Comstock and other zealous lay religious leaders. These laws extended an 1842 ban on importing obscene books and pictures to include the sale of contraceptives. After being appointed a postal inspector, Comstock intimidated, had arrested, or prosecuted people who wished to disseminate birth-control information, collect or display depictions of nudes, write about nonmarital coitus, or advocate abortion (Bullough and Bullough, 1977; Rugoff, 1971). These laws remained in effect until recently. Though unevenly enforced, they were effective in censoring material meant for many citizens and hindered clinicians and sex researchers who wished to send or receive material through the mails.

The Supreme Court is constantly testing and arguing cases, and national priorities change; federal laws reflect these tests and changes. The following two sections highlight two areas of current concern.

Reproduction and Reproduction Control

From Comstock's days until 1965, the distribution by mail of contraceptive information, even by physicians, was illegal. Then the U.S. Supreme Court decided (*Griswold* v. *Connecticut*, 1965) that for federal or state governments to prevent married couples from using contraceptive devices violated their right to privacy. This was a landmark decision in two ways. First, it returned to individuals the right to decide whether or how to control their reproductive capacity. Second, it declared marital sex behavior a private matter. Sexual privacy had not until then been a declared legal right; it has been the basis of most subsequent challenges to legal control of voluntary adult sex behavior. The right to privacy act was formalized in 1974 by Congress, in the so-called Privacy Act (Public Law 93–579).

In 1973, the Supreme Court ruled (*Roe et al.* v. *Wade; Doe et al.* v. *Bolton*) that a state cannot deny a woman the right to an abortion, reversing prohibitions that had existed since this nation's early years. It subsequently ruled that the woman may be of any age and need not have her parents' consent or, if married, her husband's. However, Congress responded to antiabortion pressures in 1977 with the Hyde amendment, denying federal funds to those who can't afford abortion—a law that especially affects disadvantaged minorities and the young (Lincoln et al., 1977). The unintended but dramatic result was an upswing in maternal deaths caused by illegal abortions, which had been decreasing since the decriminalization of abortion in 1973. The Hyde amendment and other legislation dealing with abortion is continually being challenged both in the courts and in Congress.

Abortion involves many issues of public morality (Steinhoff and Diamond, 1977). One is whether society is obliged to subsidize, let alone sanction, what a substantial number consider immoral, though a majority (75 percent) consider it acceptable (Gallup, 1978a). Another is whether a fetus has a right to life. Still another is whether a woman has the exclusive right to control her own body and babies; must she be forced to bear a child because others believe it immoral for her to abort? Should the father have a say? If society has no right to regulate sexual and reproductive activity, is it obliged to be responsible for their results and pay for contraception and abortion, pregnancy counseling, child and maternal care, and aid to unwed mothers? These issues are not easy to decide (see chapter 19), and proposed solutions often depend not only on ethical positions but

467

on psychological, religious, pragmatic, and political factors. There has been a dramatic shift toward accepting abortion in recent years, especially among Roman Catholics; three-fourths of them say they would have (or advise their wives to have) abortions (Greeley, 1978), and nearly half want the church to change its policy on abortion (Gallup, 1978b).

Pornography: The Background

The definitions of *pornography* (Greek: writing about prostitutes) and *obscenity* (Latin: what is offstage) are constantly debated. In Pennsylvania, in 1815, the first obscenity case in America charged several men with exhibiting a painting of a nude man and woman *(Commonwealth* v. *Sharpless,* 1815). Government prosecution of people selling or exhibiting sexual material, including contraceptives, kept increasing into this century; condoms were tolerated to prevent disease, not to prevent pregnancy. Havelock Ellis's landmark *Studies in the Psychology of Sex* (1936) was banned. So were scientific writings about contraceptives, abortion, and sterilization, and books construed to have immoral influence. The Comstock laws led to action against Margaret Sanger, the pioneering advocate of birth control and women's rights. The publication of her pamphlet *Family Limitation* (1914) led to her arrest and then her flight from this country (Bullough and Bullough, 1977). Many books now acclaimed as major literary works—for example, James Joyce's *Ulysses,* D. H. Lawrence's *Lady Chatterley's Lover,* and Henry Miller's *Tropic of Cancer*—were banned.

Legal and ethical arguments about pornography have revolved around attempts to define it. In the 1800s, pornography meant almost any nude, erotic description, or contraceptive information. The so-called Hicklin definition, which was legally dominant till the end of World War II, defined pornography as anything meant to deprave and corrupt public morals—although how to decide such intent or effects was unclear.

A breakthrough occurred in 1933, when James Joyce's *Ulysses* was declared worthy of importation by a New York district federal court *(United States* v. *"Ulysses").* The reasons were that it had literary merit, was not written to deprave, and must be judged by its over-all purpose and effect. Similar court rulings followed, and in 1957 the landmark U.S. Supreme Court Roth decision (*Roth* v. *United States*). defined pornography and obscenity as sexually explicit material that offended contemporary community standards and whose dominant intent was prurient (purely erotic). In 1966, another Supreme Court ruling regarding the eighteenth-century erotic classic *Fanny Hill (Memoirs* v. *Massachusetts)* added a third consideration; pornography was without redeeming social value.

Difficulties in applying these criteria soon became evident. In a nation as diverse as the United States, which community should provide a standard? Rural or urban? Religious or atheistic? Did contemporary mean this year or this decade? How could one be sure of an author's or artist's motives? Who would have to find material arousing? Does something lack social value if it provides entertainment or "marital enrichment"? It became difficult to find almost anything pornographic. Some joked that pornography was "anything that turned the Supreme Court on."

In 1970 there appeared the report of the Commission on Obscenity and Pornography, created in 1967 by Congress and appointed in 1968 by President Lyndon Johnson. It said, in effect, that erotic material was not harmful to society or individuals. The report was rejected by President Richard Nixon, but the gates seemed to open wider for the distribution of erotic material. Total nudity was occurring in Hollywood films and on Broadway. Much erotic material was produced for every heterosexual taste, and some for people with homosexual, fetishistic, sadomasochistic, and other sexual interests.

A backlash became evident in 1973. A more conservative Supreme Court ruled (*Miller* v. *California*) that the federal three-part definition of pornography need no longer apply; local communities could now judge for themselves what is pornographic and prosecute the producers, distributors, or anyone else involved with the material, even if it originated outside the community and was desired by some people within the community. Actors in a movie judged pornographic have been found guilty even though the movie was produced in another state and the actors had never been in the prosecuting state. The effect has been prior censorship. Few want or can afford to risk prosecution by a distant district attorney, who may be out to impress his community and build a political career.

We can report firsthand an instance of such prior censorship and its inhibiting effects. In the early Seventies, one of us (Diamond) prepared for the Public Broadcasting System (PBS) a series of thirty television programs on human sexuality. All thirty were broadcast in 1973. After the 1973 Supreme Court decision, lawyers recommended to PBS that it not show five of the programs, for fear of possible lawsuits. Not one letter had been received by PBS objecting to the series' content, it had won a national award for continuing education, and the entire series had been (and still is) widely accepted in many communities, high schools and colleges (Diamond, 1973, 1976, 1977a).

The federal government acted against pornography again in 1977. In response to public concern about an increase in "kiddy porn," erotic material using children as models or participants, Congress made it illegal for anyone under sixteen to participate, voluntarily or not, in the production of sexually explicit material. Anyone associated with the production, even a parent who gives permission for a child's appearance, is liable to prosecution.

Pornography: Factual and Ethical Issues

Pornography raises the ethical issues of privacy, harmfulness, free choice, censorship, and public morality. Almost any legal decision about sexual matters seems to satisfy some segments of this society and outrage others. However, the right to privacy in sexual matters is recognized: one has the right, affirmed by the Supreme Court (*Stanley* v. *Georgia*, 1969), to privately view or own any erotic material.

The majority of studies reviewed by the Commission on Obscenity and Pornography (1970) suggest that viewing sexually explicit material, even intensively and for long periods, does no apparent harm. Subsequent studies have reached the same conclusion (Goldstein and Kant, 1973). In fact, the use of pornography has been advocated for many individuals,

469

married and single, to aid erotic fantasy, sexual satisfaction, and tension release, especially if they have nonphysical difficulties in sexual arousal or orgasm (Diamond, 1973; Money, 1973; W. Wilson, 1978). It is also considered helpful by many sex educators and clinicians for increasing sexual comfort and communication between spouses.

The First Amendment right to free and unabridged speech lies at the heart of the pornography issue. Does the government have a right to deny a citizen access to reading or viewing any material? And, some ask, if any limits should exist, why should fantasized sexual pleasures be banned when depictions of crime, murder, and mutilation are common?

A questionnaire study of readers of the magazine *Psychology Today* found that 92 percent of the men and 72 percent of the women had voluntarily obtained or seen sexually explicit material (Athanasiou, Shaver, and Tavris, 1970). About 85 percent of men and 70 percent of women in the United States have voluntarily done so, and 20 to 25 percent of males have done so somewhat regularly (Commission on Obscenity and Pornography, 1970). We have noted that women as well as men can respond to erotica, although they often prefer other kinds of material (Stoller, 1975); more women prefer romantic themes, while more men respond to direct sexual activity and fewer women than men say they identify with erotic material, although they may become physically aroused (Schmidt and Sigusch, 1970).

Many people still consider pornography dangerous or immoral. However, polls have shown that the majority of people feel adults should be allowed to read or see any sexual material they wish (Dannemiller and Shirley,

Figure 22-1 / *Some people have fought the increasing display of erotic films and publications (below), but the definition of pornography remains problematic (right). A depiction of a nude woman may be considered art rather than erotica. Yet a picture of a woman partially clothed or one adorned in "bondage" paraphernalia may arouse viewers more than the nude. Apparently nudity and arousal, like "community standards," are ambiguous or arguable as tests for what is "pornographic."*

470

471

1978). Children, however, are thought to require protection through censorship. The public also favors restricting unsolicited pornography in the mail and prefers a national to a local standard (Gallup, 1977).

Opponents of explicit material offer little evidence that antisocial activity results from seeing it, but several points deserve mention. The report of the Commission on Obscenity and Pornography was not unanimous. Several dissenting members felt that the majority report "deliberately and carefully avoided coming to grips with the basic underlying issue . . . the prevention of *moral* corruption and *not* the prevention of overt criminal acts and conduct, or the protection of persons from being shocked and/or offended." Others felt some findings were suppressed or misused. For example, they cited a study for the Commission (K. Davis and Braucht, 1970) finding that "exposure to pornography is the strongest predictor of sexual deviance among those exposed to it at an early age." Society, they said, need not wait until a crime has been committed or society has been drastically changed before it moves to protect itself, and certain moral values deserve as much protection as the right to obtain or view erotica. However, they conceded that there is "no evidence for a detrimental effect of exposure to pornography on character." A study in Denmark (Ben-Veniste, 1970) found that after erotica became publicly available, the number of sex offenses (including rape) significantly declined. A subsequent study (Kutschinsky, 1970a,b) found no change in attitudes or willingness to report such crimes to account for the decrease.

These committee members (Hill, Link, and Keating, 1970) wanted to protect "chastity, modesty, temperance, and self-sacrificing love.

The obvious evils [to inhibit] are lust, excess, adultery, incest, homosexuality, bestiality, masturbation and fornication."

Much of the public also object to pornography. More than 40 percent of the people in one survey (Abelson et al., 1970) feel it degrades women, makes them sex objects for men's exploitation, and tends to incite rape or sexual abuse. Evidence for this, however, is meager and inferential. In fact, Mosher (1970) found that after exposure to erotic films, "calloused" attitudes toward women decreased; he concluded that such material does not dispose people to exploitive or manipulative behavior.

Others have argued that erotic material may adversely affect individuals or society by creating unhealthful or improper models; society, they say, should not only prohibit undesirable behaviors but provide a guide for desirable ones (Cline, 1974). The problem, we feel, is deciding whose idea of desirable behavior shall be a model. There is no clear evidence that pornography leads to aggressive criminal behavior or to psychosexual impairment, and some evidence that it does not. There is evidence that erotic material is helpful to many (W. Wilson, 1978); certainly it brings pleasure to millions. We believe that people (certainly adults) should have access to any erotic material they want; this is a First Amendment right that is easily and arbitrarily abused.

Sex Discrimination and Women's Rights

The issue of sex discrimination has demanded national attention since the women's movement began working for equal rights and opportunities. This movement was started in the United States by Elizabeth Cady Stanton and Lucretia Mott in 1840. Eighty difficult years of fighting for the right to vote led to the Nineteenth Amendment, granting that right (Babcock et al., 1975; Flexner, 1968). More than a century ago, the movement also began pressing for women's right to choose any occupation; they were then virtually unable to enter law, medicine, and most positions of prestige and nondomestic responsibility. In 1873, one Myra Bradwell was denied admission to the Illinois bar by that state's supreme court although she had passed the required examinations (*Bradwell* v. *Illinois*). This case is considered the forerunner of all major legal cases against sex discrimination in occupation (Babcock et al., 1975).

Many early feminists worked for the abolition of slavery and demanded equal rights for both women and blacks. As today, they sought to add "sex" to the Fourteenth Amendment prohibition of discrimination "on account of race, color or previous condition of servitude." Many feminists pointed out that the issues were different (like those of lesbian rights and other women's rights today), and the movement had to deal with the rift that resulted. Elizabeth Cady Stanton and Susan B. Anthony were adamant in not separating women's and blacks' rights and lobbied against the Fourteenth Amendment because it did not include sex. The women's movement then split into the National Woman's Suffrage Association, which they led, and the American Woman Suffrage Association, led by Lucy Stone and Henry Ward Beecher. (The two groups merged into the National American Woman Suffrage Association in 1890.) The Fourteenth and Fifteenth amendments (the Fifteenth prohibited slavery) were later used unsuccessfully in the fight for women's rights. Facing this linkage of complex issues, the U.S. Supreme Court began to find the interpretation of equal-rights principles more and more difficult and finally left decisions to the states (Babcock et al., 1975).

Sex discrimination also became an issue in labor laws. After the Civil War, working hours and work conditions were, by modern standards, appalling. Eventually laws were passed to protect all workers, and children and women were barred from many jobs considered too dangerous or burdensome. This improved working conditions, but it perpetuated discrimination. While many in the labor movement wanted to enlist women members and improve their lot, most unions were relatively unsympathetic to working women's problems (Falk, 1973; Rowbotham, 1973). Therefore many women formed their own unions; the International Ladies Garment Workers Union is probably the best known.

Discrimination due to sex persists. In 1977 male high school dropouts earned, on the average, $1600 more a year than women with college degrees (*U.S. News and World Report*, 1979). Women now ask not only "equal pay for equal jobs" but for "equal pay for work of equal value." Typically women's jobs are considered less valuable than men's.

Women have continued to fight for equal employment opportunities and rewards; one result has been federal rulings that bar job discrimination on the basis of sex. Some people see equal-rights amendments as the best way to secure such rights; others fear that these would deprive both women and men of aids and protections specifically suitable for them. The issues involved are too numerous and complex to be dealt with in this book, but we wish to bring them to readers' attention for further study and thought.

THE AGE OF BRASS.
or the triumphs of Woman's rights

Figure 22-2 / *In the early decades of the feminist movement, many people feared that it would bring total gender-role reversal, as portrayed in a Currier and Ives print of 1869 (top left). Three years later, the famous cartoonist Thomas Nast portrayed the conflict that split the movement when Victoria Claflin Woodhull added "free love" to its aims (bottom left). In recent years, one of the movement's major efforts has been winning the right to "abortion on demand" (top right). Another has been the proposed Equal Rights Amendment to the Constitution (bottom right); it has met with resistance as well as support from people of both sexes.*

"Get Thee Behind Me, (Mrs.) Satan!"

WIFE (*with heavy burden*). "I'd rather travel the hardest path of matrimony than follow your footsteps."

State Laws

We cannot review here all state laws governing sexuality or even genital behavior. We will concentrate on three subjects that reveal much about how our society deals legally with sexual matters—rape, prostitution, and certain nonreproductive sex behaviors.

Rape

Aggressive Rape. By law, all sexual relations except those between spouses must be consensual. One might hope marital relations would be consensual as well; new laws are indeed challenging traditional marital sexual rights. The first case testing such traditional rights ended in acquittal of rape charges brought by a wife against her husband (*Rideout* v. *Rideout,* 1979).

After murder and kidnapping, aggressive (assaultive) rape is treated by law as one of the most serious crimes. It is allowed in virtually no society, and all fifty states prescribe very harsh punishments. In some states, such as Hawaii, it was considered a crime committed only by men, against women or other men. In others, such as California, it is a crime committed by or against either sex.

Women may rape men through threat of force, but this is rare, prosecution more rare, and conviction almost nonexistent. In 1977, a former Miss Wyoming was charged with kidnapping and shackling her former boyfriend to a bed and repeatedly raping him. He argued that her threats to shoot him with what turned out to be a fake gun kept him from running away.

A crucial issue in most rape trials is determining what constitutes force or consent. An-

other is that usually there are no witnesses, so it is a matter of one person's word against another's. These are two reasons for rape being underreported and difficult to prove in court. Other problems are embarrassment about revealing details and the possibility of harrassment by police and legal authorities investigating the case, although harrassment is less common now than in the past.

Estimates of the incidence of rape vary greatly. Some think that only 5 percent of aggressive rapes are reported (Bloch and Geis, 1963), others 50 percent (Sutherland, 1950). It has been estimated that 20,000 women were raped in 1960, of which about 7,000 cases were reported (about 30 percent). In 1973, 51,000 rapes of an estimated 100,000 to 500,000 were reported (Offir, 1975) (10 to 50 percent). The increase of rape crisis centers and of sympathetic authorities may account for part of the increase in reported rapes; it is not known if, in fact, more rapes are being committed.

The rape of males by other males draws much less public attention, and data on incidence and circumstance are even thinner. Such rapes occur routinely in prisons, but very few are reported; many penologists, journalists, and homosexual groups are concerned with the issue. Males outside prison report rape still less often; probably they are even more ashamed and embarrassed than females about doing so.

Rape is often very brutal, both psychologically and physically. We know no evidence for Brownmiller's view (1975) that the threat of rape is "a conscious process of intimidation by which all men keep all women in a state of fear." Rather, we believe it a crime most men and women unite in condemning. However, it is fantasized about with both fear and pleasure by both sexes, if only because sex and aggression are ubiquitous facts of real and of psychic life.

The motive for rape often seems to be aggression or power more than eroticism (Lief, 1977). Groth and Burgess (1977), after studying almost 200 convicted rapists and 100 rape victims, reported that only one-quarter of the rapes involved penetration and ejaculation. About one-sixth of the rapists were unable to ejaculate during rape, though they could usually do so in nonassaultive sexual relations. A study (Abel et al., 1977) of rapists' sexual response to verbal accounts of rape showed that the aggressive aspect stimulated them more than the sexual aspect.

Aggressive rape has therefore been described as a pseudosexual act motivated less by sexual desire than by uncontrolled hostility, a sense of inadequacy, or a quest for power (Nadelson, 1977). Other evidence supports this idea. The incidence of rape is as high where prostitutes are available as where they are not (Kinsey et al., 1953), and where there is no shortage of partners (Amir, 1970; Svalastoga, 1962). Male rape is common in prisons and adolescents' detention centers, although willing homosexual partners are often available there.

The values behind rape laws have been debated. One view is that a male chauvinist culture is protecting its female property; another is that women need more protection than men, since most cannot adequately defend themselves against an assaultive man. A more legalistic view is that rape laws protect a woman's right to freely bargain or barter her sexual capacity, in order to buttress monogamy (*Yale Law Journal*, 1952); if a woman's "service" can be forcibly taken from her, she loses value as a potential spouse. We would add another reason for rape control laws—that in virtually all higher species, there are greater biosocial inhibitions of aggression against females than against males (Moyer, 1976).

Statutory Rape. Statutory rape is nonassaultive sexual intercourse with a person below the legal age of consent, which varies among states from twelve to eighteen, or with someone whose judgment is legally considered impaired. Many cases of statutory rape and child molestation arise from sexual relations between consenting minors and adults, but the act is still legally rape, even if the minor instigated the activity. Statutory rape of postpubertal youngsters is generally considered a lesser crime than forcible rape. In some states, the girl's age alone determines whether the act is rape. In others, the age difference between partners is considered. For example, in some states, if a twenty-year-old male has coitus with a girl more than four years his junior, it is statutory rape; if she is four years or less younger than he, it is not rape.

Acquaintance Rape (Date Rape). These terms (DeLora and Warren, 1977) are used for forced sexual relations between people who know each other, especially if they were previously sexually intimate to any degree (Kanin, 1957). Often the man says he thought the woman wanted coitus or that she was sexually accessible but wouldn't admit it. Some attempts at going past initial sexual limits are expected in many dating or social situations. This often makes the ethical and legal problems of such rape less clear than those of assaultive rape.

477

The Rapist and the Victim. Social and psychological descriptions of assaultive rapists vary; much that follows comes from the work of Amir (1970, 1972), Gebhard et al. (1965), Hyde (1976), and Offir (1975).

Many rapists and victims are fifteen to twenty-four years old. More are black than white, and interracial rape is rare. About 40 to 60 percent of rapists are married, but only about 25 percent of victims are. The majority of both come from lower social classes, in this and other Western nations. Some 60 percent of rapists come from broken homes.

Rapists are the most sexually active of all sex offenders; they have the highest frequencies of marital coitus, masturbation, and oral-genital acts and are unusually given to sexual fantasy. They have had more premarital coitus than other sex offenders and are markedly low in homosexual activity. About one-fifth have been previously convicted of exhibitionism, although the majority of exhibitionists probably don't rape. The commonest type of rapist (25 to 33 percent) in the study by Gebhard et al. (1965) were men to whom violence was the gratifying part of the rape. Others had committed rape because they were heedless of anyone else's wishes; these have been called amoral delinquents. Some raped when drunk, some for no apparent reason. Some had a double standard; they only rape "the bad ones." Still others raped opportunistically, while committing robbery. Reports differ on whether there is a high degree of recidivism, or repetition of the crime; it depends on which type of rapist is being considered.

The majority of adult victims are raped by strangers, but many are assaulted by acquaintances, neighbors, or friends. We saw in chapter 12 that in cases of child-adult sexual contact, the majority of the adults (75 percent) are known to the child or the child's family; 27 percent are members of the child's household.

By legal definition, consent is absent in rape, but allegations of rape often raise questions of enticement or willing involvement. Was the victim seductive? Was her clothing or behavior provocative? It may be argued that a woman should be able to act in any manner she likes, but in all crimes, circumstances are taken into account, and sexually provocative dress or behavior does seem to increase the chance of rape (Gebhard et al., 1965). One study (Amir, 1970) found that almost one-fifth of the victims had previous arrest records, and 38 percent had records of "promiscuity" or prostitution.

Some rapists, however, seek out women who are alone, intoxicated, handicapped, or in need of assistance, such as hitchhikers. Women whose occupations or life-styles lead them to night work or unusual routines (nurses, waitresses, students) are also more likely to be targets.

The Ethics of Rape-Control Laws. While the law is clear, its administration is difficult, and the ethical situation sometimes complicated by the relationship between rapist and victim, for the voluntary sexual obligations of mates, lovers, and dates vary enormously. Sometimes people have coitus willingly and then deny it out of guilt or vengefulness; false accusations of rape and perhaps unjustified convictions are not rare (Gebhard et al., 1965). In one of the most quoted passages in law, Lord Chief Justice Hale wrote that rape "is an accusation easily to be made and hard to be proved, and harder to be defended by the part accused, tho never so in-

Preventing or Reporting Rape

There are many lists of measures to avoid rape. The key word is *caution*. When it is possible:

1. Avoid known problem areas and persons. Tell local authorities about these problems if they are unaware of them.
2. Travel well-known and well-lit public routes rather than secluded or dark ones. If you can't, carry a whistle.
3. Avoid pickups by strangers.
4. If approached, be brief and to the point in declining. Act confident in your walk, talk, and actions.

IF ATTACKED

There is debate about whether to resist and risk injury or death or to submit and seem to consent. Recall that there are different varieties of rapists and consider these guidelines:

1. Fighting physically is not wise when the attacker is armed or threatens harm.
2. State your lack of interest and consent in a clear but unchallenging way. Try to talk your way out of the situation.
3. Seem to go along with the attacker until there is an opportunity to flee or yell for help. To attract attention, it may be better to yell "fire" in a building than to yell "rape."
4. Try to talk the attacker into entering a place where help is available.
5. Vomiting on yourself or an attacker may put him off. Put a finger down your throat.
6. If rape becomes inevitable, do everything possible to reduce your emotional tension, attain calm, and avoid physical harm.
7. Notice the assailant's features (eyes, hair, approximate height and weight, age, scars) so that he can be clearly identified by the police. If possible, obtain some pieces of his hair, clothes, or other items that can be used as evidence. Some victims have made arrangements to "date" their attackers at a later time so that they could be apprehended.

AFTER ATTACK

A person who reports being raped runs the risk of humiliation, ridicule, and harrassment, but may also receive very helpful medical, psychological, social, and legal services. Each individual must decide whether to report the rape to the police and see a physician or just see a physician. We do not recommend that one just try to forget it. First, a woman should be sure she is not injured, pregnant, or given a sexually transmitted disease. Second, few people easily forget; they only repress painful feelings, which have effects much later. Third, reporting rape alerts the police to someone who may go on to attack others.

If a person does report the incident, he or she should do so as quickly as possible, to the police, a rape crisis center, or other social agency. Workers there will see that medical and other needs are met and ask for a detailed description of the event and the assailant. Many raped women want to first cleanse themselves physically and emotionally, but washing, douching, or changing clothes destroys evidence essential to prosecuting the rapist.

After rape, most women experience guilt at being raped, rage at the assailant, and helplessness and frustration, all interspersed with periods of calm and of depression. Many benefit from sessions with a psychotherapist, women's group, or social service. Eventually most rape victims return to normal lives (Hyde, 1976).

nocent." According to the *Uniform Crime Reports* (1976), the FBI concluded that in the 1970s one of five reports to the police of forcible rape proved on investigation to be unfounded (MacNamara and Sagarin, 1977).

How is a court to distinguish whether rape has occurred if there are no witnesses? Most often it does so by evidence of force or resistance, such as scars or bruises. Is there a history of sexual aggression or of "promiscuity"? The likelihood of a misunderstood message? Because of these difficulties, it has been argued that rape should be dealt with as is any assault; there is then no need to prove resistance or consent. The problem would remain of weighing two people's testimonies, but this exists in any case of actual or threatened assault.

The harsh punishments for rape, far greater than those for other kinds of physical assault, require that care be taken to avoid unjust prosecution and conviction. Since a harsh punishment makes conviction less likely for any crime (MacNamara and Sagarin, 1977), some say that reducing the punishment, though it might seem to trivialize the crime, may gain more convictions. They point out that even death penalties have not reduced rape. We concur with the recommendation of many legal and women's groups that the punishment be reduced, but we are uneasy about another suggestion—completely dropping the requirement of corroborating testimony or evidence. True, it hardly seems ethical to require more than verbal resistance of a person threatened with injury. But male desire and feigned female resistance (and subsequent guilt), even when coitus is mutually desired, is common (Shope, 1975) and will doubtless continue to produce unfounded charges of rape. A large dilemma remains.

It seems that the more close and intense a relationship, the more likely is pressured or unconsenting coitus (Kanin, 1957; Kirkpatrick and Kanin, 1957). However, it is often especially difficult in such situations to establish what constitutes rape. Some women and men play at sex from adversary positions; the women are supposed to be hard to get, and the men are to keep trying. The woman may want to play at or have the illusion of being forced into coitus, to reduce her feelings of guilt or for other reasons. This presents practical and ethical problems to which no one, so far, has fully satisfactory answers.

Prostitution

Kinds of Prostitution. Prostitution is the exchange of sexual services for money. The act is voluntary, and neither participant is a complainant, so prostitution is a victimless crime. It is society that complains, more against the prostitute than the customer, for it considers such activity immoral and perhaps threatening to social order. There is widespread acceptance that men biologically need sexual outlets more often and more urgently than women do, so their occasional resort to prostitutes is commonly considered, if not praiseworthy, at least natural.

Prostitution has occurred under the protection of religion in the ancient Near East and medieval Europe (Henriques, 1965). In many places today, as in the past, prostitution is regulated by the government. Prostitution is not illegal in Great Britain, Germany, Sweden, Holland, Korea, and many other nations. In the United States it is legal only in some counties of Nevada.

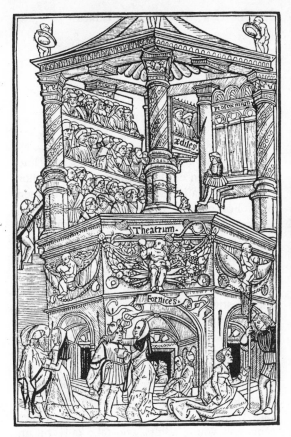

Figure 22-3 / *Western nations have long tried to ban, tolerate, or regulate prostitution. A French woodcut of the late sixteenth century (top left) shows prostitutes inviting men into their quarters on the ground floor of a theatre; at that time, many cities (and even churches) allowed prostitution on property they owned. Today, police in many cities, such as New York, harass and periodically arrest prostitutes (top right), somewhat limiting their visibility. In other cities, such as Amsterdam, a "red light" district operates with little official interference (bottom) as long as it more or less "polices" itself to minimize other illegal activity and sexually transmitted diseases.*

The great majority of prostitutes (whores, "hustlers," "hookers") are women who service men, but there are also many male prostitutes, almost all of whom service men. Male prostitutes for women are rare, and female prostitutes for women rarer still. Prostitutes may be classified as street prostitutes, house girls, and call girls. All offer essentially the same services, but they do so somewhat differently, and society views them somewhat differently.

Street prostitutes ("streetwalkers") are most common. They walk the streets or frequent bars or hotels to find customers ("tricks," "Johns"), whom they usually take to nearby hotels or, sometimes, to cars or customers' homes. The cost is standardized in most cities and neighborhoods, but some bargaining takes place. The sexual activity is usually brief and ends as soon as ejaculation occurs. A street prostitute may have three, five, or more customers a night. Working illegally in public and coping with the physical and emotional strains of the job take a toll. Many streetwalkers have short professional lives; five to ten years is a long career for them.

Most street prostitutes work for a *pimp*, a man who offers protection from police, abusive men, and competing prostitutes, some degree of emotional security, and access to customers. In return, he usually demands all of the streetwalker's income, from which he provides for her needs and gives her an allowance. A pimp may have a "stable" of several women. He may become threatening or violent should one try to leave his stable or quit prostitution.

Prostitutes are often arrested on charges of soliciting, prostitution, disturbing the peace, or other misdemeanors and receive fines or short jail sentences. For some women, these brushes

with the law are merely nuisances, the fines business expenses. For others, frequent short jail terms are a life sentence on the installment plan. For society, the pressure of such legal actions seems a way of trying to keep prostitution from being flagrant. The social reaction to streetwalkers is often very hostile; their public soliciting seems to offend more than their sexual activity. In some places, such as Great Britain, prostitution is not illegal, but soliciting is.

Male hustlers, like their female counterparts, walk the streets or work bars looking for male customers. They work without pimps and keep all their earnings (Harris, 1973). They are more likely to vary their fees, depending on the customer and their own financial needs. They vary from effeminate homosexuals to adolescents and young adults who take only the insertee role, consider themselves heterosexual or bisexual, and resort to hustling only when they need money (A. Riess, 1961).

Lesbian prostitution is rare. It is more a matter of occasionally obtaining meals, favors, or a contribution to living expenses than of active hustling. This little-studied activity was described in Émile Zola's novel *Nana* (1942).

House girls work in *brothels* ("whorehouses"). There is usually a madam, or house manager, with whom they split their earnings (from 40 to 60 percent goes to the madam). The house offers protection from some of the problems of the streets, a place to meet customers, rooms for sexual activity, and protection from offensive clients (Woolston, 1969). Some "massage parlors" work the same way. Many or most house girls today are of lower-class origin, though some are middle class. Their status seems to depend partly on how tolerant the community is.

Call girls are the least visible and best paid prostitutes. Most work alone, keep all their income, and are selective about clients. Often they serve as escorts or companions as well as sexual partners and spend the entire evening and night with a customer. Many come from middle-class backgrounds and, with their high income, maintain that status or rise above it. These women are rarely involved with the law and may continue their work for many years.

The Lives of Prostitutes. The majority of prostitutes are of lower-class origin. A drug habit, poverty, or social circumstances make some turn to prostitution ("the life," "the game"), but according to Gebhard (1969), fewer than 4 percent are forced into it. Most call girls enter prostitution and make contacts on their own (Jackman, O'Toole, and Geis, 1963) or hear of it from a friend or acquaintance. Adolescent rebellion, desire for money, a hope for glamor and adventure, sexual desire, and urging by pimps or by friends who have already become prostitutes may combine to entice a person to enter the life. They then tend to develop a defensive ideology that justifies and glamorizes their work despite its deviant status (N. Davis, 1978).

Nearly two-thirds of the prostitutes in one study expressed no regrets about their choice of work (Gebhard, 1969). Nevertheless, many of them, particularly streetwalkers, live in a criminal subculture of violence, theft, blackmail, drug abuse, and misfortune. Some find it

---

Parlor Houses

During the 1850s, New York physician William Sanger studied prostitution in America as part of his study of venereal disease. He classed brothels as parlor houses, second-class houses, third-class houses, and slum basements. Parlor houses were for the well-to-do, and one needed an introduction to enter. There was time for small talk, good food, and drink. The women were educated, sophisticated, and from middle- or upper-class homes. Second-class houses were less dignified and less exclusive. The men and women were middle class; the women were not sophisticated, and many were foreign born. Venereal disease was common in these houses. Third-class houses were usually associated with bars or beer gardens. Many were run by a husband and wife and served a neighborhood trade. Some had accommodations for streetwalkers. In the slum basements, older, worn-out prostitutes continued their trade. Old meant twenty-five. Dr. Sanger said: "The average duration of life among these women does not exceed four years from the beginning of their career! . . . it is a tolerably well-established fact that one-fourth of the total number of abandoned women in this city die every year."

— Mary Cable et al., *American Manners and Morals* (1969)

---

exciting. However, depth interviews of call girls (Greenwald, 1958) revealed a high degree of anxiety, emotional conflict, and self-destructive behavior beneath reports of self-satisfaction. Family instability, early teens use of coitus to win attention or status, and isolation from conventional home and social supports mark the histories of many women who turn to prostitution (N. Davis, 1978).

Some writers stress the financial incentives for prostitution and minimize psychological problems, especially for call girls. Millet (1971) quotes one call girl as saying:

With most uptown call girls, the choice is not between starvation and life, but it is a choice between $5,000 and $25,000 or between $10,000 and $50,000. . . . psychologically I've suffered so much more in other situations. . . . I was in tears so much more in graduate school, infuriated and sick. I didn't get an ulcer when I was a prostitute. That happened when I was in graduate school.

Whether research would confirm such self-perceptions is not known.

For a century or more, penologists and researchers have reported that many prostitutes dislike men, are anorgasmic with them, and often prefer lesbian contacts (H. Ellis, 1936). Gebhard (1969) reports that there is great variation. For instance, almost 25 percent of the younger prostitutes in his study claimed they almost always reached orgasm with clients; only about 20 percent said they never did. With their husbands (about 75 percent of the women were or had been married) or male friends, many were more orgasmic than a comparable group of women, and from one-quarter to one-half experienced multiple orgasm. More than 30 percent of prostitutes had had homo-

sexual experience, a figure far above average. However, not all prostitutes are especially knowledgeable about sex. Many have had no training and possess no techniques unknown to many experienced women.

Some prostitutes are linked with organized crime, but The Commission on Law Enforcement and Administration of Justice (1967) and the Commission on Crime in the District of Columbia (1966) deny that organized crime is involved in most prostitution. Prostitutes and pimps may use money for other illegal activities, such as dealing in drugs, but mostly on their own and often to cover their income for tax or other purposes. The large number of freelance prostitutes, their transience, and the relative privacy of their work all make prostitution difficult to organize and discipline.

Many prostutes and pimps do, however, pay for police protection, practice blackmail or extortion, and sometimes rob, threaten, or beat customers (McNamara and Sagarin, 1977). These practices, too, seem to be more random than organized, but several large blackmail rings using heterosexual and homosexual prostitutes have preyed on rich and prominent people in the past decade.

The Clients. Society, police, and law officers rarely show much interest in prostitutes' clients. In many jurisdictions, clients could be fined or jailed for fornication or using a brothel, but usually they aren't. These laws, when applied at all, are usually used to intimidate them into testifying against prostitutes (Babcock et al., 1975). Similarly, male prostitutes are harassed and prosecuted, their clients not as often (Harris, 1973).

Many customers are unmarried or away

from their wives, on business trips or in military service. Kinsey et al. (1948) found that about 70 percent of white American males had had at least one experience with a prostitute, and 15 to 20 percent had had several over a period of up to five years. Contact with prostitutes may be declining, but is still significant.

Men visit prostitutes for many reasons. A common one is quick, anonymous release from sexual tension while away from regular sexual partners. Another is to engage in acts a wife or partner won't permit; oral-genital and anal-genital intercourse are the services most often requested (Kinsey et al., 1948). Other reasons are novelty and adventure. Occasionally a man goes to a prostitute with a group of friends. Some men experiment with prostitutes to overcome embarrassment or ignorance or for coital initiation. To some men who are shy, physically handicapped, or have difficulty finding partners, prostitutes offer sexual relief. There are prostitutes who allow or even specialize in fetishistic, sadomasochistic, or other unusual practices.

Some men claim that considering the time and money spent on a date and the uncertainty of the outcome, it is cheaper to visit a prostitute. Other men visit prostitutes partly or primarily for companionship—someone to talk with who will provide them with kindness and deference. A small number of women obtain any or all of these services from a gigolo (a paid male companion) or male prostitute.

Ethical and Legal Aspects of Prostitution. Our society is inconsistent about prostitution. Though it maintains laws against prostitution, it rarely punishes prostitutes harshly and almost never bothers clients at all. It often urges that criminal law be used to control open commercial sex, but those who enforce and administer the law find it difficult in both practical and humanitarian terms.

Historically, the women's movement has opposed prostitution on the grounds that it degrades women (Pivar, 1965), but recently some feminists have reversed that position. Why, they ask, can't women do as they wish with their bodies? Such a view is defended by an organization of prostitutes called COYOTE (Call Off Your Old Tired Ethics).

Some people fear that decriminalizing prostitution would subject all women to harassing or degrading public sexual approaches. This is possible but unlikely; it hasn't happened where prostitution is permitted. Furthermore, some women find public attention complimentary rather than degrading, but others feel outraged by it (Babcock et al., 1975). There are also other serious problems, such as the use of young runaways by experienced pimps, that may not yield easily to regulation.

Those who favor decriminalizing prostitution claim it would allow monitoring of the medical, financial, and civic aspects of prostitution. They also point out that since people participate in prostitution voluntarily and privately, it should remain their private choice. Decriminalization has been relatively effective in some nations, and serious public problems seem not to have arisen.

Other Illegal Sex Behaviors

Most states have laws against *fornication* (nonmarital coitus), adultery, incest, and many nonreproductive sex behaviors, such as oral-genital and anal-genital intercourse, homosexual acts, pedophilia, and bestiality. The punishments range from a reprimand to a fine to many years in prison.

In many states, a number of nonreproductive activities are not specified but included in so-called sodomy laws. Strictly speaking, *sodomy* is anal-genital intercourse, but in many jurisdictions the word refers to any homosexual act and to heterosexual oral or anal intercourse. Other terms are also used, such as "unnatural acts." Sodomy laws have been challenged for vagueness (Barnett, 1973), on the grounds that every person should be able to know what is or is not legal.

Some sex behaviors are widely illegal although they involve no genital contact—exhibitionism, indecent exposure, voyeurism, and transvestism—since both laws and custom limit nudity and sexual activities almost entirely to private places. These acts are performed mostly by men, except for exposing the breasts, and because most men probably would not object if women exhibited themselves or peeped at them. Women are rarely charged. Also, women now commonly wear traditionally masculine clothes, whereas a man who wears a dress is subject not only to ridicule but in many states to arrest.

The punishments for exhibitionism and voyeurism are usually relatively light, but often they dramatically exceed the crime. Women or young girls may be frightened, shocked, or merely surprised by the act (Gebhard et al., 1965); it does violate the right to privacy, but does flashing the genitals on a streetcorner or watching someone undress through a window merit years in jail and a felony conviction record that follows one for life? In many states, a peeper or flasher is officially listed as a sexual psychopath and offered psychiatric treatment, which seems a mixed blessing.

Virtually all societies forbid sexual contact between adults and those defined as sexually immature (see chapter 20). However, child molestation laws in the United States have been called vague, harsh, and biased against men. A man who fondles a child is much more likely to be charged with assault and prosecuted than a woman who does so (Gebhard et al., 1965). A study of legal records (Anderson, unpublished) revealed that while 4,000 men were prosecuted for molestation, only four women were, although the author of the study believes women may perform the same behavior almost as often. If a man hugs, kisses, or fondles a child, it is more likely to be considered assaultive than fatherly. If a woman does so, it more likely to be thought motherly or grandmotherly.

Kinsey et al. (1953) found that some 24 percent of women recalled a sexual experience (commonly exhibitionism, rarely coitus) with an adult before age thirteen. In only one case of 4,441 did serious physical injury occur. Gagnon (1965) found that of 333 women who reported such events, only three thought it had caused damage in adult life. Much remains to be learned about early-life sexual contact with adults.

Ethical Issues

The basic ethical and legal issues involved in sexual activities are privacy, consent, and the welfare of individuals and society. Traditionally, our society has allowed private acts between consenting adults more by custom then by law. The Constitution doesn't explicitly guarantee privacy, sexual or otherwise, but increasingly courts are deciding that privacy is an implied right (Barnett, 1973). It seems to us, as to many others in the United States today, that what occurs consensually in private does not warrant public review. Even many traditionally devout people feel that a free choice is the most meaningful one. More than a century ago, the right to privacy and control of one's body was argued thus by philosopher John Stuart Mill (1956):

That the only purpose for which power can be rightly exercised over any member of a civilized community, against his will, is to prevent harm to others. His own good, either physical or moral, is not sufficient warrant. Each person is the proper guardian of his own health, whether bodily, or mental or physical.

The issue is problematic, however, when one considers minors, certain handicapped people, and the mentally incompetent. To be sure, they should be shielded from coercion and deception, but are they entitled to give consent? Or must they remain frustrated, waiting for a guardian or the state to decide if and when they may express their sexuality? A right to sexual expression for those formerly denied it is now being defended for the first time in our society's history (Gochross and Schultz, 1977).

Ethically, one might think that a person has a right to decline any sexual activity, but the law does not say so. In most states, spouses are legally entitled to sexual access. Oregon was the first state to reverse the automatic acceptance of this access. New Jersey followed suit, and other states are considering similar legislation. However, this right is so strong that in every state, if an accidental injury makes coitus impossible for someone, the spouse may sue the person who caused the accident for loss of *consortium* (sexual association) and sue the spouse for divorce. However, our society's traditional disapproval of noncoital acts complicates the picture. For a couple unhindered by physical problems, the law in all states protects a wife if she doesn't want anal intercourse; but the law does not guarantee to protect her (except per-

---

Cause for Annulment

The Roman Catholic church has long held that marriage is a sacrament and has forbidden divorce. Annulment, or dissolution of marriage without divorce, has been possible on sexual grounds, though difficult to obtain. One justification for annulment has been marriage based on a lie or a false promise. Another has been that marriage that was never consummated (confirmed by coitus). This might occur if the man was impotent or the woman had vaginismus. In the Middle Ages, there was a test meant to prevent men from using false claims of impotence to win annulment. A local court in England would select and deputize seven "honest women" (it is not known exactly how they were chosen) to tease and tempt the man, to test whether he was indeed impotent. It was assumed that potency in that situation reflected potency in the marriage—though modern research shows that impotence may occur only with a certain partner or partners (Helmholz, 1974).

haps in one state) if she doesn't want vaginal intercourse. Only relative ethics can resolve the problems of a couple whose sexual desires differ. The law does, in some states, allow divorce for sexual incompatibility.

Many sex acts are now being *decriminalized.* This is different from legalizing them. To legalize a behavior is to approve and regulate it; drinking laws, for example, say who may purchase alcohol, where it may be sold, and where consumed. When a state decriminalizes something, it withdraws its concern and remains neutral. This does not necessarily make personal decisions easier; in fact, the responsibility for decisions falls increasingly on each individual, and not everyone feels comfortable with that. Some people who argue for keeping sex laws on the books contend that even adults want certain decisions made for them or at least want formal guidelines.

Overview

We started by distinguishing absolute and relative values and by noting that most laws more or less reflect social values. Where formal laws do not regulate sex, there are other constraints, and ethical conflicts often arise for individuals and couples whose desires do not coincide with law and traditional values.

We have recently seen some changes in laws meant to govern several sex behaviors. Only a few decades ago, it was illegal in many states to

---

Moral Decisions

The essence of morality lies in the quality of interrelationships which can be established among people. Moral conduct is that kind of behavior which enables people in their relationships with each other to experience a greater sense of trust, and appreciation for others; which increases the capacity of people to work together; which reduces social distance and continually furthers one's outreach to other persons and groups; which increases one's sense of self-respect and produces a greater measure of personal harmony.

—Lester A. Kirkendall,
*Searching for the Roots of
Moral Judgments* (1967)

Whatever is hateful unto thee, do it not unto thy fellow. This is the whole Law; the rest is but commentary.

—Hillel, *The Talmud,* c.550 B.C.

There are no simple solutions, only intelligent choices.

—Anonymous

---

have an abortion, obtain contraceptives through the mail, own pornography, marry someone of a different race, wear a bikini, or show pubic hair in a magazine or book. Religious ideas of morality have not changed as much, but many clergymen and devout laymen are now resigned to the facts that the majority of couples aren't virgins at marriage, noncoital sex practices are common, pleasure is a common motive for coitus, divorce and remarriage are widespread, and the double standard is less strong. Probably more of them accept situational rather than absolute standards for sex behavior. However, many laws and moral restraints remain as restrictive as ever (Coleman, 1978).

In a society that has, in a few decades, seen masturbation change from a problem to an answer, the use of surrogates change from illegal to therapeutic, and homosexual acts be decriminalized or recriminalized in many states, no one can know where society is heading. We can only decide what to do ourselves.

We must add that sex education, research, and therapy, like other types of research and therapy, always involve ethical issues. The right to privacy and consent must be protected, and the researcher and therapist must not psychologically or physically harm their subjects or patients (Masters, Johnson, and Kolodny, 1977).

Most sexual decisions have ethical considerations, not only about the possible right or wrong of a sex act but about the personal and interpersonal consequences. Guilt and doubt often follow a decision that involves conflict over strongly felt values. Knowing that one is not alone in facing difficult decisions often helps to relieve this burden. We agree with E. C. Kennedy (1972) and others who stress that to help persons make good judgments on their sexual behavior, the best course is not quick advice or cutting them loose to do what they feel is right; it is rather to help them to grow totally so that all their power of judgment can be brought to bear on an aspect of their life which cannot be successfully isolated from the rest of their personality.

Review, Discuss, Decide

1. Would you describe your own moral or ethical beliefs about sex behavior as absolute, relative, or a combination of the two?
2. Give some examples of laws reflecting traditional attitudes and customs. How closely do they match current attitudes and behavior?
3. What do various religions have to say about the issues presented in this chapter?
4. Considering the material in this chapter and the chapter on what societies say, how much do you think laws influence sex behavior?

5. How would you resolve the question of sexual consent? How are the issues different between strangers, acquaintances, friends, spouses?
6. What are some of the ethical conflicts over sexual matters that you have experienced. Has your view of them changed since they happened?
7. How, if at all, would you change the laws in your nation, state, or community governing pornography, prostitution, rape, homosexuality, oral-genital acts, or any other kind of sex behavior?
8. Given the opportunity, how would you deal with the double standard in ethics, law, and daily life?
9. How might your decisions change if you were making them for yourself, your partner, a child, friend, or society?

Glossary

abortion. Termination of pregnancy. It may happen spontaneously *(miscarriage),* be done to protect the mother's health or life *(therapeutic abortion),* or be chosen as a form of postconception birth control.

absolute morality. The belief that certain acts are right or wrong for all people in all situations. Compare RELATIVE MORALITY.

abstinence. Voluntarily not performing an act; choosing to be sexually inactive.

accessory organs. The prostate gland, seminal vesicles, and bulbourethral glands. These specialized glands produce seminal fluids, sugars, and prostaglandins, which nourish sperm and promote their survival after ejaculation.

achieved role, achieved status. A role or status resulting from one's own behavior or others' attitudes toward it. Compare ASCRIBED ROLE.

acid phosphatase. A component of semen produced by the prostate gland; its presence in the vagina is taken in some jurisdictions as legal evidence that coitus has occurred.

adolescence. The time between reaching physical sexual maturity (puberty) and reaching social maturity (acting and being treated as an adult). It varies greatly among individuals and societies.

adrenal glands. Paired glands, one atop each kidney, that produce testosterone in females and adrenalin and other hormones in both sexes.

adrenogenital syndrome. A rare genetic condition in which a female is exposed to excess androgens before birth and is born with masculinized genitals.

adultery. A legal and general term for extramarital coitus.

affectional system. The network of bonds, or relationships, that exist in humans and some higher social species.

afterbirth. The placenta and the membranes that surrounded a fetus; they are normally expelled soon after childbirth.

agape. In ancient Greece and in philosophy, spiritual and altruistic love; distinguished from *eros,* erotic and romantic love, and *philia,* nonerotic love or comradeship.

alternate life-style. A phrase now used by some to describe relatively uncommon patterns in sexual and marital behavior, such as homosexuality and "group marriage."

ambisexual. See BISEXUAL.

ambivalence. Having contrary feelings or attitudes at ..e time, such as love and hate.

amenorrhea. Absence of menstruation.

amniocentesis. Removing and studying the amniotic fluid, which surrounds a fetus in the uterus, to test a fetus for genetic defects. Also see GENETIC SCREENING.

amyl nitrate. A medication for heart disease that is sometimes inhaled to produce a brief high or light-headedness during sexual activity. The slang terms are "amies" and "poppers."

anal eroticism. Erotic responsiveness in the anal area; erotic stimulation of the anus. According to psychoanalytic theory, anal eroticism marks a normal stage of early childhood, and many erotic and

491

nonerotic feelings associated with it persist throughout life.

anal stage. See ANAL EROTICISM.

anaphrodisiac. A substance meant to turn off love or sexual desire or to decrease sexual response or performance.

anarousmia. Inability to be sexually aroused.

*androgen-insensitivity syndrome (*also *testicular feminizing syndrome).* A rare genetic condition that makes a male unable to respond to androgens. He does not develop male genitals or typical male behavior patterns; looks and acts as a female.

androgens. "Male" sex hormones produced primarily in the testes and in the adrenal glands of both sexes, but also, in smaller amounts, in the ovaries. They maintain the male sexual and reproductive systems, help create male physical and behavioral traits, and activate sexual drive in both sexes.

androgynous. Having both male and female characteristics.

anilingus. Oral stimulation of the anal area.

annulment. Invalidation of marriage without divorce.

anorgasmia. Inability to reach orgasm. It may be *primary* (lifelong), *secondary* (occurring in someone once able to reach orgasm), or *situational* (occurring only with a certain partner or in a certain situation).

anovulation. Absence of ovulation.

anus. The orifice between the buttocks where the digestive system ends. In some people it is erotically sensitive (see ANAL EROTICISM).

aphanasis. See CASTRATION ANXIETY.

aphrodisiac. A substance meant to arouse love or sexual desire or to enhance sexual response or performance.

*areola (*pl. *areolae).* The pigmented area around the nipple.

arousal. Widely used as synonymous with excitement, although some distinguish excitement as physical and arousal as psychological. There are *arousal mechanisms* and an *arousal stage* in the sexual response cycle.

artificial insemination. Placing sperm in the vagina or uterus without coitus, to raise the chances of conception. The sperm may be that of the husband, a donor, or both.

ascribed role, ascribed status. A role or status resulting from visible, unchangeable traits, such as biological sex. Compare ACHIEVED ROLE.

aspect, sexual. Aspect: a view or part of something. Sexuality can be thought of as having *psychological aspects,* both *cognitive* and *instinctive,* and so-

matic *(physical) aspects,* both *phenotypic* (in appearance) and *situational.*

autoeroticism. Sexual self-stimulation; masturbation and erotic fantasy.

autosome. See CHROMOSOME.

Bartholin's glands. See VULVOVAGINAL GLANDS.

basal body temperature. A woman's body temperature at rest. One rhythm method of birth control involves calculating the basal body temperature every day to try to determine when ovulation occurs, so that the woman refrains from coitus when most likely to conceive.

berdache. Any of several social roles in Plains Indian, Eskimo, and other cultures in which men are variously transvestites, homosexuals, priests, magicians, or combinations of these. Used loosely for an effeminate male homosexual.

*bestiality (*also *zoophilia).* Sexual contact between a person and an animal.

*biased interaction theory (*also *biosocial interaction theory).* The theory of sexual development that biological forces set potentials (ranges and biases) for development, and that social influences and individual experience determine the extent to which these potentials are realized.

birth control. Controlling reproduction by sexual abstinence, contraception, abortion, or other means.

birthrate. Number of births per thousand women, usually per year.

bisexual. Having organs or traits of both sexes; not to be confused with HERMAPHRODITE. Also less precisely used for having erotic partners of both sexes. The slang terms are "bi" and "AC/DC."

bladder. A hollow organ that stores fluid, such as the urinary bladder.

"blue balls." Pain in the testes caused by excessive vasocongestion, usually caused by extended sexual excitement. See CHRONIC PELVIC CONGESTION.

bondage. Being tied or shackled for erotic excitement or satisfaction. This form of masochism, when accompanied by "domination" (being humiliated or enslaved), is called "B and D."

bonding. The forming of a relationship. See AFFECTIONAL SYSTEM.

Bovaryism. Exaggerated romantic expectations; from Gustave Flaubert's novel *Madame Bovary.*

brothel. House of prostitution.

bugger. To perform anal intercourse; the act is called *buggery* or *sodomy.*

492

bulbourethral glands (also Cowper's glands). A pair of small glands within the male's pelvic diaphragm, under the prostate gland. Early in sexual excitement they produce a clear fluid that appears at the urethral meatus.

butyl nitrate. A drug with effects similar to those of AMYL NITRATE.

caesarean delivery. Delivery of a child through an incision *(caesarean section)* in the abdomen and uterus. Named for Julius Caesar, said to have been delivered this way.

calendar method. A rhythm method of contraception in which a woman keeps track of the days she menstruates to determine when ovulation occurs and refrain from coitus when most likely to conceive.

call girl. An expensive prostitute who is contacted by appointment and may provide social companionship as well as sexual services.

candidia (also monilia). A yeastlike fungus that causes a vaginal infection called *candidiasis (or moniliasis).* Produces thrush.

carpopedal spasm. Curling or flaring of the fingers and toes, as during orgasm.

castration. Removal of the testes or ovaries. Sometimes also used for removal of the penis.

castration anxiety. Fear of castration or loss of the penis. More broadly, conscious or unconscious fear of damage to vulnerable parts of the body. The female counterpart, a generalized fear of mutilation or annihilation, is called *aphanasis.*

celibacy. Remaining unmarried. The word is usually applied to men or women members of the clergy. Incorrectly used as a synonym for sexual abstinence.

cervix. The neck of the uterus.

chancre. An ulcerlike sore caused by syphilis. (Pronounced shan'-ker.)

chancroid (also soft chancre). One of the five classic venereal diseases. It causes a sore resembling a chancre.

change of life. See MENOPAUSE.

chastity. State of virginity; sexual abstinence.

chauvinism. Exaggerated patriotism; often implying prejudice and hostility toward people of other nationalities. Now sometimes loosely used for such attitudes toward the opposite sex.

chromosome. A body within the nucleus of a cell that contains genes, or genetic messengers. A human cell has twenty-two pairs of similar chromosomes *(autosomes)* and one pair of *sex chromosomes,* which are different in men and the same in women. A female's two sex chromosomes are called *X chromosomes;* a male has one X chromosome and a smaller *Y chromosome.* All human cells have twenty-three pairs of chromosomes except mature sperm and egg cells, which have twenty-two unpaired autosomes and one X or one Y sex chromosome (X in all egg cells, X or Y in sperm cells). Sex chromosomes determine an offspring's sex.

chronic pelvic congestion. Prolonged vasocongestion of the female pelvis, often resulting from extended sexual excitement. See "BLUE BALLS."

circumcision. Removal of the foreskin from the penis or, more rarely, from the clitoris. In our society, the male foreskin is now routinely removed in infancy; in many others, it is done in childhood, at puberty, or not at all.

climacteric. See MENOPAUSE.

climax. See ORGASM.

clitoris (pl. clitorides). The female phallus; a small hooded body above the vagina and between the labia. Unlike the penis, or male phallus, the clitoris is not truly erectile in most women and has no urinary function. Its function seems wholly erotic. Slang terms are "clit" and "button."

cognitive development theory. A theory of psychological development that stresses how mental capacities grow through childhood and how new knowledge and feelings develop at each stage.

cohabitation. Living together sexually. Usually used of unmarried heterosexual couples.

coitus (also coition). Genital intercourse; entry of the penis into the vagina. Slang terms are "balling," "screwing," "making it," "fucking." (Pronounced co'-i-tus.)

coitus-dependent/coitus-independent. Terms describing contraceptive methods. Some methods, such as the condom, must be used with each coition; they are *coitus-dependent.* Others, such as the IUD, remain in effect regardless of whether coitus occurs; they are *coitus-independent.*

coitus interruptus (also withdrawal). Attempting contraception by withdrawing the penis from the vagina before ejaculation.

coitus reservatus. The technique of coitus without having an ejaculation.

colostrum. A fluid produced by the breasts, usually soon after childbirth and before lactation begins. It is high in protein and antibodies.

commitment. Pledging or binding oneself to a person or a relationship.

493

commune. A community that aims to equally share property, labor, authority, sexual partners, or any combination of these.

complementary needs theory. The theory that one tends to be attracted to people whose needs complement one's own: for instance, that nurturing people are drawn to those who seek nurture. Compare HOMOGAMOUS NEEDS THEORY.

conception. The fertilization of an egg by a sperm cell, to form a zygote.

concubine. A woman who is part of a man's household and is his sexual partner, but does not have the full rights and status of a wife.

*condom (*also *prophylactic).* A sheath, now commonly made of rubber, plastic, or animal gut, that is rolled over the penis before coitus to prevent both conception and the transmission of disease. The slang term is "rubber."

consanguine kin. Biologically related ("blood") kin. Compare DESIGNATED KIN.

consummation. Affirming the marriage bond by performing coitus.

contraception. Preventing conception, by a device or behavioral means.

contraceptive. A device, such as the condom, IUD, or vaginal diaphragm, or a substance, such as hormone or foam, used to prevent conception.

coprophilia. Erotic interest in or arousal by feces or defecation.

copulation. Coitus.

corona. The rim at the edge of the glans penis.

corpora cavernosa. Paired cylinders of tissue in the penis and in the clitoris; the large spaces between the cells fill with blood (vasocongestion) during sexual excitement, causing erection of the penis and swelling of the clitoris.

corpus luteum. A yellow body in the ovary that develops after ovulation from a mature follicle and produces progesterone.

*corpus urethra (*also *corpus spongiosum).* A cylinder of spongy tissue in the penis that cushions the urethra.

courtship. In biology, the stereotyped behaviors by males and females that lead to copulation. More loosely, a person's attempts to interest another in sexual contact or marriage.

couvade. The custom, existing in many societies, of a man ritually imitating some aspects of his wife's delivery of a child.

Cowper's glands. See BULBOURETHRAL GLANDS.

crab lice. Parasites related to body lice that infest pubic and other body hair. They are easily trans-mitted by sexual or other physical contact. The slang term is "crabs."

critical period. A genetically determined period when the capacity for developing a trait or learning a behavior is greatest. There are, for instance, critical periods in humans for sexual differentiation and developing a sexual identity.

*cryptorchidism (*also *undescended testicles).* A condition in which the testes remain in the body cavity instead of descending into the scrotum.

*cultural adaptation theory (*also *neo-Freudian theory).* A theory of psychosexual development rising from psychoanalysis and ego psychology; it uses many psychoanalytic concepts but stresses adaptation to the family and social environment rather than instinctive drives as influences on personality and behavior.

cultural relativism. The view that one society's beliefs and practices should not be judged according to another society's values.

cunnilingus. Oral stimulation of the female genitals.

curettage. Using a curette (scraper) to remove the endometrial lining of the uterus and, sometimes, growths or an embryo implanted there. Often preceded by dilation of the uterus and called *dilatation and curettage (D and C).*

cyclic. Happening in a recurrent pattern.

cystitis. Inflammation of the bladder, often caused by infection and involving the urethra.

"day-after pill." Pills containing estrogens that are taken for several days after coitus to prevent implantation of a zygote that may have formed.

decidua. The portion of the endometrium, or uterine lining, that is shed during menstruation.

designated kin. People who are related according to custom or law rather than biologically. Compare CONSANGUINE.

determinism. A belief or theory that most events or acts, even those apparently based on decisions, have predetermining causes. Some theories of human sexuality reflect *biological determinism,* others *social determinism.*

detumescence. A lessening of swelling (tumescence), especially of that caused by vasocongestion in the sexualia during sexual response.

deviance. Different from the mathematical average; in social science, a behavior or identity that is disapproved or only tolerated. Often used for untypical sex behaviors, as is the word *deviant* for those who perform them. Although neutral in

494

scientific use, these words are sometimes charged with social or moral values. See PARAPHILIA.

diaphragm, vaginal. A contraceptive rubber cap placed over the uterine cervix, usually used along with spermicidal cream or jelly.

differential socialization theory. The theory that many or most differences in males' and females' behavior result from social stereotypes, the sex-typing of tasks and behaviors, and the different rearing of boys and girls by their families and society.

dildo. Artificial penis used in heterosexual play or for masturbation by females and some male homosexuals. In Greek, an *olisbos (pl. olisboi)*; in French, a *godmiché.*

dimorphism. The existence of two forms. *Sexual dimorphism* is the existence of two forms of a species, male and female, that must carry out a sexual act to reproduce.

divorce. The legal termination of marriage.

divorce rate. The number of divorces per thousand marriages, usually per year.

Don Juanism. A man's compulsive need to seduce women. Like many terms for allegedly excessive sex behavior, it has no precise, scientifically accepted definition.

dorsal. On or toward the back of the body or any part of it.

double standard. Different standards of sex behavior for males and females.

dysfunction. Less than full or desirable function, physically or psychologically or socially.

dysmenorrhea. Painful menstruation.

dyspareunia. Pain in or near the vagina caused by coitus.

ectopic. Out of place. An *ectopic pregnancy* is implantation and development of a zygote outside the uterus—for instance, a *tubal pregnancy,* in the oviducts.

effacement. Thinning of the uterine cervix as childbirth nears.

effeminacy. A male's expression, imitation, or parody of feminine behavior in place of masculine behavior. Some effeminate men are homosexual and some are not.

ego. In psychoanalytic and several other theories of development, the conscious self. Also, sense of individual identity.

ego psychology. The study of personality, development, and relationships as a continuing adaptation, using psychodynamic concepts. See CULTURAL ADAPTATION THEORY.

ejaculation. The expulsion of semen from the penis; it normally occurs during orgasm from puberty on. It has two stages: *emission* (emptying of the contents of the accessory glands into the urethra) and *ejaculation proper* (the propelling of semen from the penis).

ejaculatory duct. The portion of duct that links the vas deferens and seminal vesicles to the urethra.

Electra complex. A female's erotic attachment to her father and rivalrous feelings toward her mother. Compare OEDIPUS COMPLEX.

embryo. A developing offspring from the time of implantation until eight weeks later; after that it is called a *fetus.*

emission. See EJACULATION.

endocrine. Relating to hormones. The *endocrine glands,* or *ductless glands,* are those which produce hormones.

endogamy. The tendency to marry within one's class, caste, religious or other social group.

endometrium. The layer of tissue lining the uterus where implantation occurs. The cyclic shedding of part of it (the decidua) produces menstruation.

eonism. See TRANSVESTISM.

epididymus. A mass attached to each testicle consisting of a long, coiled tube for storing sperm and carrying it to the vas deferens.

episiotomy. A surgical incision in the perineum, to enlarge the vaginal outlet, often used in standard childbirth to ease delivery.

erection. Swelling and hardening of the phallus or nipples, caused by vasocongestion; it may be reflexive or a result of sexual excitement.

erogenous. Erotically responsive. In Freudian theory, *erogenous zones* are areas of the body that normally become sexually responsive during childhood—first the mouth, then the anus, then the genitals.

eros. See AGAPE.

erotic. Sexually arousing; referring to sexual desire or response.

estrogens. "Female" sex hormones, produced primarily in the ovaries, the adrenal glands of males and females, and in small amounts, in the testes. They maintain the female sexual and reproductive systems, help create female physical and behavioral traits, and in large amounts reduce sexual interest and responsiveness in males.

estrus. The cyclic period of sexual receptiveness that occurs in females of many species. Human females' erotic responsiveness is not limited to an estrous period.

ethics. Beliefs about morality, or right and wrong behavior. See ABSOLUTE MORALITY and RELATIVE MORALITY.

eunuch. A male who has been castrated.

exchange theory. The theory that in relationships people weigh costs against benefits and tend to do what brings the most gain or requires the least cost.

excitement phase. See AROUSAL PHASE.

exhibitionism. Compulsively seeking sexual gratification from exposing the genitals to unwilling viewers. The slang word is "flashing."

extended family. See FAMILY.

extramarital coitus. Coitus between a married person and someone other than his or her spouse. Compare NONMARITAL COITUS.

Fallopian tube. See OVIDUCT.

false pregnancy. See PSEUDOCYESIS.

family. The *nuclear* family consists of spouses (in some societies more than two) and their children, both biological and adopted. Other biological or socially designated kin comprise the *extended* family.

fantasy. An imagined scene or event.

fellatio. Oral stimulation of the male genitals. Slang terms are "blow," "give head," "go down on."

female. One of the two biological sexes, characterized by female gonads (ovaries). Adj., characteristic of females; as distinguished from FEMININE.

feminine. Culturally associated with females; not to be confused with *female,* which refers to biologically determined traits. The comparable terms are masculine and male.

feminism. An ideology and social movement that aims at fostering women's interests and equalizing the rights and opportunities of both sexes.

fertility. Relative capacity for reproduction.

fertilization. The fusion of an ovum and a sperm cell (gametes) to form a zygote.

fetishism. Compulsive or exclusive sexual interest in an inanimate object or in a part of the human body rather than in a partner.

fetus. A developing offspring from about nine weeks of age until birth; for the first eight weeks it is called an *embryo.*

fidelity. Exclusive relations in love, sex, or both with one partner. Legally, the sexual exclusiveness expected of the married.

fimbriae. The fingerlike projections at the upper ends of the oviducts that sweep ova into the oviducts.

flaccid. Limp; used to describe the nonerect penis.

flirting. The give and take of erotic invitations.

follicle. A small cavity or capsule. See OVARIAN FOLLICLE.

follicle stimulating hormone. See FSH.

foreplay. See PETTING.

*foreskin (*also *prepuce).* The hood of skin that covers the head (glans) of the penis and the clitoris. See *circumcision.*

fornication. Legally, coitus by unmarried people. The word often has overtones of disapproval.

"French." "To French" is sometimes used for French kissing, but more often for oral-genital intercourse.

*French kiss (*also *deep kiss).* A kiss in which one or both partners reciprocally thrust the tongue inside the other's mouth.

French tickler. A device, usually of plastic or rubber, attached to the penis or to a condom to increase vaginal stimulation or psychological arousal.

frenulum. A thin band of skin. There is an erotically sensitive frenulum on the underside of the penis, near the corona, and on the underside of the clitoris.

frequency. How often an event occurs.

Freudian. Referring to the work and ideas of Sigmund Freud and sometimes to that of other early psychoanalysts. See PSYCHOANALYSIS.

frigidity. A word for lack of sexual interest, anarousmia, anorgasmia, or even emotional unresponsiveness. Now widely in disfavor among sexologists.

FSH (follicle simulating hormone). A gonadotropic hormone released from the pituitary gland that stimulates spermatogenesis and the growth of ovarian follicles.

functionalism. The principle that physical structures, behaviors, traits, and social institutions evolved to help an individual, culture, or species adapt to its environment.

fundus. The uppermost part of the uterus.

gamete. An ovum or sperm cell; a male and a female gamete must unite for reproduction to occur.

game theory. Calculating odds and studying strategies and alternate scenarios in human behavior. Inaccurately used to describe manipulations in relationships.

gender. The social concomitants of being biologically male or female; as distinguished from biological sex. The adjectives for gender are *masculine* and *feminine* (for sex, male and female).

gender identity. A sense of oneself as masculine or feminine. Sometimes inaccurately used for sexual identity, the conviction that one is male or female.

gender roles. The social roles for and expectations of males and females; masculine and feminine roles.

gene. The basic unit bearing hereditary messages; genes are in the chromosomes of all cells.

genetic screening. A genetic study of prospective parents to discover the existence of conditions that might be passed on to their offspring.

genital apposition. Pressing or rubbing the genitals together while clothed or unclothed, without vaginal penetration.

genitals (also genitalia). The pelvic organs usually involved in erotic activity. Some are external (penis, scrotum, clitoris, labia) and some internal (testicles, uterus). Sometimes defined as external pelvic organs involved in reproduction.

gestation. An offspring's development in the uterus; gestation usually takes about 266 days.

glans. The head of the penis or the clitoris.

gonad. One of the paired glands that produce gametes and sex hormones: in males the testes, in females the ovaries. The gonads define a person's biological sex.

gonadotropic hormones (or gonadotropins). Hormones, such as LH, ICSH, and FSH, produced by the pituitary gland that stimulate gamete development and sex-hormone production in the gonads.

gonorrhea. One of the five classic venereal diseases, and among the most common and dangerous sexually transmitted diseases. Slang terms are "clap" and "morning drip."

Graafian follicle. A mature ovarian follicle; the last stage in the development of an ovum and the follicle surrounding it.

granuloma inguinale. One of the five classic venereal diseases; also known as *Donovan's disease.*

granulosa cell. A cell that, as part of an ovarian follicle, surrounds an ovum and aids its development.

gravid. Pregnant. Women who have had no pregnancies are called *nulligravida;* one pregnancy, *primigravida;* more than one pregnancy, *multigravida.* Gravidity describes only pregnancy, not birth; see PARITY.

group marriage. A self-defined (but not, in our society, legally valid) marriage among three or more people.

gynecomastia. Enlarged breasts in a male.

hemorrhoid. A varicose (swollen) vein in the rectal area; it can be painful and of medical concern.

hermaphrodite. Strictly defined, someone with both male and female gonadal tissue (a pair of ovaries and a pair of testes or one of each). Hermaphrodites are very rare; not quite as rare, though still uncommon, are *pseudohermaphrodites,* whose external genitals differ from their genetic sex or from their internal sexual and reproductive organs. Do not confuse hermaphrodite with BISEXUAL.

herpes genitalis. A sexually transmitted disease caused by a virus of the herpes type.

heterosexual. Noun; someone whose erotic desire and behavior are largely or entirely oriented to people of the other sex. Adj.; indicating such desire and behavior. Slang term is "straight."

homogamous needs theory. The theory that one tends to be attracted to people whose needs are the same as one's own. Compare COMPLEMENTARY NEEDS THEORY.

homosexual. Noun; someone whose erotic desire and behavior are largely or entirely oriented to people of the same sex. The orientation, called *homosexuality,* should be distinguished from hermaphroditism, transvestism, transsexualism, and effeminacy. Female homosexuality is also called *lesbianism* and *sapphism.* A slang term for homosexual is "gay." See BISEXUAL; HETEROSEXUAL.

hormone. A substance produced in one part of the body and carried by the bloodstream to other parts of the body to have its effects. The glands that produce hormones are called *endocrine glands.*

HPG axis (hypothalamic-pituitary-gonadal axis). Interactions among the hypothalamus, pituitary gland, and gonads that regulate the female reproductive cycle and male reproductive functions, and which influence some sexual behaviors and responses in both sexes.

hydrocoele (also hydrocele). A fluid-filled cyst in the testes or spermatic cords.

hymen. A membrane that covers part or much of the vaginal opening. Although its presence is widely associated with virginity, it can be pierced, stretched, or almost absent in a virgin or partly present in a nonvirgin.

hypothalamic-pituitary-gonadal axis. See HPG AXIS.

hypothalamus. A part of the brain that governs many basic physical and emotional responses, some of which are sexual or sex-related.

hysterectomy. Surgical removal of the uterus; the

operation ends fertility but need not end sexual desire or response. *Radical hysterectomy* includes removal of the ovaries and other internal reproductive organs as well.

ICSH (interstitial cell stimulating hormone). A hormone produced by the pituitary gland that in males stimulates production of sperm cells and testosterone in the interstitial cells. In females, the same gonadotropic hormone is called *LH.*

id. In psychoanalytic theory, the part of the mind that consists of basic, primitive desires, needs, and impulses.

identification. A feeling of being like or at one with another person. This psychoanalytic concept has been adopted in many social-learning theories of psychosexual development.

implant (also implantable). Something placed within the body, such as a contraceptive drug (synthetic progesterone) inserted under a person's skin, where it remains effective for many months.

implantation. The attachment of the ball of cells resulting from a developing zygote, normally to the endometrial wall of the uterus, where the cells will develop as an embryo.

impotence. Inability to reach or maintain penile erection; the opposite of potency. Impotence may be *primary* (lifelong), *secondary* (occurring in someone previously potent), or *situational* (occurring only in certain situations or with certain partners).

incest. Sexual contact with any member of one's nuclear family except one's spouse, and with certain other kin (variously designated in different societies). It is forbidden in all societies.

incidence. In the study of sex behavior, the number or proportion of people who have performed an act. *Cumulative incidence* is the percentage who have ever done something; *active incidence* is the percentage doing something at a given time.

infertility. Relative inability to reproduce; complete and permanent inability to reproduce is *sterility.*

infidelity. Sexual contact with someone other than a partner with whom there is an agreement to have an exclusive relationship.

infundibulum. The funnellike section of the oviduct, close to the ovary.

instinctive. Reflexive; normally occurring in response to a stimulus whether one wills it or not. Instinctive behaviors are largely hereditary, but some can be modified by learning.

interaction trait. A behavior or response that results from the interaction of a genetic predisposition and environmental influences.

intercourse. Sexual contact involving the genitals of at least one participant. *Genital intercourse,* or penile penetration of the vagina, is properly called *coitus* and, more loosely, *sexual intercourse.* Intercourse may also be *oral-genital, anal-genital, intermammary* (penis between the breasts), or *interfemoral* (penis between the thighs).

interfemoral intercourse. See INTERCOURSE.

intermammary intercourse. See INTERCOURSE.

interpersonal. Occurring between individuals; often used in a phrase coined by Harry Stack Sullivan, *interpersonal relations.*

interstitial cell stimulating hormone. See ICSH.

interstitium. Interstitial tissue, composed chiefly of interstitial cells (also called *Leydig cells*), around and between the seminiferous tubules of the testes. Also the stroma, or main nonfollicular tissue, of the ovary.

intrapsychic. Within the mind; often used in the phrase *intrapsychic conflict* to describe conflict between feelings or ideas within one person.

intrauterine device (IUD). A contraceptive device inserted by a physician into the uterus, where it remains.

intromission. Insertion, especially of the penis, into the vagina.

isthmus. The narrow region between the body and the cervix of the uterus.

IUD. See INTRAUTERINE DEVICE.

"jock itch." See TINEA CRURIS.

Klinefelter's syndrome. A genetic anomaly in which an individual is born with XXY chromosomes. The presence of the Y chromosome leads to the development of testes and basically male appearance, but there may be a somewhat feminized physique, low sex drive, and relative infertility.

labia majora. Parallel rolls of tissue extending from the mons veneris almost to the anus, bordering the labia minora, clitoris, and vaginal entrance.

labia minora. Rolls of tissue parallel to and medial to the labia majora; in most women they are erotically sensitive.

labor. The passage of a fetus from the uterus to outside its mother's body.

labor pains. Waves of muscle contractions in the uterus and surrounding areas that accomplish labor.

lactation. Milk production. It usually goes into full swing a few days after childbirth.

Lamaze method. A popular alternative to the standard method of childbirth; the woman learns to relax and help herself in the delivery, anesthesia is used sparingly or not at all, and the husband participates.

laparotomy. An incision made in the abdominal wall to allow diagnosis or further surgery.

latency period. In psychoanalytic theory, the preadolescent period, when sexual drive is channeled into social and mental development; this is now thought, to the extent that it does occur, to be largely a result of sexual restrictiveness.

latent homosexuality. According to early psychoanalytic theory, an instinctive homosexual drive that exists in everyone, but which is sublimated or repressed in those who develop heterosexual behavior and identity. The concept, like that of instinctive bisexuality, has been questioned.

learning theory. Any of several theories asserting that sexual development, like other aspects of development, depend largely or entirely on learning, conditioning, reinforcement, and similar processes.

Leboyer method. An alternative to the standard method of delivery that emphasizes the infant's physical and mental comfort, and also considers the mother's ecstatic and erotic feelings. It aims at reducing the presumed shock of leaving the uterus and entering the world outside the mother's body.

lesbian. See HOMOSEXUAL.

leukorrhea. A whitish discharge from the vagina, caused by infection or irritation.

levirate. The custom in many societies that a woman marry one or more of her husband's brothers, before or after the first husband's death. Compare SORORATE.

Leydig cell. The interstitial cell of the testes, which produces testosterone.

LH (luteinizing hormone). A hormone produced by the pituitary gland that aids the formation and growth of the corpus luteum. In males, this same gonadotropic hormone is called *ICSH*.

libido. In psychoanalytic theory, an instinctive drive toward erotic pleasure, reproduction, and well-being. More loosely, sexual drive.

life-table analysis. A way of rating a contraceptive method's effectiveness; it includes method effectiveness, user effectiveness, and how often the method is started, stopped, or resumed.

lightening. A fetus's descent, in a head-down position, into the pelvis during the last weeks of pregnancy. Also called *dropping* or *engagement*.

lochia. A discharge from the uterus and vagina that occurs for some days to a few weeks after childbirth.

lordosis. The crouching presentation of the hindquarters characteristic of females in most mammalian species. This posture allows copulation and is used for both sexual and nonsexual communication.

luteinizing hormone. See LH.

lymphogranuloma venereum. One of the five classic venereal diseases, affecting lymph glands in the genital region.

machismo. A complex of masculine attitudes and behaviors originally described in certain Latin American and Mediterranean cultures. It is now loosely used for almost anything assertively or distinctively male or masculine; in such usage there is no precise, agreed-on definition. Adj., *macho.*

macromastia. Unusually large breasts.

madame. A woman who manages a house of prostitution.

male. One of the two biological sexes, characterized by male gonads (testes). Adj., characteristic of males; as distinguished from MASCULINE.

mammae. Breasts. Adj., *mammary.*

marriage. The social institution binding a male and female as husband and wife; it universally ensures certain rights and responsibilities, such as sexual access, socially approved reproduction, and childrearing. In some societies, a person may have only one spouse at a time *(monogamy),* in others more than one *(polygamy).* Having more than one spouse, but only one at a time, is *serial monogamy.*

masculine. Culturally associated with males. Compare MALE.

masculine protest. In the theory of psychoanalyst Alfred Adler, some women's tendency to undervalue femaleness and femininity and to overvalue and envy maleness and masculinity. Some writers use the term *feminine protest* for a male's rejection of the masculine role and envy of feminine and female traits and prerogatives.

masochism. Erotic desire for or gratification from

pain and humiliation. Often used in both an erotic and a broad psychological sense. Masochism may coexist with sadism; hence the term *sado-masochism*.

mastectomy. Surgical removal of a breast; usually done to remove cancerous growth. *Radical mastectomy* involves removing chest muscle and axillary (armpit) lymph glands as well.

masturbation. Sexual self-stimulation, most commonly by using the hand but also in many other ways. The term is also used for one person's manual stimulation of another's genitals; when two people so stimulate each other, it may be called *mutual masturbation*. Also called onanism (incorrectly), "playing with oneself," and in males "jerking off."

matriarchy. A supposed stage of social evolution when women held greater authority than men; however, no matriarchy is known to have ever existed. Sometimes loosely used for a family or a cultural group in which women have relatively strong influence or decision-making power. Compare PATRIARCHY.

matrilineal descent. Descent reckoned through the mother and her family.

matrilocal residence. The tradition, found in some nonwestern societies, of a married couple living with or near the wife's family.

mature follicle. See GRAAFIAN FOLLICLE.

mean. What is popularly meant by an average; the result of adding figures and dividing the sum by the number of figures. See MEDIAN.

meatus. The opening of a duct; the urethral meatus is at the tip of the penis in men, on the floor of the vaginal vestibule in women.

mechanisms, sexual. Physical processes involved in sexual response. Sexual mechanisms can be classified as *arousal*, *copulatory*, or *orgasmic*, corresponding with the stages of the sexual response cycle.

median. The midpoint in an array of figures; often used rather than a mean (an average) to find the most representative figure, since it is less affected by extreme highs and lows. See MEAN.

ménage à trois. A sexual and domestic arrangement among three people; sometimes loosely used for a married person keeping a secondary partner.

menarche. The advent of a female's first menstrual period. (Pronounced meh-nar'-ky.) See SPERMARCHE.

menopause (also change of life, climacteric). The mid-life end of menstruation, reduced estrogen production, and resulting physical and psychological changes (including sterility). It most commonly occurs at about ages forty-five to fifty. There is no equivalent dramatic hormonal and reproductive change in men.

menstrual extraction (also menstrual induction and menstrual aspiration). Removing the endometrium (the lining of the uterus) and with it an embryo that may be present, by using suction through a thin tube inserted into the uterus. A method of abortion.

menstruation (also menses, period, monthly). The cyclic (almost monthly) breakdown of the endometrium, or lining of the uterus, and its discharge through the vagina along with blood from small uterine blood vessels.

method effectiveness. The effectiveness of a contraceptive method if always used properly; a measure of the method's theoretical effectiveness. Compare USER EFFECTIVENESS.

micromastia. Unusually small breasts.

miscarriage. Spontaneous abortion.

mittelschmerz. Abdominal pain associated with ovulation.

monilia. See CANDIDIA.

monogamy. Marriage to only one spouse; also, loosely, sexual exclusiveness. See MARRIAGE.

mononucleosis. A viral infection that can be transmitted by deep kissing as well as nonsexually. Slang terms are "mono" and "kissing disease."

mons veneris, mons pubis. The mound of protective fatty tissues that covers the pubic symphysis in both sexes. The term *mons veneris* is used more for females, *mons pubis* for males.

mores. Customs and traditional attitudes, standards, and beliefs. They may be *overt* (open) or *covert* (unspoken or secret).

morning sickness. Nausea and discomfort felt by many women during pregnancy and by some who take oral contraceptives.

Müllerian ducts. A set of ducts in the fetus. Between the seventh to twelfth weeks, they normally atrophy and disappear in a male, and in a female develop into the internal reproductive organs. Compare with WOLFFIAN DUCTS.

multiple orgasm. See ORGASM.

myometrium. The muscular wall of the uterus.

myotonia. Muscular tension. Myotonia and vasocongestion are the basic physical elements of sexual response.

natural childbirth. A method intended to allow delivery without pain or anesthesia by preparing the mother to understand and help the labor process. The term, coined by Dick-Read, is also sometimes used for related methods, such as the Lamaze and Leboyer, and sometimes mistaken to mean childbirth without medical assistance or facilities.

navel. See UMBILICUS.

neo-Freudian theory. See CULTURAL ADAPTATION THEORY.

nipple. The protuberance on the breast that, in females, contains the openings of the milk ducts.

nocturnal emission. An ejaculation that occurs by reflex during sleep, sometimes accompanied by an erotic dream and awareness of orgasm. The slang term is "wet dream."

nondemand. Giving a partner sexual pleasure without expecting any to be given in return at that time.

nonmarital coitus. Coitus by someone not yet married (called *premarital*) or widowed or formerly married (called *postmarital*). Compare EXTRAMARITAL COITUS.

*nonspecific urethritis (*also *NSU, NGU, nongonococcal urethritis).* A disease with symptoms like those of gonorrhea but of unknown cause; it can be transmitted sexually or nonsexually.

norm. Mathematically, an average; socially, a standard of or rule for behavior. Loosely, common beliefs and standards. See NORMAL.

normal. Mathematically, close to average. Socially and medically, the word is variously used to mean healthy, free of disorder, natural, or mathematically average. All of the meanings except the mathematical one has been debated, as has the opposite term, *abnormal.*

nuclear family. See FAMILY.

nymphomania. The judgment that a woman is sexually overactive, the female equivalent of satyriasis. As with satyriasis, there is no agreement on how much is overactive. Sometimes used to describe female sexual activity that appears compulsive or pleasureless or violates society's or the woman's own role expectations. Compare SATYRIASIS.

obscenity. Language about things sexually or socially offensive, or that falls outside social or legal limits.

Oedipus complex. A male's erotic attachment to his mother and rivalrous feelings toward his father. Compare ELECTRA COMPLEX.

onanism. Coitus interruptus. Incorrectly used as a synonym for masturbation.

*oogonium (*pl. *oogonia).* A primitive egg cell, which through a series of divisions produces ova.

open marriage. A marriage in which partners agree that each may engage in sexual or nonsexual relationships outside the marriage.

oral contraceptive. A contraceptive pill, consisting mostly of synthetic estrogens and progesterone. The slang term is "the pill."

oral eroticism. Erotic responsiveness in the mouth and lips; erotic stimulation of the mouth. According to psychoanalytic theory, oral eroticism marks a normal stage of infancy, and many erotic and nonerotic feelings associated with that stage may persist throughout life.

oral-genital intercourse. Oral stimulation of the male genitals (fellatio) or female genitals (cunnilingus).

organizing effect. See SENSITIZING EFFECT.

*orgasm (*also *climax).* A phase of the sexual response cycle marked by a peak of myotonia, vascongestion, psychological tension, and erotic pleasure. A couple may reach orgasm at the same time *(simultaneous orgasm).* Some women and a very few men have two or more orgasms without returning to the resting phase of the response cycle *(multiple orgasm).* The slang term is "coming."

orgasmic platform. The outer third of the vagina, which narrows, tightens, and rises during sexual response.

ovarian follicle. A follicle containing a developing ovum; it develops near the surface of the ovary. An egg's release from the ovarian follicle is ovulation.

ovary. One of the paired female gonads, which lie near the floor of the pelvis. Their chief functions are producing ova and female hormones, especially estrogens and progesterone.

overt transference. Sexual contact between patient and therapist, with the belief that it helps the patient. It has been declared unethical by many professional organizations.

*oviduct (*also *Fallopian tube, uterine tube).* The tube that carries eggs from the ovary to the uterus, and sperm upward from the uterus. It consists of fingerlike *fimbriae;* the funnellike *infundibulum;* the *ampulla,* where fertilization normally occurs; the narrow *isthmus;* and the *intramural* portion, which enters the uterus.

ovogenesis. A series of cell divisions by which an oogonium becomes ova.

ovulation. The release of an ovum, enclosed in a mature follicle (Graafian follicle), from the surface *(stigma)* of the ovary.

ovum (pl. *ova*). The female gamete, or egg cell.

oxytocin. A hormone released by the pituitary gland that stimulates lactation and uterine contractions during childbirth; it is sometimes administered to hasten the onset of delivery.

"panty itch." See TINEA CRURIS.

"Pap" test (Papanicolaou smear test). A test to detect cancer of the uterine cervix early in its development. It should be a routine part of a woman's genital examination.

paraphilia. A relatively neutral term for a sexual behavior that is deviant in both scientific senses of that word—not done often by most people and socially disapproved or only tolerated. Paraphilia are also called *deviations, perversions,* and *sexual alternatives.*

parity. How many children a woman has borne. Women who have had no children are *nullipara* (adj. *nulliparous*), one child *primipara,* two or more *multipara.* See GRAVID.

partialism. Being especially aroused by the sight of some part of the body or by a kind of clothing. Some degree of partialism exists normally in many men; in some it borders on fetishism.

parturition. Childbirth.

patriarchy. A supposed stage of social evolution when men took from women the preponderance of social privilege and authority (compare MATRIARCHY). Loosely used for a family or cultural group in which men have relatively great power and influence.

patrilineal descent. Descent reckoned through the father and his family.

patrilocal residence. The tradition in many societies of a married couple living with or near the husband's family.

Pearl index. A way of rating a contraceptive method's effectiveness by calculating the ratio of pregnancies among sexually active women using the method to the number of pregnancies theoretically possible without contraception.

pederasty. In ancient Greece, the love of boys by men—variously erotic, romantic, educational, or all of these. Loosely, male homosexual feelings or behavior of any kind.

pedophilia. Compulsive sexual attraction to or activity with prepubertal children.

pelvic diaphragm. The muscular floor of the pelvis; it supports the bladder and internal sexual and reproductive organs.

pelvic inflammatory disease (PID). A painful and dangerous inflammatory condition resulting from untreated infection (usually gonorrhea) in women.

pelvis. The area cradled by the hip bones and other nearby bones, containing the sexual and reproductive organs, kidneys, urinary system, and other organs.

penis. The male phallus, or copulatory organ; in slang called "cock," "prick," "peter," "tool." It is the chief focus of erotic sensation in most men and the outlet of the male urinary and reproductive systems. It consists of a shaft, glans, foreskin, and frenulum, and internally of two corpora cavernosa and a corpus spongiosum.

penis envy. A female's conscious or unconscious desire to possess a penis; in the broader sense, a woman's resentful association of physical sex differences with male's greater aggression, higher status, social roles and prerogatives. See MASCULINE PROTEST.

performance anxiety. Anxiety about sexual performance, especially fear of impotence, anorgasmia, or inability to please a partner.

perineum. The pelvic floor; more specifically, the region between the anus and the vagina or scrotum.

period. See MENSTRUATION.

peristalsis. Wavelike muscle contractions.

permissive. Tolerating or encouraging sexual expression. Compare RESTRICTIVE.

perversion. See PARAPHILIA.

petting. Kissing, caressing, and other erotic play other than coitus; sometimes extended to include oral-genital contact. When it precedes coitus, it is sometimes called *foreplay.*

phallus. The penis, the clitoris, or the embryonic organ from which both develop.

phase. Part of a cycle or pattern; especially a stage of the sexual response or menstrual cycles.

pheromone. An airborne substance that seems to act like a hormone. In many species, pheromones signal sexual readiness and help induce or synchronize mating and reproductive processes.

philia. See AGAPE.

phimosis. Constriction of the foreskin that prevents its full retraction.

PID. See PELVIC INFLAMMATORY DISEASE.

"pill". See ORAL CONTRACEPTIVE.

502

pimp. A man who manages prostitutes and lives on their earnings.

pituitary gland. The small gland at the base of the brain that produces many hormones regulating growth, sexual development, reproduction, and the action and interaction of other endocrine glands. See HPG AXIS.

placebo. A neutral substance taken in the belief that it is medically or chemically effective. It may produce a *placebo effect,* a response resulting solely from belief in its effectiveness.

placenta. The structure that develops in the uterus along with the embryo to bring nourishment to and remove wastes from the fetus through the mother's bloodstream. It is attached to the infant by the umbilical cord..

plateau phase. The phase of the sexual response cycle that follows excitement and precedes orgasm, characterized by high, relatively sustained levels of myotonia and vasocongestion.

polyandry. Having more than one husband at a time.

polygamy. Having more than one spouse at a time.

polygyny. Having more than one wife at a time.

pornography. Writings about or depictions of sexual activity that exceed legal or social limits. When the erotic becomes pornographic is a matter of continuing debate.

postmarital coitus. Coitus after marriage. See NON-MARITAL COITUS.

postorgasmic period. The part of the sexual response cycle that follows orgasm, marked by decreased vasocongestion and myotonia. In most men and some women it continues to the resting phase; in some women it proceeds only to the plateau phase, and the woman reaches orgasm again.

postpartum. After childbirth. *Postpartum depression,* or "baby blues," is the depression that sometimes follows childbirth; in severe form it can lead to *postpartum psychosis,* a severe emotional disorder.

potency. Ability to reach and maintain penile erection; inability to do so is *impotence.* Adj., *potent.*

preadolescence. The period between early childhood and adolescence, usually the years from about seven to about thirteen. The change from preadolescence to adolescence is marked by the appearance of puberty.

pregnancy. The bearing of an embryo or fetus. Full-term pregnancy, from conception till childbirth, takes about nine months.

premarital coitus. Coitus before marriage. See NON-MARITAL COITUS.

premature ejaculation. Early ejaculation; how early remains a matter of debate. Some common standards are: in seconds rather than minutes after vaginal entry; too soon to satisfy a responsive partner at least half the time; too soon for the man's own satisfaction.

premenstrual tension. Tension, irritability, depression, anxiety, becoming accident-prone, and other states that affect most women sometimes, and some women always, in the days before and at the start of menstruation. The possible physical, psychological, and social sources of such tension are debated.

prepuce. See FORESKIN.

priapism. A physical disorder in which erection persists for extended periods of time; the erection is pleasureless or even painful, and medical treatment is necessary.

primal scene. Parental coitus witnessed by a child.

progesterone. A female hormone present in high levels during pregnancy and the luteal phase of the ovulatory and menstrual cycles. It tends to reduce sexual interest in both sexes and, in men, to inhibit arousal, potency, and sperm production.

prolactin. A hormone produced by the pituitary that stimulates milk production.

promiscuity. The judgment that a person has too many sexual partners; but there is no agreement on how many are too many.

prophylactic. A device, substance, or method for prevention of disease; especially a condom.

proportion of sexual outlet. The proportion of a person's sexual activity comprised of a given sexual activity; sometimes measured in proportion of all acts leading to orgasm, especially in males.

prostaglandins. Hormones produced by the seminal vesicles, prostate gland, and endometrium that stimulate smooth-muscle activity, thus increasing orgasmic contractions and aiding gamete transport. They are sometimes used to induce menstruation or abortion.

prostate gland. A gland that surrounds part of the male urethra and empties into it, supplying much of the fluid that constitutes semen. It also produces prostaglandins.

prostitute. A person who exchanges sexual services for money. They range from streetwalkers to expensive call girls. The largest number are women; some are men, the great majority of whom serve homosexual clients.

pseudocyesis. False pregnancy; the delusion that one is pregnant, and physical symptoms of pregnancy that may accompany it.

pseudohermaphrodite. See HERMAPHRODITE.

503

psychoanalysis. A theory of psychological and sexual development and a related method of psychological therapy, originating in the work of Sigmund Freud. It says that libido, or sexual energy, progressively charges the mouth, the anus, and the phallus during infancy and childhood, and that sexual and nonsexual feelings associated with these oral, anal, and phallic stages affect personality and sexual development throughout life.

psychosomatic. Referring to physical changes and symptoms caused by the emotions.

puberty. The extended period of sexual development and reproductive maturation, signaled by the arrival of menstruation in girls and ejaculation in boys, and by the development of many secondary sex characteristics.

pubic. Referring to the area above the pubic symphasis, which after puberty is normally covered with hair.

pubic symphysis. The juncture of the pubic bones. At parturition, this union relaxes to aid delivery.

pubococcygeus muscle. Muscle around the vaginal entrance, involved in vaginal contractions, orgasm, and childbirth.

pudendum (also mons veneris). The part of the external genitals, especially of a female, that can be seen from a normal front view.

Puritanism. Sexual shame, prudery, and restrictiveness. Although commonly associated with the period of rule by the Puritan sect in England, it was not characteristic of all Puritans or limited to Puritans as a group. See VICTORIANISM.

quickening. The time in pregnancy when fetal movements are first felt.

rape. Coitus with an unwilling partner. *Assaultive (aggressive) rape* involves force. *Statutory rape* is coitus with someone too young or mentally immature to give responsible consent. *Acquaintance rape (date rape)* is rape of someone with whom there has been social acquaintance or emotional or erotic intimacy.

rectum. The lower part of the large intestine, leading to the anus.

refractory. Unresponsive to sexual stimulation. A *refractory period* usually follows orgasm; more common in males than in females.

relative morality, relative ethics. The belief that what is right or wrong depends on circumstances and motives, not on unvarying rules of behavior. Compare ABSOLUTE MORALITY.

resolution phase. The phase of the sexual response cycle that follows orgasm and leads to the resting stage.

resting phase. The state of sexual inactivity with which the SEXUAL RESPONSE CYCLE begins and ends.

restrictive. Limiting; in terms of sexuality, disapproving, discouraging, or punishing eroticism. Compare PERMISSIVE.

retarded orgasm (also retarded ejaculation). Difficulty or inability reaching orgasm.

retrograde ejaculation (also dry orgasm). Ejaculating not forward through the urethra but backward into the bladder; the semen is eliminated with urine.

rhythm method. A contraceptive method based on avoiding coitus when ovulation is most likely, which is determined by using the calendar method, the temperature method, or both. See CALENDAR METHOD; BASAL BODY TEMPERATURE.

role. The behavior socially expected of someone in a given situation or relationship because of his or her characteristics or status. See ASCRIBED ROLE and ACHIEVED ROLE.

role modeling theory. The theory of psychosexual development that ascribes many important gender differences to the existence of different roles for males and females, which are taken as models by developing children.

Rubin test. A medical test to reveal blockage of the oviducts.

sadism. Erotic enjoyment from inflicting pain and humiliation. Often used in both an erotic and a broad psychological sense. Sadism often coexists with masochism: hence the term *sadomasochism.*

sadomasochism. See SADISM; MASOCHISM.

sanction. A law or custom maintaining social control of behavior, including sexual behavior; a formal or informal standard of behavior. Also, the punishment for violating such a standard or the reward for observing it.

sanitary napkin. A pad of cloth or paper products worn externally to absorb menstrual flow.

sapphism. See HOMOSEXUAL.

satyriasis. The judgment that a man is sexually overactive; the male equivalent of nymphomania. As with nymphomania, there is no agreement on how active is too active. Sometimes used for male sexual activity that seems compulsive or pleasureless or violates society's or the man's own role expectations.

scabies. Tiny skin parasites that cause welts and itching. They can be transmitted by sexual or nonsexual contact.

*scopophilia (*also *scoptophilia).* See VOYEUR.

scripting theory. The sociological theory that gender roles and sex behavior are parts, or scripts, taught by society, and that such scripts are the major forces in sexual development.

scrotum. The sac below and behind the penis that contains the testes and part of the spermatic chord.

seduction. Persuading a person to engage in sexual activity; the word often implies doing so against the other's full or initial desire, and perhaps with an element of manipulation or deceit.

*semen (*also *seminal fluid).* The milk-colored fluid that males normally ejaculate from the penis during orgasm from puberty onward. The fluid, which carries sperm from the testes through the urethra to the meatus, is produced in the prostate gland, seminal vesicles, and bulbourethral glands.

seminal vesicles. A pair of saclike structures near the bladder and prostate gland that produce prostaglandins and part of the seminal fluid.

seminiferous tubules. Long, thin tubes coiled in compartments of the testes, where spermatogonia mature into spermatozoa.

sensate focus. Concentrating mostly or entirely on one's erotic response to determine what is most pleasurable and become accustomed to responding to it. Sometimes used in sex therapy.

*sensitizing effect (*also *organizing effect).* The action of hormones from the fetus and its mother in programming sex-linked behavior in the fetus's developing nervous system.

serial monogamy. Having more than one spouse, but only one at a time. Inaccurately called *serial polygamy.* See MARRIAGE.

sex. By narrow definition, being male or female. In a wider sense, all that results from being male or female. Also sexual activity.

sex assignment. The declaration that a newborn infant is male or female, usually because of the appearance of its external sexualia.

sex characteristics. Physical signs of being male or female. The *primary sex characteristics* are the gonads; all others are *secondary.*

sex chromosomes. See CHROMOSOMES.

sex flush. A blush (the result of vasocongestion) that appears on the chest, breasts, back, and neck of some men and many women during sexual response, especially soon before and during orgasm.

sexism. A word for hostility toward or disparagement of the other sex; the term implies that the feelings resemble racism.

sex-linked behavior. Behavior resulting directly from one's physical sex; not the same as SEX-TYPED BEHAVIOR, which is socially learned.

sexology. The study of sex in all its aspects.

sex ratio. The ratio of males to females from conception onward. The ratio of males to females conceived is the *primary sex ratio;* the ratio at birth is the *secondary sex ratio.*

sex role. See GENDER ROLE.

sex-typed behavior. A behavior socially associated with males or females; not the same as SEX-LINKED BEHAVIOR, which is biologically caused.

sexual differentiation. The development of a fetus's primitive sexual, reproductive, hormonal, and nervous systems as male or female. This is triggered genetically at the fetal age of six to seven weeks and continues through the twelfth week and probably after.

*sexualia (*also *sexual system).* The parts of the body associated with sexual expression; some are also part of the reproductive or the excretory system. The *primary sexualia* are the external genitals and, in men and women, the nipples and breasts and the internal genitals that can be erotically stimulated by touch. The *secondary sexualia* are other erotically sensitive areas, such as the mouth, skin, and anus. Excluded are the nonerotic areas of the reproductive system, or internal genitals.

sexual identity. The conviction that one is male or female; in most people it is irreversibly fixed in early childhood. Do not confuse with GENDER IDENTITY.

sexually transmitted disease (STD). A disease that can be transmitted by erotic contact; includes, but is not limited to, the five classic venereal diseases. See VENEREAL DISEASE.

sexual mechanisms. The processes involved in sexual excitement, coitus, or orgasm. These are called, respectively, *arousal, copulatory,* and *orgasmic mechanisms.*

sexual orientation. The sort of person (or object) one finds sexually attractive or arousing. The most common orientation is heterosexual (to people of the other sex); the most common atypical orientation is homosexual (to people of the same sex).

Some people are oriented to children (pedo-philia), animals (bestiality), objects or parts of the body (fetishism). Also called *sexual object choice* and *sexual preference,* although in most people orientation does not seem a conscious, neutral choice.

sexual pattern. A behavior that rises from being male or female; is primarily cultural, socially learned (which sex wears skirts), individual (erotic fanta-sies), or a combination of any or all of these.

sexual response cycle (SRC). The physical and psychic changes involved in erotic response. The com-plete cycle can be described as having five phases—*resting, excitement, plateau, orgasmic,* and *resolution* (the last phase includes a postorgasmic period). Not everyone experiences the entire cycle each time sexual response occurs, nor iden-tically from one occasion to another.

sibling. A brother or sister.

simultaneous orgasm. Both sex partners reaching or-gasm at the same time.

situation ethics. The belief that decisions should be based on what is kindest and most loving in a given situation, not on an unvarying moral stan-dard for behavior. See ABSOLUTE MORALITY and RELATIVE ETHICS.

smegma. A cheesy, odorous substance that can collect under the foreskin.

socialization. The training of a child, sometimes in-formally or by example, to become a member of society; first done chiefly by parents, then by peers and social institutions outside the family.

sodomy (also *buggery*). Anal intercourse.

sodomy laws. Catch-all laws that in some states forbid not only sodomy but other noncoital behaviors. They may apply to both homosexual and hetero-sexual contacts.

somatic. Physical.

sororate. The custom that a man marry one or more of his wife's sisters, in some societies after his first wife's death, in others if the first wife is barren. See LEVIRATE.

spectator role. Taking a spectator role, or *spectatoring,* is mentally detaching oneself from sexual plea-sure to observe one's own performance. It is a common element in many sex dysfunctions and in limited sexual response.

sperm (also *sperm cell, spermatozoan*). A male gamete. It must unite with *(fertilize)* an ovum for repro-duction to occur. The word is sometimes inac-curately used for *semen,* the fluid in which sper-matozoa are ejaculated from the penis.

spermarche (also *thelarche*). The first occurrence of ejaculation; the male equivalent of females' MEN-ARCHE. (Pronounced sperm'-ar-ky.)

spermatic cord. A structure connected to each tes-ticle that contains the vas deferens and the testic-ular artery, vein, and nerve.

spermatic duct. See VAS DEFERENS.

spermatocytes. Cells resulting from the division of spermatogonia; they mature into sperm cells.

spermatogenesis. The development, through several cell divisions, of a spermatocyte into mature sperm cells.

spermatogonium (pl. *spermatogonia*). A cell in the sem-iniferous tubules that goes through a series of divisions to become spermatocytes, which in turn divide to produce spermatozoa.

spermicide. A substance that kills sperm cells.

sphincter. A ring of muscle, such as that which sur-rounds the anus and that which controls the release of urine from the bladder.

spouse. Husband or wife.

SRC. See SEXUAL RESPONSE CYCLE.

standard delivery. The most common way to deliver a child in the United States today, done by a physi-cian in a hospital with anesthesia, antiseptic con-ditions, and the husband absent from the delivery room. See NATURAL CHILDBIRTH.

statutory rape. See RAPE.

stereotyped. In biology, directed by the genes, hor-mones, or other constitutional mechanisms. In social science, directed by custom or tradition.

sterility. Absolute inability to reproduce. See INFER-TILITY.

sterilization. Making a person incapable of reproduc-tion; the most common techniques of sterilization today are vasectomy for men and tubal ligation and hysterectomy for women.

stroma. The main body of any gland. The stroma of the ovary contains developing ova; that of the testicle lies around and between the seminif-erous tubules. The stroma is also called the *inter-stitium.*

sublimation. According to some psychoanalytic theories, the transformation of sexual drive into nonsexual drives and activities; the validity of the concept has been questioned.

substitutive homosexuality. Homosexual behavior by a person with a heterosexual orientation in a situa-tion that prevents heterosexual activity, such as imprisonment.

suppository. A drug or medication prepared in a form that can be inserted into the anus or vagina. There are contraceptives in the form of vaginal suppositories.

506

surrogate. Substitute. In some kinds of sex therapy, a trained and supervised surrogate partner is paid to help a person who lacks a regular sex partner.

swinging. The sexual involvement with each other of married couples. Once popularly called "wife swapping" and now sometimes "mate swapping."

symbolic interaction. A sociological theory that all interactions and situations are affected by how they are symbolically perceived.

symphysis. See PUBIC SYMPHYSIS.

syphilis (also lues). One of the five classic venereal diseases, and among the most common and dangerous of sexually transmitted diseases. It can be transmitted genitally, orally, or rectally and eventually affects most vital organ systems. The slang term is "syph."

temperature method. See BASAL BODY TEMPERATURE.

tampon. A cylindrical fabric plug inserted in the vagina to absorb menstrual fluids.

term. The end of fetal growth, usually at a weight of about seven pounds (3,300 grams), after nine months.

testicle. See TESTIS.

testicular feminizing syndrome. See ANDROGEN-INSENSITIVITY SYNDROME.

testis (pl. testes; also testicles). The testes are the paired male gonads. They hang below the body and behind the penis in the saclike scrotum. Their chief functions are producing sperm cells and testosterone. Slang terms are "balls," "nuts," "jewels."

testosterone. The major "male" sex hormone (androgen), produced mostly in the testes; it occurs in smaller amounts in women's adrenal glands. In both sexes it is responsible for sexual excitability and many male physical and behavioral traits.

thelarche. See SPERMARCHE.

thyroxin. A hormone produced by the thyroid gland; low thyroxin levels tend to decrease sexual desire and activity.

tinea cruris. A fungus infection of the genital area. Slang terms are "jock itch" and "panty itch."

tonic. Continuous; noncyclic.

total sexual outlet. All of a person's sexual activity; sometimes measured in acts leading to orgasm, especially in men.

transference. The psychiatric term for transferring to people in one's present life feelings associated with other people in earlier life (e.g., father figures and mother figures).

transsexualism. A sexual-identity dysfunction in which a person is convinced that he or she belongs to the other sex. As a result, a *transsexual*—a person with this condition—may desire "sex-change" surgery.

transudation. Exuding of fluids, such as sweating and the wetting of the vagina during sexual excitement. The fluid is a *transudate.*

transvestism (also cross-dressing, eonism). A gender-role dysfunction, occurring mostly in males, in which sexual gratification or relief from anxiety comes from wearing the clothes of or masquerading as the other sex. It is sometimes but not always associated with homosexuality. A person who receives gratification from cross-dressing is a *transvestite.*

trial marriage. Living together to test a relationship for formal marriage.

trichomoniasis. A common vaginal infection, commonly called "trich."

trimester. A period of three months. Full-term fetal development and pregnancy are usually described in terms of three trimesters.

troilism. Sexual contact among three people.

tubal ligation. Tying and severing the oviducts as a means of sterilization.

tubal pregnancy. See ECTOPIC.

tumescence. Swelling, such as that caused by vasocongestion of the male and female sexualia during sexual response. Incorrectly used as strictly synonymous with penile erection, which is only one example of tumescence. May refer to clitoris or nipple.

twins. Two children conceived and delivered at the same time. *Identical twins,* also called *monozygotic (MZ) twins,* develop from the division of a fertilized egg early in embryonic development; they are of the same sex and look very similar. *Fraternal twins,* or *dizygotic (DZ) twins,* develop from two different eggs fertilized by different sperm cells. They may be of the same or different sex, and they look no more alike than any other two siblings.

umbilical cord. The cord connecting a fetus to the placenta and thus its mother's bloodstream.

umbilicus (also navel). The indentation in the abdomen where the umbilical cord was once attached.

undescended testicles. See CRYPTORCHIDISM.

ureter. A tube leading from each kidney to the urinary bladder.

urethra. The tube that in both sexes carries urine from the bladder to the outside of the body, and in men also carries semen outside the body.

urethritis. Inflammation of the urethra. See NONSPE-CIFIC URETHRITIS.

urolagnia. Compulsive sexual interest in urination.

user effectiveness. The effectiveness of a contraceptive method in terms of how people use it, not merely its possible effectiveness, a measure of the method's actual effectiveness. See METHOD EFFEC-TIVENESS.

uterine tube. See OVIDUCT.

*uterus (*also *womb).* The hollow, muscular organ in which an embryo develops into a fetus and a fetus develops until birth. It has a *cervix* (neck) that protrudes into the vagina, a short *isthmus* leading to the main *body,* and an upper part called the *fundus.* Its walls consist largely of muscular *myometrium;* the lining is the *endometrium.*

vagina. The flexible, muscular sheath that contains the penis in coitus and through which an infant passes from the uterus to outside the mother's body during childbirth. The slang terms are "pussy," "snatch," "hole"; the common vernacular term is "cunt." Some of these terms are used for the external female sexualia as well.

vaginismus. Spasmodic contraction of muscles surrounding the vagina, sometimes sufficient to prevent coitus or even the insertion of a tampon.

vaginitis. Inflammation of the vagina.

vas deferens. The duct that carries sperm from the epididymus to the ejaculatory duct and urethra.

vasectomy. Tying and severing the vas deferens; now done as a means of sterilization.

vasocongestion. The swelling and reddening of tissue caused by increased blood flow. Vasocongestion of the sexualia causes penile erection and vaginal wetting (transudation), the chief signs of sexual excitement, and is involved in most of the sexual response cycle.

*venereal disease (*also *VD).* Five of the many sexually transmitted diseases: gonorrhea, syphilis, chancroid, granuloma inguinale, and lymphogranuloma venereum. As the wider term *sexually transmitted disease* comes into use, the phrase "classic venereal disease" is sometimes used for these five infections.

*venereal wart (*also *condyloma acuminatum).* A wart, caused by a sexually transmitted virus, that appears on or near the genitals. A sexually transmitted disease.

ventral. On or toward the front of the body or any part of it.

vestibule, vaginal. The basin-shaped area bordered by the labia minora; it contains the openings of the vagina and the urethra and in most women is erotically sensitive.

Victorianism. Sexual restrictiveness in behavior, attitudes, and etiquette; commonly associated with the period of the reign of Victoria of England, but not limited to that period or characteristic of all people then. See PURITANISM.

virgin. A person who has never experienced coitus; used of both sexes, though more of females. Female virginity is not always reflected by the presence or absence of a hymen.

*voyeur (*also *peeping Tom, peeper).* A person who compulsively seeks sexual pleasure from observing (especially from spying on) nudity or sexual acts. The behavior is *voyeurism.*

*vulvovaginal glands (*also *Bartholin's glands).* Small glands near the vaginal entrance. Their function is not clear, though they may provide some lubrication for the vestibule.

vulva. The external female genitals.

withdrawal. See COITUS INTERRUPTUS.

Wolffian ducts. A pair of ducts in the fetus that between the seventh and twelfth weeks normally atrophy and disappear in a female, and in a male develop into internal male reproductive organs. Compare MÜLLERIAN DUCTS.

womb. See UTERUS.

X chromosome. See CHROMOSOME.

Y chromosome. See CHROMOSOME.

*zoophilia (*also *bestiality).* Sexual contact with animals.

zygote. A fertilized egg, resulting from the fusion of a sperm cell and an ovum.

References

AASECT. *Proposed Code of Ethics.* Washington, D.C.: American Association of Sex Educators, Counselors, and Therapists, 1978.

Abarbanel, A. R. Diagnosis and treatment of coital discomfort. In J. LoPiccolo and L. LoPiccolo (eds.), *Handbook of Sex Therapy,* pp. 241–60. New York: Plenum, 1978.

Abel, G. G.; Barlow, D. H.; Blanchard, E.B.; and Guild, D. The components of rapists' sexual arousal. *Archives of General Psychiatry,* 1977, *34*(8), pp. 895–903.

Abelson, H.; Cohen, R.; Heaton, E.; and Slider, C. Public attitudes toward and experience with erotic materials. *Technical Reports of the Commission on Obscenity and Pornography,* vol. 6. Washington, D.C.: U.S. Government Printing Office, 1970.

Aberle, Sophie, and Corner, George. *Twenty-five years of Sex Research.* Philadelphia: Saunders, 1953.

Ables, B. The three wishes of latency age children. *Developmental Psychology,* 1972, *6*, p. 186.

Ackerman, Nathan. *The Psychodynamics of Family Life.* New York: Basic Books, 1958.

Acton, William. *The Functions and Disorders of the Reproductive Organs.* London: John Churchill, 1857.

Adams, Clifford R. An informal preliminary report on some factors relating to sexual responsiveness of college wives. In M. DeMartino (ed.), *Sexual Behavior and Personality Characteristics,* pp. 208–26. New York: Grove Press, 1966.

Adams, David B.; Gold, Alice R.; and Burt, Anne D. Rise in female-initiated sexual activity at ovulation and its suppression by oral contraceptives. *New England Journal of Medicine,* 1978, *299*, pp. 1145–50.

Adams, M. S., and Neel, J. V. Children of incest. *Pediatrics,* 1967, *40*, pp. 55–62.

Adler, Alfred. *The Individual Psychology of Alfred Adler,* H. Ansbacher and R. Ansbacher (eds.). New York: Harper and Row, 1964.

Adler, Alfred. *Cooperation Between the Sexes,* H. Ansbacher and R. Ansbacher (eds. and trans.). Garden City, N.Y.: Anchor, 1978.

Altmann, N.; Knowles, E.; and Bull, H. A psychosomatic study of the sex cycle in women. *Psychosomatic Medicine,* 1941, *3*, pp. 199–225.

Altschuler, Milton. Coyapa personality and sexual motivation. In D. S. Marshall and R. C. Suggs (eds.), *Human Sexual Behavior,* pp. 38–58. New York: Basic Books, 1971.

American Medical Association. *Human Sexuality.* In press.

Amir, M. *Patterns in Forcible Rape.* Chicago: University of Chicago Press, 1970.

Amir, M. The role of the victim in sex offenses. In H. L. P. Resnik and M. E. Wolfgang (eds.), *Sexual Behaviors: Social, Clinical, and Legal Aspects,* pp. 131–67. Boston: Little, Brown, 1972.

Anderson, P. Problems of transvestism. *Acta Psychiatrica Neurologica Scandinavica,* 1956, *106* (Suppl.), pp. 249–56.

Anderson, Ray. Offenders against children. Unpublished paper.

Annon, Jack S. *The Behavioral Treatment of Sexual Problems: Intensive Therapy.* Honolulu: Enabling Systems, 1975.

Annon, Jack S. *The Behavioral Treatment of Sexual Problems: Brief Therapy.* New York: Harper and Row, 1976.

Anonymous. *Onania, or the Heinous Sin of Self-Pollution.* London: n.d. (1717?).

Apfelbaum, Bernard. The myth of the surrogate. *Journal of Sex Research,* 1977, *13*, pp. 238–49.

509

Arafat, Ibtihaj; and Cotton, Wayne L. Masturbation practices of males and females. *Journal of Sex Research,* 1974, *10,* pp. 293–307.

Ard, Ben. Premarital sexual experience: A longitudinal study. *Journal of Sex Research,* 1974 *10,* pp. 32–39.

Ard, Ben. Sex in lasting marriages: A longitudinal study. *Journal of Sex Research,* 1977, *13,* pp. 274–85.

Aristophanes. *Four Comedies,* D. Fitts (trans.). New York: Harcourt, Brace and World, 1962.

Armentrout, J. A., and Burger, G. K. Children's reports of parental child-rearing behavior at five grade levels. *Developmental Psychology,* 1972, *7,* pp. 44–48.

Asken, Michael J. Psychoemotional aspects of mastectomy: A review of recent literature. *American Journal of Psychiatry,* 1975, *132,* pp. 56–59.

Athanasiou, Robert; Shaver, P.; and Tavris, C. Sex. *Psychology Today,* July 1970, pp. 39–52.

Babcock, B. A.; Freedman, A. E.; Norton, E. H.; and Ross, S. C. *Sex Discrimination and the Law: Causes and Remedies.* Boston: Little, Brown, 1975.

Bach, George R., and Wyden, Peter. *The Intimate Enemy: How to Fight Fair in Love and Marriage.* New York: Morrow, 1969.

Bachofen, Johann J. *Myth, Religion, and Mother Right,* R. Mannheim (trans.). Princeton, N.J.: Princeton University Press, 1967.

Balswick, Jack O.; and Anderson, James A. Role definition in the unarranged date. *Journal of Marriage and the Family,* 1969, *31,* pp. 776–78.

Bancroft, John. *Deviant Sexual Behavior: Modification and Assessment.* Oxford: Clarendon Press, 1974.

Bancroft, John. The behavioral approach to treatment. In J. Money and H. Musaph (eds.), *Handbook of Sexology,* pp. 1197–1225. New York: Excerpta Medica, 1977.

Bancroft, John. The relationship between hormones and sexual behavior in humans. In J. B. Hutchison (ed.), *Biological Determinants of Sexual Behavior,* pp. 493–520. New York: Wiley, 1978.

Bandura, A., and Walters, R. *Social Learning and Personality Development.* New York: Holt, 1963.

Barbach, L. G. *For Yourself: The Fulfillment of Female Sexuality.* Garden City, N.Y.: Doubleday, 1975.

Barclay, A. M. Sexual fantasies in men and women. *Medical Aspects of Human Sexuality,* 1973, *7* (5), pp. 205–16.

Bardwick, Judith. *Psychology of Women.* New York: Harper and Row, 1971.

Bardwick, Judith. Psychological factors in the acceptance and use of oral contraceptives. In J. T. Fawcett (ed.), *Psychological Perspectives on Population,* pp. 274–305. New York: Basic Books, 1973.

Barnett, W. *Sexual Freedom and the Constitution.* Albuquerque: University of New Mexico Press, 1973.

Barraclough, Charles, and Gorski, Roger A. Evidence that the hypothalamus is responsible for androgen-induced sterility in the female rat. *Endocrinology,* 1961, *68,* pp. 68–79.

Bartell, Gilbert D. *Group Sex.* New York: New American Library, 1971.

Bass-Hass, Rita. The lesbian dyad. *Journal of Sex Research,* 1968, *4,* pp. 108–26.

Baumrind, D. Current patterns of parental authority. *Journal of Developmental Psychology Monograph,* No. 4, 1971.

Baumrind, D., and Black, A. E. Socialization practices associated with dimensions of competence in preschool boys and girls. *Child Development,* 1967, *38,* pp. 291–327.

Bayer, Alan E. Early marriage in the United States. *Medical Aspects of Human Sexuality,* 1973, *7* (8), pp. 208–14.

Beach, Frank A. *Hormones and Behavior.* New York: Hoeber, 1948.

Beach, Frank A. Factors involved in the control of mounting behavior by female mammals. In M. Diamond (ed.), *Perspectives in Reproduction and Sexual Behavior,* pp. 83–131. Bloomington: Indiana University Press, 1968.

Beach, Frank A. Hormonal control of sex-related behavior. In F. A. Beach (ed.), *Human Sexuality in Four Perspectives,* pp. 247–67. Baltimore: Johns Hopkins University Press, 1977. (a)

Beach, Frank A. (Ed.) *Human Sexuality in Four Perspectives.* Baltimore: Johns Hopkins, 1977. (b)

Beach, Frank A., and Jordan, L. Sexual exhaustion and recovery in the male rat. *Quarterly Journal of Experimental Psychology,* 1956, *8,* pp. 121–33.

Beach, Frank A., and Whalen, Richard. Effects of ejaculation on sexual behavior in the male rat. *Journal of Comparative and Physiological Psychology,* 1959, *52,* pp. 249–54.

Becker, Howard. *The Outsiders.* New York: Free Press, 1963.

Behavior Today, 12 December 1977, pp. 3–4.

Beigel, Hugo G. The meaning of coital postures. *International Journal of Sexology,* 1953, *6,* pp. 136–43.

Beigel, Hugo G. Three transvestites under hypnosis. *Journal of Sex Research,* 1967, *3,* pp. 149–62.

Beigel, Hugo G., and Feldman, Robert. The male transvestite's motivation in fiction, research and reality. In H. G. Beigel (ed.), *Advances in Sex Research,* pp. 198–210. New York: Hoeber, 1963.

Bell, Alan P., and Weinberg, Martin S. *Homosexualities: A Study of Diversity Among Men and Women.* New York: Simon and Schuster, 1978.

Bell, Alan P.; Weinberg, Martin S.; and Hammersmith, Susan K. *Sexual Preference: Its Development Among Men and Women,* in press.

Bell, Robert, and Buerkle, Jack. Mother and daughter attitudes to premarital sexual behavior. *Marriage and Family Living,* 1961, *23,* pp. 390–92.

Bell, Robert, and Chaskes, Joy. Premarital sexual experience among coeds 1958 and 1968. *Journal of Marriage and the Family,* 1970, *32,* pp. 81–84.

Bell, R. Q., and Costello, Naomi S. Three tests for sex differences in tactile sensitivity in the newborn. *Biologica Neonatorum,* 1964, *7,* pp. 335–47.

510

Bellow, Saul. *Mr. Sammler's Planet.* New York: Viking, 1969.

Bem, Sandra L. Sex-role adaptability: One consequence of psychological androgyny. *Journal of Personality and Social Psychology,* 1975, *31,* pp. 634–43.

Bem, Sandra L. Probing the promise of androgyny. In A. G. Kaplan and J. P. Bean (eds.), *Beyond Sex-Role Stereotypes: Readings Toward a Psychology of Androgyny,* pp. 45–62. Boston: Little, Brown, 1976.

Bender, Lauretta, and Blau, A. The reaction of children to sexual relations with adults. *American Journal of Orthopsychiatry,* 1937, *7,* pp. 500–18.

Bender, Lauretta, and Grugett, Alvin E., Jr. A follow-up report on children who had atypical sexual experience. *American Journal of Orthopsychiatry,* 1952, *22,* pp. 825–37.

Bengis, Ingrid. *Combat in the Erogenous Zone.* New York: Bantam, 1972.

Benjamin, Harry. *The Transsexual Phenomenon.* New York: Julian Press, 1966.

Benkert, O. Pharmacological experiments to stimulate human sexual behavior. In T. A. Ban et al. (eds.), *Psychopharmacology, Sexual Disorders, and Drug Abuse.* Amsterdam: North-Holland, 1973.

Ben-Veniste, R. Pornography and sex crime: The Danish experience. *Technical Reports of the Commission on Obscenity and Pornography,* vol. 7. Washington, D.C.: U.S. Government Printing Office, 1970.

Berest, Joseph. Medico-legal aspects of incest. *Journal of Sex Research,* 1968, *4,* pp. 195–205.

Bergler, Edmund. *Divorce Won't Help.* New York: Harper, 1948.

Bernard, Jessie, *Remarriage: A Study of Marriage.* New York: World, 1956.

Bernard, Jessie. The fourth revolution. *Journal of Social Issues,* 1966, *22*(2), pp. 76–87.

Bernard, Jessie. Marriage: Hers and his. *Ms,* December 1972, pp. 46–49, 110, 113.

Bernard, Jessie. Infidelity: Some moral and social issues. In R. W. Libby and R. N. Whitehurst (eds.), *Renovating Marriage: Toward New Sexual Life-Styles,* pp. 75–94. Danville, Calif.: Consensus Press, 1973.

Berne, Eric. *Games People Play.* New York: Grove Press, 1964.

Berscheid, Ellen E.; Walster, E.; and Bohrnstedt, G. The happy American body: A survey report. *Psychology Today,* November 1973, pp. 119–23, 126, 128–31.

Bieber, Irving. Sadism and masochism. In S. Arieti (ed.), *American Handbook of Psychiatry,* pp. 256–70. New York: Basic Books, 1966.

Bieber, Irving, et al. *Homosexuality: A Psychoanalytic Study.* New York: Basic Books, 1962.

Bienvenu, Millard A., Sr. Measurement of marital communication. *Family Coordinator,* 1970, *19,* pp. 26–31.

Blackwood, B. *Both Sides of Buka Passage.* Oxford: Oxford University Press, 1935.

Bloch, H., and Geis, G. *Man, Crime, and Society.* New York: Random House, 1963.

Block, Jeanne H. Conceptions of sex role: Some cross-cultural and longitudinal perspectives. Unpublished paper. Cited in E. E. Maccoby and C. N. Jacklin, *The Psychology of Sex Differences* (Stanford, Calif.: Stanford University Press, 1974).

Block, Jeanne H. Another look at sex differentiation in the socialization behaviors of mothers and fathers. In J. Sherman and F. Denmark (eds.), *Psychology of Women: The Future of Research.* New York: Psychological Dimensions, 1977.

Blood, Robert, and Wolfe, Donald. *Husbands and Wives: The Dynamics of Married Living.* Chicago: Free Press, 1960.

Boswell, James. *London Journal, 1762–63,* F. A. Pottle (ed.). New York: McGraw-Hill, 1960.

Bower, Donald W., and Christopherson, Victor A. University student cohabitation: A regional comparison of selected attitudes and behavior. *Journal of Marriage and the Family,* 1977, *39,* pp. 447–52.

Bowlby, John. *Maternal Care and Mental Health.* New York: Schocken, 1966.

Bowlby, John. *Attachment and Loss.* New York: Basic Books, 1969.

Bradwell v. Illinois, 83 U.S. (16 Wall.) 130, 21 L. Ed. 442 (1873).

Brecher, Edward M. *The Sex Researchers.* Boston: Little, Brown, 1969.

Bremer, J. *Asexualization: A Follow-up Study of 244 Cases.* New York: Macmillan, 1959.

Brinton, Crane. *A History of Western Morals.* New York: Harcourt, Brace and World, 1959.

Broderick, C. B. Sexual behavior among preadolescents. *Journal of Social Issues,* 1966, *22*(2), pp. 6–21.

Broderick, C. B., and Weaver, J. The perceptual context of boy-girl communication. *Journal of Marriage and the Family,* 1968, *30,* pp. 618–27.

Bronfenbrenner, Uri. Some familial antecedents of responsibility and leadership in adolescents. In L. Petrullo and B. M. Bass (eds.), *Leadership and Interpersonal Behavior,* pp. 239–71. New York: Holt, Rinehart and Winston, 1961.

Bronson, Frank N. Pheromonal influences on mammalian reproduction. In M. Diamond (ed.), *Perspectives in Reproduction and Sexual Behavior,* pp. 341–61. Bloomington: Indiana University Press, 1968.

Brooks, George F.; Darrow, William W.; and Day, Janet A. Repeated gonorrhea: An analysis of importance and risk factors. *Journal of Infectious Diseases,* 1978, *137,* pp. 161–69.

Broude, Gwen, and Greene, Sarah. Cross-cultural codes on twenty sexual attitudes and practices. *Ethnology,* 1976, *15,* pp. 409–29.

Brown, J. B.; and Fryer, M. P. Plastic surgical correction of hypospadias with mistaken sex identity and transvestism resulting in normal marriage and parenthood. *Surgery, Gynecology and Obstetrics,* 1964, *118,* pp. 45–46.

Brown, Judith K. An anthropological perspective on sex

roles and subsistence. In M. Teitelbaum (ed.), *Sex Differences: Social and Biological Perspectives,* pp. 122–37. Garden City, N.Y.: Anchor, 1976.

Brown, Judith K. A note on the division of labor by sex. *American Anthropologist,* 1970, *72,* pp. 1073–78.

Brown, Sarah; Lieberman, James; and Miller, Warren. Young adults as partners and planners: A preliminary report on the antecedents of responsible family formation. Unpublished paper.

Brownmiller, Susan. *Against Our Will: Men, Women and Rape.* New York: Simon and Schuster, 1975.

Brown-Séquard, Charles. The effects produced on man by subcutaneous injections of a liquid obtained from the testicles of animals. *Lancet,* 20 July 1889, pp. 105–6.

Bryson, J., and Shettel-Neuber, J. Unbalanced relationships: Who becomes jealous of whom. Cited by James Hassett in Newsline, *Psychology Today,* February 1978, pp. 26, 29.

Buck, M. R., and Austrin, H. R. Factors related to school achievement in an economically disadvantaged group. *Child Development,* 1971, *42,* pp. 1813–26.

Buffery, A. W. H., and Gray, V. A. Sex differences in the development of spatial and linguistic skills. In C. Ounsted and D. C. Taylor (eds.), *Gender Differences: Their Ontogeny and Significance,* pp. 123–57. Baltimore: Williams and Wilkins, 1972.

Bullough, Vern L. *Sexual Variance in Society and History.* New York: Wiley, 1976.

Bullough, Vern L., and Bullough, Bonnie. *Sin, Sickness and Sanity.* New York: New American Library, 1977.

Burchinal, Lee. Trends and prospects for young marriages in the U.S. *Journal of Marriage and the Family,* 1965, *27,* pp. 243–54.

Burnap, D. W., and Golden, J. S. Sexual problems in medical practice. *Journal of Medical Education,* 1967, *42,* pp. 673–80.

Burns, R. K. Role of hormones in the differentiation of sex. In W. C. Young (ed.), *Sex and Internal Secretions,* pp. 76–158. Baltimore: Williams and Wilkins, 1961.

Burton, Richard. *The Erotic Traveler,* Edward Leigh (ed.). New York: Putnam's, 1967.

Butler, Julius C.; Reisner, Dale P.; and Wagner, Nathaniel N. Sexuality during pregnancy and parturition. In R. Green (ed.), *Human Sexuality: A Health Practitioner's Text,* 2nd ed., pp. 176–90. Baltimore: Williams and Wilkins, 1979.

Cable, Mary. *American Manners and Morals.* New York: American Heritage, 1969.

Caldwell, J. R., and Cluff, L. E. Adverse reactions to antimicrobial agents. *Journal of the American Medical Association,* 1974, *230,* pp. 77–80.

Calhoun, Arthur W. *A. Social History of the American Family.* Glendale, Calif.: Arthur Clark, 1917.

Carroll, Michael P. Freud on homosexuality and the super-ego: Some cross-cultural tests. *Behavioral Science Research,* 1978, *13,* pp. 255–71.

Carter, Hugh, and Glick, Paul C. *Marriage and Divorce: A Social and Economic Study.* Cambridge: Harvard University Press, 1970.

Catullus. *The Poems of Catullus,* Horace Gregory (trans.). New York: Grove Press, 1956.

Cauldwell, D. O. Psychopathia transsexualis. *Sexology,* 1949, *16,* pp. 274–80.

Cavallin, Hector. Incestuous fathers: A clinical report. *American Journal of Psychiatry,* 1966, *122,* pp. 1132–35.

Center for Disease Control, Department of Health, Education, and Welfare. *Abortion Surveillance, Annual Summary, 1974.* Washington, D.C.: U.S. Government Printing Office, 1976.

Changing Times. The costs of having a baby today. July 1976, pp. 13–16.

Charlesworth, R., and Hartup, W. W. Positive social reinforcement in the nursery school peer group. *Child Development,* 1967, *38,* pp. 993–1002.

Chein, Isadore; Gerard, D.; Lee, R.; and Rosenfeld, E. *Narcotics, Delinquency and Social Policy.* London: Tavistock, 1964.

Christopherson, V. A., and Walters, J. Responses of Protestants, Catholics, and Jews concerning marriage and family life. *Sociological and Social Research,* 1958, *43,* pp. 16–22.

Clanton, Gordon. The contemporary experience of adultery: Bob and Carol and Updike and Rimmer. In R. W. Libby and R. N. Whitehurst (eds.), *Renovating Marriage: Toward New Sexual Life-Styles,* pp. 95–115. Danville, Calif.: Consensus Press, 1973.

Clark, A. M.; Wyon, S. M.; and Richards, M. P. M. Free play in nursery school children. *Journal of Child Psychology and Psychiatry,* 1969, *10,* pp. 205–16.

Clark, LeMon. *101 Intimate Sexual Problems Answered.* New York: New American Library, 1967.

Clark, LeMon. Adhesions between clitoris and prepuce. In H. Beigel (ed.), *Advances in Sex Research,* pp. 233–35. New York: Hoeber, 1963.

Clatworthy, N. M. Living together. In N. Glazer-Malbin (ed.), *Old Family/New Family,* Chapter 3. New York: Van Nostrand, 1975.

Clayton, Richard R., and Voss, Harwin L. Shacking up: Cohabitation in the 1970s. *Journal of Marriage and the Family,* 1977, *39,* pp. 273–83.

Cleugh, James. *Love Locked Out.* New York: Crown, 1964.

Cline, Victor B. (Ed.) *Where Do You Draw the Line?* Provo, Utah: Brigham Young University Press, 1974.

Cochran, W.; Mosteller, F.; and Tukey, V. W. *Statistical Problems of the Kinsey Report.* Washington, D.C.: American Statistical Association, 1954.

Cole, Charles Lee. Cohabitation in social context. In R. W. Libby and R. N. Whitehurst (eds.), *Marriage and Alternatives: Exploring Intimate Relationships,* pp. 62–79. Glenview, Ill.: Scott, Foresman, 1977.

Cole, Theodore M. Sexuality and the spinal cord injured. In R. Green (ed.), *Human Sexuality: A Health Practi-*

tioner's Text, 2nd ed., pp. 242–63. Baltimore: Williams and Wilkins, 1979.

Cole, William Graham. *Sex in Christianity and Psychoanalysis*. New York: Oxford University Press, 1966.

Coleman, T. F. Sex and the law. *The Humanist,* March-April 1978, pp. 38–41.

Comfort, Alex. *The Joy of Sex.* New York: Simon and Schuster, 1972.

Comfort, Alex. *The Anxiety Makers.* New York: Dell, 1970.

Comfort, Alex. *Sex in Society.* New York: Citadel, 1966.

Commission on Crime in the District of Columbia. *Report.* Washington, D.C.: U.S. Government Printing Office, 1966.

Commission on Law Enforcement and Administration of Justice. *The Challenge of Crime in a Free Society.* Washington, D.C.: U.S. Government Printing Office, 1967.

Commission on Obscenity and Pornography. *Report.* New York: Random House, 1970.

Commonwealth of Pennsylvania v. *Sharpless,* 2 Serg. & R. 91 (1815).

Constant, Benjamin. *Adolphe,* Harold Nicolson (trans.). New York: New American Library, 1959.

Constantine, Larry, and Constantine, Joan. *Group Marriage.* New York: Collier Books, 1973.

Constantine, Larry L., and Constantine, Joan. Sexual aspects of multilateral relations. In J. R. Smith and L. G. Smith (eds.), *Beyond Monogamy: Recent Studies of Sexual Alternatives in Marriage,* pp. 268–90. Baltimore: Johns Hopkins University Press, 1974.

Constantinople, A. Perceived instrumentality of the college as a measure of attitudes towards college. *Journal of Personality and Social Psychology,* 1967, *5,* 196–201.

Cuber, John F., and Harroff, Peggy B. *Five Kinds of Relationships.* New York: Appleton-Century-Crofts, 1965.

Cuber, John F., and Harroff, Peggy B. *Sex and the Significant Americans.* Baltimore: Penguin Books, 1966.

Culliton, Barbara. Penicillin-resistant gonorrhea: New strain spreading worldwide. *Science,* 1976, *194,* 1395–97.

Culliton, Barbara. Mammography controversy. *Science,* 1977, *198,* pp. 171–73.

Curran, James B.; Neff, Steven; and Lippold, Steven. Correlates of sexual experience among college students. *Journal of Sex Research,* 1973, *9,* pp. 124–31.

Curtis, L. R. *Venereal Disease: America's Modern Plague.* Fairfield, Conn.: McKesson Laboratories, 1972.

Dahlström, Edmund. (Ed.) *The Changing Roles of Men and Women.* Boston: Beacon Press, 1971.

Dahlström, Edmund, and Liljeström, Rita. The family and married women at work. In E. Dahlström (ed.), *The Changing Roles of Men and Women,* pp. 19–58. Boston: Beacon Press, 1971.

Dalton, K. *The Premenstrual Syndrome.* Springfield, Ill.: Charles C. Thomas, 1964.

D'Andrade, Roy G. Sex differences and cultural institutions. In E. E. Maccoby (ed.), *The Development of Sex Differences,* pp. 175–204. Stanford, Calif.: Stanford University Press, 1966.

Dank, Barry M. Six homosexual siblings. *Archives of Sexual Behavior,* 1971, *1,* pp. 193–204.

Dannemiller, J. E., and Shirley, E. *A Study of Community Standards in the City of Honolulu.* Honolulu: Survey Marketing Services, 1978.

Darrow, William. Changes in sexual behavior and venereal diseases. *Clinical Obstetrics and Gynecology,* 1975, *18,* pp. 255–67.

Darrow, William W. Approaches to the problem of venereal disease prevention. *Preventive Medicine,* 1976, *5,* pp. 165–75. (a)

Darrow, William W. Social and behavioral aspects of sexually transmitted diseases. In S. Gordon and R. W. Libby (eds.), *Sexuality Today and Tomorrow,* pp. 134–54. North Scituate, Mass.: Duxbury Press, 1976. (b)

Davenport, William. Sexual patterns and their regulation in a society of the Southwest Pacific. In F. A. Beach (ed.), *Sex and Behavior,* pp. 164–207. New York: Wiley, 1965.

Davenport, William. Sex in cross-cultural perspective. In F. A. Beach (ed.), *Human Sexuality in Four Perspectives,* pp. 115–63. Baltimore: Johns Hopkins University Press, 1977.

David, Henry P., et al. Prague study of developmental consequences of unwanted pregnancies. In Y. Poortinga (ed.), *Basic Problems in Cross-Cultural Psychology.* Amsterdam: Swets and Zeitlinger, 1977.

Davis, Katherine B. *Factors in the Sex Life of Twenty-two Hundred Women.* New York: Harper, 1929.

Davis, Keith. Sex on campus: Is there a revolution? *Medical Aspects of Human Sexuality,* 1971, *5*(1), pp. 128–42.

Davis, Keith, and Braucht, G. N. Exposure to pornography, character and sexual deviance: A retrospective survey. *Technical Report of the Commission on Obscenity and Pornography,* vol. 7. Washington, D.C.: U.S. Government Printing Office, 1970.

Davis, Kingsley. Jealousy and sexual property. *Social Forces,* 1936, *14,* pp. 395–405.

Davis, Kingsley. *Human Society.* New York: Macmillan, 1949.

Davis, Nanette J. Prostitution: Identity, career, and legal-economic enterprise. In J. M. Henslin and E. Sagarin (eds.), *The Sociology of Sex: An Introductory Reader,* pp. 195–222. New York: Schocken, 1978.

Dawkins, R. *The Selfish Gene.* New York: Oxford University Press, 1976.

Debrouner, C. H., and Shubin-Stein, R. Sexual problems in the infertile couple. *Medical Aspects of Human Sexuality,* 1975, *9*(1), pp. 140–48.

Delaney, Janice; Lupton, Mary Jane; and Toth, Emily. *The Curse: A Cultural History of Menstruation.* New York: Dutton, 1976.

Delcourt, Marie. *Hermaphrodite,* J. Nicolson (trans.). London: Studio Books, 1961.

DeLora, Joann S., and Warren, Carol A. B. *Understanding Sexual Interaction.* Boston: Houghton Mifflin, 1977.

DeMartino, Manfred. *The New Female Sexuality.* New York: Julian Press, 1969.

DeMause, Lloyd. The evolution of childhood. *History of Childhood Quarterly,* 1974, *1,* pp. 503–75.

Denfield, D., and Gordon, M. The sociology of mate swapping. *Journal of Sex Research,* 1970, *6,* pp. 85–100.

Dennis, E. J., and Hester, L. L. Toxemia of pregnancy. In D. N. Danforth (ed.), *Textbook of Obstetrics and Gynecology,* 2nd ed., pp. 397–416. New York: Harper and Row, 1971.

De Rougemont, Denis. *Love in the Western World,* M. Belgion (trans.). New York: Fawcett, 1966.

Deutsch, Helene. *The Psychology of Women,* vol. 2. New York: Grune and Stratton, 1945.

Devereaux, George. Institutionalized homosexuality of the Mohave Indians. In H. Ruitenbeek (ed.), *The Problem of Homosexuality in Modern Society,* pp. 183–226. New York: Dutton, 1963.

Devereaux, George. A psychoanalytic study of contraception. *Journal of Sex Research,* 1965, *1,* pp. 105–134.

De Vore, Irven. Male dominance and mating behavior. In F. A. Beach (ed.), *Sex and Behavior,* pp. 266–89. New York: Wiley, 1965.

De Vries, Peter, *Comfort Me with Apples.* Boston: Little, Brown, 1968.

Dewhurst, C. J., and Gordon, R. R. Change of sex. *Lancet,* 1963, *2,* pp. 1213–16.

Diamond, Milton. Sexual activity of women in Hawaii. Unpublished paper.

Diamond, Milton. A critical evaluation of the ontogeny of human sexual behavior. *Quarterly Review of Biology,* 1965, *40,* pp. 147–75.

Diamond, Milton. Genetic-endocrine interactions and human psychosexuality. In M. Diamond (ed.), *Perspectives in Reproduction and Sexual Behavior,* pp. 417–43. Bloomington: Indiana University Press, 1968.

Diamond, Milton. Intromission pattern and species vaginal code in relation to induction of pseudopregnancy. *Science,* 1970, *169,* pp. 995–97.

Diamond, Milton. Vaginal stimulation and progesterone in relation to pregnancy and parturition. *Biology of Reproduction,* 1972, *6,* pp. 281–87.

Diamond, Milton. *Human Sexuality.* (Television cassette series.) Washington, D.C.: Public Broadcasting System, 1973.

Diamond, Milton. Sex and the handicapped. *Rehabilitation Literature,* 1974, *35*(2), pp. 34–40. (a)

Diamond, Milton. Transsexualism. *Medical Journal of Australia,* 12 January 1974, p. 51. (b)

Diamond, Milton. Diamond's rules (axioms) of sex education and counseling. *Sex News,* 1975, *6*(12), p. 1. (a)

Diamond, Milton. *Human Sexuality.* (Audio cassette series.) New York: Jeffrey Norton, 1975. (b)

Diamond, Milton. Human sexuality: Mass sex education —student and community reaction. *Journal of Sex Education and Therapy,* Fall-Winter 1976, pp. 1–11.

Diamond, Milton. Education sexuelle de masse: La télévision au service de la santé publique. *Médicine et Hygiène,* 1977, *35,* pp. 2418–21. (a)

Diamond, Milton. Human sexual development: Biological foundations for social development. In F. A. Beach (ed.), *Human Sexuality in Four Perspectives,* pp. 22–61. Baltimore: Johns Hopkins University Press, 1977. (b)

Diamond, Milton. Sexual identity and sex roles. *The Humanist,* March-April 1978, pp. 16–19.

Diamond, Milton. Sexual identity and sex roles. In V. Bullough (ed.), *The Frontiers of Sex Research,* pp. 39–56. Buffalo: Prometheus Press, 1979. (a)

Diamond, Milton. Sexual reproduction: Conception and contraception. In R. Green (ed.), *Human Sexuality: A Health Practitioner's Text,* 2nd ed., pp. 58–80. Baltimore: Williams and Wilkins, 1979. (b)

Diamond, Milton; Diamond, A. L.; and Mast, M. Visual sensitivity and sexual arousal levels during the menstrual cycle. *Journal of Nervous and Mental Diseases,* 1972, *155,* pp. 170–76.

Diamond, Milton, and Henderson, Marcia. Oral-genital activity in the male hamster: Glossectomy and sexual performance. *Behavioral and Neural Biology,* 1980, *28,* pp. 1–8.

Diamond, Milton; Palmore, James A.; Smith, Roy G.; and Steinhoff, Patricia G. Abortion in Hawaii. *Family Planning Perspectives,* 1973, *5,* pp. 54–60. (a)

Diamond, Milton; Steinhoff, Patricia G.; Palmore, James A.; and Smith, Roy G. Sexuality, birth control and abortion: A decision-making sequence. *Biosocial Science,* 1973, *5,* pp. 347–61. (b)

Diamond, Milton; Smith, Roy G.; Steinhoff, Patricia G.; and Palmore, James A. *Report to the Legislature, State of Hawaii: Abortion in Hawaii; The First Year.* Honolulu: State of Hawaii, 1972.

Diamond, Milton, and Young, William C. Differential responsiveness of pregnant and nonpregnant guinea pigs to the masculinizing action of testosterone propionate. *Endocrinology,* 1963, *72,* pp. 429–38.

Dickinson, Robert L. *Human Sex Anatomy,* 2nd ed. Baltimore: Williams and Wilkins, 1949.

Dick-Read, Grantley. *Childbirth without Fear,* 2nd rev. ed. New York: Harper and Row, 1944.

Diderot, Denis. Supplement to Bougainville's "Voyage." In *Rameau's Nephew and Other Works,* J. Barzun and R. Bowen (trans.), pp. 183–239. Garden City, N.Y.: Anchor, 1956.

Dinitz, S.; Dynes, R. R.; and Clarke, A. C. Preferences for male or female children: Traditional or affectional? *Marriage and Family Living,* 1954, *16,* pp. 128–30.

Ditzion, Sidney. *Marriage, Morals, and Sex in America.* New York: Norton, 1978.

Dobzhansky, Theodosius. *The Genetics of the Evolutionary Process.* New York: Columbia University Press, 1970.

Doe et al. v. *Bolton,* 410 U.S. 179 (22 January 1973).

514

Dollard, John. *Caste and Class in a Southern Town.* New Haven: Yale University Press, 1937.

Dorner, G.; Rohde, W.; Seidel, K.; Haas, W.; and Schott, G. On the evocability of a positive oestrogen feedback action on LH secretion in transsexual men and women. *Endokrinologie,* 1976, *67,* pp. 20–25.

Doty, R. L.; Ford, M.; Preti, G.; and Huggins, G. R. Changes in the intensity and pleasantness of human vaginal odors during the menstrual cycle. *Science,* 1975, *190,* pp. 1316–18.

Doty, R. L., and Silverthorne, C. Influence of menstrual cycle on volunteering behavior. *Nature* (London), 1975, *254,* pp. 139–40.

Drinan, R. F. The right of the foetus to be born. *Dublin Review,* Winter 1967, pp. 365–81.

Dytrych, Zdenek; Matějček, Zdenek; Schüller, Vratislav; David, Henry P.; and Friedman, Herbert L. Children born to women denied abortion. *Family Planning Perspectives,* 1975, *7,* pp. 165–71.

Edmiston, S. How to write your own marriage contract. *Ms,* Spring 1972, pp. 66–72.

Ehrhardt, Anke A. Prenatal hormonal exposure and psychosexual differentiation. In E. J. Sachar (ed.), *Topics in Psychoendocrinology,* pp. 67–82. New York: Grune and Stratton, 1975.

Ehrhardt, Anke A.; Evers, K.; and Money, J. Influence of androgen on some aspects of sexually dimorphic behavior in women with late-treated adrenogenital syndrome. *Johns Hopkins Medical Journal,* 1968, *123,* pp. 115–22.

Ehrhardt, Anke A., and Money, John. Progestin-induced hermaphroditism: IQ and psychosexual identity in a study of ten girls. *Journal of Sex Research,* 1967, *3,* pp. 83–100.

Eibl-Eibesfeldt, Irenäus. *Love and Hate,* G. Strachan (trans.). New York: Schocken, 1974.

Elias, James, and Gebhard, Paul. Sexuality and sexual learning in childhood. *Phi Delta Kappan,* March 1969, pp. 401–5.

Elias, Veronica. A cautionary note on sex studies. *The Humanist,* March–April 1978, pp. 23–25.

Ellenberg, M. Impotence in diabetes: The neurological factor. *Annals of Internal Medicine,* 1971, *75,* pp. 212–19.

Ellenberg, M. Sex and the female diabetic. *Medical Aspects of Human Sexuality,* 1977, *11*(12), p. 30.

Ellinwood, Everett H., and Rockwell, W. J. Kenneth. Effect of drug use on sexual behavior. *Medical Aspects of Human Sexuality,* 1975, *9*(3), pp. 10, 14, 17, 18, 23, 26, 31, 32.

Ellis, Albert. *Reason and Emotion in Psychotherapy.* New York: Lyle Stuart, 1962.

Ellis, Albert. *Sex and the Single Man.* New York: Dell, 1963.

Ellis, Albert. Masturbation. In M. DeMartino (ed.), *Sexual Behavior and Personality Characteristics,* pp. 255–57. New York: Grove Press, 1966.

Ellis, Albert, and Abarbanel, Albert. (Eds.) *Encyclopedia of Sexual Behavior.* New York: Aronson, 1973.

Ellis, Albert, and Brancale, Ralph. *The Psychology of Sex Offenders.* Springfield, Ill.: Charles C. Thomas, 1956.

Ellis, Albert, and Harper, Robert. *A New Guide to Rational Living.* Englewood Cliffs, N.J.: Prentice-Hall, 1975.

Ellis, Havelock. *Studies in the Psychology of Sex.* New York: Random House, 1936.

Ember, Melvin, and Ember, Carol. The conditions favoring matrilocal versus patrilocal residence. *American Anthropologist,* 1971, *73,* pp. 71–94.

Engels, Frederick. *The Origins of the Family, Private Property, and the State.* New York: International, 1972.

Epstein, R., and Leverant, S. Verbal conditioning and sex role identification in children. *Child Development,* 1963, *34,* pp. 99–106.

Erikson, Erik H. Identity and the life cycle. *Psychological Issues,* 1959, *1,* pp. 18–171.

Erikson, Erik H. *Childhood and Society.* New York: Norton, 1963.

Erikson, Erik H. *Identity: Youth and Crisis.* New York: Norton, 1968.

Espenshade, Thomas. The value and cost of children. *Population Bulletin 32*(1). Washington, D.C.: Population Reference Bureau, 1977.

Evans, Jerome R.; Selsted, Georgiana; and Welcher, W. H. Teenagers: Fertility control behavior and attitudes before and after abortion, childbearing or negative pregnancy test. *Family Planning Perspectives,* 1976, *8,* pp. 192–200.

Evans, T. N. Infertility and other office gynecologic problems. In D. N. Danforth (ed.), *Textbook of Obstetrics and Gynecology,* 2nd ed., pp. 798–825. New York: Harper and Row, 1971.

Ewing, J. A. Students, sex, and marijuana. *Medical Aspects of Human Sexuality,* 1972, *6*(2), pp. 100–17.

Exner, M. J. *Problems and Principles of Sex Education: A Study of 948 College Men.* New York: Association Press, 1915.

Falk, Gail. Women and unions: A historic view. *Women's Rights Law Reporter,* Spring 1973, pp. 54–65.

Fawcett, James T. *Psychology and Population: Behavioral Research Issues in Fertility and Family Planning.* New York: Population Council, 1970.

Federal Bureau of Investigation. *Uniform Crime Reports: Crime in the United States, 1975.* Washington, D.C.: U.S. Government Printing Office, 1976.

Fee, Elizabeth. Science and the woman problem: Historical perspectives. In M. Teitelbaum (ed.), *Sex Differences: Social and Biological Perspectives,* pp. 175–223. Garden City, N.Y.: Anchor, 1976.

Feldman, M. P. Aversion therapy for sexual deviations: A critical review. *Psychological Bulletin,* 1966, *65,* pp. 65–79.

Feldman, M. P., and Macculloch, M. J. *Homosexual Behaviour: Therapy and Assessment.* Oxford: Pergamon Press, 1971.

Ferenczi, Sandor. *Sex in Psychoanalysis.* New York: Basic Books, 1950.

515

Ferenczi, Sandor. *Further Contributions to the Theory and Technique of Psychoanalysis.* New York: Basic Books, 1952.

Figes, Eva. *Patriarchal Attitudes.* Greenwich, Conn.: Fawcett, 1971.

Finch, B. E., and Green, Hugh. *Contraception Through the Ages.* Springfield, Ill.: Charles C. Thomas, 1963.

Finger, Frank W. Changes in sex practices and beliefs of male college students over 30 years. *Journal of Sex Research,* 1975, *11,* pp. 304–17.

Fisher, Seymour. *The Female Orgasm: Psychology, Physiology, Fantasy.* New York: Basic Books, 1973.

Fisk, Norman. Five spectacular results. *Archives of Sexual Behavior,* 1978, *1,* pp. 351–69.

Fitz-Gerald, D., and Fitz-Gerald, M. Sexual implications of deafness. *Sexuality and Disability,* 1978, *1*(1), pp. 57–69.

Flacelière, Robert. *Love in Ancient Greece,* J. Cleugh (trans.). New York: Crown, 1962.

Flaubert, Gustave. *Madame Bovary,* F. Steegmuller (trans.). New York: Modern Library, 1952.

Fletcher, Joseph. *Situation Ethics.* Philadelphia: Westminster Press, 1966.

Fletcher, Joseph. *Moral Responsibility: Situation Ethics at Work.* Philadelphia: Westminster Press, 1967.

Flexner, Eleanor. *Century of Struggle.* Paterson, N.J.: Atheneum, 1968.

Fling, S., and Manosevitz, M. Sex typing in nursery school children's play interests. *Developmental Psychology,* 1972, *7,* pp. 146–52.

Ford, Clellan. Culture and sex. In A. Ellis and A. Abarbanel (eds.) *The Encyclopedia of Sexual Behavior,* pp. 306–12. New York: Aronson, 1973.

Ford, Clellan, and Beach, Frank A. *Patterns of Sexual Behavior.* New York: Harper and Row, 1951.

Fordney-Settlage, Diane S. Treating sexual dysfunction: The solo female physician. In R. Green (ed.), *Human Sexuality: A Health Practitioner's Text,* pp. 213–21. Baltimore: Williams and Wilkins, 1975.

Fordney-Settlage, Diane S.; Baroff, S.; and Cooper, D. Sexual experience of younger teenage girls seeking contraceptive assistance for the first time. *Family Planning Perspectives,* 1973, *5,* pp. 223–26.

Forrest, Jacqueline D.; Tietze, Christopher; and Sullivan, Ellen. Abortion in the United States, 1976–1977. *Family Planning Perspectives,* 1978, *10,* pp. 271–79.

Forssman, Hans, and Thuwe, Inga. One hundred and twenty children born after application for therapeutic abortion refused. *Acta Psychiatrica Scandinavica,* 1966, *48,* pp. 71–88.

Foucault, Michel. *Madness and Civilization,* R. Howard (trans.). New York: Random House, 1973.

Fox, C. A. Orgasm and fertility. In R. Gemme and C. C. Wheeler (eds.), *Progress in Sexology,* pp. 351–55. New York: Plenum, 1977.

Fox, C. A., and Fox, Beatrice. Blood pressure and respiratory patterns during human coitus. *Journal of Reproduction and Fertility,* 1969, *19,* pp. 405–15.

Fox, C. A., and Fox, Beatrice. A comparative study of coital physiology, with special reference to the sexual

climax. *Journal of Reproduction and Fertility,* 1971, *24,* pp. 319–26.

Fox, C. A.; Wolff, H. S.; and Baker, J. A. Measurement of intra-vaginal and intra-uterine pressures during human coitus by radio-telemetry. *Journal of Reproduction and Fertility,* 1970, *22,* pp. 243–51.

Frank, Anne. The diary of a young girl. In *The Works of Anne Frank,* B. M. Mooyaard (trans.), pp. 25–240. New York: Doubleday, 1959.

Frank, Deborah; Dornbush, Rhea; Webster, Sandra; and Kolodny, Robert C. Mastectomy and sexual behavior: A pilot study. *Sexuality and Disability,* 1978, *1*(1), pp. 16–26.

Frank, Ellen; Anderson, Carol; and Rubinstein, Debra. Frequency of sexual dysfunction in "normal" couples. *New England Journal of Medicine,* 1978, *299,* pp. 111–15.

Frank, R. T. The hormonal causes of premenstrual tension. *Archives of Neurology and Psychiatry,* 1931, *26,* pp. 1053–57.

Franzblau, Susan; Sprafkin, Joyce; and Rubinstein, Eli. Sex on TV: A content analysis. *Journal of Communication,* 1977, *27*(2), pp. 164–70.

Freedman, Daniel G. *Human Infancy: An Evolutionary Perspective.* New York: Wiley, 1974.

Freedman, Mervin B. The sexual behavior of American college women. *Merrill-Palmer Quarterly,* 1965, *11,* pp. 33–48.

Freedman, Ronald. Theories of fertility decline: A reappraisal. *Social Forces,* 1979, *58,* pp. 1–17.

Freud, Anna. Homosexuality. *Bulletin of the American Psychoanalytic Association,* 1951, *7,* pp. 117–18.

Freud, Sigmund. *The Basic Writings of Sigmund Freud,* A. A. Brill (trans.). New York: Modern Library, 1938.

Freud, Sigmund. *Totem and Taboo,* J. Strachey (trans.). New York: Norton, 1952.

Freud, Sigmund. *A General Introduction to Psychoanalysis,* J. Riviere (trans.). New York: Doubleday, 1953.

Freud, Sigmund. *Collected Papers,* 5 vols., J. Strachey (ed.). New York: Basic Books, 1959.

Freud, Sigmund. *Three Essays on the Theory of Sexuality,* J. Strachey (trans.). New York: Avon, 1967.

Friday, Nancy. *My Secret Garden: Women's Sexual Fantasies.* New York: Trident, 1973.

Fried, Edrita. *The Ego in Love and Sexuality.* New York: Grune and Stratton, 1960.

Friedan, Betty. *The Feminine Mystique.* New York: Norton, 1963.

Friedl, Ernestine. *Women and Men: An Anthropologist's View.* New York: Holt, Rinehart and Winston, 1975.

Frisch, E. E., and McArthur, J. M. Menstrual cycles: Fatness as a determinant of minimum weight for height necessary for their maintenance or onset. *Science,* 1974, *185,* pp. 949–51.

Fromm, Erich. *The Art of Loving.* New York: Harper and Brothers, 1956.

Fuller, John, and Thompson, William. *Behavior Genetics.* New York: Wiley, 1967.

Gadpaille, Warren. Cross-species and cross-cultural con

tributions to the understanding of homosexual activity. In press.

Gadpaille, Warren J. Infertility and amenorrhea in the hysterical character. In *The Collected Award Papers*, p. 131. Port Chester, N.Y.: Gralnik Foundation, 1966.

Gadpaille, Warren J. *The Cycles of Sex*. New York: Scribner's, 1975.

Gadpaille, Warren. A consideration of two concepts of normality as it applies to adolescent sexuality. *Journal of Child Psychiatry*, 1976, *15*, pp. 679–92.

Gagnon, John. Female child victims of sex offenses. *Social Problems*, 1965, *13*, pp. 176–92.

Gagnon, John, and Simon, William. (Eds.) *Sexual Deviance*. New York: Harper and Row, 1967.

Gagnon, John, and Simon, William. *Sexual Conduct: The Social Sources of Human Sexuality*. Chicago: Aldine, 1973.

Gallup Organization. Seventy-five percent back abortions, but most say only in certain circumstances. *The Gallup Poll*, Princeton, N.J.: January 1978. (a)

Gallup Organization. U.S. Catholics and the Catholic Press. Princeton, N.J.: January 1978. (b)

Gallup, George. Public concerned about porn, but divided over Court decision. *Gallup Opinion Index*, 1977, *142*, pp. 1–6.

Garai, J., and Scheinfeld, A. Sex differences in mental and behavioral traits. *Genetic Psychology Monographs*, 1968, *77*, pp. 169–299.

Garrett, Thomas, and Wright, Richard. Wives of rapists and incest offenders. *Journal of Sex Research*, 1975, *11*, pp. 149–57.

Garris, Lorie; Steckler, Allan; and McIntire, John. The relationship between oral contraceptives and adolescent sexual behavior. *Journal of Sex Research*, 1976, *12*, pp. 135–46.

Gavron, H. *The Captive Wife*. London: Routledge and Kegan Paul, 1960.

Gebhard, Paul H. Factors in marital orgasm. *Journal of Social Issues*, 1966, *22*(4), pp. 88–95.

Gebhard, Paul H. Human sex behavior research. In M. Diamond (ed.), *Perspectives in Reproduction and Sexual Behavior*, pp. 391–410. Bloomington: Indiana University Press, 1968.

Gebhard, Paul H. Misconceptions about female prostitutes. *Medical Aspects of Human Sexuality*, 1969, *3*(3), pp. 24–30.

Gebhard, Paul H. Female sexuality. In H. Giese (ed.), *The Sexuality of Women*, pp. 10–43. New York: Stein and Day, 1970.

Gebhard, Paul H. Human sexual behavior: A summary statement. In D. S. Marshall and R. C. Suggs (eds.), *Human Sexual Behavior*, pp. 206–17. New York: Basic Books, 1971.

Gebhard, Paul H.; Gagnon, John H.; Pomeroy, Wardell B.; and Christenson, Cornelia V. *Sex Offenders*. New York: Harper and Row, 1965.

Gebhard, Paul H.; Pomeroy, Wardell B.; Martin, Clyde; and Christenson, Cornelia V. *Pregnancy, Birth and Abortion*. New York: Harper, 1958.

Geddes, Donald. (Ed.) *An Analysis of the Kinsey Reports*. New York: New American Library, 1954.

Gelder, Lindsy Van, and Carmichael, Carrie. But what about our sons? Ambivalence toward a man child. *Ms*, October 1975, pp. 52–56, 94–95.

Gerassi, George. *The Boys of Boise*. New York: Macmillan, 1966.

Giallombardo, Rose. *Society of Women: A Study of a Woman's Prison*. New York: Wiley, 1966.

Giese, Hans. The sexuality of women. In H. Giese (ed.), *The Sexuality of Women*, pp. 97–134. New York: Stein and Day, 1970.

Gillespie, W. H. The psycho-analytic theory of sexual deviation with special reference to fetishism. In I. Rosen (ed.), *The Pathology and Treatment of Sexual Deviation*, pp. 123–45. London: Oxford University Press, 1964.

Gilmartin, Brian. Swinging: Who gets involved and how. In R. W. Libby and R. N. Whitehurst (eds.), *Marriage and Alternatives*, pp. 161–85. Glenview, Ill.: Scott, Foresman, 1977.

Gilmartin, Brian, and Kusisto, Dave. Some personal and social characteristics of mate-sharing swingers. In R. W. Libby and R. N. Whitehurst (eds.), *Renovating Marriage*, pp. 146–55. Danville, Calif.: Consensus Press, 1973.

Ginsberg, George; Frosch, William; and Shapiro, Theodore. The new impotence. *Archives of General Psychiatry*, 1972, *26*, pp. 218–20.

Glick, Paul, and Norman, Arthur. Frequency, duration and probability of marriage and divorce. *Journal of Marriage and the Family*, 1971, *33*, pp. 307–17.

Gochros, Harvey, and Schultz, L. G. (Eds.) *Human Sexuality and Social Work*. New York: Association Press, 1977.

Goffman, Erving. *Stigma*. Englewood Cliffs, N.J.: Prentice-Hall, 1968.

Goldberg, Martin. Current thinking on sexual norms in marriage. *Medical Aspects of Human Sexuality*, 1978, *12*, pp. 122–23.

Goldberg, Steven. *The Inevitability of Patriarchy*. New York: Morrow, 1973.

Goldberg, Steven, and Lewis, M. Play behavior in the year-old infant: Early sex differences. *Child Development*, 1969, *40*, pp. 21–31.

Golden, Joshua; Price, S.; Heinrich, A. G.; and Lobitz, W. C. Group vs. couple treatment of sexual dysfunctions. *Archives of Sexual Behavior*, 1978, *7*, pp. 593–602.

Goldfoot, David; Essock-Vitale, Susan; Asa, Cheryl; Thornton, Janice; and Leshner, Alan. Anosmia in male rhesus monkeys does not alter copulatory activity with cycling females. *Science*, 1978, *199*, pp. 1095–96.

Goldsen, R. K.; Rosenberg, M.; Williams, R. M., Jr.; and Suchman, E. A. *What College Students Think*. Princeton, N.J.: Van Nostrand, 1960.

Goldsmith, A.; Brenner, W. E.; and Edelman, D. A. *I.U.D.s Present and Future*. Buenos Aires: World Congress on Fertility and Sterility, 1974.

Goldstein, M. J., and Kant, H. S. *Pornography and Sexual*

Deviance. Los Angeles: University of California Press, 1973.

Goleman, Daniel, and Bush, Sherida. The liberation of sexual fantasy. *Psychology Today,* October 1977, pp. 48–53, 104–7.

Goode, William J. *After Divorce.* Glencoe, Ill.: Free Press, 1956.

Goode, William J. *The Family.* Englewood Cliffs, N.J.: Prentice-Hall, 1964.

Goode, William J. *World Revolution and Family Patterns.* New York: Free Press, 1970.

Goodlin, R. C. Genetic considerations. In D. Danforth (ed.), *Textbook of Obstetrics and Gynecology,* 2nd ed., pp. 25–45. New York: Harper and Row, 1971.

Goodlin, R. C. Coitus during pregnancy. In H. Lief (ed.), *Medical Aspects of Human Sexuality: 750 Questions Answered by 500 Authorities,* p. 165. Baltimore: Williams and Wilkins, 1975.

Goodman, M. J.; Grove, J.; and Gilbert, F. Jr. Menopause and lifecycle variables. University of Hawaii Women's Studies Program Working Papers Series, *1*(3), pp. 1–13.

Gordon, Sol. Freedom for sex education and sexual expression. In S. Gordon and R. Libby (eds.), *Sexuality Today and Tomorrow,* pp. 330–39. North Scituate, Mass.: Duxbury Press, 1976.

Gordon, Sol, and Libby, Roger. (Eds.) *Sexuality Today and Tomorrow.* North Scituate, Mass.: Duxbury Press.

Gove, Walter, and Tudor, Jeannette. Adult sex roles and mental illness. In J. Huber (ed.), *Changing Women in a Changing Society,* pp. 50–73. Chicago: University of Chicago Press, 1973.

Goy, Robert, and Jackway, Jacqueline. The inheritance of patterns of sexual behavior in female guinea pigs. *Animal Behavior,* 1959, *7,* pp. 142–49.

Greeley, Andrew M. Findings on Catholic abortion views shattering. *The Anchor,* 26 January 1978, p. 6.

Green, Richard. Children of the atypical: Psychological and political implications. Unpublished paper.

Green, Richard. *Sexual Identity Conflict in Children and Adults.* Baltimore: Penguin Books, 1974.

Green, Richard. "Sissies" and "tomboys." *SIECUS Report,* 1979, *7*(3), pp. 1–2, 15.

Green, Richard, and Money, John. Stage-acting, role-taking, and effeminate impersonation during boyhood. *Archives of General Psychiatry,* 1966, *15*(5), pp. 535–38.

Green, Richard, and Money, John. (Eds.) *Transsexualism and Sex Reassignment.* Baltimore: Johns Hopkins University Press, 1969.

Greenberg, Jerrold, and Archambault, Francis. Masturbation, self-esteem and other variables. *Journal of Sex Research,* 1973, *9,* pp. 41–51.

Greenwald, Harold. *The Call Girl.* New York: Ballantine, 1958.

Greer, Germaine. *The Female Eunuch.* New York: McGraw-Hill, 1971.

Greer, Germaine. Interview. *Playboy,* January 1972, pp.

61–64, 66, 68, 70, 72, 74, 76, 78, 80, 82.

Griswold v. *Connecticut.* 381 U.S. 479, 484 (1965).

Gross, N., et al. *Exploration in Role Analysis.* New York: Wiley, 1958.

Groth, N. A., and Burgess, A. W. Sexual dysfunction during rape. *New England Journal of Medicine,* 1977, *297,* p. 764.

Guerro, R. Type and time of insemination within the menstrual cycle and the human sex ratio at birth. *Studies in Family Planning,* 1975, *6,* pp. 367–71.

Guyon, René. *The Ethics of Sex Acts,* J. C. Flugel and I. Flugel (trans.). New York: Knopf, 1934.

Guyon, René. *Sexual Freedom,* E. Paul and C. Paul (trans.). New York: Knopf, 1950.

Haeberle, Erwin L. *The Sex Atlas.* New York: Seabury Press, 1978.

Hale, E. B., and Schein, M. W. The behavior of turkeys. In E. S. E. Hafez (ed.), *The Behavior of Domestic Animals,* pp. 531–64. Baltimore: Williams and Wilkins, 1962.

Hall, Edward. *The Hidden Dimension.* New York: Doubleday, 1966.

Hall, J. E. Sexuality and the mentally retarded. In R. Green (ed.), *Human Sexuality: A Health Practitioner's Text,* pp. 181–95. Baltimore: Williams and Wilkins, 1975.

Hall, J. E., and Sawyer, H. W. Sexual policies for the mentally retarded. *Sexuality and Disability,* 1978, *1*(1), pp. 34–43.

Halleck, Seymour. The physician's role in management of victims of sex offenders. *Journal of the American Medical Association,* 1962, *180,* pp. 273–78.

Haller, John S., and Haller, Robin M. *The Physician and Sexuality in Victorian America.* New York: Norton, 1974.

Hamburger, Christian. The desire for change of sex as shown by personal letters from 465 men and women. *Acta Endocrinologica,* 1953, *14,* pp. 361–75.

Hamilton, Gilbert V. *A Research in Marriage.* New York: Boni, 1929.

Hanby, J. P. Male-male mounting in Japanese monkeys. *Animal Behaviour,* 1974, *22,* pp. 836–49.

Hare, E. H. Masturbatory insanity: The history of an idea. *Journal of Mental Science,* 1962, *108,* pp. 1–25.

Hariton, E. Barbara. The sexual fantasies of women. *Psychology Today,* March 1973, pp. 39–44.

Harlow, Harry. *Learning to Love.* New York: Aronson, 1974.

Harris, Mervyn. *The Dilly Boys: Male Prostitution in Piccadilly.* London: Croom Helm, 1973.

Hart, Gavin. Sexually transmitted diseases. In J. Head (ed.), *Carolina Biology Readers No. 95,* n.p. Burlington, N.C.: Carolina Biological Supply Co., 1976.

Hartman, William E. Interview. In M. Diamond, Marriage in *Human Sexuality.* Washington, D.C.: Public Broadcasting System, 1973.

Hartman, William E., and Fithian, Marilyn A. *Treatment of Sexual Dysfunction.* Long Beach, Calif.: Center for Marital and Sexual Studies, 1972.

Hartup, W. W., and Moore, S. G. Avoidance of inappropriate sex-typing by young children. *Journal of Consulting Psychology,* 1963, *27,* pp. 467–73.

Hastings, D. W. *A Doctor Speaks on Sexual Expression in Marriage.* Boston: Little, Brown, 1966. (a)

Hastings, D. W. *Impotence and Frigidity.* Boston: Little, Brown, 1966. (b)

Hastings, Donald R., and Markland, Colin. Post-surgical adjustment of twenty-five transsexuals (male to female) in the University of Minnesota study. *Archives of Sexual Behavior,* 1978, *7,* pp. 327–36.

Hatfield, J. S.; Ferguson, L. R.; and Alpert, R. Mother-child interaction and the socialization process. *Child Development,* 1967, *38,* pp. 365–414.

Hatterer, Lawrence. *Changing Homosexuality in the Male.* New York: McGraw-Hill, 1970.

Hatterer, Lawrence. *The Pleasure Addicts.* New York: A. S. Barnes, 1979.

Hawkins, Charles H. The erotic significance of contraceptive methods. *Journal of Sex Research,* 1970, *6,* pp. 143–57.

Heiman, Julia R. The physiology of erotica: Women's sexual arousal. *Psychology Today,* April, 1975, pp. 90–94.

Heiman, Julia R.; LoPiccolo, Leslie; and LoPiccolo, Joseph. *Becoming Orgasmic.* Englewood Cliffs, N.J.: Prentice-Hall, 1976.

Heller, C. G.; Laidlaw, W. M.; Harvey, H. T.; and Nelson, W. O. Effects of progestational compounds on the reproductive processes of the human male. *Annals of the New York Academy of Science,* 1958, *71,* pp. 649–65.

Helmholz, R. H. *Marriage Litigation in Medieval England.* Cambridge: Harvard University Press, 1974.

Hembree, W. C.; Zeidenberg, P.; and Nahas, G. Marijuana effects upon human gonadal function. In G. Nahas et al. (eds.), *Marijuana: Chemistry, Biochemistry and Cellular Effects,* pp. 521–32. New York: Springer Verlag, 1976.

Hendin, Herbert. *The Age of Sensation.* New York: Norton, 1977.

Hendin, Herbert; Gaylin, Willard; and Carr, Arthur. *Psychoanalysis and Social Research.* Garden City, N.Y.: Doubleday, 1965.

Henriques, Fernando. *Love in Action: The Sociology of Sex.* New York: Dutton, 1960.

Henriques, Fernando. *Prostitution in Europe and the Americas.* New York: Citadel, 1965.

Herold, E.; Mottin, J.; and Sabry, Z. The effect of vitamin E on human sexuality. *Archives of Sexual Behavior,* in press.

Hertig, A. T.; Rock, J.; Adams, E. C.; and Menkin, M. F. Thirty-four fertilized human ova, good, bad, and indifferent, recovered from 210 women of known fertility: A study of biologic wastage in early human pregnancy. *Pediatrics,* 1959, *23,* pp. 202–11.

Heston, L. L., and Shields, J. Homosexuality in twins. *Archives of General Psychiatry,* 1968, *18*(2), pp. 149–60.

Hill, M. A.; Link, W. C.; and Keating, C. H., Jr. Position report. In *The Report of the Commission on Obscenity and Pornography,* pp. 456–78. New York: Bantam Books, 1970.

Hirschfeld, Magnus. *Die Transvestiten.* Berlin: Pulvermacher, 1910.

Hite, Shere. *The Hite Report.* New York: Macmillan, 1976.

Hite, Shere. Interview. *Macmillan Preview,* 1977.

Hochshilde, Arlie. A review of sex role research. In J. Huber (ed.), *Changing Women in a Changing Society,* pp. 249–67. Chicago: University of Chicago Press, 1973.

Hoffman, Martin. *The Gay World.* New York: Basic Books, 1968.

Hoffman, Martin. Homosexuality. In F. A. Beach (ed.), *Human Sexuality in Four Perspectives,* pp. 164–89. Baltimore: Johns Hopkins University Press, 1977.

Hoffman, Martin L., and Levine, Laura E. Early sex differences in empathy. *Developmental Psychology,* 1976, *12,* pp. 557–58.

Hoffman, Martin L., and Saltzstein, H. D. Parent discipline and the child's moral development. *Journal of Personality and Social Psychology,* 1967, *5,* pp. 45–57.

Holden, Constance. House chops sex-pot probe. *Science,* 1977, *192,* p. 450.

Homans, G. *Social Behavior.* New York: Harcourt, Brace, Jovanovich, 1961.

Homer. *The Odyssey,* E. V. Rieu (trans.). Baltimore: Penguin Books, 1946.

Hooker, Evelyn. The adjustment of the male overt homosexual. *Journal of Projective Techniques.* 1957, 21, pp. 18–31.

Hooker, Evelyn. Male homosexuals and their worlds. In J. Marmor (ed.), *Sexual Inversion: The Multiple Roots of Homosexuality,* pp. 83–107. New York: Basic Books, 1965.

Horenstein, Simon. Sexual dysfunction in neurological disease. *Medical Aspects of Human Sexuality,* 1976, *10*(4), pp. 7–11, 17, 18, 22–24, 29, 31.

Horney, Karen. *The Neurotic Personality of Our Time.* New York: Norton, 1937.

Horney, Karen. *New Ways in Psychoanalysis.* New York: Norton, 1939.

Horney, Karen, *Self-Analysis.* New York: Norton, 1942.

Huang, Lucy J. Some patterns of non-exclusive sexual relations among unmarried cohabiting couples. *International Journal Review of Sociology,* 1976, *6.* Cited in C. L. Cole, Cohabitation in social context, in R. W. Libby and R. N. Whitehurst (eds.), *Marriage and Alternatives: Exploring Intimate Relationships* (Glenview, Ill.: Scott, Foresman, 1977).

Hubbard, L. Ron. *Dianetics.* New York: Hermitage House, 1950.

Hudson, John L., and Henze, Lura F. Campus values in mate selection: A replication. *Journal of Marriage and the Family,* 1969, *31,* pp. 772–78.

Hull, C. L. *Principles of Behavior.* New York: Appleton-Century-Crofts, 1943.

519

Humana, Charles. *The Keeper of the Bed: A Study of the Eunuch.* London: Arlington Books. 1973.

Humphreys, Laud. *Tearoom Trade: Impersonal Sex in Public Places,* rev. ed. Chicago: Aldine, 1975.

Hunt, Morton. *The Natural History of Love.* New York: Knopf, 1959.

Hunt, Morton. *The World of the Formerly Married.* New York: McGraw-Hill, 1966.

Hunt, Morton. *Sexual Behavior in the 1970s.* New York: Dell, 1974.

Hunt, Morton, *Prime Time.* New York: Stein and Day, 1975.

Hutt, Corinne. *Males and Females.* Baltimore: Penguin Books, 1972.

Hyde, M. O. *Speak Out on Rape.* New York: McGraw-Hill, 1976.

Imperato-McGinley, J.; Guerrero, L.; Gautier, T.; and Peterson, R. E. Steroid 5 α-reductase deficiency in man: An inherited form of male pseudohermaphroditism. *Science,* 1974, *186,* pp. 1213–15.

Imperato-McGinley, J.; Peterson, R. E.; Gautier, T.; and Sturla, E. Androgens and the evolution of male-gender identity among male pseudohermaphrodites with 5 α-reductase deficiency. *New England Journal of Medicine,* 1979, *300,* pp. 1233–37.

Ivey, M., and Bardwick, J. Patterns of effective fluctuation in the menstrual cycle. *Psychosomatic Medicine,* 1968, *30,* pp. 336–45.

J. (Pseud.) *The Sensuous Woman.* New York: Dell. 1969.

Jackman, Norman; O'Toole, Richard; and Geis, Gilbert. The self-image of the prostitute. *Sociological Quarterly,* 1963, *4,* pp. 150–61.

Jackson, Erwin, and Potkay, Charles. Precollege influences on sexual experiences of coeds. *Journal of Sex Research,* 1973, *9,* pp. 143–49.

Jaffe, Frederick S. Toward the reduction of unwanted pregnancy. *Science,* 1971, *174,* pp. 119–27.

James, Henry. *The Bostonians.* New York: Modern Library, 1964.

James, Wendy. Sister-exchange marriage. *Scientific American,* December 1975, pp. 84–94.

Jayaram, Bangalore N.; Stuteville, Orion H.; and Bush, Irving M. Complications and undesirable results of sex-reassignment surgery in male-to-female transsexuals. *Archives of Sexual Behavior,* 1978, *7,* pp. 337–45.

Jöchle, W. Current research in coitus-induced ovulation. *Journal of Reproduction and Fertility,* 1975, *22* (Suppl.), pp. 165–207.

Johnson, David N., and Diamond, Milton. Yohimbine and sexual stimulation in the male rat: *Physiology and Behavior,* 1969, *4,* p. 411–13.

Johnson, Virginia E., and Masters, William H. Intravaginal contraceptive study: Phase I, anatomy. *Western Journal of Surgery, Obstetrics, and Gynecology,* 1962, *70,* pp. 202–7.

Johnson, Warren R. Masturbation. In C. E. Vincent (ed.), *Human Sexuality in Medical Education and Practice,* pp. 485–95. Springfield, Ill.: Charles C. Thomas, 1968.

Jonas, Doris, and Jonas, David. *Sex and Status.* New York: Stein and Day, 1975.

Jones, Hardin, and Jones, Helen. *Sensual Drugs.* New York: Cambridge University Press, 1977.

Jongbloet, P. N. Month of birth and gametopathy: An investigation into patients with Down's, Klinefelter's and Turner's syndrome. *Clinical Genetics,* 1971, *2,* pp. 315–30.

Jost, A. Embryonic sexual differentiation. In H. Jones, Jr., and W. W. Scott (eds.), *Hermaphroditism, Genital Anomalies and Related Endocrine Disorders,* pp. 15–45. Baltimore: Williams and Wilkins, 1958.

Joyce, James. *Ulysses.* New York: Vintage, 1961.

Jung, Carl. *Two Essays on Analytical Psychology,* G. Adler et al. (eds.), R. Hull (trans.). Princeton, N.J.: Princeton University Press, 1972.

Justice, Blair, and Justice, Rita. *The Broken Taboo: Sex in the Family.* New York: Human Sciences Press, 1979.

Kaats, G. R., and Davis, K. E. The dynamics of sexual behavior of college students. *Journal of Marriage and the Family,* 1970, *32,* pp. 390–99.

Kagan, Jerome. Psychology of sex differences. In F. A. Beach (ed.), *Human Sexuality in Four Perspectives,* pp. 87–114. Baltimore: Johns Hopkins University Press, 1977.

Kallmann, Franz J. Comparative twin studies on the genetic aspects of male homosexuality. *Journal of Nervous and Mental Diseases,* 1952, *115,* pp. 283–98. (a)

Kallmann, Franz J. Twin and sibship study of overt homosexuality. *American Journal of Human Genetics,* 1952, *4,* pp. 136–46. (b)

Kallmann, Franz J. *Heredity in Health and Mental Disorder.* New York: Norton, 1953.

Kaminski, L. R. Looming effects on stranger anxiety and toy preferences in one-year-old infants. Unpublished master's thesis, Stanford University. Cited in E. E. Maccoby and C. N. Jacklin, *The Psychology of Sex Differences* (Stanford, Calif.: Stanford University Press, 1974).

Kanin, Eugene J. Male aggression in dating-courtship relations. *American Journal of Sociology,* 1957, *63,* pp. 197–204.

Kaplan, Alexandra G., and Bean, Joan P. (Eds.) *Beyond Sex-Role Stereotypes: Readings Toward a Psychology of Androgyny.* Boston: Little, Brown, 1976.

Kaplan, Helen S. *The New Sex Therapy.* New York: Bruner/Mazel, 1974.

Kardiner, Abram. *The Individual and His Society.* New York: Columbia University Press, 1939.

Kardiner, Abram, and Preble, Edward. *They Studied Man.* New York: World, 1965.

Karlen, Arno. Troilism: The variety of sexual threesomes. Unpublished paper.

Karlen, Arno. The unmarried marrieds on campus. *New York Times Magazine,* 26 January 1969, pp. 29, 77–80.

Karlen, Arno. *Sexuality and Homosexuality.* New York: Norton, 1971.

Karlen, Arno. Discussion of "Homosexuality as a Mental

Illness." *International Journal of Psychiatry,* 1972, 10, pp. 108–13.

Karlen, Arno. Everything the doctor didn't know about sex (and was often too afraid to ask). *Human Behavior,* July 1964, pp. 16–22.

Karlen, Arno. Homosexuality: The scene and students. In J. Henslin and E. Sagarin (eds.), *The Sociology of Sex: An Introductory Reader,* pp. 223–48. New York: Schocken, 1978.

Karlen, Arno. The soiled pinafore: A sexual theme in psychiatric history. In T. Karasu and C. Socarides (eds.), *Sex and Psychoanalysis.* New York: International Universities Press, 1979.

Karlen, Arno. Homosexuality in history. In J. Marmor (ed.), *Sexual Inversion,* 2nd ed., in press. (a)

Karlen, Arno. Why couples fight over coital positions. *Sexology,* in press. (b)

Karpman, Benjamin. *The Sexual Offender and His Offenses.* New York: Julian Press, 1954.

Katchadourian, Heran A., and Lunde, Donald T. *Fundamentals of Human Sexuality,* 2nd ed. New York: Holt, Rinehart and Winston, 1975.

Kaye, B. L. Micromastia vs. macromastia. *Medical Aspects of Human Sexuality,* 1973, 7(8), pp. 96–123.

Kegel, A. M. Sexual functions of the pubococcygeus muscle. *Western Journal of Surgery, Obstetrics, and Gynecology,* 1952, 60, pp. 521–24.

Kempton, W. *Guidelines for Planning a Training Course on Human Sexuality and the Retarded.* Philadelphia: Planned Parenthood Association of Southeastern Pennsylvania, 1973.

Keniston, Kenneth. *The Uncommitted.* New York: Dell, 1967.

Kennedy, E. C. *The New Sexuality: Myths, Fables and Hang-ups.* New York: Doubleday, 1972.

Kephart, William M. Some correlates of romantic love. *Journal of Marriage and the Family,* 1967, 29, 470–81.

Kern, Stephen. Freud and the discovery of child sexuality. *History of Childhood Quarterly,* 1973, 1, pp. 117–41.

Kern, Stephen. Explosive intimacy: Psychodynamics of the Victorian family. *History of Childhood Quarterly,* 1974, 1, pp. 437–62.

Kessel, N., and Coppen, A. The prevalence of common menstrual symptoms. *Lancet,* 1963, 2, pp. 61–64.

Kimura, D. Functional asymmetry of the brain in dichotic listening. *Cortex,* 1967, 3, pp. 163–78.

Kinsey, Alfred C.; Pomeroy, Wardell B.; and Martin, Clyde E. *Sexual Behavior in the Human Male.* Philadelphia: Saunders, 1948.

Kinsey, Alfred C.; Pomeroy, Wardell B.; Martin, Clyde E.; and Gebhard, Paul H. *Sexual Behavior in the Human Female.* Philadelphia: Saunders, 1953.

Kirby, Douglas. Methods and methodological problems of sex research. In J. DeLora and C. Warren (eds.), *Understanding Sexual Interactions,* pp. 563–86. Boston: Houghton Mifflin, 1977.

Kirkendall, Lester. Characteristics of sexual decision-making. *Journal of Sex Research,* 1967, 3, pp. 201–11. (a)

Kirkendall, Lester. Searching for the roots of moral judgments. *The Humanist,* January-February 1967, pp. 20–23. (b)

Kirkpatrick, Clifford, and Kanin, Eugene. Male sex aggression on a university campus. *American Sociological Review,* 1957, 22, pp. 52–58.

Klaus, M. H.; Kennell, J. H.; Plumb, N.; and Zuehlke, S. Human maternal behavior at the first contact with her young. *Pediatrics,* 1970, 46, pp. 187–92.

Klemer, Richard. *Marriage and Family Relationships.* New York: Harper and Row, 1970.

Kline-Graber, Georgia, and Graber, Benjamin. *Women's Orgasm.* Indianapolis: Bobbs-Merrill, 1975.

Kline-Graber, Georgia, and Graber, Benjamin. Diagnosis and treatment procedures of pubococcygeal deficiencies in women. In J. LoPiccolo and L. LoPiccolo (eds.), *Handbook of Sex Therapy,* pp. 227–39. New York: Plenum, 1978.

Knaus, H. Die periodische Frucht- und Unfrucht-barkeit des Weibes (Periodic fertility and infertility in women). *Zentralblatt für Gynäkologie,* 1933, 57(24), p. 1393.

Kohlberg, Lawrence. Cognitive development and analysis of children's sex role concept and attitudes. In E. E. Maccoby (ed.), *The Development of Sex Differences,* pp. 82–173. Stanford, Calif.: Stanford University Press, 1966.

Koka Shastra. New York: Ballantine, 1965.

Kolodny, Robert C., et al. Depression of plasma testosterone levels after chronic intensive marijuana use. *New England Journal of Medicine,* 1974, 290, pp. 872–74.

Kolodny, Robert C., et al. *Ethics Guidelines for Sex Therapists, Sex Counselors and Sex Researchers.* St. Louis: Reproductive Biology Research Foundation, 1978.

Komarovsky, Mirra. *Blue-Collar Marriage.* New York: Vintage, 1967.

Krafft-Ebing, Richard von. *Psychopathia Sexualis,* H. Wedeck (trans.). New York: Putnam's, 1965.

Kubo, S. Researches and studies on incest in Japan. *Hiroshima Journal of Medical Sciences,* 1959, 8, pp. 99–159.

Kupfer, David; Rosenbaum, Jerrold; and Detre, Thomas. Personality style and sexual functioning among psychiatric outpatients. *Journal of Sex Research,* 1977, 13, pp. 257–66.

Kutschinsky, Berl. Pornography in Denmark: Studies on producers, sellers and users. *Technical Reports of the Commission on Obscenity and Pornography,* vol. 4. Washington, D.C.: U.S. Government Printing Office, 1970. (a)

Kutschinsky, Berl. Sex crimes and pornography in Copenhagen: A study of attitudes. *Technical Reports of the Commission on Obscenity and Pornography,* vol. 7. Washington, D.C.: U.S. Government Printing Office, 1970. (b)

Lacey, F. K. *The Family in Classical Greece.* Ithaca, N.Y.: Cornell University Press, 1968.

Lallemand, Claude-Francois. *A Practical Treatise on* . . .

521

Spermatorrhea (1853). Cited in J. Haller and R. Haller, *The Physician and Sexuality in Victorian America* (New York: Norton, 1974).

Lamaze, Fernand. *Painless Childbirth,* L. Celestin (trans.). Chicago: Regnery, 1970.

Lambert, W. E.; Yackley, A.; and Hein, R. N. Child training values of English Canadian and French Canadian parents. *Canadian Journal of Behavioral Science,* 1971, *3,* pp. 217–36.

Lambiri-Dimaki, Jane. Dowry in modern Greece. In C. Safilios-Rothschild (ed.), *Toward a Sociology of Women,* pp. 73–83. Lexington, Mass.: Xerox College Publishing, 1972.

Lancaster, Jane. Sex roles in primate societies. In M. Teitelbaum (ed.), *Sex Differences: Social and Biological Perspectives,* pp. 22–61. Garden City, N.Y.: Anchor, 1976.

Landis, Paul H. *Making the Most of Marriage,* 4th ed. New York: Appleton-Century-Crofts, 1970.

Lansdell, H. A sex difference in effect of temporal-lobe neurosurgery on design preference. *Nature,* 1962, *194,* pp. 852–54.

Lansky, L. M. The family structure also affects the model: Sex-role attitudes in parents of preschool children. *Merrill-Palmer Quarterly,* 1967, *13,* pp. 139–50.

Lapidus, D. Differential socialization of male and female preschoolers: Competition versus cooperation. Honors thesis, Stanford University. Cited in E. E. Maccoby and C. N. Jacklin, *The Psychology of Sex Differences* (Stanford, Calif.: Stanford University Press, 1974).

Laplanche, J., and Pontalis, J.-B. *The Language of Psycho-Analysis,* D. Nicholson-Smith (trans.). New York: Norton, 1973.

Laschet, Ursula. Antiandrogens in the treatment of sex offenders. In J. Zubin and J. Money (eds.), *Contemporary Sexual Behavior: Critical Issues in the 1970's,* pp. 311–20. Baltimore: Johns Hopkins University Press, 1973.

Lätz, L. *The Rhythm of Sterility and Fertility in Women.* Chicago: Lätz, 1932.

Lätz, L., and Reiner, E. Further studies on the sterile and infertile periods in women. *American Journal of Obstetrics and Gynecology,* 1942, *43,* pp. 74–79.

Lawrence, D. H. *Sons and Lovers.* New York: Kennerly, 1922.

Lawrence, D. H. *Lady Chatterley's Lover.* New York: Grove Press, 1969.

Lea, Henry C. *History of Sacerdotal Celibacy in the Christian Church.* New York: University Books, 1966.

Leacock, Eleanor B. Introduction. In Frederick Engels, *The Origins of the Family, Private Property, and the State,* pp. 7–67. New York: International, 1972.

Leboyer, Frederick. *Birth Without Violence.* New York: Knopf, 1975.

Lederer, William J., and Jackson, Don D. *The Mirages of Marriage.* New York: Norton, 1968.

Legman, Gershon. *The Rationale of the Dirty Joke.* New York: Grove Press, 1968.

Leon, J. L., and Steinhoff, P. G. Catholics' use of abortion. *Sociological Analysis,* 1975, *36,* pp. 125–36.

Levin, Robert J., and Levin, Amy. The surprising preferences of 100,000 women. *Redbook,* September 1975, pp. 51–58.

LeVine, David L.; DeVesa, Susan S.; Godwin, J. David, and Silverman, Debra T. *Cancer Rates and Risks.* National Cancer Institute, Department of Health, Education, and Welfare, Publication No. (NIH) 75-691). Washington, D.C.: U.S. Government Printing Office, 1974.

Levitt, Eugene; Albert, D., Jr.; and Klassen, E. Public attitudes toward sexual behaviors. Unpublished paper.

Lewis, Lionel, and Brissett, Dennis. Sex as work. *Social Problems,* 1967, *15,* pp. 8–18.

Lewis, M. State as an infant-environment interaction: An analysis of mother-infant interaction as a function of sex. *Merrill-Palmer Quarterly,* 1972, *18,* 95–121.

Lewis, W. C. Coital movements in the first year of life. *International Journal of Psycho-Analysis,* 1965, *46,* pp. 372–74.

Leznoff, Maurice, and Westley, William. The homosexual community. In H. Ruitenbeek (ed.), *The Problem of Homosexuality in Modern Society,* pp. 162–74. New York: Dutton, 1963.

Libby, Roger W. Sexual behavior as symbolic exchange. Unpublished paper.

Libby, Roger W. Adolescent sexual attitudes and behavior. *Journal of Clinical Child Psychology,* Fall-Winter 1974, pp. 36–42.

Libby, Roger W. Creative singlehood as a sexual lifestyle. In R. W. Libby and R. N. Whitehurst (eds.), *Marriage and Alternatives: Exploring Intimate Relationships,* pp. 37–61. Glenview, Ill.: Scott, Foresman, 1977. (a)

Libby, Roger W. Today's changing sexual mores. In J. Money and H. Musaph (eds.), *Handbook of Sexology,* pp. 563–76. New York: North-Holland, 1977. (b)

Libby, Roger W., and Nass, Gilbert. Parental views on teenage sexual behavior. *Journal of Sex Research,* 1971, *7,* pp. 226–36.

Libby, Roger W., and Whitehurst, Robert N. (Eds.) *Renovating Marriage: Toward New Sexual Life-Styles.* Danville, Calif.: Consensus Press, 1973.

Libby, Roger W., and Whitehurst, Robert N. (Eds.) *Marriage and Alternatives: Exploring Intimate Relationships.* Glenview, Ill.: Scott, Foresman, 1977.

Licklider, S. Jewish penile carcinoma. *Journal of Urology,* 1961, *86,* p. 98.

Lief, Harold. Sexual health. In press.

Lief, Harold. Sexual survey #4: Current thinking on homosexuality. *Medical Aspects of Human Sexuality,* 1977, *11*(11), pp. 110–11.

Lief, Harold. Rape: Is it a sexual or an aggressive act? *Medical Aspects of Human Sexuality,* 1978, *12*(2), pp. 55–56.

Lief, Harold, and Karlen, Arno. (Eds.) *Sex Education in Medicine*. New York: Spectrum, 1976.

Lief, Harold, and Mayerson, Peter. Psychotherapy of homosexuals: A follow-up of nineteen cases. In J. Marmor (ed.), *Sexual Inversion: The Multiple Roots of Homosexuality*, pp. 302–44. New York: Basic Books, 1965.

Lincoln, Richard; Döring-Bradley, Brigitte; Lindheim, Barbara; and Cotterill, Maureen. The Court, the Congress and the President: Turning back the clock on the pregnant poor. *Family Planning Perspectives*, 1977, *9*, pp. 207–14.

Linnér, Birgitta. *Sex and Society in Sweden*. New York: Pantheon, 1967.

Lipsitt, L. P., and Levy, N. Electrotactual threshold in the human neonate. *Child Development*, 1959, *30*, pp. 547–54.

Looft, W. R. Sex differences in the expression of vocational aspirations by elementary school children. *Developmental Psychology*, 1971, *5*, p. 366.

LoPiccolo, Joseph. Treatment of sexual concerns by the primary care male clinician. In R. Green (ed.) *Human Sexuality: A Health Practitioner's Text*, 2nd ed., pp. 264–75. Baltimore: Williams & Wilkins, 1979.

LoPiccolo, Joseph, and Lobitz, W. Charles. The role of masturbation in the treatment of orgasmic dysfunction. In J. LoPiccolo and L. LoPiccolo (eds.), *Handbook of Sex Therapy*, pp. 187–94. New York: Plenum, 1978.

LoPiccolo, Joseph, and LoPiccolo, Leslie. (Eds.) *Handbook of Sex Therapy*. New York: Plenum, 1978.

Luckey, Eleanor. Marital satisfaction and its association with congruence of perception. *Marriage and Family Living*, 1960, *22*, pp. 49–54.

Luckey, Eleanor, and Nass, Gilbert. A comparison of sexual attitudes and behavior in an international sample. *Journal of Marriage and the Family*, 1969, *31*, pp. 364–79.

Luschen, Mary, and Pierce, David. Effect of the menstrual cycle on mood and sexual arousability. *Journal of Sex Research*, 1972, *8*, pp. 41–47.

Lynd, Robert, and Lynd, Helen. *Middletown*. New York: Harcourt, Brace, 1959.

Lynd, Robert, and Lynd, Helen. *Middletown in Transition*. New York: Harcourt, Brace, 1963.

Lynn, David B. *Parental and Sex Role Identification*. Berkeley, Calif.: McCutchan, 1969.

McCaghy, Charles. Child molesting. *Sexual Behavior*, August 1971, pp. 16–24.

McCance, R. A.; Luff, M. C.; and Widdowson, E. E. Physical and emotional periodicity in women. *Journal of Hygiene*, 1937, *37*, pp. 571–605.

McCartney, James. Overt transference. *Journal of Sex Research*, 1966, *2*, pp. 227–37.

McCary, James. *Sexual Myths and Fallacies*. Princeton, N.J.: Van Nostrand, 1971.

McCary, James. *Human Sexuality*, 2nd ed. New York: Van Nostrand, 1973.

McCary, James. *Human Sexuality*. New York: Van Nostrand, 1967.

Maccoby, Eleanor E., and Jacklin, Carol N. *The Psychology of Sex Differences*. Stanford, Calif.: Stanford University Press, 1974.

McCracken, Robert. *Fallacies of Women's Liberation*. Boulder, Colo.: Shields, 1972.

MacDougald, Duncan, Jr. Aphrodisiacs and anaphrodisiacs. In A. Ellis and A. Abarbanel (eds.), *The Encyclopedia of Sexual Behavior*, pp. 145–53. New York: Hawthorn, 1961.

McFalls, J. A., Jr. Impact of V.D. on fertility of U.S. black population 1880–1950. *Social Biology*, 1973, *20*, pp. 2–19.

McGill, Thomas E. Studies of the sexual behavior of male laboratory mice: Effects of genotype, recovery of sex drive, and theory. In F. A. Beach (ed.), *Sex and Behavior*, pp. 76–88. New York: Wiley, 1965.

McGlone, Jeannette. Sex differences in functional brain symmetry. *Cortex*, 1978, *14*, pp. 122–28.

McGrew, W. C. *An Ethological Study of Children's Behavior*. New York: Academic Press, 1972.

Macklin, Eleanor D. Cohabitation in college: Going very steady. *Psychology Today*, November 1974, pp. 53–59.

McLennan, John. *Primitive Marriage*. Chicago: University of Chicago Press, 1970.

MacLeod, John. The semen quality in relation to male infertility. In C. Joël (ed.), *Fertility Disturbances in Men and Women*, pp. 127–34. Basel, Switz.: Karger, 1971.

MacNamara, Donal. The criminal signature concept in *modus operandi*. *Journal of Offender Therapy*, 1961, *5*, pp. 3–4.

MacNamara, Donal, and Sagarin, Edward. *Sex, Crime, and the Law*. New York: Free Press, 1977.

Madorsky, Martin; Drylie, D. M.; and Finlayson, B. Effect of benign prostatic hypertrophy on sexual behavior. *Medical Aspects of Human Sexuality*, 1976, *10*(2), pp. 8, 11, 15, 16, 21.

Mair, Lucy. *Marriage*. Baltimore: Penguin Books, 1971.

Maisch, Herbert. *Incest*, C. Bearne (trans.). New York: Stein and Day, 1972.

Malinowski, Bronislaw. *The Sexual Life of Savages in North-Western Melanesia*. New York: Halcyon House, 1929.

Malinowski, Bronislaw. *Sex and Repression in Savage Society*. New York: Meridian, 1955.

Malla, Kalyana. *Ananga Ranga*. Paris: Librairie Astra, n.d.

Malthus, Thomas. *An Essay on the Principle of Population*. New York: Macmillan, 1929.

Mantegazza, Paolo. *The Sexual Relations of Mankind*. North Hollywood, Calif.: Brandon House, 1966.

Marcott, D. B., and Weiss, D. S. An alternative to the squeeze. *Journal of Sex Education and Therapy*, 1976, *2*, pp. 26–27.

Marcus, Steven. *The Other Victorians*. New York: Basic Books, 1964.

Margolis, R., and Leslie, C. H. Review of studies on a

mixture of nux vomica, yohimbine and methyl testosterone in the treatment of impotence. *Current Therapeutic Research,* 1966, *8,* pp. 280–84.

Marks, Isaac; Gelder, Michael; and Bancroft, John. Sexual deviants two years after electric aversion. *British Journal of Psychiatry,* 1970, *117,* pp. 173–85.

Marmor, Judd. Impotence and ejaculatory disturbances. In B. Sadock, H. Kaplan, and A. Freedman (eds.), *The Sexual Experience,* pp. 403–11. Baltimore: Williams and Wilkins, 1976.

Marrou, H. I. *A History of Education in Antiquity,* G. Lamb (trans.). New York: Sheed and Ward, 1956.

Marshall, Donald S. Sexual behavior on Mangaia. In D. S. Marshall and R. C. Suggs (eds.), *Human Sexual Behavior,* pp. 103–62. New York: Basic Books, 1971.

Marshall, Donald S., and Suggs, Robert C. (Eds.) *Human Sexual Behavior.* New York: Basic Books, 1971.

Marshall, J., and Row, B. Psychological aspects of the basal body temperature method of regulating births. *Fertility and Sterility,* 1970, *21,* pp. 14–19.

Marshall, J., and Row, B. The effect of personal factors on the use of the basal body temperature method of regulating births. *Fertility and Sterility,* 1972, *23,* pp. 417–21.

Martin, D., and Lyon, P. *Lesbian Women.* San Francisco: Glide Publications, 1972.

Martin, N. G. Genetics of sexual and social attitudes in twins. In W. E. Nance (ed.), *Twin Research: Psychology and Methodology,* pp. 13–23. New York: Alan Liss, 1978.

Martinson, Floyd. *Infant and Child Sexuality: A Sociological Perspective.* St. Peter, Minn.: Gustavus Adolphus College, 1973.

Maslow, A. H. *Toward a Psychology of Being.* Princeton, N.J.: Van Nostrand, 1962.

Maslow, A. H. Self-esteem, dominance-feeling, and sexuality in women. In M. DeMartino (ed.), *Sexual Behavior and Personality Characteristics,* pp. 71–112. New York: Grove Press, 1966.

Masters, William H., and Johnson, Virginia E. *Human Sexual Response.* Boston: Little, Brown, 1966.

Masters, William H., and Johnson, Virginia E. Human sexual inadequacy and some parameters of therapy. In M. Diamond (ed.), *Perspectives in Reproduction and Sexual Behavior,* pp. 411–15. Bloomington: Indiana University Press, 1968.

Masters, William H., and Johnson, Virginia E. *Human Sexual Inadequacy.* Boston: Little, Brown, 1970.

Masters, William H., and Johnson, Virginia E. *The Pleasure Bond.* Boston: Little, Brown, 1975.

Masters, William H., and Johnson, Virginia E. *Homosexuality in Perspective.* Boston: Little, Brown, 1979.

Masters, William H.; Johnson, Virginia E.; and Kolodny, Robert C. Sexual aversion: A diagnostic entity. Unpublished paper.

Masters, William H.; Johnson, Virginia E.; and Kolodny, Robert C. *Ethical Issues in Sex Therapy and Research.* Boston: Little, Brown, 1977.

Matějček, Z.; Dytrych, Z.; and Schüller, V. Children from unwanted pregnancies. *Acta Psychiatrica Scandinavica,* 1978, *57,* pp. 67–90.

May, Dean L. People on the Mormon frontier: Kanab's families of 1874. *Journal of Family History,* 1976, *1*(2), pp. 169–92.

Mayo, Julia. The new black feminism: A minority report. In J. Zubin and J. Money (eds.), *Contemporary Sexual Behavior: Critical Issues in the 1970's,* pp. 175–86. Baltimore: Johns Hopkins University Press, 1973.

Mazur, Ronald. *The New Intimacy: Open-Ended Marriage and Alternative Life Styles.* Boston: Beacon Press, 1973.

Mead, George Herbert. *Mind, Self and Society.* Chicago: University of Chicago Press, 1934.

Mead, Margaret. *Coming of Age in Samoa.* New York: William Morrow, 1928.

Mead, Margaret. *Sex and Temperament in Three Primitive Societies.* New York: William Morrow, 1935.

Mead, Margaret, *Male and Female.* New York: William Morrow, 1949.

Mead, Margaret. Marriage in two steps. *Redbook,* July 1966, pp. 48–49.

Mead, Margaret, and Bateson, Gregory. *Balinese Character.* New York: New York Academy of Science, 1942.

Medical Aspects of Human Sexuality. Current thinking on sexual dysfunction. 1977, *11*(8), p. 69.

Meigs, Anne. Male pregnancy and the reduction of sexual opposition in a New Guinea Highlands society. *Ethnology,* 1976, *15,* pp. 393–407.

Meiselman, Karin. *Incest.* San Francisco: Jossey-Bass, 1978.

Melamed, M. R.; Koss, L.; Flehinger, B.; Kelisky, R.; and Dubrow, H. Prevalence notes of uterine carcinoma in situ for women using the diaphragm or contraceptive oral steroids. *British Medical Journal,* 1969, *3,* p. 195.

Memoirs v. *Massachusetts.* 383 U.S. at 441 et seq. (1966).

Mendelson, Jack H.; Kuehnle, J.; Ellingboe, J.; and Babor, T. F. Plasma testosterone levels before, during and after chronic marijuana smoking. *New England Journal of Medicine,* 1974, *291,* pp. 1051–1055.

Merriam, Alan. Aspects of sexual behavior among the Bala (Basongye). In D. S. Marshall and R. C. Suggs (ed.), *Human Sexual Behavior,* pp. 71–102. New York: Basic Books, 1971.

Mesnikoff, A.; Rainer, J.; Kolb, L.; and Carr, A. Intrafamilial determinants of divergent sexual behavior in twins. *American Journal of Psychiatry,* 1963, *119,* pp. 732–38.

Messenger, John C. Sex and repression in an Irish folk community. In D. S. Marshall and R. C. Suggs (eds.), *Human Sexual Behavior,* pp. 3–37. New York: Basic Books, 1971.

Meyer-Bahlburg, Heino F. L. Sex hormones and male homosexuality in comparative perspective. *Archives of Sexual Behavior,* 1977, *6,* pp. 297–326.

Meyer-Bahlburg, Heino F. L.; McCauley, F.; Schenck, C.; Aceto, J., Jr.; and Pinch, L. Cryptorchidism, development of gender identity and sexual behavior. In

R. Friedman, R. M. Richart, and R. L. Vande Wiele (eds.), *Sex Differences in Behavior*, pp. 281–99. New York: Wiley, 1974.

Meyerson, Bengt J., and Malmnäs, Carl-Olof. Brain monoamines and sexual behaviour. In J. Hutchison (ed.), *Biological Determinants of Sexual Behavior*, pp. 521–54. New York: Wiley, 1978.

Michael, Richard P., Bonsall, R. W., and Zumpe, Doris. Evidence for chemical communication in primates. *Vitamins and Hormones*, 1976, *34*, pp. 137–186.

Michael, Richard P., and Zumpe, Doris. Potency in male rhesus monkeys: Effects of continuously receptive females. *Science*, 1978, *200*, pp. 451–53.

Mill, John Stuart, *The Subjection of Women*. London: Dent, 1929.

Mill, John Stuart. *On Liberty*. Indianapolis: Bobbs-Merrill, 1956.

Millar, Mervyn. Apollonians and Dionysians: Some impressions of sex in the counterculture. In R. W. Libby and R. N. Whitehurst (eds.), *Renovating Marriage: Toward New Sexual Life-Styles*, pp. 192–207. Danville, Calif.: Consensus Press, 1973.

Miller v. *California*. 413 U.S. 15 (1973).

Miller, Henry. *Tropic of Capricorn*. New York: Grove Press, 1961.

Miller, Henry. *Tropic of Cancer*. New York: Random House, 1975.

Miller, Sherod; Nunnally, Elam W.; and Wackman, Daniel B. *Alive and Aware: How to Improve Your Relationships through Better Communication*. Minneapolis: Interpersonal Communication Programs, 1975.

Millett, Kate. *Sexual Politics*. New York: Doubleday, 1970.

Millett, Kate. Prostitution: A quartet of female voices. In V. Gornick and B. Moran (eds.), *Women in Sexist Society*, pp. 60–125. New York: Basic Books, 1971.

Milton, John. *Complete Prose Works*, 3 vols., D. Wolfe, E. Sirluck, and M. Hughs (eds.). New Haven: Yale University Press, 1953–62.

Minton, C.; Kagan, J.; and Levine, J. A. Maternal control and obedience in the two-year-old. *Child Development*, 1971, *42*, pp. 1873–94.

Minturn, Leigh; Grosse, Martin; and Haider, Santoah. Cultural patterning of sexual beliefs and behavior. *Ethnology*, 1969, *8*, pp. 301–18.

Mischel, Walter. A social-learning view of sex differences in behavior. In E. E. Maccoby (ed.), *The Development of Sex Differences*, pp. 56–81. Stanford, Calif.: Stanford University Press, 1966.

Monahan, Thomas P. How stable are remarriages? *American Journal of Sociology*, 1952, *58*, pp. 280–88.

Monday, L. A.; Hout, D. P.; and Lutz, S. *College Student Profiles*. Iowa City: ACT Publications, 1966.

Money, John. *Sex Errors of the Body*. Baltimore: Johns Hopkins University Press, 1968.

Money, John. The therapeutic use of androgen-depleting hormones. *Journal of Sex Research*, 1970, *6*, pp. 165–72.

Money, John. Pornography in the home: A topic in medical education. In J. Zubin and J. Money (eds.), *Contemporary Sexual Behavior: Critical Issues in the 1970's*, pp. 409–40. Baltimore: Johns Hopkins University Press, 1973.

Money, John, and Ehrhardt, Anke A. *Man and Woman, Boy and Girl*. Baltimore: Johns Hopkins University Press, 1972.

Money, John; Hampson, J. G.; and Hampson, J. L. Hermaphroditism: Recommendations concerning assignment of sex, change of sex and psychologic management. *Bulletin of the Johns Hopkins Hospital*, 1955, *97*, pp. 284–300.

Money, John, and Tucker, Patricia. *Sexual Signatures: On Being a Man or a Woman*. Boston: Little, Brown, 1975.

Montagu, M. F. Ashley. *Touching: The Human Significance of the Skin*. New York: Columbia University Press, 1973.

Mooney, Thomas O.; Cole, Theodore M.; and Chilgren, Richard A. *Sexual Options for Paraplegics and Quadriplegics*. Boston: Little, Brown, 1975.

Moos, R. H., et al. Fluctuation in symptoms and moods during the menstrual cycle. *Journal of Psychosomatic Research*, 1969, *13*, pp. 37–44.

Morgan, Edmund. *The Puritan Family*. New York: Harper, 1966.

Morgan, Henry Lewis. *Ancient Society*. Cleveland: World, 1963.

Morgan, Marabel. *The Total Woman*. Old Tappan, N.J.: Revell, 1973.

Morgan, Robin. (Ed.) *Sisterhood Is Powerful: An Anthology of Writings from the Women's Liberation Movement*. New York: Vintage, 1970.

Morris, Desmond. *The Naked Ape*. New York: Dell, 1969.

Morris, N. M. The frequency of sexual intercourse during pregnancy. *Archives of Sexual Behavior*, 1975, *4*, pp. 501–7.

Mosher, D. L. Psychological reactions to pornographic films. *Technical Reports of the Commission on Obscenity and Pornography*, vol. 8. Washington, D.C.: U.S. Government Printing Office, 1970.

Moss, H. A. Sex, age and state as determinants of mother-infant interaction. *Merrill-Palmer Quarterly*, 1967, *13*, pp. 19–36.

Mountjoy, P. Some early attempts to modify penile erection in horse and human. *Psychological Record*, 1974, *24*, pp. 291–308.

Moyer, K. E. *Psychobiology of Aggression*. New York: Harper and Row, 1976.

Muncy, Raymond. *Sex and Marriage in Utopian Communities*. Baltimore: Penguin Books, 1974.

Munson, Martha L. Wanted and unwanted births reported by mothers 15–44 years of age, United States, 1973. *Advance Data from Vital and Health Statistics*, *9*(10), August 1977.

Murdock, George P. The social regulation of sexual behavior. In P. H. Hoch and J. Zubin (eds.), *Psychosexual*

Development in Health and Disease, pp. 256–66. New York: Grune and Stratton, 1949. (a)

Murdock, George P. Social Structure. New York: Free Press, 1949. (b)

Murdock, George P., and Provost, Catarina. Factors in the division of labor by sex: A cross-cultural analysis. Ethnology, 1973, 12, pp. 203–25.

Myrdal, Alva. Foreword. In E. Dahlström (ed.), The Changing Roles of Men and Women, pp. 9–15. Boston: Beacon Press, 1971.

Nabokov, Vladimir. Lolita. New York: Putnam's, 1972.

Nadelson, C. C. Rapist and victim. New England Journal of Medicine, 1977, 297, p. 784.

Nahamias, A. J., et al. Genital infection with type 2 Herpes virus Hominis. British Journal of Venereal Disease, 1969, 45, pp. 294–98.

Nefzaoui, Sheik. The Perfumed Garden. New York: Lancer Books, 1964.

Nelson, E. A., and Rosenbaum, E. Language patterns within the youth subculture: Development of slang vocabularies. Merrill-Palmer Quarterly, 1972, 18, pp. 273–85.

Neubeck, Gerhard. (Ed.) Extramarital Relations. Englewood Cliffs, N.J.: Prentice-Hall, 1969.

Neubeck, Gerhard, and Mason, Sally. Five years of a college human sexuality course. Unpublished paper.

Newman, G., and Nichols, C. R. Sexual activities and attitudes in older persons. Journal of the American Medical Association, 1960, 173, pp. 33–35.

Newman, Herbert F. Vibratory sensitivity of the penis. Fertility and Sterility, 1970, 21, pp. 791–93.

Newson, J., and Newson, E. Four Year Olds in an Urban Community. Harmondsworth, England: Pelican Books, 1968.

Newton, N., and Newton, M. Psychological aspects of lactation. New England Journal of Medicine, 1967, 277, pp. 1179–88.

New York Times. No progress seen in sexual problems. 27 June 1971, p. 21.

Norris, Kenneth Stafford. The Porpoise Watcher. New York: Norton, 1974.

Novak, Edmund R.; Jones, Georgeanna; and Jones, Howard W., Jr. Textbook of Gynecology, 9th ed. Baltimore: Williams and Wilkins, 1975.

Noyes, R. W. Perspectives in human fertility. In M. Diamond (ed.), Perspectives in Reproduction and Sexual Behavior, pp. 177–86. Bloomington: University of Indiana Press, 1968.

Ochsner, A. Influence of smoking on sexuality and pregnancy. Medical Aspects of Human Sexuality, 1971, 5(11), pp. 78–92.

Offer, Daniel. Psychological World of the Teen-ager: A Study of Normal Adolescent Boys. New York: Harper and Row, 1973.

Offer, Daniel, and Offer, Judith. From Teenage to Young Manhood. New York: Basic Books, 1975.

Offer, Daniel, and Simon, William. Stages of sexual development. In A. Freedman, H. Kaplan, and B. Sadock (eds.), Comprehensive Textbook of Psychiatry, 2nd ed., pp. 1392–1400. Baltimore: Williams and Wilkins, 1975.

Offir, Carole. Don't take it lying down. Psychology Today, January 1975, p. 73.

Ogino, K. Ovulationstermin und Konzeptionstermin (Time of ovulation and time of conception). Zentralblatt für Gynäckologie, 1930, 54(8), pp. 464–79.

Oliven, John. Sexual Hygiene and Pathology. Philadelphia, Lippincott, 1965.

Oliven, John. Clinical Sexuality. Philadelphia, Lippincott, 1974.

O'Neill, Eugene. Mourning Becomes Electra. New York: Random House, 1959.

O'Neill, Nena, and O'Neill, George. Open Marriage. New York: Evans, 1972.

O'Neill, Nena, and O'Neill, George. Open marriage: The conceptual framework. In J. R. Smith and L. B. Smith (eds.), Beyond Monogamy: Recent Studies of Sexual Alternatives in Marriage, pp. 56–67. Baltimore: Johns Hopkins University Press, 1974.

Orgebin-Crist, M. C. Sperm age: Effects on zygote development. In W. A. Uricchio and M. K. Williams (eds.), Proceedings of a Research Conference on Natural Family Planning, pp. 85–93. Washington, D.C.: Human Life Foundation, 1973.

Osofsky, Joy D.; Osofsky, Howard J.; and Rajan, Renga. Psychological effects of abortion. In H. J. Osofsky, and J. D. Osofsky (eds.), The Abortion Experience: Psychological and Medical Impact, pp. 188–205. New York: Harper and Row, 1973.

Ounsted, C., and Taylor, D. C. (Eds.) Gender Differences: Their Ontogeny and Significance. Baltimore: Williams and Wilkins, 1972.

Ovesey, Lionel. Homosexuality and Pseudohomosexuality. New York: Science House, 1969.

Ovid. The Art of Love, R. Humphries (trans.). Bloomington: Indiana University Press, 1957.

Owen, Steven; Blount, H. Parker; and Moscow, Henry. Educational Psychology. Boston: Little, Brown, 1978.

Packard, Vance. The Sexual Wilderness. New York: David McKay, 1968.

Pakter, Jean; Nelson, Frieda; and Svigir, Martin. Legal abortion: A half-decade of experience. Family Planning Perspectives, 1975, 7, pp. 248–55.

Panken, Shirley. The Joy of Suffering. New York: Aronson, 1973.

Parlee, M. B. The premenstrual syndrome. Psychological Bulletin, 1973, 80, pp. 454–65.

Patai, Raphael. Sex and Family in the Bible and the Middle East. Garden City, N.Y.: Doubleday, 1959.

Pavlov, Ivan. Conditioned Reflexes. New York: Dover, 1960.

Pederson, F. A., and Robson, K. S. Father participation in infancy. American Journal of Orthopsychiatry, 1969, 39, pp. 466–72.

Persky, H.; Lief, H.; Strauss, D.; Miller, W. R.; and O'Brien, C. Plasma testosterone level and sexual behavior of couples. *Archives of Sexual Behavior,* 1978, *7,* pp. 157–73.

Peterson, James R. The Public-Sex Breakthrough. *Playboy,* 1978, *25* (5), pp. 152–60, 222–24.

Petras, John. *Sexuality in Society.* Boston: Allyn and Bacon, 1973.

Pfeiffer, Eric; Verwoerdt, Adriaan; and Wang, Hsioh-Shan. Sexual behavior in aged men and women: I. observations on 254 community volunteers. *Archives of General Psychiatry,* 1968, *19*(6), pp. 753–58.

Phoenix, C. H.; Goy, R. W.; Gerall, A. A.; and Young, W. C. Organizing action of prenatally administered testosterone propionate on the tissues mediating mating behavior in the female guinea pig. *Endocrinology,* 1959, *65,* pp. 369–82.

Phoenix, C. H.; Goy, R. W.; and Resko, J. A. Psychosexual differentiation as a function of androgenic stimulation. In M. Diamond (ed.), *Perspectives in Reproduction and Sexual Behavior,* pp. 33–49. Bloomington: Indiana University Press, 1968.

Pius XI. *Casti Connubii. Acta Apostolicae Sedis 22.* New York: Paulist Press, 1930.

Pivar, David J. The new abolitionism: The quest for social purity, 1876–1900. Unpublished doctoral dissertation, University of Pennsylvania, 1965.

Plato. *Symposium,* B. Jowett (trans.). Indianapolis: Bobbs-Merrill, 1956.

Pocs, Ollie; Godow, Annette; Tolone, W. L.; and Walsh, Robert H. Is there sex after 40? *Psychology Today,* June 1977, p. 54–56, 87.

Poe, Edgar Allan. The fall of the House of Usher. In *Complete Tales and Poems.* New York: Vintage, 1975.

Pohlman, Edward. *Psychology of Birth Planning.* Cambridge: Schenkman, 1969.

Polsky, Ned. *Hustler, Beats, and Others.* Garden City, N.Y.: Doubleday, 1969.

Pomeroy, Wardell B. Homosexuality, transvestism and transsexualism. In C. E. Vincent (ed.), *Human Sexuality in Medical Education and Practice,* pp. 367–87. Springfield, Ill.: Charles C. Thomas, 1968.

Pomeroy, Wardell B. *Dr. Kinsey and the Institute for Sex Research.* New York: Harper and Row, 1972.

Population Reports. Oral contraceptives: OC's update on usage, safety, and side effects. Series A, No. 5, January 1979.

Population Reports. Series B, No. 2, January 1975. Intrauterine devices: IUD's reassessed—a decade of experience.

Population Reports. Series C, No. 7, May 1976. Sterilization: Tubal sterilizations—a review of methods.

Population Reports. Series D, No. 1, December 1973. Sterilization: Vasectomy—old and new techniques.

Population Reports. Series D, No. 2, January 1975. Male sterilization.

Population Reports. Series D, No. 3, May 1976. Sterilization: Vasectomy reversibility—a status report.

Population Reports. Series F, No. 3, June 1973. Pregnancy termination: Uterine aspiration techniques.

Population Reports. Series F, No. 5, September 1976. Pregnancy termination in midtrimester: Review of major methods.

Population Reports. Series H, No. 2, May 1974. Barrier methods: The modern condom—a quality product for effective contraception.

Population Reports. Series H, No. 3, January 1975. Vaginal contraceptives: A time for reappraisal?

Population Reports: Series H, No.,, 4, January 1976. Barrier methods: The diaphragm and other intravaginal barriers—a review.

Population Reports. Series J, No. 4, July 1975. Breast feeding: Aid to infant health and fertility control.

Population Reports. Series J, No. 8, November 1975. Effects of child bearing on maternal health.

Population Reports. Series K, No. 1, March 1975. Injectables and implants: Injectable progestogens—officials debate but use increases.

Powdermaker, Hortense. *Stranger and Friend.* New York: Norton, 1966.

Powdermaker, Hortense. *Life in Lesu.* New York: Norton, 1971.

Praz, Mario. *The Romantic Agony.* New York: Meridian, 1956.

Prescott, W. James. Phylogenetic and ontogenetic aspects of human affectional development. In R. Gemme and C. C. Wheeler (eds.), *Progress in Sexology,* pp. 431–57. New York: 1977.

Prince, Virginia. Transsexuals and pseudotranssexuals. *Archives of Sexual Behavior,* 1978, *7,* pp. 263–72.

Prince, Virginia, and Butler, P. Survey of 504 cases of transvestism. *Psychological Reports,* 1972, *31,* pp. 903–17.

Raboch, Jan. Studies in the sexuality of women. In H. Giese (ed.), *The Sexuality of Women,* pp. 47–94. New York: Stein and Day, 1970.

Raboch, Jan, Mellan, J., and Stárka, L. Klinefelter's syndrome: Sexual development and activity. *Archives of Sexual Behavior,* 1979, *8* (4), pp. 333–40.

Rader, Dotson. The feminization of the American male. *Harper's Bazaar,* November 1970, pp. 106–7, 156.

Radin, M. A. A comparison of maternal behavior with four-year-old boys and girls in lower-class families. Unpublished manuscript. Cited in E. E. Maccoby and C. N. Jacklin, *The Psychology of Sex Differences* (Stanford, Calif.: Stanford University Press, 1974).

Rado, Sandor. *Adaptational Psychoanalysis.* New York: Science House, 1969.

Rainer, J.; Mesnikoff, A.; Kolb, L.; and Carr, A. Homosexuality and heterosexuality in identical twins. *Psychosomatic Medicine,* 1960, *22,* pp. 251–59.

Rainwater, Lee. *And the Poor Get Children.* Chicago: Quadrangle, 1960.

Rainwater, Lee. *Family Design: Marital Sexuality, Family Size and Contraception.* Chicago: Aldine, 1965.

Rainwater, Lee. Marital sexuality in four "cultures of poverty." In D. S. Marshall and R. C. Suggs (eds.), *Human Sexual Behavior,* pp. 187–205. New York: Basic Books, 1971.

Ramey, James. *Intimate Friendships.* Englewood Cliffs, N.J.: Prentice-Hall, 1976.

Ramsey, G. V. The sex information of younger boys. *American Journal of Orthopsychiatry,* 1943, *13,* pp. 347–52. (a)

Ramsey, G. V. The sexual development of boys. *American Journal of Psychiatry,* 1943, *56,* pp. 217–33. (b)

Rapoport, Anatol. *Fights, Games and Debates.* Ann Arbor: University of Michigan Press, 1960.

Rapoport, Rhona, and Rapoport, Robert. The dual-career family: A variant pattern and social change. In C. Safilios-Rothschild (ed.), *Toward a Sociology of Women,* pp. 216–44. Lexington, Mass.: Xerox College, 1972.

Rasmussen, A. Die Bedeutung sexueller Attentate auf Kinder unter 14 Jahren für die Entwicklung von Geisteskrankheiten und Charakteranomalien (The comparative sexual attainment of children under 14 years old in the development of mental illness and character anomalies). *Acta Psychiatrica et Neurologica,* 1934, *9,* pp. 351–434.

Rathmann, W. G. Female circumcision, indications and a new technique. *General Practice,* 1959, *20,* pp. 115–20.

Reik, Theodor. *The Psychology of Sex Relations.* New York: Grove Press, 1961.

Reinisch, J. M., and Karow, W. G. Prenatal exposure to synthetic progestins and estrogens: Effects on human development. *Archives of Sexual Behavior,* 1977, *6,* pp. 257–88.

Reiss, Albert J. The social integration of queers and peers. *Social Problems,* 1961, *9,* pp. 102–20.

Reiss, Ira L. *Premarital Sexual Standards in America.* New York: Free Press, 1960.

Reiss, Ira L. The sexual renaissance: A summary and analysis. *Journal of Social Issues,* 1966, *22*(2), pp. 123–37.

Reiss, Ira L. *The Social Context of Premarital Sexual Permissiveness.* New York: Holt, Rinehart and Winston, 1967.

Reiss, Ira L. Premarital sex codes: The old and the new. In D. L. Gruman and A. M. Barclay (eds.), *Sexuality: A Search for Perspective,* pp. 190–203. New York: Van Nostrand, 1971.

Reiss, Ira L. Heterosexual relationships of patients: Premarital, marital and extramarital. In R. Green (ed.), *Human Sexuality: A Health Practitioner's Text,* pp. 36–52. Baltimore: Williams and Wilkins, 1975.

Renwick, Patricia A., and Lawler, Edward E. What you really want from your job. *Psychology Today,* May 1978, pp. 53–65, 118.

Rideout v. *Rideout. 5 Family Law Reporter,* 2164, 2 January 1979.

Riemer, Svend. A research note on incest. *American Journal of Sociology,* 1940, *45,* pp. 566–75.

Rimmer, Robert. *Proposition 31.* New York: New American Library, 1968.

Rimmer, Robert. Come Live My Life. New York: New American Library, 1977.

Robbins, Mina B., and Jensen, G. D. Multiple orgasm in males. *Journal of Sex Research,* 1978, *14,* pp. 21–26.

Roe et al. v. *Wade.* 410 U.S. 113, 93 S. Ct. 705 (1973).

Rogers, Carl. *Client-Centered Therapy.* Boston: Houghton Mifflin, 1951.

Rogers, Jane B.; Van Campen, H.; Uono, M.; L'Ambert, H.; and Hale, R. Analysis of human sperm fertilizing ability by using zona-free eggs. *Fertility and Sterility,* in press.

Romney, A. Kimball. Variations in household structure as determinants of sex-typed behavior. In F. A. Beach (ed.), *Sex and Behavior,* pp. 208–20. New York: Wiley, 1965.

Rose, Robert M. The psychological effects of androgens and estrogens: A review. In R. Shrader (ed.), *Psychiatric Complications of Medical Drugs,* pp. 251–93. New York: Raven Press, 1972.

Rosebury, Theodore. *Microbes and Morals.* New York: Ballantine, 1973.

Rosen, Ismond. (Ed.) *The Pathology and Treatment of Sexual Deviation.* London: Oxford University Press, 1964.

Rosenbaum, Maj-Britt. Treatment of sexual concerns by the primary care female clinician. In R. Green (ed.), *Human Sexuality: A Health Practitioner's Text,* 2nd ed., pp. 276–86. Baltimore: Williams and Wilkins, 1979.

Rosenbaum, Marsha. Clarity of the seduction situation. Unpublished master's thesis. Extract in J. Wiseman (ed.), *The Social Psychology of Sex,* pp. 50–57. New York: Harper and Row, 1976.

Rosenberg, B. G., and Sutton-Smith, B. A. A revised conception of masculine-feminine differences in play activities. *Journal of Genetic Psychology,* 1960, *96,* pp. 165–70.

Rosenthal, Bernice G. Love on the tractor: Women in the Russian Revolution and after. In R. Bridenthal and C. Koonz (eds.), *Becoming Visible: Women in European History,* pp. 370–99. Boston: Houghton Mifflin, 1977.

Rossi, Alice S. Maternalism, sexuality and the new feminism. In J. Zubin and J. Money (eds.), *Contemporary Sexual Behavior: Critical Issues in the 1970's,* pp. 145–73. Baltimore: Johns Hopkins University Press, 1973.

Roth v. *United States.* 354 U.S. 476 (1957).

Roth, Phillip. *Portnoy's Complaint.* New York: Random House, 1969.

Rotkin, I. D. A comparison review of key epidemiological studies in cervical cancer related to current searches for transmissible agents. *Cancer Research,* 1973, *33*(6), pp. 1353–67.

Rowbotham, Sheila. *Hidden from History: 300 Years of Women's Oppression and the Fight Against It.* London: Pluto Press, 1973.

Roy, Della, and Roy, Rustum. *Honest Sex.* New York: New American Library, 1968.

Royal College of General Practitioners. *Oral Contraceptives and Health.* New York: Pitman, 1974.

Rubin, Emmanuel; Lieber, C. S.; Altman, K.; Gordon, G. C.; and Souther, A. Prolonged ethanol consumption increases testosterone metabolism in the liver. *Science*, 1976, *191*, pp. 563–64.

Rubinstein, L. H. The role of identifications in homosexuality and transvestism in men and women. In I. Rosen (ed.), *The Pathology and Treatment of Sexual Deviation*, pp. 163–95. London: Oxford University Press, 1964.

Rugoff, Milton. *Prudery and Passion*. New York: Putnam's, 1971.

Russell, Phillips. *Benjamin Franklin: The First Civilized American*. Philadelphia: R. West, 1926.

Ryder, Norman B. Contraceptive failure in the United States. *Family Planning Perspectives*, 1973, *5*, pp. 133–42.

Sacher-Masoch, L. von. *Venus in Furs*, F. Savage (trans.). New York: Belmont Books, 1965.

Sade, Marquis de. *Philosophy in the Bedroom and Other Writings*, R. Seaver and A. Wainhouse (trans.). New York: Grove Press, 1966.

Safilios-Rothschild, Constantina. Companionate marriages and sexual inequality: Are they compatible? In C. Safilios-Rothschild (ed.), *Toward a Sociology of Women*, pp. 63–70. Lexington, Mass.: Xerox College, 1972.

Sagarin, Edward. Prison homosexuality and its effect on post-prison sexual behavior. *Psychiatry*, 1976, *39*, pp. 245–57.

Saghir, M. T., and Robins, E. *Male and Female Homosexuality: A Comprehensive Investigation*. Baltimore: Williams and Wilkins, 1973.

Sagin, Edward. Swinging through the VD tree. *Physician's World*, April 1974, pp. 70–74.

Saint Augustine. *City of God*, G. McCracken (trans.). Cambridge: Harvard University Press, 1957.

Salmon, U. J., and Geist, S. H. Effect of androgens upon libido in women. *Journal of Clinical Endocrinology*, 1943. *3*, pp. 235–38.

Salzman, Leon. Latent homosexuality. In J. Marmor (ed.), *Sexual Inversion: The Multiple Roots of Homosexuality*, pp. 234–47. New York: Basic Books, 1965.

Sanger, Margaret. *Family Limitation*. Cited in V. Bullough and B. Bullough, *Sin, Sickness and Sanity* (New York: New American Library, 1977).

Sappho. *Lyrics*, W. Barnstone (trans.). Garden City, N.Y.: Anchor, 1965.

Sarrel, Philip M. *Teenage Pregnancy*. New York: SIECUS, 1971.

Savel, L. E. The present status of contraception. *Journal of the Medical Society of New Jersey*, 1971, *68*, pp. 635–41.

Sawyer, Ethel. A study of a public lesbian community. Unpublished thesis, Washington University, St. Louis, 1965.

Sayre, Nora. Ahh, how-to books on sex. *New York Times Book Review*, 11 February 1973, pp. 3, 10.

Scales, P. How we guarantee the ineffectiveness of sex education. *SIECUS Report*, 1978, *6*(4), pp. 1–3.

Schäfer, Sigrid. Sexual and social problems of lesbians. *Journal of Sex Research*, 1976, *12*, pp. 50–69.

Schapera, I. *Married Life in an African Tribe*. New York: Sheridan House, 1941.

Scheflen, Albert. *How Behavior Means*. New York: Aronson, 1974.

Scheinfeld, Amram. *Twins and Supertwins*. Baltimore: Penguin Books, 1973.

Schiavi, Raul C. Sexuality and medical illness: Specific reference to diabetes mellitus. In R. Green (ed.), *Human Sexuality: A Health Practitioner's Text*, 2nd ed., pp. 203–12. Baltimore: Willams and Wilkins, 1979.

Schiller, Patricia. *Creative Approach to Sex Education and Counseling*, 2nd ed. New York: Association Press, 1977.

Schmidt, Gunter, and Sigusch, Volkmer. Sex differences in response to psychosexual stimulation by films and slides. *Journal of Sex Research*, 1970, *6*, pp. 268–83.

Schmidt, Gunter, and Sigusch, Volkmer. Patterns of sexual behavior in West German workers and students. *Journal of Sex Research*, 1971, *7*, pp. 89–106.

Schneider, Harold K. Romantic love among the Turu. In D. S. Marshall and R. C. Suggs (eds.), *Human Sexual Behavior*, pp. 59–70. New York: Basic Books, 1971.

Schofield, Michael. *The Sexual Behavior of Young People*. London: Longmans, Green, 1965.

Schull, W. J., and Neel, J. V. *The Effects of Inbreeding on Japanese Children*. New York: Harper and Row, 1965.

Schur, Edwin. *Crimes Without Victims*. Englewood Cliffs, N.J.: Prentice-Hall, 1965.

Schvaneveldt, Jay D. The interaction framework in the study of the family. In F. I. Nye and F. M. Berardo (eds.), *Emerging Conceptual Frameworks in Family Analysis*, pp. 97–129. New York: Macmillan, 1966.

Schwartz, Pepper. Female sexuality and monogamy. In R. W. Libby and R. N. Whitehurst (eds.), *Renovating Marriage: Toward New Sexual Life-Styles*, pp. 211–26. Danville, Calif.: Consensus Press, 1973.

Seal, Herb. *Alternative Life Styles*. Adelaide, Australia: S. A. Growth Press, 1973.

Sears, Robert R. Doll play aggression in normal young children. *Psychological Monographs*, 1951, *65*, No. 6.

Sears, Robert R. Development of gender role. In F. A. Beach (ed.), *Sex and Behavior*, pp. 133–63. New York: Wiley, 1965.

Sears, Robert R.; Maccoby, E. E.; and Levin, H. *Patterns of Child Rearing*. Evanston, Ill.: Row, Peterson, 1957.

Sears, Robert R.; Rau, L.; and Alpert, R. *Identification and Child Rearing*. Stanford, Calif.: Stanford University Press, 1965.

Seemanova, E. A study of children of incestuous matings. *Human Heredity*, 1971, *21*, pp. 108–28.

Semans, James. Premature ejaculation: A new approach. *Southern Medical Journal*, 1956, *49*, pp. 353–57.

Shainess, Natalie. Psychiatric evaluation of premenstrual tension. *New York State Journal of Medicine*, 1962, 62, p. 3573.

Shepard, Martin M. *The Love Treatment*. New York: Wyden, 1971.

Sherfey, Mary Jane. *The Nature and Evolution of Female Sexuality*. New York: Random House, 1966.

529

Shettles, Landrum B. Predetermining children's sex. *Medical Aspects of Human Sexuality*, 1972, *6*(6), pp. 172, 177–78.

Shope, David. *Interpersonal Sexuality*. Philadelphia: Saunders, 1975.

Shuttlesworth, G., and Thorman, G. Living together: Unmarried relationships. Unpublished paper. Cited in C. L. Cole, Cohabitation in social context, in R. W. Libby and R. N. Whitehurst (eds.), *Marriage and Alternatives: Exploring Intimate Relationships* (Glenview, Ill.: Scott, Foresman, 1977).

Siegelman, M. Evaluation of Bronfenbrenner's questionnaire for children concerning parental behavior. *Child Development*, 1965, *36*, pp. 163–74.

Sigusch, Volkmar, and Schmidt, Gunter. Teenage boys and girls in West Germany. *Journal of Sex Research*, 1973, *9*, pp. 107–23.

Silbergeld, S.; Brast, N.; and Noble, E. P. The menstrual cycle: A double blind study of symptoms, mood and behavior, and biochemical variables using enovid and placebo. *Psychosomatic Medicine*, 1971, *33*, pp. 411–28.

Simner, M. L. Newborn's response to the cry of another infant. *Developmental Psychology*, 1971, *5*, pp. 136–50.

Simon, William; Berger, A. S.; and Gagnon, H. J. Beyond anxiety and fantasy: The coital experiences of college youths. *Journal of Youth and Adolescence*, September 1972, *1*, pp. 203–22.

Simon, William, and Gagnon, John. Psychosexual development. *Trans-action*, 6 March 1969, pp. 9–17.

Simpson, George. *People in Families*. Cleveland: World, 1966.

Simpson, M. Parent preferences in young children. In *Contributions to Education*, No. 652. New York: Columbia University Teacher's College, 1935.

Singelmann, Peter. Exchange or symbolic interaction: Convergences between two theoretical perspectives. *American Sociological Review*, 1972, *37*, pp. 414–24.

Singer, Irving. *The Goals of Human Sexuality*. New York: Schocken, 1973.

Singer, June. *Androgyny: Toward a New Theory of Sexuality*. New York: Doubleday, 1976.

Šipová, I., and Stárka, L. Plasma testosterone values in transsexual women. *Archives of Sexual Behavior*, 1977, *6*, pp. 477–81.

Skipper, James, Jr., and McCaghy, Charles. Teasing, flashing, and visual sex: Stripping for a living. In J. Henslin and E. Sagarin (eds.), *The Sociology of Sex*, pp. 171–93. New York: Schocken, 1978.

Skolnick, Arlene. *The Intimate Environment*. Boston: Little, Brown, 1973.

Sloane, Paul, and Karpinski, Eva. Effects of incest on the participants. *American Journal of Orthopsychiatry*, 1942, *12*, pp. 666–73.

Slovenko, Ralph. *Sexual Behavior and the Law*. Springfield, Ill.: Charles C. Thomas, 1965.

Smith, James R., and Smith, Lynn B. (eds.) *Beyond Monogamy: Recent Studies of Sexual Alternatives in Marriage*. Baltimore: Johns Hopkins University Press, 1974.

Smith, Richard W., and Garner, Brian. Are there really gay athletes? *Journal of Sex Research*, 1977, *13*, pp. 22–34.

Smith, Roy G.; Steinhoff, Patricia G.; Palmore, James A.; and Diamond, Milton. Abortion in Hawaii: 1970–1971. *Hawaii Medical Journal*, 1973, *32*, pp. 213–20.

Smith, Stuart L. Mood and the menstrual cycle. In E. J. Sachar (ed.), *Topics in Psychoendocrinology*, pp. 19–58. New York: Grune and Stratton, 1975.

Socarides, Charles. *The Overt Homosexual*. New York: Grune and Stratton, 1968.

Socarides, Charles. *Beyond Sexual Freedom*. New York: Quadrangle, 1975

Solberg, D. A.; Bulter, J.; and Wagner, N. N. Sexual behavior in pregnancy. *New England Journal of Medicine*, 1973, *288*, pp. 1098–1103.

Sommer, B. The effect of menstruation on cognitive and perceptual-motor behavior: A review. *Psychosomatic Medicine*, 1973, *35*, pp. 515–34.

Sonnenschein, David. The ethnography of male homosexual relations. *Journal of Sex Research*, 1968, *4*, pp. 69–83.

Sorensen, Robert C. *Adolescent Sexuality in Contemporary America*. New York: World, 1973.

Sotile, W. M., and Kilmann, P. K. Effects of group systematic desensitization on female orgasmic dysfunction. *Archives of Sexual Behavior*, 1978, *7*, pp. 477–92.

Spitz, René. *The First Year of Life*. New York: International Universities Press, 1965.

Stanley v. *Georgia*. 394 U.S. 557 (1969).

Steinhoff, Patricia G. Background characteristics of abortion patients. In H. Osofsky and J. Osofsky (eds.), *The Abortion Experience: Psychological and Medical Impact*, pp. 206–31. New York: Harper and Row, 1973.

Steinhoff, Patricia G. Premarital pregnancy and the first birth. In W. B. Miller and L. F. Newman (eds.), *The First Child and Family Formation*, pp. 180–208. Chapel Hill, N.C.: Carolina Population Center, 1978.

Steinhoff, Patricia G., and Diamond, Milton. *Abortion Politics*. Honolulu: University Press of Hawaii, 1977.

Steinhoff, Patricia G.; Smith, Roy G.; and Diamond, Milton. Characteristics and motivations of women receiving abortion. *Sociological Symposium*, 1972, *8*, pp. 83–89.

Steinhoff, Patricia G.; Smith, Roy G.; Palmore, James A.; Diamond, Milton; and Chung, C. S. Women who obtain repeat abortions: A study based on record linkage. *Family Planning Perspectives*, 1979, *11*, pp. 30–38.

Stekel, Wilhelm. *Sexual Aberrations*, 2 vols., S. Parker (trans.). New York: Grove Press, 1964.

Stendhal [pseud. of Marie Henri Beyle]. *On Love*. Garden City, N.Y.: Anchor, 1957.

Stephens, William N. *The Family in Cross Cultural Perspective*. New York: Holt, 1963.

Stephens, William N. Predictors of marital adjustment. In W. N. Stephens (ed.), *Reflections on Marriage*, pp. 119–29. New York: Crowell, 1968.

Sterling, T. D., and Kobayashi, D. A critical review of

reports on the effects of smoking on sex and fertility. *Journal of Sex Research,* 1975, *11,* pp. 201–17.

Stevenson, A. G.; Johnston, H. A.; Stewart, M. I.; and Golding, D. R. *Congenital Malformations.* Geneva, Switz.: World Health Organization, 1966.

Stoller, Robert. *Sex and Gender.* New York: Science House, 1968.

Stoller, Robert. *Perversion.* New York: Dell, 1975.

Stoller, Robert. Sexual deviations. In F. A. Beach (ed.), *Human Sexuality in Four Perspectives,* pp. 190–214. Baltimore: Johns Hopkins University Press, 1977.

Storr, Anthony. *Sexual Deviation.* Baltimore: Penguin Books, 1964.

Streissguth, A. P. Maternal drinking and the outcome of pregnancy: Implications for child mental health. *American Journal of Orthopsychiatry,* 1977, *47,* pp. 422–31.

Stukert, R. Role perception and marital satisfaction. *Marriage and Family Living,* 1963, *25,* pp. 415–19.

Sturgeon, Theodore. If all men were brothers, would you let one marry your sister? In H. Ellison (ed.), *Dangerous Visions,* pp. 346–89. New York: Doubleday, 1967.

Suggs, Robert. *Marquesan Sexual Behavior.* New York: Harcourt, Brace and World, 1966.

Sullerot, Evelyne. *Women, Society and Change.* New York: McGraw-Hill, 1971.

Sullivan, Harry Stack. *The Interpersonal Theory of Psychiatry.* New York: Norton, 1953.

Sutherland, E. H. The sexual psychopath laws. *Journal of Criminal Law, Criminology, and Police Science,* 1950, *40,* p. 543.

Svalastoga, L. Rape and social structure. *Pacific Sociological Review,* 1962, *5,* pp. 48–53.

Symonds, C. Pilot study of the peripheral behavior of sexual mate swappers. Unpublished master's thesis, University of California at Riverside, 1968.

Szmuness, Wolf, et al. On the role of sexual behavior in the spread of hepatitis B infection. *Annals of Internal Medicine,* 1975, *83,* pp. 489–95.

Tacitus. *On Britain and Germany,* H. Mattingly (trans.). Baltimore: Penguin Books, 1948.

Tagliamonte, Alessandro; Tagliamonte, P.; Gessa, G. L.; and Brodie, B. B. Compulsive sexual activity induced by p-chlorophenylalanine in normal and pinealectomized male rats. *Science,* 1969, *166,* pp. 1433–35.

Talmon, Yonina. Mate selection in collective settlements. *American Sociological Review,* 1964, *29,* pp. 491–508.

Tasch, R. J. The role of the father in the family. *Journal of Experimental Education,* 1952, *20,* pp. 319–61.

Taylor, D. C. Differential rates of cerebral maturation between sexes and between hemispheres: Evidence from epilepsy. *Lancet,* 1969, *2,* pp. 140–42.

Taylor, Gordon R. *Sex in History.* New York: Vanguard, 1954.

Taylor, Gordon R. *The Angel Makers.* London: Heinemann, 1958.

Teitelbaum, Michael. (Ed.) *Sex Differences: Social and Biological Perspectives.* Garden City, N.Y.: Anchor, 1976.

Terman, Lewis M. Psychological factors in marital happiness. *Psychological Bulletin,* 1939, *36,* pp. 191–203.

Terman, Lewis M. Correlates of orgasm adequacy in a group of 556 wives. *Journal of Psychology,* 1951, *32,* pp. 115–72.

Thamm, Robert. *Beyond Marriage and the Nuclear Family.* San Francisco: Canfield Press, 1975.

Thibault, C. Normal and abnormal fertilization in mammals. *Advances in the Biosciences,* 1970, *6,* pp. 63–85.

Thibaut, John, and Kelly, Howard H. *The Social Psychology of Groups.* New York: Wiley, 1959.

Thompson, Clara. Changing concepts of homosexuality in psychoanalysis. In H. Ruitenbeek (ed.), *The Problem of Homosexuality in Modern Society,* pp. 40–51. New York: Dutton, 1963.

Thompson, Clara; Mazer, Milton; and Witenberg, Earl. *An Outline of Psychoanalysis.* New York: Modern Library, 1955.

Thoreau, Henry David. *The Writings of Henry David Thoreau,* vol. 3, B. Torrey (ed.). Boston: Houghton Mifflin, 1906.

Tietze, Christopher. *The Condom as a Contraceptive.* Publication No. 5. New York: New York National Committee on Maternal Health, 1960.

Tietze, Christopher. Induced Abortion: 1977 supplement. *Reports on Population and Family Planning,* No. 14, 2nd ed., 1977. (a)

Tietze, Christopher. New estimates of mortality associated with fertility control. *Family Planning Perspectives,* 1977, *9,* pp. 74–76. (b)

Tiger, Lionel. *Men in Groups.* New York: Random House, 1969.

Tiger, Lionel, and Shepher, Joseph. *Women in the Kibbutz.* New York: Harcourt, Brace, Jovanovich, 1975.

Time. The Law: *Housen* vs. *Duke.* 31 May 1976, p. 45.

Tinbergen, Niko. *The Study of Instinct.* Oxford: Clarendon Press, 1951.

Tinbergen, Niko. Some recent studies in the evolution of sexual behavior. In F. A. Beach (ed.), *Sex and Behavior,* pp. 1–33. New York: Wiley, 1965.

Tissot, Samuel. *L'Onanisme.* Lausanne, Switz.: Chapuis, 1760.

Tolstoi, Leo. Family happiness, J. Duff (trans.). In *The Death of Ivan Ilych and Other Stories.* New York: New American Library, 1960.

Toufexis, Anastasia, and Karlen, Arno. The Lolita syndrome. *Physician's World,* January 1974, pp. 53–56.

Trethowan, W. H., and Conlon, M. F. The couvade syndrome. *British Journal of Psychiatry,* 1965, *111,* pp. 57–66.

Trivers, Robert L. Parental investment and sexual selection. In B. Campbell (ed.), *Sexual Selection and the Descent of Man,* pp. 136–79. Chicago: Aldine, 1972.

Turgenev, Ivan. *First Love,* I. Berlin (trans.). London: Hamilton, 1956.

Tuttle, W. B.; Cook, W. L., Jr.; and Fitch, E. Sexual behavior in postmyocardial infarction patients. (Abst.)

531

American Journal of Cardiology, 1964, *13,* p. 140.

Tylor, Edward. *Primitive Culture.* London: Oxford University Press, 1963.

U.C.L.A Law Review. The consenting adult homosexual and the law. March 1966, pp. 644–832.

Udry, J. Richard. *The Social Context of Marriage,* 3rd ed. Philadelphia: Lippincott, 1974.

Udry, J. Richard, and Morris, N. M. Distribution of coitus in the menstrual cycle. *Nature,* 1968, *220,* pp. 593–96.

Udry, J. Richard, and Morris, N. M. The distribution of events in the human menstrual cycle. *Journal of Reproduction and Fertility,* 1978, *51,* pp. 419–24.

Ullerstam, Lars. *The Erotic Minorities.* New York: Grove Press, 1966.

United States Bureau of the Census. Population by age, race and sex: 1960 to 1977. In *Statistical Abstracts of the United States, 99th Annual Edition,* p. 29. Washington, D.C.: U.S. Government Printing Office, 1978.

United States Department of Health, Education, and Welfare. *Syphilis: A Synopsis.* Public Health Service Publication No. 1660. Washington, D.C.: U.S. Government Printing Office, 1968.

United States v. *"Ulysses."* S. Fed. Supp. 182 (S.D.N.Y 1933).

Updike, John. *Couples.* Greenwich, Conn.: Fawcett, 1968.

U.S. News and World Report. Working women: Joys and sorrows. 15 January 1979, pp. 64–74.

Van Buren, Abby. Dear Abby. *Honolulu Star-Bulletin,* 20 April 1977, p. E3.

Vandervoort, Herbert E., and McIlvenna, Theodore. Sexually explicit media in medical school curricula. In R. Green (ed.), *Human Sexuality: A Health Practitioner's Text,* pp. 234–45. Baltimore: Williams and Wilkins, 1975.

Van de Velde, Theodoor. *Ideal Marriage.* New York: Covici Friede, 1930.

Varni, Charles A. An exploratory study of spouse-swapping. *Pacific Sociological Review,* 1972, *15,* pp. 507–22.

Vātsyāyana. *Kama Sutra,* R. Burton and F. Arbuthnot (trans.). New York: Capricorn Books, 1973.

Verwoerdt, Adriaan; Pfeiffer, Eric; and Wang, Hsioh-Shan. Sexual behavior in senescence: II, Patterns of sexual activity and interest. *Geriatrics,* 1969, *24,* pp. 137–54.

Vessey, M.: Doll, R.; Peto, R.; Johnson, B.; and Wiggins, P. A. A long term follow-up study of women using different methods of contraception—an interim report. *Journal of Biosocial Science,* 1976, *8,* pp. 375–427.

Vesterdahl-Jørgensen, J. Persisting human blastocysts. *Danish Medical Bulletin,* 1970, *17,* pp. 33–38.

Vieth, Ilza, *Hysteria: The History of a Disease.* Chicago: University of Chicago Press, 1965.

Vincent, Clark. *Sexual and Marital Health: The Physician as a Consultant.* New York: McGraw-Hill, 1973.

Vollman, R. F. The degree of variability of the length of the menstrual cycle in correlating with age of women.

Gynaecologia, 1956, *142,* p. 310.

Wabrek, Alan; Wabrek, Carolyn; and Burchell, R. C. Marital and sexual counseling after mastectomy. In R. Green (ed.), *Human Sexuality: A Health Practitioner's Text,* 2nd ed., pp. 214–45. Baltimore: Williams and Wilkins, 1979.

Wagner, Nathaniel N. Sexual activity and the cardiac patient. In R. Green (ed.), *Human Sexuality: A Health Practitioner's Text,* pp. 173–79. Baltimore: Williams and Wilkins, 1975.

Wagner, Nathaniel N.; Fujita, Byron; and Pion, Ronald J. Sexual behavior in high school. *Journal of Sex Research,* 1973, *8,* pp. 150–55.

Walker, J. E. The germicidal properties of soap. *Journal of Infectious Diseases,* 1926, *38,* p. 127.

Walker, Paul A. Antiandrogens in the treatment of sex offenders. In C. B. Qualls, J. P. Wincze, and D. H. Barlow (eds.), *The Prevention of Sexual Disorders,* pp. 117–36. New York: Plenum, 1978.

Waller, Willard, and Hill, Reuben. *The Family: A Dynamic Interpretation.* New York: Dryden Press, 1951.

Wallin, Paul, and Clark, Alexander L. A study of orgasm as a condition of women's enjoyment of coitus in the middle years of marriage. *Human Biology,* 1963, *35,* pp. 131–39.

Walsh, Robert. Cited in *Behavior Today Supplement,* 2 September 1970.

Ward, David; and Kassebaum, Gene. *Women's Prison.* Chicago: Aldine, 1965.

Ward, Ingeborg L. Prenatal stress feminizes and demasculinizes the behavior of males. *Science,* 1972, *175,* pp. 82–84.

Waxenberg, Sheldon E.; Drellich, M. G.; and Sutherland, A. M. The role of hormones in human behavior. *Journal of Clinical Endocrinology and Metabolism,* 1959, *19*(2), pp. 193–202.

Weinberg, Kirson. *Incest Behavior,* rev. ed. Secaucus, N.J.: Citadel, 1976.

Weinberg, Martin S., and Williams, Colin J. *Homosexuality in the Military: A Study of Less Than Honorable Discharge.* New York: Harper and Row, 1971.

Weinberg, Martin S., and Williams, Colin J. *Male Homosexuals: Their Problems and Adaptations.* New York: Oxford University Press, 1974.

Wendt, Herbert. *The Sex Life of the Animals,* R. Winston and C. Winston (trans.). New York: Simon and Schuster, 1965.

Westermarck, Edward. *The History of Human Marriage,* 3 vols. New York: Allerton, 1922.

Westoff, Charles; Bumpass, L.; and Ryder, N. B. Oral contraception, coital frequency, and the time required to conceive. *Social Biology,* 1969, *16,* pp. 1–10.

Westoff, Charles F., and Jones, Elise F. Contraception and sterilization in the United States, 1965–1975. *Family Planning Perspectives,* 1977, *9,* pp. 153–57. (a)

Westoff, Charles F., and Jones, Elise F. The secularization of U.S. Catholic birth control practices. *Family Planning Perspectives,* 1977, *9,* pp. 203–7. (b)

Westoff, Charles F., and Rindfuss, R. R. Sex preselection in the United States: Some implications. *Science*, 1974, *184*, pp. 633–36.

Westwood, Gordon. *A Minority*. London: Longmans, 1960.

Whalen, Richard E. Differentiation of the neural mechanisms which control gonadotropin secretion and sexual behavior. In M. Diamond (ed.), *Perspectives in Reproduction and Sexual Behavior*, pp. 303–40. Bloomington: Indiana University Press, 1968.

Whitam, Frederick L. Childhood indicators of male homosexuality. *Archives of Sex Research*, 1977, *6*, pp. 89–96. (a)

Whitam, Frederick L. The homosexual role: A reconsideration. *Journal of Sex Research*, 1977, *13*, pp. 1–11. (b)

Whitam, Frederick L. Rejoinder to Omark's comments on the homosexual role. *Journal of Sex Research*, 1978, *14*, pp. 274–75.

White, Gregory L. Cited in Newsline (Unbalanced relationships: Who becomes jealous of whom?), *Psychology Today*, *11* (9), pp. 26–27.

Whitehurst, Robert N. Changing ground rules and emergent life-styles. In R. W. Libby and R. N. Whitehurst (eds.), *Renovating Marriage: Toward New Sexual Life-Styles*, pp. 309–20. Danville, Calif.: Consensus Press, 1973.

Whiting, Beatrice B., and Whiting, John W. M. *Children of Six Cultures*. Cambridge: Harvard University Press, 1975.

Whiting, John. *Becoming a Kwoma: Teaching and Learning in a New Guinea Tribe*. New Haven: Yale University Press, 1941.

Wickler, Wolfgang. *The Sexual Code*, F. Garvie (trans.). Garden City, N.Y.: Doubleday, 1973.

Wiechman, G. H., and Ellis, A. L. Study of effects of sex education on premarital petting and coital behavior. *Family Coordinator*, 1969, *18*, pp. 231–34.

Williams, K. Father-child interaction in cooperation and competition with preschool children. Honors thesis, Stanford University, 1973. Cited in E. E. Maccoby and C. N. Jacklin, *The Psychology of Sex Differences* (Stanford, Calif.: Stanford University Press, 1974).

Williams, Peter, and Smith, Martin. Interview in "The First Question." London: British Broadcasting System Science and Features Department film, 1979.

Wilson, Edward O. *Sociobiology*. Cambridge: Harvard University Press, 1975.

Wilson, Ronald S. Synchronies in mental development: An epigenetic perspective. *Science*, 1978, *202*, pp. 939–48.

Wilson, W. Cody. The distribution of selected sexual attitudes and behaviors among the adult population of the United States. *Journal of Sex Research*, 1975, *11*, pp. 46–64.

Wilson, W. Cody. Pornography and the prevention of sexual problems. In C. B. Qualls, J. P. Wincze, and D. H. Barlow (eds.), *The Prevention of Sexual Dis-*orders, pp. 159–79. New York: Plenum, 1978.

Winch, Robert F. *Mate Selection*. New York: Harper and Brothers, 1958.

Wiseman, Jacqueline P. (Ed.) *People as Partners: Individual and Family Relationships in Today's World*. San Francisco: Canfield Press, 1971.

Wisner, Paul. Letter: Center for Disease Control, 18 October 1978, p. 3. Atlanta: United States Public Health Service, 1978.

Witelson, S. Sex and the single hemisphere: Right hemisphere specialization for spatial processing. *Science*, 1976, *193*, pp. 425–27.

Wollstonecraft, Mary. *The Rights of Women*. London: Dent, 1929.

Woolston. H. B. *Prostitution in the United States*. Montclair, N.J.: Patterson Smith, 1969.

World Health Organization. *Seventh Annual Report: Special Programme of Research, Development and Research Training in Human Reproduction*. Geneva, Switz.: World Health Organization, 1978.

Yale Law Journal. Forcible and statutory rape: An exploration of the operations and objections of the consent standard. 1952, *55*, pp. 70–73.

Yalom, Irvin. Aggression and forbiddenness in voyeurism. *Archives of General Psychiatry*, 1960, *3*(3), pp. 305–19.

Yalom, Irvin; Green, R.; and Fisk, N. Prenatal exposure to female hormones: Effect of psychosexual development in boys. *Archives of General Psychiatry*, 1973, *28*(4), pp. 554–61.

Young, William C. The hormones and mating behavior. In W. Young (ed.), *Sex and Internal Secretions*, vol. 2, pp. 1173–1239. Baltimore: Williams and Wilkins, 1961.

Zarrow, M. X., and Clark, J. H. Ovulation following vaginal stimulation in a spontaneous ovulator and its implications. *Journal of Endocrinology*, 1968, *40*, pp. 343–52.

Zborowski, Mark, and Herzog, Elizabeth. *Life Is with People*. New York: Schocken, 1974.

Zelnik, M., and Kantner, John F. Sexuality, contraception and pregnancy among young unwed females in the United States. In *U.S. Commission on Population Growth and the American Future: Demographic and Social Aspects of Population Growth*. Washington, D.C.: U.S. Government Printing Office, 1972.

Zelnik, M., and Kantner, John F. Sexual and contraceptive experiences of young unmarried women in the United States, 1976 and 1971. *Family Planning Perspectives*, 1977, *9*, pp. 55–71.

Zilboorg, Gregory. *A History of Medical Psychology*. New York: Norton, 1941.

Zitrin, Arthur; Dement, W. C.; and Barchas, J. D. Brain serotonin and male sexual behavior. In J. Zubin and J. Money (eds.), *Contemporary Sexual Behavior*, pp. 321–38. Baltimore: Johns Hopkins University Press, 1973.

Zola, Émile. *Nana*. New York: Pocket Books, 1942.

Name Index

Subject Index

TO THE OWNER OF THIS BOOK:

All of us who worked together to produce *Sexual Decisions* hope that you have enjoyed it as much as we did. If you did — or if you didn't — we'd like to know why, so we'll have a better idea of how to improve it in future editions. We appreciate your comments.

School:_____

Instructor's name: _____

Department in which course was given: _____

Other required reading:_____

1. Please give us your reaction to the following elements of the text by ranking them from 1 (excellent) to 5 (poor).

	1	2	3	4	5
Overall impression	☐	☐	☐	☐	☐
Level of difficulty	☐	☐	☐	☐	☐
Explanations of terms and concepts	☐	☐	☐	☐	☐
Writing style/interest level	☐	☐	☐	☐	☐
Learning aids (questions at beginning and end of chapter)	☐	☐	☐	☐	☐
Appearance (cover, layout, use of illustration)	☐	☐	☐	☐	☐

2. Were all the chapters assigned? _____

   If not, which were not assigned? _____

3. Which chapter did you like best? Why? _____

   _____

4. Which chapter did you like least? Why?_____

   _____

5. Please comment on illustrations. Were they helpful? How might they be improved?

   _____

6. Do you think the instructor should continue to assign this book? Why or why not?

_____

_____

_____

7. Will you keep *Sexual Decisions?* _____

8. Please add any comments or suggestions on how we might improve this book.

_____

_____

_____

_____

9. (Optional) Your name: _____

Address:_____

Date:_____

10. May we quote you, either in promotion for this book or in future publishing ventures?   Yes ☐   No ☐

Please mail to:

SEXUAL DECISIONS
College Division
Little, Brown and Company
34 Beacon Street
Boston, Massachusetts   02106

WESTMAR COLLEGE LIBRARY